PIMLICO

829

DOWNING STREET DIARY

Bernard Donoughue taught at the London School of
Economics from 1963 to 1974, when he moved to
10 Downing Street as Senior Policy Advisor to Harold
Wilson and then to James Callaghan. His books include
Herbert Morrison: Portrait of a Politician, Prime Minister,
The Heat of the Kitchen and *Downing Street Diary:*
With Harold Wilson in No 10.

Also by Bernard Donoughue

British Politics and the American Revolution
Herbert Morrison: Portrait of a Politician (with G. W. Jones)
The People into Parliament (with W. T. Rodgers)
Prime Minister
The Heat of the Kitchen
Downing Street Diary: With Harold Wilson in No. 10

DOWNING STREET DIARY

With James Callaghan in No. 10

———

BERNARD DONOUGHUE

PIMLICO

Published by Pimlico 2009

2 4 6 8 10 9 7 5 3 1

First published in Great Britain in 2008 by Jonathan Cape

Pimlico
Random House, 20 Vauxhall Bridge Road,
London SW1V 2SA

www.rbooks.co.uk

Addresses for companies within The Random House Group Limited can be found at:
www.randomhouse.co.uk/offices.htm

The Random House Group Limited Reg. No. 954009

A CIP catalogue record for this book is available from the British Library

ISBN 9781845950941

Typeset in Ehrhardt by
Palimpsest Book Production Ltd, Grangemouth, Stirlingshire

Printed and bound in Great Britain by
CPI Mackays, Chatham, Kent ME5 8TD

To Rachel, Kate, Paul and Stephen

Contents

Introduction   I

I James Callaghan Settles In (April–July 1976)   11

II Policy Initiatives, especially on Education
(September 1976–July 1977)   63

III Calmer Waters (August 1977–July 1978)   229

IV Things Begin to Fall Apart (September–December 1978)   351

V Nemesis: The Winter of Discontent (January–May 1979)   409

List of Persons Mentioned in the Diary   505

Index   537

Introduction

This second volume of my Downing Street Diary covers the premiership of James Callaghan from 1976 to 1979 and so completes the story of the Labour government of 1974–79 as seen from inside No. 10.

Its predecessor, published in 2005, dealt with Harold Wilson's final two administrations and particularly retailed the colourful battles and scandals of the personal team surrounding Wilson. The events described in this present diary are different in tone and emphasis, reflecting the different character of the new man in charge, being more concentrated on public issues. The individuals advising James Callaghan, including the author, are, as they should be, more often in the background – though not without their recorded whims, prejudices and influences for good or for ill. The centre stage is now rightly occupied by the Prime Minister, his Cabinet ministers and their policies. James Callaghan is seen quickly to establish greater dominance over his ministerial team than was ever achieved by Harold Wilson. Callaghan had over the years become tougher, almost intimidating, taking colleagues and issues head-on, whereas Wilson was ever the soft manipulator, avoiding confrontation whenever possible.

The location of most of the action described below remains No. 10 Downing Street, always the central theatre of British politics. The atmosphere of that house stays in the memory of anyone who has worked there for any significant period of time. But No. 10 does not produce an unchanging performance regardless of the shifting cast of actors present in office there. This volume demonstrates a different style of conduct of central government in Downing Street under James Callaghan from that previously shown under Wilson. The diary of the early days of his premiership shows Callaghan clearly feeling for his prime ministerial style, exploring different rooms in the house from which to conduct his business and ways in which to process his papers and to handle his ministers and advisers. He was, however, the most experienced high-level minister in modern British politics, having uniquely served as Chancellor of the Exchequer,

Home Secretary and Foreign Secretary. He soon established his own natural style.

Above all he used, enjoyed and nourished the traditional Cabinet form of government to which he and his colleagues were accustomed. These years 1976–79 were probably both the peak and the final performance of classic British Cabinet government. After Callaghan, Margaret Thatcher began the process of bypassing Cabinet, a process which was accelerated so spectacularly and possibly damagingly under Tony Blair.

Personally, James Callaghan emerges from these pages as a quite different character from Harold Wilson, even though they shared remarkable political skills. I wrote my conclusions on Callaghan's personality and style, which dominate these diaries, in my recent memoirs, *The Heat of the Kitchen*, (pp. 235–7) and will repeat them here:

> Watching James Callaghan over the coming months and years, I observed a very commendable man, quite different in style and character from Harold Wilson, not just in that he was nearly a foot taller (and walked with a curious gait, tilted towards one side as if compensating for the lurch of one of the ships on which he served during the war). Most different from the previous regime was his strong sense of values – really like those of a nonconformist Victorian, with deep feelings of responsibility towards the under-privileged and a strong sense of right and wrong (where Harold was often ambivalent).
>
> When in the Unit we produced a paper for his first Easter holiday reading about the restoration of responsible values in our society, another of my personal concerns, he telephoned me from his farm to say how much he liked it and asked me to join in the writing of his future speeches to incorporate this dimension. Sometimes these 'values' emerged as a touchingly old-fashioned prudery. He once cautioned Tom McNally and me not to tell bawdy stories in front of his wife Audrey (not that we had any such intention). He told me that he had been totally unaware of homosexuality until well into adult life, adding, 'It all puzzles me. There have always been so many pretty girls.' But he was more comfortable in male than female company and was not as good as Harold in promoting women.
>
> Although apparently an agnostic, his Baptist upbringing showed through when, especially during a crisis, he would suddenly burst out singing hymns. Before he left his Commons room for the big debate on our pay sanctions policy, he sang to us one of his favourites – 'We'll meet again with the Lord'. I often heard him humming a hymn to himself as he set off for a critical meeting. But he was partly

Irish by descent and his long political memory and private pleasure at cold revenge for long-distant grudges was a very Irish trait.

He was much more of a family man than Harold. Audrey played a key role in his life and we always knew that a parliamentary situation was serious when he asked her to travel with him in the car over to the Commons from No. 10. We were aware that his children and grandchildren mattered greatly to him. On Trooping of the Colour day in 1976 – different from our experience the previous year when our children were deprived of drinks! – Jim toured the reception room and talked with each messenger, waitress and child in turn. My children still remember it with affection. He also had more of the common touch than Harold, helped by his tougher upbringing and his time in the navy as well as a trade unionist. He also shared many of the pleasures of ordinary people, often going to the popular theatre and watching television, on which he was very knowledgeable about the various series and the actors who starred in them.

My observation over the coming three years was that James Callaghan had three layers of personality. On the surface was the familiar bluff and avuncular Jim. Below that was a shrewd, secretive and even wily politician. And beneath those layers was an authentic and very decent person who really did believe in the straight honest values in life. By comparison, Harold Wilson had only two main layers. On top was Tricky Harold, the clever and devious political manipulator. Below that was a kindly, weak and insecure man. But I am not sure that there was anything at all beneath that: perhaps just a void where Jim had his root values. To me as his personal adviser, what mattered most about the Callaghan regime was that it was sane, sensible and balanced, with none of the hysteria (though of course less of the colour and fun) which afflicted the fringes of Wilson's reign.

Callaghan's style of working as Prime Minister was quite different from Harold's. He needed a lot of time and space for his working process. He did not like a crowd of advisers around him, preferring them to approach him singly, by prior arrangement and having sent in a paper in advance so that he could prepare mentally. He often took a while to return papers – some of mine were found under his bed. He told me that he did not like too much sudden pressure and that he did not like 'all the problems to come together. I like to take issues one at a time.' That may be why he sometimes appeared to be overwhelmed by the avalanche of problems in the pay crisis in 1979. In such crises he tended to withdraw into himself and cut off communication with his team, instead of involving them even more to share the burden. That perhaps reflected his insecurities and that he did not have a freely outgoing personality. He did not pretend to be 'cosy' and did not often chat openly as Harold did, disapproving of what he saw as 'gossip'. He usually played his cards close to his chest.

I admired the way that he took serious issues seriously and had an acute sense of the likely public and political reaction to any proposal. He could be extremely severe and I would not have wanted to be on the wrong end of one of his critical rebukes. Having been Chancellor, Foreign Secretary and Home Secretary, he knew how to make Whitehall deliver. He once told me that he viewed No. 10 as an old-fashioned railway signal box: he had to pull the right levers to make the policy trains reach the right Whitehall destinations on time.

He was also skilled at using the appropriate civil servants for the appropriate tasks. On one occasion, I thought that I had a wonderful idea in the social policy area which would have great political benefits. I explained it to Jim on paper and he ticked it and arranged a meeting in the study to discuss it. When we gathered, I saw that a senior civil servant, Ken Stowe, was present. I politely questioned this since, although Ken was a good friend, I felt that my proposal was very political and civil servants should not be present. Jim disagreed, explaining: 'You see, Bernard, I have been around in government for a long time and I have been tempted by a lot of very clever political wheezes like yours. Sadly they don't all work as well as it looks at first sight. So I have found it is better to have someone present who says "wait a minute". Ken is my "wait a minute" man.' Ken did indeed say wait a minute to my clever wheeze, spotting a fundamental flaw, and I was pleased that it was allowed to die without further embarrassment. That was the Civil Service at its best – not being simply obstructive but detecting a genuine downside in a proposal.

Callaghan's personal political style was magisterial (helped by his height), even authoritarian at times, and his occasional grumpiness and severity meant that some colleagues and staff could be nervous in dealing with him. But he was good at handling his ministerial colleagues and he was not afraid to confront them and their political problems head-on. He was said to be anti-intellectual (some of his early political allies were not impressive), possibly arising from having left school in his early teens, being then the only British Prime Minister born in the twentieth century not to have been to university. I like to think that he was simply impatient with the pretentious arrogance with which some self-professed intellectuals surrounded themselves. His mind was powerful, based on practicality and honed by very great experience. He had a devastating capacity for asking simple but central questions which did not allow for anything but simple and straight answers – which I often did not quite have.

He was always nervous before a big speech, telling me that he felt 'terrible, for two days it is like a big black cloud. I get irritable and say to Audrey, "I cannot do it. I've nothing to say." But she keeps me at it. Then ten minutes beforehand I feel OK.' In delivering his speeches, he was a true professional, always dominating and yet involving his audience. He had a strong and commanding style in the House of Commons and it is now often forgotten how he usually dominated Mrs Thatcher there. Even in the depths of the Winter of Discontent he was personally well ahead of her in the polls, when his party trailed the Tories by up to 20%. He told me that from his experience of the Commons it was essential 'always to be accurate, always understate, never exaggerate. Remember there is always somebody who knows better than you do.' This was typical of his natural modesty, shrewdness, prudence and caution. He never wanted to show off or to 'showboat'.

Like Harold Wilson, he grew to dislike Commons Questions. He said to me, 'This is my worst fifteen minutes of the week. I hate this silly game we have to play.' At first he abolished our pre-Questions briefing on Tuesdays and Thursdays, preferring to take his post-prandial nap instead. He said, 'It is better to be well rested than well briefed.' But he found that he could not do without his briefings for Questions and he soon resumed them. Jim was also good on television in a solid, reassuring and old-fashioned way. Before broadcasting about the Winter of Discontent in 1979, he asked me, 'What demeanour should I adopt?' I replied, 'Be natural, be yourself.' He said, 'Yes, that is the only way. There is no point in trying to adopt a false style.' That was authentically Jim. He was quite unsuited to modern 'spinning' or presentation with a 'celebrity' style. I always liked the fact that he was just himself.

Although the events described in this diary are only a generation ago, many current media commentators show little interest in and even less knowledge of them. This is sad because that decade of the 1970s contains matters of great significance for our nation's history. Among them, the negotiations over the IMF loan to the UK in 1976 were both a national humiliation and a prime example of Cabinet government operating at its best. The 1979 Winter of Discontent, when the left-wing trade unions brought this country to a virtual standstill for many weeks, cutting off transport, heat and water, preventing the sick from entering hospital and the dead from being buried, was probably a unique example of modern Britain's social structures in virtual collapse and its elected government rendered impotent. During that latter dreadful experience citizens realised that the conventions of orderly democratic government are a precious national asset which should be valued and not taken for granted.

The relentless sequence of economic and monetary crises which resound through these pages is a reminder of how weak was the British economy at that time – we were viewed from across the Channel as the 'sick man of Europe' – and how comparatively easy has so far been the economic life in office of Tony Blair and Gordon Brown, benefiting from the radical reforms of Margaret Thatcher in the 1980s.

Inevitably, some of the heated policy battles recorded here have proved to be of ephemeral interest (and constitute the main part of the cuts made in editing the diaries). It seems odd today to be reminded that so much Whitehall time and effort was then devoted to preparing (never implemented) legislation for industrial democracy and on how many trade union officials should serve on the proposed complex boards of major companies; or that among the main focuses of economic policy were giving support to the daily exchange rate of sterling and to protecting our declining manufacturing industries. Which newspaper today, as often then, has this month's trade balance as one of its front-page stories? Above all, the government's then obsession with reducing the rate of inflation through direct state intervention in the intricate processes of wage negotiations, which runs through these pages, seems from a different age.

Other policy issues described below were, however, of more long-term consequence: the decisions to offer devolved government to Scotland; to continue fighting the IRA in Northern Ireland; to pay child benefits directly to mothers; to remain outside the new European monetary mechanism; to rush the exploitation of North Sea oil while neglecting our nuclear power industry; and especially to focus British school education back on to the basic values of learning. All of these policy decisions were of significance to Britain's future – as were the government's policy failures: such as the failure to adopt a properly diverse energy policy; failure to invest in the transport infrastructure; failure to implement my Policy Unit's proposal to sell council houses to tenants long before Mrs Thatcher took that immensely popular initiative; failure to confront the excessive and irresponsible trade union power which ultimately destroyed the Labour government; and above all, the failure to appreciate that the state alone could not solve the basic economic problems of pricing and resource allocation and that the free market, properly conducted, to a greater extent could.

Taking a longer perspective, one interesting aspect of the Callaghan government was its historical position as a bridge between the end of the post-war era of collectivism, valuing social cohesion and political moderation, and the subsequent 1980s decade of material individualism and extreme ideological confrontation. This 1976–79 government played – and sometimes staggered – on the cusp between the era that was termed 'Butskellism' (indicating the overlap of beliefs between the two main parties and their leaders) and the later period often personalised as 'Thatcherism'. Callaghan, his ministers and his advisers all grew up as 'Butskellites' – basically Keynesian social democrats – always seeking compromise and viewing the public sector as a prime social 'good'. But by 1976–79 the problems and the political opponents now facing and ultimately defeating them were increasingly of a more extreme kind. The economic problems were not soluble, and sometimes made worse, by Keynesian state intervention and inflating the public sector. Callaghan's political adversaries were deaf to appeals for social cohesion: the hard left showed no interest in political compromise while the new right wing preferred individual material interest to a collectivist common approach. Neither opposing side could be reconciled by the familiar old political formulae. So in these pages we see the Prime Minister and his colleagues looking bemused as their efforts at compromise and conciliation failed. Well before his election defeat, James Callaghan looked a sad figure, recognising that there was nothing he could do to control or oppose the 'sea change' which was occurring in British politics towards Thatcherite individualism.

The devasting Winter of Discontent in 1979 both reflected and accelerated the geological shift which was occurring in the British political and social landscape, converting many in the electorate to the need for a harsher market approach to our economy. But in fact the signs of that transition are present earlier in these pages. We see increasingly that the previous Keynesian model was failing to deliver either sufficient economic growth or adequate social services. James Callaghan gave that model its final test. Its failure prepared the way for the 'Thatcher revolution'.

Not all of the politicians figuring below emerge as major ministerial figures. The author comments that Callaghan's government, both in Cabinet and especially in its middle ranks, contained too many mediocrities – 'marshmallows' – certainly not of the calibre needed to master the immense challenges then facing them. The place of some in the government was explicable only in terms of being party 'worthies' or as loyal personal supporters of James Callaghan during his rise to the top of the political greasy pole. Such is usually the case with any government – though Wilson's later administrations had been blessed with major figures from the outstanding post-war parliamentary generation. The quality weakness in Callaghan's team was accentuated early in his premiership as the post-war Labour giants began to fall away – either as a sacked enemy, like Barbara Castle, or from career choice, as Roy Jenkins move to Brussels, or by death, as with Tony Crosland. They together consituted a deficit of political stature which the new Prime Minister was never able to replace. The pool of political talent was now more shallow – and at times I felt that James Callaghan's personal inclination was to value loyalty above ability.

Some of Callaghan's colleagues would, however, have shone in any administration. Tony Benn and Michael Foot, from Labour's otherwise dismal left wing, displayed remarkable communication skills. The younger right-wing group contained the most promising ministers: Shirley Williams, Bill Rodgers, David Owen, John Smith and Roy Hattersley. None was later to enjoy the full bloom of a political career because Labour soon went into opposition for their prime next eighteen years, while the first three of them left the party, alienated by what they understandably saw as intolerable left-wing fanaticism.

Apart from the Prime Minister himself, who stood a tall head and shoulders above his Cabinet, its outstanding member was undoubtedly Chancellor Denis Healey. He features combatively throughout this volume and, representing the Treasury with which my Policy Unit was often in disagreement, is frequently treated unfairly in the battle heat of these pages. Denis carried for five years an incredible burden. It was a tribute to him that when Callaghan is seen contemplating moving him to the Foreign Office, the Prime Minister planned to replace him with two ministers at the Treasury, because he knew there was no other colleague who could carry that burden alone. Denis was a remarkable Chancellor facing the most difficult, sometimes overwhelming, problems faced by any British Chancellor since 1950.

This volume follows the format of its predecessor, providing a daily and continuous narrative of British politics and government during those years as seen from inside No. 10 and usually written on the night or early morning following the day's events. It is again the single view of one observer from one privileged position. As with most diaries, it is not written with the balanced fairness of later hindsight. It is unbalanced, often unfair to individuals and subject to the exhaustions and temporary irritations of the author on a particular day. Hopefully it also conveys the virtues of immediacy and direct personal involvement at the time.

This diary has, unlike its predecessor, been substantially edited for length. The original typed script (based on scores of handwritten notebooks) contained over 1,300 pages. That would have been too great a burden on the reader. For similar compassionate reasons there are no footnotes, but small biographies of most characters are appended.

Contrary to current fashion, I have delayed the publication of both volumes of diaries until all the participants have left the public stage –

many, including James Callaghan, now sadly dead – so they can no longer be affected by what is written. Keeping and publishing diaries is in fact a delicate moral process. The other people involved in the events described are usually unaware that a record is being kept and so, in a sense, their confidence and trust is being exploited. They might have spoken and acted differently had they known they were 'on the record'. There is actually no real and total solution to that moral dilemma, unless it is never to keep diaries – which would leave historians and others interested in life at a particular time very deprived. The traditional compromise, sadly recently abandoned, was to wait a decent period of time before publication and I have tried to do that. Some three decades seems to me a decent length of time, even though it runs the commercial risk of finding too few readers remaining interested in those times a generation ago. I prefer that risk to the certainty of giving offence by the discourtesy of instant publication.

I particularly wish to express gratitude to Sandra Lee and Della Brotherstone for their assistance and discretion in the complex process of converting my almost illegible diaries into modern word-processing technology. I also thank my loyal friend Graham Greene for his unfailing friendship and support over this prolonged project. My deepest retrospective appreciation goes to Carol and my children who put up with a great deal during the exciting and exhausting years described in this book.

I

James Callaghan Settles In (April–July 1976)

Tuesday 6 April 1976

Jim Callaghan's* first full day. He had a diary meeting at 9.30 with John Hunt* and Ken Stowe* [the Cabinet secretary and principal private secretary] who complained afterwards that Tom McNally* [Jim Callaghan's political adviser] had attended. I don't think this was a Civil Service shut-out: just that Jim does not like many people with him at the same time. On the other hand his personal aides need to make sure they get in there from the beginning.

I went up after the meeting and said I wanted a formal decision on the Policy Unit. He did not know the Unit advisers had been officially sacked when Harold Wilson* resigned. He said, 'I want the Unit to continue. Bring them back in, double-fast.' So I went off and did that. He later came down and worked in the Cabinet Room – including seeing Michael Foot* and Roy Jenkins* (though him in the study I think). Harold Wilson never worked in the Cabinet Room in my time.

We had lunch in the small state dining room. Back to where we were two years ago – except no PM and no Marcia [Williams]*. Several times this morning I walked in to see Tom McNally in Marcia's room, just to enjoy the pleasure of having a nice person in there.

Jim ate in his study, the same food as us. He has decided to share our lunches on Tuesdays and Thursdays, and then to have sandwiches on other days in the study. He doesn't want to pay especially for a cook on other days – he has a reputation for being 'tight' on money. And he doesn't seem to want to go to eat in the Commons – which was the only way HW kept in touch with the Parliamentary Labour Party. Jim also has a sleep every day after lunch. He said to us, 'Better well rested than well briefed.'

We assembled for Questions briefing in his room at the Commons – the same one Wilson had down the corridor behind the Speaker's Chair. He arrived around 1.45. It was a very good session. He brought everybody in, and listened with interest to all suggestions. He admitted to being bewildered by PM's Questions. As a departmental minister at the Foreign

Office he simply had to know the departmental policies and then he could handle it. Here it is impossible to predict. Supplementaries can be on anything, despite the new Speaker Thomas's attempts to make them more strictly relevant. We tried to make predictions from previous experience. The private secretary responsible for PQs – Nick Stuart* – is so good at this that Jim has asked him to stay on longer (he was already prolonged by HW). Nick is depressed since he wants to get back to his own Department of Education.

Question Time itself was easy. Lots of congratulations – and [Margaret] Thatcher*, remembering her earlier mistake, was much more gracious this time. Jim handled everything else easily. He is more general and emollient, more avuncular than Wilson. Less teasing to the Opposition. The real problems will arise if he gets caught out and loses his temper and his confidence.

Afterwards he came back to No. 10 and went on a tour of the house allocating rooms to his staff – including the room I had reserved for my lads in the Cabinet Office. He was also deep in discussions with Tom McNally and John Cunningham* on how to set up a Political Office. He decided to ask two moderate unions and Transport House to finance a secretary each. This way it would be open and institutional – with none of HW's shady private individuals paying money in anticipation of future honours. He asked me about it later, and I stressed the need to have 'no backstairs money'.

When I went home he was still in the Cabinet Room talking to Tom McNally and John Cunningham who are both first class and with each of whom I am co-operating very closely.

Wednesday 7 April 1976

I went in early and was sitting in Tom McNally's office with Tom when the PM called in. He said he wanted to see me later.

Yesterday he asked for my views on the junior ministers, so I was just dictating this when Jim sent for me. I went up to the study with half a Green Paper! He told me that he had now 'just finished putting the pieces together' in his new Cabinet. He sat at the desk – something HW never did – and asked me to draw up a chair. We talked for a while about the job of Prime Minister. He said he felt 'lost', 'isolated', 'bewildered' and 'a prisoner'. He was used to sitting in a departmental office with the door open and the private secretaries next door, with work flowing in and out. Now he felt isolated. That is why he had at first tried working downstairs in the Cabinet Room.

Actually HW dealt with this situation by encouraging an endless flow of people up to him in his study. We all went in, if only to say hello, and he was never left alone. Jim does not like to be crowded, and prefers people to come only if sent for or by appointment. So he has long gaps on his own. He does not yet know how to make the house work – he has not even started to use his 'buttons' to buzz for the secretaries. So he feels isolated but is not by personality somebody who encourages others to diminish the isolation. Yet all will be made better once the Cabinet committees begin. His days will soon fill up.

The only question is whether that will leave any time for access to his personal staff. I am not somebody who likes making formal appointments with my boss. Yet it is clear that Jim will not stroll around in Private Office holding court, or stand for hours chatting near the ticker tape as Harold did. They were very valuable occasions, especially for clearing smaller bread-and-butter questions too trifling to put on paper – or for fixing a formal interview.

Jim also said he was not quite clear how he should make his mark as a Prime Minister. He admitted he did not have HW's capacity for imaginative interventions. I said I was preparing a paper on just this problem. I also raised the role of the Policy Unit. He said he was very keen on keeping it, but was not too clear on how it slotted in. I described its functions and we discussed its membership.

He concluded by saying, 'Bernard, I want you and the Unit to stay on. I am not very clever, as you will know from the newspapers. I don't have Harold's brain for bright ideas. But in fact I need the Unit more than Harold did. And although I don't get many bright ideas of my own, I am good at spotting the bright ideas of others and know whether they will work or not. I want you to feed in a lot of ideas, I won't take them all, so I want a lot of intellectual input.'

Quite impressive and reassuringly self-aware.

We then discussed junior ministers – where I recommend Edmund Dell*, Roy Hattersley*, Bill Rodgers* and John Smith* for immediate promotion to the Cabinet. He showed a lot of interest in John Smith. We discussed devolution and I said it needed somebody with some charisma – I suggested Smith if he wanted a Scot, but said it depended who was in charge – Ted Short* or somebody else. He asked me whether it needed to be with the Lord President. I said yes – or at the Home Office. He said, 'The Scots won't be happy about that.' I got the impression that Ted Short would go.

He said he needed some good left-wingers. I named Albert Booth*, Stan Orme* and Eric Deakins*, but pointed out that the first two were not brilliantly intellectual (he obviously resented that) and Deakins a bit trendy. He asked who I preferred of Booth and Orme, I said marginally Booth, though I loved Stan Orme. He said what job could they do and I said their present jobs. He said, well Orme won't do Northern Ireland. I added that Booth had been a good Minister of State at Employment, but that might be his natural level.

We then discussed other younger ones. I recommended especially David Owen*. Bob Maclennan* (though Jim said 'he is bad in the House'). And a list of backbenchers including Phillip Whitehead*, Ray Carter, Betty Boothroyd*, Neil Kinnock* and just possibly Brian Sedgemore* – who Jim clearly did not trust. I also pressed for promotion for Alf Morris* and Jack Ashley*. He queried whether deaf Jack could do it. I said yes and put the symbolic arguments of having a disabled minister looking after the disabled at a time when we have no money to spend. He grinned and said, 'I can see you do think politically.' I left after an hour and a quarter feeling much more in touch with how he thinks – though he will never be as revealing as HW was, despite all the latter's hilarious attempts to be secretive.

But I did learn that Jim did not reveal details of his appointment intentions, as Wilson would have done. He only revealed to us his intention not to let Jenkins have the Foreign Office. When Tom McNally said he disagreed and this would mean Jim being described as 'the PM who drove Jenkins from British public life at the behest of Michael Foot', Jim said he thought that was 'impertinent' – and then froze up. That is all very different. Harold did not mind what we said. He had his compensations!

Thursday 8 April 1976

JC was forming his Cabinet this morning, seeing a stream of senior people. First Jenkins and Foot. Apparently Jenkins was very upset at not getting the Foreign Office. Foot tried for forty-five minutes to persuade Jim to keep Barbara Castle*, and to make various other left-wing appointments, but Jim was firm on most points. He would not have both Booth and Orme in the Cabinet and forced Foot to say which one was better – Booth. Jim insisted Barbara must go.

Shirley Williams* was waiting downstairs while Foot was with the PM. I talked to her, and said that Jim wanted to promote her and make great use of her. She said she was worried about the Roy rumours and did not mind either way whether she stayed or went. She said, 'There are some Cabinets I would rather not be a member of.' Then she told me she had told Jim she would not wish to serve if there was 'a lurch to the left' and he slapped her down, saying, 'I make my own Cabinet.'

Tony Crosland* and Willie Ross* were in by then. Willie was quite amusing beforehand, saying that he had been reading his own sacking for ten years, though he correctly did suppose this was finally it. He also commented on how the Cabinet feels different with somebody different in the chair, then going on to say how good Wilson was with the Scots – implying that Jim was not so good. Tony Crosland was looking very pleased with himself and clearly delighted with the Foreign Office.

Barbara Castle was glowering coming down the stairs but on seeing me put on that familiar cosmetic smile and said, 'Isn't it a lovely day?' Later we heard that she ranted a bit at Jim, saying she wanted to complete her NHS legislation. There must have been a hint of a peerage, because she later issued a press statement saying that she had firmly refused Jim's offer on socialist principles that she wanted to be a commoner. [She later happily took a peerage.]

Jim saw these senior people upstairs in his study. He then saw the younger ones – Albert Booth, John Smith, Stan Orme – downstairs in the Cabinet Room. I saw Albert Booth beforehand. He said he felt very nervous and always felt nervous in No. 10. He is a good solid man, but no flier.

I spent a lot of time chatting to Tom McNally. We had lunch and then went over to Questions. The PM did not spend much time on the briefing, and commented, 'It must be boring for you all, going over the same ground again and again.' Very true. He did well and hammered Mrs Thatcher. But no jokes.

Afterwards I went for a walk in the corridor and met Roy Jenkins. I told him how sad I was that he is going to Europe. He said that Jim left him with no option. I said that it was a pity to go when he felt down. He said he did not feel down but very up – but he did not look it. I said that Jim was really quite impressive. Roy said he had not impressed him at all, not at all – particularly because Jim had appeared to firmly offer him the Treasury on their first meeting (on Tuesday), and then to retreat from that twenty-four hours later. (He saw Roy a second time on Wednesday.) I felt very down as we parted. I admire Roy greatly. It was sad to have him attacked so often by HW and now disliked by Jim. But to have him leave altogether is terrible.

I went back to No. 10 and slowly got drunk over Roy's departure. I rashly told the Press Office, McNally and [Tom] McCaffrey*, that Jim had made a mistake about Roy, and I tended to exaggerate the likely consequences. I went to the House of Commons and drank more and did not get home till very late, very depressed.

Incidentally during the Cabinet appointments all the left played the game of saying that they wanted time to think over Jim's offers – as a tactic to humiliate him and stress his dependence on Foot. Jim got fed up with this, and towards the end when John Silkin* said he wanted twenty-four hours, Jim said, 'You've got two minutes, or you are out.' Slimy Silkin, who is lucky to be in any Cabinet, immediately accepted.

[Tony] Benn* said that he wanted to consult his wife – exactly as he did over his Energy appointment in 1975. He said he wanted 'a political ministry'

not a technological one like Energy. Jim told him to 'take it or leave it' –
and he took it. Benn looked very sour when he left at about 5 p.m. Jim is
much tougher on the left than Harold was and they soon cave in.

Friday 9 April 1976

Jim away in Wales. I worked in the Unit preparing a long brief for him for
Easter.

The atmosphere in No. 10 is different. Jim is slower. Likes less paper.
Gets tired easily – he looked old and grey last night. He has left everybody
jumpy. He plays his cards close to his chest so we have difficulty in inter-
preting his wishes except when he has given a straight instruction. Yet he
is refreshing in many ways after Wilson and more direct, and with no hidden
influences (or none we have seen so far).

Monday 12 April 1976

By the time I got in to No. 10 this morning the PM was already in. He
saw the Chancellor and they had a general discussion of the economic situation – just a tour de horizon. Nothing dramatic came up.

After his meeting with the private secretaries, around noon, the PM sent
for me. We had some small chat – including his wish to meet the members
of the Unit – and then he said he did not want me to go on my planned
trip to Israel with my travel paid for by the Israeli Labour Party. He said
we must find a different way of doing it and he had asked the Foreign Office
to produce some money. I was due to go next Saturday so feel a bit jumpy
about my Easter plans, needing to know one way or the other. He was very
friendly and direct – and I find him easy to talk to.

Lunch in the Cabinet Office mess with Patrick Wright* from Private
Office, trying to sort out the Israeli dilemma. I sense that the climate towards
Israel has definitely cooled with the new regime.

Worked on my Easter brief to the PM. Then saw the secretary of the
charity Gingerbread – One Parent Families – to see if it is possible to help
them more. The PM spent a lot of time in the Commons for the last day
of the Budget debate. He was particularly keen to be there supporting when
Michael Foot was winding up. Home 9.30.

Tuesday 13 April 1976

I had decided overnight to call off the Israeli trip – although PM authorised it last night. Prefer it this way. He had Cabinet. Nothing on the agenda
but he took the opportunity to push the counter-inflationary policy.

Tom McNally – who is a very nice lad – told me that JC had said to him, 'You should keep close to Donoughue – he is politically shrewd.' From an old pro like him that is a particularly generous comment.

Lunch at No. 10 – we all waited around afterwards not knowing if there was to be a briefing or not. Finally when he woke up he called a quick meeting in his study and that was that. He has a quite different routine from Wilson. He reads his briefs over lunch in the study; then asks for notes on certain extra questions. Then when he gets them from Nick Stuart he is content. He does not want a crowd of people around him generally chatting in the way Harold did.

Questions went easily again, with JC presidentially tough. He does not mind ˙admitting saying that he does not know and will find out – something Harold could never bring himself to do.

The Unit had a meeting on economic policy. I spent some time with Andrew Graham*, who is sadly leaving us to return to his Oxford college, Balliol. He has been a great stalwart in the Unit, a crucial support to me when setting it up.

The PM gave a reception for the Labour MPs who had supported him in the first round of the ballot – a nice but undistinguished lot. His speech was excellent. He keeps saying that he means to restore some 'values' to politics – and I believe it.

Afterwards we had a dinner for Prime Minister [Robert] Muldoon* of New Zealand – an amiable but crude man. Jim again was superb, ignoring his written speech and talking off the cuff for fifteen minutes. Absolutely right in tone, and coming over with great conviction. All of us at No. 10 feel uplifted by his firm touch and sense that we have to get things right.

Home at 12.30 a.m.

Wednesday 14 April 1976

The PM did his junior appointments today. He sacked Alex Lyon* and then Bill Rodgers refused to take his job (there is nothing in the Home Office for Bill, without promotion and with a departing Roy). Subsequently Jim had another ill-tempered telephone exchange with Roy Jenkins. Things and relations are going very badly there.

The changes were not impressive – mainly rewards to Jim's own mediocre supporters, which is necessary in politics. Both Lovell-Davis and Crowther-Hunt* are out as 'Wilson lackeys'.

Had lunch with Joe [Haines]* and Margaret Jackson* [Beckett]. She is obviously doing well at Education and will go far. Joe is preparing to write his memoirs. He saw Harold Wilson for lunch yesterday and found him very cool.

Later in the day I worked on our big brief for him to study over the coming holiday, not leaving the office till 10 o'clock, very tired, and then having supper. But the brief looks good – a development of his TV theme on the restoration of responsible values in society – and it offers him a strategy and a style as Prime Minister, while nudging him to take up education as a policy theme.

Thursday 15 April 1976

JC saw Jack Jones* of the Transport Workers and Ron Hayward* from Party headquarters this morning, as part of the policy of maintaining good relations with the Labour movement. Also had his first Cabinet committee – energy, with a long agenda, including the tricky question of bribery involving BP and Shell. Lots of the new ministers were there and they seemed a bit grey – Tony Benn dominated them. The PM was well informed but spoke too much (beginner's nerves?). Joel Barnett* was uncharacteristic-ally weak and had to be rescued by Edmund Dell putting the Treasury position (from his own at the Board of Trade). The ministerial problem is that the government has lost a lot of weight and personality at the top – Castle, Jenkins (soon), Ross and Short gone. The new men lack charisma and magic.

I left in the middle and chatted outside to Sam Silkin*. He said that [Reginald] Maudling* is still not in the clear over the [John] Poulson* corrup-tion scandal.

Lunch at No. 10. I put in my brief and got away to Suffolk for a rest.

So the opening round is over. Jim has formed the new government. Not bad. Good political balance. But it lacks personality – and I suspect [David] Ennals* is not a good appointment at Health, a critical post for a Labour government. Jim must bring on the young men. Personally he has done well, giving an impression of being a Prime Minister in a way that Wilson often was not. He won't be as active – he complains about too much paper, and in the evening often looks tired, old and very grey. Nor does he yet understand the central machine as Harold did, but he will learn that. He is less accessible and does not chat or show his hand. None of us know what he is up to. McNally and McCaffrey don't know much more than the rest of us. But when we get to him he is straight and tells us exactly what he wants. Above all he does seem to have a stronger moral position than HW. He has a sense of wrong and right (as opposed to prejudices and senti-ments). That is refreshing.

A sad story. Earl Mountbatten came to the front door today, was let in, and was found wandering around the corridors. He said he was 'looking for Muldoon' who was here on Tuesday! They say his mind is going.

Easter 1976

I was on holiday in Suffolk, each day full of glorious sunshine, sleeping and reading in the garden, when the police car arrived from Bury St Edmunds. A message to say that the PM had asked me to supervise a speech he is giving the following week at Blackpool to USDAW.

So up I went to London on Tuesday morning, leaving our little thatched cottage at Wickhambrook at 7.25 a.m. and hitching a lift to Audley End. Arrived at No. 10 at 9.45 and started work on the speech – David Piachaud* from my Unit and Nigel Wicks* from Private Office had already done drafts. Worked all day (lunch with Nigel at the Reform) and finally finished and left for home at 10.30 p.m. Need not have taken that long really. Parkinson's Law. But also keen to get it right.

The PM telephoned me from the country at 11 a.m. We had a long talk. He said how much he liked the brief we put in last weekend. Wanted to talk about it. Also wanted me to come with him to Blackpool next Monday. He told me what he wanted to go into this speech.

Also asked about the reaction to his ministerial appointments. He said he was feeling a bit sorry about how he had treated Roy Jenkins and would look for ways to make up for that. But Roy was difficult. Jim was very nervy about the whole appointments business. He also said he had been pressed hard by the left to put Judith Hart* or Eric Heffer* in the Cabinet but he did not want to. He was sorry Norman Atkinson* had turned him down.

It was so good to have a long conversation about serious matters. And Jim obviously listens to what one says. An encouraging start for the Unit. We should have no difficulty finding a role.

Wednesday 21 April 1976

Worked on the Blackpool speech in the morning – it begins to look good. Finally cleared it with departments in the late afternoon. Lunch alone at the Reform. Beautiful sunny day. Not much happening really. Carol and children in the country.

Visit to Blackpool to make the speech is rearranged for Sunday.

Evening with our close friends Nori and Philip Graham*.

Thursday 22 April 1976

The PM came up from the country at about 10.45. I went up to him near the PA tapes and he asked me to come upstairs. We talked about the speech – he was using our draft, but he wanted to do his own speech in his own words.

Lunch in at No. 10, after a long Unit meeting discussing top pay policy. The PM saw his 'new' Cabinet ministers – Dell and Booth (Ennals abroad). Not because he had anything to say to them but so that he could appear to be busy. He also had a long chat with Merlyn Rees* about Ireland. Then he went back to the country. I went home early.

In my chat with him this morning I suggested he should invite 'disenchanted' backbenchers to dinner. He agreed – but objected when I mentioned David Marquand*, saying, 'What has he ever done in the House?' But he supported my suggestion of Phillip Whitehead.

Friday 23 April 1976

Worked all day in the Unit on the paper on top pay policy, criticising some very poor official papers, and on the PM's version of his speech. Also on a brief on the second round of wages policy. [Denis] Healey* met the TUC today and they rejected his 3% package. They asked for 6–7% on wages; a 5% ceiling on prices; and the full package of tax concessions. This is just not possible and would finish sterling – which remains under terrible pressure. But it is clear that Jack Jones and Len Murray* do want a helpful deal. Whether they will come down to a 3–4% package though remains in doubt. Healey was a bit depressed tonight and the PM was very jumpy when he phoned Private Office around 9.

I shall take our pay brief with me on the plane on Sunday to give it to the PM then. The duty clerk did not want to send it down because he complains if papers arrive unannounced in advance. This is very different from Wilson, who gobbled up all paper. Jim does not want too many papers, and likes to be warned in advance that they are coming. He also allows the private secretaries to 'take him through' the contents of boxes in the day, explaining verbally and getting a verbal reaction. Harold read it all late at night and scribbled his instructions on the papers.

We worked till after 10 p.m. and I came home very tired.

The Private Office is depressed. They had arranged a nice dinner for Harold Wilson with all his twenty-four private secretaries from his career as Prime Minister. For next Thursday. Marcia has sent a message cancelling it.

Joe Haines told me today that Wilson is upset by the *Sunday Times* investigation into his peerage lists and that Arnold Goodman* has told him that I am 'behind it'. Joe was worried. I am not. These echoes of that old paranoia just make me glad it is all over and behind me. Ironically of course it was not me who told Harry Evans* the details.

Sunday 25 April 1976

Went with the PM to the USDAW Conference at Blackpool. We flew in the HS125 jet from Gatwick at around 1.30 p.m. Jim was jumpy at first – said he did not like flying (but was pleased it was this jet and not the horrible old Andover) – complained we were not flying high enough – was upset that no arrangement had been made to take him to a hotel to settle down when we arrived: he doesn't like to go straight to a conference or speech. But he soon worked on his speech, writing in link sentences and making it more of a speech, less a script.

Over lunch on the plane I briefed him about problems with the arithmetic of Healey's pay package offer – and my worry that it is too long until the TUC Conference in June to approve the package. He listened, but then made it clear that was enough. He does not want too much new stuff fed to him in advance of a speech.

Blackpool looked unusually delightful with the tide out as we skimmed in to land over the sands.

On landing he said that he did not want to be whisked off straight away. He wanted to stand around a bit 'and get the feel of the ground'. And he did that, standing on the runway and chatting to the RAF staff. He also reacted against the No. 10 car waiting for him, saying that it was a waste of petrol to send up a car all the way from London in advance. This is for security, because the No. 10 Rover has special glass and a special floor against bombs. He apparently dislikes the whole paraphernalia of security.

Private Office is also troubled by his style of dealing with his overnight boxes. He doesn't write his wishes and instructions on the documents as Harold did. He says verbally what he wants to do – to whoever is around, who may be the foreign affairs secretary being instructed on complex economics, or often is just the garden-room girl. But the worst thing is that he actually loses papers, sometimes into his pockets. He does not send them back in an orderly fashion. So Private Office cannot find his economic papers for Tuesday's economic strategy meeting. None of my briefs have reappeared, although he does refer to them in detail verbally. He is not yet slotted in to the processing needs of the No. 10 machine. But he will.

I was in the sitting room at the Imperial alone with Jim – the same room in the same suite which Harold Wilson had at last September's Labour Party Conference. He was standing for some time looking nervously out of the window towards the sea. I said, 'It will go well. It's a good speech and they are a good union.' He replied, 'I'm pleased you said that. I needed somebody to tell me it would be OK. Audrey usually does that.' Then he marched out and we set off for the conference. As we entered the hall there was a spontaneous outburst of clapping and we all went up on to the platform.

Jim's speech was very powerful. He is an orator. He amended the speech as he went along, with a lot of ad-libbing. He feels for the audience reaction and then amends his text accordingly. Quite different from Harold who just read off the text like the football results. The audience was very attentive and gave him a standing ovation at the end.

We drove straight off to the airport. We were in the air by 4 o'clock.

He was obviously quite pleased. He said, 'I think I like being Prime Minister. Better than being Foreign Secretary.'

We read newspapers, had sandwiches and tea, and then landed at Northolt. I travelled back with him to his dingy flat in Kennington, along a dirty corridor with two policeman sitting guard on wobbly old wooden chairs. We chatted about improving arrangements for visits; about the incomes policy; about farming and how important it was to him to be able to relax. He said he could forget about everything on his Sussex farm. And that it meant he did not need to be PM. He said he could 'take it or leave it'. He had done all the big jobs now, and at 64 he was prepared to give it all up and retire to the farm. If there was any nonsense in the Party he would do that. He said he had told Michael Foot last week that it would no longer be said that MPs had to join the left-wing Tribune Group to get promotion. He was not going to put up with that kind of pressure.

He means to be tougher than Wilson – but he did not think HW was wrong. At that time it was necessary to conciliate. Now people wanted a tough lead.

At one point, just as we were going around Hyde Park Corner, he asked with genuine doubt: 'Well, Bernard, do you think I can do this job?' I reassured him, also genuinely. He is quite refreshing.

The car then drove me back to No. 10 and home – by 5.30 p.m., ready to watch the conference speech on TV. Amazing in five hours.

A lovely spring evening and I went for a long walk on the Heath to clear my head of aeroplane fatigue.

Monday 26 April 1976

The PM spent the morning at the liaison committee and the afternoon at the Commons. He went home to his flat by 7.30 p.m. Private Office closed down early and we all went home early. It is still not what we used to consider a full-time regime.

I worked in the Unit all day on papers, and discussing some economic briefs to put in to the PM. Had interesting lunch at the Gay Hussar with David Basnett, leader of the GMW union, and with Ken Griffin*, who is working to improve the relations between No. 10 and the trade unions. Basnett left early but was clearly interested.

Home by 8.15 p.m.

Harry Kissin* phoned to tell me that Lord Goodman told him that Harold is convinced I am behind the *Sunday Times* inquiry into his honours list and is getting paranoid about it. And that people are gossiping about HW's new office set-up. Echoes of another regime, now happily past! No. 10 seems incredibly sane by comparison now.

Tuesday 27 April 1976

At the EY [Cabinet Economic committee] at 10.30 on top pay the PM did not take our line – which was to reject all big increases for top earners. He said that the top chairmen in the nationalised industries had a 'real grievance'. Healey supported him. Foot and Booth took a line similar to ours – it would be crazy to jeopardise the second round of the incomes policy by doing anything provocative on top pay. Foot suggested that we put the problem to the TUC and CBI and ask for their help in solving it – and this gave the PM his compromise.

I left before the item on the debts of less developed countries. Outside I chatted to the Lord Chancellor about the proposed new chairman of the Royal Commission on the Law for which I had pressed – Henry Benson*. Elwyn Jones* claimed to have no knowledge of it, though there is a paper on file from his office claiming that the Lord Chancellor is strongly in favour of Benson – so he won't be for the kind of radical reform which the reactionary lawyers need.

I worked on papers and prepared the Unit for this afternoon's meeting with the PM. Lunch at No. 10, discussing speeches.

I went over for Question Time itself; where JC was totally dominant, squashing Tories like [Robert] Adley*, [Norman] Tebbit*, etc. JC is serious and magisterial; the Tories will have to put up somebody similar to reply.

I walked back to No. 10 and saw Roy Jenkins there, he having come to the wrong place for a meeting on direct elections. He was upset to be wrong and late and shouted at his driver. But he asked me to walk back with him and claimed to be feeling very happy.

Jim asked me in for five minutes before his meeting with the Policy Unit and we discussed how to handle the meeting. Then he was first class with the Unit, explaining his aims and philosophy, and greeting each person in turn. The Unit was delighted and came away refreshed and committed to work with enthusiasm. We sat for two hours afterwards, discussing work implications.

I was so involved that I walked to Charing Cross and took the Tube home, and had to turn round at Warren Street, remembering that I had left my car at Horse Guards Parade. Not home till 10 p.m. Feeling the pressure of a new regime.

Wednesday 28 April 1976

Drove in. Jim was at the NEC until midday and in the Unit we discussed briefs on child benefits (especially taking them away from Asian immigrants with children abroad) and on the Contingency Reserve, which has been totally spent in the first month of the financial year.

Jim came back in and had a secret meeting in the Cabinet Office with the ministers negotiating the new wage round with the TUC (Foot, Willams, Healey, Booth). They entered from No. 11 so that nobody saw them come in.

Out to lunch with Robin Butler*, previously in Private Office and now at the Treasury, at the Anglo–Belgian club. He said there is still great tension and rivalry between the Treasury and the Cabinet Office, personally between Douglas Wass* and John Hunt.

Back to a Cabinet committee meeting on BP bribes. Benn wanted a big inquiry, but most ministers felt that what had happened was part of the export world and we would damage ourselves if we set standards which nobody else would follow. Benn, who has never done a real job outside the public sector, was very much the Boy Scout in this.

Jenkins looked happy and relaxed, and I believe he has decided to resign early.

Feel that we did not get the immigrants child benefits questions quite right. Partly my desire to resist woolly Liberal 'nonsense' (most of these 'non-resident' children are 'non-existent'); partly I had a terrible headache, going home and straight to bed at 9.30 with a lot of Disprin. Will bring in Tom McNally, who is very sensible, earlier in future.

Thursday 29 April 1976

Went in early to the Economic Strategy Cabinet committee discussion on the wage negotiations with the TUC. Clearly they are not as well advanced as the newspapers believe. The TUC have put up a counter-package of around 5% total – but spread between minimum of £2.50 and up to £3.50. Plus prices ceiling of 5% (which is impossible) and all the tax reliefs.

Healey thinks this is too high, and so do most others, especially since we have spent $2.5 billion of our reserves in the past two months – not maintaining a parity rate, but simply smoothing out its fall. This is over one-third of our total reserves. This is crazy incompetent currency management by the Bank. What they needed was a single step devaluation – $2 to $1.80 as we recommended – and then use the reserves to defend that realistic rate. It is terrible. If there is a run now, after disappointment with the TUC agreement, then we have totally inadequate reserves to defend sterling. Most ministers – and especially PM – defended this view. But Albert Booth was very concerned we could push the trade unions too hard. If we don't, we are all bust.

Cabinet followed. On child benefits they decided to give benefits to non-resident (non-existent) children. Because they are afraid of being called racist and because Peter Shore* and John Silkin made emotional appeals from alleged principle (each having half their constituents from Pakistan).

Went for lunch with Will Plowden*. We each are thinking about the next job, eternally restless.

No briefing, just straight in to Questions, where Jim's authoritarian side begins to emerge more and more. He really lectures the Tories.

He saw Sydney Jacobson* of the *Mirror* about publicising counter-inflation policy – and Benn to tick him off for not supporting government policy at the NEC.

In the evening I went with Tom McNally and Carol to the premiere of the film *All the President's Men*. Entertaining but naive bit of humbug. Home midnight.

Friday 30 April 1976

Worked in the Unit in the morning. Also saw Anthony Lester*, who is preparing to go back from the Home Office to the Bar when Jenkins leaves in July (Jim has now formally offered Roy the European job, and talked to Helmut Schmidt* about it last night). Anthony said that Roy was considering leaving politics even before the Foreign Office question came up. He is fed up with the Party. So the denial of the Foreign Office simply acted as a catalyst.

Apparently Roy approached Jim before the leadership ballot and was brushed off. Roy apparently said that Jim is 'like a pretty girl at a dance, she seems desirable and you approach her, and then you find she has bad breath'.

Jim explained to us his excellent ideas for seeing ministers from each department individually and that he wants the Unit to brief him in advance of each meeting.

Had lunch with Tom McNally and we planned our future work together.

Worked in the Unit in the afternoon – particularly troubled about future staffing. Need people on the social policy side, but not 'bleeding hearts' who will bankrupt the country.

I stayed till 8 p.m. Then saw Harry Evans who told me about his *Sunday Times* stuff on the honours list. I tried to keep him to the serious side and away from attacking Wilson. Home at 9.30.

My daughter Rachel came back from her holiday in the West Country so we had a nice supper together.

Monday 3 May 1976

The PM was in a grumpy mood when he came in. Ken Stowe was running around about honours, so it was clear that Harold Wilson had pushed Jim when he saw him yesterday. Tom McCaffrey said he was for a leak inquiry and that it looked as if No. 10 was the source. In fact the *Sunday Times* has the full list – I don't know where from. Not from me, since I haven't seen it yet. But Lord Crathorne, a privy councillor on the scrutiny committee, who Harry Evans mentioned as a source yesterday, has clearly spilled the beans to the newspaper.

I went to the City to lunch with Grieveson Grant [the stockbrokers, with whom I had earlier contact as a client and a consultant]. They worryingly were expecting a pay settlement well below 5%. No hope!

Had long talk with Jack Straw* in the afternoon – I find him very nice, amusing and immensely well informed. Then for drinks and supper with Alf Morris and Jack Ashley discussing the disabled. Marvellous company as usual.

Tuesday 4 May 1976

Just missed the Economic Strategy committee this morning. Furious. But Nigel Wicks gave me complete debriefing afterwards. Lunch with Ralf Dahrendorf*, who is going to make a 'final offer' to me from the LSE about my future there, if any.

In the afternoon worked with Gavyn Davies* on a brief on the possible sterling crisis if we make a wage settlement that is too high. (Our reserves are perilously low.)

The ministers gathered at 10 p.m. to discuss pay policy. Healey reported, very pessimistically, that he was still trying for 4½%, but the TUC would not budge and wanted 5%. Jim was terrifically firm. He said 5% would damage the government's credibility and might destroy the currency. So the ministers went off to see the TUC again and we went back to No. 10.

We reassembled in the Cabinet Room (with Healey, Foot, Shirley Williams and Booth). They reported progress. The TUC would not shift. Healey wanted to settle for 5%. Jim said no – go away again and tell them that 5% would damage the currency. We sat there chatting and Healey came back alone. No progress. He wanted to settle at 5%. Jim said no – it would destroy the credibility of his government. So Healey went off again.

We sat there talking. Jim said he was prepared to resign. It would be the end of his government. He was not prepared to do what he thought was wrong. John Hunt and Ken Stowe were for settling, because to break off negotiations would be fatal. Tom McCaffrey and I were for taking a firmer line and trying to the end to beat the TUC down. Jim finally concluded that he would make an appeal to the TUC. But he would not threaten to resign. And if they would not come down from 5% he would have to accept.

This is what happened. At 1.30 a.m. the TUC Six came through from No. 11, where they had been negotiating with the Chancellor. We officials left the Cabinet Room except for John Hunt.

But I could clearly hear the discussion through the doors which lead from Ken Stowe's office through into the side of the Cabinet Room (I was standing near the doors, one of which was not properly closed). They went around the table. Jim made his appeal. Murray, Jones and the rest of the trade unionists said that 5% was the least that they could sell. They were not willing to bargain. So Jim said OK that is that. They broke up at about 2.30 a.m. I talked to the PM afterwards. We agreed that we could not finally have defended breaking off the negotiations over the difference between 4.6% and 4.8% – or 5% and 4½% depending on how one presents the sums. Nobody could predict which figure would be intolerable, which straw would break the City camel's back.

I stood in the hall of No. 10 talking with the PM for ten minutes before he left. He was clearly not happy with 5%, but was finally convinced that we had no alternative. What impressed me was his desire to do the right thing, and his willingness to resign if need be. That is very encouraging.

Home by taxi at 3.15 a.m.

Wednesday 5 May 1976

Went in at midday, missing the devolution Cabinet committee – which seems to have gone quite well and constructively.

The point about Jim is that he has three layers: on the surface is Simple Honest Bluff Jim. Below that is a very cunning and secretive politician. But beneath that is somebody who does believe in the simple and honest virtues.

Harold had two layers. On top was a devious clever political manipulator. Below that was a kindly timid insecure man. But nothing beneath that.

Saw adviser Chris Foster* about transport and housing policies. Not very encouraging about the DoE, who at official level want to do nothing, including about our plan to sell council houses. He says that Peter Shore gives the impression of being frightened of the immense tasks in that too-big department – and that Crosland left all the difficult problems behind unsolved.

Dinner with the new American ambassador, Mrs Armstrong. Sat between Lady Carver, wife of CIGS and very delightful – with whom I discussed India and the army – and the new American lady ambassador to Nepal (a divorcee from California, rather like Mae West, very rich but not very subtle).

Home at 11.45.

Thursday 6 May 1976

Cabinet discussed child benefits and decided to delay the introduction of the new scheme replacing tax allowances to fathers with actual payments to mothers. This is a bad decision which will upset the Party. It is terrible how it happened. Last week Cabinet decided to give benefits to children living overseas – which basically means half a million children of Asian immigrants. A crazy decision, since most of these children are non-existent as well as non-resident ('a fiddler's charter' as Tom McNally said). That cost £45 million and was decided because of an emotional speech by Peter Shore (whose constituents are Asian). Having decided to waste that £45 million, they then could not afford the full rate of child benefits under the excellent new scheme since it all comes out of the Contingency Reserve, which is already exhausted.

They dare not announce a lower rate for the new scheme than for the old, so they decided not to announce the scheme at all – one of the major planks in our election manifesto. What a cock-up.

I worked in the Unit in the morning. Had lunch with publisher George Weidenfeld*, who wants me to write all sorts of books, but did not mention peerages or Marcia. George is a natural Viennese 'courtier'. I am wary of him, although he is charming and energetic.

Incidentally Joe had lunch with Harold Wilson yesterday. He reported they chatted amiably but with little purpose. Harold hinted I was responsible for the press leak on his honours list. As evidence, he cited the fact that I had been at a *Daily Mail* lunch on Monday talking about Jarvis Astaire's* prospective honour. This is actually evidence of his sickness. In fact it was Bernard Delfont, showbiz brother of Lew Grade, at the *Daily Mail* lunch. He has converted Bernard Delfont into Bernard Donoughue! Despite the fact that I have never and would never set foot in the evil *Daily Mail*.

Question Time went as before, with Jim completely dominant.

I went back to the deputy secs meeting on next week's government business, and then started work on the speeches. Jim has put McNally in charge, but it is clear that he won't have time to do them. So in the Unit we have to do three distinct drafts – for the CBI, for the Inland Revenue Conference, and for the trade union MPs. Gavyn Davies did a first draft on one of them this evening.

Went home at 9 p.m.

Friday 7 May 1976

Spent all day sweating away on the speeches. Tom did not manage to do anything at all in the end. We produced a full and good draft for the CBI. A sketchy piece for the Inland Revenue. And a detailed note for the trade union group. It was a gloriously hot day – over 80° – and very irritating to have to sit in a hot office for twelve hours. Still the speeches had to be done for the PM's weekend box.

I did not see him today. Apparently he was in a very bad mood after the bad local election results. He has clearly snapped at Private Office – which is still not working smoothly. His instructions are still not clear and his paperwork is erratic. So the machine is not smooth.

Went home and ran into local friends and went for drinks until 1.15 a.m. Very hot and difficult to sleep. Woke at 5 a.m. and read – finishing William Clark's *No. 10*.

Monday 10 May 1976

These daily diary pieces should now hopefully be much shorter. I no longer feel the incentive or need to record all the details as I did with the Wilson regime. Callaghan is more regular, less Byzantine and extraordinary.

Went to lunch at *The Economist*. A young team. Dick Leonard* nice as ever. The two women – Sarah Hogg* and Anne Lapping* – are bright. But I got no sense of the editor, Andrew Knight*, who is clearly a very smooth young man.

Home quite early, to look after the children – Carol away at an NUT conference.

Tuesday 11 May 1976

Spent the morning working on our education paper, which was intended to go in today but is now delayed till Friday. JC's programme of seeing ministers individually about their work has aroused great interest among ministers – an excellent idea. But he is getting frightened of it, and keeps delaying his first meeting (with Fred Mulley* on education).

After lunch in No. 10 JC suddenly announced he was going to have a Questions briefing at 2.30 (despite his earlier cancellation of this Wilsonian practice). Apparently John Cunningham had recommended it. But Jim really resented it and arrived very grumpy. He began picking on us all, challenging us to make some 'sensible points'. We were unprepared – some had been summoned dashing back from posh restaurants. We were convinced that he did not really want a briefing. He looked tired and kept rubbing his eyes while complaining that we had deprived him of his sleep. It was not a happy occasion. But he was OK in Questions, still dominating the chamber.

I went to watch football at Wembley in the evening with [Sports minister and friend] Denis Howell*, who told me that the DoE had a discussion on our Unit's proposal for the sale of council houses that morning. Peter Shore is feeling his way carefully. Nobody told Shore that the whole issue had already been thrashed out and agreed at Cabinet committee level.

In the afternoon I attended a senior Treasury meeting with the top public expenditure officials Leo Plietzky* and Fred Jones*. They are very worried. They said the local authorities' spending was still out of control and unless we devised ways to harness them we would be bust.

Wednesday 12 May 1976

Began with 9.45 Statistics committee – mixed ministers and officials under Edmund Dell – in the Cabinet Office to discuss proposed cuts in statisticians to save money. I disliked the way the permanent secretary at the Board of Trade, Thornton, kept referring slightingly to statisticians as if they were completely irrelevant to government.

JC was all day at the NEC, fighting off a mad left-wing policy paper from Transport House.

We had a working lunch in the Unit. Then I saw Joe Haines at the Commons. He had been to a press lunch for Wilson who had sounded off again about South African conspiracies. The point is that HW suffered these paranoid delusions while PM, but his advisers restrained him from displaying them too much in public. Now he has no such restraint.

Albert Murray* joined us and told us that HW is working from Lord North Street, Albert and the secretaries are in the Embankment office, and Marcia is at home in Wyndham Mews.

Wilson has now formally seen the people on his honours list – some of whom are disappointed at being downgraded following press criticism. James Goldsmith* is now only a knight! Goldsmith is furious, threatening to leave the country.

I went to a curious dinner at the Coq d'Or given by some Americans from Georgetown University for 'distinguished' Britons – Peter Jay*, John Mackintosh* MP and myself. I smelled the CIA even before the lady next to me revealed that she did work for them. Peter Jay spoke brilliantly and pessimistically.

Thursday 13 May 1976

Worked in the Unit in the morning. The PM had Cabinet, mainly on the proposed cuts in Civil Service numbers which had been agreed in Cabinet last year – in the end they reversed the earlier decision and decided no cuts, just no increases. Typical victory by the Whitehall machine.

In the afternoon went to a meeting in John Hunt's palatial room in the Cabinet Office to discuss the new monthly report on economic indicators. It is terrible. A banal covering note by Bryan Hopkin* of the Treasury, and then a lavatory roll of statistics, with no selection or emphasis. Try to sort it out and the Central Statistical Office graciously accepted our (Gavyn Davies's) suggestions for improvements.

Home feeling very exhausted.

Friday 14 May 1976

Went in to the office with my brother Clem, who was off to live in my house in France. Had a meeting with the Unit and Tom McNally at 10.30 on education and on council house sales, both for this evening. I sat till lunch redrafting our brief.

Lunch with old *Times* friend Mike Cudlipp* at Wheelers. Feeling quite ill, with tonsillitis and a temperature.

Finally left at 5 p.m. and went home briefly to bed leaving our two drafts ready. In the evening had a nice dinner with Ralf Dahrendorf from the LSE, and Sheila and John Hale* (he was my Oxford tutor on the Italian Renaissance). When they left at midnight I collapsed into bed feeling very ill.

On Saturday I felt just as bad.

Monday 17 May 1976

Ron Spiers*, political counsellor from the US Embassy, came in this morning. Said everybody assumes that the Democrats will win the presidential election and then they will all be moved, including the new ambassador, so there is a touch of 'lame duck' about everything here.

Lunch with my friend Graham Greene* who is head of publisher Jonathan Cape at the Garrick. Discuss Joe Haines's explosive book and how to handle it. Afternoon working on Unit papers. Feeling tired and very in need of a holiday.

Phoned Joe – who is as puzzled as everybody why Wilson is pushing his 'South African plot' so hard. When he was here there was no evidence. The intelligence people looked at it and found nothing. Some people think HW is setting up a smokescreen for when something is revealed about him.

Tuesday 18 May 1976

Defence committee discussed Chile and Iceland (where Crosland opposed his own official Foreign Office paper recommending total and ignominious withdrawal from Iceland's waters).

Cabinet took child benefits and decided to defer the new scheme for three years. Mainly because it means a transfer of cash out of the man's wage packet to the mother's purse – and will therefore mean a real cut in the wage-earner's take-home pay. Jim thinks that is bad. Most of the Cabinet thought the same. So he is taking the risk of abandoning a major manifesto commitment within six weeks of taking office. That could be dangerous.

Had Policy Unit lunch, discussing future briefs – and new staff. Questions went easily as usual.

Interviewed Liz Arnott from Transport House for the social policy position in the Unit to replace David Piachaud, who to my great sadness is returning to the backwaters of the LSE.

Home very tired and strained.

Wednesday 19 May 1976

The PM was away all day giving speeches at Scarborough. I worked in the Unit.

Lunch at the Reform.

Home 9 p.m. Still feel unwell.

Thursday 20 May 1976

Put in a brief with some radical names for membership of the new Royal Commission on Legal Services, especially Michael Zander* and Joe.

Lunch with David Basnett of the GMW union at the Etoile. Discussed better liaison between No. 10 and TUC (he complained that we had relaxed the price code without consulting the trade unions).

JC asked me to travel over to Questions in the car with him. Mainly discussed child benefits, and he was very nervy that he will be rightly blamed for abandoning the manifesto.

At the deputy secs meeting today John Hunt revealed his intention to spring massive increases in nationalised board salaries on 10 June – six days before the TUC Conference. It is mad and I said so. Afterwards Ken Stowe said, 'John Hunt has too many dinners with the nationalised board chairmen. He is trying to look after them.' It could wreck the pay policy. I returned and warned Tom McNally. If Jim ignores politics and relies on the Cabinet secretary he will end up where Ted Heath did – out.

Home at 9 p.m.

Friday 21 May 1976

The meeting on education with Mulley was delayed an hour because of a sudden Defence committee decision to authorise Crosland to do a fishing deal with the Icelanders. Mulley came at 11. JC asked me and Ken Stowe to attend. He quizzed Mulley for a solid hour, very cleverly, innocent questions, but absolutely on the ball. The weaknesses of the DES – and Mulley – were exposed. The PM never looked at his brief, but used every point. His style is always the same – he absorbs the points, digests, and then regurgitates in a totally different form. Afterwards he said how good the briefs were – ours and the Cabinet Office's.

Then held a meeting on his future regional visits. Tom McNally and I managed to insert some politics into the choice – and I suggested my favourite India for an overseas visit.

Home at 8.45 p.m.

With Cyprus in the air – the select committee has attacked JC for his handling of it – I can only laugh at those who now say we should have taken military action when the Turks invaded. At the time of the crisis, on the key Saturday morning, Defence secretary Roy Mason's* private secretary failed to arrive. Mason was unable to operate his 'hotline' telephone. The Ministry of Defence got the time of the Turkish invasion wrong – they knew it was 'dawn' but failed to allow for the time difference in the eastern Mediterranean. And the Phantom aircraft we sent lacked the essential equipment to give good support. So JC was quite right not to get militarily involved with such a mess!

Monday 24 May 1976

Dentist in the morning. Lunch with David Shapiro, an old Oxford friend. Afternoon clearing papers.

6 p.m. to JC's meeting with junior ministers. Many ministers took the

opportunity to make their big speech to impress the new PM. But some good ideas emerged – especially concern with the inner-city problem.

Afterwards I worked on a brief on huge salary increases to nationalised industry chairmen. The official paper is a disgrace, completely ignoring the PM's summing up at the last Economic Strategy committee (MES). We are pressing for rejection. The idea of announcing £100 a week rises for chairmen of bad nationalised industries at the same time as asking the miners to accept £4 seems crazy to me. But the civil servants have made promises to the chairmen – some of whom are former civil servants.

Tuesday 25–Thursday 27 May 1976

The top-pay issue dominated these days. At one point the PM sent for Hunt and Ken Stowe. Apparently he gave Hunt a real rocket for trying to bounce the increases through before the holiday. Told him that the proposals were bad and contrary to what he had asked for and called off the Cabinet committee meeting arranged for the following day. Hunt went away with his tail between his legs.

Next day – Thursday – after Questions Tom McNally told me that Jim had said he did not like Hunt and was thinking of sacking him. Tom asked if I wanted to put the boot in. I replied that I was not interested in just Hunt-baiting. Actually Hunt is very efficient at delivering policy and an effective Whitehall machine operator. The problem comes when he tries to run policy his own way. Providing Jim runs him, he will do as well as any. But Jim has got to control him – which Harold Wilson rarely ever did.

The honours list was finally published – with all those original names except Jarvis Astaire, Illtyd Harrington* and David Frost* (who was struck off because of his direct financial involvement with Wilson through the Yorkshire TV contract due to be announced next week). Jimmy Goldsmith had at first been totally struck off the list because of objections from several official quarters, including the Inland Revenue and the Bank of England (I saw the files), but was restored with simply a knighthood which infuriated him.

The Philip Allen* inquiry into the 'leak' of the honours produced no result. Wilson, although he demanded that the inquiry take place, refused to allow Allen to interview anybody in Harold's own office.

The list was properly denounced by all and sundry. HW issued a statement saying that the list was 'his'. Harold told me that he 'did not know half the people' on the list.

Friday 28 May–Sunday 6 June 1976

I was in France with my brother Clem.

   There was a sterling crisis. The Treasury and Bank decided to go to the International Monetary Fund and get a six months loan swap facility. The PM resisted a Treasury attempt to bounce through a package of public expenditure cuts without ministerial consideration. Healey had arranged for the Governor to come to see the PM – but he refused and sent a message telling him not to come. Jim said that he knew what the Governor would say and he did not want to hear it. He also said that they should try to get a loan without cuts. And this they did – though only six months of swap facility and not the long-term loan which is needed. Still it was a bounce which was well resisted.

Monday 7 June–Friday 11 June 1976

I went to see Jim on Wednesday evening **[9 June]** and discussed the sterling crisis. We had a good half-hour talk. I said that I was worried about the attempted 'bounce' in last week's crisis. I am sure that the Bank will spend the new swap facility quickly and we will be forced to go to the IMF for a full loan and then will have the cuts forced on us. This will damage or destroy the wages policy and that could be the end of his government.

   He listened hard and made a few points – including that we must make cuts. I agreed, but said that the cuts must be politically chosen by him and Healey, not imposed by foreign bankers. He said he would see Healey tomorrow after Cabinet.

   This Wednesday evening was also the day of the great vote of censure. Jim had made a splendid speech – much of which he wrote himself at home alone in his little flat in Kennington this morning. Thatcher made a poor speech and was in great disarray. I was there drinking with Labour backbenchers till 1.15 a.m. and their spirits were high. Enormous praise for Jim.

   After the vote (we won by 19) we gathered in Jim's room – the two Toms, John Cunningham and myself, and we discussed the general situation. We all praised Jim for his speech, but then warned him that it could go wrong before the autumn. He has got to handle the politics very carefully. I pointed out that even the Puerto Rico summit was a political occasion – a reference to the fact that he was not taking there any of his political staff. Afterwards he asked McNally to come with him!

   It was a very hot summer night and I drank on the terrace with various MPs – talking with Gerry Fowler* about overseas students; with Margaret Jackson about Jim attending an NUT conference; with George Cunningham* about the government's volte-face on child benefits; with Tom Pendry* and

Arthur Bottomley* socially; with Michael English* about his select committee on the Civil Service; with various others socially. The House was alive and fascinating and I loved being there. But not as an MP, thank God!

Next day I had a long talk with Healey, walking through to No. 11 with him. He was very pleased with himself, but critical of his official advisers. I gathered from him and from the private secretaries that Jim had put to him all the points I put to him.

Earlier in the week a Cabinet committee discussed a proposal to raise public sector pensions in line with the historic RPI. This will give them 15% when everybody else has 4½%. I strongly briefed Jim opposing this. In the committee every minister spoke in favour of doing it. Summing up Jim said, 'The committee is unanimous. Except for me. I think you are wrong. This is a question of politics. I want it to go to Cabinet where I will minute my dissent.' I was pleased he followed our brief.

Friday 11 June was an all-day Cabinet on Europe. I did not attend, but I was at the lunch upstairs, sitting next to Roy Jenkins. We discussed the affair of his not getting the Foreign Office. He said, quite correctly, that Jim had already decided this in advance. He said that actually he did not want to go back to the Treasury. He also said that his personal preference all along had been to take the European presidency. He said that 'others persuaded me that I ought to have the Foreign Office. I always really preferred Europe.' He would not say when he was going to resign, and has not told Jim, but hinted it would be rapidly after the European Council in July.

Saturday 12 June was Trooping the Colour. It was strikingly different from previously in one respect. Jim came down from the flat at 10.40 a.m. and wandered into the reception rooms where the children were (all the VIPs had gone on to the stand). He spoke first to every single child in the room, and to the messengers and waitresses. He was friendly and relaxed and a proper host. My daughter Katie said, 'Famous people don't usually talk to children,' and 'He is friendlier than Mr Wilson, he is a family man.'

At dinner with Sir Pat Nairne* on Friday at his Surrey home was Philip Moore*, assistant secretary to the Queen. He was trying to arrange for Prince Charles to spend a year in the Civil Service learning about government – he said, 'Prince Philip has never understood how government works.' He then revealed that in recent years the Queen has ceased to give audiences to individual ministers. She had begun to see permanent secretaries – after twelve months in office and then on retiring. That is a real symbol of the changing balance of power in our system – away from ministers towards the civil servants.

Monday 14 June 1976

Last week Jim slept one night in No. 10 – and hated it. He went around moaning all day. The private secretaries say that it is a calculated game by him to prove that they should not live in the No. 10 flat. He does not want to do so because he does not want people – especially his sister – to come and stay with him. While they are in Kennington he can argue that that flat is too small!

This afternoon Jim had another individual ministerial meeting – with [Eric] Varley* on industry. He asked me to attend. He was very good, using our brief, but bringing it out quite differently.

Varley was very nervous at first. Apparently Mulley had warned him it was a very testing occasion. But he did quite well – except he did not seem to realise the scale of financial assistance from the government to industry – about £4 billion. Jim pushed him towards greater selectivity, and asked him to come back with some precise proposals. Afterwards Jim thanked me for the Unit paper, which he said was very good.

Tuesday 15 June 1976

Attended the Cabinet committee on imports, based on a paper by Peter Shore calling for import controls and various papers from the Chancellor, officials, etc. opposing them. It was a good, intelligent discussion. This particularly pleased the PM, who is keen to defuse this issue. Healey and Dell opened by speaking against. Supported briefly by Roy Jenkins. Shore put his case for import controls well and moderately. He said that if Healey's present strategy worked that was fine. But if it failed, we had a crisis and were forced to go to the IMF, then he wanted this alternative to be considered. Crosland said he sympathised with Shore, and rejected many of the arguments of those opposed to imports, but at this time it was simply not on – it was not acceptable internationally. Varley was also ambivalent. He was against, but warned that the erosion of our industrial base was not stopping, and that the TUC would continue to be interested in import restraints.

Benn put his case for a siege economy without compromise. He rejected Shore as too modest. He said one should do all or nothing – he was for all. He said we should 'rebuild behind a full tariff wall . . . we need a big scheme – something on the trade balance, something to control currency transactions, and import controls'. He was clearly convinced the economic revolution would come anyway.

JC summed up against import controls but he said there should be no minutes of the meeting. Then he said that the government probably would have to cut public expenditure. But it must be done by the Cabinet, not by the IMF (which is what I told him last Wednesday). So he authorised Healey to bring his public expenditure cuts to this committee whenever he was ready. He is preparing the way for a cuts package. In a relaxed atmosphere, with no atmosphere of hysteria. And he is excluding 'bounces' by authorising Healey to do it regularly and calmly.

Afterwards I chatted with Jim at the telex. He was very pleased especially with how calmly they had discussed imports – 'without rancour'. This is what he wants, calm discussion.

Wednesday 16 June 1976

In the morning I attended an Energy Cabinet committee. Discussed changes in our nuclear programme – abandoning our 1974 decision to build steam generators. What emerged was we don't have an energy strategy. Each section of it goes ahead (or stagnates) quite independently. Benn as minister was being fairly slippery but Jim kept him well under control. Benn basically wants to stop the nuclear programme to please the left.

Lunch with Michael and Hugh Cudlipp* at the Reform.

Afterwards to House of Commons to see the new Palantype machine which would enable Jack Ashley and all deaf people to follow the proceedings of the Commons on a kind of small television set on his lap. Very pleased because I influenced Wilson to support this for Jack.

Then to the DES to talk to the chief inspector of schools, Miss Brown, a small birdlike woman, very bright, but with something grey and barren about her. Inevitably unmarried. All these people who run our education system, ministers or civil servants, are unmarried or married without children. We clashed sharply on several issues but ended up getting on quite well. I had first met her at Oxford when, as Dean of Somerville College for women, she found me there early one Sunday morning having stayed illicitly overnight. She kindly took no action.

Went to the pub with Tom McNally and then home at 9 p.m.

Thursday 17 June 1976

Before Cabinet I chatted to Edmund Dell about British cars. He said that when British Leyland brought out the new Princess, the Board of Trade ordered one. In the past year three of them have gone completely wrong and had to be withdrawn.

Went over to the Treasury at 11 a.m. to see Joel Barnett on fees for overseas students. This has got into a terrible bog. The Treasury asked for fees of £1,800 p.a. DES put up a scheme for £600 for home and overseas, but it is such a bad paper that it was thrown out in Cabinet committee a few weeks ago. They have now refined it. I saw Gerry Fowler about it on Tuesday afternoon and we now have the makings of a compromise (fees of £650 for undergraduates, £750 for graduates, but no quota). Discussed this with Joel Barnett who was very helpful and constructive. Seems to have agreement, so won't have to go to Cabinet, thank God, where nobody would understand the details.

Cabinet ended around noon, but the PM had a meeting in his study after that to discuss today's leak of a Cabinet document on child benefits to *New Society*. Everybody is very agitated. I got angry because the civil servants in Private Office began to talk about the special advisers being responsible for the leak – with no evidence at all. Then I learned that the duty clerk had actually told the PM that they thought it was Tony Lynes (the special adviser in DHSS). I was fuming at Question Time and told Private Office that I hoped we were not going to have a repetition of last time, when there was suspicion of special advisers and the PM was told he would have to sack the culprit and announce it publicly – until a regular civil servant confessed and then nothing more was heard of it.

This evening, after the meeting of deputy secretaries, Ken Stowe came to see me. He said that they now suspected a regular civil servant in DHSS! I told him that I was a bit unhappy, sensing a general squeeze on special advisers. And that Tom McNally was annoyed at being left off the trip to Bonn (he has now been put on; but this exclusion comes immediately after a row he had about being left off the trip to Puerto Rico). These small battles for inclusion and for status are very boring and irritating. But Ken is a good straight man with whom I can discuss these problems openly.

Finally went home at 8.30.

Joe Haines telephoned – I had lunch with him and Graham Greene today about his book, *The Politics of Power*. He said that H. Wilson had sent for Janet Hewlett Davies, Joe's former assistant at the Press Office under Harold, this afternoon. He was worried about the book Joe was writing. He said he had spoken to Barnetson of United Newspapers about a job for Joe and Barnetson would be approaching Joe. But it depended on the book . . . In other words – Joe only gets a job if he plays ball on not writing about Harold and Marcia in the book.

Joe said, 'That is the wrong way to treat me. You know my reaction to that.' He is quite fed up with Wilson now.

Friday 18 June 1976

PM away in the North for the day.

The atmosphere in No. 10 is very jumpy because of the *New Society* leak of Cabinet minutes on child benefits. Everyone going around putting the finger on everybody else – and especially on the special advisers. Douglas

Allen, the helpful head of the Civil Service, sent for me – as 'head' of the special advisers – at 5 p.m. to discuss it in general. He did not seem to have much idea who the culprit was. He said he did not believe it was Tony Lynes (the *Sun* is going to name him as the culprit tomorrow, but without evidence). Journalists tell me that the Civil Service briefing is to blame special advisers.

Had lunch with David Jones*, the new deputy sec on industry questions, in the Cabinet Office. Seems very capable. Afterwards we did a brief for the Puerto Rico summit on funding the sterling balances/debts.

Home at 8.30, very depressed. Feel that we special advisers are very vulnerable, and nobody is defending us.

Monday 21 June 1976

The PM was at the TUC Labour Party committee at the Commons most of the morning.

Joe Haines came in to No. 10 at 11.30 and we discussed his book – he is making remarkable progress, already 40,000 words, and it is very good. All the flavour of Downing Street politics.

I went to lunch with David Basnett, the boss of the GMWU (my union), at the Reform. He was very late arriving from the liaison meeting, but he said it had gone well and Jim was good. He told them that if they wanted to bring down the Labour government, so be it, but he was not going to compromise. We also discussed public expenditure. Basnett said that cuts must not be sprung on the TUC. They must, be put first to the Neddy Six to consider how best to handle them. ['Neddy' was the popular name for the National Economic Development Council, a forum for consultation between government, management and trade unions. There were six union leaders on the Council.]

Went back to an Energy Cabinet committee meeting at No. 10. Discussing BP partial privatisation and how to get it to give the state 51% participation. Benn is for a tough line, with threats. [Harold] Lever* for a softer line. In the end the PM backed Benn, though forbidding any threats. He wants to keep Benn sweet for public expenditure cuts next week!

Went to the LSE in the evening to see the new Strand House library building. Encouraging. Dahrendorf is still very good.

Tuesday 22 June 1976

I worked in the Unit. Had lunch at No. 10. Then to Questions, which went easily as usual. Jim completely dominates them.

After tea went to a meeting in Leo Plietzky's room in the Treasury. He revealed his schemes for public expenditure cuts next month. Leo is good in that he does bring us in. But he does ramble on interminably, never letting his assistants speak. In the end it was clear that he had decided we could get away with about £1 billion cuts and so he would go for that. He never said whether it was for reasons of confidence, reserves shortage, money supply, etc. It was a figure, with no rational base other than that he was convinced they could get it.

Afterwards I went to the North St Pancras Labour management committee. Terrible. Constantly passing mad motions denouncing the government. If ever the Party – and government – is really controlled by these middle-class, left-wing neurotics, who represent and are typical of nobody but themselves, then that is the end of either the Labour government or of Britain.

Home at 11.30 p.m., had a cold snack before bed. It was terribly hot – over 90° today and 70° in the evening. Too hot to sleep.

Wednesday 23 June 1976

The PM was occupied this morning with French President Valéry Giscard* – and while he and others were away, the Labour National Executive committee voted against the new social contract. (Later Jim said, 'It doesn't matter, what has this NEC got to do with a Labour government anyway.')

The Giscard lunch was pleasant, though unbearably hot. Jim was relaxed, affable, clearly wanting to improve relations with the French. Giscard was polished, elegant and witty. He spoke in French after lunch, though beforehand I talked with him in his excellent English. I said that my Policy Unit was based on the French 'Cabinet' system. He replied that he thought they had gone too far – and that the political appointees came between the ministers and the civil servants.

In the evening I went across to the Commons for a drink on the terrace. Had a long talk with David Owen. He is locked in battle with his Health Department trying to get them to cut staff numbers. They are refusing – though he has found out that in recent years their number at under-secretary level and above has increased by 35%! We agreed that the bureaucracy is now beyond control, and that ministers won't do anything because they enjoy the comforts too much.

Then back to the Unit where David Piachaud, Gavyn Davies and I worked until nearly midnight preparing our brief on public expenditure.

Thursday 24 June 1976

Cabinet, mainly on 'Parliamentary Business'. It is quite striking how, compared to two years ago, this item has expanded in Cabinet business. Discussing how to manage our Commons minority now sometimes takes over an hour. The only 'business' item was the counter-inflation White Paper, mainly on modifying price controls, and that went through fairly easily.

Lunch with Robert Armstrong* at the Athenaeum. Pleasant as ever. He said that his Home Office is getting a bit slack now Roy Jenkins is leaving. Things are left to slip, which is never good. He also told me that Max Rayne*, who got a peerage on HW's notorious list, only received his letter from HW on the Tuesday asking for a reply by return of post since the announcement was on Thursday. It was a last-minute inclusion to give the list respectability – as was Anne Crossman, who declined to give this façade.

At the deputy secs meeting John Hunt revealed the Treasury's public expenditure plans and the proposed timetable – three Cabinets between 8 and 22 July.

The Treasury wants agreement on detailed cuts at the first meeting. Hunt rightly thinks that is crazy; much better to get the principle and the global figure agreed. Then the detail follows. Hunt has put in a good brief to the PM pointing out that the worst outcome is to go openly for a July package and then fail. But the PM has brushed him aside, and sent a telegram to Healey in Paris on Wednesday (for the OECD) saying that we must push ahead and get the cuts now. A meeting has been arranged for Chequers on Saturday afternoon before they all take off for Puerto Rico. The PM has asked me to attend. This puts even more pressure on us for our brief, which must be good.

In the early evening went to see Victor Rothschild* at his flat in St James's. About the Royal Commission on Gambling. He wants to recommend a football levy, but thinks the pools cannot bear much more, and doesn't know how to distribute it. I put to him my plans for a Sports Levy Board, like the horse-racing levy. We had a plateful of smoked salmon and a large gin fizz, and finished by discussing whether I should go to work for Rothschild. He thinks I would be bored.

Walked back in the stifling heat across St James's Park, already parched brown. Worked till 11.15 in No. 10 on our briefing. Appallingly sticky in No. 10. But can now see the way through – and Gavyn has proposed a brilliant brief. Home at midnight.

Friday 25 June 1976

The PM had his Puerto Rico briefing, and then Henry Kissinger* called on him. I saw Hal Sonnenfeldt*, Kissinger's aide, separately. Discussed the currency. I stressed that the US must back us and sterling with patience while we got public expenditure straight. And in Puerto Rico they should try to deal with funding the sterling balances. We agreed to meet tomorrow at Claridge's for breakfast. I cancelled lunch with journalist Peter Jenkins* and worked right through till evening finishing the brief.

Then had two pints at the Reform with Douglas Wass from the Treasury, discussing tomorrow's Chequers meeting. He agrees that the only ground for cuts is sterling confidence, but says Healey has told them he cannot sell them that so they must make an economic case on resource grounds, even if it doesn't exist. Wass as always is very frank and open, though not always strong. One understands why the Treasury has so many views. But I like him.

Home at 8.30 – then off to Brian Knox's* party in his lovely garden by the Heath. Home at midnight, but still too hot to sleep (the temperature in London today was 96°). A bit nervous about tomorrow's Chequers meeting but looking forward to it. It could destroy the government.

Saturday 26 June 1976

The car collected me immediately after lunch on Saturday and we drove to Chequers in enormous heat – the last stretch of winding country road was melting and the sticky tar slowed the car and made an odd tearing sound.

I arrived early – round 3.05 – but John Hunt was already there closeted with the PM. They were discussing the child benefits leak. The PM said, 'At first I thought it was a special adviser, but I have gone cold on that.'

We gathered in the downstairs lounge – the PM, Healey, Wass, Derek Mitchell*, John Hunt, Tom McNally, Tom McCaffrey and myself. Tony Crosland was an hour late and missed much of the discussion.

The PM opened. He had our Green Paper on his knee, and expressed our view that there was little case for cuts on resource grounds.

Healey replied for about twenty minutes. His arguments slid from 'resource' reasons to 'currency confidence' reasons. He also quoted the latest medium-term assessment in support of cuts, saying it showed a rise in manufacturing output next year of 9½%, which needed cuts to make more 'resource space'. Yet when we asked what extra unemployment this involved, he dodged it and said that he did not believe the unemployment forecast. He had a list of proposed £1 billion and £2 billion cuts and said he would hand copies round, but never got round to it.

The PM commented that it seemed to mean that 'our economic strategy is not viable'. Healey bridled at this. The PM added that we could probably make the cuts and get them through the Cabinet, but he was 'not sure whether we would have a Party at the end of it'. Crosland was there by then and made the same points on resource arguments which we had made. He was gently sceptical.

John Hunt then asked a key question – could the £1 billion cuts carry over from 1977–8 to 1978–79?

The Treasury team looked bewildered. They had clearly not thought of this. Crosland came in here and pointed out that if true, it implied big deflation in 1978–80, when nobody believed there would be resource pressures.

Jim summed up that the debate had been opened. In fact he is firmly in favour of cuts. But he preserved an appearance of open-mindedness and by criticising the Treasury arguments retained his own authority – and freedom to change his mind if he wished.

My own final conclusions were that there are arguments for cuts now – decisively on currency grounds, and also, but not decisively, on grounds of administrative convenience, since if you are going to cut, then the sooner the better, or else the savings do not come through quickly enough. There are also grounds for cuts on money supply basis; and possibly because of the expected big rise in output. But neither of these needs cuts now – the autumn would do.

I suspect a strong motive with Jim is that he wants this cuts issue out of the way this session, before the holiday, so we can start the next session with a clean sheet.

We broke and had tea at about 5.15, served in the main lounge. I chatted with Crosland and the PM. Both Crosland and I made points critical of the Treasury case. Jim said, 'Those are good destructive points – but what do we do?' Jim went into a side lounge to discuss sterling 'intervention policy' privately with Healey. I walked round the garden and passing an open window heard the PM say loudly and firmly to Healey, 'Never mind if sterling drops four cents, don't throw all the reserves away defending it.'

It was a glorious June evening. I thought of going for a swim in the Chequers swimming pool. But Healey had swum before the meeting and said it was so warm it was not in fact refreshing. At six o'clock there was a sudden buzz of activity and they all dashed into their cars, some to go off to London Airport and by Concorde to Puerto Rico. I felt a bit left out. I miss the excitement and movement of the foreign trips. But I really did not want to go to South America and back within twenty-four hours.

In the evening Carol and I went to a nice party with Naomi and Andrew Macintosh* in Highgate. Ken Berrill* was there. He told me he is fed up. He is not enjoying running the CPRS, and does not think he is getting on with Jim. He said that he intends to go and earn some money – and that

I should have his job. He spoke to Carol and said, 'Bernard is serious about policy; I am an operator.'

Monday 28 June 1976

The PM away in Puerto Rico. I went in late morning, briefed the staff about Saturday. Then to Grieveson Grant for lunch and home with Joe Haines in the afternoon.

Nice story about dear Fred Mulley. Tony Crosland said he went up to canvass Fred before the first round leadership vote, and said, 'What are you going to do about the leadership election, Fred?' – meaning who would he vote for. Mulley replied, 'Well I have not put my hat in the ring yet, but if there is a deadlock I will move in.' Fred would get only one vote – his own. Politicians have little self-awareness.

Tuesday 29 June 1976

The PM slept much of the morning, having arrived at London Airport at 6 a.m.

I went to lunch with Ted Short at the Reform. I always like him. He says he is miserable at being underemployed (having been dropped by Jim) and is clearly keen to get a job. He wants to go to the Lords as soon as possible. He told me that after the general election in 1964 Derek Mitchell, then principal private secretary at No. 10, came to see him to say that Marcia must not be allowed to come to No. 10. But Wilson insisted. Ted said he had always steered clear of her.

Walked back through the Park with Ted and then to No. 10. The PM was at the tapes and he asked me to travel with him in the car to the Commons to report on the general situation. At Questions he gave some broad hints on public expenditure – though he is angry with the Treasury over the massive leaking they are doing to the press on public expenditure cuts.

He saw the Chancellor at 4.45 and the Governor of the Bank at 5 p.m. at No. 10. Ken Stowe told me that the PM said his problem was that he could not get much more than £1 billion cuts through the Party, but he thought that was not enough to do the trick. The Governor said it would – because it would alter the trend of ever-rising public borrowing and start bringing it down.

Incidentally just before lunch Sir Douglas Allen* sent for me. He said there were 'odd discrepancies' in David Piachaud's evidence on the child benefits leak. David had also written to Frances Morrell*, Benn's political adviser, in Energy, expressing concern about child benefits in the middle of May. None of this had anything to do with the basic question of who leaked the confidential annex in mid-June. But it has provided another opportunity for the Civil Service to get at the special advisers so that the machine can undermine Jim's trust in the Policy Unit – and also justify excluding us from sight of the papers.

It is all such a bore and these highly paid bureaucrats should not spend so much time on such trivial games.

Wednesday 30 June 1976

I went in late again, because the PM was off to Bonn, and I went to order some cheap suits from Burtons. I have nothing to wear for official dinners.

Home early. The heatwave continues and it is lovely to sit in the garden in the evening, drinking and talking with Carol and the children.

Thursday 1 July 1976

Cabinet this morning, but no important business except the continuing problem of getting our business through the House of Commons without a majority.

We are briefing tonight on public expenditure for tomorrow's EY Cabinet committee and had a long Unit meeting discussing the shape of our brief.

Lunch at No. 10 then I left early at 2 p.m. to attend a Social Affairs Cabinet committee under Shirley Williams to discuss vehicles for the disabled. We should phase out the trike-car because it is unsafe. But the intention is simply to give £5 mobility allowance instead. This will provide very little – therefore it means we are actually immobilising some people, and in many cases it may deprive them of their jobs which depend on their being able to drive to work. Not right.

The meeting was very poor, with bad preparation by officials. Nobody raised the political problem of immobilising the disabled – Alf Morris is privately considering resigning on this, but he could not mention it because his Secretary of State Ennals was there as well and supports the line of his officials that the £5 mobility allowance is a sufficient substitute for a car. Ennals was not very impressive. He was scribbling while Joel Barnett declared his intention to make more cuts in disabled services, and he did not question this. Afterwards I asked Shirley to get something done about it.

I went back to the office to see Philip Williams*, my old friend from Nuffield College, and then to the deputy secs meeting – where they discussed the compromise agreement on overseas students' fees and kindly acknowledged that it was due to my intervention with DES and Joel Barnett. Then

Gavyn Davies and I worked on finalising our brief on public expenditure for tomorrow and put this in at 7.15 p.m.

Home and then out to supper with Karel and Betsy Reisz* and Haya Harraree from the film industry. In a noisy Italian restaurant in Highgate. Very pleasant evening.

Friday 2 July 1976

Long EY Cabinet committee on public expenditure. Healey did a better presentation than at Chequers arguing for £1 billion cuts, based wholly on maintaining confidence in sterling. Crosland and Benn led the opposition from different points of view.

Shirley Williams looked very down and fell asleep once – as did Michael Foot, in the middle of Healey's opening statement. The late nights in the Commons are clearly getting them down.

Afterwards Jim talked to me and was clearly pleased with the meeting, especially the relaxed style and lack of animosity. Then he said I must not tell anybody in the Unit about it – 'because I am told they leak'. I was furious and denied this. I then spoke to Tom McNally and we fixed a time in his diary for Monday to raise the whole question of special advisers and the Civil Service campaign against them. As Tom said, 'He has got to decide whether he wants them or not.' Certainly there is no point in our going on if we cannot get information.

I was very angry. I went off to a filthy lunch alone in the Cabinet Office canteen, and then came home to sell my old Cortina car for £135. Am very short of money on my £8,000 a year salary.

Nice dinner with our friends the Grahams in the garden in the evening. To bed at 1 a.m. – still very hot. My girls slept in the garden all night in a tent – I took them tea at 7.30 this morning.

Monday 5 July 1976

The PM was in Northern Ireland. This was the first I had read or heard of it. There are good security reasons, but this serves to emphasise the feelings of exclusion from information which we all have. Tom McNally and I have arranged to see Jim this afternoon about this lack of access. We were both angry and decided to put the boot.

I put in a brief for tomorrow's Cabinet on public expenditure. Jim went to his study on returning from Ireland and read it immediately, prior to seeing Michael Foot, who came in to warn him against acting too precipitately on public expenditure.

Tuesday 6 July 1976

The heatwave blazes on, with temperatures in the 90s. It is intolerable in town. When I drive in, I wear a cotton vest to drive. It is soaking wet on arrival. I then change into my shirt for the day – otherwise it is ruined before I get into No. 10.

Went for an early morning run. The Heath is completely brown from lack of rain and the ponds are low. But the scents from the trees and shrubs are marvellous.

Before Cabinet Jim came over to me (he had just seen Healey for a pre-Cabinet chat). He said how good the Unit briefs were – this was a great tribute to Gavyn Davies. He also asked why Tom McNally and I had asked for a formal meeting with him – 'Are you going to resign?' he asked. I laughed and said, 'No, we are not resigners.' Not necessarily true; but it is always a mistake to threaten Prime Ministers with resignation. Firstly, they do not care very much. Secondly, they can never give in.

Cabinet went on all morning until after 1.

At lunch in No. 10 we had a full debriefing on Cabinet from the private secretaries. There had been a large majority in favour of the Chancellor's proposals for cuts. Peter Shore was (apart from Benn, who resubmitted his paper) the chief spokesman against. The PM could have secured a firm majority there and then, but decided to play it gently, have talks with the PLP and the TUC, and then get a decision from the Cabinet a week on Thursday. He is playing this much more slowly and confidently than HW ever did – the complete reverse of the 'bounce' procedure. Much better. By next week everybody will have learned to live with the prospect of cuts.

Parliamentary Questions went as comfortably as usual. But interestingly Jim has grown to hate it as much as HW. He said today, 'This is my worst fifteen minutes of the week. I hate this silly game we have to play.'

At 5.50 Tom McNally and I went to see him in the garden of No. 10. We sat under the big tree drinking lime juice in the afternoon sunshine. He asked what was wrong. I did most of the talking. I said it was now three months since he came in and we might review how it was going. My main complaint was of the squeeze on special advisers in general and on my Unit in particular. The incidents were trivial in themselves, but added up to a 'salami operation'. Papers are withheld from us. Also general information. And there was the attempt by John Hunt to stop me from going to the Social Affairs committee. I outlined the machine's use of 'leaks hysteria' as a tactic to attack and squeeze out special advisers – Lynes, the honours, the Joint Approach on Social Policy, now Piachaud. I said that in a small place like No. 10 there could not be two classes of trust – with less for those politically committed to his government. He must either decide to have special advisers – and support them – or get rid of them.

He responded sympathetically and questioned me closely for nearly an hour. Tom supported me totally. I concluded by saying that he must leave the machine in no doubt.

Now we wait and see. But if he does nothing I will go.

Wednesday 7 July 1976

National Economic Development Committee (NEDC) all day. I only stayed for the morning session – over three and a half hours in one sitting. But it was going well. JC is very strong in the chair, and gives an impression of caring.

I had a quick drink and chat with David Basnett before lunch and then left to have a delicious fish salad with Margaret Jackson [Beckett] at Sheekey's. She is obviously doing well, but finding it hard going against a bunch of civil servants whose view is that education has nothing to do with the Department of Education and especially not its ministers.

Returned to No. 10 and prepared a brief on Civil Service manpower cuts for the PM. Then to hear Tony Benn give the Herbert Morrison memorial lecture at Caxton Hall. Very interesting – fair to Herbert and kind to George Jones* and me as authors of Morrison's biography.

Thursday 8 July 1976

Cabinet went on for hours about European direct elections and the Civil Service cuts. In the end they have failed to get £45 million of the £140 million cuts. So once again bureaucracy is spared. The Civil Service is the only subject in last winter's £3.5 billion cuts to be let off – because they have the chance to bring every single proposed cut back again to Cabinet. That doesn't happen to Health or Housing investment. So they can brief ministers and always save something – while the teachers are being put out of work on to the streets!

Jim was grumpy when I saw him afterwards, because it had gone on too long.

Friday 9 July 1976

PM went to Wales for the day. I worked all morning on the Scottish brief for his meeting with [Bruce] Millan* next Tuesday. Lunch at the House of Commons by myself. Chatted with Gerry Fowler and then Alf Morris. All the MPs look shattered from heat and late nights

Worked in the afternoon with Gavyn on a public expenditure brief, then home at 6.30 to look after the children – Carol has gone away to Bath for another NUT weekend conference.

Monday 12 July 1976

The PM went off to Brussels for the council of the heads of government at noon today. Before, the Toms and I discussed Uganda and the murderous President Amin. Agreed that the Foreign Office were being too appeasing as usual. The PM agreed and sent appropriate messages to the FO.

I worked in the office all day, I stopped another move by the Civil Service Department against special advisers. With David Lipsey* they have said special advisers can only have increases in salary when they move departments, i.e. if they remain in a department they never get promoted or get an increase. Incredible. Part of the squeeze on special advisers, driving a few more out.

Lunch at the Reform with Tom McNally and Roy Hattersley.

Saw Alma Birk*, junior minister at Environment in the evening and she told me how at DoE to meet the cuts they are sacking dozens of disabled custodians in provincial museums (which earn revenue from tourists) but there is no question of touching any official in central headquarters.

Home at 9.15.

Tuesday 13 July 1976

The PM was still away in Brussels until teatime. I went in late to the office, then to lunch at the Etoile with David Higham, a grizzled but remarkably alert literary agent of 80. He wanted to sign up my future books. I wanted to hear about his experiences in the 1916 Battle of the Somme when he was wounded.

On returning from Brussels the PM saw Anthony Crosland about the dreadful situation in Uganda. The PM thinks that the FCO is 'up to Appeasement' again. He says he had to fight it all the time when he was there. Their prime objective in diplomatic life is to make sure that their flow of invitations to cocktail parties is uninterrupted. For this end they would kiss the ass of Hitler and Amin on every odd day of the month (handing over Jewish hostages to the Arabs for execution as sacrificial offerings on the even dates). The PM is furious. Crosland has taken the office advice and refuses to break off diplomatic relations. The PM pressed him but said he refused actually to overrule his Foreign Secretary.

Crosland incidentally looked terrible. His face was puffy and ashen grey. He admitted to feeling exhausted and when walking with Patrick Wright suddenly stopped, closed his eyes and leaned on the wall to rest, saying, 'It's jet lag.' Roy Jenkins once told me that 'Tony is not well.'

Ken Stowe told me that when Wilson talked of having Crosland as a successor, John Hunt strongly warned him off – 'He is only capable of one decision a day.' Apparently he sleeps a lot, even more than JC. [Crosland died six months later.]

We did the PM a brief for tomorrow's pay and trade union meetings.

Wednesday 14 July 1976

The PM went early to the TUC Economic committee – where Healey took the lead in explaining the case for the cuts. They then went on to the PLP meeting, which apparently went surprisingly well.

Incidentally I went to lunch yesterday at the Reform with Roy Hattersley and Tom McNally. Roy told me that when the CPRS report arrived at the FCO recommending some cuts in FCO staff etc., Crosland said he had no time to read it until the public expenditure discussions were out of the way. [Michael] Palliser*, the head of the FCO, then produced a twelve-page letter criticising the CRPS report, written by the FCO officials. Crosland said he had no time to read that either. Palliser said that the PM was asking for a quick response so Crosland was persuaded to sign an (unread) rebuttal of an (unread) report.

In fact it was quite untrue that the PM had been asking for a quick response. A good example of how the Civil Service, when they are to be cut, use every device to protect themselves. But of course nurses and teachers, the sick and the disabled get cut by the civil servants without any chance to protect themselves.

Michael Foot came to agonise about public expenditure. Finally the PM saw Joel Barnett for nearly an hour getting a full briefing on the public expenditure situation. He sees much more of his ministers than Wilson ever did. In fact he is better at Party management, something on which HW always prided himself. Because he is not afraid of direct confrontations. HW was always trying to avoid direct discussion of difficult situations.

In the evening I had dinner with Alf Morris and Jack Ashley at the Commons. We are very concerned with the proposed statement on ending the issue of invalid trikes. I intervened with DHSS to persuade them to give some reassurance about replacing trikes with other vehicles – otherwise disabled people who now have transport to work will lose it and become unemployed. The mobility allowance of £5 a week will certainly not cover daily transportation. So we stopped the proposed statement until DHSS would give better reassurances.

Went home at 11.30.

Thursday 15 July 1976

The big Cabinet today at 9.30 on public expenditure. They went round the general arguments and began getting some of the smaller cuts – defence, etc. The PM curiously said he would exclude overseas aid. Don't know why. [Reginald] Prentice[*] has threatened to resign – but I believe that the PM will drop him in the next reshuffle anyway. I don't see why aid should be exempt, when so many vital domestic policies are being cut.

In the Unit we discussed the CPRS report on reforming the Diplomatic Service. I included Tom McCaffrey – who as a career civil servant was against the report – and Tom McNally, who sees it as a good opportunity to modernise and democratise the FCO. We shall take it slowly, but I want to involve the two Toms since they have actual experience of the FCO.

After Cabinet the PM asked me and the two Toms to go upstairs to the study with him and he gave us a full debriefing on expenditure. He seemed content with the way things are going. He said Tony Benn had a problem as chairman of the Party's Home Policy committee which had predictably come out against all cuts. The PM said if he – Benn – was associated with the report he would have to leave the government. 'But that is a problem for Tony, not for me.'

Lunch at No. 10. Afterwards to the Commons for PM's Questions. Beforehand I saw Roy Jenkins – who said it was 'the most boring Cabinet he had ever attended' though he thought Jim was 'handling it all very well'. Then I saw Crosland who said it was 'the turning point, the beginning of the end'. He said it was 'the least justifiable public expenditure exercise he had ever taken part in'. He thought it would finish us for the election. He still looked in poor shape to me, and had a large cut on the bridge of his nose, apparently suffered in Washington at the White House reception for the Queen, when his lovely wife Susan fainted at the dinner table, he carried her to her bedroom, and walked into the door.

Questions went fairly quietly. But business questions afterwards were in uproar when Michael Foot announced our scheme to guillotine five bills in one day next week! Foot and the chief whip Michael Cocks still have not got the proper feel of the House. Speaker Thomas had great difficulty in controlling it. It was the worst disorder I have seen, with the Tories chanting 'Cheat' and '*Sieg Heil*'. Foot kept commendably cool. But he is in a weak position, having opposed so many guillotine motions in his backbench career.

Returned to No. 10 for the deputy secs meeting in the Cabinet Office on the government's future timetable. Hunt in the chair reported that the permanent secretaries have met and 'decided' to implement the Franks

Report in full, as the best way to deal with the Official Secrets Act/Official Information problem. Quite a volte-face this. Also interesting that they 'decided' this in advance of the ministerial meeting. Hunt did say they were wondering whether to delay the ministerial meeting 'until after Jenkins has gone'. Also the Treasury is very unhappy with this morning's Cabinet, because it has not made much progress. Really it is just quite different from a traditional 'Treasury bounce'. This time the PM is taking ministers on a route of what this lunchtime he called 'familiarisation'. Ministers 'are consulted so often they come to believe that they have taken the decision already'.

Afterwards Tom Connelly, from the Community Relations Commission, came in to discuss working with me. His stories from the CRR are hair-raising. Just a bunch of black pressure-groupers milking the state.

Home at 8.30 p.m. to watch Hitchcock's *North by Northwest*. USA in 1959 – when I was there. Seems far away.

Friday 16 July 1976

The PM went away this morning to the Durham Miners Gala. I worked on our inner-cities brief. Then lunch at Stones Chop House for Nick Stuart, formerly an excellent private secretary, now returned to DES. He said he finds the change of work very striking – now home much earlier! He clearly does not think much either of the department or of minister Fred Mulley.

Cleared my papers and began work on the brief for the PM's meeting with Peter Shore.

Home at 7.30 to go to Rachel's school party.

Monday 19 July 1976

Cabinet met again on public expenditure cuts at 9.30 a.m. They made quite good progress, agreeing about £250 million cuts – £100 million from spend-thrift Defence, about £130 million from Industry and £25 million from Employment. The PM seemed content afterwards. The atmosphere was apparently good with plenty of laughter.

Worked all afternoon on environment questions – inner-city problems, etc. Jonathan Charkham* came in from the Cabinet Office for drinks and to discuss our plans for improving procedures for public appointments.

Home at 9.45, tired and straight to bed to sleep. (Cabinet met again at 8 p.m. this evening. I waited for the start of it. Was told it was going more slowly, but I left before the end.)

Tuesday 20 July 1976

Again an early Cabinet to continue the public expenditure saga until
1.30 p.m. Getting bogged down. Peter Shore being very sticky. He
has been asked to produce £250 million but is finding it difficult to do
so.

One problem is that all the ministers have large additional bids, extra
claims to spend in 1977–78, which have to be eliminated first. So although
Shore cuts £400 million, it only comes to £150 million net because he has
£250 million overspend to eliminate first. In fact because of £1 billion extra
bids, we have to cut £2 billion to get £1 billion off the last expenditure
survey figures.

Shore and Benn are putting up a spirited resistance. Foot won't allow
anything off food subsidies. And Crosland is being very sour – the PM has
really gone off Crosland.

We had lunch at No. 10 and decided we must try to do a paper for the
PM showing the way through – they have now got about £800 million
savings in all.

After Parliamentary Questions Jim asked the civil servants to leave. He
then talked to John Cunningham, Tom McNally and me for over an hour
about the politics of the cuts. He said he is very worried about the Party's
reaction. He also expressed concern that the cuts always affected the sharp
end of services and never the tail of bureaucracy. He looked tired and fed
up with it, but determined to see it through and to carry the Party with
him.

I went back to No. 10 and worked on a brief paper indicating the areas
where he might get another £200 million of cuts. Home at 9.30.

Wednesday 21 July 1976

Again Cabinet pushes on to the £1 billion with a few more odds and ends.

I had lunch with Arthur Bottomley at the Reform. A decent man, who
clearly feels bitter at how badly he feels Wilson treated him, dropping him
after his long and loyal support. He asked if I wanted his safe Middlesbrough
seat.

In the afternoon the PM made his statement on the IRA murder of our
ambassador in Dublin.

In the evening Cabinet met and finally cleared the £1 billion – by the
inclusion of phoney reduced 'debt interest' – and then the Chancellor
produced his bombshell – an extra £1 billion from Employer's National
Insurance Contributions.

Thursday 22 July 1976

The PM spent the morning in the study. He was trying to telephone President Ford* but the Washington Embassy got the time difference wrong! So when Ford was ready (at midday) we were not phoning, then when we phoned (at 1.30) Ford was not there. But the PM finally got through at 3 p.m. and they had a general chat. Ford was mainly interested in the implications of Defence cuts. By then the PM had talked to Schmidt and to Giscard.

At midday JC had a meeting with the junior ministers. It went very well. He handles these meetings superbly, very honest, no attempt to deceive.

Lunch at No. 10.

After Questions Healey made his statement, which he did extremely well. I returned to No. 10 and went to the deputy secretaries meeting. One thing which emerged was that the 'machine' has decided to try to let the National Health Bill on private pay beds 'run into the sand' – not get through this session. I do not like the bill, but it does not seem right that officials who also do not like it should decide to sabotage a major government proposal.

At 6.30 I went with Tom McNally across to John Smith's room and we discussed devolution for next session. He is confident we still have a majority of over thirty for it. This depends on some Tories 'fraying' over to our side. He also expects the Nationalists to support us, but accepts that some of our regional MPs will oppose. It is proposed to allocate half of next session – thirty days – to devolution, giving the government more time to think and to govern.

Then had supper with Denis Howell and Carol. Home very tired at 11.30 p.m.

Friday 23 July 1976

The general reception to the cuts package is not bad, though the City seems a bit disappointed – the pound was weak this morning and the Bank actually spent a few millions in support. The problem is that the more clever it is politically, so that the left do not complain, then the City thinks the cuts are not real – which in some cases is true.

Travelled by train to Cardiff in the afternoon for the PM's honorary degree at Cardiff University. Dinner with the Lord Mayor – and back on the early train to London next morning.

On Friday morning around noon I went up to see Jim in the study before going to Wales (he went in the car). I said that we should deal with some of the longer-term problems which had emerged during the public expenditure exercise – especially excessive local authority current expenditure. He agreed and in fact had already done so, having told Cabinet Office to prepare some papers. I also asked for his support for the purchase of this new machine which will help Jack Ashley to follow proceedings in the chamber.

While I was in there Tony Benn phoned. He is going to see his constituency GMC and proposes to ask them whether to resign or not over the cuts. He had also prepared a press statement announcing this. Jim told him he could not do it. He must make up his own mind whether to resign. And he must not issue press statements saying that he would continue to campaign against the government's policy even if he was still in the government – which is what he was proposing! Jim warned him clearly. Afterwards Jim said to me, 'If he does it, I shall sack him.' We should be so lucky!

Monday 26 July 1976

I came up from a weekend in Suffolk, driving to Audley End and taking the train. Went to the Reform and lunched alone. The PM was at the liaison committee all morning – again the trade unions stood by him to defeat the left on public expenditure cuts etc.

Worked in the Unit in the afternoon, then went to the annual private secretaries party in the garden of No. 10, my third such party. Nobody remained from the first party in 1974 – when John Hunt told me that Ken Berrill was replacing Victor Rothschild running the CPRS. JC did not come to this one – he was in the House seeing Tony Benn, who is apparently going to toe the line as always. (But he wants another job – 'more political' than Energy.) It was a pleasant sunny evening, but rather a drab party. People really want to get away on holiday. We have all seen enough of one another.

Going home, I went around the corner to the Grahams for a snack and to watch the Olympics on TV, and then home to bed by 10.30. Nori and Philip are our closest friends, she from Oxford twenty years ago.

Tuesday 27 July 1976

Carol, I and the children should have been going to France today, but I had to postpone because of a balls-up over parliamentary business.

The Devolution committee was very boring. Highly technical. With long wrangles about 'override' and Scottish private law. John Smith was very good – well informed, clear and strong in argument.

Jim took them through the long agenda at a good pace. He is now much more assured in the chair. But Michael Foot seemed perplexed by the detail. I talked to Jim about it afterwards. He agreed Smith was good, but added,

'I'm not so sure about his political position.' Jim simply does not like devolution.

Lunch with Gerry Fowler at St Stephen's Tavern. He told me terrible tales about his Education department – three out of four of the deputy secs are incompetent. One important issue concerning further education was sent to the deputy sec last September and sat on his desk till last week! He is also appalled by local government extravagance and quoted some frightening examples from his Wrekin constituency.

Went to Prime Minister's Questions, where Jim put on the most dominant performance I have seen in two and a half years. Totally relaxed and amusing, putting Thatcher down gently but with patronising contempt. Even the Tories were roaring with laughter. Our side were in excellent spirits. It is clear that this matters. They are more likely to swallow public expenditure cuts because their general morale is high from seeing their leader so much in charge.

Jim was obviously pleased with himself afterwards. He said that he always feels like a bullfighter when he goes 'into the ring'.

William Plowden came in. The CPRS is deeply dissatisfied. They know they are having too little influence. On many big issues they do not intervene at all – e.g. on the £5 billion of public expenditure cuts since last November. They feel that Ken Berrill is too easily persuaded not to interfere by the other permanent secretaries. They want me to attend a CPRS meeting and advise on how they should proceed – with Ken there. This will be delicate and embarrassing, but I agreed. I like Ken. But the fact is he is too locked in to the official network. The CPRS must be used independently by ministers or it has little function.

Afterwards I went to the Commons for supper. Had drinks on the terrace with John Smith and Donald Dewar* (what a nice man, and what a pity he cannot get back into the Commons). Later we were joined by Bill Rodgers and by Giles Radice*. Everybody is impressed by Jim's performance. I also chatted to one of the young whips, who said that discontent over the cuts is widespread and there is much threat of abstentions. I told him they must choose whether they want a Labour government or not. Jim is not one to bend.

Had quick fish and chips in the cafeteria. Margaret Thatcher, whom I have respected since I covered her Finchley constituency campaign in the 1964 election, was there with Bob Mellish*, complaining about the prolonged parliamentary session and saying how much better things were under Mellish as chief whip. Margaret turned on me and said it was my fault and it was a good thing that my family holiday had been delayed. I said this was hard. She said, 'I have had to learn to be hard.'

Sitting down at the next table after she had gone, Mellish began to abuse me, as paid for doing nothing, and to abuse the government as incompetent. He was a bit drunk and very boring. Bitter old men are not a pleasant sight, especially third-raters like Mellish.

I had a long talk with Peter Shore on the terrace. We agreed that we disliked the Layfield Report on local government and it would be intolerable to give our profligate local authorities any more autonomy. Home at 11.30 p.m.

Wednesday 28 July 1976

The PM was at the NEC this morning – where the trade unions again smashed the left.

I went to lunch with Donald Trelford*, editor of the *Observer*. He is a nice and straight man. He told me that it was Harold Wilson himself who leaked to the *Observer* the story that a leaks inquiry was to be set up into the honours list. Wilson – a former Prime Minister – went personally to the *Observer* twice to see Trelford and to try to mobilise them into attacking the *Sunday Times* for running the honours story. He gave them this leak partly as a bribe, partly to bounce Jim into setting up the inquiry.

Worked in the Unit in the afternoon, and put in a paper for tomorrow's Cabinet on creating more jobs. Officials have come up with some harebrained 'job-swap' scheme, which is really just early retirement at 59.

Had supper at the local Southampton Arms, and then sat up watching the Olympics till 1 a.m.

Thursday 29 July 1976

Worked all morning in the Unit during Cabinet – where the PM took our line on job-swaps, but where sadly they decided not to abolish vehicle excise duty. The Cabinet had already decided twice to abolish it, but the Treasury simply comes back again and again till people are worn down and give way. The Treasury never gives up any source of revenue, however expensive to collect by hordes of civil servants.

Had lunch in No. 10.

At PM's Questions, viciously bad relations between our side and the Tories because Mrs Thatcher had last night cancelled all pairing of the sick. This meant two of our 'dying' – Alex Lyon and Alec Jones* – had to be brought to the House, and Frank McElhone* who is crippled with a slipped disc had to be flown down from Scotland. The PM and others went 'sick-visiting' to them and returned looking shocked and angry. The Speaker had great difficulty controlling the House. Tempers are really bad now.

I went to dinner with John Lyons* of the Power Engineers. Lyons, an ex-communist and highly intelligent, is a tough trade union 'pro'. We clashed on several issues but I liked him very much. He warned me that his members would not settle for another pay deal which eroded pay differentials. He said they would bust the whole thing up – and they can. If they pull the switches we are finished. He was very firm and I would not risk trying to call his bluff.

After, dinner I went back to the House of Commons for the shipbuilding vote, into the distinguished Strangers' Gallery with some tickets from John Cunningham. Could not hear a word the weak [Gerald] Kaufman*, trembling like a jellyfish, said because of the braying by the Tories. But we won by 3 votes – the three sick! I sat next to beautiful Elizabeth Harrison, Rex Harrison's separated wife, whom I last met with Peter O'Toole eighteen years ago when she was married to the wild actor Richard Harris and I then occasionally shared Gordon Snell's* Earls Court flat with Gerry Fowler and O'Toole. She was there with Jonathan Aitken*. The Tories always do better with women. Because of money, I suppose.

Home in John Smith's car at 12.30.

Friday 30 July 1976

10.30 we had a Cabinet committee on the Franks Report on Official Secrets. The PM was quite open that he wants 'reform' in order to tighten the law and make it more effective. Jenkins wanted something more liberal than Franks, and quoted my (original) phrase about replacing the blunderbuss with the Armalite rifle (which I gave to Peter Hennessy* of the *FT* and now keeps cropping up everywhere). Actually the balance of the committee was more liberal than last time – Edmund Dell, Denis Healey, Sam Silkin and Shirley Williams (who was not on the committee before) all supported Jenkins. But Crosland took a conservative line, reading out his Foreign Office brief on why every FO telegram must be protected by the criminal law (not even John Hunt believes that: in fact he put in a fair and moderate brief).

They decided to go for Franks basically, with perhaps the extra protected Defence and FCO stuff to make it less liberal, and easing the position on economic matters to make it more liberal. Healey was very good.

The atmosphere was good, and the PM said, 'What a relief after public expenditure.'

I went to lunch at Grieveson Grant. They were as friendly as ever but all a bit sheepish about the City having given our public expenditure cuts such a sour reaction.

Beforehand in No. 10 we had a reception for those members of the No. 10 staff who were in the honours list. Harold Wilson was there, and he came over and chatted to me for at least half an hour. He was very cheerful and friendly and told me all about his new book on the governance of Britain. No mention of me leaking his honours list – since he knows I did not.

But he was shifty about Joe Haines. He told me that he was 'in regular contact' – in fact he has not communicated with Joe for three months. He also said he had 'spoken to Barnetson' about getting Joe a job. This was in fact months ago and Harold knows that Barnetson has done nothing about it. HW then said, 'Joe may come back to work for me. A certain distinguished lady assistant has suggested it.' When I told Joe later, he exploded (Joe's book is now nearly finished and does not pull any punches).

Home by 8.45 p.m. The family is back from Suffolk. We go to France next Tuesday. I should go into the office on Monday – we have an Economic Cabinet committee, and I also want to put in a brief on inner cities. But I shall not record that here, as I want to get this latest notebook of the diary safely away into the vaults of the National Westminster Bank. Scores of illegible notebooks reside there.

So the summer term ends. Much more relaxed at the end – though personally I am exhausted. I have got Jim's rhythm now. I much prefer his style to Wilson's, and look forward to the autumn. The PM is dominating Cabinet and Parliament. But the question is will the government, without a parliamentary majority, be able to survive next session? I think so, but most commentators disagree.

II

Policy Initiatives, especially on Education
(September 1976–July 1977)

Monday 6 September 1976

Back in to No. 10 after my wonderful holiday in Ceret. (We returned from France on Saturday.) I worked till very late reading papers – a large backlog over the summer.

The PM came in just before lunch from Balmoral. He had enjoyed his weekend with the Queen immensely. He says what a 'natural family' they are. But he is not keen on Philip. I had a talk with him at the news tape machine outside the private secretaries' office at the bottom of the stairs about the unemployment figures. Gavyn Davies had already done a brilliant paper on this.

Had lunch with Tom McNally and caught up on the holiday news.

Henry Kissinger came in at 5 p.m. to discuss South Africa and Rhodesia with the PM. I did not bother to go in the talks, but Tom McNally did. He told me that Kissinger seemed very vague on details.

I went home at 10 p.m., feeling exhilarated to be back in the middle of things.

Tuesday 7 September 1976

The PM had a meeting in the study at 9.30 with the two Toms, Ken Stowe and myself. We ranged over the whole field of problems ahead. A long time on unemployment, and he asked for more figures from the Unit. We also discussed journalists, his press and TV relations. Tom and I wanted him to appear more often. He said he 'hated' journalists. He wasn't 'going to suck up to the media', etc. Perhaps all Prime Ministers decide not to have anything to do with our awful media. But we made him compromise a bit.

I also raised the question of the *Observer* newspaper. It is in terrible financial trouble. The PM's first reaction on paper was that he was 'inclined to let it go'. I pressed him to try and save it and McNally and McCaffrey supported me. So he agreed to see Lord Goodman, and Pickering, a creepy man from the *Mirror*, and he talked with them before lunch, getting very interested and sending for Jack Jones to try to get a trade union interest.

In passing he said something which suggested that he was losing his enthusiasm to go to Canada next week. At lunch in No. 10 Ken Stowe predicted we would not go (it is really Mrs Callaghan who wants to go).

Tom McCaffrey told me that just before the holiday the PM had asked him if he was 'getting pompous'. It is a danger, but encouraging that he is aware. JC also expressed irritation with Crosland because he gave no support over public expenditure. He indicated that he now won't send Crosland to the Treasury to swap with Healey. Presumably Healey will have to soldier on. He is really irreplaceable.

One curious incident concerned the coming Cabinet changes. Jim had told Ken Stowe his ideas and Ken wrote them out in longhand – to be implemented on Tuesday 21 September. These were put in a very secret envelope. But the PM lost them at the weekend and they came back in the ordinary box and were put back in his tray – the tray called 'information and reading' which is not at all urgent. I read it there and wondered what the hell was going on. Anybody could have seen it. Ken rescued it and took me privately into the Cabinet Room to beg me not to say a word. Jim doesn't yet know how to process paper properly.

Home late again – after going to a reception at the Brazilian Embassy, where I chatted with the Governor of the Bank [Gordon Richardson*] and with Tory Geoffrey Howe*, who seems very decent.

Wednesday 8 September 1976

My 42nd birthday. Cannot believe it. Still feel young and inexperienced.

The PM saw Healey and the Governor of the Bank of England this morning, with Douglas Wass. The Bank had already spent £175 million defending the currency by the time they met at 10 a.m.! The PM, according to the private secretary's notes, criticised all this intervention by the Bank. He said that either we had a floating rate or we did not. At present we were supposed to have a floating rate, but the Bank always intervened at great cost to fix it at $1.77. The Chancellor gave the arguments for and against and ended on balance by agreeing with the PM that we should *not* intervene any more. Richardson opposed this and gave the reasons for supporting the rate.

I took Ken Berrill to lunch at the Reform. Did not learn very much.

In the evening I went to a dinner at Guildhall with thirty educationalists and careers officers to discuss problems of 16- to 18-year-olds. The PM was good in his opening remarks and so were several of the speakers, though it went on after 11 p.m. and Jim got very touchy and called it to an end.

I got home about 12.30.

Thursday 9 September 1976

The seamen's strike announced for Saturday hits the headlines. Sterling fell like a stone to $1.73. The Bank threw away $100 million in the first ten minutes and then withdrew support, following Tuesday's instructions from the PM which were given *without any thought* of the strike. Everybody thought this was a 'revenge' tactic, to frighten the seamen by showing the effect on sterling. In fact it was a quite separate decision.

I waited in the hall of No. 10 till the PM came in at 9.45 and asked to talk to him. We went up to the study and the two Toms joined us. I said I was afraid of overreaction to the strike. (Private Office had been enquiring about recalling Parliament and issuing states of emergency.) I told Jim that he must avoid Harold Wilson's hysteria in the 1966 strike. In fact a seamen's strike was not a catastrophe. We could survive it. The only danger was that if *we* reacted as if it could destroy sterling, then it *would* destroy it because foreign holders would sell following our attitudes.

He agreed. I produced some figures showing how little damage the 1966 strike did. He decided to play it coolly: to leave the negotiating to the TUC and if there was a strike he would make a TV broadcast on Sunday saying that we would not give way to it. I was very pleased – since this is exactly what later he told the Cabinet in his statement.

But one disappointment. He decided not to go to Canada. So I would lose another trip! Tom McCaffrey was pressing him not to go – because Tom does not want to go, his wife is ill. Tom McNally supported this, since he is not going anyway.

For the rest of the day McCaffrey and I clashed. He insisted there would be a strike and therefore Jim must not go. I said there might not be one, and if there was, there was nothing Jim could do once it started. We were both arguing from personal interest, but I was convinced my self-interested case was better.

In the evening both Toms declared, 'There is no way Jim is going to Canada.' We will see.

Friday 10 September 1976

I came in early and found Private Office working flat out, summoning ministers, telephoning ministers in foreign countries. Jim was not going to Canada and had decided to do his reshuffle.

Roy Hattersley came in first. He looked delighted afterwards. I thought he had Education – that was on the list in the PM's box on Monday. Instead he got Prices and Incomes. He said to me, 'It doesn't matter what I got, so long as my feet are under that Cabinet table on Thursday mornings.' He is right.

Merlyn Rees came in, still talking in great detail about Northern Ireland. He is obsessed with it – that is why it is right to move him to the Home Office. But a nice man who had done an honourable job in Ireland.

Roy Jenkins came in from Paris, he thought it was about the seamen's strike. When he was told it was 'appointments', he looked agitated – it was the end for Roy, his final visit to No. 10 as a minister, done in a rush, with him not knowing what it was about. We talked briefly. I watched him go out for the last time after his interview with the PM, head down, arms swinging, somehow not happy.

Bill Rodgers came in, and we talked before, and had coffee in my room afterwards. He was pleased – would have preferred Education but was delighted to be in the Cabinet. Jim had sworn him to silence so we did not discuss what he had got, but I knew it was Transport which is completely right for him. A few more ministers came but most of the others were dealt with on the phone. Fred Mulley complained but reluctantly agreed to go to Defence, replaced at Education by Shirley Williams.

I was very sad about dropping Gerry Fowler, which seems a mistake. I put this to the PM when he talked to McNally and me in the Cabinet Room afterwards. But Jim obviously does not like Gerry – perhaps because of his alleged drinking.

Jim said that neither John Silkin nor Stan Orme were really Cabinet material, but he had to have people from the left and they were the 'least harmful'. He also said that Shirley Williams had stated there were several ministries she would not take – I wonder which? Perhaps Ireland and DHSS because of her Catholicism? And the Home Office, which she hated before?

Throughout the day we discussed the seamen. McCaffrey still thought/hoped that there would be a strike. We all assumed there would be no Canada visit.

Went home via Bill Rodgers, where we had a drink to celebrate his promotion.

Woke on the Saturday morning to find the strike off – we are going to Canada in the evening at 9.15!! McCaffrey wrong again.

Canada: Saturday 11–Saturday 18 September 1976

Quick impressions:

Flew all Saturday night in the VC10. Drank too much wine and felt queasy. Slept about two hours – then it was Saturday night in Calgary when we arrived (they are seven hours behind). Terrible jet lag. Woke at 3 in the morning and watched TV. Could not sleep.

Sunday morning in Calgary. Grey. Drizzly. And not beautiful. Lunch with Jim, Mrs Callaghan and Canadian protocol man in the hotel. In the afternoon went with the PM to Banff – seventy miles, beautiful. Rockies. Barbecue with the Alberta PM. Home to bed at 10.

Monday – took the plane to Regina, small prairie town. Straight to a farm for lunch. Endless plains. Large tidy farms. Evening terrible meal at the hotel.

Tuesday – morning four-hour flight to Toronto – exciting and clean city. Evening to dinner at the Empire Club. PM made big and good speech.

Wednesday – morning to Ottawa. Big military reception. Lunch at the Governor General's. Good food and nice people. Watched the ice hockey game on TV – Canada beat Czechoslovakia.

Thursday – all morning in government offices discussing incomes policy with officials. Then lunch at Rideau Gate with the PM, Pierre Trudeau*, Paul Martin and four of us. Trudeau still sharp, but clearly absorbed in his own domestic political problems (reshuffle yesterday) and young wayward wife. Big official dinner.

Friday – I went off privately to visit my friend Mike Kirby in beautiful Halifax, Nova Scotia. Had a marvellous time with him, Bonnie and the boys. I was so late to the airport on Saturday evening that I nearly missed the plane home to London.

Monday 20 September 1976

Still a bit sleepy from missing Saturday night's sleep flying back from Canada. Also have a cold. But as always feel revived to be back.

Caught up on my papers and correspondence in the morning. In the afternoon had a Cabinet committee on the drought – which is now the worst in 250 years. Denis Howell is doing a good job as troubleshooter. Home early. But before leaving the PM sent for the two Toms and me to discuss bank nationalisation. The NEC has put up a terrible document for Party Conference on nationalising the clearing banks. Jim wants to outflank it. He is clearly inclined towards a Royal Commission. To bash the City for its failure, but oppose nationalisation. Tom McNally was very sound in his advice.

Tuesday 21 September 1976

Came in early for a Cabinet committee discussing stage three of incomes policy. Everyone agreed we must have one – but difficult to get. The inflation projections are very depressing.

Michael Foot made the most interesting suggestion – for a new national plan, worked out with the trade unions, so that they would see the need and benefits of an incomes policy – and the cost of not getting one. I immediately decided to pursue this.

Shirley Williams came to my room for coffee. Shirley commented on how tough Jim has become, which she welcomes. She also said that she proposed to pursue a 'hard' line at Education – where she was 'depressed to see the same old dead-beat civil servants' as when she was there before. (Not the new permanent secretary, who is very good.) She added that 'it would have been worse at the Home Office'. She also said she was *astonished* at the dropping of Gerry Fowler. She asked me to find out from Carol if there were any members of the NUT executive who were worth talking to, and I arranged to see her again in Blackpool at Party Conference.

Lunch in No. 10. Afterwards to a permanent secretaries meeting in the Cabinet Office on redefining public expenditure. Leo Plietzky gave us his usual lecture on restoring the integrity of the Treasury by re-establishing tight financial control. Correct, but boring.

Jim left for Birmingham in the late afternoon so I again took the opportunity to go home at a reasonable hour.

Wednesday 22 September 1976

Jim away all day.

I worked in the office in the morning – we put in a paper on import controls, which is more and more becoming an issue. (Jim sees that it is politically essential to do something, especially against Japan, but the Board of Trade is against.)

Had lunch with John Hunt at the Reform. We talked mainly about central government reform. He believes that the troika of top permanent secretaries – Civil Service Department (Allen), Treasury (Wass) and himself – will have to be reduced to two. And that CSD staffing will have to go back to the Treasury which pays the bill. I agree with him.

He is a curious mixture. Incredible energy. Sharp. Keeping an eye on a vast field. Persistent. Yet deeply insecure which makes him not trust anybody – making it difficult for them to trust him. He is the only person I work with to whom I do *not* show my hand fairly openly. I have this curious feeling it will get cut off. Perhaps unfairly. He told me that the Cabinet Office feels I do not co-operate enough with them. I do try.

In the evening Jack Straw came in to tell about his boss Peter Shore's housing plans – which still seem cautious to me. We discussed the new inner-city policy as well – the key to which is jobs. Jack is a very able and sensible man. He also talked about Barbara Castle – she was angry with Jim for dropping her because she wanted to retire anyway – but 'gracefully' in August; that she did not like old-age pensioners because she feared old age.

Thursday 23 September 1976

I saw Bill Rodgers before going in to his first Cabinet, glowing with excitement. And Fred Mulley, who said he was astonished at Jim dropping Gerry Fowler, who he said was 'the best supporting minister I ever had'.

A settlement is imminent on Rhodesia, and Kissinger is due at No. 10 tonight. Ironical that Jim has so quickly presided over the Rhodesian settlement which HW worked at for years and never got.

At 3 o'clock I went to a fascinating Cabinet committee on economic strategy. First discussing import controls against Japan. At present we limit Japanese imports by *voluntary* controls negotiated by government and industry. But this is illegal under the EEC. So we have to give up that – in the hope that the EEC will do something better, which they might, but certainly not soon. Jim pressed Dell very hard, but got nowhere. Peter Shore was eloquent – happy that all predictions about the dire consequences of joining Europe were coming true.

The arguments were taken up again over the Chancellor's paper 'The Next Steps'. This painted a very gloomy future, and stated that we should have to go to the IMF for another loan next month. Even that would only tide us over till the end of 1977. He is preparing for import *deposits* on a seven-day basis. But he rejected import controls. His strategy looks very right now. Our reserves are down to £4 billion – and the deficit this year and next will absorb that. Sterling is at an all-time low. Inflation is no longer falling. The incomes policy is lacking. We have record interest rates to protect sterling and finance the PSBR. Our import content is rising all the time. There is no prospect of unemployment falling.

The siege economy looks a little nearer. Benn and Shore sit and wait for it. We may just avoid it by the skin of our teeth. But I see no chance of winning an election before 1979 – and we shall lose some more by-elections before then.

Harold Wilson came in to see Jim. I had a brief chat with him. He talked about his book on the governance of Britain and said that Lord Blake had 'given him an alpha for it'. (He still sees everything in terms of passing Oxford examinations.) He looked well, but gave an impression of being out of it.

He came to see Jim about some Israeli complaints that Jim was responsible for the recall of the Israeli ambassador. Total nonsense of course. Jim saw him briefly – for no more than five minutes – and was irritated by it.

Friday 24 September 1976

The *Financial Times* had the whole story about import deposits and import controls – certainly from the Treasury. Yesterday the *Guardian* had Jim's plans for an inquiry into the banks – and Healey had lunch with Peter Jenkins, the author. Ministers leak!

Jim was away in Blackpool for the NEC and Party Conference. I worked in the morning, had lunch with a Canadian civil servant, and then went to Suffolk for a short weekend before going to Blackpool Conference on Sunday afternoon.

Sunday 26 September 1976

Went up on the train with Joe Haines. Discussed my job – where Joe's inclination is that I should leave. And his book, which is ready for the printers. And N. Ireland – where a lot of information has come through on Protestant murder expeditions from Glasgow to Belfast. I realised how much I miss him at No. 10. The two Toms are friendly, especially McNally, but it is not the same. Joe was a comrade in arms. Without him there is much less sense of mission and of teamwork. We always worked together, keeping an eye on one another's interests, telling one another everything. Now the new team is friendly, but private, and each of us is left to look after ourselves – I can do that OK but I don't enjoy it as much.

Had dinner at the Imperial Hotel and hung around the rest of the evening. The PM went off, as each evening, on a social tour. We were all invited, but I was not keen just to be a hanger-on. Have done all that with HW.

Monday 27 September 1976

Off to the conference for the first session – and five of the first eight speakers were Trotskyites. (The PM had a private list prepared beforehand of all the Trots who were due to move or second motions.) Jim came off the platform at around 11.30 and I went to join him in the back room with John

Cunningham. Jim was very annoyed with the Trots. He was also jumpy about his speech, which was finished, but we were waiting for Tom McNally to bring the final copy.

Lunch back at the hotel and then returned to the conference. I suggested to the PM that he should include a paragraph on import controls – he agreed, saying that he had simply forgotten.

In the evening we hung around the suite, but he did not have a 'gathering' in his room the way that Harold Wilson used to. He went to bed early. I was late, sitting up drinking with Margaret Jackson till after 3 a.m.

Tuesday 28 September 1976

Jim had made a number of changes in his speech this morning. He seemed quite relaxed. We knew that Atkinson had beaten Eric Varley for the treasurership and that Shirley Williams had lost the AEU votes for the NEC. After these were announced Jim made his speech. It was nearly an hour. No humour. Few cheers. Straight down the line. It also had some remarkably courageous words about the impossibility of simply reflating back to full employment – so the campaign by the monetarist economists has made an impact. [Son-in-law Peter Jay had drafted this section.] No standing ovation, but the moderates and the PLP liked his attack on leftist infiltration. In the room afterwards he was relieved that they had taken it so well.

We were also very worried abut sterling, which has been plunging to new lows. Jim talked on the phone to Healey who decided not to go off today to the international finance talks in Manila. In the afternoon there were emergency talks in the Treasury with Healey, Lever and the Bank of England people. The Bank wanted to resume intervention to support sterling. But it was decided we could not until we had fresh loans. The PM asked me what I thought we should do. I said get the IMF in as soon as possible – accelerate the timetable. He did not respond, but later he told Healey to do that.

In the evening I sat up drinking with the Granada TV people till 3.30 a.m.

Wednesday 29 September 1976

Up at 7.00 a.m. and went for a three-mile run along the front towards Fleetwood. I had half arranged to run with Hattersley, but he did not show up: too early and too fat! Back in the hotel, sweating, I ran into David Owen and made him feel very guilty. A great proponent of preventive medicine, he conceded he did not do much about it.

Spent the morning in the conference hall, moving around, taking to MPs, talking to Joe, out to coffee, back to the PM's room when he came off the platform, discussing sterling – we announced the application for £2.3 billion of IMF loan at 11 a.m.

I also talked to Gerry Fowler and strongly advised him to make a generous speech from the rostrum tomorrow, with no show of bitterness for being sacked. He agreed completely. But he dislikes Jim. Actually it is clear that Jim *is* anti-intellectual. People like Gerry Fowler and Roy Jenkins, and David Marquand – and *me* really – worry him. It is his educational insecurity not having been to university. In fact he is *very* intelligent. Lack of a formal education does not matter and is almost a strength in Labour politics.

We returned to the Imperial for lunch with the *Daily Mirror* in a private room. They are a nice, but not very dynamic, lot.

Also went to the *Daily Mirror* reception in the evening. They threw out ex-Wilson men Terry Pitt* and John Schofield Allen* as gatecrashers – or at least physically prevented them from getting in. It was symbolic of the end of the Wilson era.

Later I went to 'Scots Night'. I linked up with Frank McElhone and his Glasgow party and enjoyed myself so much that I stayed on till 1 a.m. and let the PM go off to 'Welsh Night' – which I gather was appalling.

Sat around in the lounge of the Imperial until 4 a.m. gossiping. The lack of sleep – approx. three and a half hours a night – is beginning to hit me. But I am enjoying the circus atmosphere so much more than last year. I eat a lot and drink little and so get through. Also I bathe three times a day, which keeps me awake.

Thursday 30 September 1976

Did not run as I intended because it was raining so hard.

Spent the morning at the conference. Back to the hotel for lunch – with the PM and Audrey. We discussed what tone to take in his TV broadcasts this evening.

The afternoon in conference was very exciting. Denis Healey flew up to speak in an emergency debate on the IMF loan. He made a crudely powerful speech and won the support of conference. But earlier they had voted to nationalise the banks. Most of the votes went against the platform. The easiest way to win votes and cheers was to attack the Labour government. It was really terrible and everybody was depressed. Jim said to me that it was worse than ever before. Afterwards he went for his TV interviews, which he did very well.

We had supper and then I accompanied him on his evening's social round. First to the NUR. Then to the Tailor and Garment Workers, which was sad: a dozen nice elderly Jewish men and women in the basement of a small hotel. Then to 'Israeli Night'. The food and drink were delicious, and lots of nice people there. Finally, we went to 'Lancashire Night' at Tiffany's. Barbara Castle came up and asked me to dance – saying loudly, 'This will ruin your career.'

So we returned home at 11. It had rained all evening and the cavalcade of cars and police escorts flashed through the wet streets.

Back at the hotel I stayed up until 5 *a.m.* and talked with countless people.

Friday 1 October 1976

Up at 7.30 for a morning run and travelled in to the conference in Jim's car. Rather a boring morning, except for a nice walk to coffee at Lewis's with Jean Corston, the able SW regional assistant organiser. Back to the hotel for lunch.

Then flew down on the plane to Gatwick – falling asleep the moment we took off. Out to dinner with Nick Deakin – whose brother told Carol he is making a programme on Harold Wilson's 1974–76 government. He had not bothered to contact Joe or me.

Must decide whether to stay or leave No. 10. Strong sense of being at a watershed. Less excitement and novelty. And the conference shows the appalling mess in the Labour Party – full of lunatics. Yet no desire to go back to part-time work as an academic. Incapable of decision.

Monday 4 October 1976

Worked all morning in my office on the backlog of papers and correspondence.

Went to see John Hunt about industrial democracy. It is going badly and Hunt wants me to sit on Douglas Allen's co-ordinating committee. It seems that the Bullock committee will have a minority report, opposing industrial democracy.

During the afternoon I became aware that the Bank and Treasury were up to something. They are constructing a big monetary package – minimum lending rate at 15%, mortgage rate at 14%, long-term interest rates 16%, special deposits, import deposits, all giving a massive deflation. Aimed to sell gilts, and to keep money supply down to the target of 12% increase. But it will increase unemployment a further 250,000 minimum. And will give further *decrease* in output – and living standards. They concede it means further bankruptcies of banks and insurance companies.

The justification is clear. They cannot sell gilts, and so finance the public deficit, and control money supply, while sterling is so weak. So they are

going for a brutal squeeze. It will deal the economy another terrible blow
– construction and manufacturing will bear the burden. It is mad, however
logical. This government could not survive it – two million unemployed in
1978, with zero growth in output 1975–78, and reduced living standards
all round.

The problem is our propensity to import. It seems that we cannot balance
our payments on anything less than two million unemployed. So the Treasury
set about producing the two million. And the left sit and wait with the
alternative strategy of a siege economy – certainly more attractive – which
keeps out the imports by tariffs and quotas.

The Treasury has had a secret meeting with Yeo of the American Treasury,
and he has preached rigid monetarism at them. I have seen all the minutes
and papers. Our Treasury is having a critical meeting with Healey tomorrow,
when they will try to convert him to the squeeze. They say we cannot get
a loan without such a squeeze, and certainly some of the IMF people are
saying this. But our Treasury and Bank people are encouraging them to
say it.

I had a long meeting with Gavyn Davies of the Unit and Nigel Wicks
of Private Office. They were fairly depressing and could see no alternative
to the squeeze. I was not so sure. We have to find another way – or we
might as well go out now. I began to think of a different package – a big
loan to fund our sterling balances/debts plus a selective squeeze on the
public sector bureaucracy plus a national plan to invest for regeneration of
our industry. They were sceptical. But I mean to follow it up.

I dashed off to see Harold Lever at 7 p.m. in Eaton Square. He was very
upset. Since 1974 he has predicted this would happen and has urged the
Treasury to borrow long-term money. They did not try because they did
not want to. They are puritans and think borrowing is corrupting. They
want a bloodletting. He is still convinced we can get loans. Certainly without
loans our present policy is not viable now.

Drove home at 8.30. Tomorrow I see Jim about my career. And about
this crisis.

Tuesday 5 October 1976

A very exciting day. I worked this morning on economic matters, preparing
for this afternoon, when I was to have a meeting with the PM – and he
was to see the Chancellor.

I summoned the Unit economic consultants – Andrew Graham from
Oxford, David Gowland from York, David Piachaud from LSE. We
discussed through the late morning and through a terrible lunch in the
Cabinet Office canteen. The majority view was that something needed to

be done on the economic front – because we cannot finance next year's external deficit and we won't meet this year's 12% money supply target. Therefore sterling will weaken again. So they accept the Treasury concern, and agree a monetary squeeze is necessary. Andrew Graham disagrees. He thinks we are still on course, and the devaluation plus incomes policy means a reduction in real living standards and more competitive exports – which is what is required.

However, we went for the squeeze, but decided it must not be the traditional Treasury one, indiscriminately high interest rates bashing industry and mortgage rates. So Gavyn and David concocted a package which would reduce money supply without raising interest rates.

I went to see the PM in the study at 2.45. John Hunt dashed in ahead of me with a handwritten note setting out the Tresury plan (which I had known since last night). I walked in and said, 'That is quite a bombshell you have there.' The PM looked quite impressed when I told him what it contained. I warned him not to swallow it all straight away. That 15% MLR would hit our industrial policy; 14% mortgages would hurt us politically. I urged him to see Harold Lever and to give Lever the chance to raise long-term loans to fund the sterling balances/debts. He nodded and made some notes.

The main point of our meeting was my need to decide whether to resign or not. LSE have given me an ultimatum. I must resign from No. 10 *today* (not have leave till 5 January 1977 as earlier promised) or resign my life tenure at LSE. I am inclined to go back to the LSE which I have always loved. Those right-wing professors in the LSE Government department are making me give up my life career and job security – something they would never dream of doing themselves. As if this work here is not relevant to my future research as a teacher of British politics and government. Typical academic humbug and envy! But the PM argued very strongly for me to stay – though he would not give me any promise of finding me a job afterwards. Really deep down I wanted to stay on in the middle of this great economic battle. And I resented the LSE pressure and crude ultimatum. It is one of my rules, never bend to pressure. So I decided to stay.

The PM then saw the Chancellor and apparently put all my arguments against the Treasury package – mustn't bash industrial investment, mustn't have 14% mortgages, must give Lever a chance to get long-term money. Healey apparently looked worried and completely abandoned the Treasury position.

The PM then sent for Lever, with John Hunt and Palliser, and gave full authority for him to try to get the long-term money to fund the balances. So it was quite a triumph.

Douglas Allen asked me to come over to talk about the Civil Service college. He has excellent ideas – to make a college for the whole public *sector*, to train and examine, to make it in fact like a services *staff college* and not like a second-class university. I support him on all this. Douglas Allen asked if I would go on the college governing council and I agreed.

In the evening we worked on a brief for the PM setting out our alternative strategy for a monetary squeeze without the usual disadvantages.

I then phoned Professor [Elie] Kedourie* and told him I was leaving the LSE. Having done it I wasn't sure it was the right thing to do. I could be unemployed at 44. [I was!] But I either take a risk now or never.

Wednesday 6 October 1976

The PM had a meeting at 10.30 with Lever, Healey, John Hunt, Michael Palliser from the Foreign Office and Alan Lord* from the Treasury. He sent Ken Stowe to tell me he wanted me to attend as well, which was nice.

We met in the Cabinet Room and the meeting went on till 12.15. Healey put the case against trying to borrow long-term money to fund the sterling balances. He thought we would not get it and we needed to put on the squeeze first anyway. The PM told Healey that he lacked political sense and should realise that once we did the package we would have no leverage for getting the long-term money.

Lever was very emotional in putting the case for funding the balances and spent too long criticising previous policy on currency management. Healey began to lose his temper, shouting, 'Why don't you keep quiet?'

Palliser made a good case for appealing to Schmidt on the basis of maintaining a strong Britain in Europe. But Healey continued to resist and in the end the PM said that he was not prepared to push it against total Treasury opposition – or they would make sure it failed anyway. But it was agreed to put it to a wider group of ministers. At the end of the meeting the PM called me over and asked me to send a copy of our brief to him to the Chancellor.

Lunch with my stockbroking friends at Grieveson Grant, with their gilt dealers and Peter Cook from the Bank of England. Interestingly they believed we would have no problem in selling gilts and financing the PBSR deficit.

Spent the afternoon on papers. Told the Unit I had resigned from the LSE (I still feel that may be a mistake). Afterwards I walked along Pall Mall to have a drink with Harry Evans. He has been approached about becoming Director General of the BBC. I told him I might need a job from him!

Thursday 7 October 1976

Wake up depressed by the drift of economic events. It was pouring with rain and I did not go for my usual morning run.

The PM sent for Healey before the Defence Cabinet committee and they discussed the Unit paper. Healey apparently intends to ignore it and proceed on a crude rise of 2% in MLR and special deposits. In fact he had promised Ed Yeo – the appalling American redneck – last week at a Treasury lunch that he would raise interest rates today. So the whole consultation process, even with the PM, had been a charade.

Healey got the PM's permission last night. The PM still thinks it is wrong, and said so, but has got to stand by his Chancellor.

In Cabinet, only Shirley Williams spoke against. The rest were mesmerised. I asked Varley afterwards why he didn't protest, and he said, 'Well we have to rally round the Chancellor.' He did not seem to have grasped what it meant for his industrial strategy. Industrial investment will be smashed. I also asked him what he thought of 13% house mortgage rates. He blinked and said, 'Nobody mentioned mortgage rates.'

The left just sat quietly, not at all displeased. This policy will bring our central policy – the social contract plus incomes policy plus industrial investment – into complete disrepute. Then they hope to slip into the siege economy of import controls – that is why they are completely happy with what Healey is doing.

Healey is in the hands of primitive monetarists at the Treasury, the Bank of England, and Yeo and Simon in the US.

The point about Denis is that he has no fixed policy preferences. He is very impressive and effective because of his strength and stamina. But it all depends in which direction this tank is going – he is capable of driving away in any direction and crushing the opposition, friend or foe, along the way.

Lunch with Ken Berrill. He did not know that the measures had been announced – he and the CPRS seem to be withdrawing from short-term policy altogether. But his analysis of the situation is always very incisive.

The PM saw Lord Goodman this afternoon about the *Observer* crisis – no great hope of rescue there; and the Northern Ireland trade unions about the recession in Ulster; then the miners about early retirement.

I was supposed to go to a party at the American Embassy but I never got there. Home at 12.30.

Friday 8 October 1976

Very depressed about the whole economic nonsense. The full horror in terms of interest rates (16½%) and mortgage rates (12¼%) emerged today.

But the pound did not strengthen much. We issued a new gilt tap and sold £250 million – but that is not much at 16%.

Worked on the PM's speech for Monday's emergency debate and I drafted his important speech on education at Ruskin College, Oxford.

The PM was in this morning, just fiddling around, before going off to Ringmer [his farm] around noon. He also invited Schmidt to dinner on Sunday. They hope to discuss sterling balances. It is the last hope to rescue our economic policy – if we fund the balances then this week's nonsense won't matter – we will be able to get rates down quickly. The Foreign Office is doing a splendid job on this. They have found the Germans very receptive. Lever and I agree that we must now use the Foreign Office much more. Palliser is very good. And they at least think internationally.

The reality is that the Treasury and the Bank do not *want* us to get the loans. They think it will corrupt us. They want us to be forced to cut borrowing by £6 billion in one year, even if it kills off industry and produces five million unemployed. They are Cromwellian dogmatists, without Cromwell's humour, radical nature or flexibility.

David Owen also phoned to say that he would not go along with it. He has obviously had an impact at the FCO, pushing his interest in international monetary questions. And of course his Secretary of State, Crosland, could make a big impact too if he would only mobilise himself. He has been away at the UN and was not there at Cabinet yesterday.

Had lunch in the Cabinet Office mess and worked hard all afternoon and evening.

Finally back home at 9.30 – to dinner with the Grahams till 1.30 a.m. Have a deep feeling that the Labour government has taken steps this week which will make its defeat inevitable – unless it reverses direction very soon. The officials have taken over. We have slumped into Conservative policies – always the prelude to Conservative government as in 1950–51.

Monday 11 October 1976

The Times this morning ran a piece about my leaving the LSE – on the front page. Very favourable. But am still sad at being forced to leave the LSE. Quite an emotional break.

The PM saw Schmidt off this morning and then went into hiding to work on his speech in the debate on the economic situation, which marks the reopening of Parliament. He did not debrief us on Schmidt. All that Jim would say was that 'it went well'. The crucial question is whether Schmidt has really committed himself to helping us over the sterling balances. That nobody knows.

I had lunch at the Reform with Jimmy Margach of the *Sunday Times* (though he is now retired). He said I was right to leave the LSE and that now I would be treated as my own man. He has been working on Barbara Castle's diaries – over a million words on the period 1964–70. She is apparently quite vitriolic about Harold Wilson and about Jim. But Margach says they are much better than Crossman's diaries because they are more immediate – a page typed every night, whereas Crossman sometimes did not write his till the holidays and with hindsight!

My favourite Irish cousin, Margerie, arrived for tea and I took her home for supper – and then returned to the Commons at 9 to hear the debate. Thatcher was *very* good. She made her own speech, not reading somebody else's text, none of those awful aphorisms which her speech-writers used to give her. The best performance I have heard her give and she had her backbenchers behind her. They are clearly still intoxicated by the heady air of their Brighton Conference (we are still depressed by ours at Blackpool – a poll taken at the end of that week by ORC shows us 11½% behind!).

Jim wound up quite effectively, scoring some points, trying to educate the House in the problems, but he did not have much to say. He did not have a speech – just a series of paragraphs and some economic statistics. Really he does not believe in Healey's present policy and this showed through. (Keith Joseph* looked absolutely *mad*, arms waving, head and eyes rolling, when he interrupted to speak up for monetarism.)

We won the vote comfortably.

Went to the Strangers Bar afterwards and drank till nearly 1 a.m. With Gerry Fowler, Mark Hughes* [the three of us were at Oxford together], Robin Corbett*, who seems very nice, with John Cunningham and with John Smith, who is still very confident on devolution. Phillip Whitehead took me on one side to press me that Shirley Williams must stand for the deputy leadership. Wants to demonstrate that the left is not having it all their own way. The word is being put about that Jim is against Shirley and wants Foot to win. I doubt that and promise to check.

Shortly before I left the Strangers Bar a Labour MP standing next to me at the bar – Colin Jackson, the pro-Arab – ordered a whisky, slowly drank it, and then slowly fell over backwards on to the carpet. Other people just looked quickly, said things like, 'Oh, it's Colin,' and then continued drinking. A large policeman arrived and carried him away.

Tuesday 12 October 1976

There were committee meetings on EEC direct elections and devolution. Before then I spoke to Shirley Williams. She still did not know whether to stand for the deputy leadership or not. It is clear that personally she would prefer *not* to, feeling she will lose – it suits many people to have an *old* man like Foot, since he does not close options for other people. She has time to wait. But she is under great pressure from the right and correctly feels that she must not be accused of 'running away'. I told her that Jim was not 'against her' – he simply would prefer there to be no contest. She felt that if there was to be a fight it should be her, because she would do best and she did not want the right to be beaten heavily by the left.

Question Time went smoothly enough.

I saw Harold Lever briefly, and he told me that Tony Crosland was prepared to help on the economic side, to try to get an alternative to the present policy of 'drift and squeeze'. Lever had supper with Crosland last night.

Worked on the environment brief for the PM's Thursday meeting with Peter Shore. Then attended a reception for our disabled athletes at No. 10.

Continued work until 10 p.m.

Wednesday 13 October 1976

Terrible Tube journey into town so I missed the EY Cabinet committee. It decided once again to delay increases for nationalised industry chairmen. They were also due to discuss import deposits, and Healey's curious proposal to do a scheme for only three months – which would mean we would suffer the 'unwinding' early next year. But there was not time to discuss this before they had to go off to the meeting of the PLP on the economic situation. This was apparently fairly drab, nobody happy, but nobody with any alternatives.

I went to Harold Lever for lunch in Eaton Square. We went over the situation. He was at first opposed to any public expenditure cuts, because they are deflationary, but when I revealed some of my plan for cutting the public sector and switching the resources into investment he was favourable.

In the afternoon the PM had a meeting with editors – where he let slip that he was 'not wholly intellectually convinced' of the Treasury's arguments for higher interest rates.

I worked all evening and did not go home till 11 p.m. We put in Gavyn Davies's paper on cuts in public expenditure. And at the same time Liz Arnott and I were working on a draft for the PM's important education speech at Ruskin College next Monday. The press is speculating that Jim is going to come out with some revolutionary statements about going back to the '3Rs'. So we have had to tear up the original draft, which had some interesting thoughts but was in no way 'major', and we are having to write the 'major' speech which the press expects. This is a marvellous chance to feed in some of my personal prejudices.

Home very tired. It is proving a tough week.

Thursday 14 October 1976

Before Cabinet I went up to see the PM. He was delighted about the way the advance publicity was going for the Ruskin education speech.

Ralf Dahrendorf came in at 10.30. We discussed LSE and the future of his 'European Brookings Institute'. He can obviously get a lot of money for it.

Lunch with Peter Gibbings* of the *Guardian*. We discussed rescuing the *Observer*. He is against Murdoch as rescuer because Murdoch is a 'monster' who does not understand quality papers. Agree with that.

Parliamentary Questions went quickly as usual.

At 5.15 the PM saw Peter Shore about his work at DoE. I sat in – and Jim brought me in regularly to the discussion. Jim told me beforehand that he had not had time to read the long Cabinet Office brief. So he followed our Unit brief throughout. It was very satisfying. Shore was good and lively. Jim was adequate, but clearly his mind was not completely on it.

In the evening we continued to work on the education speech. Finally cleared the draft with Ken Stowe – who had made some brilliant additions – at about 10 p.m. and then went home.

Friday 15 October 1976

The PM was away in Wales today.

In the morning the Unit worked on our proposals for a new 'national plan' – or a 'Stabilisation and Recovery Programme 1977–80' as we prefer to call it. An alternative to the Treasury recession.

At midday I went with Gavyn Davies across to the Treasury to discuss public expenditure in Leo Plietzky's room. Leo mentioned the possible need for yet further action – extra cuts or extra taxes. We did not react but simply said that the PM must see any proposals in good time.

I went to lunch with Michael Butler*, from Ottawa, at the Cavalry Club in Piccadilly. Then back for more work on our national plan. Cleared my papers and home by 8.30.

Saturday 16 October 1976

To Cardiff on the new high-speed train in the afternoon. [It travelled faster than trains do in 2008.]

Dinner at the Callaghans' flat with the PM and Audrey, Merlyn Rees and his wife, Ron Hayward and his wife, myself, Jim's secretary, Ruth, and Jean Denham from the Press Office. We all united to attack Ron Hayward about the Trotskyites in the Party. A nice meal and very good company.

Off to the big reception at Sophia Gardens to celebrate Jim becoming PM.

1,000 guests. A cabaret. Marvellous spirit. Music and singing till 2 in the morning. Quite different from Conference. A reminder that there really are nice people in the Labour Party. Decent working-class supporters of Labour, not those guilt-ridden middle-class Trots at Blackpool.

I stayed till 1.45 a.m., then caught a sleeper train to Paddington, got off at 7 a.m., went home for breakfast, and then played a good game of football for two hours.

Monday 18 October 1976

Off to Ruskin College, Oxford, for the big education speech – it has been trailed and discussed so much in the papers that it was impossible to meet expectations.

The official car failed to arrive at home to take me to Paddington for the train, so I had to go all the way to Oxford in the car. It was the PM's reserve 3.5 Rover, full of radio equipment and anti-bomb defences. We thundered up the motorway at 114 m.p.h. I shut my eyes. We went from Northolt to Nuffield in twenty-five minutes! I was petrified. But it was rather funny to arrive at Nuffield gate in the big car, and Warden Chester and the Dean (David Butler*) to step forward and greet me – a long way from when I was a student of theirs. We had drinks in the SCR and then a simple lunch. The PM was very relaxed and chatted nicely to all the students.

He rested after lunch and Tom McCaffrey and I went for a walk around Oxford, including looking into Lincoln College, where I was a very happy undergraduate.

Then out to the Rookery of Ruskin College where Jim delivered his big education speech. He had modified it quite a bit over the weekend, softening some of the criticisms of current education methods, making sure he did not end up in the Rhodes Boyson/Tory camp. He read the speech rather hurriedly and was interrupted by a crowd of student Trot militants, protesting about education cuts. I sat on the platform with Audrey. We are all conscious that these were the *privileged* students protesting. Jim's speech was about the underprivileged in education.

Afterwards we had tea. The PM went to discuss the issues with some student representatives, all – including the girls, I'm sure – with beards.

Then home to the office to clear papers. Among them was the report of the inquiry into the child benefit leak. The police inspector said quite openly that he had concentrated on (i.e. been directed towards) special advisers. But he had found nothing. Yet this conclusion was lost. The Attorney General's report was mainly about how the special advisers talked together about policy decisions and how wrong this is.

But what is ridiculous is that even this report, by police into a criminal leak, is turned into an attack on the political activities of special advisers which has nothing to do with the original reason for the inquiry. Tom McNally and I are both fed up with it, and mean to see the PM to bring it to an end.

Home at 9.00 p.m.

Tuesday 19 October 1976

The PM spent all morning at a meeting of the Cabinet and NEC in the state dining room. I chatted with various ministers going in – Bill Rodgers, Roy Hattersley and Shirley Williams. Shirley says she has plans to follow up the PM's education speech with some hard policy initiatives. She thinks she won't win the deputy leadership.

Spent the morning working on my papers. Then to lunch at the American Embassy with Ron Spiers. We discussed the UK economic situation and the need to finance our sterling balances. He said it is necessary to get the question taken over from their Treasury by the State Department and thinks that Kissinger would help. He also said that the US wants us to take the lead over Rhodesia, since if the US takes the lead that will force the Russians to interfere. But I know that we want the US to lead, since we don't want to carry the can if it fails.

Back to Parliamentary Questions. Almost boring. No tension at all.

Rumours of a prosecution of a minister by the DPP over the Poulson scandal – but I don't know who it is.

I saw and attacked Attorney General Sam Silkin for his child benefit brief, turning it into an attack on the special advisers. He seemed very woolly on it. Obviously it had been drafted for him by officials and he simply signed it without reading it.

Wednesday 20 October 1976

At 3.30 p.m. the PM made a statement on the 'end of the Poulson affair'. Afterwards we had two Cabinet committees, one on small matters of devolution. The PM looked very bored and inclined towards an 'anti-devolution' position. Healey said we must 'take stands now or else too much will be given away to appease the Scots'. Another on the so-called Alternative Economic Strategy ran around the import controls course, with two Cabinet Office papers setting out the pros and cons. No further progress.

Thursday 21 October 1976

Cabinet spent most of its time deciding whether to set up a Commons inquiry into corruption of MPs connected with Poulson. The PM had decided against yesterday – mainly under pressure from the whips who did not want to give away a day's debate to it. But we all felt this was wrong. So they changed their minds today.

Afterwards PQs – quiet as usual (or am I just bored with it?). Then worked in the office till going to Rachel's school in Camden in the evening.

Friday 22 October 1976

The PM in Southampton and Sussex all day.

I went in early to the 9.30 deputy secs meeting. Then spent the rest of the morning discussing our scheme for public expenditure cuts in the public sector. Lunch at the Canadian High Commission to celebrate our Canadian visit. Afternoon to an LSE seminar on French planning – not much for us to learn. They are different. Anyway their Civil Service believes in it.

Off to Suffolk in the pouring rain late at night, very cold and tired.

Monday 25 October 1976

Woken by Harold Lever on the telephone, deeply depressed by yesterday's article in the *Sunday Times* saying that the IMF wanted sterling down to $1.50. This was bound to produce a run on the pound: Lever could now see little hope of us winning through. The impact on domestic inflation will be terrible. The social contract will collapse and we won't have a third round of wages policy.

I am depressed too. We had got domestic policy into good order. Now it is always external pressure on sterling which defeats us. We don't know who planted the *Sunday Times* article. It was from America – but possibly from our Treasury representatives there? So that they can create the kind of sterling crisis in which they can bounce through another deflationary package?

In to No. 10 just before the PM arrived from the TUC/NEC liaison committee. Sterling had fallen 7 cents this morning – the biggest percentage fall ever!! The PM sent for the Chancellor straight away. Just before he saw Healey I talked to him and told him not to be panicked. No more dribs and drabs of policies. Wait for the IMF and then produce a proper final package. This was the line the PM put to the Chancellor and they agreed 'steady as she goes' for the Chancellor's statement to the House this afternoon.

This afternoon worked on papers. Masses of them – the flow is as bad as ever under Harold Wilson. Also went to the committee of permanent secretaries on industrial democracy. Most of them were totally opposed to greater participation by workers and intend to brief their respective ministers accordingly. The Board of Trade man described the Bullock proposal – likely to be very mild – as 'dangerously extremist'. But Douglas Allen summed up very sensibly and we now wait to see what the paper is like.

Worked on clearing papers till 9.30 p.m.

Also watched *Panorama*, where the PM was marvellously indiscreet, again distancing himself from the Treasury and the Bank of England.

Tuesday 26 October 1976

In early. Dealt with papers and then went down to see ministers outside the Cabinet Room before the 10 a.m. Cabinet. I talked to Bill Rodgers and to Shirley Williams and warned them that I had learned that Healey would try to slip through formal approval for more public expenditure cuts – not because I disapprove of these, I don't, but because I don't like the dishonest way the Treasury does it, completely contemptuous of the Cabinet. He did exactly as I predicted, as Bill Rodgers later confirmed on the telephone. But only Shore and Benn spoke up. Bill must wait till he is less 'new'.

I worked on papers all morning – the flow has increased enormously of late, back to Wilsonian proportions, up to 300 pages of typescript a day. It puts a great physical strain on me, especially on my eyes. I also had to make a lot of telephone calls.

Everybody is depressed by the sterling crisis. It has thrown us completely off course. One can sense the feeling that we might lose the next election. It affects everybody. The civil servants are more difficult. The CBI is less co-operative. The Tories are more intransigent. We must re-establish the feeling that we are the only credible government – which means that Healey must get on top of the Treasury again.

Had lunch with [the head of the Civil Service] Douglas Allen. We reached agreement on how to handle industrial democracy. He was also very critical of the Treasury. He said that Douglas Wass did not have 'the grit' to run the Treasury. And that John Hunt was 'not very subtle'. He said that if he had known that the head of the Civil Service would be excluded from access to the PM – because of how William Armstrong* had behaved with Heath – then he would not have taken the job but would have stayed at the Treasury. He had a low opinion of Armstrong, who he felt got on by flattery and who he held responsible for Heath's failure. He was much more open and human than previously, less cynical, and I liked him a lot.

Back to the Commons for PQs – dull as ever. Afterwards Jack Ashley spoke to me about the left's manoeuvres to keep him off the NEC now that Foot has moved to deputy leader.

Back to No. 10. So much paperwork that I could not attend the meeting with the TUC Economic committee. Worked on our 'Public Sector Bureaucracy Cuts' till 9.30 p.m., then drove home.

Wednesday 27 October 1976

There is now a pervading sense of crisis. Sterling remains very weak. The Chancellor is said, by Douglas Wass, to be exhausted and near the end of his tether. We are reported to be doing very badly in the three by-elections due on 4 November. The Treasury forecasts are terrible – PSBR *up* £2 billion above the previous borrowing forecast to £11 billion. Unemployment up above 1.75 million till 1979.

In all this climate the PM went to the Labour National Executive this morning, and that bunch of imbeciles voted 13–6 to support a demonstration *against* the government organised by some trade unions – four of which are not even affiliated to the TUC or the Labour Party. The fatuous irresponsibility of these people is only comprehensible if you have actually met them. The PM sat through it all and then left for a lunch with the shipping owners. Afterwards the press carried headlines that 'Jim storms out'.

I went into the office as usual before 9, since I have to drive Carol into work early.

Lunch with Brian MacArthur* of *The Times*, an old friend of many years. He told me that the *Daily Express* has a story on the police investigating Denis Howell which they are waiting to run. In fact there seems to be some delay on that. Ken Stowe hinted to me that it might not happen since there is a lot of exaggeration. It is Denis's enemies in Birmingham who are trying to get him so there may be a lot of malice and misrepresentations in these rumours.

Went to the Economic Cabinet committee – now called EY, used to be called MES – at 4 p.m. Discussed (again!) increasing top salaries for nationalised industry board chairmen. But it was clear there was no majority for an increase. So the PM summed up saying that the Chancellor must talk to the TUC without a remit.

I went to see Harry Evans for a drink in the flat of his lovely new girl-friend – Tina Brown. He told me that the *Sunday Times* got its story that the IMF would insist on a sterling parity of $1.50 from Washington – first from a *British* Treasury source there, and then confirmed from an American source. Finally they confirmed it with Peter Middleton* in the Treasury here.

Harry is still angling for the Director Generalship of the BBC.

Home at 10 p.m. feeling exhilarated by the crisis, but very tired deep down. Still it is a marvellous opportunity to try to steer things in the right direction. I decide to put in two papers this weekend: (1) on our plan to cut public expenditure by £6 billion in 1977–80 by freezing staff recruitment and salaries in the public bureaucracy, and (2) our proposal for a new national plan 1977–80.

Thursday 28 October 1976

Went in at 9 a.m. The atmosphere still full of crisis and doom, talk of Callaghan not surviving and a coalition around the corner. Some of this phoney – Thatcher had dinner at the Tory Conference in Brighton with Alastair Burnet* of ITN, Ian Trethowan of BBC, the appalling Shrimsley of the *Mail* and Fatty Butt of *The Times* to discuss and co-ordinate this media attack on the government. Even so we are in a bad way at the moment, with inflation turning up again, and it looks like an odd time for me to have left the LSE!! Yet, oddly, I think we will survive through to an election in 1978–79. Whether we would win it, is impossible to tell from this distance in time.

There was a Cabinet committee on Ireland at 9.30. The meeting was difficult for Roy Mason on his first appearance as Secretary of State. His department had drafted a reply to a PQ which showed a swing towards the Protestant position – no mention of 'participation by the minority', etc. The Irish had been shown the draft reply, as usual, and had gone through the roof. Their Cabinet discussed it in Dublin and [Liam] Cosgrave* first approached Thatcher and then telephoned Jim to protest. So Mason was reprimanded and sent off to draft another reply.

I went down before Cabinet – I say 'down', in fact is only half a dozen steps down from my suite of offices to the Cabinet Room and the private secretaries' offices – to see what was going on. I talked to Lever and Varley – who was complaining that the latest investment forecasts are appalling and that our 'industrial strategy is just words'. Then saw Stan Orme, who is trying to appoint a special adviser and is consulting me about it. I suggested Tessa Jowell* from Camden, who is brilliantly able and very nice, and he immediately agreed to see her on Monday. I arranged that straight away.

Worked in the Unit in the morning, getting our two papers into final form, though Gavyn Davies had done much of the hard drafting on them.

The PM also discussed with me my information to him on the role of Glasgow Protestants in Northern Ireland terrorism. He said that the information is good. I still have not told him my Irish source.

Had lunch at No. 10, for the first time in some weeks.

Then PQs. Very riotious. In the gallery was a Russian delegation led by Pomavivev, the murderous ex-Stalinist. The Tories attacked on this from the beginning, which was a ridiculous mistake. There are so many policy areas where we are weak at the moment; it is ridiculous for them to waste their ammunition on this – especially since Jim won in the end.

The Tory attack has been spearheaded by Winston Churchill. Yet he visited Russia in 1974 and wrote articles arguing the need for and benefits from such contacts. Jim had dug out one of the articles. He also dropped a personal note to the Speaker asking to him call Churchill – very improper, but happens, especially among the 'Welsh Mafia'. The Speaker left Churchill till the end. Churchill quoted Bevin against having dealings with the Russians. Jim rose slowly. He said he had a quote too. From Churchill himself. Arguing in favour of the maximum amount of contact between our politicians and the Russians. Our benches cheered. Churchill was crushed (lots of Tories looked pleased at this). And that was the end of Question Time.

The PM saw Lord Bullock to get a preview of his report on industrial democracy, which is apparently running into lots of trouble, with the CBI representatives writing a minority report against worker representatives on the boards. Actually the commission was fated to fail from the beginning because: (1) it was specifically required to look at trade union (not 'workers') representatives on *boards*, and (2) the industrial representatives were known hardliners.

In the evening I went to dinner with Israeli Yoram Peri*. Among his guests was Hans Koschnik, deputy leader of the German Socialist Party. He was very funny, intelligent and immensely well informed. He is mayor of Bremen, but knows a great deal about international politics.

At midnight Koschnik and I went privately into the bedroom and discussed Germany's attitude to Britain's financial position. He said that he had been in the German Cabinet on Monday morning, with Schmidt, Genscher, Apfel, etc. when they discussed Britain, and all agreed Germany must help because it would be terrible for *Europe* if Britain collapsed. Koschnik said he firmly believed that many of the financial community, and especially the Americans, *wanted* the Labour government to fall. The Germans wanted to preserve it. We agreed to keep in touch.

I went home to bed at 1 a.m. Carol was still out to dinner with the NUT.

Friday 29 October 1976

Woke early and heard that sterling was very strong in the Far Eastern markets on rumours of a German loan to Britain! Phoned Gavyn Davies at 7.45 and then drove quickly to the office. Cleared my papers by 9.10 and then went upstairs to see the PM, who had just come down from the flat, where he slept last night.

We discussed the 'loan' story – the PM did not confirm it or show any knowledge. He is very tight on information. We also discussed the press and the apparent campaign by the Tories and the press to crack his nerve. He said he did not feel that his nerve was cracking (though he did personally telephone Robert Carvel of the *Standard* yesterday to point this out – a great mistake, since journalists suspect that a PM's nerve *is* cracking when he telephones them personally to complain!).

I briefed him verbally for his meeting with the Chancellor. The Treasury plans now are to cut £3 billion from the PSBR – half by tax and half by public expenditure cuts. I wanted to press him that *cuts* are better than taxes. Healey looked *exhausted*, his eyes small and red from lack of sleep. No wonder Wass says that he is 'cracking'.

I went back to the office for a while then to deputy secs meeting in John Hunt's room to plan next week's business. I went home before lunch, picked up the four children, and drove in the rain to Suffolk, which was grey and soggy. Carol stayed in London on NUT business. I won't get much rest cooking for four children, but it will be a change.

Monday 1 November 1976

Went in early and spent all morning reading through an enormous pile of papers. Taking off half a day, as on Friday, leaves me terribly behind. There was a good paper on the third pay round from the Treasury – 5% plus a little margin for differentials.

Lunch at the Reform. Ate alone and badly. Coffee with Bob Worcester*, the pollster, who is still convinced that Jimmy Carter* will win in the USA. The PM has said throughout that Ford would do it. [Bob was right.]

Back through the Park and the rain to No. 10. The weather has been appalling, grey and wet every day. It begins to get people down. I am tired, tense and overworked. Exhilarated by the excitement, but a bit nervy. I still feel sore with the LSE and have intervened to cut the public expenditure on university teachers' pay. Silly tit for tat, but it eases my annoyance.

Good news was the very positive reaction by the PM to our weekend paper on a new national plan 1977–80. He wrote a full separate note to say how much he approved the approach and asked me to process it with John Hunt. I went to see Hunt at 4 o'clock. He was a bit jumpy, because the CPRS are doing a paper on the same subject and he clearly wanted the Cabinet Office to make the running. He therefore pressed me not to take our paper to the Treasury or to ministers. But he responded positively and said he hoped to have a Green Paper – which we propose – out by Christmas.

I agreed to go along with him, but warned him that I was very committed on this, and if there was any delay I would push ahead with it myself. I would go to ministers direct. However, if Hunt will work with us, that will be smoother and more efficient, since he is a remarkably effective operator on the Whitehall machine.

David Lipsey, Crosland's clever special adviser, came in to see me at 6.30 p.m. to liaise over economic policy, where our plan of mobilising Crosland and the Foreign Office to counter the Treasury is coming along nicely. Crosland has put in an excellent memo to the PM (David Owen helped in the drafting) suggesting that we work through the EEC to get long-term funding of our sterling balances. Crosland is going to appoint an economic adviser to strengthen him on the economic side. He is thinking of getting Michael Stewart*. I talked to Crosland when he came in before lunch and we agreed it was time to have another drink.

Lipsey and I agreed to keep in touch, and to try to get a common economic position – accepting *some* cuts, but opposing Treasury negativism, and trying to push our industrial strategy.

The PM called a secret and emergency meeting of the ministerial group discussing the economic situation – Healey, Crosland, Lever and Douglas Wass. I chatted with Healey beforehand, and went into the lavatory for a pee with him. I said that things would be better from the end of the month, and we must stick to the existing strategy. He said, 'If things are not better, we shall really be in the shit.'

Then Crosland came into the lavatory for a pee as well. Healey began to pull his leg about press leaks that Crosland was fighting Healey in Cabinet. I then left the lavatory and slipped into the waiting room to tell Lipsey to keep hiding since we did not want the Treasury to know that we were meeting – and in fact not even Crosland knew he was coming to see me.

At around 9 p.m. I saw the PM and walked to the front door with him. He said, 'Well, Bernard, as my spiritual adviser, don't you think we should make our next big speech on violence, vandalism, law and order, etc.?' I agree and we will start working on it.

Home at 10 p.m.

Tuesday 2 November 1976

Feeling worryingly tired and tense. Most of the morning spent on the enormous flow of papers. The PM was in the study all morning, reading and relaxing. He also telephoned Schmidt in Germany. It went well but nothing conclusive. One thing he said was that the Tories, and especially Keith Joseph, had been persuading the American bankers *not* to loan Britain money.

I had lunch with Joel Barnett at the House of Commons. We discussed the possibilities for further cuts. He is pessimistic. He cannot see us getting more than £700 million. He said that Denis had been depressed by reports that the PM was not supporting him – and that the officials blamed me and said that I had briefed the press accordingly. This is ludicrous. I believe that Healey is the best Chancellor around. I disagree with some of the particular policies which he has pursued of late, but still think he is the best man we could have there.

I didn't go to Questions because I had a meeting in the Treasury with Leo Plietzky. Plietzky lectured us in customary fashion on his dedication to keep public expenditure under control. On cuts, he says they must come from changes in social security legislation – ending the commitment to uprate in line with the *gross* rise in earnings – and from the housing area. Curiously Plietzky does not seem to feel we can get savings from Defence.

Later Stella Greenhall, Mulley's adviser, phoned me from Education to say that the DES blames me for giving the notorious DES policy document to *The Times* and the *Guardian*. Incredible. I only had one copy, which I still have. This is all ridiculous. Typical of the Civil Service. They are as suspicious of leaks as Harold Wilson. It seems that I am the target for all their smears. But it is pathetic that these overpaid bureaucrats do not have something better to do.

In the evening Joe Rogaly* of the *FT* dropped in with his and my daughters and he said his colleague Michael Dixon was specially told by the DES Press Office that I had handed out the documents to its usual newspapers. Crazy.

Exhausted and came home to bed at 10.30 p.m.

Wednesday 3 November 1976

Went to NEDC in the morning. Discussed industrial strategy, etc. I did not stay for lunch, but went off with Robert Armstrong to a nice restaurant in St Martin's Lane. He is waiting quietly to take over as permanent secretary at the Home Office. He told me that Harold Wilson had involved Charles Curran* of the BBC in his mad pursuit of South African spies. Wilson had sent for two BBC/freelance journalists and told them he, as ex-PM, knew of a big scoop story, but he would only give it to them if they got the full and open support of the head of the BBC. So Curran stepped in. Now they have discovered there is nothing to discover. They all look fools. And the BBC is furious.

We walked back down to St Martin's Lane and then hailed a lift with Harold's doctor Joe (now Lord) Stone*. He was going to the Lords. This is amusing since this morning's *Guardian* had attacked Wilson's list of peers because they rarely voted to support the government. Marcia has still never voted. Joe has obviously decided he had better turn up.

At 4 o'clock there was a fascinating EY Cabinet committee to discuss the latest depressing Treasury national income forecast, and the resulting stance we should take with the IMF negotiators, now here. The four 'import controllers' – Foot, Benn, Shore and Booth – persuaded no new recruits. Shore was very honest in facing up to the massive deflation that must go with protection. Benn does not admit it. For the others it was a question of how to reinforce and modify the existing strategy. Hattersley and Varley wanted cuts in the social programme so that we can concentrate on jobs and getting unemployment down.

Healey at first looked depressed. Yet the number of ministers who accepted firm measures – and 'cutting the social programme' – made him realise that he was not too isolated. So in his concluding summary Healey was much more buoyant.

Afterwards Jim came out and chatted with the two Toms and me. He was still in good form, joking and confident. He told me to keep working away on the public sector cuts. 'You won't get away with it,' he said, 'but keep at it. It's right.'

I went back to the Unit and Gavyn Davies and I discussed our next papers. Then home – with a cold coming on.

Thursday 4 November 1976

Today is by-election day – Workington, Walsall and Newcastle – and we are expecting to do badly. Reports from the constituencies by MPs and canvassers reveal that morale is low and Party organisation is deplorable. The general secretary, Ron Hayward, spends his time exhibiting his vanity on TV, while the Party machine collapses.

Tom McNally told the PM that he thought we would just hold on to all three seats. I am not so sure. A lot of things have gone wrong lately. There is an air of mismanagement about the government, especially in the financial field.

While waiting for Cabinet I talked to several ministers. Stan Orme asked me to send him an economist as special adviser – I suggested David Metcalf* from the LSE. Michael Foot was back after his illness, still looking poorly, a bad colour, and with 'wraparound' spectacles to protect his eyes after the shingles. We discussed the economic situation, on which he is very pessimistic.

I also had a long talk with the chief secretary of the Treasury, Joel Barnett, about public expenditure. Joel is still pessimistic about getting any cuts. I urge him to continue along the line of *restructuring* and *redistributing* public expenditure – away from the bureaucracy, and to some extent away from its more extravagant social programmes, towards industrial investment. The problem is how to get the industrial investment to *actually happen* when we provide the funds. In fact the banks have funds *now* – though at high interest rates – and nobody is investing. Joel does not believe direct state intervention will work. Only a restoration of confidence and profit margins. Maybe right but I would still like to launch an investment programme.

I spent most of the rest of the morning in the Unit and then went to lunch at the Reform with Robin Butler, who has just finished a task of setting up the computer monitoring of the new cash limits system in the Treasury. He is next going off to be secretary of the Public Expenditure Survey Committee (PESC).

Robin and I spent much of the time discussing the Treasury. Clearly he is responsible for persuading Plietzky to include me in his discussions on public expenditure. Robin sensibly believes that the Treasury should be opened up. He said that they are fairly demoralised in there. Their trouble is that they take such a narrow view. And on City market questions, e.g. sales of gilts, they leave it to the Bank of England.

I worked in the Unit in the late afternoon, suffering more and more from a bad cold. We were all supposed to go off to a reception at the Russian Embassy, but we called it off.

There was a dinner for the Fabian Society in the evening. It was a mixed bunch of guests. A very eccentric publisher who talked about Nigeria. John Cleese* the comedian and Melvyn Bragg* the novelist (who talked good sense), plus some Labour councillors from the North, and economist J.K. Galbraith* who dropped in from the USA at the last minute. Tom and I tried to persuade the Fabians to work more closely with the constituency parties to defeat left-wing claptrap, but they seemed a bit afraid of this. The PM spoke some good sense, and Audrey, who was 'allowed' to come along, intervened very intelligently on the Health Service. I like her more and more.

I went home at midnight and listened to the first by-election result. Newcastle, Ted Short's old seat, where there was an appallingly low poll, but we held on, and the Liberals pushed the Tories into third place. This was not too discouraging. But then between 1 and 2 a.m. came the hammer blows at Walsall and Workington. Both lost – swings of 13% and 22%. I drank some more whisky and went to bed.

Friday 5 November 1976

Went in by 9 a.m., cleared my papers, and then went to see the PM for the meeting McNally and I had scheduled a week ago to discuss the aftermath of the by-elections. Jim looked a bit glum. The press was terrible, blowing up the jubilation of Mrs Thatcher and writing us off as finished. He was a bit worried that Thatcher's morale and personal popularity might increase, and he sent for and listened to a tape of her broadcast interview on the radio this morning.

But he soon cheered up. We discussed improving relations with the Party – and particularly sorting out the left-wing hacks and deadbeats on the NEC and in Transport House. McNally believes it needs a counter-revolution. To persuade the unions to send good men to the NEC – and not to vote for horrors such as Ian Mikardo* (whom the PM hates).

I went back to the Unit where they were meeting to revise our paper on a new national recovery programme 1977–80. Andrew Graham had come up specially from Oxford and David Gowland was there from York. David Piachaud came in from the LSE later, so all our loyal consultants were present.

The meeting was broken up by the arrival of my lunch guest, John Lyons, the general secretary of the Power Engineers. We went to the Reform for lunch. He is clearly going to build up that union into something big. If they pull the switches, the country comes to a halt. He told me that the next pay round is very much in doubt because his people will insist on getting bigger differentials – not just a straight percentage. He thinks that Jack Jones has pushed the egalitarianism too far. He suspects that the *present* pay round will begin to crumble next spring. It is worrying because he is a responsible man, no idle talker, and his union has big clout.

More encouraging, he agrees wholly on the need to reduce the public sector bureaucracy. He says that the government should stand up to any strikes from the public sector trade unions – the rest would not support them. If only the politicians had the nerve to do it.

Back to the Unit where we were working on two papers. One on the IMF negotiations, stressing to the PM that the Treasury must insist to the IMF that there is no case whatsoever for deflation. The other is our revised national plan. This produced a great flutter in the Cabinet Office. There the CPRS has produced a paper which is really just a bleak statement of our hopeless economic position. This is scheduled to go to ministers on Monday, for Wednesday's ministerial discussion at EY. The problem was, what about our paper, which was more political, quite different from the CPRS paper, and which the PM liked and has already approved? We wanted it to go to ministers. Hunt did not and intervened with Ken Stowe to try to stop this. Ken finally reached a sensible compromise. He put *both* papers to the PM and asked *him* to choose.

Another vivid and exhilarating week. I am enjoying it immensely. I still feel the government will get through till 1978. But by then it may have lost several more by-elections and could be defeated in the Commons. It is a tightrope, but I am enjoying walking it.

Monday 8 November 1976

Carol dropped me off in Kentish Town to visit my doctors to get inoculations against typhoid, cholera, smallpox, etc. for my visit to India. Began to feel poorly afterwards. I already had a cold and this made it worse.

The PM had liked our Policy Unit paper on a new national plan and instructed that it be distributed to ministers at EY on Wednesday. That is satisfying, but also worrying. The regular Civil Service will resent this intrusion by 'outsiders'.

Jean Corston*, the excellent Labour Party organiser from the South-West region, came in during the afternoon and reported on the horrors of canvassing in Walsall for last week's by-election – apparently there was no organisation whatsoever: no canvass cards, no postal votes, no cards, no committee rooms.

Dinner in the evening at the Reform Club.

Tuesday 9 November 1976

I decided not to attend this morning's two Cabinet committees – Gen 45 on the *Observer* (ministers are still *against* rescuing it) and Gen 12 on Rhodesia (Ivor Richard* was here from Geneva to report on the conference: he seemed confident and said that the blacks were just making a public fuss 'for the record').

Had lunch at the Reform with Alan Lord, a permanent secretary at the Treasury, to discuss the current economic proposals. He tried to bully me a bit on regional policy and investment incentives to industry. But at coffee we began to agree on a broad 'package'. He liked my idea of getting big cuts through a freeze on public sector bureaucracy recruitment. I liked his idea of keeping the savings on the shelf and re-spending much of them on the second stage of the industrial policy, which Neddy [the NEDC] should have ready by Christmas. So the net result would be fairly neutral in demand and unemployment terms.

Lord dashed off back to the Treasury. I went outside into Pall Mall and ran into Douglas Wass. He said that Healey is very down at the moment, and implied that the PM and No. 10 were not giving him enough support. He also strongly denied that any Treasury officials had been against us getting long-term loans to fund the sterling balances. It was clear that they are feeling sore and oppressed in Great George Street.

Actually what Healey needs is some *personal* staff – a policy unit and some special advisers who he can let his hair down with. He is completely on his own with that departmental machine. Yet when I put this to Alan Lord he reacted very sharply, saying that the private secretaries can provide everything a minister needs.

I returned to the Commons for Question Time. The PM was in an aggressive mood. He said that 'the time for statesmanship is over. Now is the time for Callaghan the heel.' I did not go into the chamber, but the others said it went very well and that he knocked Thatcher around pretty hard.

I went off to see Victor Rothschild at his flat in St James's Place, overlooking the Park, which looked lovely in the winter sunshine. He told me about the first stage of his Royal Commission on Gambling. He also told me that Harold Wilson had been to dinner with him, had been full of praise for me, and had asked if Victor would ask me if I would be 'nominally' associated with his inquiry into City financial institutions. How strange that he should approach so indirectly.

I dashed to a meeting at LSE to discuss Ralf Dahrendorf's idea for a 'British Brookings'. Quite a high-powered meeting: Douglas Wass, Belgrove of BP, Mark Bonham Carter*, Peter Parker* of British Railways, Frank Macfadean of British Airways, Anthony Part*, formerly of the Department of Industry, and Edward Boyle*. We made a lot of progress, and clearly Ralf has access to quite big funds. It could just happen.

We ate a buffet supper at the table and then Douglas Wass drove me to No. 10 and came into my room to talk. Wass very excited and felt that the next ten days would decide our financial fate. He told me that the IMF people are afraid that if they impose their customary 'stern' monetary regime they will bring down the government here – as they feel they have already done in Italy! Well that is encouraging, at least.

I worked in the office and then left at 9 p.m.

The PM has a secret meeting tomorrow morning with all the top Treasury people about the IMF.

Wednesday 10 November 1976

Went in feeling nervous about this morning's Cabinet committee on economic strategy (EY) which is discussing our Policy Unit paper as well as the CPRS paper on the national recovery programme. The PM asked me to speak. I was nervous addressing a Cabinet committee. Ken Berrill had just introduced the CPRS paper, so I pointed out the differences – basically that ours was more political and involved more participation by the trade unions, etc. I saw John Hunt's brief to the PM, which was quite disgracefully biased. Only one line reference to our paper, saying it 'may be criticised for lack of credibility'.

The discussion went heavily our way with support especially from Benn and Crosland. John Hunt looked very black and started to nudge the PM into taking the next item (third round of incomes policy). The only dissenting voice was Peter Shore, who does not want *any* national recovery paper, since it would presumably exclude his protection strategy. That is precisely why we should have one.

Overall it was a great triumph for us. But we must watch out to make sure that John Hunt does not torpedo it along the way.

Ken Berrill took all the criticism of his CPRS with a shrug and a wry smile. He is incredibly cool and detached. It reminded me of a conversation I once had with him when he said, with slight surprise, 'You actually *care* about these things, don't you, Bernard.'

Afterwards we had lunch for [François-Xavier] Ortoli* of the EEC. Only thirty guests, including Roy Jenkins as the new president of Europe. Roy looked very nervous beforehand and was flapping a bit. As a friend, I just wish he would seem more relaxed. I sat with John Hale, my former tutor at Oxford, and Mark Hughes, who was also at Oxford with me as an undergraduate. I have been trying to get Hale an appointment in the arts world. Dahrendorf sat next to the PM, who asked him to arrange a seminar of sympathetic economists so that he could hear some alternative strategies.

Afterwards Art Hartman – US State Department – came to see me and we discussed our problems for an hour. He is very impressive, and seems to be more confident now that he knows Kissinger is about to be off his back.

I went over to see Tony Crosland in his room at the Commons at 7.15 p.m. We discussed economic policy, and he was very critical of Healey, and said straight out that he could do it better. He will clearly attack if further deflation is proposed. But I suggested to him some tolerable cuts in the public sector, providing the money is spent elsewhere to maintain demand.

Crosland did not seem to me to have any new ideas or particular suggestions. Just that it was 'a good thing' to maintain public expenditure, and we 'must not lose sight of our principles'. He seemed tired and without any drive. There were a couple of bottles of medicine on his desk. I felt that he now depends very much on David Lipsey for economic facts and detailed arguments. And my estimate of Lipsey has seriously gone up. He is a very clever young man. But Crosland is near the end of the road physically and politically – though he will intellectually still frighten Healey in Cabinet.

I drove home quite late – 10 o'clock, and sat up talking domestic problems to Carol till 11.30 p.m.

Thursday 11 November 1976

David Ennals had asked to see me before Cabinet at 9.45 a.m. I took him up to my room and he immediately began to complain about a letter I had sent to a Labour backbencher in which I had shown concern for the problems of the handicapped in getting dental treatment. He said that by saying that I and the PM were concerned we were implying that he was not concerned. It was partly his *amour propre*; he wanted a monopoly of concern. But it was also his department, which was trying to steer us away from interfering in their territory. I was feeling tired and influenza'd anyway, so I got a bit impatient with him and told him he was being oversensitive. We parted on less than friendly terms. His predecessor, Barbara Castle, with all her faults, would never have been as silly as that.

I also had a quick word with Harold Lever. Yesterday morning's secret meeting with Healey, Lever, the Governor of the Bank, Derek Mitchell and Douglas Wass had decided to send Lever to Washington to see Arthur Burns* and others to try to raise some big loans. This is Healey's idea. He realises that anything Lever can get is useful. But the officials are against Lever, and will certainly spread some poison against him in advance. I noticed today that one of our private secretaries, and [Kit] McMahon* from the Bank of England, made gratuitous attacks on Lever. This only happens when the 'machine grapevine' is pushing out the poison.

Once Cabinet had begun I went through to the Cabinet Office to see Ken Berrill about the national recovery programme. It was clear that they were not very interested now that their draft had been rejected. But Ken and I reached an agreement, which basically meant the Policy Unit doing the work – and having the control.

Worked desperately to clear my papers before lunch. Lately I have had too many meetings, and the volume of paper is getting on top of me, especially as I feel unwell from my smallpox, typhoid and cholera injections.

Lunched at Wheelers with Kit McMahon of the Bank of England. He is very clever and interesting. They feel very touchy about the PM's criticisms of their technical competence in managing the currency. He repeatedly tried to reassure me that the Bank was not against the Labour government politically. I accepted this, while suggesting it would help if all the Governor's speeches did not totally coincide with the current policies of the Tory Opposition.

We had a long argument about economics. He said that public borrowing must be got down, but could not answer my question of how to get it down without causing more unemployment – which increases the PSBR. We discussed the vicious circles – every policy to improve problem X always makes worse problems Y and Z. It got heated at times but was interesting. We agreed that we should meet again – though I felt he really wanted me to suggest that the PM sees the Governor more often. Actually what the Governor needs is a policy adviser!

One serious point he made is that defending a fixed sterling rate with large reserves is quite different, and easier, than, as we do, defending a floating rate with inadequate reserves. The floating rate always encourages the speculator that he can make a *quick* profit – and the lack of reserves means that he *will*.

I again missed Question Time – this time in order to attend John Hunt's deputy secretaries meeting. We agreed the timetable for the next draft of the national recovery programme. Hunt admitted that he is against the programme and that he was going to try to talk to the PM against it in Paris. I warned him off trying to torpedo it. Ministers may wish to drop it, but that is for them, not for civil servants.

The PM went off to see Giscard in Paris, to get his support for our international monetary needs. I am pessimistic since the French oppose Britain on everything.

At dinner in the Commons dining room with Harold Lever, Harold ordered sweet white Sauternes to go with all the courses. It really did not go with the hors d'oeuvre, but it was such a superbly luscious Sauternes that I drank it regardless – and so did he. His beautiful wife Diane told me that she hunts around to find wine shops selling *half* bottles, since they find full bottles wasteful. It was a happy meal, with lots of gossip, and surrounded by some odd characters, including the Duke of Kent.

John Biffen* came over to me to say that 'a friend of mine' [Enoch Powell*] says he is going 'to keep your show on the road'.

I ran into Bill Rodgers downstairs and he gave me a lift back home. He said he had eaten with Denis Howell, who had told him all about his troubles with Bryants, the Birmingham builders, and how he knew the police were investigating him for corruption. Denis is clearly worried. But Bill is convinced Denis will be OK – because he has always declared his interest. Everybody knew he worked for Bryants. Still I ought to have a drink with Denis to give him some support.

I felt very tired when I got home at 11.30 and a bit 'fluey'. These inoculations have affected me badly.

Friday 12 November 1976

Ill in bed all day.

Monday 15–Wednesday 17 November 1976

This is written quickly and in one go. I am off to India for a long weekend on Thursday morning – tomorrow – and the last few days have been a fantastic rush.

Everything has been dominated by the IMF visitation. Massive secrecy is being maintained, but I pick up information from every possible contact and end up with a fairly full picture. A large number of people know what is going on – many more than the politicians realise.

Nobody has ever written properly about Whitehall's doctrine of secrecy, and the way in which all Prime Ministers are deliberately worked up about 'leaks'. It is a device that is used to freeze out the 'political' side – ministers as well as special advisers. Here are decisions being taken which could decide the fate of this Labour government. Yet the Labour members of it are frozen out of the decision making. Apart from the PM and the Chancellor, only civil servants are informed. Tom McNally and Tom McCaffrey do not know. I only know because I have learned ways of finding out and spent most of my day 'snooping'. I read all the papers going into the PM's 'dip', overhear telephone conversations in Private Office, keep a close eye on the PM's diary, talk to a 'friend' in the Cabinet Office, plus special advisers and ministers who may know pieces of the jigsaw without realising their full significance. I also ask Ken Stowe direct questions which he generally answers, partly because he has always preferred to be open and helpful, mainly because it would be ridiculous not to. I also telephone garrulous Leo Plietzky in the Treasury and he usually spills the beans. But it is a hard and silly process. Ridiculous that we are not told automatically. Ridiculous that we are always suspected of leaking to the press. In fact I do occasionally talk with three old friends on newspapers without giving anything secret away – one on the *Sunday Times* (Harold Evans), one on *The Times* (Peter Hennessy) and one on the *Financial Times* (Joe Rogaly). *Each* tells me that *most* of their frequent leaks of *secret* information comes from regular civil servants.

Although I spent the time *gathering* information, there was little I could do. The situation is still fluid. No precise figures have been put on the table. The Treasury was not authorised to *negotiate*, only to explore, until Wednesday's EY Cabinet committee.

Harold Lever was in Washington since Saturday. He telephoned me late on Wednesday night to say that the American position was softening and that we need not impose massive and suicidal deflation. But that evening's Cabinet committee authorised the Treasury to go ahead on a basis of getting the PSBR down by quite a big figure.

This EY was delayed over two hours because there was a privilege debate and Foot had to be in the chamber. I hung around getting agitated because of my departure tomorrow morning to Bombay – and still no packing done, etc. When we finally assembled the PM said that we have to get the PSBR down. But he wanted to do other things at the same time – get the sterling safety net and push the industrial strategy. He also expressed doubts about holding the Party together. This seemed both to satisfy and to mute the rest of the meeting, which was very restrained.

Healey seemed uncertain, but was not hard-pressed. Shore said he was not interested in the figures of cuts in the PSBR, but only in what amount of deflation that added up to. Hattersley said that he suspected that in seven years' time we would look back and consider ourselves mad to have mutilated ourselves for the sake of the PSBR fetish. Like others he said he was prepared to proceed only because of the reassurance from the PM at the beginning. Crosland intervened early but failed to hit the point. He sounded very academic.

Healey was probably pleased with this outcome. Without being too precise, he managed to flash around PSBR figures such as £8.5–9 billion – which is a commitment to quite considerable cuts. His case is now resting solely on the 'market reaction'. There is no resources case, he admits. His final position, and the PM has some sympathy with it, is that it will do us no good to twist the arm of the IMF to give us a 'soft' settlement – because if the markets know that they will give the settlement the thumbs-down and sterling will collapse. That is why we must *persuade* the IMF and the City that the 'soft' option is *correct* economically. But of course officials at the Treasury and the Bank are unlikely to do that.

In the Unit we briefed the PM, as we had throughout so far, that there was no resources case for deflation, and that the only sensible thing to do was to cut some social expenditure and re-spend it on industrial investment.

Tuesday evening I went to the farewell party for lovely Janet Hewlett Davies from our Press Office. It was a touching occasion (she is going off to work with Bill Rodgers). Joe Haines and Albert Murray were there and we three sat in the corner of the pillared room and gossiped like in the old days. Albert made a little speech (frequently interrupted by Joe and me). I left at about 9.30 to supervise our brief for tomorrow's EY.

Apparently Albert and Joe went downstairs later to sing to the garden-room girls. Joe took the last train home to Tonbridge but fell asleep and went all the way to Hastings. He had to take a taxi back which cost him £16. When I phoned him next morning he had a bad head.

Wednesday was spent preparing for the EY, clearing papers before India and generally catching up.

Thursday 18–Monday 22 November 1976

This was the most fantastic trip of my life. To Bombay, Delhi, the Taj Mahal, Agra, Fatipur Sikri. First class, as a guest of Stephen Wheatcroft of British Airways, colour and flowers and beautiful women. (Carol came too.) I was bitten by the East and will go there again.

Inevitably the flight back went wrong. The British Airways plane was delayed so I switched and flew all night to Paris, changed, and arrived in No. 10 by 10 in the morning – by when the Cabinet had just begun.

Tuesday 23 November 1976

I was feeling enormously exhilarated despite my lack of sleep. India had an extraordinary effect on me, as if I could devote the rest of my life to her. Sadly that won't happen. The swirl of events here will soon sweep me up and engulf me again.

Cabinet was discussing the IMF. Originally it had been intended to hold a Cabinet committee (EY) but now it is switched to a full Cabinet. The Chancellor's paper showed the 1977–78 PSBR now forecast at £10.5 billion. He set out the implications of getting it down to 'below £9 billion' – the IMF suggest £8.5 billion. But of course the forecasting techniques are anyway totally unreliable. For 1977–78 Healey's proposals mean GDP rising only 1% – i.e. creating 100,000 more unemployed. He was suggesting £1 billion in real expenditure cuts, plus some financial rearrangement including £450 million from selling our Burmah/BP shares. He then set out a borrowing target for 1978–79 of £6.5 billion, i.e. down a further £2 billion, partly because of reduced debt interest. This would all get the balance of payments into surplus a bit earlier.

From my talks with ministers afterwards it is clear that Healey had a rough ride. The majority of ministers said that it was not on. Only Dell and [Reginald] Prentice support him. The PM was detached.

Crosland led the attack much more effectively than last week. He demolished Healey's case – and then conceded £1 billion of cuts simply to meet the 'irrationality of the foreigners'. Bill Rodgers had been in caucus beforehand with Shirley Williams, Hattersley and Ennals and they had decided to be very tough. So the Cabinet adjourned to think again. And the Treasury decided that it did not want Thursday's scheduled Cabinet. Later I heard from the Cabinet Office that the Treasury still had not got the message, and proposed to go ahead as if nothing had happened in Cabinet.

In the afternoon the PM saw Len Murray, who apparently told him that the TUC would support the government whatever we do, but they could not hold the support of individual union conferences in the spring if we had another big squeeze.

The Eve of State Opening party at No. 10 was useful, as usual, for me to talk to ministers. Especially to Rodgers, and to David Owen who is very involved in the FCO's economic activities.

Went home at 9.30 to get my first full night's sleep in nearly a week – in India I got up at 4 or 5 o'clock every morning, and last night was on an aeroplane.

Wednesday 24 November 1976

The EY Economic Cabinet committee was cancelled. I took my daughter Rachel in to No. 10 and then to the State Opening of Parliament. We stood in the central lobby and watched the Speakers' parade. She loved it. Lots of MPs came up to us and chatted.

The afternoon was an incredible rush. David Lipsey came in to discuss the IMF package. I also ran into marvellous Paul Sarbanes*, from my Oxford days, now senator for Maryland. In between we were trying to draft our paper on a suggested compromise package for the IMF. In the evening I was supposed to go to see Harold Lever, but I was so tired by the time we had finished at 9.30 p.m. that I went home.

Thursday 25 November 1976

To the office early, clear papers, then off to the CPRS in the Cabinet Office to discuss our national recovery programme. Not much progress there.

This morning's Cabinet had a brief discussion of the IMF, but nothing serious and no papers. The Treasury had decided not to expose its hand for a while.

Lunch upstairs with the private secretaries.

Spent the afternoon with Gavyn Davies drafting our 'compromise package'. He had thought of clever ways of getting £3 billion off the PSBR with little deflation – mainly through import deposits and investment expenditure to boost the industrial strategy. We put this in to the PM at 8 p.m.

Then I dashed off to the Reform to have dinner with Mike and Mrs Kirby from Canada. Very pleasant. Home at 11.30.

Friday 26 November 1976

What a day! Went to the weekly deputy secretaries meeting in the Cabinet Office at 9.45. Came back and was about to see Peter Bourne, Jimmy Carter's aide, when the PM phoned to say he wanted to talk to me about our paper last night. I took up Gavyn and Tom McNally.

Jim took us through the paper paragraph by paragraph. He quizzed us on every detail, showing a remarkable grasp of the technical detail, clearly an inheritance from his Treasury days. Gavyn was stunned by this grilling, though he coped and answered brilliantly on questions where I was stumped.

At the end the PM said he thought it did give him a way through and he authorised us to send it to the Treasury. Then he sent for the Chancellor and, with only Tom McNally in the room, took the Chancellor through it and according to Tom was very tough on Healey. The PM pushed our suggestions very hard.

It was very pleasing for us. This is the second time that the PM has used one of our papers to grill the Chancellor. Gavyn was delighted, if petri-fied. Now we wait for the Treasury's revenge.

Went to lunch with the French cultural attaché – a lunch for a visiting French director of the budget, who was giving a lecture at the LSE, which I attended (it was in French and very technical!).

Then back to No. 10 to complete our revised paper to send to the Chancellor. And another paper on import controls to refute a very crafty paper from Tony Benn (drafted by his adviser Francis Cripps) saying that *now* is the time for the alternative strategy. This latter will go to Cabinet next week, so the PM wanted some answers this weekend.

In the evening I went to dinner with the French economic attaché. Delightful. Marvellous food and beautiful ladies. Home at 1.30 a.m. Exhausted. And tomorrow we give a big dinner party!

Monday 29 November 1976

The pouring rain continues, pelting down day after day, just as I remember from my childhood. Days of puddles and wellingtons. I went in late to the office, because the PM is at the European Heads meeting at The Hague. Masses of paper to read – and too many visitors.

I was trying to find out what was going on with the IMF. I was told that the Chancellor had personally read our minute and that the Treasury was 'actively considering it'. I gather from Private Office and from the Cabinet Office that the Treasury was still at sixes and sevens. Healey has still not made up his mind. Different officials incline to packages of different sizes.

Went to lunch with Professor Hilde Himmelweit* at LSE.

At 5 went with Gavyn to see Leo Plietzky in the Treasury. He made his usual long opening speech, on his triumphs in cutting public expenditure, but it was still too high. He added that he had been personally authorised by the PM to talk with the IMF. He said that the IMF wanted £1.5–2 billion in real public expenditure cuts. He said that the Chancellor would put to Cabinet a paper containing alternative packages ranging from £1.5–2.5 billion cuts, with a range of ways of getting them. Plietzky said that we needed to get our total of spending down by about 2% and then all would be well. I protested that this meant adding massively to unemployment. He said that if we did not do it we would run out of money like Turkey once did.

The Treasury is aiming particularly at school meals. There are now nearly 700,000 ancillaries in education (mainly part-time) and thousands of expensive luxurious kitchens which are used for only a couple of hours a day – an incredible waste.

We went through our paper. Clearly they had little objection to our proposals – except that they came from us, outsiders; and that they did not contain enough public expenditure blood. Above all the Treasury is insisting on the need to reduce social security benefits upratings. This is political dynamite and almost certain not to get through the Commons, but they are not interested in such practical and political considerations. To be fair, they are proposing to suspend public service pension upratings for two years.

Then we turned to public service manpower and our proposals to freeze recruitment. Present was Sir John Herbecq* from the Civil Service Department who announced that such a scheme was impossible and totally impractical because it involved *more work* and less jobs for the Civil Service. The civil servants would not have that. He threatened that civil servants 'will be on the streets protesting. We can bring the country to a halt faster than the miners.' I blew up with anger and contempt and told him that the prospect of this government offending the Inland Revenue, the social security payers-out and the pen-pushers was almost the only hope we had of winning the election.

But the appalling thing was the arrogance of these privileged people. I asked Herbecq why public servants should have total protection from the burdens of the recession, why Civil Service advisers should advocate to ministers recession and unemployment for others in the private sector while insisting that their own kind have total protection.

Herbecq and I exchanged very angry remarks. Plietzky said that my desire to reduce the public sector bureaucracy arose from prejudice. So we ended in a bad mood all round. I was furious. And I clearly offended most of the people round the table, which won't advance our paper. But it was appalling. The first thing we must do is abolish the Civil Service Department which is an appalling waste of men and money, and put its functions back into the Treasury who would run it more efficiently at a third of the cost.

Home at 10 p.m. very tired and edgy. It seems to be slipping away again, and the government is now in real trouble. Not only because of the big differences in Cabinet over the IMF. But also our legislative programme continues to run into trouble in Parliament – shipbuilding nationalisation is 'hybrid', occupational pensions cuts produces a revolt on our side. On devolution, the latest polls show a swing to Scottish nationalism. It will need nerve and luck to get through till next summer.

Tuesday 30 November 1976

The PM in The Hague.

Had a sense that the economic thing was slipping. No reaction from the PM to our papers. Rumours of the IMF still taking a hard line. Ralf Dahrendorf reported to me his breakfast in Germany yesterday with Chancellor Schmidt who was very hawkish and said that President Ford and he had decided to push Callaghan 'to the brink'. It looks as if the PM will *have* to take the side of Healey because the foreigners won't yield.

I heard of a meeting this evening in Crosland's room – Crosland, Lever, Shirley Williams, Bill Rodgers, Roy Hattersley and David Ennals. Lever and Crosland were talking of resigning against *any* deflation and were pressing the others to take an equally hard line. Rodgers was sceptical and said to me later that he did not believe they would stand up to the PM. Rodgers's judgement of people is generally right. He knows Crosland and Lever well. They are very clever, but have no steel in them. I am sure he is right. They will fold up in the end. Then Hattersley will move over to the PM's side. Therefore the Treasury will win. Rodgers is sensible not to go out on a limb for this particular clever and charming but unfrightening Keynesian army.

I did not get to bed till midnight – very depressed and apprehensive. The government could break up.

Wednesday 1 December 1976

Cabinet was put back to 10.30 because the PM was seeing [H. Johannes] Witteveen* and [Alan] Whittome* from the IMF. Witteveen had been flown in early this morning to put last-minute pressure on the PM and to stress that we must concede a big package of cuts – they would not accept a compromise. In other words, it is nothing to do with a purely financial problem of financing the deficit, with getting the PSBR down, as they claim. It is politics – they want blood out of the Labour programme, cuts in public expenditure, even if it goes straight through into unemployment. They want to take this opportunity of our weakness to impose on us Tory policies. Their 'technical' analysis always concludes in a position identical to that of the Tory Party.

Shirley Williams told me she was still convinced the Crosland/Lever line of minimum deflation would work and get a majority in Cabinet – and then get the IMF support. I briefed her a bit, showed her our paper criticising Benn on import controls, and advised her to get an economist as special adviser. Because only by taking a leading role in economic matters can she take up the leadership of the right. I pointed out how Hattersley's economic innocence was compensated by Maurice Peston's* excellent economic briefing to him; she decided to put a paper for Cabinet tomorrow. She supports cutting social security benefits, to bring them into line with wage rises, and she wants to make some cuts to finance tax cuts at the bottom of the scale. She sat in my room, on the settee drinking coffee. I hope she is tough enough for what lies ahead.

In Cabinet various ministers introduced their papers. The main emphasis was on the Shore/Benn alternative strategy papers. These were given a full run – and a harsh grilling. The PM was reading out the list of 'questions to Mr Benn' which we had put on a Green Paper for him. Shirley and Bill Rodgers and David Ennals also had copies of our paper so there was a fairly concerted attack. This delicate private 'circulation' was done without the PM's authority, but not without his knowledge. Crosland made a statement against Healey which many felt was disappointing. Perhaps the PM had nobbled him in The Hague – they travelled back together on the plane. Today the largest *number* – about ten – were with Healey. But they were still a minority overall. *If* the alternative-strategy people compromise and unite with the Croslanders, they have a clear majority. While the alternative strategy is on the table, the anti-Treasury majority is split. With it now out of the way, the left has to decide what to do – resign, support the Crosland compromise, or support Healey on the basis that it is more likely to destroy the present leadership and policies and so leave a vacuum for them to fill.

The TUC told Jim at a meeting this afternoon that they had no idea such a severe package was in prospect. They had been led to believe by the newspapers that it would be mild. They were pessimistic about the social contract holding up. The PM was apparently quite open about the possibility of the government falling.

It is noticeable that the ministers making the running against the Treasury – Crosland, Lever, Williams, Ennals, Hattersley, Shore, Benn – *all* have special advisers. This means that the Treasury can no longer get away with nonsense and mumbo-jumbo.

We were very depressed in the Unit at the Treasury victory. So were the other special advisers. I don't think that the two Toms realise what has happened. Maybe Shirley's paper will help, which came round late this evening, with proposals *very similar to ours* (she saw our paper this morning) plus a switch from direct to indirect tax. It reads very well.

The enigma is Varley. While the rest of us have been pressing the industrial strategy, he, as Industry minister, has been silent. The PM commented on this today. Varley's private secretary says that he is unwilling to show his hand until he knows where the PM stands – NB he was brought up as HW's and Marcia's protégé. I believe that he has never recovered from the

Chrysler episode, when he went out on a limb, and was cut off by Wilson and Harold Lever.

Went home at 9 p.m. very tired and a little anxious.

On Horse Guards Parade I ran into David Lipsey. He said, 'We have lost.' At a meeting in Crosland's room in the House of Commons this evening, Lever had 'defected', supporting a Treasury proposal for massive public expenditure cuts now and 'possible' tax cuts later. Presumably the PM had spoken to him. Apparently the PM has told Crosland three times in the past twenty-four hours that he won't compromise, but is supporting the Chancellor.

The PM has so far spoken to President Ford five times on the telephone; spoken to Schmidt, visited him for breakfast in The Hague, telephoned him and received two letters; and has had two meetings with the IMF, including one this morning with Witteveen present. All this to try to open up the financial situation at the 'highest political level'. But he has found them all very hawkish.

At Wednesday's Cabinet, those for *Crosland* and against cuts were: Lever, Williams, Hattersley, Rodgers, Ennals, Millan. Those for the *Benn/Shore alternative strategy* were: Benn, Shore, Booth, Foot, Orme, Silkin. Those for *Healey* were: Dell, Prentice. Those *with the PM*, and therefore implicitly with Healey, were: [Fred] Peart*, Rees (did not speak), Morris, Elwyn Jones, Mason. Varley did not speak but is thought to go with the PM.

Thursday 2 December 1976

Ken Stowe told me that yesterday the PM and Witteveen of the IMF had a very tough meeting. Witteveen insisted on £2 billion of public expenditure cuts. The PM said that was not economically sensible or politically possible. He would do £1 billion – or it meant a break with the IMF. The PM then phoned President Ford and told him this. He was tough with Ford – 'He put the boot into Ford,' said Ken, who overheard the call.

But the basic position is that the IMF wants £2 billion cuts. Healey *really* wants £1.5 billion. The PM has brought Healey down to £1 billion and then sticks at that, refusing to compromise towards Crosland's £500 million.

Before Cabinet Eric Varley came in for coffee. He is still depressed. He confessed that the Chrysler episode had been a big blow to his morale. He blamed Healey, who he said kept encouraging him to take a strong stand and saying that the tough line would prevail, and then left Varley to be massacred at the end. I pointed out that Wilson was the real guilty party, sacrificing Varley because he did not want Chrysler to go bust three months before he retired. Varley seemed rather petulant and feline. I tried to persuade him to fight more vigorously for his industrial policy.

After they had gone into Cabinet I talked to Joel Barnett, who was waiting to be summoned in to item three of the Cabinet agenda. He said that the IMF had put us in a position with no alternatives. He said, 'Jim must make his position clear this morning.' This is the general Treasury view – that the PM must declare for their side. Of course we think he has. But he has not agreed to the 'joint declaration' with the Chancellor which they were asking for. That could have been foolish. The PM should stand by his Chancellor, but he need not make 'joint declarations' which completely stop his capacity to be flexible in managing and holding together his Cabinet.

We had lunch – and a full debriefing upstairs. In Cabinet Crosland and Hattersley had announced predictably that they were switching to support the £1 billion cuts for 1977–78 simply because it was wrong for the PM and the Chancellor to be in a minority. This effectively finished it, though everybody spoke. The secretaries said the 'voice count' was 14–9 for £1 billion – NB the PM said at the beginning that he was supporting the Chancellor. Lever made an ambivalent statement, saying he regretted the high figure of cuts.

This afternoon after Questions, another crisis was provoked by the Treasury. They wanted the Cabinet minutes to be rewritten to add that Cabinet had also decided the subsequent year's 1978–79 cuts at the Chancellor's proposed £1.5 billion – despite the fact that Cabinet had *not* discussed 1978–79. John Hunt and the Cabinet Office refused. So Healey went to see the PM in his room at the Commons to insist. He had Whittome from the IMF waiting outside. But the PM said he refused to rewrite Cabinet minutes with a lie. The Treasury's contempt for Cabinet and Cabinet government has to be seen to be believed.

Now Healey will negotiate with the IMF on 1977–78 firm, and 1978–79 as possible, and if the IMF agrees it will be put to the Cabinet as attractive because already agreed.

Friday 3 December 1976

Last night's meeting between the Chancellor and Whittome of the IMF apparently went badly. The IMF say £1 billion is not enough and still want £2 billion – in hard and real cuts. This exposes the truly *political* nature of this operation. As a friend in the Cabinet Office said to me this morning, 'They are actually saying that a Crosland version of democratic socialism is not be to be allowed.' In fact they are saying that a Labour government must carry out the policies of Mrs Thatcher.

Went to the weekly deputy secs meeting. Little emerged. Then spent the morning in the office, more relaxed than for some time. Despite the fact the government is very precarious. Jim is not confident he can hold it together. And he is right. I had lunch with Margaret Jackson and afterwards she came back to my room and said that the left knew of possible 'cuts in social security benefits' and this could cause the resignations. I told her that nobody should do anything until they see the *final* package, where the positive items might make the cuts swallowable. She agreed. We also arranged to keep in close touch over the next few days.

The rest of the afternoon I was working on papers.

Things are still in doubt and disarray. There are fresh problems with the cuts – including whether it counts simply to carry over cuts from 1977–78, or if they want *new* ones in 1978–79. The Chancellor has told the PM first one thing and then another, and the PM is worried and says we have to start again.

Home at 9.00 p.m.

Monday 6 December 1976

The final week of decision on the IMF public expenditure cuts. I am conscious of being nervous and tired because of the threat to the government. If a single Cabinet minister resigns, that probably means the end of the government.

The PM was at Transport House all morning on the liaison committee, where he warned them of the tough decisions ahead. Tom McNally took me to the Finnish Embassy for a reception at lunchtime. He is thinking of going in for David Marquand's seat at Ashfield. Jim has tried to persuade him not to stand till after the next election, but that is a big sacrifice. Tom would be an excellent MP.

I returned to No. 10 in time to see people assembling for this afternoon's Cabinet. Today they get down to details of the £1 billion cuts in 1977–78 – and at some point they must approve the £2 billion for 1978–79 (that has not been seriously discussed). The Cabinet went on for nearly three hours, till after 6. Occasionally the private secretaries would come running out of Cabinet to phone up some department to pursue some figures for some potential cuts – this afternoon it was mainly Environment, with suggestions for all kinds of marginal savings on maintenance of public buildings.

The PM has said he will let them run till Tuesday, and then if they cannot agree the Chancellor's list he will produce his own list and if they won't have it he will go.

It was a glorious winter's day, frosty and golden sunshine.

Gavyn Davies has done a brilliant memorandum on the IMF's Letter of Intent which I have put in to the PM today. It points out the numerous ways in which the Treasury can try to commit us to further public expenditure cuts by agreeing to tight targets for domestic credit expansion and money supply growth, which cannot be met even with the present cuts. The paper sets it out so that when the Letter of Intent comes the PM can immediately test the implications of the figures.

Stayed in the office till 9 p.m.

Tuesday 7 December 1976

As Cabinet assembled this morning I talked to Tony Benn about a paper (nineteen pages!) he is proposing to circulate to the NEC on the historic influence of Marxism. He has taken some quotes from our Herbert Morrison book, from 1907 when Morrison was a Marxist in the SDP, to demonstrate that it is legitimate to have Marxists in the Labour Party. His purpose is to defend the appointment of the dangerous Trotskyite, Andy Bevan, as National Youth Officer. I went back to my room and wrote Benn a letter pointing out that things had changed since 1907, and especially since Lenin/Trotsky/Stalin. I gave him this letter after Cabinet.

I also talked to Eric Varley about an incident yesterday involving his department. John Lyons of the Power Engineers had written in to No. 10 arguing powerfully for an inquiry into the engineering profession. I had given it support but industry officials have opposed it. After yesterday's Cabinet I asked Varley about it and he looked astonished, saying that he had held a meeting in his department and had decided to respond favourably. This morning Varley told me that he had blown up his officials. But they had completely ignored his decision and afterwards reinserted a final paragraph to a letter signed by him recommending against an inquiry. Bounces in all directions!

The explanation of course is that the civil servants do not want to upset the engineering profession who, like the lawyers earlier his year, are totally opposed to having an inquiry into their own outdated practices and training. The professional establishment at work again.

The Cabinet went on until nearly 1.30 and was still a long way from final success. The PM apparently exploded towards the end and said they had to settle it one way or the other *today*, and they would meet again this evening at the Commons.

I walked out after Cabinet with Shirley Williams and we chatted about her need for more economic advice. She is obviously pleased with having put her paper in.

We had lunch in No. 10 but got no information. Ken Stowe was being very tight and refused to answer several direct questions from Tom McCaffrey, which is ridiculous since Tom has to deal with the press and must not reveal that he is ignorant. It is the old crazy fear of 'leaks', which leads to only the civil servants having the information. So we get in the crazy position where McCaffrey, who must answer the press, McNally, who is Jim's closest adviser, and I, who briefs him on these Cabinets (all of whom will be unemployed if the decisions are wrong), are not told what is going on. I of course have my own ways of finding out and in fact I know all the public expenditure decisions. There are always ways of finding out.

Incidentally Joe Rogaly told me at the weekend that the *Financial Times* had the Chancellor's paper to Cabinet on the cuts *before* it was circulated to Cabinet – and from the Treasury!

After lunch to Questions. The PM was a bit subdued. He has a bad cold and is husky and coughing.

I went to tea with Alf Morris and Jack Ashley in the Commons tea room. In there I saw Helene Hayman* sitting with the appalling fellow travelling battleaxe Joan Maynard* and very angry because the PM had said that he did not like the script of Labour's Party political broadcast (which Helene appeared in). Maynard said that all Labour Party people liked its overt 'class warfare' propaganda and its critics were not from the Party. I'm not sure that she is from the Party – or not our Party at least.

In the evening Henry Porchester*, the Queen's racing manager, came in with his wife to take Carol and I out for dinner. We had a drink and a quick chat, but I was very jumpy because tonight's Cabinet in the PM's room at the Commons began at 8 p.m. This is the final crunch. They could go on until the midnight vote if need be (the Tories refused to pair the PM). The government could fall tonight if Benn or Orme decided to break on this issue. I don't think so, and the PM seems quietly confident. He has now come out completely for Healey and has carried the Cabinet decisively over to that side. But it is *his* majority. To the end Healey persuaded only Dell, Prentice and Mulley. The rest were the PM's men.

The Porchesters took me to a nice restaurant in Sloane Street and we had an excellent meal. Henry is a marvellous person, totally devoted to the public weal. His wife Jeannie is a beautiful American, but after a while one takes the beauty for granted and simply appreciates her fundamental niceness.

I left them early and drove back to the House of Commons. Cabinet was over and the PM sat in his room reading his papers. He looked tired – grey, with little voice left, and constantly coughing. He said he was pleased they had tied up the package and he had got the figure he had gone for. He thought the Party would hold together on it, but he was less confident about the reaction in the markets. I said that we could now set about the recovery programme, and plan on an election in 1979. He said, 'I will be dead by then, given how I feel tonight.'

I felt immensely relieved that the Cabinet had held together. Providing we get the sterling safety net as well, this will be an enormous achievement for the PM. He has done it. Without him, Healey would have been lost.

Next day – Ken Stowe told me that towards the end of last night's Cabinet, when they had not quite reached the required figure for cuts, Jim gave them a choice. He said that either they could go for it *all* in cuts, which meant they had to concede the Treasury's list. Or the extra had to come in tax. He would go round the table and count heads. He called on Roy Mason, who was for the tax. He then moved to Benn, who wriggled, ducked and weaved, and said he could not answer the questions or take the choice. Apparently he looked very cowardly and diminished before his colleagues. The others all gave their views openly and clearly and went for £200 million tax to pay for the £200 million to be spent on industrial investment.

Wednesday 8 December 1976

Felt tired but relieved that the ordeal is apparently over – though we still have to get over the IMF hurdle and land the safety net safely. The PM had a meeting with the whips to prepare them and the PLP for the cuts package – again his skill at handling the Party, much more open than Harold would ever be. He went off to lunch at Times Newspapers, which he did not enjoy – too many pompous people, too much hectoring and lecturing.

I had the quietest day for some time, mainly in the office. Harold Lever dropped in for half an hour. He is very optimistic and thinks everything will be fine, with the safety net making sterling safe, interest rates coming down, etc., etc. [He was right.]

Information was very tight. We – the two Toms and I – have not been allowed to see the minutes of yesterday's Cabinet. This is 'leak' madness again. As if Tom McCaffrey, after twenty years in the service, is going to start leaking Cabinet minutes! For myself, I don't care, since the decisions are all taken. In that sense I have no 'need to know' – though I do know everything that went on anyway and the PM knows this. But it is ridiculous that the Toms and I always have to go to *ask* for information in papers which are automatically circulated around the Private Office, even to principals and to a very young executive officer. I learned that the IMF here has accepted the package in principle. They now have to take it to Washington, and the Group of Ten bankers meet to approve the borrowings.

The safety net for sterling is coming along, and Healey hopes to announce next week that there is 'agreement in principle', but it still seems worry-ingly vague. If we get it, it will be almost wholly due to Jim, with a bit of help from Lever. The Treasury has been a positive obstacle. Jim has constantly communicated with Schmidt and Ford to maintain their support; without that it would never have got this far.

In the evening I went home at 9 and to bed early.

Thursday 9 December 1976

Cabinet met this morning with a much more routine agenda – devolution, dispersal of civil servants (the PM resisted dropping this).

I had another quiet day. Lunch at No. 10, and again nothing was revealed – about the IMF. Ken Stowe produced two bottles of wine and it was a delicious meal. I had two helpings of mince pies and felt bloated for the rest of the afternoon – but I had been for my usual morning run at 7.30 over the frosty Heath so I still felt virtuous.

Question Time was uneventful. The PM was clearly more relaxed with the public expenditure behind him. But still very tired.

In the evening I went to the annual Jonathan Cape party at 9. Always a pleasure. But Carol was tired so we left before midnight. It was a bitterly cold night, clear with a full moon, and car windows were already completely frosted over.

No leaks of the IMF package in the press so far.

Friday 10 December 1976

The PM was in bed in his flat this morning with his cold much worse – in fact it sounds like bronchitis or pneumonia. He sent for his doctor.

Graham Day of British Shipbuilders came in, furious with the Department of Industry which had not communicated with him at all during the days leading up to the defeat of the Nationalisation Bill. Ken regretted Varley insisting on proceeding with nationalising ship repairing which is what led to the bill's defeat. He also mistrusts Kaufman whom he describes as a 'snake'. But he is an excellent man who was really whipping up ship-building orders. He said that the phone stopped ringing the day the bill was defeated. Apparently many of the firms are technically bankrupt and have been waiting for the new nationalised corporation to bail them out. Now they will go bust and he expects 50,000 redundancies.

Spent most of the afternoon at the LSE, at a meeting on French economic planning, then back to No. 10. Later Gavyn had overheard Nigel dictating a covering note to the draft Letter of Intent which had just been sent over by the Treasury for the PM's quick approval. It was in fact, as we had feared all along, the Treasury 'bounce' of all time. It apparently contained no figures for the targets on money supply, borrowing and credit expansion, to which the Treasury was going to commit us over the next two years. The Treasury would fill them in later. The paper also said that the figures were not ready, would not be ready till Sunday night, and then the Chancellor would not bother to show them to the PM unless they were 'radically different' from expectations. So No. 10 excluded!

It is inexplicable that they 'cannot' have the figures ready by Sunday. They have had the decisions since Tuesday night. Gavyn says it takes no more than a day to run them through the computer. Our suspicion is that they will not be ready before Sunday night because they want the minimum time available for others to consider them. And it is typical of the Treasury's contempt for the PM and the rest of Cabinet that they send him a document with blanks instead of figures, when this document will constrain the government's economic policy over the next two years up to the general election.

Nigel Wicks, who is usually very good on these matters, but is of course from the Treasury, did not tell us that the document was in, though he knew we were interested and I went in several times to talk to him. His own covering note to the PM was very 'Treasury', describing the omission of figures as 'unavoidable'. I was quite angry, but said nothing to him. I alerted the two Toms upstairs at a dinner Jim was giving for Henry Kissinger who was passing through London for the last time as Secretary of State. I also wrote a handwritten note to the PM warning him that he must insist on seeing the figures. I then went home.

Hal Sonnenfeldt, who is Kissinger's number two, dropped in to see me at 5.30. He told me he was convinced from all he had heard in Washington that the US Treasury and our Treasury were 'in cahoots' to get more deflation. I took him through to No. 11 to have a drink with Healey. I stayed while Healey finished his bath, but then left when he arrived.

Saturday 11 December 1976

I was lying in bed with the children, on a cold and frosty morning, thinking about whether to play football this afternoon, when the telephone rang. It was the Prime Minister. He wanted me to come into No. 10 to study the IMF Letter of Intent. It did not indeed have any figures. He was a bit worried but he did not have time to study it himself. He was preparing his 'lefta' speech and his 'devolution' speech and was in bed with bronchitis.

I got up, phoned Gavyn, and set off by public transport, since I must leave the car for Carol and the children, after a quick bowl of cereal. I arrived just after Gavyn, made some coffee, and we read the letter. It was very long – about a dozen pages. All the key figures had been omitted. But

what was there was pretty awful. It did have a commitment to a PSBR of
£8.7 billion and if we missed it – because of higher unemployment – then
we have to deflate further, causing more unemployment, and so on down
the vicious spiral. It said in the appendix that the BP shares sold would
not, as Cabinet assumed, count off the PSBR.

There was a commitment to cut a further £1-plus billion off in 1978 if
growth exceeded 3½%. These further cuts will produce more unemployment, then there is no prospect of getting unemployment down by the next
election. Finally it quite specifically excluded import controls in the future,
and import deposits.

We wrote a minute to the PM along these lines and sent it up to his
room. At 1.15 Carol and the kids came in to collect me to go to Crystal
Palace to play football for the House of Commons against the Belgian
Parliament. It was a gloriously sunny, though freezing afternoon. Afterwards
I went home with the family.

Gavyn phoned me at home. He had had an incredible afternoon.
At 4 o'clock the PM sent for us. Gavyn went up to the flat, where the
PM was lying ill in bed. He was grumpy and coughing, snapping at Audrey
when she tried to bring him tea and comfort.

But he had now read the Letter of Intent and our paper. He was furious
with the Treasury. He took Gavyn through the paper – and then phoned
the Chancellor. Apparently he tore strip after strip off him. He told him
he did not believe he could not produce the figures and that this was a
bounce. He wanted to call a Cabinet on Monday and to circulate the Letter
of Intent to ministers. He said that this went far beyond what had been
agreed. Jim said it was far worse than the 1968–69 loan. Denis said it was
the same. The PM put his hand over the phone and asked Gavyn what the
1969 Letter of Intent had been like. Gavyn said it was shorter with less
constraints. The PM said to Healey, 'Denis, I have it here in my hand, it
is shorter and has many less restraints.' There would be a row when this
was published. He insisted on seeing the figures. He said that the domestic
credit expansion must not be below £7.5 billion – Healey said 'that will be
difficult to negotiate'. The PM said he shouldn't have put in such a tight
restraint against import deposits. Healey said that the 'IMF insisted on
that'. The PM said that was not true because he had specifically talked to
the IMF about it, and they were relaxed about it.

By the end, according to Gavyn, Healey was sounding very deflated. In
fact this is down to his officials and Healey has not been close to the drafting
of the letter – the covering note from his secretary suggested that as of last
night Healey had still not seen it. The PM was clearly pleased with our
work on this, and Gavyn has every reason to be proud.

Nigel Wicks, who listened in to the conversation and took a record, must have been worried. The PM said to Gavyn that Nigel's brief had not warned him sufficiently of the problem. In fact Nigel has temporarily become completely 'Treasury' and this time he went too far, joining in the Treasury manoeuvre to slip it past the PM. The PM knows this. It is the old problem – that Treasury civil servants in No. 10 find it difficult to give all their loyalty to any other boss, especially since they have to go back to the Treasury in a couple of years. But apart from this inevitable problem, Nigel is an excellent man.

The PM has asked Gavyn and me to be ready for duty tomorrow. He has also asked John Hunt to prepare for a Cabinet. The machine has failed him here. But they will never forgive us for exposing it.

Sunday 12 December 1976

I played football again in the morning (scoring three goals!), had lunch at home with my brother and his prospective bride, and then went in to No. 10.

Shortly after arriving Jim phoned down and invited me up to tea. He was lying in bed in the flat, surrounded by his boxes, and Audrey was producing tea and cakes. The doctor had been in the morning and given Jim some antibiotics, some vitamins and some cough mixture. Certainly his chest and cough sounded much better.

We first discussed the IMF. He showed me the latest figures of monetary targets which the Treasury were proposing – and negotiating – to put in the Letter of Intent. I said they were a great improvement and the PM yesterday had made a great impact. He said he noticed that they were virtually the same as the likely figures we had put to him in our brief at the beginning of the week. I pointed out that this was because the Treasury already had the figures then, although they had denied this. They had subsequently tried to tighten them. When we had mobilised the PM they had simply gone back to their original figures.

On the Cabinet he expressed disappointment with Dell, over import controls, and with Varley, over industrial strategy in general. He was obviously feeling perkier and expressed firm confidence that we 'would survive till Christmas'. He also asked me to draft 'some passages' for tomorrow's speech on devolution. I went away and did this – very slowly because I am a reluctant speech drafter.

Nigel Wicks told me that the Letter of Intent was mainly the work of officials. As I was leaving at 9 p.m. I saw Nicholas Monck*, the Chancellor's private secretary, whom I have known for many years, in Private Office. He was waiting for the Chancellor to arrive to see the PM. Presumably he had the revised letter, but he did not show me. In fact he was very nasty, accusing me of being a 'conspiracy theorist' and saying that the Treasury had behaved 'decently and openly throughout'. He said to Gavyn Davies, 'I strongly resent being accused of cheating.' Gavyn said, 'The Treasury only gets what it deserves.' I decided not to put the boot in, since he had clearly been working terribly hard and had had a rough time. But one saw the Etonian bureaucrat resenting the interference by upstarts such as me. Too bad. They deserve to lose this one.

Nigel Wicks said that the problem with the Treasury is that it has *no* political feel. 'They are writing the letter for Gordon Richardson, not for Jack Jones or Jim Callaghan at all.' Spot on.

I went home very tired.

Monday 13 December 1976

Came in still feeling tired, having worked through the weekend. Saw Jonathan Charkham about improving public appointments. While he was there, the PM phoned and asked me to write his speech on the parliamentary motion for an Attlee statue.

I learned the 'safety net' negotiations were going badly. Although Healey virtually announced the net last week the Americans won't agree to anything now. Arthur Burns is simply refusing to do what President Ford has asked him. At the same time, the Bank of International Settlements in Basle is putting together a quite different scheme but the Germans are reluctant to proceed without the Americans. The Governor of the Bank of England, Gordon Richardson, has gone out today to negotiate, but it does not look promising. Without the net, sterling will look very fragile and may go. So the PM's original 'three-legged stool' – IMF cuts plus import deposits plus safety net – has collapsed. The import deposits are excluded in the Letter of Intent. Now no safety net. As I said, the three-legged stool has become a shooting stick, and we are sitting on it upside down! The PM has been sending messages to Ford and Schmidt, but so far without effect. Derek Mitchell from the Treasury has gone to Washington to negotiate but we doubt it that will help since we are not sure that he is on *our* side!

In the afternoon we had the devolution debate. The PM opened in a very low key and read his speech without conviction. He read my peroration, but he was obviously troubled by the objections of his own Welsh backbenchers. Mrs Thatcher put on a remarkable performance. A brilliant barrister's dissection of our bill. She had been thoroughly briefed. She obviously knew the bill inside out, which is more than you can say of Jim – or of me. But in the end she did not say where she stood on Scotland and devolution. She said what was wrong with our bill, but not what she would replace it with. It is not even clear whether or not she opposes devolution totally. She simply hopes to bring down the government on devolution.

[She did.] Then the Scot Nats will take Scotland, and she will take power as the largest English party. Afterwards Jim seemed relieved to be done with it. He is not really interested in devolution. I went back to work in the office, where we are struggling to produce a new national recovery programme. Private Office – which after the weekend crisis is showing me *everything* – showed me the Chancellor's draft statement, and the final Letter of Intent, which is much improved, with looser targets on monetary aggregates.

Home at 9 p.m. to watch *Madigan*, an excellent cops and robbers film.

Slept badly. Had my flu jab today, and it left me feeling feverish and with a stiff arm.

Tuesday 14 December 1976

In early. Still bad news on the sterling safety net. No hope of a firm settlement. Ministers were invited half an hour before the 11.30 Cabinet, to go upstairs and read the Letter of Intent.

The Unit had a meeting about the national recovery programme with William Plowden and Steve Powell of the CPRS. This was quite tough, with the CPRS wanting to recover control of the draft, but I would not have this, and in the end we reached an amicable compromise. But it is going to be tough, getting the draft done by Friday.

Lunch upstairs. Learned little – except that Cabinet agreed to drop the proposed suspension of the uprating of public service pensions! Inevitable. The same old story. The CSD came up with all kinds of stories of how difficult it would be – would affect the miners, and everybody in the public sector. All ministers were briefed yesterday, by their officials, who are prospective public service pensioners, on how catastrophic the consequences of suspending would be. Moreover two departments had been briefed on how to offer compensating cuts on the spot – Trade gave something on airport charges and Industry and Energy gave a lot on telephone and gas prices – so old-age pensioners will now pay higher gas prices so that William Armstrong and other retired mandarins keep their inflation-proofed pensions. I was neither angry nor surprised. I am almost gratified to see the greedy privileged bureaucracy behaving in character. Ministers are just fools to be conned in this way. In the last two public expenditure cuts exercises only two decisions have been *revoked* after special Cabinet discussions – the £140 million cuts in the Civil Service, and the £120 million savings on public service pensions. Each was put back on to a further Cabinet agenda to make sure they were revoked and that finally less of the burden of sacrifice fell on the Civil Service.

This afternoon's Questions passed mundanely. Afterwards I worked in the Unit on the recovery programme and then till 9 p.m. on the draft speech on [Clement] Attlee*.

The PM saw Len Murray and Jack Jones about tomorrow's Budget secretly in No. 10, with them coming in from the Cabinet Office.

Wednesday 15 December 1976

The PM went off to the NEC at Transport House. Terrible! They voted 15–12 to support the appointment of an overt Trotskyite to be in charge of the Labour young socialists. This is the state of the Labour Party.

I worked in the Unit on the national recovery programme, and on a speech Jim is giving next week in honour of Attlee.

Went to lunch with Carol's Uncle Louis at the Trattoria Pescatore (lovely fish!) and then back to No. 10. The final version of today's statement by the Chancellor was there. Flabby and rambling. In an earlier version there were almost no *figures* for the cuts. Apparently, so Ken Stowe told me, a Treasury official advised the Chancellor that 'backbenchers would be happier if there were no figures'! The PM thought it was 'terrible'.

I watched the TV coverage of the statement. All the comments were bad. So we expected sterling to collapse tomorrow. Everyone was gloomy.

In the evening I went to the state dinner for the Poles. Very pleasant. Jim left poor old Tony Crosland as Foreign Secretary to receive the guests while he did some work. Then when Jim came in, he said to Tony C, 'You are doing a splendid job, Tony, carry on,' and walked into the reception. Poor old Crosland looked black, since he hates these official things anyway. [He died a few weeks later.]

We stayed until about 11.30. I sat near John Mendelson, the left-wing MP, who seemed surprisingly sensible. He claimed not to know Polish or much about the Poles, but after the dinner the Polish ministers all came and shook hands with him as with an old friend. Maybe they get useful information from him as from several left-wing MPs.

Thursday 16 December 1976

Before Cabinet this morning Tony Benn came over to me, beaming about his paper on Marxism. I told him that I could get him a job as a lecturer at the LSE if he ever wanted it. (The PM today described Benn as 'a canting hypocrite'. Everybody is still furious with yesterday's NEC vote 15–12 for the appointment of the Trotskyite Bevan.)

I talked to Joel Barnett waiting outside Cabinet for his item on the agenda to come up. He said that the Treasury plan was to do huge increases on indirect taxation – VAT up to 12½% etc. – and then to make cuts in direct taxation. Cabinet discussed devolution and agreed to Michael Foot's suggestion of a referendum on Wales and Scotland.

I saw more papers on the sterling safety net. It was clear that the Americans were unhelpful to the end. The Germans and others were prepared to help, but not without the US. The Bank of International Settlements scheme is going ahead quite well. The Dutch are taking the lead, helpful as ever. Their plan is to present it to the Americans as a fait accompli, saying that the US must not sabotage it at the late stage. But that won't be until well after the New Year. We watched the exchange rate nervously, but it held up remarkably well. The PM became increasingly optimistic about it. I worked on the draft of our paper on the national recovery programme. This is coming along well, and Gavyn Davies has written about twenty-five pages. I did the final restructuring and correcting.

It is absolutely clear that the CPRS want nothing to do with the recovery programme. I had a very sharp letter from Berrill setting out all his objections to our approach. Curiously he made a savage long attack on our section on 'anti-inflation policies' – which we had lifted wholesale from the CPRS's own paper. Clearly Ken had not read their paper.

The heart of their difference from us is psychological/political. They do *not* believe there is *any* hope of recovery over the next five years. They believe that the British people are incorrigibly lazy and incompetent and – as Will Plowden and Steve Powell specifically said – most of the CPRS believe that only a 'political cataclysm' can shake up Britain into recovery. They see our recovery programme as one more step in 'deceiving the people' into believing that there is 'a soft option' way out. I worked hard to keep the CPRS in play – because I want to minimise the Whitehall attack on us, at least until we have actually got to the stage of circulating to ministers. Nigel Wicks took me on one side this morning and warned me that 'we had enemies' on the recovery programme. So it is going to be a hard slog.

We worked quite late on the recovery programme – till about 9.30 p.m. – then Carol came from an NUT party to collect me in the car and drive me home.

Today Ken Stowe said to me that I must not believe this is a Treasury 'conspiracy' to make trouble for the PM and the government. 'There is no Treasury conspiracy,' he said. 'There is just an incredible depth of Treasury stupidity.' That is the view of an experienced senior civil servant.

Friday 17 December 1976

I was working all morning on the recovery programme and on the PM's speech on Attlee for Monday. So I did not go to the first part of the 10 o'clock EY on Energy policy – which was apparently pretty shambly. Benn has totally failed to produce a coherent Energy policy, although that was his main task when sent there fifteen months ago. He makes great speeches on energy, calls conferences, suggests Green Papers – but never actually takes any decision on policy.

EY also discussed the new policy on prices suggested by Hattersley – for a new Prices Board. Apparently Hattersley made a long and windy speech introducing it. Two-thirds of the way through the PM interrupted him and asked, 'What does it mean, Roy?' saying it will help develop the government's broad economic strategy. 'What is your point?' Hattersley flannelled a bit. The PM interrupted again and said, 'It is all right for the despatch box, Roy. Not right for in here.' Took Hattersley's ego down a peg or two. But he is very able and will learn.

At around 3.30 the PM sent for me to discuss my Attlee speech draft. He was very pleased, which was satisfying. We discussed Attlee and Morrison and the 1945–51 government. And his own political style. He identified with a lot I said about Attlee – which I had in mind when writing it. I also mentioned to him the problem of Glasgow and Ulster violence. I mentioned that action had been taken on my previous information – but only against the Roman Catholics. He noted it, but obviously did not want to get involved.

David Lea* of the TUC came in around 6.30 p.m to discuss industrial democracy. Full of the Bullock Report, parts of which he has written. He said that after the cuts, there is little left of the social contract for the unions except industrial democracy. We must give it a positive and fair wind. Yet Whitehall is against, and the officials' paper is very negative. This will be a big battle. It comes to Cabinet committee next Wednesday.

I left the office shortly after 8. At least the worst of the pressure is now over. The cuts behind. Sterling fairly stable. The recovery programme is written. But it always seems as if 'the worst is over'. Then the next day/week always has a new set of 'worsts'.

Monday 20 December 1976

The pressure remains off. I spent a gentle morning, clearing off papers and going around the house seeing what was going on. Met Robin Butler back visiting his old haunts in Private Office and went to the Cabinet Office mess with him. Only the third time I have eaten the filthy food there in three years – and the first time was with Robin Butler and Nick Stuart back in the spring of 1974.

Jack Rampton*, the permanent secretary from Energy, came to join us. He talked freely about the defects of Tony Benn as minister – that he *never* takes decisions, never commits himself, never forms a firm policy – because he doesn't want to offend any political interests, especially the unions. He said that much of the time of Benn and his special advisers is spent dealing with these outside interests, in the unions and in the Party.

In the afternoon I went over to the Commons to hear the PM move the motion for the Attlee memorial statue. He used my draft as a basis, but had made a number of changes which were definitely improvements. Thatcher and Jeremy Thorpe* were both good as well, though it was a fairly empty House. Bob Mellish gave an emotional and silly speech.

In the evening we had the Christmas party for disabled children. It went very well. Good entertainment and well organised.

I did not stay for all the party since the Unit had a final meeting with the CPRS about our national recovery programme. They are still keen to demonstrate that they have nothing to do with it, and feel we are incorrigibly optimistic in believing that Britain could recover economically while retaining its democratic political system.

Tuesday 21 December 1976

Came in early and read papers. Roy Jenkins came in at 11.30 to have a final chat before he goes to Europe. I met him at the door and we walked up the passage together. He seems much slimmer, but just as nervous and jumpy. He said he had come for a 'very brief' talk, though in fact he stayed some time.

In the Unit we were completing our national recovery programme paper, for circulation to ministers over Christmas. It was decided to put it out from No. 10 – because of a feeling that the Cabinet Office would not give it a fair wind.

I had lunch at the Reform. A grey damp day. Then back to deal with the Department of Industry who had sent the PM a brief for a newspaper interview, saying that the PM had ruled out having an inquiry into the engineering profession. Despite the fact that two weeks ago Varley decided they should have an inquiry and No. 10 supported that. They never give up. And they have no respect for their minister's decisions.

Spent the latter part of the afternoon drafting our brief on industrial democracy. Then went to the whips' party, here in No. 10, and on to the Lord President's party in his office, where I picked up Gerry Fowler to go over to the Commons for a drink – and then to meet Carol and her employer Alan Evans.

We had quite a jolly time and then went upstairs to see Shirley Williams in her room at 10.10. She was reading the papers from her box when we entered. She poured us a drink and then gossiped a while. We discussed the 'Black Mafia' (Roman Catholics), partly in relation to John Hunt, whom she admires. Shirley was in a marvellous mood, having just played a role in the Transport House Christmas review. But I had to leave the other two to talk Education shop with her. I went downstairs and ran into David Owen and we discussed the IMF. He said that he had been shut out at the last stages. The American Embassy people keep telling us (David and I and Tom McNally have each heard this separately) that the degree of disloyalty in what our Treasury and Bank people say to their American counterparts is 'unparalleled' in their experience.

Harold Lever came up and we discussed the general situation. This was in the corridor at the back of the Speaker's Chair and there was a constant flow of people into and out of the chamber and the lobbies. Margaret Jackson and Helene Hayman came and reported what the Labour left were planning – it now seemed that less than thirty would vote against us on tonight's big vote on the economic package. But a lot would abstain. Judith Hart took me on one side to discuss her dismissal from the government last year. She blames Harold Wilson. She said she had discussed it with him recently in Geneva. He apologised and said it was because he had 'just had a row with Roy Jenkins'. Then I went to Roy Hattersley's room – he said his civil servants were demoralised and thought the government was about to collapse. Then to Bill Rodgers's room, where we discussed politics generally. Finally back to Shirley's room to collect Carol and Alan Evans at 12.30. On the division, twenty-six of our people voted against, and over fifty abstained – including Gerry Fowler! (He is thinking of leaving Parliament!)

Wednesday 22 December 1976

Came in for the important EY committee on industrial democracy. It was clear that we did not give the PM what he wanted in our brief. He is acutely aware of the TUC position. He wants a way to hold the CBI as well.

I went to lunch with Joe Haines, acutely depressed to be still unemployed; he said that the strain is beginning to tell at home. He also told me a remarkable story – that he knew on the very best authority, that Jim had *offered somebody the chancellorship* in November during the IMF crisis. He preferred not to say who. But who? I tried the Jenkins story, but he seemed to deny it. I wonder if it was Harold Wilson? He said I would be very surprised. So Jim was willing to get rid of Denis. That makes the whole IMF story even more complex. We ate at Lockets, and then walked to the Army and Navy Stores together, where I bought some Christmas toys for the children. On the way, we were nearly run over by Robin Butler on his bike. We had a nice 'old times' chat. I am very struck by how Private Office has changed. Under Robert Armstrong they were all prima donnas, with charisma and character. Now they are all much greyer, sound and decent machine men, like Ken Stowe. Presumably the private secretaries do reflect the character of the principal PS.

Before the staff Christmas party, Joe Haines came in to see Tom McNally, at Tom's request. Tom is very fed up. He thinks that Jim has fallen completely into the hands of the civil servants and that he personally is having too little influence. He said the same to me at the party. He kept repeating, 'I am not happy.' He feels he is being squeezed out of everything. And of course economic matters are not his field anyway. He is clearly having adjustment problems. McCaffrey feels a bit the same. No. 10 is not a completely happy ship this Christmas.

Joe told me that somebody has been feeding Jim with the view that I am leaking to the press – the *Sunday Times* as usual. How boring they are.

Thursday 23 December 1976

Went Christmas shopping this morning with Carol. Not till today had we seriously started to prepare for Christmas. One's family certainly suffers in this job. So we went to Selfridges – and I failed to get to Questions this morning.

We had a delightful Christmas lunch in the small dining room at No. 10. The usual staff plus the PM, Mrs Callaghan and his personal secretary Ruth Sharpe. It went very well, very relaxed, with the PM obviously enjoying it. He does have a marvellous way of putting people at their ease.

One thing he discussed was his memoirs. I said he should do them. He said he wanted help and pressed me. I did not respond. He then said he would perhaps get somebody from Sussex University, since it was nearby. I intend to take this up again with him – but not around a large dinner table!

After lunch the two Toms and I retired for a whisky in McNally's room. He was still fed up. But we discussed positive ways of recovering – mainly by focusing on the 1978–79 election. Tom is going to prepare a strategy paper over Christmas. We hope to focus the PM on a two-year view – holding on over the next six months, then stabilising with the trade payments going into balance in early 1978, then recovery up to a 1979 election. This cheered Tom up a bit.

He was also much agitated by having been shown a very secret paper from inside the board of the National Westminster Bank. It states quite categorically that some of the serious financial difficulties which faced the NetWest Bank in the final quarter of 1976 arose from policies pursued by the Bank of England – policies which were specifically described as being 'political'. These were to attempt to bring about cuts in public expenditure by 'failing to sell gilts'. Tom has now joined the 'conspiracy school' – because there *is* one! Not surprising. Most of the institutions in our pluralist society are run by people who do not support a Labour government and strongly resent its tax and income policies towards the middle classes. It is no surprise that they will pursue policies contrary to the interests of a Labour government. They justify them as being in the national interest.

I went out in the late afternoon and did some last-minute shopping for presents in Victoria Street. Then back to No. 10 for final drinks with the staff. And off to the National Theatre to see Stoppard's *Jumpers* with Will Plowden. Quite enjoyable, and an essential break between Downing Street politics and tomorrow to Suffolk for a simple Christmas at the cottage, with no telephone, no television.

The end to a very hard year. I still resent having been forced to leave the LSE. It is very hard in the Unit, with the Civil Service clearly more hostile than at any time since we came in. 1977 will be a tough year – if I am at No. 10 on 23 December 1977 then we will go and win the next election. [I was – and we didn't.] But I don't look forward to it very much. Some of the fun has gone out of the job. And fighting the machine is tedious and exhausting. That of course is why they always win in the end.

Tuesday 4 January 1977

To work after an incredible eleven-day holiday – by when I was very keen to get back.

The PM is down on the farm at Lewes and won't come in till Thursday. I went through my accumulated papers and began discussions on our next project – the PM's initiative on unemployment for the World Economic summit in the summer.

Another stage in the saga of the national recovery programme. Before Christmas I had heard that Ken Berrill was going to send a minute of dissent to the PM. It was not too heavy, but basically says that the CPRS do not wish to be associated with the project because it is mainly aimed towards the government's Labour Party supporters (and the trade unions). This seems to me an incredible doctrine, that civil servants should not work on White Papers mainly aimed towards the government's supporters – after all *most* White Papers concern proposed legislation based on the government's election manifesto, drawn up by the Party and aimed at the Party. In fact the CPRS just want to back off. Ken thinks this government is going to fall and he doesn't want to be associated with it.

I sent a minute to the PM about his memoirs. He raised this at the Christmas lunch. I did not respond because others were present, but I have written offering help.

At lunch we had an argument about access to papers. Tom McCaffrey was complaining bitterly that he is not shown papers which are circulated to even the most junior private secretary. He was quite heavy with Ken Stowe. I also asked Ken what kind of papers could be shown safely to an assistant principal, but not to me. Ken had no answer and looked embarrassed.

The private secretaries told me that the PM's meeting with Roy Jenkins was terribly stiff and unrelaxed. It had been arranged through a long line of intermediaries, at Jenkins's instigation. Apparently there were long silences and it was very embarrassing all round, with Roy at his most inhibited. They are just like oil and water. Sad really, because they are naturally on the same political side, against left claptrap and cheap gimmicks and soft options. They both believe in honesty and integrity and old-fashioned virtues. They are both right wing, from poor family backgrounds. Yet they are worlds apart, Roy a Balliol Edwardian with a taste for claret, Jim a clerical civil servant with a preference for hymns and a cup of tea. Jim has won because he is dogged and has never lost contact with the broad bottom of the Labour movement. He knew that the Labour leader is elected in the tea rooms of the House of Commons and not in the salons of Belgravia. Even so I am sure that Roy Jenkins, with his strong historical sense, and personal ambition to be Prime Minister, must still find it hard to visit another Labour Prime Minister, like Wilson, whom he despises but could never beat.

Tom McNally told me that Jim resented that Roy always pronounced Callaghan with a hard 'g' – as I dislike Donoughue with a hard 'g'. The Irish always pronounce both Irish names with a soft 'g'.

Left for home by 7.30 p.m.

Wednesday 5 January 1977

Shortly after arriving at the office the PM phoned from Sussex. He said he was very pleased with my minute on his memoirs and would be very happy to have me help him with them. He felt we got on personally – he said I 'have this knack of sparking me off'. He was very cheerful and said he felt that the general atmosphere was now much less pessimistic.

Went to the Cabinet Office canteen and had lunch with the staff.

Spent the afternoon working on papers. There were eight papers on unemployment for the new Cabinet Office committee preparing the way for the PM's initiative at the World Economic summit. They virtually all argue that there is nothing new about the present unemployment – it simply arises from the world recession, plus increased productivity.

At 6.30 I went to the Carlton Club to have dinner with Lord (Edward)

Boyle. We had dry martinis for an hour before supper, discussing universities and students. Then we went in to eat and talked about the Reith
Lectures which he is giving next year. For hours we went over the whole
field of political institutions. I pressed my theories about the increased and
overt power of the bureaucracy. He is very well informed and liberal in his
views, though fairly orthodox. He also talked about his time as a minister.
He thought some of the senior officials around in the mid-1950s – he named
Rowan and Makins – were terrible. He also pointed out that the trouble
Heath got into with the miners was only a replay of what he did over resale
price maintenance in 1963, boxing himself in, convinced he was right, not
leaving any way to get off the hook.

We talked afterwards over coffee and port and I did not leave till 11.30.
A delightful evening. He is a very good man.

Thursday 6 January 1977

Very cold morning. I ran on the Heath, and strained a calf muscle, which
is annoying. Then walked from Leicester Square Tube station through St
James's Park to No. 10. Foreigners everywhere, buying up our 'sales bargains'.

At 10.45 a meeting of special advisers on our national recovery
programme. It is clear that ministers have reservations. 'Too many hostages
to fortune.' I thought that the points made especially by David Lipsey
were perceptive and generally convincing. So I decided to do a tactical
retreat and brief ministers that this paper was only one approach to a White
Paper.

Had a meeting with the PM, who had come up to town just before lunch.
He discussed his memoirs and said he would like me to work with him
after retirement. He asked me about publishers and I suggested Collins or
Cape. He asked if he could expect £50,000 and I said 'minimum'. We agreed
to start collecting documents and that he would debrief me on meetings he
had with interesting people and I would keep notes. I was also to check on
the No. 10 'archives' to make sure they were adequate for him. But we would
not tell anybody – just say to Ken Stowe that I was doing an 'archives job'.
He said he preferred not to do a full autobiography 'starting with my first
memories of the Germans bombing Portsmouth in 1916'. He thought he
would just write about themes 'like sterling, Ireland, etc.'. I suggested he
might do a mix of 'life' and 'themes', perhaps starting with coming into
Parliament in 1945. We agreed that he would talk to me about his memories and we would tape it. Then I would edit the material. He was very
keen and friendly.

We went downstairs at 4.30 and he went into the Cabinet Room for a
meeting on the sterling balances. Also there were Healey, Gordon Richardson

and Kit McMahon from the Bank, John Hunt and Ken Stowe. The PM had been sent a paper by the Treasury this morning which set out their bargaining position on the sterling balances. The PM was not too pleased with this and told me in our meeting that he thought their position was 'defeatist'. I said that we should try to get more – a bigger loan over a longer term. He said he would rather wait a month or so until Yeo was out and the new Carter regime was in.

At the meeting Healey declared that we had now agreed the sterling safety net. The PM was furious, especially since he had asked for this meeting to be last Monday and had been persuaded by the Treasury to wait. He felt he had been held off until it was all over. Ken Stowe later told me he had heard that the Treasury and Bank wanted to demonstrate that officials could negotiate the deal 'without interference from ministers'. The PM grew ever more angry and sent for Healey to give him a dressing-down.

Later it emerged that nobody knew the deal would be done. McMahon and Mitchell went to Washington for 'consultations'. On arrival they found that [Michael] Blumenthal, the new Treasury secretary, had told Burns and Yeo to settle the safety net *before* he took over on 20 January. It was a sudden take it or leave it. They took it and returned on the Concorde this afternoon, with no time to brief No. 10 in advance. Well that is their story anyway. The PM was cooled down by it and seemed reasonably happy when he left.

Came home at 8.45.

Friday 7 January 1977

Woke feeling very uncomfortable from a large and very sore bump on my stomach. It was painful to sit or walk. So I did not go for my usual morning run on the Heath.

Went to the Cabinet Office for the first meeting of the new interdepartmental committee on unemployment. This was a curious affair. The papers were quite good – all showing that the main cause of this unemployment is the savage downturn in the demand cycle. It *is* cyclical unemployment, not structural – and yet, and yet . . . Most people agreed that although it is cyclical, it is somehow new. Michael Butler from the FCO was quite good in talking about the 'post-industrial society's problems' and David Dirkes from Employment pointed out how little could be done by international action. The Treasury was obviously *against* any action against unemployment because it might worsen inflation. In fact [Geoffrey] Maynard*, in a long and boring exposition, argued that the best thing to do was to cut real wages. It was very rambling, but well meaning. I had some sympathy for John Hunt, though, who has the problem of putting this together into a paper for action.

Late for lunch at Grieveson Grant who were nice as usual, very fair to the government, and enjoying the continuing rise in the markets. Back in the afternoon feeling very sore, with a large carbuncle growing on my stomach. And an argument with Private Office about special advisers. The Civil Service Department is refusing the pay Michael Stewart the salary which the FCO had agreed with him. This means that the CSD has objected to *every* special adviser appointed since Jim took over, either on pay or political grounds.

Saturday 8 January 1977

To Northampton to open my old art teacher David Gommon's art exhibition at the Guildhall. Lovely day, but feeling very poorly. Bought painting *Grasshopper in a Storm*.

Monday 10 January 1977

In bed with a terrible carbuncle on stomach.

Tuesday 11 January 1977

Still in bed.

Wednesday 12 January 1977

Learned that the PM had *never* received our recovery programme paper. Private Office 'forgot' to send him a copy. He read it last night and thought it was too *pessimistic* – although the CPRS think it is too optimistic.

My worry is that on reflection our paper is just not good enough. I regret having circulated it.

Thursday 13 January 1977

Harold Lever phoned. The press this morning is full of reports that the PM is taking over the direction of more economic policy, including sterling and external policy. This is the result of No. 10 briefing. Lever is delighted to see the Treasury getting its nose rubbed. (Me less so – I don't want Healey to get demoralised.)

Apparently last night Fleet Street was buzzing with the PM's initiative in directing the economy – some thought it might mean a reorganisation of the Treasury, with a 'Bureau of the Budget' to do the pay and rations side. I know John Hunt has some such scheme, and he is right. (Under the Hunt scheme, the Treasury Bureau of Budget side would run internal budgetary matters, including the Civil Service, with Ian Bancroft* doing it when Douglas Allen retires. The wider monetary fiscal issues would be under Wass, and this is the side that the Chancellor would be concerned with. He would not then be bogged down on budgetary details. It would also mean the end of the scandal of the Civil Service Department which is overstaffed, underworked and just acts as a spokesman for the Civil Service unions.)

Tom McCaffrey phoned to say that the PM was worried by the press coverage, especially the suggestion of demotions for Healey and Varley, and was trying to retreat from it. He blamed the lobby for 'blowing it up' and said that maybe there should not be press lobbies. I said that 'No. 10 had been down that road before'. (Wilson and Joe Haines abolished the lobby in 1975.)

Actually the Treasury have handled the PM as if he were still the broken Chancellor of 1966–67 – for whom they had contempt. They had not realised that he has matured and toughened since then; and he remembers the games they play.

Monday 17 January 1977

My first day back at work. I needed the car to get to work, since my stomach was too painful to join the Tube crush, but Carol had taken the car keys with her. So I went in late and by bus. I felt very low and weak.

At 3.00 p.m. John Hunt's committee on unemployment in the Cabinet Office Room A, the lovely Old Treasury Room. Unfortunately I was in some pain and had to sit with my trousers undone in order to ease the pressure on the carbuncle. The discussion was rambling and academic with long and pedestrian exchanges between Geoffrey Maynard of the Treasury and Christopher Dow* of the Bank of England. Maynard seems to have one idea – that we must cut real wages – and brings this in to every discussion. Hunt is handling it well, letting them run out of wind on theories of diagnosing the problem, and then will come down to the hard stuff. I left early.

Back to No. 10 for the PM's meeting with the seven LSE economists I had proposed and arranged. The meeting was basically disappointing. They were not madly incomprehensible and irrelevant as I had feared. But they did not spark at all, and said little that was new. Only [Denis] Sargan caught the PM's attention with some research he had been doing which demolished much of the monetarist theory. He claimed that there was no evidence that the rate of inflation diminished with higher unemployment – or that lower unemployment would produce higher inflation.

We ended shortly after 6 and then went upstairs to a party for the left-wing Tribune Group. I had a long chat with Stan Orme, who has appointed my friend and suggestion, David Metcalf, as special adviser.

Tom McNally and I also talked to Healey about the national recovery programme. He revealed no hostility, but when I said that it would be useful in Party terms he replied, 'Well, bugger the Party, frankly.' I understand the sentiments. But Healey is so non-political. As Nigel Wicks said, 'He is really a techno-bureaucrat – originally in Transport House as a functionary, then a technocratic Minister of Defence, which he understood well, and now a bureaucrat at the Treasury, which he understands less well.' But he carries a huge ministerial burden well.

Tuesday 18 January 1977

A big morning. EY on industrial democracy, and then on the recovery programme.

The industrial democracy meeting was serious and good-tempered, but very hard to see a clear consensus. So at the end the PM said he would have to take it over and do a draft. Basically he wanted to win the CBI away from a campaign of total hostility to *any* scheme for industrial democracy. So he wants no commitment to Bullock specifically; and to beef up our commitment to greater industrial democracy in general.

This seems good politics, given his desire to keep the middle ground. We must be seen to be seeking compromise, not railroading industrial democracy through only to get repealed later. He is right, and we were wrong in our Unit brief to him to push for total and immediate commitment.

The PM then said he wanted half an hour on our national recovery programme. He called on Hattersley first. He spoke in favour of a programme, though not our paper. Healey then intervened and spoke strongly against the paper, the project, the lot. He said that we must not have any targets, or commit ourselves to any plans, for fear of 'giving hostages to fortune'. He was completely negative, and was clearly reading from a Treasury brief. The PM then called on Ken Berrill – who admitted the CPRS was responsible for most of the troubles the Policy Unity had faced. And then Michael Foot came in afterwards and spoke strongly in support of me. So did Harold Lever.

The PM summed up. Our paper was not the answer, but the project still attracted him. He would go away and think how to handle it next. Afterwards, near the tape machine, I spoke to him. He said, 'The Chancellor is quite wrong on this. We will go ahead. I will take away the papers and decide how best to proceed.' He then went upstairs to have lunch and to prepare for this afternoon's Questions.

Question Time went reasonably well – except for the PM referring to his being 'saddled with this albatross' of the story about his taking over the economy.

I stayed very late – till after 10 o'clock, working on a draft brief on immigration for tomorrow's Gen 24. The situation is awful. Immigration is rising yearly – probably by 60,000 last year, more this, with no prospect of ever stopping it. That is a new black town every year. And this is all to be published, with projections of a 10% black population, before the end of the month. Basically it is necessary to stop *dependants* and *marriages*; without this, nothing else touches the numbers.

Wednesday 19 January 1977

At 10.45 we left for the National Enterprise Board. I travelled with the PM in his car. We mainly discussed industrial democracy, which is dominating his mind at the moment. But I also spoke to him about interest rates, which are ruinously and unnecessarily high. We are selling masses of gilts. The choices are either just to let sterling rise or to cut interest rates. The latter is much better from nearly every point of view.

When we got to the NEB it emerged that the private secretary had forgotten to bring the PM's brief. So I wrote down some questions on some scraps of paper and gave them to him in the meeting. He wove them into a brilliant off-the-cuff analysis of our industrial problem.

At lunch I sat next to union leader David Basnett and we had a long chat. He also talked a bit to the PM about industrial democracy. He agreed to support the PM if he broke from Jack Jones and Len Murray did not support Bullock.

In the afternoon the PM saw Roy Mason about Ulster. I put a brief to him pointing out that nothing has happened on Ulster – no papers or meeting of IRN since October. Apparently the PM did raise the general point which I suggested – where are we going? And where does Mason want to get to? And he told Patrick [Wright] to tell me this and show me a minute of the meeting.

At the Gen 24 on immigration, Rees was long-winded but short on proposals. Shirley Williams tried to maintain her liberal principles by not facing up to the problem. And Ennals was dreadful, complaining with that meaningless liberal cliché, that 'we must not play the numbers game'. The PM shut him up and told him that 'numbers are now the name of the game'. At the end Rees was sent away to think again and to come up with some more impressive proposals to contain the explosion which will occur when these figures are published.

Jack Ashley came in to see me. He told me about his excellent visit to Germany. We drank a lot and laughed a lot. It is always good to see him. In between I was interrupted several times to try to decide what to brief the PM on his meeting with the Chancellor tomorrow. In the end we decided not to. It is an opening shot on the Budget, and we can have another bite at that cherry later.

Home at 9.30.

Thursday 20 January 1977

I worked in the office all morning (last night I finally finished the backlog of papers from last week – nearly two feet high!).

We had lunch upstairs and discussed this morning's Cabinet. They had spent hours on devolution and the PM had finally got the compromise he wanted. During Cabinet Healey came out for a chat. He told me about his attack of shingles last year, which was very painful. He said he cured it 'by painting it'.

We are all discussing the proposals to cut down Scottish and Welsh Commons representation after devolution. Tom McNally briefed the PM against, but it was lost in Cabinet.

Questions went comfortably. Beforehand I saw Michael Foot and thanked him for his support over the recovery programme. He said he meant to follow it up.

In the afternoon after Questions the PM saw the Chancellor to have a first run over the Budget. They discussed the tax switch – with 12% VAT, but were unsure how to give the rebate on direct tax. He also pressed Healey hard on interest rates. Nigel Wicks, who was taking the note, said he 'heard' my 'voice' in the PM's arguments.

I went to the deputy secretaries at 5.15. It is clear we are running into trouble over our industrial strategy. It all reflects a situation in which the Treasury *controls* industrial strategy but does not *believe* in it, while Varley – though not his department – believes in it, but has no initiative or influence. We got home by 1.

In the evening we went to an inaugural ball for President Carter, held by the Democrats Abroad at the Europa Hotel. Bob Worcester organised our table – McCaffrey, McNally, wives and some Americans. Carol danced with David Owen and found his ambitions showing very strongly.

Friday 21 January 1977

I went to John Hunt's Unemployment committee in the morning and it did not finish till after one. The Treasury was bad as ever, trying to avoid any discussion of recycling of OPEC petro-dollars, but Hunt managed it well. I made some suggestions on reorganising the paper. In the afternoon the PM went off to Cardiff. I wrote a note on industrial strategy, four official papers finally came round. I suggested to the PM that they should be rewritten, merged and shortened.

Our *currency inflow* so far *in January*, till the 18th, was $1.2 billion. So the lending rate was cut by ¾% today. In fact the Bank cannot control interest rates and keep sterling low and have a policy of not building up the balances. It means selling masses of gilts at suicidally high interest rates.

I went to confidential filing this afternoon to discuss keeping documents for the PM's future memoirs. Sheila Wright is the key figure, an old hand. She told me that HW did not write his book on the 1964–70 government from his famous 'phenomenal memory'. She said most of it was written by officials in draft, with the documentary sources checked, while *he was at No. 10* in 1967–70! So it was already in a raw state, and he took it away and finalised it with Joe afterwards.

Monday 24 January 1977

Went to the clinic – the carbuncle has not healed, leaving a large hole, and I have to have it 'packed'. Disgusting and painful.

Arrived at No. 10 just before the PM and Schmidt. They then went into the Cabinet Room for talks – the Japanese threat featured very large in it. Before the Schmidt lunch upstairs, I stood talking for twenty minutes with Foot, Lever, Varley and Benn. Benn was talking of the stamina needed for politics. He said he had taken no exercise since leaving the RAF, but the excitement of the job kept him going. He thought those who dropped out of politics were either lazy or lacked stamina.

At lunch – held in the pillared room at four small tables, the first time we had done that, and very pleasant – I sat at table with Tony Crosland, Fred Mulley and three Germans. Crosland was preoccupied with Rhodesia, where our initiative collapsed today. He said that Ivor Richard, our man at the UN, is talking wildly to the press. Crosland left early, as usual, muttering about a press conference, but looking exhausted and probably going to sleep.

Afterwards I worked in the Unit, did another note on industrial strategy, and then saw Tessa Blackstone* for a drink. She told me of the hostility aroused by her CPRS study of the Foreign Office. She is not very keen on Ken Berrill.

To the LSE to see my old friend Hilde Himmelweit, who fears the Annan Report on Broadcasting would be too bland – because Annan is terrified of offending the Establishment.

Home at 9.30.

Tuesday 25 January 1977

To the clinic and then to Cabinet committee EY on industrial strategy. The PM said he wanted to know how to get action at firm level. Benn met that by proposing the *Company* working parties.

I went to lunch at the *Guardian*. With Peter Gibbings, Peter Preston*, David McKie – and John Methven of the CBI, who was the other guest. Discussed industrial democracy. Methven said he had launched his campaign against Bullock because he thought it was wrong, and he knew he could not restrain his members.

Came back and went straight to a meeting of John Hunt's committee on unemployment which went on for *three* hours. But a lot of progress. A promising draft. Yet the Treasury man continues to talk about the need for a 'once and for all' cut in real wages, whatever the subject matter at the time.

Then straight into a meeting on immigration with the two Toms. Slow progress. We are going to have to be very tough – on marriages, on dependants, on job vouchers – if we are to get the numbers down at all. Will continue tomorrow.

This afternoon the PM saw Hattersley and asked him to write the next draft of the national recovery programme. Hattersley said OK – but the PM will have to support him against Treasury opposition. Jim gave him a total assurance of this, saying, according to Tom McNally, 'You know I am not going to be economic supremo, I am going to be Denis's political adviser. That's what he needs. I know what it's like in the Treasury. Those knights bachelor keep coming up to you and saying, "You must behave like a Chancellor." In fact you need somebody to come and say, "You must behave like a politician, Chancellor."'

I read papers till 8.30, went to have a drink with the two Toms, and then home by 9.30.

Wednesday 26 January 1977

Late in from the clinic; my stomach is slowly getting better. From 11–1 had a Unit meeting on immigration with the two Toms present, where we slowly came to grips with difficult and complex steps necessary to restrain the flow of immigrants. Without them there will be a self-perpetuating flow of 100,000 every year. But I doubt if this government will grasp the nettle – though Jim alone would.

Thursday 27 January 1977

More work on immigration – we had a lunchtime meeting in the Unit with the two Toms.

To the West German Embassy for drinks. Then to the dinner for the new US Vice President Mondale – very jolly. Mondale sang 'Glasgow Belongs to Me', the PM sang 'Jerusalem'. The young men with Mondale seemed very impressive – much better than the Ford crowd, optimistic and full of that marvellous excitement on first taking office. Home at 12.30.

Friday 28 January 1977

Up at 7 to get to Northolt to fly to Leeds with the PM. The driver got lost on a short cut and we nearly missed the plane. Cold and icy. We spent the morning at Allied Textiles, lunch at Huddersfield Polytechnic, and the afternoon at David Brown tractors. The PM took the opportunity to talk about industrial democracy, which has clearly scared the life out of British management. One man at David Brown tractors became quite hysterical. They are frightened – and therefore must be handled carefully.

I loved it. The provinces attract me more and more. We drove in the evening to Harrogate over fell-land covered in snow, with miles of old stone walls. Harrogate is very handsome, though the hotel was poor, with very grumpy service.

At dinner we sat with the PM and Audrey – myself, Philip Wood* from Private Office and beautiful Clare from the garden room. Over coffee the PM began to discuss politics and history. He was completely relaxed. We discussed Macmillan, Home, Churchill. He then talked about being Home Secretary – and how the worst decision was whether to release on parole a life-sentenced murderer, always afraid he might do it again. He also talked of his visits to prison and talks with bank robber McVicar, the criminal Richardson brothers, baby-faced Probyn and various other villains. He had enormous respect for McVicar – described as 'the most dangerous man in England'. The PM said he was very intelligent, of great character and courage.

I did not sleep well, and went out again for a walk around Scarborough under a frosty moon. I walked right out of the town and on to the moors above, where the snow was six inches deep.

Saturday 29 January 1977

To the conference hall at 9.15. Interestingly, the floor speakers were generally loyal, if troubled, and when one man attacked the government he was hissed. We left at 12.30, drove to Leeds and took the plane back, having sandwiches on the plane.

Saturday night went to Tonbridge for Joe Haines's party. He had his book there which looks very attractive – I read it on the train going back at midnight. I miss him still at No. 10.

As yet no signs of writs against Joe's book. Just one more week to go to serialisation in the *Mirror*.

Monday 31 January 1977

Went in early to meeting of John Hunt's committee on unemployment. We went through the final draft, line by line. A long hard slog – finishing at 1 p.m. We do not have a great deal to suggest, but I think they have done the best possible, thanks to a positive attitude from Employment, Industry and the FCO.

Lunch at the Reform with my old friend Clifford Barclay*.

In the Unit we continued the long tortuous agony of finishing our immigration paper. We have a reasonable balance now, although it is a bit too wishy-washy liberal for my liking.

I went home to dinner with Bruce Grant*, an Australian journalist friend from my Harvard days. To bed at midnight.

Tuesday 1 February 1977

I went to the clinic for a final dressing of my carbuncle hole, which is finally beginning to heal up. Then to No. 10, where the PM saw Witteveen of the IMF with Healey. Apparently Witteveen was very bullish and said we were well on target.

Lunch at No. 10. The officials began to talk deprecatingly of Tessa Blackstone, who is doing the CPRS study on British representation overseas. Ken Stowe said there were 'too many wild young radicals' in the CPRS – I wish it were true. But this is all familiar to me, an early alert that the machine is preparing the way to discredit the CPRS report on the FCO in advance.

At about 6.30 Frank McElhone came in to talk about his plans for involving the community in helping to solve Glasgow's problems. We agreed to meet again, and that I would visit his Glasgow constituency in March. He is depressed about the SNP and thinks they will take ten to twenty seats from us next time.

Home at 9.30. Tired but not exhausted. Now the immigration battle in the Unit is over, I feel much better.

Wednesday 2 February 1977

Into No. 10 before 9, then off to National Economic Development Council (NEDC) with the PM for the big meeting on industrial strategy. There was a sharp exchange between Jack Jones of the T&G and Watkinson of the CBI at the beginning, but otherwise it went very constructively.

I stayed for lunch and had a long chat with David Basnett. He is very depressed about the wage policy prospects. Last night's meeting with the Chancellor was sticky. The trade unionists told him they were not interested in a tax deal. Basnett said they were having great difficulties in holding the rank and file. He does not see how a deal can be made – he even asked me what would be the result of a return to free collective bargaining. I said higher inflation and unemployment.

Back to No. 10 into the Gen 24 on immigration. Jim handled it well, only putting the boot in at the end and telling them to face up to the problem. In fact Merlyn Rees was all over the place, passionately against new controls at the beginning, but quickly swinging when Jim showed his hand at the end.

Jim revealed his resentment at Roy Jenkins. He told the committee that in 1967 Roy had delayed acting on immigration for months, and then when Jim took over the Home Office Jim was saddled with doing it in a rush – and getting the blame for it.

Went to supper with Tessa Blackstone at a Greek restaurant in Islington, and home early at 9.30.

Thursday 3 February 1977

Before Cabinet I chatted with Lever and Healey. Healey said that Tuesday's meeting with the trade unions on wages was 'pretty bloody' but no worse than last year. He said that Basnett puzzled him. He thought that Basnett *looked* impressive but in fact was intellectually much slower than Jones or Scanlon* – and because he did not come from the shop floor he lacked their confidence.

After Cabinet the PM had Parliamentary Questions briefing. These are much better *before* than *after* lunch – when we are all too sleepy. The PM said he does not think much of Carter's folksy start, with fireside chats, etc. He said, 'The reality, the pressures, will soon push them off all of that.'

Went to the LSE for lunch with Dahrendorf. We get on very well. We discussed the Brookings Institute for London. He said he had thought of John Mackintosh or William Plowden to run it. I am still interested.

He is a bit worried about the Royal Commission on the Law. Says it has become too 'Zanderish' (my friend Michael Zander is on it) – too obsessed with providing more legal services employing ever more lawyers. He is convinced that Britain must not become 'over-juridicised' like Germany.

Home by 9.

Life is quieter at the moment – and very welcome. I am recharging my batteries.

Friday 4 February 1977

To meeting with the PM on overseas visits. He is keen to make these 'political' – e.g. he pressed for India and Pakistan because of our large immigrant communities. Probably next Christmas.

Lunch of sandwiches in the office. Did a minute for the PM on the Unemployment committee – and sent a copy to John Hunt since he had shown me a copy of his.

Had a long drink in the evening with Patrick Wright, the private secretary on foreign affairs. He is the last of the 'old team' and I have a friendship and bond there which is missing with the new lot – who are anyway less 'charismatic' than Robert Armstrong's team. I told him a bit about Joe's book. He said he was always a bit afraid of Joe.

Home at 9 p.m. for a quiet weekend.

Joe's book begins serialisation in Monday's *Mirror*. I shall go to dinner with him on Sunday to launch it off.

Monday 7 February 1977

Today Joe's 'memoirs' had their first instalment in the *Mirror* – and caused a sensation. Every newspaper took it up. The journalists again besieged Falkender's home in Wyndham Mews – shades of 1974!

The newspapers were enjoying it all because they wanted revenge on *everybody* involved – including Joe. He will take a battering from it, and it will be a pity if the serious side of his book does not get through.

The PM did not say anything to me, but he apparently told two private secretaries that 'there will be nothing like this when I go'.

Had lunch at the Reform with *The Economist* journalist Dick Leonard – who told me that somebody from the FCO had got the editor of *The Economist* to 'doctor' an article so it was savagely critical of the (still unfinished!) CPRS report on the FCO. The machine is absolutely unprincipled in defending its interests.

I worked in the Unit for the rest of the evening, apart from a long talk with Michael Foot about India. He shares my love for it, and for the same reason, the movement and the colour. We get on very well.

Home at 9.

Tuesday 8 February 1977

I went to Gen 24 on immigration. A boring meeting and Merlyn was sent back and asked to do better next time. Then the draft statement on the Franks Report on Official Secrets. John Hunt and the PM had completely rewritten Rees's draft. Not a good day for the Home Office.

At lunch in No. 10 Tom McCaffrey started again to attack Joe Haines for writing the book. Tom always speaks warmly of Joe, but I think really he dislikes him and is jealous of him. I defended Joe strongly, but could feel all the others, except McNally, who is a good man, backing off. Everybody is buzzing about it, and Bill Rodgers told me it was impossible to lay hands on a copy of the *Mirror* in the Commons.

In the evening, I went to the opera with Carol, hosted by Claus Moser*, with some lively fellow guests – the Humphrey Burtons and the Mostyn-Owens. To hear *Un ballo in maschera* – poor performance, but the delightful company made it all worthwhile.

Home by midnight.

Wednesday 9 February 1977

I went in early to go with the PM to the Royal National Institute of the Deaf Conference on problems of the deaf. I arranged this with the secretary of the RNID to give them a boost. We are doing very little on social policy at the moment and it is necessary to show the flag wherever possible. I sat with Jack Ashley at the conference. The PM spoke very slowly so that he could be 'interpreted' to the audience, many of whom were deaf. It was impressive and moving.

The newspapers still full of Joe's 'revelations'. The reaction – and the *Mirror* treatment – has been much more sensational than we expected. Nothing of the 'serious' material has been used so far. The trouble is that, used day by day, very personal anecdotes, some trivial, it begins to look like a vendetta. I felt particularly sensitive because today's *Mirror* had my picture on the front page. McCaffrey still behaves oddly, suspiciously towards me, and with barely concealed hatred towards Joe Haines.

We all came back straight to a Cabinet committee on unemployment.

After the committee I went for lunch with Harold Lever. We each felt victims in the present '*affaire*', being thought of as part of the Wilson kitchen Cabinet. How does one *prove* one was different from toadies like John Scholefield, Allen and Kaufman?

In the evening Tessa Jowell arrived – she is still hoping to go to Stan Orme, as a special adviser, but I would like to keep her as a reserve for the Policy Unit if he does not take her. She lives locally and drove me home before 9.

I feel depressed by the publicity. Taking the lid off the Wilson regime has reminded me of some of the stink and brought back many of those awful memories. What really upset me was the *Evening Standard* beating on my door at 7.30 this morning – and my daughter, aged 11, having the shock of dealing with these gutter predators.

Thursday 10 February 1977

A quiet morning – although the press is still full of the Joe and Marcia battle, with the journalists taking every opportunity to kick *both* of them.

Lunch in No. 10. McCaffrey made a snide remark about this morning's piece in *The Times*, sympathetic to Joe, as if he resented it. Apparently he thought I had briefed for it. There is no doubt that *all* the staff at No. 10 – except McNally – are taking cover and putting on record their disapproval of what Joe has done. The finger is pointing at him and they wish it to be known they disapprove. (If of course he returns to favour, and public employment, they will all display his book on their desks.) The machine is a total jungle, breeding loyalty only to itself.

Briefing for Questions went very well. Cledwyn Hughes* sat in – I don't know why, perhaps to demonstrate there is no 'kitchen Cabinet'.

I went home early, still tired in that way one is by *pressure* rather than work. I hate the public spotlight myself. And the sight of Terry Pitt (quite drunkenly incoherent on television), Kaufman, Lovell-Davis*, Illtyd Harrington and a whole regiment of other of Marcia's lap dog bit-players with a sad past and no future was demoralising. There is still Sunday to come. The *Sunday Times* is doing a big 'Insight' piece – as well as the 'Treasury' section of the book. I am bound to figure in each.

Carol and I have decided to go to the country this weekend. No television. No newspapers!

Friday 11 February 1977

In early to the deputy secretaries meeting. I did not intervene, until called on by John Hunt. I said, 'Nothing. A quiet week.' Others laughed. Hunt said, 'Oh, quietly writing your memoirs.' Indeed.

I took in my copy of Joe's book, at Ken Stowe's request, and sent it to the PM. I enclosed a letter saying I didn't expect him to like it, but pointing out that Joe was loyal to him, the Party and to me.

The Unit was working on a piece on the Budget. Gavyn Davies worked most of the day dictating it.

Had lunch at the Reform. James Margach joined me. He said that the *Sunday Times* had been ambivalent towards Joe's book because the chairman had received a rushed knighthood from Harold.

Michael Stewart, Tony Crosland's new economic adviser, came to see me. He told me how miserable he had been at Trade in 1974, completely frozen out by the civil servants and *not* defended by Peter Shore.

In the evening to a nice dinner with the Grahams, civilised friends. I took a good bottle of wine and relaxed by midnight.

Off to Suffolk Saturday morning.

Saturday 12–Sunday 13 February 1977

The weekend was lovely, beautiful early spring sunshine, mild, blue skies. We went for a long walk to Denston on Saturday and to the lovely hamlet of Somerton on Sunday. I was supposed not to see the Sunday papers, but I sneaked a *Sunday Times* – Harry Evans had done a good job, with the minimum of gossip and trivia.

Nice to sit by the fire with the children listening to the radio. Always the same, when under pressure I withdraw to the family and dream of a quiet country and academic life.

Monday 14 February 1977

Got up at 7 and drove to Newmarket to catch the early morning train to Cambridge and London. The newspapers were still full of Joe's book – with far too many references to me. I am now fed up with it all – but there is much more to come, with Joe and Harold on TV.

I arrived just after Jim, and he invited me up to the study to have coffee. We discussed the book. He had read chunks of it and seemed to be enjoying it. He said he needed 'somebody who could write as well as Joe Haines. He is a brilliant phrase-maker.' He referred to Joe's response to Peter Lovell-Davis – 'look before you creep' – and said, 'That sums up Peter perfectly.' But he was serious about needing a speech-writer. He said that 'the Toms cannot write like Joe'.

He seemed fairly confident that we would get a pay deal of some sort. I queried whether it was worth getting a bad one. He said, 'Yes. We have to wind this down slowly.' He has said all along that the pay policy could not be maintained for very much longer.

Had a quick lunch upstairs with Gavyn in the Cabinet Office canteen. Fiddled the afternoon away while the PM had his talks with [Adolfo] Suarez and the Portuguese.

Everything was overshadowed by the tragic news that Tony Crosland is dying. He had a stroke yesterday on returning from a walk. It was a deep stroke, which slowly paralysed him and he went unconscious with no prospect of recovery. Susan apparently asked the doctors not to resuscitate him. She had discussed it with Tony and they had agreed not to do anything to keep him alive as a vegetable.

The PM talked to Susan on Sunday evening but she kept from him the full seriousness. He then telephoned David Owen and told him he would have to take over the FCO for a while, but it wasn't till this morning that he realised it was very serious, and this afternoon we were told that the doctors said there was no hope. The brain damage is deep and spreading and he is deeply unconscious.

Tony has not looked well for some time. When I have visited him in the evening he has had medicines on his desk – I believe for blood pressure and for blood clots and hardening of the arteries. He had a minor heart attack two years ago. So now it all looks inevitable. Actually last Wednesday when he arrived for the Cabinet committee on unemployment, straight from an all-night sitting in Brussels, he looked terrible, his face puffy and purple. Apparently he had an unnaturally high colour that night when he gave a dinner for Anne Armstrong, the outgoing American ambassador. Somebody at the dinner was so struck by it that they asked Tony whether he had been skiing. This high colour continued on Thursday and then on Friday he looked pale and drained.

All very sad. The brains and quality and style has gone out of the moderate wing of the Party now, with Roy Jenkins departed and Tony Crosland gone in the space of four months. Added to Harold Wilson, Barbara Castle, Ted Short, Willie Ross, it means that the big figures have all been swept out of the Cabinet in the past year. Now there are too many second-rankers, decent but without charisma – Morris, Mulley, Peart, Ennals, Millan. It would be better to have young hopefuls than old never-has-beens.

The dinner for Suarez in the evening was overshadowed by the Crosland tragedy, a shadow across the Party. Jim commented to Tom McNally afterwards that he could sense the anxiety of the political wives there – Edna Healey, Audrey Callaghan, Molly Hattersley – that it could have been them in Susan Crosland's place.

Healey kept looking at me in a very glinty way, and making references to how terrible Joe Haines's book was. He clearly resented publication in the *Sunday Times* of the Unit's role in the pay policy. I stood my ground.

Home at 12.30.

Tuesday 15 February 1977

Had a bad night, suffering from anxiety over domestic matters.

I did not go to the Devolution committee this morning – they discussed the referendum and agreed it should *not* be binding, so as not to offend parliamentary sovereignty. Everyone now agrees that devolution is dead. The whips estimates show 22–46 deficit on any vote on a devolution guillotine. Still they have decided to go ahead with it next week to show the Scots that we tried.

Questions went well – though we were saved by an uncharacteristic slip by Dennis Skinner* about Wilson's honours. He said that Jim should consult his political advisers and get a piece of lavender paper on which should be written . . . then he paused, fatally, and somebody shouted, 'Skinner.' So the attempt to expose the honours collapsed in laughter.

I went back to No. 10 and worked with Gavyn on his Budget paper for the rest of the afternoon. Decided not to put it in till the weekend, although it is very good. And went home at 9 o'clock.

Jim is thinking of splitting the Treasury in the way that John Hunt has advocated to the parliamentary select committee, and he has Dell in mind for the public expenditure/CSD part and Shore for the Ministry of Finance part (neither first-division players). But he is worried about Healey moving to the FCO now. I don't want Healey to go. He is the only big man we have, apart from Jim.

Wednesday 16 February 1977

The PM was all morning at a joint Cabinet-NEC meeting in the dining room of No. 10. I had a meeting nearly all morning with Meinolf Dierkes* of the Berlin Social Research Institute, discussing research to be done under the EEC auspices. It was a good brainstorming session, made me think how much I would enjoy going back into that world. I get good ideas in conversation – but do not put them often enough to the PM. This is a hangover from HW, who was not interested in policy ideas anyway.

The Haines story has now spilled over very dangerously, with the press on to the contributors to Party funds – most of whom later got peerages. Typically, the press does not mention that Heath was financed in opposition by private contributors – or that Thatcher does not have to be because we passed legislation providing £150,000 p.a. for the office of the leader of the Opposition.

Had an excellent lunch at Grieveson Grant. What a nice and intelligent lot they are.

The 4 p.m. Economic committee was in the PM's room at the Commons. The Chancellor reported on the pay policy situation. He said that the trade unions would not do a deal ahead of the Budget – 'They want to see the colour of our money on the table'. But he was confident they would move rapidly after the Budget. He reported he had a meeting with foreign bankers, who are monetarists and do not believe an incomes policy has any utility in their own country, but insist it is essential to Britain. The PM said, 'Perhaps we need an autumn Budget to complete the deal' – which is what I suggested to him on Monday – 'but we must get a pay policy of some kind.'

I went to the Gay Hussar for the *Daily Mirror* celebration dinner for Joe's book. I felt tired and not well. I did not enjoy it at all. The food was good but the constant discussion of Marcia and the kitchen Cabinet bored me. Joe's blood is in the circulation of the *Daily Mirror*. At the end I expressed this view, and said bluntly that they should give him a job.

I felt I had had enough of sensationalism and publicity and said so. It is a lesson for me. When I leave No. 10 I shall not immediately take a peerage and will not write any 'personal' memoirs for a long time [twenty-four years till The Heat of the Kitchen in 2003] though I would like to write something serious.

Arrived home at 12.45 a.m. Carol was away again for the NUT. I was miserable, tired and did not sleep well.

Thursday 17 February 1977

Attended the Gen 17 Cabinet committee on the problem of allowing our captured SAS soldiers to go to court in Dublin. This is very delicate. If they are jailed and/or assassinated we shall suffer a backlash. Mulley took a firm Defence line and said don't risk sending them. Mason said that they had to go, otherwise co-operation on the Ulster border would totally cease. He said that since the incident *fifty* of our troops have wandered into Ireland and been arrested, but all have been quickly and friendlily handed back. He preferred to rely on the Irish President or Minister of Justice to pardon any prison sentence and send the men back. But he admitted that if they were imprisoned they would be killed by the IRA within days.

At the end the PM decided to have a secret talk with Garett Fitzgerald*, the Irish Foreign Secretary, and then decide what to do. At one point the

PM referred to the fact that 'I have Irish blood in my veins'. I have never heard him say that before. I went to see John Smith about the future of devolution. It all sounds very grim. Smith is much less optimistic than nine months ago. The whole thing has gone very sour in the House.

We had lunch upstairs in No. 10. I put my thoughts on Ireland – a Dominion in the North, jointly guaranteed by the UK and the Republic, with a Bill of Rights, and some population movement, plus massive financial aid. Ken Stowe rejected it and said Ulster was 'our responsibility'. But for how long? And how 'responsible' is it not to have a long-term policy?

Question Time went OK with the PM confidently on top – though there was uproar afterwards when Michael Foot announced the devolution guillotine for next week. Incidentally, the Tories have told us that they refuse to pair Crosland for next week's debate while he is still Foreign Secretary. In other words they will pair him as Foreign Secretary, but not as a dying MP. Very cruel.

I went off to the American ambassador's house in Regent's Park in order to meet Nelson Rockefeller again. I had an interesting talk with Donald Trelford, editor of the *Observer*. I reminded him that I had refused the *Observer*'s approach to take money for my future 'memoirs'. An American Embassy official said it was remarkable that I had 'survived the battle without a single bullet hole in my flak jacket'. Perhaps. I will wait and see. I certainly feel scarred.

I went home to bed, very tired. This is turning into a bad week, stressful and exhausting.

Friday 18 February 1977

I saw John Hunt about his evidence to the parliamentary select committee – where he floated the idea of a split Treasury divided into a Bureau of the Budget, with CSD and public expenditure; and a proper Ministry of Finance. This had fascinated me, because three weeks ago Peter Hennessy wrote an article in *The Times* floating such an idea – and he told me that John Hunt and Douglas Allen had floated it towards him. Now it has re-emerged and been floated towards the select committee – just at the time when a big reshuffle is due, and the PM might want to do something with the Treasury. John Hunt told me that the Treasury was hopping mad. What I would like to know – and don't – is whether the PM authorised Hunt to fly the kite. It is hard to believe that the Cabinet secretary would put up a proposal to carve up the Treasury without higher authority.

The PM was away all day today.

Lunch with Douglas Wass at the Reform. Very interesting. He is as nice, intelligent and open as ever. I went out of my way to rebuild my fences with the Treasury – somewhat damaged since Joe wrote about our incomes policy episode. I told him that I wanted to work closely with the Treasury, and gave him several policy areas we could build on. Afterwards at coffee upstairs he got me on the subject of splitting the Treasury. He was very upset. He said that John Hunt had told him that he would mention the matter but *not* that he would *advocate* it, and had sent him no draft of his statement in advance. He assumed that the PM had approved it. I told him, truthfully, that I had been told nothing.

In the afternoon I worked with Gavyn on our pay policy brief. Went to Private Office around 9 p.m. First we had a message from Oxford saying that Crosland was going to die very soon. So preparations for the PM's statement went ahead. Then Giscard d'Estaing came through on the phone to talk to the PM. It was relayed over the radio in Private Office – and taped. He said how sad he was about Crosland and what 'a fine man' he was.

Then he went on – all in English – to make suggestions for the Economic summit. He wanted a private meeting of the Big Four – himself, Callaghan, Carter and Schmidt. He suggested 'a *long* evening', and the PM said that No. 10 was the best place for it. So they agreed. Giscard made it clear he had already discussed it with Schmidt.

At the end, Jim said, 'I hope you are in the country?' 'No,' said Giscard, 'I am in Paris. But I am shortly flying to the Alps for a skiing weekend.' Very different from Jim.

I came home at 10.45, dreading the weekend press, and decided to go to Scotland soon to get away from London.

Monday 21 February 1977

The PM did not go to Birmingham because of Tony Crosland's death – at 5 o'clock on Saturday morning. Today is the private funeral and the tributes in the Commons.

Michael Foot, Rees and John Smith came in to see the PM about devolution. The vote tomorrow looks very dicey. At one point the chief whip has indicated a majority of three, but during the day people grew more pessimistic.

I had a quiet morning, and then lunch at the Reform.

Incidentally Tom McCaffrey told me that the PM did authorise John Hunt to float the idea of splitting the Treasury to the parliamentary select committee. John Hunt had minuted the PM with his ideas on this on 11 February, and the PM commented 'very good' on the 14th. McCaffrey said, 'Something will happen – but not yet.'

I still feel very tired. But at least the Marcia nonsense seems about over. HW continues to issue statements denying various true allegations, but people are understandably getting bored with it all.

Tuesday 22 February 1977

I came in early, and saw the Chancellor on his way up to his 9.30 meeting with the PM to discuss the Budget. He seemed cheerful. I said I was pleased he was staying on at the Treasury. He said how pleased he was about David Owen getting the FCO; he had worked well with him at Defence in the previous Labour government.

The Defence and Overseas committee (DOP) met at No. 10 to discuss Cyprus. I chatted to David Owen beforehand. He seemed pale and strained, completely bowled over by being made Foreign Secretary. He did not know about it till Monday afternoon at 4 p.m. – after the Commons tributes to Crosland. On Cyprus, there is some fear of a spy somewhere high up – something has got out. These Cyprus papers – not circulated to me – have been 'observed' in a foreign embassy, i.e. within forty-eight hours of circulation!

I went to the Gen 24 on immigration. They focused on options to get the numbers down – mainly preventing marriages to foreigners who then came in. I felt unwell, my stomach is still painful and bleeding, and I left halfway through to rest.

Lunch at the Oxford and Cambridge Club with Pat Nairne from Health. He shares my negative view of Ennals, though completely loyal. He was rather critical of David Owen, partly because Owen fought them to get DHSS staff numbers down.

Back to Parliamentary Questions, which Jim continues to dominate.

Afterwards I saw Ron Spiers of the American Embassy. They are fascinated by the Owen appointment. They wonder if this is not a downgrading of the Foreign Office – a thought which had clearly crossed Sir Michael Palliser's mind when I met him in Downing Street at lunchtime. Perhaps there is something in that. Jim has often said he enjoyed the FCO, but Downing Street is different 'because being PM is for real', i.e. foreign affairs is a bit of a game.

In the early evening I sat for a long talk with Tom McNally and we cooked up a plan for the NEC – to get two good right-wingers on to the women's section (Williams and Boothroyd), two responsible left-wingers (Jackson and Hart) and [Lena] Jeger*. Younger and better balanced. And then to get the big trade unions to support this package. A long shot, but it could just win.

Then I went over the Commons for the end of the debate on the

devolution guillotine. I went to the Strangers Café for supper and joined
David Owen and his wife Debbie at their table. I told him I had absolute
faith in his ability to do the FCO job. He is going to keep on all the Crosland
team to stress continuity – though we may well take on David Lipsey in
here, to help with the speech-writing.

I went and stood in the passage behind the Speaker's Chair while the
votes were counted through the division lobbies. It was clear that we had
lost by more than anyone expected – 22 rebel votes against, many more
abstentions. The Tories were jubilant.

I went to Jim's room and he was telling McCaffrey to brief the press
that this was 'a hollow victory'. I stressed the need to get the blame on the
Tories – 280 of whom had voted against devolution! Jim agreed, and when
Michael Foot and Bruce Millan dropped in he stressed this point to them.
Jim said afterwards that Millan 'has no politics in him'. We discussed alternative Secretaries of State for Scotland. It is John Smith or Dickson Mabon*
(who Jim says is good but has 'other problems').

The PM was quite relaxed. He said he does not mind losing the bill
providing we get the credit in Scotland for 'having tried to get devolution'.
I think that is his preferred outcome.

McCaffrey told me that Jim's original idea was to put Judith Hart at the
FCO beneath Owen, but the security services objected, and Tom suggested
putting her at Overseas Development and Judd to FCO.

I travelled back in the car to No. 10 with Jim at 11 p.m. He said, 'We
have not lost anything providing we handle it right.'

In the committee on immigration today, the PM said he is 'a supporter
of Brazil'. Wants immigrants to marry UK natives, 'decent white Britons',
and let us have a coffee-coloured community, but one single community, not this inflow of different cultures into a so-called 'multicultural
society'.

Wednesday 23 February 1977

The PM was at the NEC this morning. I saw him when he returned. He
confirmed that my friend Helen Liddell* had been appointed secretary of
the Scottish Labour Party, adding that not everybody seemed happy with
it. She is too tough and sensible for most in the Party.

I went to lunch with David Basnett at the Reform. We discussed pay
policy – he is not as pessimistic as before, but says that the PM will have
to jolly along some of the TU leaders. He said that one could almost physically see the power ebbing away from Jack Jones and Hugh Scanlon at the
T&G and the Engineers.

Robert Armstrong came in to tell me about the Agee and Hosenball 'secrets' case. Two other journalists have got hold of a lot of classified information on our military intelligence and are thinking to publish it. They have been arrested and things are bubbling up rather ominously.

Robert also told me the incredible story of William Armstrong's crack-up during the last days of the Heath administration in 1974. William Armstrong came through to No. 10 to see Robert, looking very distraught, and said they must talk somewhere 'not bugged'. Robert took him to the waiting room where WA lay on the floor, chain-smoking, and talking 'very wildly' about the whole system collapsing and the world coming to an end. In the middle of this, Gordon Richardson, Governor of the Bank, walked in and 'took it all calmly'. Robert then took William upstairs and tried to calm him down but he was still fairly mad.

Next day WA summoned a special meeting of all the permanent secretaries and told them all to go home and prepare for Armageddon. He was babbling incoherently. Douglas Allen led him away, phoned his wife and the hospital and WA was taken off to hospital for treatment. Robert phoned Heath, who was out of London, and told him that the head of the Civil Service had been locked up. Heath was not surprised, saying that he 'thought William was acting oddly the last time I saw him'.

Home at 9.30.

Thursday 24 February 1977

Felt as if I have used all my reserves of nervous energy. So I decided not to go to the meeting of special advisers. I just sat and read, and then went upstairs for lunch.

Cabinet decided to have talks with the Opposition parties about devolution – Tuesday's defeat has been very demoralising, and most political commentators think that the government is now collapsing. I don't. But we just do not have a legislative programme any more. And today's Westminster by-election means that we will become a minority government again. Back to 1974!

After lunch went upstairs and slept until after 4 o'clock. Woke feeling much refreshed. Really what I most need is a few nights' good sleep and to start getting exercise again – my stomach is still bleeding and I cannot play football yet.

Went to see Frank McElhone at 4.30 and took Liz Arnott and Jim Corr to hear his philosophy of the inner-city problem, and all his schemes for Glasgow. He is certainly on to something and if his ideas for using people and the community, rather than money, institutions and social workers, were put into action, I am sure that our social problems would be lessened. I shall try to see him in Scotland. Home at 11 p.m.

Friday 25 February 1977

The Cabinet met on European direct elections, all morning, through a buffet lunch at No. 10, and then afterwards. There was a lot of disagreement, so they decided to produce a White Paper which merely sets out the options.

I went to the Civil Service College, where I am on the advisory council, and we discussed how to reorganise it in the future. Had lunch there, and then a two-hour meeting afterwards. Douglas Allen was very good, as were other mandarins Jim Hamilton and Peter Carey.

When I got back to No. 10 at 4.30 the PM had already gone off to Sussex for the weekend. I worked on clearing up my papers and then home at 8.30, and took Carol out to the pub for a couple of drinks. We needed it.

Incidentally, this week Robert Armstrong told me that Joe Kagan* has KGB contacts. And Joe Haines told me that the *Mail* has discovered Kagan has illegal Swiss bank accounts. Joe confirmed that Jim apparently offered Harold Wilson the *Treasury* in November! – and Anthony Lester told me that he also approached *Roy Jenkins*. So Jim was clearly seriously considering replacing Healey, but from outside the present Cabinet. Harold was a strange thought, burnt out.

Monday 28 February 1977

I worked in the Unit in the morning, and did not see the PM.

Went to lunch with David Higham, the literary agent. He is 81. He claimed that he has been Harold Wilson's literary agent since 1951. He said that he negotiated for *The Governance of Britain* back in 1971–72. But when HW published it he was omitted – until he got very firm with HW, and received his money.

This afternoon Douglas Wass told me that John Hunt was getting very heavy about this question of splitting up the Treasury. Wass said, 'What a curious man John Hunt is.' But the Treasury is very worried; and Healey joined in the conversation, saying, 'We are now embarked on the dismantling of John Hunt.'

My position is that I don't really know what to do with the Treasury. I have long supported *two* Treasury ministers in the Cabinet. And I think the Civil Service Department should be abolished. Beyond that I am not sure.

Tuesday 1 March 1977

So now it is three years since I came in to No. 10. I am older, tireder, tougher, more serious, sadder, more cynical and more devoted to my family as a result.

To EY, which went on for over two hours. The item which interested me was on the unemployment initiative. The PM was clearly looking for imaginative ideas, and the proposals of the John Hunt committee – on the European Investment Bank, etc. – were clearly not good enough. He was very taken by some of what Booth and Shirley Williams said about guaranteeing employment to young people. The unemployment question is becoming much more overt, and Benn correctly warned that it could become an explosive issue quite soon.

To Questions after lunch upstairs. Jim was splendid in defence of Joe. He slapped down Tebbit and foolish Jeremy Thorpe, who joined in the witch-hunt. But then after Questions Speaker George Thomas agreed to allow an emergency debate on British Leyland tomorrow. Jim was furious, stormed back to his room and wrote a letter of protest to the Speaker. Then he obviously felt better. We all went back to No. 10.

Came home early – by 9 p.m.

Feeling much better this week – because my stomach is healing and I am running over the Heath again in the mornings. Makes all the difference.

Wednesday 2 March 1977

A quiet day. The PM away on a visit to Essex. I read in the office, then to lunch with [Sports minister] Denis Howell and [old friend] Clifford Barclay. We discussed football. It is ten years since we were on the Chester Football Inquiry together – I have aged the most.

In the late afternoon I went to see Margaret Jackson to discuss our 'plot' to get her on to the NEC – along with an extra right-winger (Boothroyd) and as part of getting rid of 'Stalin's grannies' Joan Maynard and Renée Short*.

Then to dinner with Jack Ashley at the Reform. Nice to see him as always. He is very involved in the whooping cough vaccine problem. The DHSS are handling him roughly and, he claims, Ennals is not playing it straight.

Thursday 3 March 1977

The PM has now decided to fly to the States on Concorde. At first he decided against, preferring the VC10 on grounds of cost, etc. But pressure from all sides forced him to change.

I went to see Douglas Wass at the Treasury at 11.30 to discuss Budget strategy. The most interesting thing he told me was that the Chancellor is thinking of doing the big giveaway *now*, before the pay deal, gambling on the trade unions then feeling obliged to do a pay deal in return. A bit optimistic.

I had to dash back for briefing on PM's Questions because Cabinet had finished unexpectedly early. He got through Questions quite well, saved by an absolutely wild intervention by Keith Joseph, arms waving and eyes staring.

I had lunch with the German Embassy staff, Jack Ashley and Alf Morris, on the question of co-operation over disablement.

I came home early in the evening to help Carol. This morning she got a telephone call from her sister in Israel – Markie, Jill's eldest son, was killed last night in a car accident. We are all saddened beyond belief. A young boy of 22, just married. We were so exhausted by it we went to bed and to sleep at 10 o'clock.

Friday 4 March 1977

After a lovely dawn run over the Heath I went in early to the meeting of deputy secretaries. The usual things were buzzing – devolution, where the government certainly has *not* decided to give up its bill; Tony Benn, who is trying to make a big political issue out of opposing nuclear power (Windscale, nuclear waste, etc.), in fact he wants to kill off the entire nuclear energy programme (so we will be fully in the hands of the mineworkers' union); and British Leyland, which goes from bad to worse, though we simply cannot afford to close it down because of the resulting burden on our balance of payments.

Went to lunch at dear old Mon Plaisir with journalist Maureen Cleave*, who I fancied greatly at Oxford – I've only seen her twice since 1957. Delightful reminiscences. She reminded me how carefree I used to be, and quite properly told me off for now being pompous at times. I need that often.

Home early again.

Monday 7 March 1977

The PM had an early meeting with the police over their pay. There were already hordes of police reps there when I arrived at 9.15 a.m., including Robert Armstrong from the Home Office – always nice to see him back on his home territory. I knew the PM was going to take a tough line.

At 2.30 we met for briefing for Washington – this time on the international and defence questions – a little bit of trade (Concorde and Air Services). Not much for me. But an interesting discussion on Rhodesia, where Owen is proposing a new initiative, with the black leaders. The PM gave him full support – and Owen was excellent at presenting the case, brief, lucid and forceful. Ivor Richard is to be left playing his own Rhodesia game at the UN, with little hope. 'If Ivor has to be sacrificed . . .' said the PM.

The PM kept expressing doubts how to approach Carter. He said he was afraid the President was in daily communication with God. He did not want to appear to tell him to suck eggs. David Owen said it would be a mistake to treat Carter as a naive new boy. In fact he is a very capable and experienced politician.

In the late afternoon the PM went to talk to Mrs Thatcher about devolution. Apparently it was a polite and bland meeting. She did not show her hand at all, and the PM did not press her as hard as he had pressed the Liberals and the Nationalists in his earlier meetings.

I had Leo Plietzky in for drinks. He was open and funny as usual. Interestingly he told me that the Treasury 'had got the message' and would be co-operating with the Unit in future.

I drove home early to look after the children, as Carol was away working till late.

Tuesday 8 March 1977

EY discussed Budget strategy. This is quite a revolution. It is the first time a Chancellor has opened up his budget to a Cabinet committee of this size – though he did not say which taxes he would change, or give any numbers to particular items. The discussion was of a high level, with Shirley Williams very good, and Roy Hattersley political in his suggestion of a new prices freeze policy.

At 5 p.m. the PM saw Wilson about his decision to take Marcia off the proposed Film Industry committee. HW was apparently very unpleasant. Jim was firm and quiet, regretting that 'this cloud has come between us'. It was decided that HW would go away and think about it for a week. Jim is not very keen to announce another public plum for Marcia.

I worked in the Unit and then came home early at 8 p.m. to pack for Washington tomorrow.

Washington and Ottawa: Wednesday 9–Sunday 13 March 1977

We left No. 10 at 6 p.m. and went to London Airport and then on to the Concorde. It is longer than I expected and cigar-shaped – only two seats each side and a narrow gangway. We took off in the dark. As we left the Welsh coast it accelerated with a surge of power which pinned me back in my seat. Like being on a motorcycle.

The PM held a briefing meeting on the issues for the visit. He asked everybody to write down their six themes on a piece of paper, then we gathered in the rear compartment of the plane, which is empty of seats, rather like a luggage wagon, and *very* noisy. We stood around in a circle, and read out our issues, having to shout to make ourselves heard. The PM wrote them down on his paper.

Then we went back for supper. David Owen asked me to join him and his wife Deborah. Tom McNally sat with the PM and Audrey. The food was good and we all drank a lot of champagne. The sun was rising as we swooped in over the Potomac to Washington. We landed at 6 US time, an hour before we left, and swept off in a long cavalcade to Blair House.

My room was next to the Prime Minister's, the only other room on that first landing. I lay and rested on the four-poster bed and watched a little television – the news was dominated by some kidnappings by Muslim extremists and police sieges of three buildings close to the White House. It all seemed typically American. As somebody commented, they should not be worried by the noise of Concorde, it would be drowned by the sound of gunfire.

By the time I came down the briefing meeting had started. A bad mistake – never leave the scene of action. So I sat in the big reception room eating fruit and drinking iced Coca-Cola – it was very hot outside. John Hunt joined me, being too late for the briefing also, so I didn't feel too bad.

Apparently a message had arrived from Schmidt saying that the Germans were going to send Carter a message (Jim had a copy, twenty-five pages long in German!) to the effect that they opposed any further reflation. Inflation was the enemy, not unemployment. This was a bit of a blow to Jim, but we decided to press on with our line.

Afterwards Jim went for a walk around the square opposite the White House – with Tom McNally, Jim's PPS, Roger Stott*, and myself. We walked back with the PM to Blair House, surrounded by policemen. He mentioned that he would have lived here had he got the IMF job in 1972 but 'Audrey did not want to come'.

After we had seen him off to bed we nipped off to McCaffrey's room and drank whisky with the press. We came back to Blair House to bed at about 11.30 – which was really 4.30 a.m. British time. I had been up twenty-one and a half hours and was running around Hampstead Heath twenty-one hours earlier.

Thursday 10 March 1977

I woke at 4.30 (9.30 British time) and, although tired after only less than five hours sleep, I could not get to sleep again, so read my briefs, then got up for a big breakfast, and went out for a walk with McNally and Stott. It was already hot at 8 a.m. Washington looked beautiful in the sun, with the blossoms and buds just beginning. The sieges continue, with over a hundred hostages, all within half a mile of where we slept and walked, but it was hard to believe in them. Generally Washington seems less tense than a couple of years ago. America is getting back to normal, with Vietnam and Nixon left behind.

We walked down towards the Washington Memorial and then around the back of the White House. Then back to Blair House for a briefing session with the PM, the ambassador, and the people from the FCO, Treasury and Trade. It was mainly on international monetary matters and was dominated, as usual, by Michael Butler of the FO, who seems to know the facts on virtually everything.

Then we all whisked off to the White House lawn for the opening ceremony. Glorious sunshine and crowds of children waving flags, a naval band and splash of uniforms just like with Wilson two years ago. But different. No nineteen-gun salute – for fear of frightening the Muslim guerrillas into shooting their hostages! No Joe to help look after me. Both leaders are new, and both made a much better speech than Ford and Wilson. Carter, who is not as small as he appears, made a very warm and gracious welcome, Jim an equally warm reply.

We all trooped up into the White House for coffee. Jim and Carter went off for their talks. We staff were leaving by the front path when an American suggested we go down to the Cabinet Room, where the meeting was taking place. We went – and joined in the meeting, with McNally, Stowe and I sitting at the oval Cabinet table. This was a marvellous occasion for me to be at.

The Cabinet Room is as I remember it. Two flags behind the President. Five flags in the corner. Pictures of Truman and Lincoln on the walls. Four full-length windows (behind where the President sits), looking out on to gardens, neat lawns and hedges and the trees just beginning to break into bud or blossom. The sun was shining and it was very peaceful.

The main feature of Carter is the alertness of his eyes. He smiles a lot, but that is a diversion. His eyes show his real reactions. He was tentative in many of his replies but justifiably so, early in his administration. Also he is clearly new to international questions, but he is interested and his instincts seem good. He was very snappily dressed, smart blue suit, blue shirt, red tie.

Cy Vance from the State Department was heavy and loud in his interventions, and interrupted Zbigniew Brzezinski*, clearly aiming to dominate him. Carter said, 'We have an extraordinary close relationship with Japan. They are almost blood-brothers of ours.'

Afterwards we went back to Blair House for a quick change before going off to the congressional lunch. Interestingly, at Blair House, Jim said to me, 'I hope you took a few notes of that, Bernard,' his first acknowledgement of my 'memoirs role'. As we left for Capitol Hill, I mentioned to him my idea for an exchange scheme of people involved in our schemes for training the unemployed – careers and training officers. He said he liked it and asked me to travel to Capitol Hill with him in the lead car.

The lunch was a bit of a shambles – there were three votes during the speeches and questions, and people were constantly drifting in and out. But I enjoyed it. I sat next to Senator Dick Clarke from Ohio, a most intelligent and attractive man. I also saw my old Oxford friend Paul Sarbanes, now senator for Maryland.

After lunch we went back to Blair House. The PM had a series of meetings – with Blumenthal, Brzezinski and [James] Schlesinger*. I sat in my room and drafted a paper on youth unemployment and also some defensive points on the UK economy.

We went off to the White House at 7.10 – me in my very tight old 1953 Oxford dinner jacket. It was very similar to our 1975 visit: a naval band playing as we entered, everybody gathering in the big reception room to drink and talk (I was with Peter Jay, who was invited at the PM's request); then lining up to shake hands with the President.

Dinner was at a dozen small tables. I sat next to Governor Harriman's wife (Pamela Churchill, Winston Churchill Jr's mother), a beautiful television lady, and adviser Brzezinski. The food was poor – they produced roast beef and Yorkshire pudding (with Californian wine) and it just didn't work. But the speeches were terrific. Carter was brilliant – witty, serious, delivered with perfect timing. The PM was good as well, ignoring most of his typed speech. Then we retired for 'entertainment' – some lovely Stephen Foster songs by a lady mezzo, and other Victorian songs by a marvellous young tenor, Robert Whyte. Very moving. We hung around a little afterwards. I chatted with the Hartmans, the Owens, various American friends. Finally, after midnight, I walked back from the front door, along the drive to the front gate, and across the road to Blair House. It was a very warm night and Washington was alive with cars and people and lights. Lovely.

Ken Stowe and Patrick Wright and I went for a walk around town and came back in to bed at around 1.

When we got back to Blair House we talked to the PM about Carter. He was very impressed, but almost overwhelmed by the warmth of this reception. Jim said, 'He seemed so impressed, and said he had always wanted to meet me – and he meant me!' Jim still doesn't quite believe he is now a famous man. He was also a bit worried that Carter was setting so much store by the Anglo-American relationship. He said, 'I am not sure we can deliver anything for them. I am worried that they will be disappointed.' Above all he was puzzled by Carter. Was he naive? Had he thought it all through? Was he religious, in touch with God? – that especially worried Jim. On balance the PM thought he was a shrewd politician, but some doubts lingered on. Though he had to admit that Carter handled this morning superbly.

One nice touch. Jim said, defensively, 'He kissed Audrey goodnight, so I kissed Mrs Carter – that was all right, wasn't it?'

Friday 11 March 1977

Up early and off for a walk after breakfast. Then a long briefing meeting upstairs in the PM's bedroom, mainly on international politics questions: nothing of domestic and little of economic significance. We all went off to the White House in cavalcade, but this time the PM had his session with Carter alone. So I went off with McNally and Stott to see Stuart Eisenstadt, the President's domestic affairs adviser, and we discussed youth employment. They have the same problem as us – only worse – and Carter's new measures are very similar. His office was a basement room in the White House, where there is a whole network of offices. This is the territory where Kissinger, Erlichman, Haldeman, Dean, etc. all held sway under Nixon. Now it feels very clean.

We all went to lunch at the National Press Club. The food was a bit better than last time. I sat on the top table, and we had the usual business of introductions to the audience, rather like boxers at Madison Square Garden. Our roll call of Irish names – Callaghan, Donoughue, McNally, McCaffrey – sounded particularly funny in American.

The PM's speech was good, and his answers to questions brilliant. In fact he peaked out here, and seemed quite exhausted afterwards.

On return I went to tea in Georgetown with gorgeous Liz Stevens, to whom I am strongly attracted. She is the wife of famous film producer George. We went for a walk and a talk. It was lovely, all the wooden houses, the sun and the blossoms. We ran into Governor Harriman in N Street, walking in his shirtsleeves. He is 85 and very deaf, but still in the middle of the Washington social scene.

I returned late and had to change in a hurry to go to the embassy party and dinner. The party was the better – the Sabanes, lovely Teresa Heinz, and several of the Carter aides were there. Then on to the embassy dinner. I was at the ambassador's table, though sitting between Senator Frank Church's wife and ancient Arthur Burns of the Federal Reserve. Burns was pontificating about the sins of the British, but I shot him down a few times. He is full of admiration for the PM.

It broke up after midnight when the PM and Mrs Carter left. David Owen then put his wife Debbie to bed – she had a stomach bug – and came out with me in the ambassador's Rolls-Royce to Georgetown. We visited Teresa Heinz's house. She had put her husband to bed, the better for drink, and still had with her two amusing men who had consumed a great deal of wine. One was David's friend and they had an argument upstairs, while Teresa and I chatted happily downstairs. I love her Portuguese accent and in a different world would fancy her strongly.

David took me back to Blair House at 2 a.m. He said that the new job was incredibly exhausting.

We also discussed the CPRS report on the FCO. He wants to do something about foreign service extravagance – he says that the waste in the embassy is 'obscene' – but he is also worried about 'morale' in the service. I like Ambassador [Peter] Ramsbotham* very much, and also Tom Bridges the Commercial minister – but they are both straight out of the nineteenth century.

It had been a marvellous day and I was sorry to think of leaving tomorrow. Ridiculous to leave the sun for the snow.

Saturday 12 March 1977

Another glorious morning. The TV and papers full of the end of the Muslim sieges. I was up at 7.15 a.m. to put my case out ready for the plane, and then went for a long walk with McNally, McCaffrey and Stott. Right along Pennsylvania Avenue, down past government buildings and back around behind the White House. The sky was full of aeroplanes coming in to land at the domestic airport and the noise was constant.

We set off in cavalcade and then switched to the President's helicopters to fly to Dulles Airport – certainly the best way to get there, landing right close to Concorde. The flight to Ottawa was only an hour. Soon there was snow below, and it was cooler when we landed, but quite sunny and not as cold as I had anticipated. We drove straight to Rideau Gate and waited for Prime Minister Trudeau to come to collect us. He looked tired. The newspapers were full of the story of his hippie wife

Margaret Trudeau going to New York this week with the Rolling Stones and spending two wild nights with one of them. Apparently she has problems and this puts a great strain on her husband, who is anyway thirty years older.

Trudeau and Callaghan decided to walk down Sussex Drive to the Lester B. Pearson Building. We walked behind and soon the path was full of photographers. The traffic skidded to a halt and drivers gaped at the Prime Ministers. Lunch was upstairs. I sat between veteran diplomat Paul Martin (who was next to Trudeau) and Pierre Dupuy, who is the Overseas Development minister. We mainly talked economics. I also discussed machinery of government with Michael Pitfield, their 39-year-old whiz-kid secretary of the Cabinet who sat opposite.

We broke up at 3.30. The PM went to the TV studios – where he got some hostile questioning on Britain's faults, especially the impossible trade unions.

I rested, and then went out in the evening to the French part of Ottawa to eat with [friends] Gordon Smith and Gerry Varracatt. A delightful evening with delicious food and charming wives. Back at the hotel Chateau Laurier I waited in the bar till Stott and McNally arrived, having several beers along the way, and finally going to bed at 2.30 a.m.

Sunday 13 March 1977

We rose at 7 a.m. and handed in our luggage at 7.30. There was no breakfast available, the restaurant being closed on a Sunday, so we drove off to the airport. It was wet and foggy and there was talk of delay. We finally took off, landed at Montreal for more fuel, and spent an hour in the waiting room having a briefing session with the PM. We discussed the tone of his statement to the Commons, and how to face the issues back home – especially British Leyland which is going disastrously wrong. I told the PM to stay out of it.

The rest of the flight was marvellous: excellent food and drink. I had dinner again with the Owens. Then we all had a briefing session with the PM on prices – which are rising and again becoming the dominant issue at home. We all want the government to act, though we could not agree among ourselves. Some wanted a total freeze, some selective freezes, I wanted to freeze the public sector. The PM listened, asked a few questions, and then told us to go off and work it out.

He was marvellous to his personal staff throughout the trip, bringing us into everything. Tom McNally thanked him for this. Jim said, 'The mandarins don't like it. But that is good for them.'

He told us that Mrs Trudeau was not at his private dinner with Trudeau last night. She had returned to Ottawa, but not to Trudeau, who discussed the whole problem with Jim, saying he had nobody in Canada he could discuss it with, but felt he could do so with Jim.

Landed at 9 p.m. and then home. Took the presents to the children's bedrooms and left them there by their beds, like at Christmas time.

Monday 14 March 1977

I was woken early by the children, who loved their presents – especially the packages of Concorde mementoes. But it was still the middle of the night American time, so I felt tired, fell asleep, and woke up at midday in an empty house. I made lunch, went for a haircut, and then did not get in to No. 10 till teatime. It was very quiet. The PM had held a meeting on Leyland this morning, and was resting in the afternoon. I reported to the Unit, read through my papers and then went home for an early night.

Tuesday 15 March 1977

This was the first time that a Chancellor had opened up the Budget to Cabinet a fortnight before Budget day – though of course he did not tell them any specific details of taxes, just the overall strategy, and options. It went very quietly.

After Cabinet I went with David Owen to the Foreign Office, where we had a light salad lunch and discussed the Budget. He was thinking of sending a memo to Healey and the PM setting out his views – which are basically reflationary and expansionist. We discussed the Budget strategy – whether to give away £1.5 billion now; or to give it away in two stages, half before and half after the pay policy; or to give it all away now, but to slow down the Finance Bill so that if we don't get a pay policy the relevant clauses can be withdrawn. We both inclined to the last option.

David Owen is keen to put down a marker showing his interest in economic policy. But we are not convinced at the end that he has enough to say. That Foreign Secretary's room is very glamorous – much better than anything the PM or the Chancellor has.

Judith Hart came in to see me at 6.45 and we talked for two hours, consuming a lot of gin and tonic along the way. She had brought a long agenda of items, mainly about the NEC.

She was being very 'responsible' for a so-called left-winger and quite right wing. She obviously did not enjoy being a backbencher and wants to get back into the ministerial mainstream by showing Jim she can be responsible. She spoke very disparagingly about Harold Wilson. So does everybody now.

They all refer to his having 'shrunk' physically, as well as in reputation. A sad, but inevitable end. Everybody uses the word 'shabby'.

I took a taxi home at 9 o'clock.

Wednesday 16 March 1977

I worked in the Unit in the morning. The PM remained in the flat until quite late – then he went off to the PLP meeting (on the Budget).

Went to lunch with Bill Woestner from the American Embassy at the Inigo Jones at lunchtime. He told me that all the reports from Washington were that our visit had been a tremendous success. He is a great supporter of this Labour government, and thinks the Tories are appalling, but obviously feels we might fall quite soon.

Harold Lever came in to see the PM about something 'personal' – I assume it is that he does not want to stand at the next election and would like a peerage. He is getting fed up with the militants in his constituency. Also the prospects of his getting the Treasury have finally gone and he begins to hanker after private life and business again.

Incidentally Tom McCaffrey told me that the PM had no intention of putting Tony Crosland to the Treasury had he lived. He knew of Tony's health problems and had decided he could not do it – that is why in November he played with the idea of Wilson and Roy Jenkins as Chancellor.

The PM had Albert Booth in for one of his 'ministerial' meetings and I sat in. Booth was quite good, obviously enjoying his job and very much in touch with the detail. The PM likes him and said afterwards how pleased he was with how 'Albert has grown in the job'.

Jim then went off to a meeting with the Ulster Unionists, to see if there was any basis for future Commons co-operation. Curiously they did not bring Enoch Powell – but the awful [Ian] Paisley* insisted on coming.

An Australian friend Bruce Grant came to see me at 6.30 and we went out to dinner at the Reform, walking back afterwards through Soho to Charlotte Street for a drink in the Fitzroy Tavern. Then we took a bus together to Camden Town, where he lives, and I went home at 11.15.

Thursday 17 March 1977

The Cabinet discussed what to do about this evening's vote on the last public expenditure White Paper. We will lose – the left won't vote. Jim has thought up some scheme to *abstain* on our own motion. So we will be humiliated but not defeated. It looks a bit silly, but it is part of the reality of *minority* government. We have to live with the fact that we can be beaten whenever the Opposition chooses to unite and beat us.

I went off to the Treasury at 11.30 for a meeting with Derek Mitchell.

He nearly got the sack over the IMF negotiations and has clearly decided to make peace with No. 10. He wrote me a nice letter before we went to Washington and suggested this meeting. On the Economic summit, he said that nothing serious could come out of it. The Germans would not reflate. The American and Japanese mini-reflations did not add up to very much. I said we must come out of the summit with something. So I pressed my scheme for youth unemployment. He was sceptical – he is a totally sceptical man, though very amusing – but said he would give it a run. Actually like most frustrated mandarins, he enjoys the failures of politicians, and is very tempted to push the politicians gently towards the banana skin.

I returned for lunch at No. 10. I met the ministers coming out of Cabinet. Hattersley told me that the last meeting with the TUC on pay policy went very stickily, and Jack Jones lost his temper with Healey. I saw the minutes and they don't encourage me very much. Jones and Scanlon simply said that it was not on.

The PM was very worried about Questions, thinking it would go very badly – especially with all the bad news on prices, now rising up to 16½% again. But it was OK. The Tories somehow seem inhibited from joining in a real attack. But tonight is the big test on public expenditure.

I was supposed to be going out to dinner with Harry Evans and some guests, but I was tired and he did not mind my calling it off.

Tonight the government did abstain on its own motion. The PM decided not to put down a government motion of confidence, but to challenge the Opposition to do so. (There is a difference. None of the Opposition has confidence in the government, but they may not all wish to join in with the Tory Opposition.) It is bluff and brinkmanship. We do not have a majority in the House.

Friday 18 March 1977

In mid-morning Thatcher announced that she would put down a no-confidence motion next Wednesday. So this will be the crunch. The messages coming in are not hopeful. The Irish and the Scots and Welsh Nationalists won't support us. The Liberals are talking privately about voting against. They are all in a suicidal frame of mind – at least eight Liberals would lose their seats, but there is a hysterical atmosphere. I still think that the Liberals will abstain, because they have more to gain from a deal with us than from an election. They must play hard to get and hope we will do a last-minute deal with them. I won't mind. But it may be the end – ironical just as things could be getting better.

The PM is cool, though not very well. He has another attack of bronchitis. We were all thinking about the draft for his confidence speech, with

Tom McNally supposed to be doing a draft, but he did not get round to it. Nigel Wicks began a draft.

I had lunch at the Reform with Robert Armstrong, who has now taken over as permanent secretary at the Home Office. We get on very well together, and enjoyed strolling back though the Park.

William Plowden dropped in for a drink in the evening. He is leaving the CPRS today, going off to the USA for a lecture tour and then returns to get a job in the Department of Industry. He openly admits that no job outside the Civil Service has the same high salary, pension and security. He said he 'could not afford to leave'. The privileges of the public sector!

I left for home at 8.15. My car battery was flat so I had to leave the car on Horse Guards Parade and go home by bus. Perhaps next Friday we shall be in an election campaign. But somehow I think not.

Monday 21 March 1977

This is a decisive week. We have no majority in the Commons. *All* the Opposition parties say that they will vote against us. So we will lose unless we get some kind of coalition/arrangement. And at absolutely the wrong time for us – with prices rising and before the North Sea oil comes in. If the Tories get in now it will be just like 1951 – inheriting a bonanza. The weekend press, radio and TV have been full of it. Curiously I feel very relaxed. I enjoyed my football yesterday. I don't look forward to being unemployed – even less to an election. But it does not worry me. I have done over three years. I am ready to call it a day. But in fact I do not believe it will happen. Governments do not fall from parliamentary procedures. We are not yet ready to go. We may be by the autumn, but not yet.

At 2.30 the PM saw the Ulster Unionists, who were represented by [James] Molyneaux* and Enoch Powell (looking as always like a prosperous barrister) and it went very well. They agreed to support the government *until the end of this Parliament* providing we put Ulster Representation at Westminster to a Speakers Conference and 'consider' giving a new tier of local government to Ulster. On this basis they could offer six abstentions on Wednesday and afterwards. The PM was pleased. He likes the Ulster Unionists – much more than the Liberals – because they are his kind of straight, tough old-fashioned conservative people.

While we were sitting outside this meeting, Party chairman Cledwyn Hughes arrived. He had been liaising with the Liberals and was quite optimistic. Clearly he was very much in favour. But he is on the right. I saw Stan Orme who was against. He preferred an election. The Benn faction also prefer an election – if we lose, then Jim will resign and they will go for the leadership again.

I went back to No. 10 for a while to clear my papers. The Unit is totally paralysed, waiting to see the outcome of Wednesday. I tried to reassure them – in fact Gavyn Davies has bet £100 on our victory.

Then David Steel* came at 6 p.m. to discuss a Lib–Lab pact. He stayed an hour and a quarter. I sat in the anteroom with Tom McCaffrey and Roger Stott. We could often hear Jim's voice booming through the door.

While we waited Margot MacDonald* of the Scot Nats phoned from Scotland, trying to talk to Jim. It was not clear what she wanted. She is pressing the Scot Nats to vote against. Because she wants an election – because she is broke, unemployed, having left her husband six months ago. Her only way to get a living is to get an election and become an MP.

Steel came out at 7.15 p.m. and I walked up the passage with him. He seemed bewildered. He took me by the arm and told me to come and see him tomorrow. He obviously was not satisfied with the talks. He wanted another go. Afterwards Jim told us it was very unpromising. All too vague. He 'could not get hold of anything'. So it was a bad start.

We all went across to No. 10 for the dinner with scientists. This was a bizarre occasion, with much high talk about genetics, biology and energy, yet the PM's mind must have been on other things. Afterwards he asked the politicians present to stay behind in the pillared room. He asked them what they thought about 'doing a deal with the Liberals'.

John Cunningham, Ken Weedon and Geoffrey Robinson* said 'do a deal'. Kaufman foolishly disagreed. He argued for 'have an election immediately'. Tom McNally made an excellent attack on the silly Kaufman position.

McCaffrey, Stott, John Cunningham and I gathered in Tom McNally's room and drank a bottle of whisky while we discussed the situation. We agreed that a deal had to be done. And tomorrow we would get in on the act. This was too important for the civil servants. And too political. That is what we will go for tomorrow. So I went home after midnight, quietly confident.

Tuesday 22 March 1977

At 10.30 the PM sent for me. I went upstairs to the study and Tom McNally was already there. Jim immediately started apologising for having shut us out so far. He said, 'You know I keep these things very close.' He then went on to explain that he had done a deal with the Ulster Unionists. He had a copy of a letter to exchange. They would abstain, he explained. That would be enough. He added that he 'could talk to the Ulster Unionists': they were serious men. He found it difficult to talk to the Liberals. Steel was very 'adolescent'. He did not think he could deal with them.

Tom McNally then intervened sensibly to put the case again for a Liberal deal. He said it would be ridiculous to break off now, over some small points which would seem irrelevant in three months' time, and hand over the government to the Tories just as the economy was turning round and the oil flowing in. I supported that, adding that it was not worth doing a deal just for Wednesday night, we needed a longer-term deal; that Steel may irritate him, but he is the only Liberal leader we have. And I warned that the Ulster Unionists might not be enough. They might drive the Catholic Irish, Gerry Fitt* and [Frank] Maguire* away. And then if we lost the by-elections at Stechford and Grimsby where would we be? Jim said, 'You are right; we would be back without a majority.' We went round this course several times. Roger Stott and Tom McCaffrey joined us and agreed with us.

Jim said, 'You are a right-wing lot. I will have to carry the can with the left.' He was playing hard to get. When McNally said the only alternative was 'to lose a general election', Jim said, 'Well you know what my preference is – to go off to the farm.' We then switched to briefing him for the TV broadcast, recorded at 11.30 but broadcast in the evening.

On TV the PM made it absolutely clear that he was seeking an accommodation with the other parties. There was no equivocation. This was certainly a change of mood from earlier this morning – though then he may have been playing games with us. After the broadcast we went back to his study. Everybody was delighted with the TV. Jim knew he had done well.

Then Ken Stowe came in with a letter from Steel setting out the terms. The tone was very impertinent. Jim threw it on the coffee table and said, 'Well I cannot take that.' The rest of us agreed it was not a good negotiating letter. The PM was behaving as if that meant the end of it. We went to McNally's room. I said that what was required was for McNally and Stowe to go off and draft for the Liberals the letter which conveyed their position which we could accept. The PM agreed. Tom and Ken drafted. The Liberals agreed it all except for PR on direct elections to Europe and on elections to the Scottish Assembly. It was arranged that the PM would see Steel to negotiate this tonight. Cledwyn Hughes talked to me before Questions and said that we must now do a deal. It would be crazy to split over this one last issue.

Several left-wingers have said they would support a deal – including Heffer and Atkinson. Audrey Wise* – having considered her tiny majority as well as her Marxist principles – told a whip that she supported 'a deal at any price'.

Now it is up to Jim to out-negotiate the Liberals.

Wednesday 23 March 1977

So the big day arrives. Once more I am faced by the possible end of the government – and unemployment for me, but I don't really believe it. Steel telephoned early this morning to report that the Liberals will accept the paper agreed between Jim and Steel at two meetings last night, with a 'free vote' on direct elections. As Michael Foot said, a free vote got us out of a difficulty with our own left wing which we would have needed anyway.

The PM worked on his speech. In the Unit we did a section on prices which he accepted and used, as he did with a peroration I did on what we would do in the time gained by a coalition.

An emergency Cabinet was called at noon. I talked to people beforehand. They seemed relaxed, little tension. They were given a copy of the agreement with the Liberals when they got in there. The final vote was 20–4 – with Orme, Shore, Benn and Millan expressing doubts. Benn apparently was embarrassing, saying that he ought not to support it because it had not been put to his constituency party.

At the end the PM turned to the four dissenters and asked what they wanted to do. Stan Orme asked if he was being asked to resign. The PM said no – but was he going to insist on resigning? Stan said, 'No, no.' The others joined in and agreed to support the Cabinet decision.

The PM took us upstairs afterwards. He looked a bit tired, and said it had been a tough meeting. He had taken more criticism than he had expected. Obviously the pressure of this crisis is beginning to get at him.

After lunch at the Commons I nipped upstairs to the ministerial floor. I stood outside Roy Mason's room, preparing to go in there, but through Tony Benn's adjacent door I could hear Benn asking Ian Mikardo to organise a letter of protest and signatures from Labour backbenchers. Benn said, 'This is just like the Common Market. We need the right to dissent. We cannot be bound by this decision.' Benn was of course referring to the collective decision of Cabinet which, barely an hour earlier, he had agreed to be bound by. He was conspiring to organise a left-wing backbench rebellion against the decision he had shared in. Jim had given him the chance to resign, but he had declined. Once again he wanted the pleasure of opposing, without resigning. (And later this afternoon we learned that he had briefed the press that he was 'on the brink' of resigning. It was a brink he never meant to go over, despite all of our attempts to push him.) Benn said he 'wanted sixty to eighty signatures'. Mikardo said he would go off and do what he could.

I slipped away in order not to be observed. I waited outside the PM's room. Judith Hart telephoned me. She said she had heard of the Cabinet decision and wanted to give it her full support. She offered to sell it to the left. I said that she might be needed. I told her that somebody was organising a counter-attack. I did not name Benn, but made it clear who it was.

The House was packed for the main speeches. Thatcher was very poor. She had an ill-mannered reception from our side and often could not be heard. But it was clear that she was depressed by our deal with the Liberals and her confidence was gone. Also she made her old mistake of sticking rigidly to the text of her speech, reading paragraph after paragraph, cliché after cliché. She made no adaptation to the fluid and turbulent mood of the House. Her jokes were bad anyway, but in fact no carefully chiselled jokes could have gone down in that House. She never got on to the Commons wavelength, and the longer she went on the worse it sounded. Above all, there was no serious policy content or problem analysis. She just attacked us on the old philosophical grounds – freedom versus the state, etc.

Jim immediately spotted and reacted to this. Although he had at least three scripts with him and was shuffling them like a pack of cards, in fact his first fifteen minutes was not the opening of any of his scripts. He simply went straight into the economic problems which face Britain, the policies which the government has introduced, and all the boring statistics connected with this. In this way he not only sobered the House – although Tory interruptions were even more ill-mannered than ours – but he also painted the contrast between a government on course to recovery and an Opposition without policies. He dominated the House.

Steel was quite good in the circumstances – starting off by pointing out that if he had any doubts about the deal they were set to rest by Thatcher's speech.

We went back to the PM's room. He said it was 'the roughest House I ever remember'. He thought Thatcher 'very poor'. On Benn, he said he was never willing to go too far, but given the chance, 'perhaps I will sack him'. I suggested Judith Hart for Benn's job and the PM said, 'Not a bad idea. I may do that.'

I saw [John] Pardoe* and we sat and had a long chat about the Liberal pact. He is very keen to do a longer deal.

I went to the central lobby at 8.30 to collect Carol, and ran into David and Debbie Owen. We discussed the deal, which David is very happy with. I was very hungry by now and so we went to the Strangers Café and had a quick meal. Then again to the bar, which was quite packed. Jock Stallard was there, hanging on to a very unsteady Gerry Fitt, but complaining desperately that he had 'lost Maguire'. Apparently Jock, as a whip, had been assigned the task of making sure that the two Irishmen got into our lobby at 10 p.m. He had stuck with them and drunk with them all day. But in the past hour he had lost Maguire and had sent out search parties.

The atmosphere was jubilant and when the result was announced – a majority of 24 – our MPs burst out cheering. Neil Kinnock led them in singing a couple of verses from the 'Red Flag'. It then struck me that the Strangers Bar is a Labour bar, with rarely any Tories there.

I went upstairs to the PM's room. He was already there celebrating with Audrey and the rest of our team. He had *even* opened the drinks cupboard and provided a bottle of brandy, which is a rare historical event since Jim does not drink and is not overgenerous in encouraging others. After some jokes and chat the PM got up to go to bed. We stayed behind to finish the brandy, being unwilling to see it disappear back in the cupboard for another twelve months.

We finally went home towards 1 a.m. It had been a great day and I did not feel in the least tired.

Our next task is to make this deal last two years!

Thursday 24 March 1977

I spent the morning in the Unit, mainly discussing prices, with Andrew Graham up from Oxford and Maurice Peston from Roy Hattersley's office. We made some progress, and hope to put in a paper to Jim for Easter.

Lunch at No. 10. We discussed the machinery for implementing the 'joint consultation' with the Liberals – it will be the Lord President's office which services the meetings.

I went to supper with Edward Boyle. I took him to the Reform and we had an interesting talk, as always.

I still felt elated, and therefore not tired.

Friday 25 March 1977

The PM had gone to Rome for the European meeting.

Tom McCaffrey and Ken Stowe were left behind at the last moment – because of a new Benn move. Last night Ron Hayward phoned the PM and said that Benn was organising a letter to convene an emergency meeting of the NEC to attack the Lib pact. It needed fifteen signatures out of twenty-nine members to succeed.

The PM phoned Benn and told him bluntly to withdraw his name or resign. Benn began to flannel and said it might be too late, he had signed. 'Well you had better unsign,' said Jim. 'If you haven't done it by tonight you will have to go.' He was very heavy, according to McCaffrey who heard the phone call, and Benn sounded very frightened. Afterwards they drafted the press statement announcing Benn's resignation for McCaffrey to issue tomorrow, and he and Stowe stayed behind to handle it. Judith Hart was going to get Benn's job as I had suggested.

I went for an excellent lunch at Simpson's with Bruce Grant and Lord Harewood (who when we were both at Harvard married Bruce's girlfriend). I ate and drank too much but it was a very lively lunch. I began to feel sleepy in the afternoon. Benn had not resigned. There was sadly no sign of his letter, or of a special NEC meeting. So I went home, saw the children for the first time this week, and then went to bed early.

Monday 28 March 1977

The pre-Budget Cabinet went very easily, with little criticism.

At 6 we had a secret birthday party for Jim. He was brought back to No. 10 from the House, grumbling and complaining, on the pretence of seeing somebody at No. 10. When he entered the Blue Room we all sang 'Happy Birthday' and there was a big birthday cake. Jim looked very pleased.

I talked to the PM about the coming Stechford by-election. I had been in the constituency yesterday to play in a charity football game, and did not see a *single* Labour poster. There was a bad smell about the place. I told Jim it was essential to launch a mass attack in the last three days before polling. He agreed, and went off to telephone the chief whip.

I left at about 9 p.m. and called in for a long chat with dear Alan Bennett* in Camden Town on the way back, so I was not home till after 11 p.m. He has some weird old lady living in a van in his front courtyard, taking his electricity, but he does not seem to mind. Alan and I get along very well having been historians at Oxford together. He is a fine writer. He said that television celebrity David Frost is a great example of how in Britain one can get to the top 'with absolutely no talent whatsoever'.

Tuesday 29 March 1977

Budget day.

In the morning I went to Gen 26 on the inner-cities problem. Peter Shore presented his paper for giving special aid to five selected problem cities. Most ministers attacked it. The PM took the line set out in our paper – that Shore would upset the excluded, without satisfying the chosen five. So Shore was sent back to think again.

Had lunch at No. 10 and then to the House for Questions before the Budget. Very quiet.

I went back to No. 10 and watched the TV coverage. The reaction was hostile. As I had feared, people were upset by the indirect tax increases – which were *immediate* – and did not appreciate the direct tax cuts, which won't reach their pockets for weeks (and not at all without a pay deal). Actually it is a sensible economic Budget. But not very political. And terrible for Stechford, which is full of car workers and car drivers, who will resent increases in tax on vehicle excise duty and on petrol (5p a gallon!).

Graham Greene came in with his wife. Carol joined us, and we went to the Reform for dinner. Bob Worcester interrupted us at dinner to give me a post-Budget 'straw' poll in Stechford – showing that 50% thought they were *worse* off and only 8% better off, and a massive switch to the Tories, direct from Labour. So it looks as if the by-election is certainly lost.

I saw Douglas Wass after dinner and told him that the Budget had lost us Stechford. He properly pointed out that it was 'the Budget we had agreed together'! Fair point.

Home by 11.30 and bracing myself for more political trouble by the end of the week.

Wednesday 30 March 1977

A limbo day, waiting for tomorrow's by-election disaster.

I went out to lunch at the French Club with a Californian academic who offered me a teaching job at Berkeley, California, if the government falls. Might need it.

Went home early for a change to see the children.

Thursday 31 March 1977

The polls showed us 7% behind in Stechford today – calling back on the same people who put us only 1% behind on Monday. So it is all slipping the wrong way because of the Budget.

To make things worse, the Liberals have announced they will vote against the petrol tax next Tuesday. This is ridiculous. They have set out their conditions for the deal and we have accepted them. But now they keep adding extra items – 'flashing' their new-found virility. Having power at last after so many years, they want to unzip and show it off every other day. McNally and I agree that if they vote against the Budget resolutions on Monday then the government must resign. No compromise.

The PM took this line in Cabinet, though Joel Barnett and others (including Michael Foot!) were talking of compromise. The PM arranged to see David Steel at lunchtime and told him there could be no compromise. Steel was not encouraging, so Jim told him to go away and do something about it.

I went for lunch with Harold Lever. He had *thirteen* relations – mainly children – plus servants round the table. We both agree on the need for a new counter-inflation policy – based on getting interest rates down and getting the exchange rate up. We will each put in separate briefs on this.

It is also clear to me that Lever is ready to quit. That whole '1945' generation is passing on. Jim, Merlyn Rees and Elwyn Jones are the last, apart
from Lever.

Back to the House for Questions. We discussed Stechford. The PM said
it would demoralise our people further. He clearly thinks it will be difficult to hold on beyond the autumn.

We had a Unit meeting this morning on prices policy, with Tom McNally
there. Gavyn had done a brilliant paper, which we amended and put into
the PM this evening, calling for a new anti-inflation package to get us over
the hump till the autumn.

Once I had put this in, I went home by Tube. I didn't bother to sit up
late to hear details of the Stechford disaster. (Hattersley told me that the
Party organisation there was terrible. Six weeks ago they were told to put
committees in our main wards. This *Monday* it has still not been done.)

Friday 1 April 1977

April Fool's Day – and we did not feel too good. Defeated by 2,000. And
the National Front beat the Liberals! Does not look good for the coalition.
But we must hold on and make it work – that middle ground is still the
natural majority.

The Tories are cock-a-hoop, and the press is writing off the government
completely. We will see.

The PM was away to Oslo for a Socialist International meeting. Read
some long papers which had been hanging around. Had a delicious fish
lunch at Scotts with Bernard Nossiter of the *Washington Post*. Scallops, crab
and Sancerre. Went back and had a little sleep – a rare indulgence. Had
some Unit discussions about 'the family' – it is clear that people with children continue to do worse than anybody else. A mad policy for a Labour
government.

Went to a big party given by Claus Moser in CSO, the Central Statistical
Office. I spent most of my time talking to Treasury people – Plietzky, Byatt,
etc. I must strengthen those links.

Ken Stowe told me that the proposed Film Industry committee is in
limbo. Jim has told HW that he *won't* put Marcia on the committee. HW
then said, well in that case he would not serve as chairman. Jim said, OK,
sorry, but there you are, and suggested HW think about it for a week. It is
now *three* weeks. HW has phoned twice but refused to give an answer – he
simply accuses *Ken* of leaking stories to the press!

End of a funny week. Maybe the government is beginning to crack. But
I don't feel too worried – either way. I am battle-hardened and no longer
notice the gunfire.

Monday 4 April 1977

Felt very stiff after yesterday's football game at Reading. Aged 42, I marked Johnnie Brooks, former Tottenham and England inside forward – and it was quite stretching. I have never run so far without touching the ball.

The PM was due to see David Steel at the Commons at midday to discuss tonight's vote on the petrol tax. Jim has told Steel to his face that if they vote against this – a Budget resolution – then we will take it as a vote of no confidence. So again the government might fall. But the Liberals backed down. I was in the Private Office when Steel phoned Ken Stowe and said that the Liberals had met (as planned) and agreed to abstain tonight.

I worked in the Unit in the afternoon and then went home early because Carol went away overnight to a NUT Conference at Keele. I looked after the children, and had an early night. I was completely confident that the Budget vote would go OK – as indeed it did.

Tuesday 5 April 1977

Today is the anniversary of Jim's first year in office. It has been a hard year, with many things going wrong, and lots of H. Wilson's chickens coming home to roost. But it has been better in so many ways – cleaner, simpler, more directly concerned with policy. I have seen less of Jim than of Harold, but so has everybody. And the meetings have been purposeful, little gossip. Jim is a very cost-effective Prime Minister. He wastes little time on gossip, trivia or on secondary issues.

At an Ireland Cabinet committee, Roy Mason reported on the political/ military situation – which, as always, was better than last year.

Militarily the RUC is taking over the front line from the army. Politically Ulster is stagnant. The PM pushed Mason on this, and he said he was waiting till after the local elections in May.

Had lunch at No. 10 and then Questions afterwards. The PM decided to walk to the Commons, and we went with him – two detectives, a private secretary, McCaffrey and me. [In 2006 the Prime Minister needs a cavalcade of armed vehicles for this small journey.] It was a curious little procession, on a cold spring day. Most people in the street looked at the PM puzzled as if they had seen him once before long ago. Jim was held up at the Bridge Street lights for ages. He recalled that when he first came to the Commons there was a policeman there who held up the traffic to allow MPs to cross. Sign of the decline in their status.

Questions were again very quiet, mainly the Tories baiting the Liberals.

Afterwards I went back to No. 10 for a meeting of the Unit on the problems faced by families screwed down by inflation and by the fact that family support has not kept up with real values. We are going to put in a paper for the PM's Easter reading.

At 5.15 we went to see the PM in his study – the two Toms, Roger Stott and I. This was really an anniversary celebration which I put in his diary weeks ago. He said that it had seemed a hard year and a long one, it had not flashed by. He was also not sure we could get beyond the autumn.

I raised the question of organising for a general election – the need for polls, for a press officer, a baggage man, speech-writer, etc. Jim said he had not thought about it. He asked McNally and I to go off and draw up a plan for it including suggested names, etc.

I went home fairly early again.

Wednesday 6 April 1977

I worked on my papers while the rest of the Unit discussed the future of the British motor car industry with a young economist who used to be a student of mine at the LSE.

The PM had an early-morning meeting with the NEDC trade union-ists on pay policy – which has been going very badly with the Chancellor. The minutes of Healey's meetings are very pessimistic, with Jones and Scanlon both saying there is *no* hope of a deal. Apparently this meeting this morning went better, and afterwards David Basnett wrote in to say he thought there would be a deal in the end. In fact they like the PM to be involved and don't trust Healey, whose Budget has annoyed them again.

Went to tea with John Smith. He said that HW often comes and chats to him – and always claims, 'I have just finished today's 5,000 words.' We went back to Smith's room where he outlined his plan for the future. Basically it was to give devolution concessions to the Liberals, especially on finan-cial powers, and then we would have their support, *and* win back the Scot Nats. He had held several meetings with David Steel, who struck him as surprisingly *un*informed on devolution. Smith as always was very fluent and master of all the details, though perhaps a little over-optimistic. I think he is a future Chancellor or Party leader.

We broke up at 5.30 and I went down to the Strangers Bar to see Frank McElhone. We arranged some details for my Scottish visit, and especially for the weekend in Glasgow. When he left I joined Ted Garrett and Bob Woolf, two real North-Easterners, and discussed gardening. Ted said he would like me to have a safe North-East seat. When they went, I had some more beers with Gerry Fowler. By 9 p.m. I was feeling quite merry, so I went off home.

Thursday 7 April 1977

David Lipsey came in to fix the time for his starting in the Unit. He is also supposed to do some speech-writing for the PM, but I don't know how that will work out.

We then went across for morning Questions. The House was barely a third full. The PM went out of his way to praise David Steel. I get the impression that the Liberal pact is growing on him. It will be a fantastic achievement if he 'normalises' it and gets everybody in the Party and country to take it for granted.

We came back for lunch at No. 10 and the PM joined us. He is going to read David Marquand's *Ramsay MacDonald* over Easter – though he had said he would not read it at all. Worried about coalitions?

In the middle of lunch he said: 'Do you ever stop and think that Baldwin and Neville Chamberlain had lunch here, in this small dining room?' He was obviously touched and impressed by it. I do stop and think that often. I am pleased he takes that historical view.

In the afternoon we worked on the paper on family deprivation and put it in for Easter.

A last flood of papers came in especially on nuclear problems, where Benn is playing some strange games.

I was visited secretly in the afternoon by Quentin Morris, finance director of BP. He was worried about the operation for selling the BP privatisation shares. Q says that the Treasury and the Bank of England people are terrible innocents in the world of finance. And he is worried that ministers like Benn are on the committee for handling the marketing. I went back and saw John Hunt. He, as always, moved like lightning, sending a minute to Wass, saying that ministers should not see the commercially sensitive details of the mechanics and pricing. He is certainly the fastest and most effective operator in Whitehall.

Off to Suffolk tomorrow for Easter week. Feeling *less* tired than on any previous holiday. Partly no economics crisis this term. Partly have completed a year with Jim. If we go on, fine. If this government falls, I am ready to try new pastures.

*

Monday 18 April 1977

The PM stayed at Windsor and is having the Prince of Wales to dinner tonight.

I cleared papers. Good news from the PM – he liked our paper on the problems of families and had asked for a ministerial committee to be set up. He had also responded well to our paper on inflation, and had arranged a 'seminar' for Wednesday, including the Chancellor and the Governor of the Bank of England.

At midday I went to the Treasury to see Ken Couzens* about pay policy. He is very worried. The talks are not going well and Jack Jones is being especially difficult. We discussed alterations to the expected stage three. I favour a policy of tight control in the public sector, where the government is paymaster, and leaving the private sector to look after itself. The public sector has the job security, the private sector the wage increases. Couzens is not keen on this, because of strikes from the public sector unions. But in a crisis we may not have an alternative. He was good on public sector pay, saying that it had got out of hand and we are all over-rewarded. We agreed to keep in touch.

I talked to Tom McNally later in the day. He said that the PM is staying at arms length from stage three. The PM does not wish to get enmeshed in a losing battle.

If wages take off, inflation will quickly run to 30%, and then the government will fall. Our main claim to power is that we can deal with the unions to curb inflation. If we cannot do that, then we shall be thrown out and certainly the Liberals will quickly abandon our sinking ship.

Went to lunch with Harold Lever in Eaton Square. He is furious with the Treasury and the Bank. He says it is their handling of high interest rates which has destroyed the social contract. Inflation is now at 17%. He also told me how officials at the Bank and the Treasury had been asked by Healey for a paper on their interest rate policy last November. They had not produced it. Every month Healey and Lever asked where it was. The officials always say they expect to have it ready in a week. In fact they had no intention of producing it. Now the PM has asked for it by tomorrow. We shall see if it comes. Lever said that the officials just showed 'dumb insolence' towards the Chancellor, systematically ignoring his instructions because they have a high interest rate policy, contrary to the government's wishes, and don't intend to put it down on paper, or to change it. Lever seems resigned to us losing office before long, and talked of us going into banking together.

Tuesday 19 April 1977

Spent most of the morning planning my Scottish visit, which is now falling nicely into place. Ken Alexander from the Highlands and Islands Board came in to plan the North Scottish part.

Lunch at No. 10. There was general concern about the Eric Miller* scandal and his conduct of Peachey Property Co. It is difficult to believe that nothing will come out about his financial contributions.

I saw the papers for tomorrow's seminar on exchange rates and interest rates. They say that reducing interest rates further would increase the money supply and expose the currency. And allowing sterling to rise will destroy our export competition. These are predictable points. But completely ignore the inflation and pay policy advantages of getting the exchange rate up and interest rates down.

After an easy Questions, I went off for a stroll round the House corridors and chatted to several MPs. Also saw Harold Wilson. He looked very distracted and not quite with it.

The *Daily Express* crisis has come to a head and the talks for a merger with the *Mail* are taking place. Lord Goodman is involved, and went to see the PM at Chequers yesterday. Apparently they also discussed HW and the scandals. Goodman said that he did not think HW realised how 'shabby' were many of his 'friends'.

I went back to work in the Unit. David Lipsey has joined us and I set him to work on transport policy. He is an excellent acquisition. Home at 9.15 p.m.

Leo Plietzky is moving from the Treasury – I don't know where. This will be a clean sweep of their permanent secretaries this year – Lord, Mitchell and Plietzky.

Wednesday 20 April 1977

This morning the PM came up from Windsor and went on to a Party meeting. I worked in the Unit preparing for this afternoon's economic seminar.

The seminar was fascinating – but disappointing. Present were: the Governor of the Bank, his deputy Kit McMahon, and from the Treasury the Chancellor, Douglas Wass, Joel Barnett and Derek Mitchell, plus Harold Lever. On our side of the table were the PM, John Hunt, myself, Nigel Wicks, and a Cabinet Office secretary.

The Chancellor briefly set out the policy on the exchange rate and interest rates, basically saying the present policies work about right. The Governor said the same. Lever was then brought in. He made the tactical mistake of blaming the Bank for keeping interest rates too high and selling too much expensive gilt-edged stock, and blamed the Treasury for wanting too much devaluation of the currency. It produced an acrimonious atmosphere, and the PM clearly felt it was water under the bridge and wanted to get on to future policy. Lever then asked that interest rates should not be 'managed or manipulated up'. Broadly this was conceded. The currency discussion was less satisfactory. The Governor and Chancellor did not accept that there was any prospect of sterling rising, and the best that could be achieved was some promise not to let it fall.

Not till late did the PM introduce the political dimension, and argue that the pay policy was in doubt partly because of the price effects of our currency and interest rate policies. He said that we might lose the pay policy and should 'take some of the heat off it'. Healey conceded that the pay policy was in difficulties and said it could not be agreed with the TUC general council till July and not with the TUC Conference till September.

So we broke up. Not wholly satisfactory. But definite pressure on the Bank to get interest rates down – which is useful, since Lever told me beforehand that the Bank was giving the City the nod that it wanted rates up again. That should now be stopped. Afterwards we went upstairs to a reception for Transport House. Both the PM and Healey said to me how useful they found the meeting.

I came home at 9.

Thursday 21–Thursday 28 April 1977

Scottish visit. A delightful and interesting week.

Thursday: Edinburgh in the evening.

Friday: Afternoon to Glasgow, the Scottish Development Agency, and the East End scheme (worse than the Blitz). Evening to St Monica's Presbytery, Coatbridge, to see Father Michael Conway, Father Geraghty and a whole band of local Scots-Irish. A marvellous Catholic all-night party with lots of 'mouth music' and Irish whiskey – till 7 a.m. when Michael drove me bleary back to my hotel.

Saturday: No sleep. Morning with the Scottish Labour Party (Helen Liddell). Afternoon to Partick Thistle v. Celtic. Evening to bed.

Sunday morning to Loch Lomond. Afternoon to open day of Rangers and Celtic with Frank McElhone. Tea with Willie Waddell, Rangers winger. Evening flight to Inverness.

Monday and Tuesday in Inverness with Highlands and Islands Board. Delightful visit. Lovely people and beautiful Inverness. I could live and work there. Evening to Peterhead.

Wednesday in Aberdeen. Full of North Sea oil vitality. Overnight back to London, with little sleep, arriving at 6.45 a.m.

Thursday 28 April 1977

Rather sleepy after my night on the train. I caught up on a file of papers – little of great interest.

The Eric Miller/Peachey Property scandal saga continues. People in No. 10 begin to expect it will end up very close to Harold, on whom Eric spent some of the company's money.

Questions very quiet. We all await the by-election results at Grimsby and Ashfield – nobody is optimistic.

In the evening I went to George Jones's excellent inaugural lecture on 'Responsibility in Government' and then to dinner for him at LSE. I sat next to Sir Frank Layfield*, who seemed very wise and able. He thinks the government will be negative on his report on local government.

Friday 29 April 1977

A day of Unit meetings – on Layfield local government, on economic policy, etc. I did not see the PM, but gather that he was not too discouraged by the by-election losses. Ashfield was a case of total neglect by the Party organisation.

Everybody is busy with preparations for the World Economic summit here, with builders crawling all over No. 10. The PM is trying to resist other papers and subjects. This is very important for him – though at present it is difficult to see much hard progress coming out of it.

I came home quite early, at 7.30, and went early to bed.

Monday 2 May 1977

Spent the morning on papers, and reading the huge folder of briefs for the summit.

Went to lunch with David Owen at the Foreign Office – a very spartan salad in his office, with Michael Stewart. We ranged over economic policy. Then David and I walked to No. 10 for the summit briefing, in the Cabinet Room.

Jim was very good. Healey went on for hours about how no progress was possible, because all the other countries were against any action on growth and employment. At the end Jim said, 'What does it add up to? What message goes out from here?' Healey replied that the message was recession for years. 'Keynesianism has failed.' Jim said, 'Well it won't do. I'm not having these six leaders come here to announce that there is nothing we can do.'

So Jim suggested he send a letter to the other six saying that they must do something about recession in the West. This was agreed.

David Owen was good, putting the case that if the surplus countries won't expand their domestic demand then they should provide financing for the deficit countries. The PM obviously liked this. Owen could be Chancellor in two years.

Afterwards I walked out to Downing Street with David and he said he was very glad we had had the lunch, which focused him on economic questions. He was off to Brussels. He commented, 'Even I am getting exhausted by all this travelling.'

Tuesday 3 May 1977

Went in early to the Devolution Cabinet committee. The PM has certainly swung to a more positive line.

Afterwards I went into No. 11 with Denis Healey to discuss special advisers. He said he had always wanted to set up a cabinet of advisers, but never got round to it. He said there was a shortage of good economic advisers, and he had great difficulty in replacing Bryan Hopkin, the Treasury economic adviser. He said that he now felt on top of the job, but had been overwhelmed by it at the beginning. He said he thought of me as 'the Pope of the advisers'.

To lunch with Derek Mitchell at the Reform. He is leaving the Treasury in a week's time, and very pleased to go. He told me that during the IMF talks, John Hunt and Douglas Wass tried to squeeze him out completely, asking his subordinates to do work and excluding him. He threatened to resign and hold a press conference, and they gave way.

We swapped Marcia stories from his time in No. 10 Private Office in the 1960s.

Then to No. 10 to work on the housing finance review Green Paper (which is good) and the Layfield Green Paper (which is terrible). And cleared a Unit paper on vaccine-damaged children – where Ennals is now taking a sensible policy, but is unable to convince his department, so the PM will have to step in and rescue him.

Finished up at the House of Commons, drinking in the Strangers Bar with first Jack Ashley, and then with Geoffrey Robinson and John Smith.

Home at 9.40.

Wednesday 4 May 1977

The PM. is enormously heavily engaged in the run-up to the summit and is clearly very tired. Last night he barely did any papers at all.

I went in early for the EY committee on nuclear policy. A free-ranging discussion, over the whole area of thermal stations, fast-breeders, conservation, other forms of power generation, nuclear processing, pollution, etc. Benn wants to abandon our nuclear policy and base it all on coal (this would give him the NUM vote for life). It was a good discussion, with no hard decisions, but a clearing of the ground.

The Unit produced a paper on Layfield and local government. The

Environment draft was terribly turgid and negative. Since rates are still a big political issue we need a more positive response.

Had lunch at Reform with opinion pollster Bob Worcester criticising the Party for its lack of interest in polls. Back to No. 10 for another briefing on the summit. Good – yet depressing. All the reasons why we cannot make progress on any front. We must find a way for the PM to get some progress out of this summit.

Home at 9.30. Feeling ever more ready to go out into the real world. I would like to get out for a while. But no doubt I would quickly miss being at the middle of things.

Thursday 5 May 1977

A bad Cabinet for us. Beforehand I canvassed ministers on the Layfield Green Paper from Peter Shore. Negative in content and dreary in style. Several agreed. But in Cabinet it went through in three minutes. The PM is tired and obsessed with the summit, so domestic politics is not getting his full attention.

The vaccine–damaged children question also suffered another setback. Ennals was committed to a statement in favour of giving the compensation. We had lined up the PM and the Chancellor. But now the Law Officers came up with new objections, so they decided to delay again. Later Pat Nairne, the permanent secretary, phoned me up and said that Ennals is in a great flap. He is very afraid of Jack Ashley's campaign.

At lunch we discussed the problems of the government. Everyone agreed it is at its lowest ebb so far. Not because of the polls and the by-elections – that always happens in midterm. But because the ministers are going 'administrative'. They have lost their political feel and are behaving like permanent secretaries. The PM is always complaining about this.

In the evening I sat up till 2 a.m. listening to the local election results – a disastrous landslide against us, but not unexpected. Also saw the Frost-Nixon TV interview. How shabby.

Friday 6 May 1977

The PM away in the North-East with President Carter, having a tremendous popular success. He arrived back shortly after 4 and then spent two hours working on his boxes.

At 7.45 the heads of government began arriving at No. 10 for the informal dinner. The whole house was alive with excitement. I stood in the corridor near the front door as they arrived in turn. Roy Jenkins was early, and came over to say hello. He looked very tense after all this trouble about whether as European president he should attend or not. Tonight there was more trouble because he was put on the Foreign ministers' table instead of the top table. His appearance of continually injured dignity is not good for him.

Trudeau also came over and said hello. Then Carter came in and shook hands with everybody. He has a curious cat-like walk and an air of tremendous inner confidence. He certainly has charisma. Schmidt was looking much fitter than a couple of years ago in Dublin or Paris.

When they were all settled in and eating – not Giscard, who refused to come tonight as a gesture of Gaullist awkwardness – I went home. It is quite something to think of all that Western power upstairs in our house. Good for Jim, who is an ideal host and clearly liked by them all.

Saturday 7 May 1977

Today is the first day of the great Western summit. I set off to walk in – no car and no buses in sight – and also with no breakfast at home. A friend passed and gave me a lift to the Aldwych, where I bought a bacon sandwich and then took a bus to Downing Street – still eating my bacon sandwich as I arrived. I stood in the hall and watched the leaders arrive. Giscard was deliberately the last, and to satisfy French ego was met by the PM at the heliport.

Then I found there was little to do. The seven leaders were in the state dining room, with their Foreign and Finance ministers, but with no Civil Service advisers, just a note-taker to each delegation. There was no single agreed record. No. 10 was very quiet once they were all locked in. The seven delegations all just waited around. Nobody was wanted. Very serene, quite different from other summits in larger buildings, where everybody is buzzing around noisily. So when the leaders go to the lavatory, they do it in complete peace and quiet.

They broke at 1 p.m. and decided to walk through the Park to Lancaster House for lunch. We civil servants went upstairs to a delicious buffet lunch. I chatted with the Canadians, the Americans and Derek Mitchell – who is leaving the Treasury on Monday. He told me that Sir Anthony Rawlinson* was at first appointed as his successor, but was vetoed by the Bank because he had upset the Americans about the IMF when he was in Washington. So he was put in charge of public expenditure, and Ken Couzens, who was supposed to run public expenditure, was put in charge of international money! Thus does the deep amateurism of the Civil Service continue.

After lunch Ken Stowe and I walked back. Carter came back in a British car. Fortunately it did not break down. They all resumed again, and we all sat round again. I watched the Rugby League Cup Final on my TV.

They broke up and left around 6 p.m. The PM went to the flat and then slipped off to the Palace dinner at 7.45 p.m. The civil servants were still in the Cabinet Room drafting the communiqué.

I got home at 1 a.m.

Sunday 8 May 1977

Decided not to go in to the summit until the afternoon. I need some fresh air and normal ordinary people, so I went and played football on Hampstead Heath in the morning. No goalposts, just coats, but I scored a hat-trick and felt much better afterwards.

By the afternoon most of the agenda was completed. The house continued quiet and serene. Suddenly they broke up and went to Banqueting House for the press conference. They walked, all seven and Jenkins. I joined in and walked into Banqueting House alongside Trudeau and Jenkins.

The PM presented the main communiqué. Then each leader spoke in turn. Carter made a campaign speech. It was quite impressive to see these major figures – and they are all very impressive men – pronouncing upon the world crisis (Jenkins was not allowed to speak). It broke up towards 8 p.m. and they all filed out to their waiting limousines. A roar of engines and off they zoomed to their hotels and the airport.

I took a bus home. My weekend was lost and I shall feel tired next weekend. But it was an experience. And Jim did brilliantly.

Monday 9 May 1977

The quadrapartite meeting this morning – Jim, Carter, Schmidt and Giscard, ostensibly to discuss four-power rule in Berlin, but in fact to range over a wide field without having to bother with the other leaders. When Carter came in at 9.50, Jim took him to meet the staff and he shook hands with everybody. Schmidt came in very boisterously, laughing and shouting when he saw the PM. They spent the morning in the White Room. Just the four of them.

I had lunch with Tory MP John Biffen at the Reform. He told me about the strain he had suffered on the front bench, and how the doctor had diagnosed a chemical imbalance. He now took pills daily, and hoped to come back in the front line. He is a fair and sensible man.

In the afternoon Jim made his statement on the summit. Afterwards he said how Carter does have charisma, something no American had had since Kennedy. Then we discussed Mrs Thatcher. He said he was shocked at how brazenly she pushed herself for the job of PM. We agreed she was a bit shrill and humourless. I said she suffered from long exposure and therefore we should have a long election campaign. He agreed and said he would go for anything up to six weeks. [We did in 1979.]

Went back to No. 10 and worked till 8.30 when I went home.

Tuesday 10 May 1977

The PM was at the No. 10 meeting this morning – the succession of summits continues, and domestic policies are being allowed to slip.

No Questions today because the PM is at Lancaster House and Foot stood in at the House.

Had a Unit meeting on social security uprating in the afternoon, and then went to the Treasury to discuss the same subject with Leo Plietzky. Leo is going shortly to be permanent secretary at Trade. We shall miss him, since he has always been open with us.

This evening we discussed the DHSS proposal to uprate pensions by more than the rate of inflation in advance. The Treasury want to stick rigidly to its 13.1% forecast. The DHSS want to take 16% in advance. I fear that the DHSS will win – not afraid of pensioners doing better, but of the collapse of public expenditure control, and the crudeness of just picking 16%.

When I got back to No. 10, Carol was there, and we decide to go to eat together in the Commons. We went to the Strangers Bar and I drank again with the North-Eastern MPs, and we then had a meal with Gerry Fowler. Finally home at 11.30.

Wednesday 11 May 1977

Went in a little later than usual, having a heavy head from last night's Federation Bitter in the Commons bar.

Just before lunch Tom McCaffrey came in to tell me that the PM and David Owen have decided to make Peter Jay, the PM's son-in-law, ambassador to Washington. A political mistake. Not a big mistake, because it will soon be forgotten. And because Peter is very able. But a bad one, because the great strength Jim had was as 'Mr Clean' – the great contrast with Harold Wilson's honours list, etc. I expressed this view. McCaffrey agreed – and said McNally felt the same. But none of us had been consulted. The decision was taken three weeks ago. Owen proposed it. At first Jim said no, but Owen continued to press and Jim said OK. He told nobody.

Had lunch with Helen Liddell at the Commons. She is doing a marvellous job at the Scottish Labour Party. I wish she was in Ron Hayward's place running the whole Party.

I returned to No. 10 and worked on papers. The Peter Jay announcement came over the tapes at 5.20 – and after that the reactions came slowly in – all of disbelief. The TV news at 6 p.m. carried it very low down. It did not sink in. But later came the bitter attacks from Labour MPs.

Tessa Blackstone came in to see me about the CPRS report on the Foreign Office. It is not clear how the Jay affair will affect this. I think it will not be helpful. The FCO did say it will damage morale in the service. Above all, they like to keep the plum jobs for themselves.

Then I came home at 9.

Thursday 12 May 1977

Cabinet discussed the pensions uprating. The majority were with Ennals – for 16% – but the PM decided to hold it back.

The PM told the Cabinet what he proposed to say at Question Time about Jay – and was greeted with complete silence. We discussed all of this at lunch in No. 10. The civil servants were being very indignant that an ambassador should have been moved. Then Michael Palliser phoned from the FCO wanting the PM to make a statement in praise of Ramsbotham. All the No. 10 civil servants are now pressing for this. No civil servant must ever be criticised or punished. Anybody else can be sacked and put on the street; they are given the Bermuda governorship and they wail and whine. But Jim must have known this would happen.

After Questions we had a meeting with the Writers Guild about public lending right. I sat opposite Lady Antonia Fraser/Pinter, who mooned into space throughout. Maureen Duffy* was quite the best.

The PM went to the PLP to meet criticisms of the Jay appointment – and apparently was very grumpy and got it all wrong. This, plus the McCaffrey 'dirty briefing' of the press against sweet old Ramsbotham, has turned it all sour.

Home at 9.30.

Friday 13 May 1977

The Jay issue is in all the papers, and most of the comment is hostile, from friends as well as enemies.

Lunch with Alfred Sherman* to discuss special advisers – he works for Keith Joseph and is advising the Tories on what to do when in office.

Back to No. 10, finished my paper, then Tessa Blackstone came in again very unhappy about the vicious press attacks on her. We had a drink, then I went home early. I sat up till midnight reading the CPRS report on the

FCO – 600 pages, like an academic thesis, full of detail. Quite radical but Ken Berrill has already toned it down.

Carol was out working with her boss and did not come in till 1.15 a.m., so we were both tired next morning.

Monday 16 May 1977

There was an air of depression about No. 10. The Peter Jay affair has continued throughout the weekend and has clearly distracted the PM. Our handling of it has gone wrong and the press won't let it go. The Foreign Office is heavily briefing against No. 10, and the press diplomatic correspondents are doing what the FCO tells them, because they want to please and not to be shut out of the FCO news leaks and cocktail parties. McCaffrey is having his first row with the press. Having spent a year caressing them, and praising himself for being so much better than Joe, he now learns that there are no rewards in treating the press well. They still knife him at the first opportunity. The final laugh is that Jim is now talking of ending lobby briefings! I roared with laughter when I heard that – remembering how Joe was attacked, not least by Tom McCaffrey, for doing just that.

I went out to lunch, and then back to see Vincent Wright* from Oxford who came to urge me to apply for the Nuffield wardenship. Sadly I cannot go for it – it is to be filled this summer, and I won't be free. It would suit me well later.

The PM made a statement to the Commons about the Jay affair. McCaffrey looked very worried. The civil servants have distanced themselves completely from him, as always when a colleague is in trouble.

I went to the Devolution committee at 5.15. Foot said that he would go ahead with his offer of a select committee to the Tories, but he expected Pym to reject it, or to demand such broad terms of reference that we could reject. I chatted with John Smith afterwards and we agreed to meet one evening.

An interesting paper in the PM's box concerned a Commons proposal to set up a select committee on foreign affairs. John Hunt's minute suggested that the PM might wish to resist this because any co-operation 'would encourage the extension of the select committee system'. The Civil Service hostility to parliamentary accountability always comes through on any such issue.

I came home early, leaving at 7.45.

Tuesday 17 May 1977

Was in No. 10 shortly after 9 to clear papers before going to the long meeting of EY at 9.45. It was clearly one of the PM's main objectives to delay any decisions on industrial democracy, where Dell has put in a cautious paper which is way to the right of the trade union position and so bound to be denounced by the TUC and cause the government terrible trouble. So the PM had it changed from first item to last on the agenda, and then took the other items so slowly that he never reached industrial democracy.

They moved on to the tricky problem of reprocessing nuclear waste – with the risks of proliferating plutonium for bomb-making. We have a big commercial contract with the Japanese which Benn and Shore (who both seem to have been nobbled by Friends of the Earth) want to stop, even though it will lose us hundreds of millions of pounds and thousands of jobs. The PM and David Owen held them back and kept the contract in play.

Bill Rodgers introduced a draft transport White Paper which was described as courageous and by Healey as the 'best' he had seen. But attacked by the left because it showed some interest in car owners and was delayed.

In the evening went with Carol to the Shepherd's Bush Theatre above a pub where Harry Evans's new girlfriend Tina Brown had a sparkling new play.

Wednesday 18 May 1977

Had a series of Unit meetings – on social security upratings, which continues to split the Unit, with the 'woollies' wanting unlimited increases, and on the housing finance review, where Peter Shore is trying to bash the tax allowances of mortgage holders and I am worried that this government always seems to end up bashing groups of hard-working citizens while subsidising the idle.

I had lunch with Joe Haines, who is a bit depressed at the *Mirror*, where they don't give him much to do, but I revived him with some ideas for articles. I still enjoy seeing him and we spark one another off.

I was driven straight from Lockets restaurant to the Treasury and had a meeting with Joel Barnett about social security uprating. He admitted the Treasury lost in Cabinet last week because they underestimated the political pressures on ministers, after the local government defeats, to 'give something more away'. I told him to prepare a better fall-back position – which he did. The Ennals paper from DHSS is terrible, but it will probably win, which means that there will be no more money for child benefits.

Need a holiday. Home to bed at 9.

Thursday 19 May 1977

A bad day. Carol and I not currently in tune.

At Question Time the PM discussed the Leyland 'slush fund' scandal printed in the *Dairy Mail*. The PM was very jumpy – and snapped at me for the first time ever. I cautioned him not to condone any bribery, not to take the line that in a bad commercial world we have to be as bad as our competitors.

Home late and depressed.

Friday 20 May 1977

Went in early to a Cabinet committee on industrial democracy. Dell put his plan, which would appal the TUC because it abandons virtually everything in Bullock – single channel representation, unitary boards and parity. Booth then put his case for following Bullock almost slavishly – which would appal the CBI and not get through the Commons. So the paralysed dilemma we face on industrial democracy was personified ministerially. Jim suggested a new subcommittee to draft a White Paper, which would then be discussed with the TUC at Chequers.

I went to a good lunch at Grieveson Grant and came back to finish papers. Then home, and spent nice evening with the Grahams.

To Suffolk on Saturday.

Monday 23 May 1977

The PM went to the awful TUC/LP liaison committee at Transport House in the morning. Then he had a private session with Tony Benn – he did not have anyone in with him, not even a private secretary.

I went in the evening to the Hilton for a dinner in aid of Denis Howell as Sports minister. A nice occasion and Denis made a lovely speech. But I got sadder as the night progressed, sitting there on the top table, surrounded by sporting stars, everybody alive and cheerful. I felt very alone and sad. After the dinner finished I went to the lounge and sat alone drinking Coca-Cola till 2 a.m. It all felt very pointless.

Tuesday 24 May 1977

Last night the PM had a dinner with the Neddy Six key trade unionists. The trade unionists were all very depressed about pay policy. They said we must write off all chance of a phase three – we must cease talking about it, and just hold on to phase two, and keep to the twelve-month rule. Unless we find some other way out, such as tight money control or a public sector pay policy, then inflation will threaten worse and the pound will weaken, and we will be back on that spiral again. Not good.

I was up early this morning running my daily three miles round the Heath, and I felt a little sleepy after the Hilton dinner. Worked on papers and then to lunch with David Watt of the *FT*. He is getting fed up with journalism and looking for something else.

Back to Questions. This was easy because of the *Daily Mail* error in printing a forgery claiming that Ryder* of the Enterprise Board and minister Varley were involved in British Leyland bribery. The whole PLP is revived by their piece of good luck. Everybody loves to see this evil paper covered by shit, its own natural product. The PM really put the boot in at Question Time. Thatcher did not intervene to dissociate herself from the *Mail*, her Party propaganda sheet, which added to the fury on our side.

Afterwards the PM went to Scotland feeling very pleased with himself, to dinner with the Queen at Holyrood House.

I had drinks with John Smith at the Commons to discuss devolution. It was a beautiful sunny evening on the terrace. He is still hopeful we can get devolution on course, but we don't have any financial concessions to give to the Liberals, or anything at all to give to our North-East rebels.

Carol joined us in the Strangers Bar. Then to the café for a meal. Tony Benn joined us and we discussed the problems of fighting Whitehall, on which he and John Smith were in total agreement.

Home at 10 p.m.

Wednesday 25 May 1977

Another glorious summer morning. London was looking bright and festive with all the Jubilee flags. The PM was still in Scotland, but flew down this morning to go straight to the NEC.

I read, and drafted a paper to the PM. Off to lunch with Joe Rogaly and Sam Brittan of the *FT* at Rules. Very nice food and claret. Then I walked back down Whitehall through the sunshine and tourists.

And end-of-term feeling in No. 10.

Bill Rodgers came to my room for a drink. He is very pleased with the way his transport White Paper is going.

Then I had in Frank Cooper*, the excellent permanent secretary at Defence. I explained to him that an Irish friend of mine had been approached by an IRA gunman, who wanted to defect and then be paid to escape abroad. In return he offered a lot of information. So I took Frank Cooper to meet my friend at the RAC Club and arrange for the security forces to debrief the IRA man. I did not stay to arrange the details because I did not want to be involved.

Home to watch marvellous Liverpool win the European Cup 3–1.

Thursday 26 May 1977

The PM saw Varley about the possibility of an inquiry into Engineering, and decided in favour of the wider terms of reference which I had been pressing. The Department of Industry had mobilised other departments to write in saying how disastrously bad an inquiry would be – what Tony Benn calls 'the flood of Whitehall letters' syndrome. It used to frighten Wilson, but it did not worry JC.

Cabinet took mortgage tax rebate. Shore was in favour of abolishing all relief above 50% tax rate. We briefed Jim that this would be politically foolish. It would alienate some people without gaining anybody. The PM and most ministers took that line so it was decided not to do anything.

Lunch at No. 10. Patrick Wright was very emotional about the CPRS report on the FCO. It proposes radical changes and some redundancies – exactly what Whitehall is always proposing for private industry. But officials always assume that they themselves will be protected from the medicine they readily prescribe to others.

Friday 27 May 1977

The PM was away in Exeter opening a motorway.

We had a Unit meeting all morning discussing our Cabinet strategy paper.

Went out in the blazing sunshine to have a sandwich lunch. Then home very early. Summer has come. The Jubilee flags are flying everywhere. So I sat in the front garden and drank beer with neighbours and the children. A nice relaxation.

Monday 30 May 1977

The PM away virtually all this week – he came back this evening for the Covent Garden Jubilee. The rest of the time he was at Chequers. I spent the weekend at the cottage. The sun shone most of the time, but we all knew it would be rain for the Jubilee. Just like the royal wedding twenty-five years ago.

Had drinks with Ted Croker, secretary of the Football Association, in the evening. They are clearly thinking of sacking Don Revie, England's football manager.

Tuesday 31 May 1977

We had a Unit meeting about the shape of the paper we would put in to the PM for the Strategy Cabinet at Chequers at the end of the month.

Had an evening meeting with two people from the Central Statistical Office discussing getting computer facilities for Gavyn Davies to run a model of the economy and check his predictions against the Treasury's. We have to get Treasury permission and will be interested to see if there is any opposition from that quarter.

Wednesday 1 June 1977

Spent the morning in the Unit discussing the strategy paper. The PM has now suddenly asked for it for the weekend. Gavyn Davies and David Lipsey have done excellent economic and political sections and are starting to weave them together into a coherent paper.

To the Reform for lunch. Sat with Hans Liesners, a nice civil servant, formerly of the Treasury, now of the Department of Industry. He told me that one of his jobs is to brief three ministers – Industry, Trade and Prices – on economic questions. He is good. But that means that the Treasury view will be briefing several ministers before any Cabinet.

In the evening I took my son Stephen to the Beating of the Retreat. Absolutely lovely, especially the pipers, the Irish with their green cloaks, the Scots with their red tartan, marching across Horse Guards in the evening sun. Cold but beautifully bright.

Afterwards I went back to the office with Stephen to finish my papers. Shortly before 8 p.m., Harold Lever phoned to say that there was a special meeting with the building societies tomorrow and the Treasury was against bringing the interest rates down, mainly because of the need to build up the societies' stabilisation funds. Yet the PM – and the Chancellor – have repeatedly said that the rate must and will come down. To say that in the Commons one week, and then privately to advise the societies not to bring them down the next is crazy, and would be very damaging if it leaked out.

I lost my temper and went to the Private Office to ask for the papers about tomorrow's meeting (without revealing Lever as my source). The papers had not been sent. No. 10 always gets them, but on this occasion there had been an inexplicable omission. This may have been accidental, but I doubt it. Clearly, given the PM's firm commitment to getting rates down, they would prefer him not to see their advice to keep rates up.

It was not clear what the Chancellor's position was, though he would probably have gone along with the Treasury. But once we phoned and showed that we knew what they were up to, there was a remarkable turn-about. An hour later the Chancellor's private secretary phoned to say that Healey had had further thoughts and now was in favour of bringing the rate down – though Environment were not. This was put in the Private Office note to the PM which never revealed that the Treasury had ever had any other view! A revealing little episode.

Thursday 2 June 1977

I went in early to complete the strategy paper. We also had a special advisers meeting on family support – David Metcalf, [Brian] Abel-Smith* from Social Security and David Hill* from Prices. We had a good discussion. It revealed how badly we are doing in family support – worse than the Tories, and worse than when we came in in 1974.

I had lunch in the Cabinet Office canteen with the Unit and then came back to finish off the strategy paper. We finally got it finished and in the PM's box at about 7.

Carol and I then went to a party to welcome the new American ambassador, Brewster. David Ennals came over to express pleasure at the family support initiative but to complain that it was Orme and not him who was put on the ministerial committee. He suffers from a perpetually wounded *amour propre*, which probably reflects insecurity.

Afterwards we went on to supper at the home of David Sainsbury*. Very relaxing, with lots of old friends.

The PM has apparently been in a very grumpy mood this week.

His meeting with Fraser of Australia was, according to Frank Cooper who was present, like the 'meeting of two icebergs'. Jim is probably tired. With too many recent setbacks, so nothing buoys him up. Also ahead lies direct elections, with the Party split and the Cabinet having a free vote, industrial democracy with an unbridgeable gap between the TUC and the CBI, devolution, where we cannot find a way of giving taxation powers to the Scots without losing the North-East, and Benn and the left reopening the whole EEC question and trying to fight the next election on a platform of withdrawing from the EEC. Thank God we had the referendum – even though the left, with its contempt for democratic decisions, means to proceed regardless.

So it is a nasty outlook. A lot of blurred and complex issues, with few votes to win in them. The constant need to build and maintain a majority in the Commons. And finally the pay policy completely in the shit. Without it we shall have inflation rising from 15 to 20% late next year, and sterling under pressure again. There will not be time to recover from that.

A rational man would say we are finished. Yet somehow it still does not feel like that. With the Tories still looking bad, and North Sea oil, it is still possible to believe in survival, and hope for ultimate victory!

Personally I don't mind too much either way. It would be nice to win through in the end when everybody has written us off. But if we fall soon, I shall enjoy going back into the normal private world.

Saturday 4–Thursday 9 June 1977

4–9 June in Suffolk. Out of bed at 5.30 this Thursday morning. Piled the children and cases into the car and drove through the early sunshine of Jubilee week to London, and was in the office by 9.30.

The PM is at the Commonwealth Prime Ministers Conference at Lancaster Gate. Right through till the middle of next week, so there are no committees and few papers. I shall continue to take it easy.

The PM had reacted favourably to our strategy paper, writing on it, 'This is very helpful.' He also asked for me to go to the Chequers Cabinet. I went through the few papers there were in the morning. Then went off to St Katharine Docks to see the Queen on her Jubilee river tour. It was grey and wet but there were enormous crowds and everybody was in marvellous mood, cheering, and the boats hooting.

No. 10 was very flat in the afternoon, as always when the PM is elsewhere.

In the evening the Commonwealth heads came in for dinner. I had a long chat with Hastings Banda, who said he was opting out now and leaving it to the younger ones. After dinner everybody was driven to County Hall to watch the fireworks display on the Thames. I decided not to go. Instead I walked up Whitehall to Trafalgar Square, through hordes of people streaming towards the river. Despite the dreadful weather, there was a sense of excitement and carnival. I took a bus home and went to bed, able to hear the fireworks six miles south in Westminster.

Friday 10 June 1977

Helen Liddell came to talk about Scottish politics, and then Will Plowden to discuss leaving the Civil Service. The trouble is that nobody can afford to leave the Civil Service, since its rewards are higher than anywhere else.

I went alone to lunch at the Reform and then back to finish off my paperwork. I felt bored and tired so I left at 4 p.m. I called in at Christie's to leave a painting to sell at auction (signs of our financial straits), then to Alan Bennett in Camden Town for a delightful chat, then walked to Bill Rodgers's house in Kentish Town to discuss his Transport White Paper.

It has rained all week for the Jubilee. But the popular participation has been astonishing. I think it is because the Queen is something – perhaps the last thing – where we are the best in the world. She is doing very well even if we are not!

Monday 13–Friday 17 June 1977

I am writing this in Suffolk, at the end of the week, breaking my normal routine of writing each night however late or early the following morning. Partly because I had a week of busy evenings. Partly I was too tired. Certainly it was not a boring week. The government ran into terrible trouble and everybody was speculating that we must fall. Certainly it was more serious than previously – because the problem was within the Party. The Tories never offer a serious threat. But our own people do.

The trouble arose on several fronts simultaneously.

First direct elections. Foot, under pressure from the left, reneged on his promise to support the Government Bill in Parliament, speaking for it, providing the left in the Cabinet had a free vote. So we have the prospect of Benn and Shore campaigning against the bill. At the same time the Liberals are complaining that we have broken our promise to recommend a PR list system for Europe. Now we are simply going to offer Parliament a choice. The PM must know that he depends on the Liberals and must be more open with them.

I saw David Steel in the Commons on Tuesday and he told me he was very unhappy with the way things are going and he wanted me to tell the PM that this time he was serious that the alliance was in peril. I passed this message on. I think Steel was honest – he has received nothing back so far for his support.

The position quickly grew worse. Foot on Tuesday announced that the inter-party talks on devolution were coming to an end – as they were meant to, since the Tories simply used them as a means of delay, and disguising their own retreat from a Scottish Assembly. And the Scot Nats, who are crucial, never took part anyway. But people expected a major statement on the future of our devolution legislation. So they were all disappointed. A little pre-briefing to lower expectations would have helped them here. Instead the Nats looked furious and the Liberals dejected.

Then on Tuesday evening, two left-wingers, Audrey Wise and Jeff Rooker[*], supported the Tories on an amendment to the Budget and spent an extra £400 million on tax allowances. So it all looked very bad in Wednesday morning's press, with headlines about the collapse of the government – including in the *Guardian*. The crucial thing is that the PM was stuck away for three days with the conference of Commonwealth PMs. So while the cat was away the rats began to play. He got very fed up with it all.

We nearly had another crisis on Monday over the partial privatisation sale of BP shares. The PM with justice felt that the sale price had been fixed too low by the Bank and the brokers' commission set too high, making it a rip-off for the City.

All Jim's instincts were against disposing of this public asset and he deep down sympathised with the Benn view on City greed! The civil servants were also puritanically against a City rip-off. So it was always on the cards he would veto it if given the chance. The City, by being over-greedy, has given him the opportunity to do what he wanted to do anyway, pull out of the sale.

At a subsequent meeting with Healey the PM was very tired after having had a bad meeting on direct elections. The Chancellor put the case against cancellation of the offer – a blow to confidence and he would lose his £600 million for the borrowing requirement. The PM reluctantly gave way. He did not invite Lever to the second meeting – because Lever had supported Healey at the first: that is not what he is employed for. What is appalling is the Governor of the Bank of England coming along to the Chancellor to negotiate an extra 5p a share profit – an £8.45 price rather than £8.50 – for the underwriters. It is offensive. It will be attacked in the PLP.

The rip-off price agreed by the Governor of the Bank and his friends in the City nearly drove Jim to call it off – he did once, then caved in later. But he was right. It was a racket. The shares will be oversubscribed many times over at their low price – profits for the City at the expense of the citizen. That one is still rumbling. I went to BP to see finance director Q. Morris on Monday morning, and he told me how incompetent the Bank had been.

I came back to see David Owen at the FCO. He still hankers after a big British 'initiative' in Rhodesia – sending our troops to occupy it and our civil servants to run it – but I told him we would oppose that in No. 10. Mainly we discussed the economy, and the line he would take at the Strategy Cabinet. He will take a 'growth' line, pointing out that no government had ever won an election after a period of zero growth as now.

I then dashed to see Bob Worcester and John Smith about devolution and Scotland. Bob showed his slides from past polls – and pressed for some new polling to be commissioned – none for over a year in an area which could decide the fate of the government.

I took my Berlin friend Meinolf Dierkes to the Reform for dinner in the evening.

Tuesday 14 June 1977

I worked in the office in the morning.

Lunch with Robin Butler at his club. Great pleasure to see him again. He told me one little story. While at No. 10 there arrived on his desk a large brown envelope addressed personally to H. Wilson, and forwarded from Lord North Street. He opened it and it was a current account sheet from the offshore Swiss bank which went broke with an illegal deposit in it for Wilson. Robin just resealed it and passed it on.

I went to the Commons in the afternoon to hear Foot at Questions – quite different from Jim, more spontaneous, less prepared, but effective in the short run. Then the devolution statement, followed by Ennals's announcement of compensation to vaccine-damaged children. Jack Ashley gave me a little smile of triumph. He is a great campaigner.

Wednesday 15 June 1977

Lewis Robertson of the Scottish Development Agency came in to talk. A very impressive man, rather like a human Lord Reith.

Lunch in the Cabinet Office canteen. The weather is terrible, cold and grey, worse than any summer I ever remember. We have our central heating on at home.

We are preparing a brief on Shirley Williams's education White Paper, which we find disappointing. I went to see Margaret Jackson at 6 p.m. to discuss it. She was fairly scathing. Claims that Shirley was not sure what to say in it, especially after the PM's Ruskin speech had pre-empted the ground.

After that I went to a marvellous reception at the Royal Academy to celebrate the end of the Commonwealth Conference. I chatted to Paul Scott, my favourite novelist, whom I had suggested for the guest list.

Thursday 16 June 1977

I came in early to chat to ministers before Cabinet. They seemed in remarkably cheerful mood.

In Cabinet Jim showed his firmness by railroading Bill Rodgers's White Paper through almost without discussion. Foot had been complaining about Rodgers's plans. But Jim had his revenge on Foot by not giving him a chance to speak.

Lunch at No. 10.

Before Questions the PM worked himself up into a tough and cheerful mood. This is how he gets in the mood of 'avuncular complacency' which so infuriates the Tories and is so effective. We all tell him to forget the troubles and get on with the job, listing the progress on various issues, and he soon gets in the mood for soldiering on. Thatcher intervened immediately on collective responsibility, but Jim slapped her down imperiously and from then on all went beautifully.

Leo Plietzky came in in the evening to have a drink to celebrate his promotion to the Board of Trade. He told me that he could not get on with Alan Lord or with Derek Mitchell at the Treasury, and that he had disagreed with the Treasury policy over the IMF. He said that the IMF had demanded £3–4 billion off public expenditure in each year 1977–79. He had resisted this because it 'would destroy the government'. He implied that not everybody in the Treasury agreed with him or minded destroying the government.

Went to Brian Knox's party in the evening at his remarkable modern house in Hampstead. The Grieveson Grant stockbrokers all described the BP sale as a 'rip-off'. To bed at 1 a.m.

Friday 17 June 1977

I went in early to attend the deputy secs meeting: generally pessimistic reports on industrial democracy, where Dell and Booth are still a long way apart. We discussed the CPRS report on the FCO and John Hunt said that the Foreign Office were 'trying to strangle it at birth'.

Peter Bourne, one of President Carter's aides, came in for an hour in the morning. He said that the power of many individuals in that entourage had altered dramatically since coming to power. Stuart Eisenstadt [Carter's domestic policy adviser] is very strong.

Had lunch with Robert Armstrong at the Athenaeum. Now over two years since he left. He takes over as permanent secretary at the Home Office in two weeks. He is obviously very interested in the 'security' side of the job and talked about the spies Burgess, Maclean and Philby. He said some people may be getting worried about more revelations about 'fellow travellers' in the 1930s – probably more homosexuals in the FCO, I suspect. Robert is a big man, with more convictions than most senior civil servants. Somebody I will enjoy knowing afterwards.

Felt very tired in the afternoon. Cleared off our education brief. Waited for the Treasury's medium-term economic assessment, which came at the last moment as usual, full of gloom. But scope for £20 billion tax cuts over the five years after the next election – lucky Tories!

Home by 6, and straight off to Suffolk for a weekend decorating the cottage.

Monday 20 June 1977

Went in from the barbers to the Education Department where I had a long meeting with the excellent new permanent secretary, Jim Hamilton, about the coming Green Paper on education. I told him about our dissatisfaction and listed the main reasons. He agreed with most of them, but said that the paper had been through about fifty drafts, with never less than four people working on every paragraph. Shirley Williams had taken a very close interest, and was herself responsible for some of the compromises which were really what was wrong with it. He was, by implication, very critical of Shirley's weakness when dealing with pressure groups, and especially the awful NUT. He said he would make some more changes and they would be circulating an amended version.

I returned to No. 10 for a quick lunch in the Cabinet Office canteen and then went with Gavyn Davies to see John Hunt and Claus Moser about our proposal to set up a small model of the economy to run through the CSO Treasury computer. The Treasury already has a model, but it is huge, with hundreds of equations, built up over a long period, and it cannot do a quick uprated run-through nor is it possible to alter the main assumptions built into it.

John Hunt was helpful and sympathetic. Moser especially so. Claus came to my room afterwards and said that he and Hunt were delighted at the prospect of 'putting a stick of dynamite' under the Treasury. But he said that the Treasury were mobilising opposition. It sounds like a lovely battle ahead, and I look forward to it.

Shortly after I returned to No. 10 the PM sent for me, and I went to the study with Tom McNally. He was in bubbling mood. He had read the medium-term assessment, with its suggestion of £20 billion tax cuts in the future, and was excited by the prospect of governing Britain with good news and something to give away, after all these years of decline and depression. He was very pleased with the Unit's covering note and summary. He said it made him even more determined to soldier on for another year or more, and not to hand all this over to Thatcher.

Jim then read out to us his draft speech to the PLP tomorrow. It was very good and he knew it. Firm but not heavy-handed. Basically telling them that it was in the interests of everybody that the government went on, but that it was up to them, the whole Party, if they did or not. He was not going to nanny them. And if they continued 'playing silly buggers', that would be it. He was clearly revived and in fighting form. I was immensely cheered by this.

I went off to see Judith Hart for a drink at the Overseas Development department. We discussed the situation in the Party. She criticised the 'new left' who are much less responsible than her old left. She said she and the old Tribune Group always had agonies of conscience over whether to vote against the Party. The new ones don't care about the Party, and simply do what they want. She described Audrey Wise as 'a Trot'.

I went back to No. 10 to collect Carol and then we went out with Johnny Apple of the *New York Times* to dinner at Waltons, with a lovely lady from CBS. A delightful evening and home at about 1.30 next morning, tired but feeling in very good form.

Tuesday 21 June 1977

In early for the Cabinet committee on industrial democracy which went quite well. Still a big divide between Booth and Dell, but they have identified some areas of agreement and progress and these will go into a Green/White Paper. This has to be viewed as a ten-year job and we advance little by little.

Benn put a 'Workers' Control' view, opposing Bullock and the TUC, and saying it should all be left to the local shop stewards. Benn is increasingly influenced by Ken Coates* and that workers-control Marxist side. A curious base for a future Labour leader.

A note came in this morning saying that the City firm Slater Walker is going bankrupt tomorrow. But the Bank of England is going to put in £3.5 million of public money to rescue it (for a second time!) in order to save embarrassing the Bank and the City. This infuriated me. These Bank people go round pontificating about lame ducks and opposing any rescue of manufacturing firms in trouble, where thousands of jobs are at stake. But when it comes to their own shady financial empires they take the taxpayers' money to bail out every crook and cheapjack in the City.

Lunch with Graham Greene, who says that friends of his are thinking of buying the *New Statesman* or *Spectator*, and he wants me to be editor. Quite attractive, I suppose.

At 6.15 to the Commons to see Shirley Williams about the education White Paper. A difficult meeting, because I realised I was making a lot of trouble for her. But she made a lot of constructive concessions and agreed to rewrite chunks at the beginning.

I left her room at 7 p.m. and walked across the corridor to Tony Benn's room. We had a long talk about politics in general. He wants closer relations with the Party; asked why I was not closer to Transport House; savagely attacked Ken Berrill and the CPRS; said he would put the general secretary of the Party in the Cabinet; wants more 'strategy' Cabinet meetings; wants each minister to have a 'Cabinet' of special advisers and backbenchers. He drank tea from his big mug, but offered me whisky. He said how marvellous it was to have special advisers he could talk to. Laughingly said that taking energy policy decisions was a diversion from real politics (not a diversion he often takes); quizzed me about the organisation of No. 10 in general and the Unit in particular; was critical of Marcia for running a kitchen Cabinet – he said that he was once in it, but was 'kicked out for not being deferential enough'. I cannot help liking him personally – but not politically.

I had a quick snack in the café, and was just leaving when I met John Pardoe, who asked me to come and talk to him in David Steel's room. He said things were difficult for the Liberals. They had got nothing from the alliance, and were about to do very badly at the Saffron Walden by-election. Their polls showed them dropping to third place behind Labour. Some of his colleagues preferred to drop out and revert to their old impotent independence.

But he actually wanted to make an agreement for the long term. He suggested a pact of support for an eighteen-month session till 1979, so the government were safe. But they had to be given something. We discussed what to give them, and in the end agreed that a package of tax cuts would be better for them and us, than bits of direct elections, PR and devolution which means nothing to our supporters.

I will minute the PM on this. I left at 10 o'clock and came home slowly by public transport, having completely run out of money.

Wednesday 22 June 1977

We had a meeting of special advisers all morning in a dreary room in the Old Admiralty Building part of the Civil Service Department. I took the chair, made a brief introduction on my belief that the government could win the next election and that Sunday's Strategy Cabinet was the crucial last opportunity to change policies in order to do so. I then went round the table, keeping order very strictly. The contributions were encouragingly good – Jack Straw, Michael Stewart and Francis Cripps especially so. We went on right through till 1 o'clock and many people said how useful they found it.

The Unit had to complete our strategy paper for circulation to Cabinet by the evening, so we went back to No. 10, snatched a quick snack and then we all began work making our paper suitable for circulation.

I left at 2.45, went to Lancaster House where the PM was conducting a meeting on the industrial strategy. Before the start he came across to ask how Shirley Williams's education Green Paper was going. I said that it was much improved. He said he hoped so. I then got restless and went back to No. 10 where we redrafted sections of our strategy paper. Gavyn added a large section on the economy. I wrote some extra sections for the conclusion. Our paper will be circulated by the Cabinet Office, but not as a Cabinet Office paper – it will be on different kind of paper, and with a covering note by John Hunt. His covering note is the device whereby papers not by ministers are put to ministers.

I went home late and tired, but elated.

Thursday 23 June 1977

Went in later than intended and just missed the Devolution Cabinet committee at 9.45. They discussed – and rejected – the proposals for separate tax powers for the Scottish Assembly. Then, I was told, they agreed they could have an early guillotine on a timetable motion, and the PM would make that a motion of confidence.

Cabinet discussed the new package on youth employment, which was strongly welcomed, and then Shirley Williams's draft education Green Paper – and threw it out. There was a general feeling it was too long, too flat, and compromised too much with the teachers' unions, ignoring the wider public to which the PM had appealed in his Ruskin speech.

In fact I had briefed the PM not to throw it out, while setting out its faults. But he had attacked it and told her to do better.

I met Shirley Williams coming out of Cabinet. She looked a bit down. She clearly thought I was behind the criticisms, but was very friendly. She said that on reflection it was probably a good thing not to publish it, since it was not well written. She had been too busy chairing the subcommittee on industrial democracy and had left a deputy secretary to write the main body of the work, and he had compromised with everybody, in true Civil Service fashion. Now she would have 'to pretend to be sick' and take off four days to rewrite it properly.

I went to lunch with Harry Evans, and we had a pleasant chat at the Garrick. After Parliamentary Questions I went to call on my Scottish Nationalist friend, Margaret Bain, and then back home, where Carol's Israeli sister Jill was with us for supper.

Friday 24 June 1977

At 11, Peter Middleton from the Treasury came in to see Gavyn and me about our plan to build a model of the economy and run it through the Treasury/CSD computer. Middleton was very sympathetic, but his Treasury colleagues were less so.

I left in the middle and went to see David Owen at the FCO. We discussed our approach to Sunday's Strategy Cabinet. He had our paper, and the Treasury and CPRS paper, but had not had time to read them, having been in Europe till this morning. Michael Stewart joined us and we had an excellent meeting. David is very quick and sharp, sometimes overreacting, but he manages a lively argument which quickly identified the main points. He is going to take a firm line that we must reflate or lose the election; that pay policy is essential; and that the expansion should be via tax cuts and minimal public expenditure increases.

He also wanted to take a strong anti-bureaucracy line. In this context he moved on to the CPRS report on the FCO. He thinks 80% of the recommendations are OK, but he dislikes the underlying philosophy of pessimism about Britain's reduced role. He also does not think it is desirable to abolish the Diplomatic Service yet. He was very anti the CPRS, objected to Berrill attending Sunday's Cabinet, and said that no civil servants should be there.

Tony Benn had made the same point to me, so I went back to No. 10 and fed the thought in to Ken Stowe. I said I felt the objection was to the Cabinet Office secretariat, and ministers would be happy with No. 10 private secretaries. Since this left him and not John Hunt in charge he did not object.

I left London in mid-afternoon for Hythe, near Folkestone, to attend the Anglo-American Conference on Peace and the Law. This turned out to be excellent, fascinating people, excellent discussion. I sat up talking till 3 a.m. on Sunday morning, then went to bed for three hours, got up at 5.45, went for a walk along the front, then had early breakfast in my room with Tony Lewis of the *New York Times*, and finally left at 7.30 in a government car to drive the 110 miles to Chequers for the Strategy Cabinet.

Sunday 26 June 1977

I arrived at Chequers for the Strategy Cabinet just after 10. Michael Foot greeted me with the words 'a very fine paper if I may say so'. A lovely start. Several other ministers congratulated me on the way upstairs.

At the start the PM announced that there were no civil servants present, no John Hunt, no Ken Berrill, and there would be no minutes circulating round Whitehall. Apparently he got my message from Ken Stowe on Friday evening, and immediately gave instructions accordingly. Rumour has it that John Hunt was not pleased.

The PM then opened and went round the table, bringing in grass-roots men early – Orme, Mason, Varley. He left the 'intellectuals' – Williams, Lever, Ennals – till very late in the day. There was repeated praise for the Unit paper.

We broke for lunch at 1.15 and I met the PM upstairs. He congratulated me. He also asked for a conclusion to use in his summing up. I went down and had lunch, sitting with Healey, Hattersley and Owen. Healey was very friendly and said there was little difference between us. I chatted to several other ministers – the mood was excellent. They were uplifted and

re-dedicated to going on till 1979. But there was much criticism of the
negativity of the CPRS paper.

The PM sent Tom McNally over to collect my summary. The PM used
a lot of it in his conclusion, though as usual he wove it into his own excellent pattern.

We broke just before 5. The PM invited us to go and swim. David
Owen, Bill Rodgers and Shirley Williams dived in making the most enormous splashes. Bill had mistakenly taken the PM's swimming trunks,
which enveloped him, and led to the PM muttering loudly about 'a
reshuffle'.

I dried down and left alone to drive back. I ran into the Chancellor in
the garden, and we chatted a while. He said how tired he was feeling.
Incidentally in his summing up Healey completely conceded our programme
of reflation: £2–3 million in the summer; £1 billion in the autumn; £3
billion next year. He referred to it as the Policy Unit's programme and
explicitly accepted it as such.

I met David Owen on the way out. We agreed to drive back to London
together in his car, with mine following behind. He was very pleased with
it all – and said that the Unit had 'changed the history of this Labour
government'.

On Rhodesia, he obviously wants a grand, Kissinger-style, 'Owen settlement' of Africa. I responded cautiously and non-committally, warning him
of the danger of failure – and the financial cost. He stuck to his guns, but
obviously is worried about opposition from No. 10.

I left his car at Baker Street and took my own car home, so excited and
satisfied that I did not notice my lack of sleep.

Monday 27 June 1977

I went into work on a high cloud, still excited from yesterday's marvellous
Cabinet meeting. I did not mind at all that this morning's newspapers say
that it was a good Treasury paper which yesterday's Cabinet approved. The
only way to get the Treasury to approve of expansion is to announce that
it was their idea.

Went to a meeting in Douglas Wass's room about our proposal to have
a computer model for the economy. Douglas declared from the start that
he would go along with us, and was simply concerned to establish conditions of working co-operation. The only sour note was from Fred Atkinson*,
the new senior economic adviser. A boring old man of 58 who has not had
an economic idea for twenty years, he said that he totally opposed anybody
outside the Treasury doing anything in the economic field, but since it was
already decided he had nothing to say. It is a terrible thought that he and

his deputy, Maynard, constitute the 'Economic Advice' team in the Treasury. I would not dream of recruiting either for my Policy Unit.

Generally pottered through the afternoon and then had a meeting with McNally and McCaffrey about the organisation of the next election. We mainly discussed people to use in the team. This is especially important since McNally won't be with us at the next election – he swears he will be fighting a seat, any seat, whatever happens.

John Hunt phoned to see me at about 7 p.m. We discussed our computer meeting with Wass, since Hunt will have to process it through the machine. (Incidentally, Wass expressed great glee this morning that Hunt had been excluded from yesterday's Cabinet.) Hunt made no mention of Chequers so in the end I gave him a debriefing. He affected a studied lack of interest.

I came home at 8.30 to see Jill, Carol's sister from Israel, who is staying with us for a few days.

Tuesday 28 June 1977

The PM was away at Spithead with the Queen reviewing the fleet. This is a great moment for him, as a former sailor with a father who assisted Queen Victoria when she reviewed the fleet at her Golden Jubilee.

I had a quiet day in the office. Lunch in No. 10 and then Jill came in with her boys and I showed her the house.

I then went over to the Commons to see Michael Foot dealing with PM's Questions which he does very well.

In the evening I had a devolution dinner. Learned that Margaret Bain and the Scot Nats are putting down a motion of no confidence next Monday – so more parliamentary pressures.

Wednesday 29 June 1977

The PM was still at Spithead and did not return till late morning. There were reports from Ken Stowe of how much the PM had enjoyed going back to the navy, with lots of reminiscences and no politics at all.

Varley came to see the PM about [Don] Ryder's resignation from the Enterprise Board – there is said to be something 'unsavoury' which will emerge in mid-July but I cannot discover what.

I went to lunch with Roy Hattersley, his excellent adviser Maurice Peston and Roy's private secretary, Callum McCarthy*, a nice civil servant. Roy was late, delayed at a long meeting with Healey which he told us about. They had discussed a package of restraints on prices, partly to persuade the trade unions to give us a stage three, partly because we need it politically anyway. Healey had been much more sympathetic than usual on this and seemed to accept that something had to be done on some sensitive prices. He also said he agreed on the currency, that it must not go down (despite official Treasury policy to the contrary) and he would favour it rising if that were natural and not forced. We discussed how to handle the next round of pay policy, which is still a mystery to all of us. Healey apparently is talking in terms of concluding a deal within two weeks.

In the evening I went home to collect Carol and then drove to Winfield House, the American ambassador's residence, for a farewell party for Ron Spiers. It was a glorious evening, and we went out on to the patio overlooking the great lawns and then across Regent's Park. There were over 100 people there, with most of the 'power Establishment' (not that we seem to have much power).

It broke up at 11 and we drove home.

Thursday 30 June 1977

I went in early for a ministerial meeting on family support with Rees in the chair. Orme made an impassioned opening statement. Barnett replied saying we could not take any decisions ahead of the expenditure review. Peart said he was against but did not know why. Booth said that the trade unions wanted child benefits up. Ken Berrill came in to say there was no evidence to prove that families had been squeezed lately. I followed, saying there was evidence – and quoted it. Berrill got very angry and threw me a note. (He later said that I had broken the unwritten rule of Whitehall that one 'should not introduce new figures into any argument'. In fact the officials' paper had figures which did not take into account April's Budget!) Rees was fairly agitated in the chair and finally summed up in our favour. Ken Berrill stormed over to complain bitterly – I have never seen him to show signs of passion about anything before – about Whitehall procedure.

I went over to Lancaster House for the end of the EEC summit conference and had a very good lunch with Patrick Wright, who is leaving No. 10 today. His last day, ending with a conference. I can remember him joining us – and how I tried to stop it because he is an 'Arab'. Actually he has been marvellous, very funny, and the best of the old '1974' school. I shall miss his lovely wife, Virginia, too. All a reminder of time slipping by – my third foreign affairs secretary is now at that desk – Bridges, Wright, now Cartledge, not in the same league.

I went on to the Commons for Questions. The PM was in a grumpy mood, obviously irritated to be back from summitry to the cut and thrust of Question Time. It was a fractious session, mainly about the Grunwick strike.

Friday 1 July 1977

This morning's *Guardian* had a piece on the front page about the BP share issue, saying mainly that the Bank was unhappy with the government for having allowed the Americans only 20%, but also saying that No. 10 was unhappy with the Bank for having fixed such a low price. I sensed that this would come up when I got to the office since I spoke cautiously to Jenkins at a reception last evening.

I went straight to Private Office where they were reading the *Guardian* article and Ken Stowe was in a great flap. He said that the Governor of the Bank of England had been on the phone to complain that I had been talking to the *Guardian* criticising the Bank. The Governor said that Peter Jenkins had told him over the phone that I was the source (so much for journalists protecting their sources). The Governor wanted to come to see the PM to protest. I told Stowe that I had talked to Jenkins and would put him in a memo for the PM. We then went off to John Hunt's deputy secretaries meeting, which was mainly concerned with whether or not to serve tea at Cabinets and Cabinet committees – the decision was no.

I returned and wrote my memo – which was emollient against the Governor and did not mention (1) that the institutions authorised the Governor to go up to £8.50 and (2) that the American brokers had firm bids for 40% of the total issue at a price of £9.30 (which would work out at £8.95 to the Bank of England).

I had an official committee on the Royal Commission on the Press at 11.30, which was soon disposed of. Then I went to lunch with Quentin Morris of BP. He said that BP would never use the Bank of England again. We swapped experiences. He told me that it was a Bank broker who leaked the story of the PM's initial refusal to go ahead with the issue that Monday evening.

In the afternoon Ken Stowe told me that the Governor had had second thoughts and now did not want to see the PM.

I went home at 8.30 – still waiting to see how the Bank of England would have revenge.

Sunday 3 July 1977

The *Sunday Times* on its front page today had a piece by Kenneth Fleet accusing me of 'muck-raking' and saying it was pique because my alleged personal application for BP shares (which of course I did not make) had been scaled down. He then went on to admit that the price was too low! He is a typical gutter journalist sucking up to the Bank.

Monday 4 July 1977

Went to see Anthony Rawlinson at the Treasury. He has taken Leo Plietzky's place and wanted to re-establish relations with No. 10. We discussed public expenditure. He was worried that pre-election optimism would lead the government to throw away the hard-won financial control. The current bids for extra spending – child benefits, construction industry, public sector prices – could push us well beyond the agreed IMF targets. Therefore there would have to be more cuts to accommodate these extra expenditures. I said I agreed completely on the need not to lose financial control. He was very pleasant and modest and I think we shall have a good relationship with him.

Had lunch with Joe Haines at Lockets. Ironically, Harold Wilson, Falkender and David Frost were also there, but we had no communication. Tom McNally and I are planning to use Joe in any future election, recreating the old team, since McNally will be out fighting his by-election.

At 3.30 Ken Couzens came in for a talk about pay policy. He is due to take over Derek Mitchell's job in charge of overseas finance, but is staying on with wages policy until we can get some kind of pay agreement. He started by telling me that the Treasury has abandoned its policy of getting the sterling exchange rate down. Apparently the inflationary effect of last year's devaluation, destroying stage two of the pay policy, has had a traumatic effect on the Treasury and they have formally decided not to pursue depreciation as a policy for the rest of this year. On pay he was not very optimistic. He said they have had terrible difficulty dealing with the TUC. Jack Jones had worked to devalue the Neddy Six trade unionists and wanted the Treasury to negotiate with the whole economic council. Scanlon could not deliver his Engineers union. Others would not say what the government should give them.

The timetable is for the Chancellor to discuss the deal with the TU negotiators next Tuesday, for the TUC economic council to meet and approve/disapprove the deal on Wednesday, and for the Cabinet to agree the deal and a White Paper on Thursday. If it runs into trouble the negotiations could go on over the weekend but the following Monday, 18 July, was the last day.

Ken said that if we did not get a deal then we should withdraw some of the tax concessions and all of any promised prices package (they have in mind a £200 million price deal – small, but there are not many more public sector price rises to come). Ken, who is endearingly voluble, a kind of Charlie Chaplin figure, a grammar school boy obviously, stayed nearly two hours.

I did not go to the Cabinet committee on the CPRS report but apparently David Owen was very impassioned in his defence of the FCO and in his criticisms of the CPRS, but the PM firmly put him down. The PM quite likes the report, but above all wants a low-key reaction, and not a briefing war between the FCO and the CPRS. So he is playing it longer and quieter, setting up a committee under John Hunt to process the proposals.

My old footballing friend David Bacon came in and we went out to a nice supper at the Snooty Fox. He then drove me to the Commons, where I went in for the vote on the Scot Nats' motion of no confidence. We won easily by 29. Afterwards I went to David Owen's room and had further discussions about the CPRS and Rhodesia. He was worried whether the PM perhaps disapproved of his swashbuckling style. I reassured him this was not so. He also told me that 'Denis Healey is after your guts for promoting optimism on the economy'. Apparently the Chequers Cabinet and now the PM's Saturday speech in Wales (mainly written by David Lipsey), each lifting people's eyes to the future, have worried the Treasury. They prefer doom and gloom. Obviously there is going to be a two-pronged attack on me by the Treasury and the Bank of England. I could not have chosen better enemies!

I drove home at 11.30 on a very hot summer night – and only three weeks to go to the recess.

Tuesday 5 July 1977

Went in early to a meeting of EY Cabinet committee on problems relating to the nationalised industries – power of ministerial direction, financial targets, etc. Basically it was a very important subject, but, as the PM said, the papers were boring and made the subject seem boring. A nice moment was when Tony Benn quoted my book on Morrison about the nationalised industries.

Afterwards I phoned Jim Hamilton at Education, to congratulate him on the excellent revised draft of the Green Paper on education. He said that he had spent three days on it, but had not found it difficult to see what was wrong and to put it right.

I went to lunch with Harold Lever, taking Gavyn Davies and Andrew Graham. We sat and drank on his Eaton Square balcony, and then went to eat, and he talked all the time about interest rates, preparing for this afternoon's meeting with the Governor and the Chancellor. I left at 2.30 to go to Parliamentary Questions, and then stayed with Lever till nearly 4 p.m.

Questions went excellently. Jim put down Thatcher imperially, exposing her lack of humour. He was very pleased afterwards.

Then back to No. 10 for the seminar on the reserves with the Governor and the Chancellor (and Wass and McMahon from the Bank). The PM handled it brilliantly. Bringing in the Chancellor and the Governor on the question of the expanding reserves, and on the exchange rate (where we are automatically depreciating by linking to the depreciating dollar), and finally zoomed in on interest rates, which we had briefed him on. He brought in Lever, who immediately clashed totally with Richardson. The Governor declared himself as a total monetarist. Only the monetary aggregates mattered. He did not care if the reserves rose to £20 billion or if interest rates rose to 20%. Healey trimmed between the two of them.

In the end the PM summed up on a compromise which suited him – willing to go along with a rise in long-term rates, but the short-term rates, MLR, etc., must not go up. He also said that sterling must not go down.

Afterwards the PM called me by name and asked me to go into the Cabinet Room to chat with him. This was a tremendous gesture of support in front of the Governor. He was very pleased with the meeting and said we must have more of them. He said how under Cromer in the 1960s he and HW always saw the Governor alone. It was much better to have it all in the open. He said how grateful he was for our paper setting him off thinking about interest rates. He was also pleased with Lever's 'flanking' performance. The PM then went into the garden to read his papers before going to the Palace.

I drove home at 9 p.m. feeling very good. Am enjoying life at the moment.

Wednesday 6 July 1977

Went to dentist in the morning so in late to No. 10. Then worked on papers: read the revised draft of Shirley Williams's Green Paper on education which is very much better. Had sandwiches for lunch in No. 10 and then had a meeting with Helen Liddell about Scotland.

After tea we completed our paper on public expenditure in 1978–79. Here the Treasury is arguing for giving away nothing. We are briefing to stick generally to the IMF targets, since we do not want to shake confidence.

Graham Greene and Marie Goossens, the great ancient harpist, came in with Carol to visit me in the evening, but in fact I spent very little time with them. News came through that the T&G has repudiated Jack Jones and rejected the pay policy. Though not a total surprise, this is a bad blow.

The PM immediately sent for the Chancellor and they discussed it in the garden. In the Unit we realised that our child benefits scheme has gone through the window.

The PM came back in from the garden and we all sat down in the hall to discuss how to brief the press. The PM looked grim but did not sound it. In fact he ticked us all off for 'panicking'. He said there was no need, and we would find our way through. In a sense that is true. The difference between this and the kind of loose arrangement which was anyway the best we could hope for is not much. But it does not look good, since the social contract was a major plank in our programme.

I then went off to a delightful dinner with Graham Greene and his lively new wife in Lord North Street (which brought back memories of 1974, especially since the 'For Sale' notice was up outside H. Wilson's house at No. 5!).

Home at midnight. Have to be up at 6.30 in the morning because Carol is off to Northampton at 6 and I have to get the children off to school and then an early Cabinet.

Thursday 7 July 1977

I went to the office and cleared my papers before going off to Arnot Sutherland's memorial service. [Sutherland had been senior partner at Grieveson Grant, my stockbroker friends.] Very pleasant, but a bit too formal for Arnot who was one of the most delightfully informal of men.

I stayed for lunch with Grieveson and then came back to Parliamentary Questions. The PM said he saw no point in a briefing. It would be about pay and we could not help him there. So he went in to the chamber early. In fact it went OK – the Tories were unwilling to attack us on pay because they don't have a policy themselves. The Liberals are a bigger problem being committed to some nutty statutory policy scheme.

Had a long meeting with John Smith on devolution. He has changed the Devolution Bill considerably – shorter, less tying of every loose end, and more acceptable to the Liberals. He also told me that Enoch Powell had been to see him and Michael Foot about the Ulster Unionists promising support to this Labour government. In some ways they are firmer in their support than are the Liberals.

John Smith and I went out on to the terrace at about 6.30 p.m., and I stayed there drinking beer for the next three hours. It was a beautiful hot evening. People came and chatted and moved on. Gerry Fowler stayed with me a long time. Stan Orme came to discuss child benefits – this morning's Cabinet held the line and prevented the Treasury from using the T&G wages decision as a reason to veto all public expenditure increases. It will come back to Cabinet next week after bilaterals between the Treasury and DHSS.

I left at 9.15 and came home. There was a message from Gavyn Davies to say there was a Treasury paper on pay – on the assumption that we could get nothing from the TUC. He had briefed, quite rightly, saying that it was too early to give up all together. They are such pessimists.

Friday 8 July 1977

Yesterday the PM had a meeting with David Steel about the Lib-Lab pact. Apparently it went very easily. They agreed renewal of the pact for next year will be decided this month. It would be just an 'understanding' that Labour would take full account of the Liberal point of view in the ten chosen areas of policy and on Steel's insistence the PLP would be requested to approve.

The PM had a Cabinet committee on Rhodesia. I did not go, but I saw David Owen afterwards and we walked from No. 10 to the FCO and the Horse Guards Parade. He described the clash he had just had with Healey, saying it was 'time to get tough with Denis', since that was the only way to deal with him. David knows him well from Ministry of Defence days and says he is a bully, a tank, and the only way is to bully back.

I went back to No. 10 and had an hour's chat with Hector Hawkins of the CPRS. He is leaving this month after six years and was very critical of the CPRS, saying it had been put completely under John Hunt's Cabinet Office control.

I then went to the deputy secretaries. Little came up, except a remark by John Hunt that the Chequers Cabinet had 'caused a lot of trouble' and the permanent secretaries had reported ministers coming back and telling their junior ministers that it was time to start taking the brakes off public expenditure. This is almost certainly untrue. But Hunt resents being excluded. The Treasury resents the discussion of expansion. So the mandarins are out to smear the whole operation and to try to prevent a repetition.

Had a quick lunch with Tom McNally in a Whitehall pub. Then at teatime left for Oxford by train. Stayed in Oriel College. Had supper, then wrote my lecture, and finished the evening with a tour of Oxford pubs. At 11.30 p.m. I met Robert Armstrong in the High Street and we stopped and had a chat. He told me that Hunt was very upset by an article in last week's *Sunday Times* which said that Robert would succeed Hunt – and do it better.

On Saturday the lecture went very well. Back to London in the afternoon and good dinner party with the Rodgers, Butlers and Johnny Apple.

Monday 11 July 1977

Went to EY at 11.15 to discuss pay policy and Healey's approach to the trade unions tomorrow. A wide range of 'sweeteners' were discussed, and some agreed. Yet it was, on reflection, a most curious discussion – because there was little discussion of what Healey should actually negotiate for, whether a figure or a formula of words, and there was no discussion of why the pay policy had gone wrong – why, if the T&G Conference was crucial, nothing had been done before it. Healey did not reveal what he wanted or was going for. The PM, however, was more forthcoming. He said more than once that he did not believe that any sweeteners would make any difference to many pay claims: he said that the British Leyland workers, etc. would go for high claims this year whatever we did. He said what mattered was the level of settlements, and we must work on these. And his main point was to make sure that the Cabinet still had the fight against inflation as its main priority.

The atmosphere was good and friendly. I could not see any division between 'hawks' and 'doves' or left and right.

After the morning meeting ended, at 1 p.m., I walked out with Shirley Williams, who is very upset by leaks to the press about the education Green Paper being rejected by Cabinet because it was terrible. I told her that I did not think the leaks came from No. 10. She disagreed, saying that 'nobody in my department knew of the Cabinet objection'. This showed ignorance of how the Civil Service machine, and especially the Private Office network, works. I know that our Private Office talked to her Private Office; that when Nick Stuart came to Patrick Wright's party he knew all about it and was reporting reactions of other people in the department. It shows how ministers are ignorant of the machine. It is curious Shirley thought it was possible that the decision of Cabinet could have been kept secret from her department.

I worked in the office in the afternoon. Then we resumed the EY at 7.30. The atmosphere was much lighter, with Healey and some others clearly having had some drinks beforehand. They finished the list of 'sweeteners' for the unions to buy their support for pay policy. The only serious one was construction, where they agreed to offer £100 million. But to the end I could not see any real commitment by the Chancellor and PM to get a deal. I just don't think it was on, or was not on in a form which was worth fighting for.

I got home at 10.30 with a deep feeling that things are slipping on the wage front without us knowing quite what we are after.

Tuesday 12 July 1977

Before the Devolution Cabinet committee I talked to Peter Shore. He was stressing the need to help the unemployed in the constructions industry. When I mentioned the Channel Tunnel as a way of doing this with private finance and with European money, Shore went slightly mad. He rose to his feet, waving his arms, saying this would be the worst thing that could ever happen to Britain. How old was I? Did I not remember 1940? We would be invaded by Germans coming through the tunnel. We must not give up our island status, etc., etc. It was very worrying. He is quite mad on this European issue – in fact more unbalanced and dogmatic than Tony Benn is on any issue. He must be kept away from top power.

As I left for dinner at 8.30 Denis Healey was just arriving at No. 11. I went over and we had a long talk about his meeting with the TUC this evening. He said it had been short and made no progress. The unions were simply not prepared to go along with any structured wage policy at all, nor with any figure. Jones and Scanlon said they could not deliver their unions. Murray tried to be helpful – but had only just come back from a ten-day holiday today and seemed out of touch! They could not even agree to a helpful statement after the meeting – that had to wait till after tomorrow's meeting of the Economics committee. Healey said it was a 'non-event' and he was clearly feeling depressed. He said that he had not revealed his 'sweeteners' to the TUC because it never got that far! He could not see any reason why the unions should come back to us. It was all over. They wanted us to take over the pay policy.

Very curious. We seem to have offered nothing, and they seem to have had nothing to give in return. The only question is whether it might have been different – if we had done a big prices package before the T&G, if, if . . . we will never know. But I suspect the PM's and Healey's view is that it was never on.

Wednesday 13 July 1977

This was an exciting and incredibly exhausting day.

I went in early for the EY meeting to discuss a Treasury draft White Paper on pay policy. Denis Healey opened by reporting on his meeting with the TUC yesterday. He said it was clear unions had a meeting beforehand and decided they could offer no structured pay policy. Benn blamed it all on the Treasury for not giving in to all union demands and he and Foot attacked the paper for putting the whole emphasis on beating inflation and the whole blame on the unions.

PM said it was crucial to get the TUC to endorse our objective of reducing inflation.

He would call another meeting with the unions today and try to get a form of words on settlements which we could use and they could endorse or acquiesce in. 'I want the TUC covering my back.'

The meeting broke up and some ministers left. Others stayed for the next meeting, of ENM to decide whether to place the contract for the new Drax B power station with Parsons or with GEC. As we were settling down, Denis Healey popped his head through the Cabinet Room door and beckoned me out. He said he wanted me to take over the redrafting of the White Paper on pay. I was a bit taken aback, since I had not read the damn thing yet. But the Chancellor said he recalled that the Unit had rewritten the 1975 White Paper and he wanted the same again. He said, 'My boys in the Treasury simply cannot draft.'

He took me through into his study on the ground floor in No. 11. He telephoned his Private Office to tell them of his decision and then discussed with me the changes he wanted – mainly in the opening five pages and in the key central section on the pay targets for this year.

I agreed, but added that I wanted the Cabinet Office involved (since I knew that the Treasury would be fighting against me, I thought it best to at least neutralise, and possibly mobilise, the support of the Cabinet Office). So I went back to No. 10, went into the Private Office and summoned John Hunt out of the Cabinet Room. I told him the problem. I said I would be running the redrafting from the Unit. He sent for one of his men, Mountfield (a Treasury man and an active Tory!), to assist. Hunt also gave me the note he had already given to the PM which actually suggested that I do the rewriting of the introduction.

It was now nearly midday. We had to have the redraft done, retyped and circulated in time for a meeting of the ministerial subcommittee at 3 o'clock. So I dashed back to my offices, summoned the Unit, explained the problem and handed out the jobs. David Lipsey and I did the introduction, Gavyn the central piece on targets for next year, and Jim Corr the conclusion. All lunches were cancelled and we sent for sandwiches. It was a terrible sweat, with drafts spread all over the floor, but in the end we got it together.

The one problem was that Ken Couzens came steaming in from the Treasury at 1 o'clock to recover what he saw as lost ground. He insisted on restoring some of the original drafting and was obviously unhappy at outsiders intruding on Treasury territory.

One historical note. In my meeting with Healey this morning I asked him the central question which has been worrying me – why the package of sweeteners had not been offered to Jack Jones before the T&G vote, since that conference finally scuppered the phase three. He replied that everybody thought the T&G Conference would go OK. He and the Treasury thought so, and Jack Jones himself thought so. In fact on the Tuesday of the conference, David Lea of the TUC phoned to say he had been talking to Jack and 'it would be tough but it would be OK'. So it was a shock when it went wrong.

I went along to the 3 o'clock ministerial drafting meeting – Healey, Booth, Hattersley, Barnett and a lot of officials. They liked our introduction and went rapidly through the rest of it. Healey had spent lunchtime redrafting the central section and produced a whole new structure for it, which I could not follow. All ended happily at 4.30. Healey came up to me and said he was pleased with it now, and he had brought me in to avoid trouble with the PM later.

I went back to No. 10, and sent Gavyn off to the Treasury to join in the redrafting.

The TUC came in at 5 p.m. Before the meeting Healey told the PM that he was pleased with the redrafting.

The Cabinet Room was packed for the TUC meeting. About fifteen from the TUC, several ministers – Healey, Booth Hattersley, Foot, the PM – and a lot of officials. It went on from 5 to 7 p.m. getting nowhere, with the trade unionists explaining why they could not support or deliver a struc-tured pay policy.

Jim said in his opening, 'I want to know if there is to be a confrontation with the TUC. I don't want to end my time as leader of Labour Party like that. I've seen it all before, 1968–70. I don't want to finish my time fighting the low-paid hospital workers in September, fighting Joe Gormley in November–December. I would sooner finish now, go to the country, and say I cannot do it.

'If I hang on, with high wage claims, the credibility of this government will have disappeared. I am not going to spend twelve months fighting the Labour movement. But I believe in the common sense of you people. Democracy is not always tidy. But I believe we can work it out. It is my own firm view that the government should take a clear position: if we get 10% earnings this year, then it is worth going on. If not Mrs Thatcher will take over, with so much going well, then she will have to fight you. Now please tell me.'

He then set out 'sweeteners' – income tax reduced by 6p to 34p, substan-tial increase in child benefits, milk and school meals prices frozen 1977, gas rebate, electricity discount scheme of 25% for those on income support, petrol duty rescinded, £100 million extra on construction and a new Price Commission. A big reflation. But Jack Jones sat uninterested throughout, not taking notes. All the union leaders said they could not agree and espe-cially deliver a target figure of 10% on pay increases for the coming year –

they were having great difficulty delivering the current year's target. So it ended badly.

It was a sad meeting in many ways. The TUC looked low and chastened, having failed to deliver their conferences. Ministers looked worried at the prospect of going ahead without the TUC. The PM's contributions were good but touched with fatalism, recognising that this might be the start of the final phase. The gap between the two sides of the table was simply unbridgeable. Because they could not deliver, not because they did not agree with us.

At the end they went upstairs to have a drink in the reception rooms. The ministers stayed in the Cabinet Room. They discussed the drift the draft must take. The Chancellor went over the revised structure, which I again could not follow. The PM turned to me and said, 'You've grasped the changed drift; we've got to get it right, Bernard.' I nodded, but in fact was puzzled. I am still not sure what he wanted. Was it a more literate draft – well we had provided that. Or was it a modified policy. That is what some ministers and the TUC had called for – less rigid pay guidelines. Yet the PM had never shown much support for this, always seeming a hardliner. His position had never seemed clear to me, except where is was clearly 'hawkish'.

I then went off with Gavyn to the Treasury where we sat round Ken Couzens's table and spent four hours redrafting the counter-inflation section of the Treasury. They served bottles of white wine and some salad to keep us going.

Ken Couzens was in his usual energetic form, talking endlessly, surrounded by a mass of drafts, using scissors and paste to stick together a hotchpotch of paragraphs, with no possibility of seeing the text as a whole. People kept running in with messages, Nick Monck, the Chancellor's secretary, came in with some more bits, it was all very confusing and exhausting. The one clear theme was that single figures were the target and that was what we must say. If unions busted the policy that was their own silly fault.

We also had a small clash over the responsibilities for the latest bout of price inflation. I said it was because of sterling mismanagement, etc. They rejected this, claiming it was the sole fault of the unions for their excessive wage claims in 1974–75. Truth is a bit of both.

We left the Treasury at after midnight and went back to No. 10. We summoned a garden-room girl – Hilary – out of bed and in her nightdress she typed our brief to the PM. I finally left No. 10 at 1 a.m. and drove home, tired but as usual exhilarated by the work and excitement of the day. Whether the White Paper was any good I could not say.

Thursday 14 July 1977

I went into No. 10 feeling very low. I awoke at 6.45 and went for a morning
run to get my circulation going, and I am feeling very fit. But I am depressed
by the meeting with the TUC last night. I felt it physically as I walked in
through the front door of No. 10 – for the first time since we came in to
office in March 1974 I was going in without the TUC.

Before Cabinet I chatted with Michael Foot and Tony Benn. Ministers
were given a copy of the latest – third – draft of the White Paper just before
the meeting. They were all reading it outside the Cabinet Room. Several
people said to me that the introduction was better but it was still clear that
they were not happy with the general political balance. Nobody said what
was wrong; but I could tell that they did not think it was right.

This view was confirmed when Tom McCaffrey and Ken Stowe came
down from the study and said that the PM was in a bad mood. He had
woken up, read the draft, and said, 'It won't do.' He said that the Treasury
had 'still got it wrong and Bernard has not managed to make them get it
right'. He was not clear what was wrong, but it was 'too long, too technical
and too precise'. As he walked into the Cabinet Room he was looking very
bleak in the face.

News soon came out of the Cabinet Room that the White Paper had
been thrown out. It was decided that there would not be a White Paper at
all. Healey would make a statement, shorter and more general, tomorrow.

When Cabinet broke I talked to the Cabinet secretariat and they showed
me their formal notes of the Cabinet proceedings. (These are curious historical documents: large notebooks, written in longhand, by two people so
there is a double check. But what happens to these? They are the real historical record of what goes on in Cabinet.) It was clear that the discussion
barely got moving. Benn had just protested that the White Paper was bad
because it still seemed to blame the trade union movement. Then the PM
sank it, said it was not right, and that was that.

He then went upstairs to eat and I went off to the Reform to eat with
Peter Middleton of the Treasury. He is a very good man, very open, and
quite honest at admitting the Treasury's weaknesses. He was also highly
critical of the Bank, and warned me that the Governor was out to get more
independence, to rebuild the sterling balances, to turn the money supply
M/3 target into an IMF commitment (although it was never agreed with
the IMF last November) and finally to get interest rates up much more
quickly. He thought the institutional relations between the Treasury and
the Bank were very unsatisfactory, leaving the former with responsibility
without power. He thought Douglas Wass was worn out, with nothing more
to give, and did not like Rawlinson, but thought Couzens and Airey were

good men. He thought the economic advisers in the Treasury were 'appalling'. Dead right!

After Questions I went for a quick meeting with the Scot Nats and later I went downstairs to the Strangers Bar and bought a pint for John Smith. We went out on the terrace to drink, but it was very cold – very different from last summer (God, I am already a year older!). We discussed devolution: the only remaining problem between us and the Liberals is over the names for the Scottish executive. They want them called 'ministers' but the PM has so far vetoed this on the grounds that the only ministers are his in London!

I then went north by public transport to Camden School where I heard some lovely singing and recitation by Rachel (and others!).

Friday 15 July 1977

Into the deputy secs, where little emerged, except predictions of terrible problems on next year's legislative programme because having two bills for Scotland and Wales will run about forty-five days and direct elections and industrial democracy, etc. will take much more. Ken Stowe also reported on the plans to renew the Liberal alliance by the time of the Cabinet on the 28th.

I went over to the Commons for the Chancellor's statement. I could not get in because the box was full of Treasury knights but it was clear from the comments of MPs coming out of the chamber that it was going marvellously well. The package of sweeteners was far bigger than anybody expected, and Healey himself was in excellent form. He swept the floor with poor Geoffrey Howe. When they came out the Treasury men were all beaming and Ken Couzens said to me that he 'could barely restrain his Treasury colleagues from standing up in the box and cheering'. (He did not mention that the 'sweeteners' which had been so cheered had been in nearly every case opposed by the Treasury.)

The PM was quite pleased. He said, 'That settles the Party problem. Now we have to deal with the wages problem.' I also spoke to Benn and Shirley Williams. Each was very pleased, and stressed that it needed a Cabinet decision to alter the Treasury draft. No amount of co-drafters could have forced them to change their central policy, however slightly.

On the way out I discussed with the PM my failure to defeat the Treasury. He seemed quite relaxed about it, saying he had known what a difficult task it was. We also discussed his speech to the Durham miners tomorrow. I stressed that he must open by saying that the alliance with the trade unions was still operating. He agreed.

I went to lunch with Arnold Goodman, something we had long planned, but which has been delayed by his illness. We ranged over a wide field, but finally settled on Harold Wilson's honours list. He told me how he went to see HW and begged him not to do the list of names which was rumoured, and told him that Goldsmith was a Tory and a fascist. He told him it would 'do damage to his reputation from which he would never recover – and that has proved true'. He said that HW looked shifty and said the criticism was anti-Semitic. AG replied that on the contrary, the Jewish community above all would want these particular people not to be honoured. He got nowhere, but finished by professionally advising him not to honour anybody with whom he had a contractual arrangement – which is why Frost was struck out.

The conversation then changed and we talked about his dealings over the years with Marcia. He said that he had had virtually nothing to do with Marcia, but knew that she disliked him.

He added that 'but for Marcia, Harold Wilson would have been a good Prime Minister – not a great one, but a good one'. Implying that sadly he was not even good.

Sunday 17 July 1977

The *Observer* carries an article based on interviews with HW in which he attacked the security service – esp. MI5. He said that they gave wrong information about Judith Hart based on a bad photograph. Ken Stowe says this is untrue and that there was a tape of a phone call from Judith to King Street, Communist headquarters, in which she said something like, 'I can serve our cause much better if I don't attend this committee.'

The most incredible part of the *Observer* interview was the paranoia it revealed, all about the CIA, etc.

Monday 18 July 1977

I did not attend the 11 o'clock meeting on South Africa and Rhodesia – where David Owen's initiative for us to occupy and rule Rhodesia has been put on ice. The meeting had before them a long 'intelligence' report on the Rhodesia situation – and typically it showed no intelligence of Ian Smith's intention to call a general election, which he announced later in the day.

Had lunch with Robert Armstrong. We discussed the H. Wilson 'MI5 mistakes' story in the *Observer* yesterday. Robert told me there were suspicious things in the Judith Hart telephone tapes, but not conclusive of any bad actions, just foolish associations. And that there was never the least confusion of David Owen with Will Owen (who was prosecuted for spying in 1969). (Later Ken Stowe confirmed this: he looked up Michael Halls's record from the time and it referred to Will Owen from the beginning. HW has simply made it up.)

I spent almost the whole afternoon with Professor Cranford Goodwin from the Ford Foundation discussing setting up a European Brookings. We shall have a meeting in Paris in October.

I cleared my papers and came home early, about 8 p.m. The Liberals announced this evening that they will support the government in the economic debate on Wednesday so it looks as if we will get through comfortably till the autumn.

Tuesday 19 July 1977

Spent a relaxed morning. Cleared papers. Did some telephoning. Did some shopping ahead of the holiday.

Went to the City for lunch with Robert Fleming.

Back to the Commons for a quiet Question Time – Thatcher did not even get up. The PM was in much better spirits now he has finished with pay, did the miners speech, and thought out his 'confidence' speech for tomorrow.

I had a meeting with David Ennals and Alf Morris about mobility for the disabled. That is running into a lot of trouble – we need a higher allowance and a better vehicle available. We agree that, having got child benefits out of the way, this is the next priority. Ennals was preoccupied with the doctors, who are threatening to strike over pay.

Bright Jean Corston, from the SW Labour Party, came to see me to discuss Party matters. Then I had dinner with John Lyons of the Power Engineers. We discussed pay policy – his union will go for whatever Frank Chapple's* electricians go for – and Chapple will follow the miners. So the dominoes are all set up! He says we will have to take on somebody and beat them – he suggested the local authority workers. He did not recommend taking on his power engineers – agree there.

Home at 11.30.

Wednesday 20 July 1977

The PM spent the whole morning working on his speech. I cleared my papers
– the flow is much diminished at the moment – and then I held a Unit
meeting to discuss the general outlook. The rest are fairly depressed at the
outlook now that the trade unions have gone. Gavyn especially is pessimistic,
and thinks we shall get 20% inflation and higher unemployment.

The choices are to accommodate very high wage settlements; or to fight
them savagely by squeezing the money supply and squeezing inflation out
of the system with very high unemployment; or to try to compromise
between these, persuading some wage claims down, picking a fight with
one or two others, letting the unwinnable ones through. That seems to be
the only practical way to us. But I am not sure we can win an election on
any one of them.

I went out shopping over lunchtime, and only had time to snatch a sandwich before the big economic debate.

The PM opened very gravely to a quiet House. It was not a long speech
and he was rarely interrupted. So it was a good, serious, responsible performance, but it did not lift our people very much.

Thatcher was mixed. She was tough and good when ad-libbing, but
boring when ploughing through her text which was full of statistics.
Afterwards the PM felt he had made a mistake in being too low-key and
that he should have mixed it more.

I stayed for the vote at 10 – a clear majority of 30, and then came home
at 11 p.m.

Thursday 21 July 1977

Went in early for a 9 o'clock committee (Carol left at 7.30 for work and I
had to get the children's breakfast, lunches, etc.).

The committee was on the reform of the Official Secrets Act and the
new Official Information Bill. The civil servants had produced a draft much
more conservative than asked for by the last meeting of the committee. The
Ministry of Defence and the FCO had insisted that virtually all their documents were protected by maximum criminal sanctions – indeed some poor
clerical officer who forgot to stamp an irrelevant document as top secret
might be sent to prison for life. Also the drafters had completely changed
the basic criterion for an offence as agreed last time. Then, as with Franks,
it was agreed that only the documents classified top secret could be so
judged. Now they were suggesting that offenders could be charged irre-
spective of the classification – i.e. back to the uncertainty of the present
blunderbuss act.

Merlyn Rees introduced the main Home Office paper by dissociating himself from his own department's paper. He said it was terribly illiberal, would not stand a chance of getting through the Commons – and he would not support it. Michael Foot followed by saying that Rees's statement was the most remarkable introduction to a departmental paper he had ever heard – and he agreed with every word of it. He would rather have no bill than this one, and suggested a White Paper. He pointed out that this bill alone 'would bust the Lib–Lab pact – without even needing the help of the Chancellor'.

Healey then piled in very effectively, demolishing the Defence case for tight classification and criminal prevention. He said 'they want to lock up people because they cannot efficiently lock up papers'. David Owen supported him with a devastatingly radical attack on Defence and his own department. He said that the Foreign Office arguments were nonsense and he would deal with them.

Poor Mulley was left on his own, arguing for Defence that a more liberal case 'would create many difficulties' but unable to specify them.

In the end they decided to send it back to the drawing board, and followed Healey's argument that they should be looking for a small category that justified criminal prosecution, and ignoring the rest, rather than trying to get classifications to cover everybody. The meeting was in the beautiful Old Treasury Room in the Cabinet Office.

George Jones came in to see me and we discussed the current demoralisation of the universities.

I had lunch in No. 10. It was reported that the Tories had told us they would not support their John Cordle[*] if there was a motion down to expel him over the Poulson corruption. But Michael Foot is against expulsion. [Cordle was ultimately forced to resign from the Commons.]

Questions went very easily – the PM was in good form and Thatcher did not intervene.

Afterwards I stayed to hear Shirley Williams's statement on the education Green Paper, which she handled very firmly, then off to have drinks with Eric Roll[*] at Brooks's Club. He has now ceased to be a director of the Bank of England and is immensely critical of it for its technical incompetence. He said it is essential to replace Governor Richardson when his term is up – and not with one of his acolytes such as Kit McMahon (Blunden would do). Lever would be best.

I went back from Brooks's to the Commons and sat on the terrace with Gerry Fowler reminiscing about Northampton and discussing the education Green Paper.

Then I drove home at 9.30 to take Carol for a walk and discuss developments in the appalling NUT where she unhappily works.

Friday 22 July 1977

The PM left early to spend the day in Cardiff.

This is the end of the last full working week of the summer for me. I need a holiday. Although I have not been as hard-worked as previously, by the end of July I am always ready to go, and my temper gets very short. Also I do feel the political atmosphere has changed. It does seem that it might be too late for us to recover – going into our last full session with the wage and inflation question just breaking out again. Really we should have all the economic uncertainty behind us now. Those first eighteen months under HW were sadly wasted. I am not pessimistic, but I can see the pessimist's case.

Went to the Commons for a drink with Jack Ashley, and lunch by myself on the terrace afterwards. Everyone was talking of John Cordle's resignation – a far cry from the days when he came to No. 10 and sent the Political Office presents!

In the afternoon we worked on various briefs. Papers came in from the Bank of England and the Treasury on the exchange rate, reserves, interest rate, etc. Most interesting was a paper from the Chancellor, obviously very personal, saying that he favoured cutting sterling adrift from the dollar and letting it float upwards a bit – that is a change and very encouraging.

Came home at 8.15 and then to the Grahams for supper on the lawn on a hot and sultry night.

Monday 25 July 1977

The PM was off all morning at the TUC/Labour Party meeting – as a prelude to Wednesday's NEC meeting (for which there are 175 pages of documents: 120 pages from the Home Policy committee alone).

I went to the barbers for a very short 'summer' haircut; then to a meeting in No. 10 with Stowe and the two 'Macs' about setting up a new community service award scheme; and then to Sotheby's to sell my Epstein drawing because I am desperately short of money. Out to lunch with Edward Boyle at the Stafford. We discussed ideas for his proposed Reith Lectures – he is also coming in to No. 10 today to talk about top salaries with the PM.

Came back to No. 10 and made a series of phone calls. Then off to the ENM Cabinet committee to discuss Benn's scheme to give BNOC half a dozen licences to drill for oil ahead of the sixth round. The meeting ended at 6.15 and I went straight to the Treasury for two hours of whisky and talks with Douglas Wass. He was mainly concerned with selling the pay policy – and worried that we would lose some big settlements early on. We then got on to the Bank of England. He at first pressed the case for

Richardson to be renewed as Governor. I did not comment but did not agree. He then switched to another suggestion – John Hunt for Governor. At one stroke getting rid of the present Governor and Cabinet secretary! I liked that. I said it would all depend on how the Bank performed on interest rates – and added that I would like to improve my relations with the Bank. Wass admitted that many of his contacts in the City told him that the Bank was technically incompetent. He said the problem is that the Governor sees only great moral issues. It is no good discussing policy with him, it is all a question of honour and his dignity.

Went back to No. 10. Found another paper from the Bank. There are plans for interest rates to go up 'while ministers are away'. Another bounce.

Home at 9 p.m.

Tuesday 26 July 1977

My last day before going on holiday – and as always I feel guilty about going before the end of term. Definite looks of disapproval from some directions even though in fact the serious business ends today. I am writing this in the morning, because tonight we are at Patrick Wright's farewell dinner given by Jim and Audrey. Tomorrow we leave at 5 a.m. for France, four children, Carol and me and baggage in a small Ford Escort!

This morning was very important – an EY Cabinet committee on industrial democracy decided to delay publication of a White Paper, and then there was the 'seminar' on exchange rates and interest rate policy with the Governor of the Bank and the Chancellor. I noted that John Hunt says in his brief that the Governor views these meetings as 'for information' and 'not for decisions'. There are a mass of papers, and this could be very important, leading in fact to some crucial decisions – i.e. to stop depreciating sterling by tying it to the dollar, and to let interest rates rise. At the meeting they discussed separating sterling from the dollar and interest rates, where the Governor threatened a steep rise. The PM firmly said, 'No, that is a political decision.' And not just for information only!

Afterwards the PM said to Nigel and me, 'It is not good enough. We shall have to do something about unemployment in the autumn. Nigel, tell your Treasury friends to put their thinking caps on.'

III

Calmer Waters
(August 1977–July 1978)

Friday 27 August 1977

I returned from France on the evening of Thursday 26th after a glorious holiday in Ceret and then driving all the way home.

No. 10 was very quiet. Some of my staff and McNally and McCaffrey were still away. The PM was down at the farm at Lewes.

I spent the day reading a month's accumulated correspondence and some urgent papers. There had been a good deal of prime-ministerial activity while I was away – most of it on the wages front. The PM had chaired a ministerial committee and expressed a very firm line and still puts defeating inflation top of his list. When Albert Booth started to capitulate on the strike of air traffic controllers – Len Murray had come out in their favour – the PM put his foot down very firmly.

I heard reports of the Europe Cabinet which I missed. At the end the PM put the spotlight on Benn and asked him where he stood on Europe and if he was prepared to support the Cabinet's line, forcing him into collective responsibility. Shore apparently went along very well. So now Owen and the PM hope they have defused this and headed off the 'withdrawal' movement.

It was the late bank holiday weekend and so I was off on Monday. My brother Clem came down on Monday to discuss the sad end of his marriage. He grows more deaf and needs support.

On Tuesday I finished off a mass of papers about two feet high. Mainly detailed wage claims – there is an officials committee monitoring claims – Gavyn from the Unit attends. The rest of the week was not very exciting. Little new paper. The PM went away to Scotland for a long visit. The weather is terrible, lots of rain, but the PM is in good form and is getting a very enthusiastic reception – a great change from last year. In London I was bored and felt very flat. Mainly the lack of activity. But also other things. I need to move on. Fortunately the children are marvellous.

The political atmosphere is strikingly different from before the holiday. Our side is much more optimistic. The press is talking about us winning the next election – so are the Tories who are clearly getting jittery and warning the electorate not to be conned by a phoney economic boom. It is partly the way the economic indicators have moved our way – still massive inflows of currency (a billion dollars in August). The pound is up two cents. The payments in surplus. The tax reliefs paid this month. The PSBR well below the IMF ceilings. Massive gilt sales. But it is also the recess. Since it is in Parliament that we are weak, everything looks better when Parliament is not meeting – especially since the Liberals are all on holiday. Also the PM is doing well.

Monday 5–Tuesday 6 September 1977

The PM flew from Scotland to Blackpool for the TUC Conference. He had been working on his speech for some time but nobody knew what he was going to say. Nigel Wicks flew down on Monday evening and said that the PM had a wad of scribbled notes but he would not show them to anybody. He had been given briefs and draft sections but he was not using them. He had refused to show even Ken Stowe.

He did have a brief meeting with Healey in Blackpool on Monday and gave him some idea of his broad approach, but the Treasury had not been shown any draft. He also told Healey that we would have to reflate this autumn. They discussed announcing it either at Party Conference or when Parliament resumed.

I went to see Douglas Wass in the Treasury for two hours on Monday afternoon. We discussed the reflation, which he considered inevitable. He said he thought £2 billion between now and the end of 1978–79 would be appropriate. I said £3 billion, and we tacitly agreed it would be between the two. We agreed that we wanted it on income tax reliefs, not off in-direct tax. In fact we were very much in agreement. He particularly wanted me to help resist big pressures for increasing public expenditure, which I am happy to do.

He was jumpy about the reflation and said that 'if the economy is expanding too briskly by next autumn we shall have to claw some back'. I said that the danger seemed to me so remote, and so desirable, that if it happened I would take him out for a dinner and a bottle of wine. It was useful talk. But I still feel that Douglas is in some way burned out.

On Tuesday the PM made his TUC speech at Blackpool. It was excel-lent. Very firm. Not too long. Got the tone absolutely right. No lecturing. But no ducking. The reaction of the trade unions and in London was very favourable.

Wednesday 7 September 1977

The PM was back last night and upstairs in the flat in the morning. But as I was going out to lunch at 12.30 I ran into him outside Private Office and we had a long talk at the bottom of the stairs. We quickly got on to reflation and I pressed my point on direct taxation and against VAT cuts. I put to him the idea of a Christmas bonus for pensioners. He was not very keen – he said that you got no gratitude from those who got it, those who didn't became angry with you.

We also discussed H. Wilson and security. He asked if I thought HW really believed all he said, I said yes and no and quoted my image of the onion with many layers. I also said that I had learned that there was often something in the most bizarre things Harold said. He agreed. He told me he had had a very long talk with HW and tried to persuade him to shut up. He thought he would now do so. He also hoped that the *Observer* would call off the espionage hunt a bit.

He had been using Robert Armstrong, while John Hunt was away, and commented how equable Robert was. Back on politics, he said he was 'not going for an early election – not next year in 1978 if I can help it'. He thought we could hold on in Parliament and that the Liberals would stick with us. He then went upstairs to have lunch, and asked me to drop in and watch the TUC from Blackpool after lunch. This I did when I got back from the Connaught. I went up to the study. He was already watching. He said it was like following a Test match, ebbing to and fro. It was good entertainment, with Scanlon especially good in demolishing Clive Jenkins*. I asked him before the vote what he expected. He said Len Murray had promised a million majority. In fact it was three million, so we were very pleased.

We drank tea and chatted about other things. I asked him if he was nervous before a big speech like yesterday. He said, 'Always. Terrible. For two days it is like a big black cloud. I say to Audrey, "I cannot do it. I cannot make a speech. I've nothing to say." I also get irritable. But she keeps me at it. Then ten minutes beforehand I feel OK.'

We discussed the government. He asked who were the young people to bring in the Cabinet. I mentioned John Smith but said there was a shortage. He said the problem was he needed people with standing in the Party – there was only Foot, himself, Williams and Fred Mulley.

He then expressed concern about Shirley. He said she had lost all her steam, and several times fell asleep in Cabinet in the summer. He assumed it was something in her personal life but did not know what. He thought she would not talk to him about it.

He thought Owen was doing very well, Healey was the biggest member of the Cabinet, Foot had lost ground, Booth was very 'wooden', he liked Orme, and Shore did well but was far too wildly rhetorical. He also asked me whether I thought he bullied them too much. He thought he did and that they did not take him on enough.

He said he sacked Joan Lestor* for laziness, nothing to do with her being left wing.

I finally left after 5 o'clock.

Went to the theatre in the evening to the first night of Alan Bennett's *The Old Country*. Alan had kindly sent me free tickets. Very funny – and Alec Guinness brilliant. Sat behind Rex Harrison, whose young girlfriend coughed irritatingly throughout.

Thursday 8 September 1977

My 43rd birthday. Cannot say I feel too delighted about it.

Hal Sonnenfeldt came in this morning. He feels Jimmy Carter is about to have a very bad time politically. On Rhodesia he says we have made a mistake in pushing South Africa too hard, since we need the help of their pressure on Prime Minister Ian Smith.

Went to lunch at the Reform and then on to sell some books – sign of financial pressures and of the fact that all the bookshelves are full. Came back and found that Harold Lever was already with the PM, whose mind is clearly on the reflation.

I went with Bob Worcester to see the PM about opinion polls at 5 o'clock. The PM was at first very uninterested, but Worcester put the case quite strongly for doing polls in the whole period between now and the election. The PM agreed to try to get the NEC moving on it, but insisted he would 'not go to the kind of financial sources that Harold went to'. Apparently at the last meeting of the Campaign committee several left-wingers agreed that we did not need opinion polls but instead should consult a panel of a hundred shop stewards and Party activists throughout the country. That will guarantee we lose the next election.

In the evening the PM saw Healey about reflation. He asked him for three possible packages – direct cuts in tax, indirect and public expenditure! He did not express a preference for any one of them, but did say he wanted more expenditure on construction. Healey said there might be £1.5 billion available – which is much less than we thought.

I went to dinner with Harry Evans. He bought me a bottle of champagne to celebrate my birthday. He also told me some odd things about the case of the 'fourth man' recruiting undergraduates to communism at pre-war Cambridge. He said that they are convinced Donald Beevers was involved. He then said they had a list of other possibles – with Victor Rothschild and Maurice Dobbs high on the list.

Home at midnight.

Friday 9 September 1977

The PM was supposed to go to Bonn today to see Schmidt, but after a couple of phone calls yesterday it was called off because of the latest kidnapping in Germany.

Saw David Owen at the FCO for an hour over tea. He feels he has done enough on Rhodesia and we are in the best possible position. Even if nothing comes of it we have done the right thing and have a defensible position at the UN. He wants to get back into the economic field now, so we ranged over that one. He saw the PM this morning and they discussed it together – and David pushed the case for direct taxation cuts.

He obviously expects to replace Healey as Chancellor one day – but now thinks that this won't be before the election. He said he is fed up with the Foreign Office and does not like the smooth officials there. It was a very good meeting. I always enjoy seeing him. He is very open. And it is nice to deal with a politician who deals with one equally as of his generation, and not as a younger aide.

Went back to No. 10 and worked with Gavyn on our economic brief.

Then phoned by Harold Lever, very upset about the collapse of the Polish shipbuilding deal – we have lost £80 million of ship orders because of bureaucratic rigidity over financing in the Department of Industry, and because the FCO says we must not upset the EEC over subsidies. He said these civil servants, with their total job security, do not give a damn for unemployment in the shipyard, or anywhere else.

Home at 9.30. Off to the cottage for the weekend, and a charity football game at Cambridge on Sunday.

Monday 12 September 1977

The PM was away in Scotland. We had a quiet day in the Unit. I had a nice lunch at Grievesons, where they were extremely critical of the Bank of England.

Tuesday 13 September 1977

We spent all morning on a meeting of the Unit discussing tax reform. We concluded in favour of raising basic tax allowances rather than a reduced base rate because the latter is more regressive – harder on the lowest paid and less flexibly favourable to the married family. I spent much of the rest of the day on the Polish shipbuilding question. Harold Lever came back from Holland today and went straight in to talks with Healey and Varley and Joel Barnett to try to persuade them to do short financing in order to get the full order. I had dinner with him in the evening and he was furious with everybody. Too many are worrying about 'normal procedures' – people whose own jobs of course are totally secure.

The PM had a few meetings of no great importance and then went off to the farm – Private Office is trying to get him to take a bit more holiday before the parliamentary work begins.

Wednesday 14 September 1977

The PM away at the farm. Still very low-key at the office and I don't enjoy it.

Thursday 15 September 1977

Cabinet this morning. Beforehand I talked to Hattersley and Varley. Everybody is in a euphoric mood – today's *Telegraph* poll showed the Tory lead down from 11% to 4½%, and Thatcher falling well behind Jim. The change in the political climate is quite dramatic. This reflects the improved financial climate – currency strong, interest rates falling, high gilt sales, stock market going to new high. Even so real economy is in a bad way – high unemployment and zero growth. And massive sterling inflows over the exchanges – already over £1 billion this week. The Bank of England wants high interest rates and a low exchange rate so the money floods in.

Today the Chancellor also put to the PM his reflating plans. This was for a rise in allowances in November, backdated this year, adding up to £1 billion. But it would have to be announced almost immediately to give the Inland Revenue time. And a small public expenditure/construction package.

The PM was not happy with this. The timing was too quick. He wanted Cabinet to have time to discuss it – he said at least two Cabinets – and go over the options of direct tax and indirect tax or public expenditure. (He also objected to having this scheme bounced on him, with no paper in advance.) The PM said he wanted them to consider a reduced rate band. And said he would need time to go away and think about it.

Friday 16 September 1977

Deputy secs in the morning. Everybody clearly sore about the select committee report on the Civil Service which is highly critical of them – Hunt opened the proceedings by saying 'Welcome Wreckers' (the newspapers referred to civil servants as 'wreckers' of ministerial policies). The rest of the day was very quiet, except I was constantly on the phone about Polish shipbuilding orders.

Monday 19 September 1977

One point I forgot from Friday was that David Steel came in at 10 a.m. I had a long talk with him in the hall outside the Cabinet Room. He was quite confident about getting through his conference OK and seemed very relaxed about the Lib–Lab alliance. It was quite clear that he ought to be in the same party as us. He knows it. So does his colleague John Pardoe. I was not in the meeting between him and Callaghan but I gathered it was very friendly, with the PM showing him our latest opinion polls.

The PM was away all day today, opening the Brighton Conference Centre. I went in late and had a meeting at 11 a.m. with British Shipbuilders about the Polish shipping order. Phoned Helen Liddell in Glasgow to get some pressure from the Clyde yards.

Lunch with Richard Mayne* and Gwyn Morgan* at the EEC offices in Kensington Palace Gardens. In the evening to the American ambassador's reception. Talked mainly to David Basnett and Judith Hart about reorganising the Labour Party, and especially the NEC. The unions now mean to do something. Perhaps!

Tuesday 20 September 1977

A very quiet day. Most of the morning on the telephone about Polish shipping orders.

Lunch with William Plowden – who is not very happy with the nitty-gritty of machine tools in his new Whitehall job.

The PM came in after lunch. I heard that the three ministers – Varley, Lever and Barnett – had decided to go for the most radical solution on Polish ships – short-financing to get the maximum number of ships. This is risky, but a great triumph for Lever. I only hope it doesn't go wrong.

Delightful Gerry Fitt came in to see the PM in the afternoon and was quite hilarious. We discussed why Paddy Devlin* had resigned from the SDLP. Fitt said there were personal problems; Devlin did not get on with some of his political colleagues – 'He had thumped several of them – resorted to fisticuffs – and they did not like that.' But Gerry had a good point. Our present Irish policy is completely pro-Unionist – giving them a Speakers Conference, more Westminster representation, etc. The Catholic side had nothing. It is not getting power sharing. It has only one fallback position – the IRA. As Gerry said, 'If they are going completely orange, we can only go completely green.'

In the evening to dinner with Claus Moser. Discussed a European Brookings. He has been visiting ministers to discuss their statistical needs. Said quite the worst two in quality were Varley and Ennals.

Home at 9 p.m.

Wednesday 21 September 1977

The PM went to Italy today. Life in No. 10 still fairly low-key – and I do not like it. Not enough to do. Bored.

Had a nice lunch with Pat Nairne from Health. He was sharply critical of the English Report on the Civil Service, revealing some of the civil servant's contempt for parliamentary select committees. He was also confident that the PM was sufficiently conservative to be persuaded to ignore it. We also discussed the mobility allowance for the disabled – which I want raised to £10, the minimum level at which the disabled can actually buy mobility.

In the evening I went to dinner with Peter Hennessy of *The Times* at Odin's – a restaurant I like very much. He told me that his stories on the 'fourth man' communist spy trainer at Cambridge who had worked with Burgess/Philby, etc. had gone cold. Rees-Mogg had put him off the story. And MI5 had become scared that he had penetrated them. One possible line had led to Sir Anthony Blunt, keeper of the Queen's pictures. Another pointed towards a former head of MI5. There was a time bomb in there somewhere – and as usual a lot of public school homosexuality – including two top men sharing the same young man, one of them a fellow traveller, the other high up in our espionage service. All very messy.

Thursday 22 September 1977

My brother Clem came down from Manchester at lunchtime to discuss his marriage, which has broken up, and we spent the afternoon together.

In the evening I went out for dinner with Ted Croker of the FA, who told me some alarming corruption stories about Don Revie, England team manager.

Today Gavyn and I completed our paper on the reflationary Budget – for direct tax cuts and not either VAT or a reduced rate band.

Friday 23 September 1977

Went to the dentist in the morning, afraid that I would have to have my bad wisdom tooth out, but he did another massive filling job. Very tiring.

Lunch with Peter Gibbings of the *Guardian*. Warned me that journalist Peter Jenkins is 'a bit jealous of you'. I told him about the Bank of England affair and Jenkins fingering me as his source. Will never talk to that rat again.

Incidentally relations with the Bank are not good. The Governor is going around criticising the government and its policies, and Healey has had a row with him, telling him that all his policies are based on the assumption that the government policies will fail – hence interest rates kept too high all year, sterling too low, and a terrible price in gilt dividend costs.

News from the Polish shipping front is quite good. We have got six more big ships – because of the more flexible financing arrangements which Harold Lever and I have insisted on – this will save the Swan Hunter and Govan shipyards. The curious thing is how officials completely lost sight of the need to get shipping orders and became totally obsessed with obeying Brussels rules even if no orders were obtained. Departmental virility also came into it. Varley and Industry did not want another Chrysler defeat by Lever and No. 10. One exception was Ron Dearing* at Industry, who was helpful and enthusiastic throughout.

John Harris* came in from the Home Office to see me at teatime to get my support for a 'law and order' programme. I readily agreed, and I will start to work on the Treasury. He is curious – very able, intelligent and political. But he does a permanent personal imitation of Roy Jenkins – hands, lisp, the lot – which makes it hard to trust him as an independent person.

In the evening we were about to put in our Green Paper on reflation and have it sent to the PM in Italy when we learned there were problems with the Inland Revenue, who were refusing to do the extra work involved in cutting direct taxes – by revalorising allowances – this year (involving a back payment of £40 to the average married man in December). A great pity if trouble with the IR means that we have to cut VAT instead of direct taxes. So we kept back our paper and will put it in next week when the situation clarifies.

Incidentally, the PM had earlier decided to return today. But this morning on his way to meet the Pope, he looked up at the blue sky and said, 'I think we will go to look at the Bay of Naples' – and went off to Positano for the weekend.

Marcia's property tycoon friend Eric Miller shot himself in the early hours of Thursday morning. A sad end. He had probably done fraudulent things at Peachey Property, but he was a generous man. He was finally killed by his love of the political power stage.

Monday 26 September 1977

I went to see Anthony Rawlinson in the Treasury to discuss public expenditure next year. He is afraid that we will extract the Contingency Reserve and overspend. I told him that I wanted £10 per week mobility for the disabled and something extra on law and order. In return I offered to oppose the 'Christmas bonus'. The Treasury were also very worried about our pay policy – which is anyway running into difficulties since we cannot monitor and devise sanctions against thousands of individual settlements above the norm.

I came back and worked with Gavyn on revising our paper on the autumn Budget. We put this in during the afternoon.

I had Graham Greene in for drinks with a lovely Indian lady who was jailed by Mrs Gandhi and has now come here. Carol was in Bristol till midnight for the NUT, so I came home to be with the children at 8.30.

Tuesday 27 September 1977

Nothing happened in No. 10.

The PM read our economic paper, but asked for the tables to be redone, so we spent the afternoon on that.

Robin Butler came in at 6 and we discussed public expenditure, and I reported to him the deal I had tried to arrange with Rawlinson. He was sympathetic. But pointed out that the Treasury could never initiate expenditure – they waited for it to come from others. I said I would arrange that. Basically his fear is that if they agree to offer disabled mobility and law and order instead of a Christmas bonus, they will get the latter as well. I am afraid of getting none. So we agreed to work together. Interestingly he said that the views of the Policy Unit – and of myself – now figure continuously in internal Treasury discussions.

Then went to North St Pancras Labour management committee. What a bunch of wankers! – not a serious working person there. All part-time polytechnic lecturers. Terrible. Did not finish till 11.

Wednesday 28 September 1977

Woke up feeling as if I have incipient flu. So do not go for my regular morning run.

Attended the morning plenary discussions with the Irish. Very dull. Premier [Jack] Lynch* mainly put the complaints of the SDLP, but the Irish seemed to have few views of their own. We met at 12.20 and had difficulty in going on till 1 o'clock. Certainly Lynch and O'Kennedy, the new

Foreign minister, are not as impressive as Cosgrave and Fitzgerald were. Lunch was quite a cheerful affair, with the PM introducing his 'Irish Mafia' of McNally, McCaffrey and Donoughue. I did not bother to go to the afternoon sessions of the talks.

Took Denis Howell to supper at the Reform in the evening. Chatted about football and politics. Took a taxi home at 9 p.m. because very tired and my flu getting worse.

Thursday 29 September 1977

Feel groggy but go in early to work – still not able to take my early morning run. Wrote a section of PM's conference speech on North Sea oil.

Then Joe Haines phoned and asked me to see him. So I took a car to Kingsway and Joe and I walked around Lincoln's Inn Fields. He had *Mirror* reports that Jeremy Thorpe and ex-MP Peter Bessell had allegedly been in some conspiracy to get homosexual Norman Scott murdered 'by contract'. Bessell, who has been talking to the *Mirror*, claims to have arranged for a proposed prosecution of Thorpe – concerning an offence with a young boy – to be stopped by ministers – and this involved 'compromising' three Labour politicians – Frank Soskice, George Thomas and David Ennals. These were no more than allegations, on tape, by Bessell. But clearly the last involved the present government, and all involved the Liberals who are in pact with us. So Joe was very worried. I advised him not to say anything to anybody – though the *Observer* is going to serialise the 'Penrose' book on the Liberals and South Africa soon, and that may contain some of this.

I hope it does not damage us. Scandals are the nastiest experiences in politics: scared politicians, hysterical and self-righteous civil servants, and hypocritical lying journalists.

Went on for lunch at the Garrick with Claus Moser, whom I like more and more. He told me about three important regular senior civil servant meetings which usually determine government business: Mondays at noon with the Cabinet Office permanent secretaries, Hunt, Berrill, Moser plus Ken Stowe to discuss general matters; the top mandarins – Wass, Hunt, Allen and Palliser – who have lunch together every week; and the permanent secretaries weekly meeting on Wednesdays. I must discover what they decide.

Went back to No. 10 and Gavyn and I finished our second paper on tax changes for the next Budget. The PM has insisted that he wants a reduced rate band, even though it does not make as much sense, socially and administratively, as increasing allowances.

I saw the PM on the stairs just before he went to the country. He asked when I was coming to conference. Then I discussed taxes and pointed out that a reduced rate band must inevitably be more regressive than allowances. He said that it did not matter, it was 'only a matter of a few pennies. The important thing is the psychology of giving a reduced rate band so there is not the big jump into paying tax.'

I left at roughly the same time as him – 5 p.m. – and went home to bed, feeling very poorly. Carol was away for the night with her boss at an NUT Conference at Leicester. So the children came for a cuddle with me and then put themselves to bed.

Friday 30 September 1977

Feeling very rough. In late. Then off to Christie's where they sold my Alfred Vickers painting for £220. I am slowly and painfully cashing in my small art collection. Then lunch at Wheelers – delicious lobster – with CBS. Back to No. 10 to clear papers. Then home to bed with a fever. Does not look as if I will get to Brighton for conference tomorrow.

Joe phoned to say that the material on the Liberals scandal was even worse than expected, and much of it would be in the *Observer*. George Thomas had been alerted and said, 'So be it.' Other papers are now joining the hunt. Now there really are hordes of investigative journalists after Thorpe and HW. How sad. Blood sports.

Came home early with a heavy cold and feeling very rough.

Saturday 1 October 1977

I was due to go to the Labour Party Conference at Brighton today, but did not go because of my bronchial cold. Stayed in bed all through a lovely sunny September day. Irritating – for once I want to go to conference.

Sunday 2–Friday 7 October 1977

Labour Conference (written afterwards).

I was ill with a heavy bronchial flu on this weekend, staying in bed all day on Saturday, drinking and taking Disprins, while the rest of the family were away in Suffolk at the cottage. On Sunday morning I got up, packed, and went to Brighton on the train. It was a glorious sunny day, though I felt very groggy. We had three tables for lunch in the Grand Hotel. The food, service, weather, atmosphere – everything – was much more pleasant than last year at Blackpool. In fact I enjoyed the whole week enormously, despite my cold, and losing my voice for a couple of days, and never getting to bed before 3 a.m., twice not till 5 a.m.!

The routine was as usual for conference, nervy and tense till the PM's speech was over on Tuesday, relaxed and expansive after that. I had lunch with the PM on several days, and dinner twice, so there were many opportunities to voice points of immediate and more general interest.

One interesting discussion concerned ministers: the PM said that Varley was no good – but who could do Industry? He also criticised Bill Rodgers for being too rigid, dogmatic and provocative in dealing with opponents – 'he should be more subtle'. He regretted the lack of political sex appeal in the government – 'even the young ones are too grey' he said.

On Sunday lunchtime he came up to me and said he wanted me to work with McNally, Stott and McCaffrey on the speech. We did this in the afternoon – with John Cunningham as well. McNally had done an excellent first draft, with the help of Joe Haines. The PM asked for more on North Sea oil, so we included a piece I had written on that. When we met again late at night the PM made some more points, and dictated some parts of his own. He had worked hard on it in the evening, and makes far more changes than Wilson ever did.

At conference the left was generally very mild and accommodating. A left-wing line was being taken – no repetition of last year's militant wrecking! Brian Sedgemoor, Benn's PPS, explained to me that Benn could only make progress now if he gained support from the centre. He had captured the whole of the left and it had got him nowhere. He had no more power ministerially than ten years ago. This seemed to me a sensible analysis, and in fact all of Benn's actions and speeches during the week were in line with this.

On one occasion the PM asked everybody else to leave the room and talked to me about Civil Service reform. He asked me to do a study in great secrecy of the possible reforms in the machinery of government arising from the recent select committee/Michael English Report, and relating them to the need to replace Douglas Allen as head of the Civil Service before Christmas. I went off, phoned Gavyn to come down to Brighton immediately, bringing Fulton and the select committee report, and in the days ahead I sat for hours in my bedroom reading and writing in preparation of a brief to give the PM the following Monday.

I saw a lot of Joe Haines, who was full of the bubbling scandal about Jeremy Thorpe, and all the stories which journalists had got. Also saw a great deal of David Owen and Debbie, went to parties with them, and was sitting with him when the NEC vote was announced. He had 180,000 – very good and far more than I had expected – or the PM who predicted 'no more than 100,000'. The PM commented afterwards, 'Very good. But we must make sure he does not get big-headed.'

Every night I gossiped for hours in the Grand. The most appalling journalists were there – including the lice from *Private Eye*. But I quite enjoyed it – though till 5 a.m. on Friday was a bit late and I came home shattered. (This lack of sleep was also the reason I did not keep this diary on a daily basis as usual, or even at the end of the week – I was too shattered to do anything. But I kept notes.)

Incidentally, the PM's speech went superbly well, with a long standing ovation at the end. Afterwards he told us that he had lost the last page of his speech (it was left in his case). He said he was standing there in full peroration and in mid-sentence when he realised there was no more to come. So he made the final bits up. It sounded excellent. That is a true professional.

Monday 10 October 1977

Went into the office early to write the secret brief the PM asked for last week at Brighton – on Civil Service reorganisation and the appointment of a new head. I worked right through lunch and did not complete it till 7 p.m. I hope it is OK – it is a bit long, and I did not revise it. I am not usually a good 'first draft' man. But I was very keen to get it in tonight.

As I was leaving at 7.45 the PM came through the front door, back from Sussex where he had spent the day working on three boxes at the farm. He came in slowly, in that curious wandering way of walking he has, slightly lopsided, swinging his arms, looking vaguely around. He greeted me and I walked back with him to the tape machine. He was very pleased I had finished the paper for tonight.

Then home to supper with Carol and Rachel and to bed. Still have a cough so I am not yet back to my morning running.

Tuesday 11 October 1977

Cleared papers and then had a meeting with the Textile committee of the 1977 Industry Group – very interesting. They blamed the banks and lack of finance for much that was wrong, and for preventing them from investing and creating more jobs.

Lunch upstairs at No. 10. The PM came to join us. Told some stories. Then said he is an old-fashioned male chauvinist. He would not want a woman private secretary in Private Office (not that there is any danger!). We also discussed the problems of the falling birth rate and an ageing population, because I want to focus him on that for when the child benefits issue comes up again.

After lunch Helen Liddell phoned from Scotland and told me that the Catholic Church up there was reacting violently to the pro-abortion motion at Brighton. They are calling a conference to try to ask Catholics in Scotland to withdraw support from the Labour Party. These extreme pro-abortion women are mad, pushing it much too far, and jeopardising all our reforms in that area.

I told the PM this when we went in his study at 3.30 to discuss his future political engagements. We fixed another visit to Scotland. At one point the PM said we should plan on the basis of an election 'in autumn 1978 or the summer of 1979 – 'but of course we might be forced into one earlier'.

In the evening I read most of my backlog of paper from last week and did not leave the office till after 9.

Wednesday 12 October 1977

This morning there was a joint meeting of the Cabinet and NEC.

Bruce Millan – the Protestant Scottish secretary – came to talk to me about the Scottish Catholic situation and played it down saying there was not much in it, and nothing in the papers. In fact it is on the front page of the *Glasgow Herald* and is very serious.

Had lunch with Ken Stowe at the Reform. Discussed the Budget package – he thinks we are doing too little and should be cutting taxes more. He said Ken Berrill thinks this too, but won't be putting round a brief to that effect. Ken simply feeds it into John Hunt's brief to the PM. This is a diminution of the CPRS role and typifies the subordination of Ken to John Hunt.

Back to No. 10 where Gavyn and I discussed and finalised the brief for tomorrow's Cabinet on the autumn Budget.

In the evening to Gingerbread charity for a party to open the new One Parent Families headquarters. As a one-parent child, I try to support them.

Thursday 13 October 1977

I missed the start of an early Cabinet. But heard from Private Office that the PM is in a bad temper. He is complaining that the Chancellor's paper to Cabinet today – called 'The Next Steps' – is too detailed and tries to bounce everything through in one go. The PM wants to handle Cabinet more gently, taking them forward in stages – first the global total, then the argument of tax cuts versus public expenditure; then the particulars. As a result of his grumpiness he threw out most of the suggestions made on paper last night. He also wrote a furious note to John Hunt criticising the length – eighteen pages – of a summary of a Cabinet Office report on sanctions against Rhodesia. This report had been called for three months ago – and came in thirty-six hours before today's Gen meeting on Rhodesia. The PM said it was 'a discourtesy' to ministers and he was tempted to cancel the meeting.

Cabinet ended early at 11.45 and had accepted the broad preference for tax cuts partly because the package now contains £1 billion extra public expenditure for 1978–79, much more than we expected. The particulars of extra expenditure have not been settled – except that there will be a large slice of extra building construction (the Treasury is offering £300 million, DoE is requesting £360 million). The Home Office bid for extra on law and order, which I backed, was accepted at official level. The pensioners' bonus is still floating round, but not our bid on mobility for the disabled.

We had lunch at No. 10.

The Gen 12 on Rhodesia was at 3.15 and the PM asked for Ken Stowe and me to see him afterwards to discuss reform of the Civil Service and the appointment of a new head of the Civil Service. He first took us for a walk round the garden at No. 10. It was a lovely autumn evening. We discussed new flowers and shrubs. The PM said he did not like the big old tree which dominates the middle of the lawn and would like it cut down. I said Gladstone would have cut it down himself. We went back into the Cabinet Room to talk about the Civil Service. The PM said he felt the Civil Service Department was a failure. That a year earlier he had intended to divide the Treasury and put Tony Crosland in charge of the 'old' part and somebody else (Shore?) in charge of the public expenditure side. 'But Denis has come through his bad period now. He had not recovered all of his old bounce but he is doing much better now.' He knew about Crosland's health and knew he could not take the burden of the 'big' Treasury.

We discussed possibilities in this area, including creating a new Bureau of Budget and Manpower. We came round to a 'Prime Minister's Department' in No. 10. He said he was not happy with this because it could add to his bureaucratic burdens. Ken Stowe said he is against it and that the machine is against it. Jim asked me – and I said I was not in favour. He looked disappointed. He then explored the possibilities of strengthening the Cabinet Office, which he said really was part of No. 10. We did not oppose that in principle, but pointed out that the Cabinet secretary was already heavily worked and very powerful. Afterwards Stowe revealed that he and Hunt are out to stop Robert Armstrong becoming Cabinet secretary! – and to have Nairne there as second permanent secretary to make sure he got the succession.

In the evening Carol and I went out to dinner with Dick Ulmann, now with the *New York Times*, and enjoyed chatting of old Oxford times together – though it meant no bed till 1 o'clock.

Friday 14 October 1977

On the way to the meeting of deputy secretaries Ken Stowe showed me an explosive minute which the PM sent to the Chancellor last night. The Treasury had only informed him at 9.15 of tomorrow's issue of gilt stock, too late to do anything about it. Apparently the PM was furious. Afterwards I saw Douglas Wass in the Cabinet Office and told him they were crazy to treat the PM in this way, especially now when they need his help over the Budget. Wass said it was the Chancellor's fault – Healey had said there was no need to bother the PM!

Lunch with ex-Treasury man Derek Mitchell at Bianchi's. He was very critical of Wass – said he was dogmatic and would not listen to anybody else. That last year's sterling depreciation was entirely because Wass believed it necessary and ignored those in the Treasury who argued it would destroy wages policy. These clashes were why Mitchell left the Treasury.

In the afternoon Gavyn and I worked on a long brief on monetary policy – examining ways of controlling the inflows of foreign money and preventing it from going through into the money supply. We were finishing this right through a picnic I had in my office with the Plowdens and Carol prior to going to a lovely performance of *Bubbling Brown Sugar* at the Royalty. Home at midnight.

Monday 17 October 1977

In promptly at 9 a.m. Winter is here – foggy and cold and I still have a bronchial cough.

The PM had reacted well to both our briefs over the weekend. On monetary policy, he had asked the Treasury to come to next week's seminar prepared to discuss direct controls on inflows. He also particularly underlined and ticked our statement that higher interest rates should be the last resort. On textiles, he agreed to our suggestion that he should see the executives of the main retailers to try to get them to buy more British goods.

The rest of this morning I cleared my papers. Then had lunch at Brooks's Club with Robert Armstrong. We discussed police pay. The PM had summoned Merlyn Rees this morning to discuss it and had given him a bit of a rocket for being dilatory on this. Robert said that Rees is very afraid of the PM, is anxious to get his support on everything, and feels that he is not as close as he used to be.

Discussing Eric Miller, Robert said that the police have now discovered Miller's 'payments to clients of Goodman Derrick'. He said that the money was 'recently repaid'. On the Norman Scott social security file, part of the Jeremy Thorpe scandal, he said that Marcia had a photostat of it. Barbara Castle said that she produced it 'on higher authority' i.e. Wilson.

Joe Haines phoned and said that the Fraud Squad had asked to see him about Eric Miller.

Two officials from the Treasury's tax section came to see me about the Inland Revenue's recent crass decision to tax ocean oil divers directly instead of as self-employed. The result has been that all the divers are leaving to go abroad. A new growth industry is being destroyed. The PM has asked me to try to deal with it – so I will see the Revenue next week.

Finished my papers and came home at 9 p.m.

Tuesday 18 October 1977

Went in late – first to have a haircut, and then to look at some hi-fi equipment – Linn turntable and Naim amplifiers. I was taking advantage of the PM's absence in Germany to visit Schmidt.

A marvellous day for the PM to go – since last night the German commandos successfully stormed the hijacked plane in Somalia and killed three of the terrorists. Everybody is delighted, and the PM will be on the spot to share the Germans' pleasure. We have been advising the Germans on this and the PM told Schmidt not to give way under any circumstances.

Late on Friday night there was a secret meeting in the small dining room of No. 10 with the commander of the German commandos, who had flown in specially, and the officers of our SAS unit stationed at Bedford. Apparently they discussed tactics and weapons – and we supplied the Germans with special grenades. We also briefed them on the geography of Dubai Airport – where the plane then was. In fact they did not attack at Dubai (because the Dubai authorities insisted on taking part!), and the plane flew off to Somalia where the denouement took place.

We had lunch at No. 10 in the small dining room and heard all about the full story. In the afternoon I walked round St James's Park with Tom McNally discussing possible ministerial changes – we need some more bright young backbenchers in. Then working very hard on papers. An enormous mountain to clear.

A paper to put in on monetary policy. The Bank has sent in a very gloomy paper – money supply out of control, therefore must let sterling float quickly upwards and must push interest rates up high. This is last autumn all over again. There is a problem, but their remedies don't make sense. They always want high interest rates. Any crisis is an excuse. The heart of this crisis is massive high inflows of foreign money. The idea that this will be stopped by offering the foreigners even higher interest rates – 13% instead of 11% – shows the poverty of Bank of England thinking. Geoff Littler* told me that the Treasury is fed up with the Bank, especially because it totally ignores collective decisions and goes off and does the opposite.

Robin Butler came in to discuss public expenditure – which he is running under Tony Rawlinson. As an example of Treasury operating, he told me about last week's Treasury paper for Cabinet. The PM had asked the Chancellor not to put a paper, but to make an oral statement. Healey conveyed this order to the Treasury. But, as Robin said, 'The Treasury had a paper ready in final draft, so they decided to put it to Cabinet anyway.' They totally ignore ministerial instructions.

Had terrible typing problems. and did not leave No. 10 toll 10.15 p.m. Home very tired and looking old and grey and in need of sleep.

Wednesday 19 October 1977

I walked to Camden Town as part of my campaign to get fit again. Then slow Tube in and worked all morning on our brief for tomorrow – for the Cabinet on public expenditure and also brief for tomorrow's seminar with the Treasury and the Bank of England on monetary policy.

At lunch for Suarez and the Spaniards. I enjoy sitting next to Manchester United manager Matt Busby and talking football (more terrible stories about Don Revie). The PM made a moving off-the-cuff speech about how marvellous it is for his generation to have a democratic Spain which we can be friends with. Opposite sat Franco enemies Jack Jones, Michael Foot, Len Murray, Ted Willis, etc. all looking emotional.

Afterwards I spoke to David Steel in the corner of the pillared room. This morning's *Evening News* carried the story of the alleged Jeremy Thorpe plot to use a hired assassin to kill his homosexual ex-lover Norman Scott. I knew this was coming, but not where and when. Now it will all start rolling and God knows where it will end. I warned David that the press will exploit it in the hope of destroying the present Liberal Party and end its pact with Labour – so bringing down the Labour government. He was aware of this but thought it would be OK. I pressed him on whether any of the present Liberals had been involved in a cover-up. He insisted no. But it is clear that we shall have to give him support when the flak really starts to fly.

After lunch the two Toms and I met in the Press Office to discuss the threatening scandal. There is a journalist/police pincer at work: one prong involves the Thorpe affair, and may involve any ministers who protected him from prosecution. The other prong is the Eric Miller affair. The question is, will these pincers close, damaging the present government or not. We don't know.

A third prong is Tory MP John Cordle. Joe told me that his Fraud Squad interviewer was very interested in Cordle – apparently alerted by that *Observer* piece about Cordle. It looks like a stormy winter.

I finished off the briefs with Gavyn – more papers were coming in from the Treasury and from Harold Lever – up till the last moment. Then I went off to the reception at the Spanish Embassy. A beautiful house full of lovely pictures and tapestries. Had a long chat to Harold Wilson – the longest since 1976. He told me about his book on British government which is due out in two weeks. He looked fatter, less shrunken than of late, but with dark rings round his eyes and definitely haunted. He must sense the 'pincers' closing in. But I still like him. He was warm to me.

Home at 9.45. Carol is ill in bed.

Thursday 20 October 1977

Cabinet at 9.30 this morning on public expenditure for 1978–79. I was in at 9 a.m. and went downstairs before Cabinet where I had a long chat with Shirley Williams about the abortion issue. She thinks it is so serious that the PM will have to make a statement to reassure our Catholic voters.

Cabinet apparently was difficult. There were big pressures for more public expenditure, and Healey and Barnett did not resist very well. The PM was playing the Treasury's hard role for them. In the end there was an extra £160 million.

We all had a quiet lunch upstairs at No. 10. Ken Stowe came in late, having spent forty minutes trying to deter David Ennals from making a long statement to the press about the missing Norman Scott social security file. Apparently Ennals was very jumpy.

At 2 p.m. we assembled in the Cabinet Room for the monetary seminar, with the Governor and Kit McMahon (who used to be the PM's tutor at Nuffield and who the PM recommended to the Bank Governor Leslie O'Brien for this job. The PM said to me, 'He used to be scruffy and independent-minded, but now he is smart and does not disagree with Gordon Richardson on anything, which is a pity.') Ken Berrill also joined in for the first time – so now the Cabinet Office has Hunt and Berrill and a secretary taking minutes. They are gradually taking over. This is how a No. 10 initiative becomes 'regularised' by the Hunt machine.

It was a fascinating meeting on controlling inflows of sterling and whether to raise or lower interest rates. The general drift was towards sterling appreciation – with Berrill and Wass against (1960s Treasury devaluers?).

The PM is against appreciation of the currency and said so. The Governor is obsessively committed to sterling appreciation and higher interest rates. Most interesting was the reported clashes between Chancellor Healey and his permanent secretary Wass. They disagreed on nearly everything. One nice thing at the beginning was when the PM opened by reading my Green Paper showing a table of changes in the indicators since the last seminar and said it was very interesting and he wished I had circulated it to everybody. A lovely boost for morale – and all credit to Gavyn who put the statistics together in a flash.

We broke up at 4.15. The PM said how fascinating he found it. He then went off to Cardiff.

I went back to the office to debrief Gavyn. Read more of the Norman Scott affair as it unrolled in each edition of the newspaper. The *Evening News* editorial makes it clear that their concern is to destroy the Lib–Lab pact for political reasons. Joe phoned to say that the *Observer* might be bringing forward their stuff on Wilson and the security services. The whole of Fleet Street is buzzing and thinks it is on to a Watergate.

Then I went for drinks with Gavyn Lyall*, who is writing a novel about murder at No. 10!

Home at 9 p.m.

Friday 21 October 1977

A much easier day. I drove in to the office early in pouring rain. Cleared my papers and went to the 9.45 meeting of deputy secs in John Hunt's office. These meetings now reveal much less to me than they used to – possibly because I now know more. We arranged another monetary seminar for next Friday.

I decided to go home in the afternoon because I am very tired and still with traces of my bronchial cold so I worked right through lunchtime clearing papers and afterwards home, collecting the twins from school on the way.

It has been a fascinating week, tiring but very satisfying, and feeling much closer to the PM. He is first class. I only hope that the Thorpe business does not damage us.

Monday 24 October 1977

Went for a long run over the Heath – my first in three weeks because of this damn cold – on a glorious autumn morning. We put the clocks back yesterday, so it was quite light and sunny at 7.10 as I loped up over Parliament Hill. The trees around Kenwood were like coloured cushions. I met Michael

Foot at the top and we walked a while discussing the problem of police pay – where he does not want to give in.

I was alone at home, since Carol was in Suffolk with the children – and the car! So after breakfast I walked to Euston – two miles and then took a bus from there. I have missed my exercise.

I saw the PM in No. 10 just before he went to the liaison committee. He asked me about the 'scandals' rumoured in the press. We walked to the front door together, and he asked me to find out all that I could. So I saw Joe Haines after lunch, picking him up from Holborn station and bringing him back to No. 10. Joe told me about the police interview with him. They told him that Eric Miller's Peachey had provided – in November 1975 – big money to Goodman Derrick clients but this was repaid once Miller got into trouble. Joe also elaborated on the story about the Liberals buying honours. This is a pretty wild rumour, but may go around since Thorpe and buying honours are all topical.

I went into the Cabinet Room to brief the PM on 'scandals'. I told him of the four main stories in the Pencourt book: Thorpe murder plot; Home Office cover-up on suppressing Thorpe's prosecution; Scott's missing social security file; and the 1967 right-wing coup. Then the extra rumours about Eric Miller's Peachey and selling honours to the Liberals. He analysed them and saw little for us to worry about – unless Ennals or George Thomas really had as ministers done a cover-up at the Home Office. Nothing had come to him while he was Home Secretary. He could see no area of PM's responsibility as yet. He would not see Wilson. He found it all too incredible and could not believe it. We agreed to keep alerted and I would warn him if anything else came up.

Feeling very good today. All that exercise worked.

Tuesday 25 October 1977

The PM was off all day on a visit to Portsmouth. I saw him briefly before he set off and when he returned, but not for the discussion of anything serious.

At coffee time I had in the Inland Revenue to discuss the taxation of North Sea divers – which is driving them all offshore. Actually the Inland Revenue's case is clearly correct in law, if regrettable in its policy consequences.

Lunch at Manzi's with Graham Greene. Enjoyable as ever. He tells me that a *Telegraph* journalist named Dobson is hawking a book round Fleet Street dealing with the 'East European' Mafia and HW.

In the evening Carol came in to No. 10 and then we went together to a party in Kensington given for the group which went to India together last November.

Home at midnight.

Wednesday 26 October 1977

Budget day. We all feel cheerful because it is such a change to be giving something away at last. Though nobody will be surprised since the Treasury has leaked everything to the press – Sunday's *Observer* had every minor detail.

Had an interesting lunch with Kit McMahon of the Bank of England at the Reform. We went over the whole policy area. They have no idea where the pound will go to if we free it, and it looks like a period of instability ahead. I told him that what we above all did not want was higher interest rates and that the Bank must convince ministers that they do not want them. We agreed that we must meet regularly in order to avoid 'suspicions'. I mentioned their bad behaviour over the BP shares – he said he 'did not wish to discuss the BP shares'.

In the evening Carol and I went to a delicious supper party at the Freynes – he is economic counsellor at the French Embassy. It was given for Michel Rocard*, Mitterand's Shadow Chancellor and a very clever man [future Prime Minister of France]. Michael Foot, Roy Hattersley and Harold Lever were there. I had a long talk with Foot, who was more open and friendly than I have ever known him. When the French commented on the improved situation of the government, he said, 'Yes and we must thank this young fellow – his paper to the Cabinet at Chequers last summer lifted our morale and showed we could pull through, just when we were falling apart.' We stayed till midnight enjoying too much good food and wine. A very pleasant evening, and the high morale of the government pervaded the room.

Thursday 27 October 1977

Another glorious day. This is the best, sunniest, driest and most golden autumn I can remember. Each morning I run on the Heath and the fresh smell lifts my spirit.

The PM had a Defence committee and Cabinet this morning. I worked on papers.

Lunch in No. 10. The PM came to join us, and we had another fascinating chat. Philip Wood from Private Office said that he feared the North

Sea oil would lead to de-industrialisation, through a strong pound and our uncompetitive industry slowly being killed off by foreign competition. The PM disagreed totally. He said he thought that the new spirit of confidence and optimism would lead to more investment and better standards. He thought the country had an exciting time ahead. (Perhaps this optimism reflects the government's better prospects – today's Gallup poll shows us level pegging with the Tories and Jim miles ahead of Thatcher.)

Reaction to yesterday's Budget has been OK – nothing sensational, just another small step forward. But the foreign currency inflows are still high.

In the early afternoon Gavyn and I finished off a paper for the PM for tomorrow's monetary seminar – basically conceding appreciation of the pound, but suggesting ways of trying to modify it.

I went off to Suffolk in the afternoon to collect the children who are at the cottage for half-term. The countryside looked beautiful, and I slept overnight.

Friday 28 October 1977

Up at 6.45 at the cottage, with the sun breaking through the mist and still roses in the garden and leaves on all the trees. Drove the four children up to London, unpacked, showered and changed, and then into No. 10, arriving at 10.50 a.m. for the 11 o'clock seminar. The meeting was good, though not as fascinating as last time, because we had been over the ground before. The PM again expressed his fear and reservations about strong sterling, and said the onus was on the appreciators to put the arguments. Dell was even stronger, passionately arguing against appreciation when our economy is so uncompetitive. The Governor and Healey said appreciation was inevitable and desirable. Lever said OK – but not higher interest rates. At one point the PM was very stern in telling the Governor that he had never answered Lever's point that it was crazy to fight inflows by offering the foreigners even higher returns on their money. Finally it was agreed to let sterling appreciate – and with the gilt issue on Monday. The PM said if you are going to do it, the sooner the better.

What is interesting about this seminar was that it has now become a Cabinet committee. Today there were five ministers and Ken Berrill, John Hunt and a Cabinet Office secretary and me. This is an important constitutional development if maintained. For the first time, monetary policy has become part of collective Cabinet government.

Worked on papers all afternoon and home feeling very good. But next week Parliament meets!

Monday 31 October 1977

Today opens with gales and pouring rain, so I don't go for my normal morning run. Took my time going in to work and arrived late. The PM did not arrive from Sussex till after lunch.

No. 10 was very exercised about the *Observer* leaks of last week's decision to let sterling appreciate. Last night in Singapore and Hong Kong there was a lot of buying, and these people had made a fortune by 10 o'clock this morning – when sterling was up by six points.

I had a snack lunch in the Cabinet Office (where John Hunt's private secretary told me how active Hunt is among the Roman Catholic mafia).

Gen 89 met at 3 o'clock to discuss the CPRS report on overseas representation. I had arranged for Tom McNally to attend this – and he had put in an excellent brief for the PM supporting reform. But Tom was not back from lunch so I went in. The committee discussion was very desultory. The PM confessed he was not clear about the CPRS proposals and called on David Owen to attack them, which Owen did, but in a very low key. Edmund Dell intervened characteristically to say that the status quo was satisfactory and the FCO did a splendid job. Ken Berrill was curiously defensive and did not defend his own CPRS case at all: he simply stated that a merger of the home and overseas Civil Service was inevitable, and they might as well accept it at some point.

The PM then got a bit impatient and began to attack the FCO, saying it was over-graded and most of them worked there because they loved the expense allowances. He said, 'It is a Rolls-Royce department – which likes a Rolls-Royce style of life.' He called on Ken Berrill to make a stronger case, but he didn't. At this point David Owen picked up the ball and ran. He said that as Foreign Secretary there was a lot in the CPRS report he agreed with, many reforms he wanted to introduce in his department. He waved a list of embassies which were overstaffed, and emerged commendably as the most radical reformer in the room, a change from his initial reaction of indignant hostility. Afterwards I walked out with David and we went back together to his room at the Foreign Office. He was very angry with the decision to revalue sterling. He also thinks that pay is going wrong. We talked for twenty minutes, and then had to break off because Kissinger had arrived to see him, but agreed to meet again.

It was curious walking up the grand wide staircase of the Foreign Office with the Foreign Secretary. I have done it countless times at No. 10 with the PM. But the FCO is much more impressive, and I had never actually walked up with either David or with Tony Crosland.

Back at No. 10, the PM had the three senior permanent secretaries – Allen, Hunt and Wass – in the Cabinet Room to discuss changes in the

Civil Service. Ken Stowe reported to me afterwards that the PM never showed his own preference at all. Wass was for the status quo. Hunt made his case for a Bureau of the Budget, within the Treasury or without. Allen said that the changes post the Fulton Report had been a terrible mistake and wanted to go back to pre-1968. Allen also said personally he had been bitterly disappointed at the Civil Service Department job. He also complained of lack of access to the PM.

Home at 9 p.m. and played with the girls and then to bed to read my hi-fi magazine.

Tuesday 1 November 1977

The PM spent the morning in his study working on his speech for the Address. I worked in the office, still irritated by this chest cough. But the weather is glorious again, and was marvellous when I ran on the Heath at 7.15 this morning.

We heard the bad news that the miners had voted against the productivity scheme in mid-morning. The PM apparently said, 'That should help to keep the pound down.'

I went to lunch with brokers Grieveson Grant discussing monetary policy. They were highly critical of the Bank of England and said it kept interest rates too high. Worryingly they said that the appreciation had not deterred foreigners and their money would keep flooding in and would take the rate through $2 – which is what the PM feared.

I went home early at 8 p.m. and went to bed early to write this and to listen to music – cuddling Paul who came upstairs to join me.

Wednesday 2 November 1977

I met Michael Foot on the Heath at 7.25 this morning. It was a glorious autumn dawn, and as I ran up to the brow above the top pond I saw this familiar figure, walking with every limb waving sideways and his stick swinging, his head down forward and the long grey hair flowing. We walked some way discussing the miners. He said that in his Welsh constituency even the moderates opposed the proposed productivity scheme. But he did not think they would vote to strike. He then went on to discuss the steel problem – no demand, massive over-manning, and either big redundancies or a huge deficit.

Little to do in the office in the afternoon. I was bored and read a Brookings Institute book on 'red tape'. Some marvellous examples of appalling bureaucratic waste – sadly it is much worse here. I went to see the PM in his study at 6.30, where he was working on his speech for the Address. I informed him that the Bob Worcester poll showing us only 2% behind the

Tories has been delayed till Saturday by the *Express* because they don't want to encourage Labour.

He spoke about his attitude to the miners and his intention to stay firm. He said he would 'rather go down to defeat on a big issue like this than crumble bit by bit'. I agreed, but warned him not to get 'into a Heath position in a corner'. He said, 'I may get into a Heath position.' I warned him that it must be different – less rigid, and no question of 'teaching the miners a lesson'. He agreed. 'We are not against any union. We are against inflation.'

He then discussed his own earlier political position. Said he was totally loyal to HW in 1964–67 and believed that he was the best PM he could have. HW dropped him in 1968 and he, JC, 'felt hurt' and 'did sulk'. He genuinely opposed 'In Place of Strife', not for leadership reasons, but because he 'believed it was wrong and was not on'. When he looked as if HW was going to fall, he then decided he might as well have a go for the leadership. When HW compromised, he genuinely gave up and wanted to unite behind HW in the election. After that his relations with HW improved.

He clearly would like to make Hunt head of the Civil Service but doesn't know what that would mean for the CSD. He said that he would move Healey after the election, presumably to the Foreign Office, then we would have to do something about the Treasury being a separate Bureau of the Budget, because nobody else could carry that burden as Denis incredibly has. I suggested David Owen for Healey's successor and he did not demur.

I then went to the Eve of State Opening party to listen to the PM read the Queen's Speech. A happy occasion with high morale everywhere. The PM gave them a little talk on how well things were going; but problems ahead; must stand firm against inflation; no early election because must get devolution through.

Afterwards I left with David Owen and discussed appreciation of sterling, which he still opposes. We considered how to get him in on the act.

Then home to an early bed.

Thursday 3 November 1977

Drove in late – and hit the most terrible traffic jam resulting from the State Opening of Parliament. Finally parked off Pall Mall and walked. [Such parking was then possible and free.] Unit meeting on how to use the North Sea oil revenues and I think we will get a good paper from it.

Ken Stowe told me that Palliser and Hunt are worried about me getting on the CPRS/Foreign Office officials committee on the CPRS report because of my 'line with Tessa Blackstone and David Owen'.

In the afternoon we went across to the Commons to hear the speeches on the Address. Neither leader was at best. Thatcher was brief and thin. The PM rather verbose and avuncular. The most significant factor was the subdued tone of the Tory backbenchers. They scarcely cheered when Thatcher stood up and sat down. They have clearly lost the scent of power.

Afterwards I had tea with Margaret Jackson and we discussed her ambitions for the NEC. She had been to the T&G panel to try to get their sponsorship. She would be very good on the NEC – leftish but sensible.

Home early.

Friday 4 November 1977

I went to the Civil Service headquarters in Pimlico for a meeting of the governing body and by the time I got back after lunch the PM had left for Sussex. It was a lovely day and he must have wanted to get to the farm as soon as possible.

The Civil Service meeting was quite interesting – I continue to press for a new French ENA-style higher management training in the whole public sector.

Sat with Douglas Allen at lunch and he was quite open about his disappointment with the CSD job: he would not have taken it if he had known, and he deeply regrets not having taken an outside job in 1971. He does not want John Hunt to become head of the Civil Service 'because he wants it so much'. He blamed Wass for much of the troubles in the Treasury – 'narrow, a mathematical technician, bad with people'. Lots of jealousies among these mandarins.

I cleared my papers after lunch and then went home early.

Monday 7 November 1977

Late last night John Lyons, leader of the Power Engineers, telephoned to complain that Tony Benn is refusing to take a stand, or to declare a position, on the unofficial strike in the power stations. The union have denounced the strike. The power engineers and managers are 'blacklegging' to keep the stations running. They are doing this in defence of the government's pay policy – yet the government, or Benn, won't take a stand. This is because Benn as always is trying to play it both ways, to run government policy without offending the militants.

Early this morning I telephoned this message to the PM. He reacted immediately and telephoned Benn, telling him he had to make a statement. A meeting of ministers was fixed for this afternoon, EY (prices) which the Chancellor normally chairs but this time the PM will take it. The meeting was mainly on the miners, and how to handle the next stage now that the productivity deal has been rejected by ballot. But they also spent some time on the power strike.

Just before lunch I talked to John Lyons and he was very firm, saying that unless the government declared its position he would make a critical public statement, and possibly pull out his members. I minuted this to the PM – and he read it out at Cabinet committee. By the evening it seemed as if the unofficial strike is collapsing. A meeting is fixed for tomorrow which should see the shop stewards climb down. The Cabinet committee's decision to stand firm was conveyed to the media at the lobby briefing afterwards, and was passed on to all the trade unions at about 4 p.m.

Had lunch with Brian MacArthur, news editor of *The Times* and a very decent man. Says they cannot shift the editor, Rees-Mogg, 'who is destroying a great newspaper'. He also told me that Dick White, ex-head of MI6, was the source of Peter Hennessy's article on Donald Beevers and the Cambridge communists who trained spies pre-1939. It was clearly a delicate plant, to mislead Peter (perhaps to discredit him?), but especially to flush out some others. Blunt?

The PM saw Abba Eban* of Israel – mainly because the FCO so strongly and predictably briefed him not to. Then he went off to the Russian Embassy. I decided not to, and instead went home early, at 8 p.m., to see the kids to bed, to write this, and to read a little.

Tuesday 8 November 1977

At 10.30 there was a meeting of EY. The main item was Tony Benn's paper on energy conservation. This was very good and important. He rightly pointed out how pathetic it was to spend only £20 million on conservation, when the energy return is enormous. It is disgraceful that we have built two million council houses and have done nothing to insulate any of them.

Afterwards I went to the front door with Merlyn Rees. He said how sad it was that Herbert Morrison had so little support from his first wife – and how valuable his own wife's support is (Colleen Rees is a lovely Irish lady). He thanked me for my support over the extra Home Office law and order expenditure. He also mentioned the machine opposition to Robert Armstrong succeeding John Hunt as Cabinet secretary.

Going back in I ran into the PM and we talked for fifteen minutes on the stairs. He was going up to lunch (today Sarah our cook provides for him, but on days when Sarah is not in, and if Mrs Callaghan is not there, he actually as Prime Minister has to cook himself an egg in the flat, since there is no other help). We discussed the power workers and the firemen – who are next to go on strike. He felt the pay policy was going quite well, though we both worried that 10% is becoming a norm – so we are back with the differentials problem again. I suggested to him that we might do another social contract deal with the unions next spring when inflation will be very low – just a one-year deal to carry us over the election. He said that he would think about it. In any case he said we would have to be tough, and next year's norm would have to be about 5%.

The first parliamentary Question Time of the session. The same old charade, soon degenerating into a wrangle about procedure for questions.

I dictated a long minute on the taxation of divers; then out to sell some books in Charing Cross Road to raise a few more pounds, then to Graham Greene's for supper with the British Council. I pressed them hard on their excessive administrative tail.

Home at 11.30.

Wednesday 9 November 1977

A fairly quiet day. I went in quite early and finished the newspapers and the papers in my in tray. Had lunch upstairs in the Cabinet Office canteen. The Cabinet Office mess is now closing down for ever, except for sand-wiches. It was an elite club, subsidised on the Cabinet Office vote, and that elite subsidy can no longer be sustained in this economic climate.

Went back to the Unit to discuss my scheme for the next big Unit paper comprising a proposal for a new one-year social contract with the unions on pay for 1978–79 (5%); a price freeze in the public sector for 1978–79; and a paper on the use of North Sea oil revenues.

This could make a package which would carry us over the election in 1979, with inflation down to around 6%, and the Tories having nothing similar to offer.

The power strike took a dramatic turn this afternoon. The militants took a hard line against our hard line (the CEGB had refused to pay them while on strike and we supported that – although Benn had tried to encourage the strikers by making an announcement to the effect that their conditions (pay, etc.) 'presented no problems to the government'. I have encouraged the PM in this hard line on not paying the strikers, and if it provokes fresh blackouts I shall get some of the blame. But I do not mind. It is right not to capitu-late to unofficial strikes. And I believe that if we hold firm they will crumble.

Collected Carol from Rachel's school and home by 8.30 which was very nice and unusually early – played with the children for an hour.

Thursday 10 November 1977

Very good news on the power strike. It crumbled. The workers went back, leaving just the Yorkshire militants isolated – quite a victory. But the role of Tony Benn was appalling – actually encouraging the militants and siding with them against the CEGB. Curiously Tom McCaffrey was on the side of Benn and went round denouncing John Lyons. Tom actually supports a capitulation on virtually everything – he is taking the same line on the firemen – at any price.

Cabinet this morning is mainly on pay. The PM came away rather depressed. Lots of ministers attacked his firm line and said it was leading to confrontation. He was worried by this and came up to me afterwards and said that 'we must not get ahead of public opinion, you know, Bernard'. I think this was meant for me as a hardliner over the power strike. I agree with him on not provoking confrontation. But we cannot start giving way now.

He asked me for information on the polls from 1973–74 when Heath was fighting the miners. As expected they showed public opinion right behind the government – till it got tough and uncomfortable, then public opinion switched to wanting a settlement.

I went home fairly early in order to go on to my local ward party. Surprisingly enjoyable, and stayed till 11.30.

Friday 11 November 1977

Came in early and cleared papers before going to deputy secs. There is going to be a fresh move to get alongside the trade unions for another pay deal (I had suggested this to the PM a few days ago, and now it came up at Thursday's Cabinet). I told John Hunt that the Unit was preparing a paper and he looked agitated and asked if we could work together – 'not so that we can nobble your ideas,' he added defensively. In fact I have already set the Unit to work on a package – North Sea oil revenues diverted into jobs and industry and a price freeze in return for a pay deal next summer. Saw Douglas Allen who thinks it is very important to strengthen the quality of officials and junior ministers at the Treasury – he is very experienced.

The PM has reacted marvellously to my minute on North Sea divers' taxation. He says he wants no nonsense – the law must be changed and he wants me to sit in on all meetings between the Treasury and the Inland Revenue. That goes round in a minute and will cause some officials' blood pressures to rise.

In the Unit I did two minutes on opinion polls. David Lipsey did one on the use of North Sea oil revenues. On this, Benn and Healey have failed to agree a paper for the liaison committee. Benn wants to put in a separate paper full of socialism and alternative strategy, which can then be leaked to the Party so the activists vote for him. We are suggesting a compromise.

Then I went home to bath, change, collect Carol and go to a very nice dinner with Jack Black, my marvellous solicitor.

Monday 14 November 1977

Saturday was interesting. David Steel at his own suggestion came home to tea (with his assistant, Archie Kirkwood, who is a nice lad and seemingly a Labour sympathiser), arriving having driven from Scotland. It was not clear exactly why. Obviously he was interested in devolution, and why Jim has not made it a vote of confidence. I explained to him how that could alienate the Scot Nats and the Tory rebels. But in general we chatted with nothing precise at all – except that he was interested in doing Liberal polls and wanted to know all about mine.

He stayed for a couple of hours, drinking tea by the fire. He is very nice. He is clearly planning for the next election, and said his main problem – and interest in the polls – was how to win the Labour vote in the marginals where Labour came third. He agreed with me that there was no future in the Liberals continuing in the future as they had in the past, winning a few by-elections but never getting near power.

Monday. A quiet day. I went hi-fi shopping all morning, since the PM was not in. Returned at lunchtime and found a flood of papers. The PM had responded well to our minute on North Sea oil, and sent off a minute to Healey and Benn saying that unless they produced very low-key 'questions and options', with no answers, he would replace them with a paper by the Policy Unit. This produced a rapid phone call from Benn to the PM saying that he intended to compromise with Healey anyway and there would be no problem with the paper. So our intervention succeeded. Even so I put Gavyn and David Lipsey on to preparing a draft paper for the liaison committee in case the Benn-Healey enterprise goes wrong at the last moment.

Came home early, which I do more often now, since I particularly enjoy the rare pleasure of seeing the children before they go to bed.

Tuesday 15 November 1977

In early and cleared papers before going to the Gen Cabinet committee on the crisis in the steel industry. The Steel Corporation is £500 million in the red, over-manned by 50,000, and working at just over half capacity. Only a year ago they decided to expand some plants, and promised the workers at some old ones that they need not close till 1980. Now they come along and want to reduce everything. Varley put the case for a compromise – about 20,000 men to go, but only after full negotiations with the unions. Joel Barnett presented the Treasury case – which exposed the full financial horror and went for massive pruning. Other ministers ducked round it. The PM, Foot and John Morris all had Welsh constituencies threatened by steel closures and reacted strongly.

In the end they decided to delay it by calling for a 'full study' of the industry's prospects – which is exactly what has been done twice in the past two years without result. Just a delaying tactic. The PM then suggested that a Cabinet committee be set up to supervise this, because nearly every department was involved. Eric Varley then got very emotional and said he could not stand that, it must be him and his department alone who controlled it. This was the least good side of Eric, uptight, full of *amour propre*, feeling his virility threatened if anybody else enters his territory. It has happened before – over Chrysler, shipbuilding, the engineering inquiry. It also reflects his permanent secretary, Carey, who is very 'mandarinish'. And of course Eric's wish to protect his nasty close chum and flatmate Kaufman, whose irresponsible wheeling and dealing might be exposed by an interdepartmental committee. The PM was clearly irritated. He likes Eric but not Kaufman.

Went back to No. 10 and we finished off our brief on North Sea oil revenues, which is to be held in reserve in case the Treasury and Energy do not agree a compromise draft. We wait to see which way Benn will jump.

Then went to a delightful party in a bookseller's in Covent Garden for John Betjeman's new book. And home by 8.15 p.m., again seeing the children before they went to bed. This is one of the many blessings of the 'Callaghan regime'.

Wednesday 16 November 1977

Today is the day of the big devolution guillotine votes. The PM was away in the East Midlands most of the day. I worked on papers in the morning, but the work pressure was fairly low. Had lunch with Joe Haines, who is very miserable at the *Mirror,* who are not giving him enough to do. All journalism is a part-time trade after working in the pressure cooker of No. 10.

Most of the afternoon I worked preparing for this weekend's Ford Foundation Conference on setting up a new Brookings Institute in Europe. I am to be British representative and need to be on top of the subject. The big Scottish vote was at 7 p.m. so I went over to the House and stood just outside the lobby while the MPs voted. We won by 26. The Scot Nats were OK, so it was a much bigger majority than our whips expected.

Thursday 17 November 1977

In to Gen 107 on the Japanese threat to the Western economy. Benn made a great spiel about the need for massive import controls. The PM showed great concern about de-industrialisation.

It was concluded that the European Council on 6 December must expose the Japs' surplus problem. At a secret finance ministers meeting on 3 December Healey is to have secret discussions with EEC finance ministers on this. There should be an economic summit on this issue and the PM wants another meeting with Giscard, and wants all departmental papers.

Lunch with Joe Rogaly of the *FT* at Wheelers to discuss the proposed Brookings Institute for Europe. Afterwards to PQs – at the briefing the PM was very critical of how the Home Office was handling the firemen's strike. Afterwards the PM saw the Civil Service unions. They were complaining – they want their phoney pay research restored – but wanted to exclude scientists from outside comparison because scientists outside the Civil Service are paid less than those inside – i.e. they only want comparisons with groups earning more so their own pay will be raised. Blatant.

Did some shopping for Paris, read my briefs, then went home early to pack and catch the 10 o'clock night train-ferry.

Friday 18–Sunday 20 November 1977

Fascinating weekend in Paris, at the Trianon Palace Hotel, Versailles, at a Ford Foundation Conference to discuss setting up a Brookings Institute in Europe. Worked very hard – 9 a.m to midnight on Saturday and Friday evening and Sunday morning. But had lovely day on Friday walking across Paris in the cold sunshine, visiting the Louvre for the first time in fifteen years, and also going to the Rodin exhibition. Had a very interesting afternoon at the French Socialist Party with Michel Rocard, who has a dazzling personal assistant – there is no special adviser in Whitehall to match her. Trust the French!

We made some progress with Brookings – and now must get our governments interested. Home at midnight Sunday.

Monday 21 November 1977

In early to catch up on papers, and then was told that the PM had decided to have another monetary seminar tomorrow morning – and he wanted a paper from us by this evening. So I summoned Gavyn and we got cracking straight away. We each telephoned our contacts (Geoff Littler gave me a very good rundown on the internal Treasury positions – with Douglas Wass in a minority and the majority a more restrictive line). Then we agreed a line, and Gavyn went off to write it. We had another talk after lunch, and then he produced a marvellous draft ready by the time I returned to No. 10 from the TUC at 5.30. We made a few changes and then put it in.

I had been to the TUC to discuss planning agreements, North Sea oil revenues, the industrial strategy – with David Lea and Bill Callaghan*, the young economist who is replacing David now he is promoted to assistant general secretary.

This morning I went to Lancaster House to the press conference to announce the Polish shipbuilding order – £115 million, which in the short term will save our shipbuilding industry from annihilation. The irony is that various civil servants were there celebrating with no acknowledgement that if they had had their way there would not have been any bloody order, or certainly not such big one.

Had lunch of sandwiches in my room while I read papers to catch up on Friday's lost reading.

This evening I went to see David Owen to discuss the monetary questions which are coming up at the next two seminars – the IMF. negotiations and the question of debt repayment. We also discussed the Japanese threat, on which he is quite a hawk, and where we both see quite a lot of scope for co-operation with the French. He said the FCO officials are all total free-traders. (Though of course they do not believe in free trade and competition for FCO jobs! See their reaction to Peter Jay getting the Washington ambassadorship.) As always it was a lively and tough talk and David shows a remarkable capacity to catch up on economic issues even though he is flooded with foreign problems. If we lose the next election he will be a 'lost Chancellor'.

It was a terribly cold and wet day, depressing physically but exhilarating intellectually. I went home early – at 8.15 p.m. – and had supper with the children and then early to bed to listen to music.

Tuesday 22 November 1977

Went in early to clear papers before the seminar on monetary policy. The first trouble arose on this year's M/3 target for money supply. Here the Governor and Healey wanted a rise of 2% in lending rate to 7% straight away. Now the foreign currency inflows have ended, it is appropriate to slip upwards to a more 'natural' interest rate level at which we might sell a few more gilts. The PM said that he could accept the rise to 7% now, but he would not tolerate any rise beyond that – and he instructed the Governor not to hint to the gilt markets that higher interest rates could be expected. He was excellent – though I don't know how in practice we impose a 7% ceiling.

Lunch at the Reform with Ted Croker of the FA, who made it quite clear that Brian Clough would not get the England managership (Ron Greenwood will continue). We met Denis Howell there and sat down with coffee in the library to have a good chat about football.

A crisis arose after PM's Questions. The chief whip brought the PM a copy of a letter, signed by puppet Michael Meacher* but really from his master Tony Benn, summoning a meeting of anti-EEC ministers this evening to discuss joint action to vote against on direct elections. Benn is trying to mobilise sufficient support so that he can vote against without getting the sack. The PM was furious, but very firm. He wrote to tell Benn that he would sack him if the meeting took place. Benn will capitulate as always.

Eric Varley came in to discuss Benn. He said that when they were together at DTI in the 1960s Benn was (1) very right wing; (2) very pro-Europe: (3) in favour of closing down all coal mines and wrote a White Paper to that effect which Varley stopped him from publishing and (4) in favour of closing all the Clyde shipyards. Now he advocates the total opposite to win left-wing votes. He said Benn had little credibility.

I went back to No. 10 at around 5 p.m. and dictated several letters and cleared a great flow of papers.

Home at 9 p.m.

Wednesday 23 November 1977

The PM went away to Blackpool for the day to address the electricians union conference – and mainly to take the opportunity to lay down a hard line on the firemen's strike.

I then had a long meeting of the Unit on whether to approach the TUC with proposals for a phase four of wage policy. We will put in a paper at the weekend prior to Jim's dinner with the Neddy Six trade unionists on Monday.

I was supposed to have lunch with Joe Haines, but in the end did not because he and the *Mirror* journalists are all on strike – in a bid to breach the pay code! Journalists denounce pay rises elsewhere but, like civil servants, think that government pay policy should not apply to them.

I had lunch of sandwiches in my room and then went to an unsatisfactory meeting in the Inland Revenue Board Room at Somerset House – to discuss the taxation of divers. Only got back in time to collect Carol and go off to the American Embassy to hear David Owen lecture on UK/US relations since the war. Very Gaullist. Not a good delivery. But he held my attention throughout. Afterwards we had drinks and then off to dinner with Jack Sultzer, their political counsellor. Very pleasant. Home at midnight.

Thursday 24 November 1977

First into EY for a discussion of the Great British Steel Corporation disaster. The PM set out lines for the longer-term handling of the situation, including the maximum of consultation. They agreed on big redundancy payments and playing it slow. Nobody really knows the answers in a depression like this.

The committee finished early and Shirley Williams and John Morris asked to come and have coffee in my room. Harold Lever joined in, so we had quite a party. Then they all dashed down to join Cabinet.

After Cabinet, at lunchtime, Healey came back in to 'see His Nibs' as he put it. He was going to tell the PM that they had decided to 'talk the market up' 2% this afternoon. This is the way in which tomorrow they can announce that MLR must go up 2% because market forces expect it!

Question Time went quietly enough.

Carol came in and we went to dinner in Putney with Euen Ferguson*, David Owen's private secretary. It was a super evening, with marvellous food and lovely wine. The company was a bit right wing – Tory MP Christopher Soames*, Martin Charteris from the Palace, and Andrew Knight from *The Economist*. But it went with a swing until 1.30 in the morning. I like Euen very much.

In bed at 2 a.m. (and up at 7 to go running!).

Friday 25 November 1977

I did not see the PM today at all. Came in early for the deputy secs meeting. Then worked on my papers.

I slipped out for a quick – and appalling – lunch at the new Civil Service canteen and then back to finish off our briefs on pay policy, interest rates, and a late one on exchange controls (where Healey is suddenly proposing major relaxations without any prior warning to the PM). The Treasury are incredible: the 'bounce' is their natural weapon. So we brief the PM not to concede. In fact I support relaxation of controls, but they cannot be allowed to get away with this constant tactic of slipping things through at the last moment.

I left at 7 p.m. and had an early evening home for a change.

Monday 28 November 1977

Spent most of the morning listening to my wonderful new hi-fi, while the PM had a joint Cabinet-NEC meeting on the EEC, which apparently went very quietly. I returned for a quick lunch in the Cabinet Office canteen, with Ken Stowe. We discussed how to handle the PM on the new Brookings

Institute, now that MacGeorge Bundy has written to him supporting it. Returned to work on papers, including the PM's speech tomorrow to the Institute of Production Engineers, where the PM has asked me to harden it up.

Went home early. It is my eighteenth wedding anniversary, so I went to have a whisky and some French chocolates with Carol.

Tuesday 29 November 1977

The PM saw the firemen at 9 o'clock. They stayed for an hour but did not get much change out of the PM. He told them there was no way he could let them break the pay code. He pushed them a bit on phase four of pay policy. They agreed to start discussing it early, but did not get much beyond that.

I worked on the PM's speech for tonight, rewriting several paragraphs and felt it was much harder after that. When I saw the PM after lunch he thanked me and said the speech was much better. He asked me to go over to the House in the car with him. We discussed interest rates, since this morning the market was talking of another rise in rates. He told me to get a message through to the Governor of the Bank to say that he would not tolerate another rise.

Questions continued quiet. Beforehand at briefing the PM talked of the future on pay, and said he hoped next year to have a much lower norm and to get inflation down to about 7%.

Afterwards I went back to my room and worked through a pile of papers, Then off to the dinner of the Institute of Production Engineers. This was a lively affair. The president's speech was very sharp, included some savage, and well-justified, attacks on the Department of Industry for its neglect of engineering. The PM replied with my words of vigour and sympathy.

Came home at 11.45.

Wednesday 30 November 1977

I arrived in quite a bad temper, having read in the newspapers the reports from the City yesterday – the gilt market was very troubled because it believed that the Bank lending rate was going up again. The Bank had failed to indicate a price for the long tap and had not intervened in the stock market. This produces a vicious circle: the market thinks the Bank wants rates up (it does!); so people sell or hold off from buying and prices fall – which pushes rates up anyway. Then the Bank says alas, market forces have insisted on higher rates.

I stormed into Private Office to get something done. All the private secretaries were looking shell-shocked. The Prime Minister had exploded similarly. He told Ken Stowe to phone the Governor in New York and tell him to get moving. Ken said it was still night in New York and the Governor would still be asleep. The PM said, 'Good, wake him up in the middle of the night, he will get the message then.' Nigel Wicks was told to phone the Treasury and to get them to lean on the Bank. When Philip Wood went in to the study he was given a lecture on the 'negative treachery' of the Bank. Finally the PM came foaming downstairs and walked up and down in the Private Office swearing at the Bank. He said it was 'sabotage'. That he did not mind people who disagreed with him but he would not stand people 'trying to take him for a ride'. He told Ken Stowe to order the Bank to intervene in the market and say that it would not allow rates to rise. If not, he would arrange to answer a Parliamentary Question tomorrow and would take the opportunity to denounce the Governor and declare his intention to hold rates.

Then we went off to the South-East Planning Council. I travelled in the car with him. The meeting was at the Environment Department in Marsham Street. The excellent chairman [my racing friend] Lord Porchester met us and took us into the meeting. It was nice to see Henry again, and later we had a long chat about planning problems and about racing.

We had a buffet lunch there and then came back to No. 10 by 2 o'clock. Then I sat down and began to clear papers. The gilt market had settled down after the Bank made a public statement that it would not allow rates to rise.

In the evening Carol and I went to dinner with lawyer friend Lewis Hawser. Jimmy Goldsmith was there with Lady Annabel. He is certainly a dynamic and fascinating animal, quite a force, but dangerously right wing. Still I was interested to observe this phenomenon, who looks to me like a future newspaper tycoon, a modern Beaverbrook with the same political ambitions.

Home at 11.45 p.m.

Thursday 1 December 1977

Went in early and had a quiet morning.

Ironically the press were full of praises for the Bank of England for its firm intervention in the markets yesterday. This quietened the markets completely and the 'pressure' for a rise in interest rates completely disappeared. No mention of course that the Bank needed a shotgun to its head to do it.

Cabinet went on quite late, discussing pay and the European elections. I chatted to the PM afterwards and then went off for a quick lunch with

Harold Lever at Eaton Square. We planned our next move in dealing with the Bank. We are plotting how to sell more 'floating' bonds so interest rates won't have to go up.

At Questions the PM complained that he was tired and had not had his after-lunch nap, but he was very robust in the chamber. When pressed on phase four of the incomes policy he shrewdly left it open and simply said that we must carry the trade unions on it.

The PM took his PPS Roger Stott and me into his room. He put up his feet on the settee and chatted – about children, how much pocket money they had, what we bought them for Christmas, etc. It was a delightful talk, with the PM human and delightful, in a way that sadly HW could not have been. (JC said I was a bit tough and 'mean' in giving my children so little money!) Then I went to the Strangers Bar to have a pint with Gerry Fowler and came home at 9 p.m.

Friday 2 December 1977

In early for John Hunt's deputy secs meeting.

Some discussion for next week's monetary policy seminar. Ken Stowe said that it might not include the Bank of England. He said, 'The Governor ought not to show his face in No. 10 until relations have improved.' Afterwards Ken Berrill said to me that he was in no doubt that the Bank had tried to bounce the government into higher interest rates. He was very harsh against Gordon Richardson – but added that Kit McMahon would be no better.

I went out to lunch with Carol and bought the children some books for Christmas – cost £25 which stretches my overdraft! Came back to finish papers – but no briefs this weekend! Then went home very pleased, because the PM has put me in the list for the Indian visit – he wrote Roger Stott and me in.

Home early and then out to dinner with Karel Reisz and lovely wife Betsy who won an Oscar in *Marty*.

Monday 5 December 1977

Last night I returned from Suffolk with bad toothache and I had to go to the dentist for an emergency extraction. It was a wisdom tooth and I felt a bit groggy and sore this morning. So I went in late – and straight on to lunch with Kit McMahon of the Bank of England. We got on very well but in the end reached the crunch point – the Bank wants to hit its money supply targets regardless of the interest rates required or of the unemployment and bankruptcy which ensues. 'Our money targets are the only fixed policies,' he said. I pointed out that these targets were the Bank's and nothing to do with us, and we did have other objectives such as interest rate ceilings and lower unemployment. In such a divergence lies a danger of great conflict between the Bank and the government – and the sovereignty lies with the government, which I pointed out, though adding that I would prefer a compromise to a clash since we would all suffer from the blow to confidence in a conflict.

The Commons today passed a motion calling for a public inquiry into the Fay Report on Crown Agents. What they did not know was that the Bank of England had pushed hard to censor all reference to its own delinquent lack of supervision and the Civil Service had decided on an internal inquiry in which those taking part would be mainly from Whitehall and the Bank of England. The cry of 'cover-up' would have been deafening!

Tuesday 6 December 1977

Miserable grey December morning. I woke with my gum very sore. But I went for a run over the Heath at 7.30 – still dark – and felt better.

The PM was still in Brussels. Private Office was very occupied with the Fay Report on Crown Agents and the civil servants were still desperately trying to resist pressure for a public inquiry.

The Unit met to discuss our political and economic strategy through until the summer of 1978. We are going to do a paper for the PM setting out where our economic policy is leading us, what policy decisions must be taken in the next three months if we are to be in a position to win the next election, and what we must avoid. We shall also set out the pros and cons for October or the following spring as election choices.

Off to the CCPR party and then home to read more books about India. Am very excited about going to India again. Marvellous. I talked to Mrs Callaghan on the phone about it, and we are planning to go out together.

Wednesday 7 December 1977

I did not see the PM today. Apparently he has returned pleased with the EEC meeting, thinking it all well worthwhile, despite the fact that he did not want to go and told the press so.

Worked on papers. Most important was the draft Letter of Intent to the IMF. The Treasury had told us all that this would contain no 'targets'. On this basis the last monetary 'seminar' had let it through almost undiscussed. Now when it appeared it inevitably contained credit targets. A DCE target for the first three months of next year. Worse was a PSBR target of £8.6 million for 1978–79. This would restrain our whole economic, budgeting and election strategy for next year. It put us wholly in the hands of the forecasts. It meant that if the forecasts for the PSBR in 1978–79 suddenly went up to £8.6 billion – because of higher interest rates, etc. – then we would have no room for expansion in the Budget and would continue in total recession for the next two years.

I telephoned Geoff Littler at the Treasury and said that what was particularly suspicious was that the covering letter to the PM from Healey made no reference to this crucial PSBR sentence – and later I was told that Healey had also not been told of the target by his officials and had simply read and signed the covering letter. So it looked like another Treasury bounce. We put in a minute to the PM, suggesting alternative forms of words which did not contain any possibility of a 'target' and hinting that it might be better to pay off the IMF loan altogether. So we sit and wait to see if the PM will resist another Treasury manouevre to restrain his government in advance and without ministerial consultation.

I had lunch with Joe Haines at Manzi's. He told me more on the Jeremy Thorpe business. Cyril Smith* had told the *Daily Mail* (Greig) that the Liberals had a 'Special Seats Fund' to which all candidates for peerages contributed. Jeremy Thorpe spent it all. Most Liberal peerages had been 'sold' except for Frank Byers* and Nancy Seear. JT offered a peerage to someone for £60,000 and said he could guarantee them – this was while HW was PM.

I returned to No. 10 and continued on the IMF brief-battle.

Thursday 8 December 1977

In early to read papers before the Cabinet committee on N. Ireland at 10 a.m. There Roy Mason put his scheme for a new consultative committee in Belfast – which the PM rightly described as just a device to find a job for unemployed Ulster politicians. Nobody was enthusiastic, and Merlyn Rees was very unhappy with it, but as an alternative to doing nothing it was approved – in fact it may be worse than doing nothing. After that was Cabinet, which decided on a full public inquiry on the Crown Agents, and dealt with a lot of other fairly small things.

The PM had responded marvellously on the IMF problem and resisted the Treasury on borrowing targets. He sent a very firm letter to the Chancellor, saying that he would not have it.

I went for a lunch meeting with Leo Plietzky and his top deputy secretaries at the Department of Trade. It was really to help me get to know them, but we had a good talk on free trade and protection. That department has swung a long way away from laissez-faire of late, and Leo wanted me (and the PM) to be aware of that.

I went straight from the Department of Trade to the House of Commons, bought a piece of pie and a bar of chocolate, and swallowed them quickly before briefing for PQs. The latter was taken up almost wholly by Tory attacks on the amount of subsidy in the Polish shipbuilding deal – the PM doesn't mind this since he can attack the Tories for wanting even more unemployment.

It has been a good day on the industrial front. The miners have voted to accept the twelve-month rule and even productivity deals – which is a victory for the moderates and a big defeat for extremist [Arthur] Scargill*. Also the local authorities put in an attractive offer to the firemen, and they may well feel pressure to accept.

I went back to No. 10 at 4.30 and worked for the next four hours on papers and on writing another draft of my brief on a Brookings Institute for Britain. Then went home feeling tired – and a bit low because my gum is still infected where I had my wisdom tooth out.

Friday 9 December 1977

In early after a run before dawn over the Heath though still feeling low from this infected gum.

Cabinet committee at 10 a.m. to discuss relaxing exchange controls. The PM expressed his serious misgivings. Peter Shore exploded in a worrying mad way, clearly offended by the thought of the greater investment in the hated Europe. Benn attacked it as 'easing capital' at the time when we are 'restraining workers' pay'. The PM summed up cleverly. He reported all his doubts and worries, said he could not support easement on personal house purchases abroad, and wanted some lower limits to direct investment abroad. He then let through some other items by default. So Healey got some of what he wanted, but only with help from the PM, who ended up by neutralising the left opposition. At the end of the meeting he warmly thanked Denis Healey for bringing the issue to ministers, instead of slipping it through as in his (Jim's) days. He made no reference to the fact that he, the PM, had to beat Healey over the head to force him to put it to colleagues.

The weekly deputy secs meeting in John Hunt's office at noon was over very quickly – though I pressed them for progress on the Official Secrets Act, where the ministerial committee has only met once this year. They promised progress in the New Year.

Very interesting lunch with John Lyons of the Power Engineers at the Reform. We are both very worried about a devastating strike in the electricity supply industry. Frank Chapple's electricians are going for 30% and Lyons says they will not settle for less than 20%. Then his members – engineers and managers – will have to maintain their pay differentials. If those two unite, then that will bring the country to a standstill. So we agreed to plan in advance how to find a way through. Lyons, who is very constructive, says that if we can get Chapple's settlement down to around 15%, his people will settle for very little above the 10% guidelines.

Ken Stowe told me that the PM has asked him to stay on for another eighteen months – i.e. over the next election. Otherwise Ken would have gone to a senior policy position at Health. I am pleased with this. Ken is a real professional, and we know how to get on. He is very 'machine' – but they all are, and he certainly knows how to handle it. The PM trusts him, which is crucial.

Afterwards I finished the drafting of the Brookings brief, worked on a brief suggesting that the PM initiates an improvement in the method of public appointments – and also to cope with the latest Treasury manoeuvre on the IMF. They have resisted our suggestions, and are still trying to impose a borrowing ceiling. But they have not sent their paper yet – they are going to send it at the weekend and try to get it direct to the PM at Chequers. This is an attempt to bypass the Policy Unit and to bounce it through the PM without us having the chance to comment on it.

Home after 10 p.m.

Sunday 11 December 1977

The Treasury paper on the IMF Letter of Intent arrived by special car this afternoon. I had arranged to have it sent home. The Treasury is not giving an inch. I drafted a stiff minute of reply and dictated it over the phone to the garden-room girl at Chequers. In fact I don't expect to win, because there is a limit to how many times and on how many issues the PM can fight and overrule the Chancellor and how many times I can be allowed to beat the Treasury. Anyway the PM is not well. He is in bed with a bronchial cough and will not be in good shape for tomorrow's meeting with Giscard d'Estaing.

Monday 12 December 1977

Had to go first to the doctor's for a long list of inoculations for India – typhoid, smallpox, cholera, polio, tetanus – and still hepatitis to come.

Was delighted when I got to the office to find that the PM had come up trumps on everything with the Treasury – he approved our approach to the IMF, even stipulating that we pay them off in 1978; he approved my suggestion that we try to improve the system of public appointments; and above all he gave enthusiastic support for my Brookings proposal. He wrote a long note saying how he wanted us to get the full European Institute for London.

This is a marvellous boost. I telephoned MacGeorge Bundy in New York in the afternoon to tell him, and he was very pleased.

Back to see Gordon Downey* from the Treasury about public expenditure. He is very worried that there will be billions of pounds of extra bids in the pre-election year. I promised to support him in resisting some of them – providing we get more child benefits next autumn!

Then followed Ken Couzens from the Treasury, also to discuss the IMF. I had heard from Healey's special adviser Derek Scott* that this morning Couzens had been talking of finding some way to slip the PSBR 'limit' for 1977–79 through the PM. I pointed out that I was more interested in getting some elbow room for the autumn, not the Budget, and wanted a form of words which made it clear that that was possible. I also rebuked him for trying to 'bounce' it through us. Then he dashed off for a meeting with the Chancellor.

The next omens were not good. We were told that the Chancellor would be taking his proposed Letter of Intent direct to the PM at Chequers, where tonight they are having dinner with Giscard. When Nigel Wicks phoned the Treasury to ask for a copy at No. 10 he was told by the Chancellor's private secretary that unfortunately the Treasury did not have a copy for us. This was ludicrous. Nigel phoned me and said that it was a blatant attempt to bypass the Policy Unit. So he pressed again, and a copy duly arrived twenty minutes later. Actually it was not a bad compromise formula and I dictated a minute to the PM, accepting on certain conditions.

By the time I left the office it was 9.45 p.m. A very exhilarating day, except for those damned inoculations.

Tuesday 13 December 1977

Did some Xmas shopping for presents for the children in the morning. Then to lunch with Joe Haines. He told me that the *Mirror* were starting a series of Jeremy Thorpe articles, which expose more of the embarrassing details – but still nothing in print about selling the Liberal life peerages. Albert Murray had been to see him, and said he was willing to talk to the police if they are interested.

The IMF issue continued to bubble during the day. The PM had responded to my minute to Chequers with the comment 'I agree with Dr Donoughue's minute'. I was clearing papers till late, then to industry dinner at Grosvenor House. Did not get home until midnight.

Wednesday 14 December 1977

Went in early and cleared off the papers. Had a Unit discussion of electoral strategy and school meals policy – we have an expenditure of £400 million on terrible food which an increasing number of children refuse to eat.

To lunch at Admiralty House with the Bangladesh high commissioner. Admiralty House is lovely – fine rooms with the walls covered with eighteenth-century portraits of secretaries to the Admiralty Board.

Walked back to No. 10, down Whitehall, for the EY Cabinet committee to discuss the IMF letter. I had discussed it with Roy Hattersley's political adviser this morning – and with David Owen yesterday in his room at the Commons. They each intervened very well, making sharp points about the PSBR levels. Shore, Williams, Lever and Benn all intervened on similar lines, so the Chancellor was under severe pressure. He looked and sounded terribly tired. Suddenly all his formidable resilience has gone and he was very irritable. I hope he does not crack up now. With all his faults he is still far and away the best Chancellor to have until the next election.

The PM ended the meeting at 4 p.m. so that he could go to the Commons to meet David Steel. The Liberals have been in great turmoil over the vote on PR for Europe last night. It was heavily defeated and 120 Labour MPs – including ministers Shore, Benn, Booth and Owen – voted against. So the Liberals say we have broken the pact. However, a majority of the PLP, including most of the Cabinet, voted for PR, although many of them do not believe in it. The press is full of reports that the pact is over – this is because the Tory press want to build up pressure to take this final opportunity to force an election.

Apparently the PM took a very tough line with Steel, pointing out that we have kept our side of the bargain, meeting most of the points in the July memorandum, and showing 'best endeavours' on PR. He offered nothing to Steel, simply saying that it is a problem for the Liberals and 'they must grow up'. I saw the PM later as he was about to go over to the House. He was quite confident. He thought that the Liberals would stay with us. But he was not afraid of an election. He thought we would win. He kept saying that 'the situation is quite different from last spring'.

I finished clearing a mass of papers at 8.30 and went home very tired.

Thursday 15 December 1977

Worked on some papers and then went down to chat to one or two ministers before Cabinet. Then I slipped through to the Lord Privy Seal's office to see John Smith about devolution. He is quite optimistic since the bill is progressing well – though almost no Labour MPs are attending the debates and Smith is conducting it himself alone in the chamber.

I collected Shirley Williams and took her to Manzi's for a delicious and delightful lunch. We got on very well. I love the way she giggles. She also sounded me out on the problem of the National Theatre, suggesting that I might take a job as chief administrator, to rectify the extravagances of Peter Hall. She was delightful company and we agreed to lunch again.

Back for Parliamentary Questions. The PM was in a relaxed mood and grateful to have reached the last time before Xmas. The Tories pressed him on reports that various trade unionists were communist spies who had been named. In fact this – which comes from Frolik, the Czech defector – had all come up under HW and I saw the files with some interesting names, including MPs and journalists as well as trade unionists. In 1974–75 Wilson had denied that John Stonehouse* had anything to do with Czech intelligence. Subsequently the intelligence service told him this was wrong and there was something against Stonehouse. They also gave a bad report on Jack Jones and on appointment to NEDO he was cleared to see only low-level classified papers. Ditto the journalist Geoffrey Goodman.

To a marvellous party at *New York Times* journalist Johnny Apple's flat in Belgravia. I stayed until 2.15 a.m.!

Friday 16 December 1977

To EY Cabinet committee at 10 to discuss nuclear power decisions – Benn and others against taking the pressurised water system, which is the only system the rest of the world uses. We know that Benn is against all nuclear systems and he is supporting our AGR system simply to kill off the PWR.

Put in several brief briefs. Then to glorious *Marriage of Figaro* in the Royal Box at Covent Garden, conducted by Karl Bohm, and afterwards to a party until 2.30 in the morning. Enjoying life but looking forward to Christmas.

Monday 19 December 1977

In late, cleared papers, then to convivial lunch at Grieveson Grant. Back to a Unit meeting preparing a holiday brief for the PM on economic and electoral strategy for next year. This could be very important.

Went to the PM's Xmas party for disabled children – very moving as always. Then had drinks with Tom McNally – sadly he is not coming to India because he wants to be here and available for the vacant seat at Kettering. I hope he gets the nomination – he is a super man, and quite the best young potential MP around.

Tuesday 20 December 1977

A curious day. I did not see the PM at all – he was at Chequers with Begin of Israel. Worked on papers all morning. We are preparing two briefs, one on pay, the other on election strategy for 1978–79.

Talk with officials on special advisers' salaries. It is quite disgraceful that advisers do not get increments, whereas all civil servants do. Then to a meeting with permanent secretaries in John Hunt's room on a Brookings Institute for Britain. Ian Bancroft was very 'pro'. Wass clearly had doubts. I argued the case very strongly, and John Hunt was helpful.

Back to work on briefs and to finish reading the still endless flow of paper. (Our 'ad hoc' pay policy has left the government with hundreds of individual settlements to monitor and it is nearly killing civil servants and ministers – and me.) I fell asleep at 7.30 in my chair. So I went home before 9, and will be in early tomorrow for work on our briefs.

Wednesday 21 December 1977

The PM went to Northern Ireland today. I met him when he returned at 4 p.m. He had enjoyed it immensely – a bomb went off while he was visiting an army post. He took me into the Cabinet Room and we talked about Ireland, then about the pound, where the steady appreciation of sterling is worrying him very much.

During this morning I had a long Unit meeting on our paper on economic strategy which is coming along very nicely. Lawrence Airey came in from the Treasury at 11.45. He wanted to discuss with me the coming White Paper on the nationalised industries, and the Green Paper on North Sea oil.

Lunch with John Lippitt of the Department of Industry. An unusual civil servant – virile, positive and political. He referred obliquely to Eric Varley's 'psychological weaknesses' and his 'odd' (as a nice ex-professional footballer) and close friendship with the 'exotic and poisonous' Kaufman. They feel that Eric simply does not fight hard enough for the department.

Tessa Blackstone came in from the CPRS and we had a long chat about her problems with Ken Berrill. Then home at 9.15.

Thursday 22 December 1977

An exhausting and exciting day. Went in early to clear papers. Cabinet discussed pay – they moved slowly towards grasping the nettle of phase four, with the PM pushing our point that we must have a 'working agreement' with the TUC at election time.

The Unit worked all day on our economic strategy paper, which is long and I think good. I broke for lunch with Tom McNally and Bob Worcester at the Reform: they discussed the appalling nature of the Labour NEC and its pathetic members – including the general secretary, Hayward!

At 2.30 I went to the EY Cabinet committee to discuss industrial democracy. It was quite a good discussion. Disagreements on whether to include sanctions, how to protect confidential information, what numerical representation on boards and whether to apply it to UK subsidiaries of foreign multinationals. Benn took a very populist line, attacking the 'mandarins of the TUC' and arguing to leave the decisions to the shop floor (I have some sympathy for this). The PM said that he simply did not know what to do next – nobody supported the government's position, but nobody else agreed with one another. So he would talk to the TUC and the CBI.

Afterwards I walked back to the FCO with David Owen, discussing the timing of the next election. He is basically a 1979 man. I think November 1978 could be much better.

Went back to the office at 4.15 and for the next two hours we flogged away at the election strategy paper we were doing. It was finished just after 6 p.m., when the office Christmas party started. I stayed behind and checked it through for typing accuracy. It was a nice feeling to have it done.

The house Christmas party was marvellous. The PM had insisted that we have music, so they borrowed a record player from the Chancellor and some records from Chappell's music shop. There was dancing, plenty of drink and good food. The atmosphere was so much better than in 1974 and 1975. The PM strolled around beaming and chattering. He came over to talk to me and said what a good year it had been and how we must hold the improvement for next year. We went on until about 9.30 p.m., then I went off to a pub with Tom McCaffrey for drinks, and finally got home at midnight.

I shall go in tomorrow morning to clear up various loose ends and to see various people – Carol's cousin on a quick visit from Paris and Anthony Lester and Geoffrey Bindman* to plan a counter-attack on the people who keep taking local Labour parties to court.

Then off on Saturday to Suffolk for Christmas and the New Year – followed by India and Pakistan. A lovely winter prospect. It has been a good year, despite ups and personal downs. On the public work front, I hope next year is as good.

India, Bangladesh and Pakistan: Tuesday 3–Friday 13 January 1978

This was the most exciting trip abroad I have ever made. Fabulous India. Very exhausting schedule but I felt 'lifted' throughout. Did not have time to keep a diary – I just wanted to spend every minute actually being there, not with a pen and paper in a bedroom. A separate file of engagement diaries, invitation cards, etc. has been kept as reminder and souvenirs.

For me the highlights were:

- the lovely river trip from Dacca
- the river trip at Chittagong (memories of the war)
- the speech to the Indian Parliament by the PM
- inevitably the Taj Mahal – and a fabulous picnic at Fatipur Sikri (real shades of the Raj)
- the welcome at the university in the Gujarat countryside
- living in the old governor's house at Bombay, with breakfast on the veranda overlooking the sea
- finally dropping in at Aswan on the flight back for the PM's talks with President Sadat of Egypt – tea by the Nile and dinner with Sadat
- back at 2 a.m. and played football at 10.30 a.m. for the Commons against the German Bundestag – and scored a goal which was shown on *Match of the Day* television!

Monday 16–Friday 20 January 1978

Was too busy last week to write this diary. But it was a good week – I felt plenty of bounce.

On Tuesday there was a committee on the Annan Report on the BBC, where Merlyn Rees came along with the Home Office paper suggesting rejection of Annan, and ministers in general favoured some change.

The PM saw Healey in the afternoon. They discussed the lending rate – Healey was urging the Bank's case for detaching general interest rates from the Bank's minimum lending rate. Then they discussed the Budget, where Healey's ideas seemed OK – £2 billion tax reflation and assorted public expenditure.

After Questions on Thursday I saw David Steel briefly, and he was quite confident of victory in this weekend's Liberal Conference on the Lib-Lab pact.

The PM has been pulling my leg all week about my getting so much publicity both in India and for the football game last weekend. I promised to have a period of low profile. The weather has been very cold. I have been running soon after 7 in the morning, in the dark under the moon, on frosty paths and grass. But it is nice to think the spring is coming soon.

Monday 23 January 1978

Terribly hectic day. A private secretary came up to say that the PM had changed his mind over North Sea oil. He decided that he was not satisfied with John Hunt's draft and wants a revision by the Policy Unit – this is of a White Paper for Thursday's Cabinet, which means we must redo the draft by tonight for the PM's approval so that it can be circulated for Cabinet tomorrow.

I gathered the Unit together and we dropped all our committee engagements and sweated over the revised draft. It was thirteen long typed pages and we did not finish till 7.30 – by when we had made massive alterations in the original – including commitments to increase public expenditure and not to use North Sea revenue to repay debt. We also altered the conclusion, which originally finished on the typical Whitehall note that all our troubles were the fault of the workers.

John Hunt got very worried about us putting in an alternative draft. He sent his private secretary through three times to see if we had finished and kept phoning up Ken Stowe in our Private Office. John is so incredibly insecure, he feels threatened by anybody else operating in what he sees as his territory. No need, because he is a superb operator.

I had a quick lunch with TV presenter Robin Day at the Garrick, as payment for the bet he lost with me – that the government would fall before the end of 1977. He is a bit sad at the moment, feeling very under-utilised, wishing he were in Parliament – even the Lords – and moving well to the right. I decided to feed his name into the honours machine – he is a robust but fair interviewer.

But the rest of the day was solid drafting. I had a quick chat with the PM, who was very pleased with our work. Then home, very tired, at 9 p.m.

Tuesday 24 January 1978

I woke very tired and so did not go on my dawn run – which is always a mistake, since that is the one sure way of throwing off tiredness. The traffic was terrible going in, taking an hour to get to Horse Guards Parade.

I went almost straight into the Cabinet committee on nuclear energy. On the way I ran into John Hunt, who is not too pleased that the PM had approved of our draft on the North Sea oil White Paper, and not his. I went into the gents lavatory with him and we discussed it while we peed. He clearly didn't like it. Later in the day his brief for Cabinet arrived, full of criticisms of our draft as being too political and promising too much. No doubt the Chancellor will take this line, and other ministers will be briefed to support him. We shall see. In any case we have improved the turgid prose of the Cabinet Office immensely.

The nuclear discussion went quite well. Benn had already been forced to compromise a long way away from AGRs and towards PWRs in the joint paper with Varley. In discussion he was forced even further. He fought tenaciously, but alone. The PM cleverly ruled in his favour on all the small things, but against him on the big ones.

Lunch with Johnny Apple at the Gay Hussar discussing his info on scandals.

Straight back to the Commons for PM's Questions. The PM was in excellent humour. Indeed it is quite striking how he has been in very good form for a long time now – because everything has gone well for so long. Afterwards we had another ministerial committee on the doomed steel industry. The PM said, 'This will be at the end of the day what we used to call a shabby compromise.' In fact the collapse of our steel industry is tragic, worsened by appallingly bad management and investment decisions. Ministers are taking it carefully and sensibly: very good papers from the Department of Industry, good discussion, the PM very well briefed. There is no apparent solution, but the terrible human tragedy will at least be sensitively handled.

I came back to No. 10 from the Steel committee in the House at 5.30 and sat down for two and a half hours to read a great mass of accumulated papers – including more EEC nonsense trying to stop our anti-unemployment measures.

Then home at 8.30. I still dream of India and miss it.

Wednesday 25 January 1978

Spent all morning in my office clearing papers and doing an enormous list of phone calls which had accumulated over the past few days. Before going in I had my morning run over the Heath – cold and sunny – and met Michael Foot walking with his stick and his dog over towards Kenwood. We discussed the North Sea oil White Paper and I gave him a dawn briefing.

Went to lunch with Harold Lever and briefed him as well. He also told me that he did not want to stand for Parliament again and would go to the Lords. We discussed how to try to get his seat for Tom McNally.

Had a hectic afternoon – writing two briefs for tomorrow's Cabinet, one on renewing our temporary employment subsidies and the other on the North Sea oil paper. This took me right through into the time for the dinner with Prime Minister Karamanlis of Greece. This was quite a small and nice dinner, which ended early, but then I had a phone call from the Ford Foundation in New York about the next conference to discuss creating a European Brookings. In the end I did not get home till midnight and was very exhausted.

Thursday 26 January 1978

Cabinet started at 9.30 and they were already going in to the Cabinet Room when I arrived. I sat down in my office to try to read the endless flow of papers. Suddenly in mid-morning I got a phone call to come and sit in Cabinet – they were beginning to go through the North Sea oil White Paper paragraph by paragraph. There was quite a lot of small criticism. Also our efforts to get 'debt repayment' rejected failed. But the basic structure was accepted.

Afterwards John Hunt sat in the Cabinet Room with the PM to discuss future handling – and to establish that next time he had the last word in drafting and circulating the paper. So the PM came over and asked me to work on the initial redrafting and then to pass it on to Hunt for 'the final stamp'.

Lunch upstairs in No. 10. I was feeling tired and low, with an incipient cold – everybody seems to have one. Question Time went comfortably enough – Thatcher was also away with a cold.

Tony Benn has been behaving badly voting against the government in the NEC and making militant speeches. The PM is angry and is biding his time.

I went back to No. 10 and we had a meeting with the CPRS on their unemployment paper – a big and interesting work, taking an old-fashioned view of reflation. We are broadly sympathetic, but really our minds were on North Sea oil. We stayed on afterwards till very late discussing the Cabinet amendments to our paper – and I did not get home till 11 o'clock, feeling rough and with a sore throat.

Friday 27 January 1978

Went in early for the deputy secs meeting in the Cabinet Office, still with a sore throat. We went quite quickly through the agenda, with two points of interest. They decided to put the reply to the English select committee on the Civil Service on a Wednesday because the PM would be out making a speech the night before and 'would not have much time to read his papers' – and therefore would be more likely to follow his Civil Service brief! There was a lot of ambivalence about the CPRS report on unemployment. This takes a Keynesian, anti-Treasury view, proposing expansion of demand to reduce unemployment. For some reason the private secretaries in No. 10 are worried by this and are trying to head it off.

We also had a discussion on whether to publish the names, chairmen, etc. of Cabinet standing committees. John Hunt was fairly progressive on this, as was Ken Berrill for the CPRS, but the others were all against, feeling it was the slippery slope to open government.

I went off to a meeting and then to a lunch at the *Daily Mirror* with Joe Haines, Terry Lancaster* and Geoffrey Goodman, Toms McNally and McCaffrey and myself. We discussed organising the campaign for the next election – which they all wanted in the autumn. The *Mirror* people expressed strong hostility to the way McCaffrey has ignored them – in order to be different from Joe, he ignores them totally, which is politically crazy.

We went on till 3.30. Then back to work on redrafting North Sea oil. We completed a redraft by 7.30 p.m.

Home at 8.30.

Monday 30 January 1978

The PM was very grumpy today – not least because there was a nasty piece in the evil *Mail* suggesting that he is a rich farmer who influences the government's agricultural policies to suit his pocket.

The Unit worked all day on the North Sea oil White Paper. It is beginning to look quite good apart from some repetition. We worked on it till nearly 9 p.m. – and should finish tomorrow.

Tuesday 31 January 1978

I did not go to the EY Cabinet committee on the nationalised industry White Paper – I had to go to the Civil Service College, and needed to work on the North Sea oil draft before going. We are virtually finished on this, but are still waiting for the Treasury contributions, which are late as usual!

The Civil Service meeting – and lunch – was fairly boring though I was quite interested to see the new head of the Civil Service, Ian Bancroft, in action. Much less direct than Douglas Allen, rather 'fey' in fact, but clearly clever. I talked to him at lunch, and he told me he was disappointed in the low level of the decisions that come across his desk, as was Allen.

The two other permanent secretaries present were Jim Hamilton from Education and Carey from Industry. Hamilton is much the more impressive, lively and active. Carey is disappointing – pompous and conservative.

Back to PM's Questions, which was quite dramatic. Thatcher followed up her questions on race and immigration, cynically encouraging prejudice and blatantly courting the National Front vote. [Willie] Whitelaw*, [Edward] Heath* and Peter Walker* all looked very uncomfortable. The PM dealt with it in a deliberately statesmanlike way, reminding the Tories of their pledges and their responsibilities on race and not getting personal. I would have liked him to put the boot in, denouncing them for encouraging racism, but he deliberately chose to handle it this way. It won respect in Westminster but I fear it won't win votes in Wigan.

Then to No. 10 to work on North Sea oil again. In fact I missed the Highlands and Islands film which I was supposed to see – but I went for a drink with the Scots afterwards.

Not home until 11.

Wednesday 1 February 1978

Last night the PM made a big speech to Indian journalists on race – he again took a firm liberal line. He has been remarkably good on this. I think his recent visit to India made a big impact. What it boils down to is he is offended by the thought of prejudice against their PM Maraji Desai.

Worked all morning on the North Sea oil White Paper – and finally finished it at 1.30 p.m. It now reads very well, and everybody has contributed.

Lunch with Robin Butler. We discussed his colleagues at the Treasury – he is aware of the weaknesses at the top there. He and they are already very worried that the PM will split the Treasury after the next election – as indeed he now says he will. But in the end a lot will depend on who is Chancellor – a big man might resist the split.

I took the oil White Paper draft to John Hunt and then went off to the Commons for the Brookings discussion. The PM made it clear from the start that he wanted it and that was that. So everybody chatted encouragingly and we decided to go for one in London, with a list of buildings ready to offer. It was jovial and all over in twenty minutes. I then had tea with Shirley Williams and back to No. 10 to clear my papers and put in a brief on child benefits for tomorrow's Cabinet.

William Plowden came in for a chat – very unhappy at the Department of Industry.

A final curious vignette. The CPRS have now put in their paper on unemployment. I put in a brief supporting it. But Ken Berrill put in a minute separately in which he disagreed with much of his own CPRS's report! That must be very demoralising for them.

Home at 8.30.

Thursday 2 February 1978

Cabinet was at 9.30 and apparently was very unsatisfactory. On economic strategy they wandered all over the place. Healey spoke for thirty-five minutes and never gave a single figure! It was all very vague, so they decided to have a special Cabinet at Chequers on 19 February. I spent the morning reading and dictating letters. It was a great relief to have the North Sea oil paper off our back.

We are all still laughing at the daily episode of the 'Pencourt' book about spies in the *Daily Mirror*. Wilson comes out of it more bizarrely every day.

I saw 'M', head of the security service, in No. 10 yesterday – Sir Maurice Oldfield*. Interestingly, although I had never met him before in my life, he greeted me as we passed in a dark corridor and said, 'You have been playing some good football lately.' Obviously they have been keeping an eye on me!

Had lunch with Patrick Nairne who is running Health very well. He is obviously not too keen on Ennals.

At a meeting in the Cabinet Office John Hunt told me that he is very content with our draft of the North Sea oil White Paper. Then I finished my reading and came home.

The weather has been terrible for weeks and is getting everybody down. But I still feel a good hangover from India.

Friday 3 February 1978

Went in early for the Cabinet committee to discuss the draft White Paper in response to the English committee on the Civil Service. It was a fairly stodgy document. David Owen and Judith Hart tried to liven it up, and also to give more power to Parliament. But the PM, Healey and others all showed a clear 'executive' mentality – 'Parliament will get in the way of us governing effectively'. They attacked Owen for being too 'American'. However, the PM was very good on the special advisers. Here the draft was very anti advisers. The PM attacked this and redrafted it in a much more favourable way.

I went out for a hilarious Irish lunch with Kevin O'Shea and with Jimmy Brazil from the Irish Embassy. Home at 8 for a nice dinner with our friends the Grahams and the Reads.

Monday 6–Friday 10 February 1978

I was away ill in bed with flu. So sadly I was not there for when the Cabinet took our North Sea oil White Paper on Thursday. But it went well (David Owen phoned me at home the night before to say how much he liked it).

I went in late on Friday morning and caught up with some papers. Also discussed with Gavyn Davies our weekend papers for the PM – on the Budget stimulus for the PM's meeting with the Chancellor on Monday.

And on the dollar problem for Wednesday's seminar. Went home early in the afternoon, still flu'd, but recovering.

Monday 13 February 1978

I walked to Camden Town, had a tetanus injection on the way, and then took a bus in to work. Cleared some papers, and then the PM sent for Gavyn Davies, Nigel Wicks from Private Office and me.

We first discussed the Unit paper on the Budget stimulus and on the latest Treasury forecast – which suggests that we will move into balance of payments deficit next year and that we can only afford a modest budget expansion – about £1.5 billion. After discussion the PM said he would not have that; he would insist on over £2 billion. That was expected. And to do less was to surrender all hope of ever getting any growth.

On the election he said that although the economic indicators might turn against us next winter, that did not mean we should hold an autumn election. There was a time lag of six months before the public appreciated events. So if you wanted to capitalise on the autumn well-being you should go in the following spring. I did not necessarily believe him.

Finally we turned to incomes policy. He said that he did not think we could have a repeat of this year, with ministers involved in every detail of every pay claim. We should have to withdraw from the private sector to explain what is the percentage pay increase compatible with containing inflation; to say that we will impose that in the public sector; and to ask the private sector to follow suit.

Wicks pressed him that the government would have to be involved in the private sector. I did not agree and share the view which the PM expressed – though I don't know if he really believes it. He always flies these kites. But it is impossible to discover what he really thinks. Probably he has not yet made up his mind and is just using us to try out his ideas.

Later drafted a note proposing setting up a 'Buy British' Unit – this was the PM's idea which I pursued since I believe it is right. The problem is to achieve something without slipping into protection. And how to get people to buy British goods – e.g. cars – which are shoddier and less reliable than foreign products.

Took a taxi home because it is so cold – a terrible freeze-up everywhere. And Carol is home with flu now.

Tuesday 14 February 1978

I walked in all the way to No. 10 from Highgate – five miles in just over an hour. No transport, all on strike. A cold but bright morning.

The PM sat in the study, sending for papers and people. He had nothing on his timetable, so as usual then began to meddle round a bit. He also saw son-in-law Peter Jay, who had flown in from Washington to discuss the promised Callaghan initiative to solve the dollar weakness problem (and Peter was advising caution on this). Peter joined us for lunch upstairs and I sat next to him and chatted. The rest seemed rather overawed by him. He is very clever.

The PM was clearly worried about the immigration question and decided in advance to offer Thatcher some all-party talks – knowing she would turn it down, but thereby putting the pressure on her. He did make the offer. She did turn it down. But somehow it did not quite come off. We are still on the retreat on immigration, though most people know that Thatcher's position does not bear investigation. The problem is that nobody is investigating it – and nobody in the press will.

After Questions David Henderson, my old Oxford tutor who is now a special adviser at the Welsh Office, came in and criticised the North Sea oil White Paper. That is worrying. He is very sound.

Then my brother Clem came down from Manchester and I went to collect him at Euston. We talked until 1.15 in the morning.

Wednesday 15 February 1978

Awoke very tired. But walked in most of the way again – leaving the car for Clem.

I saw David Owen in his room at midday and we discussed the weak dollar prior to this afternoon's 'seminar'. Went to lunch with Joe Haines at the Gay Hussar. Had a very good natter. I wish he was still at No. 10.

The seminar ran from 3.30 till 5.15 and was more of a seminar than ever before – particularly because Peter Jay was there and gave a brilliant exposition on the dollar problem, mercantilism, etc. He actually dominated the meeting. I could see that this irritated Denis Healey, but it pleased the PM. Owen was also very sensible with a brief interjection. The PM clashed with the Governor and said his claim that the central bankers would not finance the dollar deficit was 'balls'.

At one point it seemed as if the PM was retreating altogether from the dollar initiative, but Lever intervened to ask him to consider it and in the end they decided to proceed preparing an initiative, and to arrange a visit to Carter, but on a more cautious basis.

Clem came in at 6.30 and we chatted till 9 about his future and then went home. I feel very close to him now, closer than anyone except Carol and the children. We came through a lot together in childhood.

Thursday 16 February 1978

Last night Tom McCaffrey had put in a note attacking our North Sea oil White Paper. So I got up very early, drafted a severe minute in reply, then travelled in to give it to the PM. He was still in the flat when I went up, so I went there and gave it to Audrey.

Around ten o'clock the PM sent for me, and McCaffrey arrived. The PM asked him to put his criticisms. He then asked me what I thought – and I said it was too late, with the paper going to Cabinet this morning. He should have made these points weeks ago. The PM then intervened and put the boot in on McCaffrey, really blasting him out of the chair. I would not want to be on the end of that. McCaffrey is a mean man and will seek revenge on me.

Cabinet went on quite late with a long wrangle about whether to have a North Sea 'Fund' using oil revenues for public puposes. The PM has swung the Cabinet against this – because he says, after thinking it through, he thinks it is phoney.

I was supposed to have lunch with Shirley Williams, but she had flu and did not come into work today. Went upstairs to lunch and then to Commons Questions, where it was clear that the Tories, and Thatcher herself, are in much better morale after her anti-immigration speeches. Two polls show them jumping up to a 9–10% lead.

I had a meeting with Helen Liddell of the Scottish Labour Party about the Scottish devolution problem and then went to dinner at the Streeters, the minister at the American Embassy. Quite enjoyable, and not home till 1 a.m.

Friday 17 February 1978

We had a strategy meeting with the PM in his study at 11.15 – Tom McNally and me. The PM said that it was very interesting how Thatcher was behaving quite different from any normal Opposition. Generally, governments upset particular minorities and spokesman groups by their decisions, and the Opposition supports them and tries to put together a majority out of these discontents. But Thatcher is actually attacking minorities – immigrants, Irish, etc. – while the government is defending them. He said it would be very interesting to see how the new strategy worked out.

We discussed immigration and law and order. The PM said that he did not think that we could ever win on these issues. They are Tory issues. We had to keep attacking on our policies – economic success, social policy, industrial relations, etc. On immigration, he ordered that ministers should meet and propose a reply immediately Thatcher produced her plans to cut immigration. On law and order, he asked McNally and me to go to see Merlyn Rees on Monday morning to arrange a big speech by Rees in Ilford. He agreed with me that we should try to turn the flank on Thatcher by asserting that her approach to race relations created violence on the streets.

I then went back to my office and worked frantically, right through lunch, on two briefs – one on the economic strategy discussion for Sunday's Chequers meeting; one on the Buy British campaign.

At 3 o'clock I had to sprint to Paddington to take the train to Oxford where I was talking to David Butler's seminar. This went quite well, but I did not stay overnight as originally intended. I came home at midnight because Carol had problems at work. She has the misfortune to work for bumbling Fred Jarvis of the appalling NUT. Poor Carol has been working for him for two years and is now in despair. She wants to leave. Jarvis is trying very petty measures to get rid of her. So I went home to give comfort. So late to bed again.

I am not going to Chequers on Sunday. I have done that often enough. Instead I have a football game for the House of Commons against a Crystal Palace professional team. Priorities!

Monday 20 February 1978

I did not see the PM today.

I went with Tom McNally to see Merlyn Rees at 10.30. He was in a large conference room surrounded by about eight civil servants. The meeting was fairly chaotic, but we managed to get over our point – that Merlyn should go to Ilford on Thursday and give a speech on law and order pre-empting Thatcher. He was anyway going to Oxford tonight, and would open the campaign by speaking on immigration – and saying that Thatcher's views actually provoke violence and disorder. These were all the points I had made to the PM on Friday morning.

We also spent some time discussing the threatened National Front march on Saturday. Everybody agreed it should be banned, but the decision lies with the Commissioner of Police, McNee, who is not very amenable. John Hunt was there and made a few intelligent remarks. Robert Armstrong was very quiet and looked a bit embarrassed by his minister's rambling style. Still, Merlyn is very nice.

Back to No. 10 where I managed to clear my desk before going to Rothschild's bank for lunch with Victor Rothschild. We chatted about mutual acquaintances.

Worked all afternoon on papers, feeling rather tired, and stiff from yesterday's football game (when I missed two open goals and gave away another penalty for overenthusiastic tackling). Apparently the Chequers Cabinet yesterday was very amiable. No rows. But no specifics – no numbers or totals. More caution than previously. It leaves the Chancellor with a fairly free hand.

Went to a nice dinner at bubbling Carla Powell's in the evening. Home at 1.15 a.m.

Tuesday 21 February 1978

Walked to Camden Town on a grey, wet and cold morning, then took the bus to work. Not many papers today so I had a fairly easy morning.

Father Michael Conway, my Jesuit friend from Glasgow, came in at 11.30, followed by Claus Moser at midday. I went shopping at lunchtime, indeed had no lunch and came back too late for PM's Questions.

All the newspaper headlines carried our attack on Thatcher – by Rees last night and by the PM this morning in a message to Tessa Jowell, our candidate at Ilford – pushing the message that the Tories are threatening law and order by their racist incitement. Thatcher was driven on to the defensive and made some statement saying she would not be bullied.

The Cabinet committee on Official Secrets met at 4.15 to discuss the proposed White Paper. The draft is terrible, stodgy, and we made no progress. Only Healey and David Owen come out of it with credit, insisting on opening up the Treasury and Foreign Office against the opposition of their officials (and of the PM!). Afterwards I finished off my papers, gave a drink to clever Bob Gavron and then home by 8.30.

Incidentally, as I was leaving at lunchtime with Claus Moser, we ran into the PM and he chatted. He particularly discussed a piece by Joe Rogaly in the *FT* which says that the CPRS is in a bad way (and that the Policy Unit is successful!). The PM asked if the CPRS's morale was low, and if so to tell them that he was fully supportive of them.

Wednesday 22 February 1978

Another quiet day. Worked on papers till 11, then the Italian ambassador, Ducci, came in to talk about the European Brookings.

The one bit of good news is that the Commissioner of Police is going to ban Saturday's National Front march. Otherwise there would have been terrible violence and disorder. It means the fascists will try to disrupt Rees' meeting in Ilford tomorrow, but that is not as bad as riots throughout the streets.

In the afternoon I went for a drink with tycoon Harry Kissin – whom I have not seen since 1976. He told me that he had recently been on a trip to Israel with Harold Wilson, and the latter drank throughout the flight, talked ceaselessly for three and a half hours in an endless flow of disconnected stories, and never spoke to Mary, sitting at his side, once. Harry also said he wished he had not taken his peerage since it was soiled by the controversy surrounding Wilson's honours list on which he figured.

Harry said that my reputation was now very high, with a 'charisma of success'. That won't last two minutes if we lose the election!

Thursday 23 February 1978

A quiet morning, clearing papers. The PM threw Rees's draft law and order speech down the stairs and said, 'Merlyn is fucking wet' – he doesn't often swear.

After Cabinet – which had nothing of interest on the agenda – Shirley Williams came upstairs for a cup of coffee and a chat. She is seeing the PM this afternoon about whether to push ahead with measures removing the tax advantages of private education. Or rather to prepare them. There is no intention to do anything before the election.

Questions was interesting but not very successful. At the briefing we all told off the PM for his 'gloomy' statement about the economy the other day – this casts doubt on Labour's image of competence. Roger Stott his PPS also told him off for not being tough enough with Thatcher. So when the PM rose, he started hitting out in all directions. He accused her of every sin in the book. It was very funny – but he did not look comfortable. There is no point in pushing him to act out of character. Calm. Statesmanlike. That is his best style.

At 5.15 we had a meeting in his room in the Commons and discussed the select committee on the steel industry, which has issued a savage attack on Varley, Kaufman and Villiers for misleading the House. The PM said he thought it was exaggerated but he is clearly expecting a rough ride on it. He thinks the real problem on this is that Kaufman is too arrogant while Varley tends to be too dismissive of any criticism.

In the evening I went to a quite mad dinner at the LSE to discuss a new Brookings Institute. It soon deteriorated into a petty squabble between the representatives of the existing institutes (Eric Roll and Charles Carter) and the SSRC. It was appalling academic pettiness. A representative of Leverhulme was there with a possible £2 million to spend on Policy Studies, but he walked out just before the end, handing Dahrendorf, who was in the chair, a note saying they would not get a penny because of these silly researchers resisting a big institute because it makes them seem inadequate.

I now see little prospect of getting any progress on this front in Britain. Everybody is too small-minded.

Friday 24 February 1978

I drove in early, after my dawn run over the Heath, and read papers and then went to the deputy secs meeting at 9.45. Nothing particularly interesting came up there.

I went out for lunch with Harry Evans at the RAC. He was full of life as ever – and offered me a job when I leave No. 10. Actually his *Sunday Times* has the story that I will get the editorship of the *New Statesman*, which is to be decided in the next week. I have denied it, which is correct, because I don't want it. But I did get a curious indirect approach. I came back after lunch (the PM had already left for the country) and fiddled around restlessly, dictating a few letters and making some phone calls. Then I got fed up and went home, picked up the family and drove to Suffolk for the weekend.

My mind has been on election strategy, focused on the Ilford by-election but really concerned with the general election.

My view is that we must establish an image of Thatcher as a dangerous woman who will divide our society and create trouble. We are doing this now over immigration. Instead of ducking this issue, as many have advised, I have pressed the PM to take it head-on and attack her for inciting racial hatred – and so causing violence on the streets. We will not win any votes on the immigration issue this way: Thatcher will gain a lot on that in the short run. But I hope that in the long run we can broaden it out to her disadvantage. So we shall show that she is abrasive and divisive on industrial relations, confronting the trade unions. And on Scottish devolution. And on social security casualties – 'scroungers, etc'. And on the unemployed – attacking redundancy payments.

It is a gamble. She may ride in on the subterranean 'fascistic' instincts which are very widespread at a time of economic depression and individual frustration such as we have had in the past three years. But I think that we might damage her in a long general election campaign. And the PM is exactly right to beat her because he symbolises all the opposite virtues – harmony on race and social issues; unity on devolution; understanding and experience on Ireland; conciliation in industrial relations. He is the great healer. Nobody knows if it will work. But at least it is a logical and coherent strategy.

Monday 27 February 1978

I did not run this morning because it was pouring with rain. So I drove in to Downing Street and cleared my papers quite early. Actually the flow of papers has been much less than for a long time; and the PM's diary has been fairly clear.

This morning he called in Peter Shore to discuss Windscale nuclear plant. Shore does not want to go ahead with Windscale and is trying to stop it even though the Committee of Inquiry has ruled for going ahead. The PM wants to go ahead, but wants to take Mrs Thatcher with him so he has talked a great deal to Shore about it.

I went to lunch at Grieveson Grant and then came back to another quiet afternoon.

In the evening I went to the Café Royal for a pleasant supper with David Webster of the BBC. He was lobbying me about the Annan Report on Broadcasting and made it quite clear that the Home Office and the BBC were completely in cahoots, officials showing him all the confidential Whitehall documents on Annan. Did not get home till 12.30.

News from Ilford is not good. There has been bad luck with the economic news, the immigrant issue, the threatened oil strike, etc. Tessa Jowell is a super candidate, but I cannot see how she can win.

Tuesday 28 February 1978

Had a long run this morning, though I felt fairly lethargic. I am going through a 'down' period at the moment. I went into the Gen 116 on the steel industry, but it was low-key so I left in the middle. That committee has agreed on closure, compensation, etc. – so there is little of interest in the ministerial discussions.

Had lunch upstairs in No. 10. Then to Parliamentary Questions briefing. We all pressed the PM to be a bit more optimistic – he resisted, saying there was nothing to be optimistic about. But he was in a good mood, and in fact performed much better, not exchanging punches with Thatcher as much as last week.

Coming back to No. 10 after Questions I first ran into Bill Housden, H. Wilson's driver. He discussed with me his prospective book of memoirs. He said he would not do it till he retired (in three years) but then wanted a publisher and a ghostwriter. He said that the thing which most influenced him was seeing how much money Harold and Marcia had made out of it all. 'So why shouldn't the peasants make a few pennies?' he said.

Then I saw Shirley Williams running round frantically in the Westminster Palace Yard. She told me she had lost her driver but when found she would give me a lift to No. 10 for the industrial democracy meeting. In desperation she suggested to her permanent secretary, Jim Hamilton, that he drive. He got in, but could not start the engine. Then the driver came running up. But Shirley discovered she had lost her brief for the meeting and went running off to try to find her secretary to see if he had got it. She came back empty-handed and we frantically set off late for No. 10.

I did not go to the industrial democracy meeting where the trade unionists rejected the PM's suggestions of a compromise, with some modest reforming legislation, demanding all or nothing. So it is nothing. Instead I went back and completed a draft on the Annan Report on Broadcasting for tomorrow's Cabinet committee.

Walter Winterbottom, the former England football manager, came in for a drink and we discussed Sports Council affairs. I don't think he knows how much I did to get him his knighthood. The PM came in to Private Office around 8 o'clock. We chatted. He said that he wanted to abolish the BBC governors. It was his revenge for the programme *Yesterday's Men*, which he thought was the most disgraceful political broadcast ever. I finally came home at 9.

Wednesday 1 March 1978

Went in early for the Gen 114 Cabinet committee on the Annan Report on Broadcasting. The PM opened by complaining about the leaking to the BBC – which he knows is from the Home Office. They discussed the proposed new fourth channel. Rees wanted to reject Annan's Open Broadcasting Authority and give it to the IBA. The PM opposed him on this, and virtually every other minister supported him. One factor which had impressed him was a table he had in an appendix, comparing the Home Office reactions to Annan with Labour and Tory policies. The Home Office views coincided with Tory policy on every issue. The PM said that he wanted to split up the BBC. There is too much concentrated power in the hands of the Director General.

But there was not a clear majority of ministers for splitting the BBC – though Hattersley, Benn and Foot supported the PM. Instead they were attracted by Bill Rodgers's compromise – to set up separate boards for TV, domestic radio and overseas radio, which would be appointed by the government. Rees had a bad time throughout the meeting and the PM enjoyed himself.

I learned today the real reason why the PM has been off form recently. He is very worried about Audrey, who has felt very poorly ever since returning from India. Her blood count is very odd. Clearly they are worried about leukaemia – though it could just be a virus.

I had lunch at the Reform with my Canadian friend Mike Kirby, who told me that Trudeau is in trouble in Canada and could easily lose his election.

The afternoon went very quietly, with few papers and no meetings.

The good news was that today's rail strike is called off. But the *Telegraph* has a Gallup poll showing the Tories 22% ahead at Ilford – which is sad for our candidate, Tessa Jowell, who has fought a terrific campaign.

In the evening I went to the Commons for drinks with Denis Howell – who is a bit worried about the Bryant corruption trial in Birmingham, where the prosecution are threatening to attack (but not to accuse) him. So the defence may have to subpoena him as a witness. I then went to the Strangers Bar and had a couple of drinks with Gerry Fowler, who is still looking round for a job outside of politics. Home at 10 p.m.

Thursday 2 March 1978

I was a little late in to Downing Street and missed the start of Cabinet. I spent the whole morning on the Brookings initiative. Douglas Allen and Michael Franklin*, the excellent FCO representative, came in to discuss our tactics in Paris this weekend, where we are attending the big Ford Conference as the official British representatives.

Went to lunch at the Midland Bank with Tom McNally – who made some lovely digs at the chairman, William Armstrong, a former head of the Civil Service. We came straight, back to the Commons for Questions briefing, which was very jolly and put the PM in a good mood. Questions itself went much better, with him seeming much more relaxed (Audrey had come to sit in the gallery and give him support). I saw him afterwards and he obviously felt more pleased with himself.

A Brookings crisis arose in the evening when I privately learned that the Germans had decided to oppose the Ford initiative for a new policy research institute in Europe. I reported this to the Cabinet Office and they frantically telephoned the FCO and Brussels but could find nothing about it. I checked back and got it confirmed – but still our massive great machine in Brussels was unable to find anything about it. Franklin said, 'I'm sorry, but it seems your sources are better than ours.' So we will have a frantic briefing session tomorrow to decide what attitude to take in response to the Germans. It is hairy – but all exciting so I shall enjoy the battle at Versailles.

I came home to have dinner with Graham Greene, whose wife has just had a premature baby on a visit to Jersey and is forced to stay there. Graham still wants me to go into banking or publishing when I leave No. 10.

I talked to Tessa Jowell in Ilford after the polls closed. She said she was bound to lose. It had rained in the evening and only 50–70% of our promises had turned out in the council estates of Hainault – elsewhere in the more middle-class areas our vote has been well up, even above 1974 standards. So it looked to her like a 5–7,000 Tory majority. Later we heard the result – 5,000 Tory majority, which is a swing of 6.9%, the lowest swing to the Tories in two years and better than anybody expected. A great relief.

Tomorrow off to Versailles. Back on Monday morning.

Monday 6 March 1978

The Ford Conference in Versailles on a Brookings Institute in Europe went very well. The Germans tried to block it, but failed. The EEC Commission moved in to merge with our initiative, being afraid they would otherwise miss the train, and they succeeded. I enjoyed it immensely, though I still do not know if we will have a European Brookings. Paris was glorious in the spring sunshine. We reached the airport so early this morning that I switched to the 9 o'clock plane and I was in London before 9 (London time). I went straight to the office and quickly got to work on papers.

I had lunch with Joe Haines. He is in good form, and gaining influence at the *Mirror*, but is very bitter about the way in which McCaffrey is excluding the *Mirror* from his No. 10 press briefings. Since they are the only Labour paper, this is a catastrophic and petty action.

Went back to the monetary seminar at No. 10 which was delayed because of Owen's statement on Rhodesia and did not finish till 6 p.m. Went well discussing a package on achieving growth and a stable dollar. The PM will go to see Carter and Schmidt about it.

Home at 8.30 pm and early to bed.

Tuesday 7 March 1978

Had a nice early morning run on a fine spring morning. In to the EY Cabinet committee on energy conservation. A very cheerful meeting, with most people in favour of further measures to save energy by subsidising insulation, etc. Then we had a meeting in the PM's study on the North Sea oil White Paper – Hunt, Stowe, the two Toms and me. Hunt had opposed (1) having an introduction, and (2) having a press conference. The PM decided to have both. Then we planned how to handle it on publication day – 22 March. He asked me to brief the Liberals and the TUC. I was pleased at this – and also when the PM said he thought our draft White Paper was really very good.

At Questions the PM was absolutely back on his best form. Relaxed. No swapping punches with Thatcher. He won easily. And the increase in morale on our side was very evident. I dashed back to the office to make some phone calls and then to write a brief on Ireland. Interrupted by Bob Worcester who reported that the next opinion poll in the *Express* would show us only 1–2% behind the Tories. I took this to the PM in his study

– he was asleep with his feet up on the table, but he didn't mind me waking him up with this news.

I came home early – 8 p.m. – because Carol was out and I looked after the children.

Wednesday 8 March 1978

I decided not to go to Gen 116 on British Steel – this was important, but was mainly on how to finance the corporation's enormous debts. I preferred to stay in the office and work with Gavyn Davies and David Lipsey on a brief on public expenditure for tomorrow's Cabinet, where there is an extra £500 million of contingency expenditure to come on British Leyland, British Steel, etc.

Went to LSE for a quick lunch with Nelson Polsby, a nice and bright visiting American professor there (how typical that only a visiting American asks me to go there).

Spent the afternoon working further on the public expenditure brief. Then went to the Cabinet committee on Ireland at the PM's room in the Commons. It was a fascinating meeting. Secretary of State Roy Mason confirmed all my worst fears – he has been so shocked by the bombing of the Le Mons restaurant by the IRA that he has become spokesman of the Protestants. He used first names – Jimmy (Molyneaux), Harry (West), Enoch (Powell) – referring to the Ulster Unionist politicians, but was offhand about the Catholics and scathing about the Republic. He repeatedly attacked Irish PM Jack Lynch, wrongly blaming him for the violence in the North (obviously he is trying to switch responsibility from himself). The PM let him go on like this and then asked him why we were not capturing more IRA men. Mason said there were about 600 Provisionals, concentrated in the big towns, and working in very small units of two or three, so they could not be caught. The PM then said to him sharply, 'So why do you expect Lynch to succeed in Dublin where you fail in Belfast?' The PM asked, 'Will we ever win this? What is your strategy?' The chief of staff said confidently, 'We will win . . . soon.' Heard that before.

Frank Judd*, from the FCO, said he was worried about the deterioration in Anglo–Irish relations and that it seemed as if we were in the middle of no-man's-land watching two sides firing at one another. The PM interrupted to say that his worry was different – 'that we are sitting in the trenches with the Protestants'. He added that he did not want any more attacks on Lynch who he thought was a good man, though getting politically weak because he probably would not stay in office much longer. The younger Irish ministers were manoeuvring to succeed him and playing politics with the North. He particularly named [Michael] O'Kennedy*, the Foreign minister.

Mason came in rather pathetically to complain that whatever we do for the Catholics, 'they don't come any nearer to Whitehall: they stay green'. He clearly does not understand the Irish at all. He often calls me 'green' to my face. I suppose I am a bit although I hate the IRA.

The committee then turned to the bill for greater Ulster representation at Westminster in response to the Speakers Conference. Mason put his case for immediate legislation, claiming that the only opposition was Gerry Fitt, and nobody else from the North had complained to him (this is because he is completely cut off from the Catholic community). Rees, Healey and Elwyn Jones all intervened to oppose legislation this session. The PM accepted this, adding that 'I'm against any more Irishmen in Parliament at any time – except for people with names like Callaghan and Healey' (or Donoughue and McNally!).

The PM then asked Mason to stay behind, and gave him firm instructions to lay off Lynch and improve his relations with the Catholics. The PM had completely taken the line in my earlier brief about not completely taking the Loyalist side and this was very satisfying. The PM then had a meeting with Merlyn Rees about immigration. He had asked the Home Office for its proposed reactions to the House of Commons immigration report. The Home Office response was totally negative on every issue. The PM told Rees off for this and instructed him to react positively. Jim has had a good day.

I went back to No. 10 to finalise the public expenditure brief and then left for home at 8.30.

Thursday 9 March 1978

Cabinet took public expenditure this morning. The PM gave them a lecture on public expenditure getting out of control. He told them to pick a few politically desirable items, but not many, and they would not decide yet. Afterwards he told me that he did not want lots of newspaper stories about big public expenditure concessions even before the Budget.

I worked in the office and had a long chat with my friend George Jones, and then lunched in No. 10, where we mainly discussed the details of the Budget. Questions went exceptionally well. The PM has re-established himself. He has decided not to attack Thatcher personally but to treat the Opposition with disdain. He does this very well, appearing prime ministerial, and she looks very poor by comparison.

I went home early feeling very tired. I am suffering the after-effects of working throughout last weekend.

Friday 10 March 1978

I went in early to clear papers before the deputy secretaries meeting in John Hunt's grand room in the Cabinet Office. There we had a long discussion on Ireland. Apparently Roy Mason and the Northern Ireland Office have still not taken the message of the Cabinet committee. They still want to attack Lynch and actually telephoned Hunt after the Irish committee to ask that there be NO reference in the minutes about establishing better relations with the Republic. I told Hunt that he must give them a hard boot, because the PM was in no doubt that Mason had got it wrong. Later in the day I heard that Mason was planning a conciliatory trip to Dublin to mend fences – but the PM was cool on this, saying that he ought to get relations better before going.

The PM had gone to meet President Tito of Yugoslavia at the airport. He returned to Claridge's with him, and then walked back across the parks. The spring sunshine was lovely and he enjoyed it, but it made our meeting late.

We met in the study at noon. First we dealt with the PM's prospective TV appearance. The PM, just like Wilson, decided to go on to ITV because of his dislike for the BBC. Then we moved on to newspapers where profiles were agreed. The worrying thing was that all of McCaffrey's suggestions were for 'posh' newspapers – the *Observer*, etc. There was nothing for a 'Labour' or a 'pop' paper. I pointed this out and the PM agreed, so something will go into a *Mirror* paper. The worrying thing is that it is all part of McCaffrey's hostility to the Mirror Group. He is out to demonstrate his difference from Joe Haines and his independence from the *Mirror*. The problem is that he is putting his own personal *amour propre* above the Prime Minister's and the government's political interests. The *Mirror* is the only paper which supports us and it is mad to alienate them.

I saw Tony Miles, managing editor of the Mirror Group, at lunchtime at the Reform. He was very bitter. He said that the *Mirror* would go its own way in the election. He claimed that McCaffrey had contacted the *Mirror* only twice since last October's Party Conference. This is a bad situation for the PM and he will have to be alerted.

I was having lunch at the Reform with Kit McMahon of the Bank of England. He expressed fears about public expenditure and took the standard current line that the existing public expenditure ceilings must not be breached. He was also a bit annoyed about the new German/American 'swap agreement' to support the dollar. It pre-empts our big initiative on the dollar, but in fact is too small to make any serious improvement.

PS. Apart from TV and press, we discussed several other items at this morning's meeting with the PM. We dealt with immigration and agreed to press Rees hard to make a positive response the moment the select committee report is announced. McNally and I then raised the abortion question and the dreadful campaign being run by SPUC. At Ilford they circulated leaflets which have been shown to the Home Office and ruled to be illegal on three counts. If sent to the DPP they would result in prosecution. The PM says he does not want a prosecution. He asked me to talk to Shirley Williams, and then to persuade the Catholic bishops to try to restrain the SPUC before we prosecute them. I talked to Shirley Williams later and we agreed to go to see bishops Butler and Mahon rather than the saintly Archbishop Hume, who she said is 'a bit unworldly' – and brother-in-law to John Hunt.

Finally we agreed the general election organisational arrangements which Tom McNally has been working on. He has put together an advisory team and the PM has agreed to see them at No. 10. But there is no speech-writer – that vacancy is being held open, possibly for Joe.

Monday 13 March 1978

The PM did not get back from Bonn till after 11. I saw him when he came in and he said it had gone well and Schmidt had encouraged him to go to Washington to see Carter. The PM then went to the Cabinet/NEC meeting – where he told them (1) the Budget would be mainly tax cuts, and (2) he was worried that unemployment was insoluble in the short run.

I cleared some correspondence and then went to the Commons for lunch with the Guinea Club. I was a guest of the *Financial Times* lobby correspondent, Richard Evans, a very nice man. We sat opposite Anthony Shrimsley of the *Sun*, who, it is rumoured, has been promised the job of Thatcher's press secretary in No. 10. I don't know if this is true, but he is certainly giving her total and craven support. I referred to a recent television programme which had criticised him and Shrimsley interrupted to warn me that he was suing the BBC and would sue me if I repeated the libel. I enjoyed this – and pointed out how journalists always complain when politicians issue writs; but they are never slow to sue themselves. He seemed a nasty man, and also very jumpy – I doubt if he has the steel to do the No. 10 job.

I came back and worked in No. 10 in the afternoon and then went to the reception for the Commonwealth Parliamentary Association upstairs. Arthur Bottomley again approached me to offer me his safe Commons seat.

Tuesday 14 March 1978

Did a full three-mile run over the Heath in a gale early this morning. Then into the Cabinet committee on the Annan Report on Broadcasting. The PM said his 'head is reeling from all the proposed bodies and initials'. On accountability, Rodgers was against change, and Williams not for much change. Benn and Hattersley put the case for letting in fresh air to the BBC – and the PM expressed sympathy with this. Benn made a superb attack on the BBC, equating them with the medieval Catholic Church, controlling thought from a middle-class Establishment position. The Labour position should be the dissenters. The PM's conclusion was that (1) we must first alter the governing structure of the BBC, and (2) also that complaints must be dealt with in a separate way.

In fact most of Annan is being rejected, so the massive BBC publicity campaign pays off – and Merlyn Rees and the Home Office successfully defend all the BBC privileges. The PM continues to press radical positions but cannot find much support outside of Benn and Hattersley, neither of whom he trusts.

After Questions, I saw Jack Ashley to discuss the Pearson Report on Compensation for Accidents, where Jack is still concerned with compensation for vaccine-damaged children. He thinks the report does not go far enough.

I was planning to go to the National Gallery for an exhibition view, but Carol phoned to say that she was ill, so I went home and saw the children to bed.

Wednesday 15 March 1978

After my early morning run, I went in to No. 10 for the latest economic seminar on monetary policy in preparation for the PM's visit to Washington next week. Very positive on a package for world growth.

The seminar broke up at 12.30 and I went to the *Guardian* Businessman of the Year lunch. I sat between amiable Tory MP Kenneth Baker* and Lady Plowden. The PM made a nice speech – quite serious about getting Britain recovering again – and when we left he asked me to travel back with him in the car. He praised his banker friend Julian Hodge's* judgement about other businessmen – the first time we have ever discussed the controversial Hodge.

I then went to the Commons to see Shirley Williams and the Catholic bishop, Konstant, about the abortion problem. The anti-abortion campaign broke the law in the Ilford by-election and we are afraid of court cases and therefore ultimately a clash between the Labour Party and the Catholic Church, which would be disastrous for us electorally and make me personally unhappy. We agreed to have a formal but private meeting with Cardinal Hume and certain other Catholics, to discuss how to put pressure on SPUC. The bishop was very nice and intelligent and took all the points.

Came back for a good meeting with Tessa Blackstone of the CPRS to discuss the NHS. Ennals, the Secretary of State for Health, has put round a dreadful paper asking for more money for the NHS. We agree with the objective, but sadly took the paper apart – a ragbag of contradictions and unsubstantiated assertions.

Worked with Gavyn on a paper for the PM for tomorrow's meeting with the Chancellor – arguing for a slightly bigger reflation than the £2 billion proposed, and for less tax concessions for the higher paid.

Went to a nice party at the Mostyn-Owens in Chelsea and not back till 1 a.m.

Thursday 16 March 1978

Worked in the office in the morning – the weather was terrible, with heavy snow. Lunch at No. 10 and then to Commons Questions. The PM is now completely back in control there – partly because Mrs Callaghan is feeling well again. The PM then made his statement on the Pearson Report on liability for accident damages. Tom McNally and I left early to see the American ambassador, to brief him for the PM's Washington visit.

The PM saw Healey to discuss the Budget. They agreed on a £2 billion Budget reflation: a reduced rate band of 25% at £750; a bit on allowances. And apparently the PM told him that they would probably have to do child allowances.

Carol came in to collect me and we went to the Covent Garden opera with Claus Moser to see Mozart's *Idomeneo*. Very lovely music, though a poor production. The Healeys were there as well. Did not get home till 1.30 because I locked our keys in the car and we had to get the police and the AA to break in!

Friday 17 March 1978

I did not see the PM today because he went off at lunchtime to Cardiff. Went to the deputy secretaries meeting in John Hunt's room. (One curious feature was that Ken Berrill arranged to take the CPRS unemployment report off the Cabinet committee agenda. This is an example of the CPRS problem – the staff do radical reports and then Ken and the 'machine' try to suppress them!)

I spent most of the rest of the day with the CPRS. The PM has asked me and Ken Berrill to comment on David Ennals's terrible paper on extra expenditure in the Health Service. So we decided to put in a joint paper. I worked most of the day with Tessa Blackstone. I produced a general introduction on the state of the NHS – whether it is really in crisis. Tessa wrote detailed comments on Ennals's paper.

Carol was feeling ill in the evening so I went home at 8.

Monday 20 March 1978

The last week before Easter – promising to be an easy week because the PM goes to Washington on Wednesday and we break for the holiday on Thursday. The PM is going for his 'summit' meeting with Carter, to try to get the world economy moving and to bridge the worrying gap between the Germans and the Americans. He is also of course going to see his grandchildren and Peter Jay and Margaret. His family is very important to him and explains why the summit was fixed for Easter time – so that the PM could stay over an extra five days with the grandchildren!

I had lunch with Robert Armstrong at the Reform and much of the discussion was about the Annan Report. He said that Merlyn Rees was badly shaken by the bashing he had taken from the PM and other ministers over the BBC. He said Merlyn had 'lost his nerve'. He suggested he should come to see the PM privately to get his support. I said that the best way was for Merlyn not to take a line totally in defence of the broadcasting establishment.

He also told me that the policeman friend of Eric Miller, who was arrested for corruption in high places, is threatening to talk about 'top political people'.

Some hi-fi people came in to No. 10 to discuss with me the plight of the British hi-fi industry. I mean to do something here to keep the Japs at bay.

Then at 6 o'clock we had the first meeting of the Election Campaign committee in the 'white' reception room upstairs. Present were: from Transport House – Hayward, Reg Underhill*, Phyllis and Percy Clarke; from No. 10 – the two Toms, Jean Denham*, David Lipsey and me, plus an advertising man, plus Derek Gladwyn* of the General and Municipal Workers Union as 'director'.

The PM opened with a little pep talk and then attacked Transport House for leaking the arrangement for the meeting. (Because of this, Mike Molloy*, excellent editor of the *Daily Mirror*, did not come.) Ron Hayward then rambled on in a most bizarre way, attacking me personally, and the H. Wilson 'entourage'. He said (contrary to all my experience) Transport House knew how to do these things and he did not want a repeat of the terrible things that went on under Harold. (McNally pointed out that we did win four out of five of the elections then!) A weakness of this set-up is that there is no permanent machinery, no provisions to meet again, no agenda for action before the autumn election.

The PM also today had a remarkable talk with David Steel about the election. They agreed the devolution referendum should be delayed, if there was an October election. On the *Budget* the PM said if Liberals opposed the Finance Bill he would *immediately* hold an election. In any case the PM thought the Liberals should disengage from the pact with us in *July*. He would then be free to go to election in October if he wanted, but could carry on if that seemed sensible. What the PM did *not* want, after July disengagement, was to prepare a legislative programme and then have the Liberals vote against the Queen's Speech, forcing a November election (i.e. he prefers to *choose* to go to an October election, disengaged from but unopposed by the Liberals, rather than to be defeated by the Liberals). *Steel* said he was 'against coming out of the pact and then fully committing himself to the Queen's Speech'. The *PM* said in July he would show Liberals the Queen's Speech. If they could not support it, he would prepare for an October election. If they did support it, though with reservations on one or two bills, he would be prepared to carry on. But this was absolutely between them.

Tuesday 21 March 1978

I did not attend the Defence and Overseas Cabinet committee this morning, but apparently it was pretty lively. David Owen wanted us to get involved in the Middle East/Lebanon UN peacekeeping operation – at a minimum by making our forces and facilities in Cyprus available to the UN as a back-up. He was opposed by Defence who, as always, are very pacifist when any suggestion arises for taking part in any military activities. They were also typically pushing the point that because of recent 'cuts' they could not put up any support facilities, and therefore they should be given more money.

The PM came down decisively *against* the Foreign Secretary – the first time he has done so on any major issue. Partly this was because he is against the UK spending large sums of money on foreign follies; partly because he thinks that the Middle East is a bog we must keep out of; partly, I suspect, because he keeps reading in the papers that he always gives David unquestioning support – so he proved to his colleagues that he does not and that he has no favourites.

I worked in the office for the rest of the morning. We had lunch in No. 10 and then to Questions, which went quietly, with Thatcher not intervening at all. Immediately afterwards the PM made his statement introducing the White Paper on North Sea oil. He was very positive, if deliberately low-key, and left the Tories totally split over whether to give all the proceeds away on tax cuts or whether to use some for investment.

We all went along afterwards to the press conference. The PM was there flanked by Healey, Benn and Millan. There wasn't a lot of excitement, as the whole thing had been leaked to the press for weeks in advance.

Wednesday 22 March 1978

The PM was in No. 10 this morning and then left at shortly after 11 a.m. for Washington. He went on a commercial flight, a British Airways jumbo – and inevitably it was half an hour late! I don't suppose he will go commercial again!

I went to lunch at the Ivy with Anthony Holden of the *Sunday Times* – a very nice and intelligent man, with much more depth than most journalists. He is writing a book on Prince Charles, from which he will make a vast amount of money.

Afterwards I worked with Gavyn Davies on a telegram to the PM commenting on a Treasury paper on the Budget. This paper had attacked the No. 10 position because we had opposed massive tax cuts for the top-rate taxpayers. It accused us of pursuing 'doctrinal redistribution' and 'cutting the living standards' of the middle class. In fact 'our' Budget proposals give a bigger percentage – and a *much* bigger absolute rebate to the upper bracket, and certainly do not involve any *cut* in living standards. It was a curiously hysterical paper (by nice Lawrence Airey) and we gently knocked it down.

In the evening I went to a film premiere with Bob Worcester – and afterwards to dinner at Manzi's. Bruce Page, the new editor of the *New Statesman*, joined us. I did not get any clear impression since he talks like he writes, very densely. Home at 12.30.

Thursday 23 March 1978

Adam Raphael of the *Observer* came in for an interview in the afternoon, and I then went home to look after the children. (Carol has gone away to Blackpool for the NUT Conference.)

Am going to Suffolk with the children and my brother Clem tomorrow. Carol will be back next Wednesday. The weather is terrible – cold, windy and wet.

Friday 24–Thursday 30 March 1978

In Suffolk with the children enjoying their rare company and painting the cottage.

Friday 31 March 1978

I came up from Suffolk yesterday evening – a lovely spring evening – on the train, but it took three and a half hours, so I was too late for Euen Ferguson's farewell party at the Foreign Office.

This morning I stayed home in Hampstead while my marvellous new hi-fi system was installed – and then one of the speakers wasn't working! Went into the office in the afternoon and put in a brief pointing out that last year's public expenditure 'shortfall' – underspending – was £4 *billion*, completely unplanned, arising from cash limits, etc., and fifteen times the sums the Treasury are now opposing spending.

Went to a delicious dinner with our neighbours the Reads, and to bed at 1 a.m.

Monday 3 April 1978

I went back to Suffolk for the weekend and came up to London this morning by train.

Worked on papers in the morning, and then lunch at No. 10 with the *Mirror* editorial people who made a lot of sensible suggestions. The PM said that he thinks that beating inflation is *politically* more important than beating unemployment (though he regrets the latter). So he will go for 5% on wages next year – and is prepared to take the trade unions on. He said that the *Liberals* ought to break with us in July, for their own good, and he had told David Steel this. He felt we could not chase the Tories 'down every hole' on issues such as immigration and law and order. We must hold to our principles, and if we lose on it 'so be it'. He did not think that the election would be decided on issues like these, but on bread and butter – prices, etc.

The PM saw Healey at 5 o'clock about the Budget and they discussed the tax proposals. The PM did not like the fact that least was given to people in the £5–10,000 bracket and he asked for something to be done about this. On public expenditure Healey said he did not want to do child benefits next November, but the PM said he thought they might not be able to avoid it because of backbench amendments to the Finance Bill. The total is now roughly £2.5 billion.

In the evening we had a reception at No. 10 for the Welsh rugby team and supporters. It was lively and enjoyable, almost riotous at times. It is the first No. 10 reception I have known where the waiters had to lock the door between the reception room and the small room where the drinks are prepared. Some of the men locked out were huge and very thirsty-looking. There was a marvellous moment when Geraint Evans and the PM led the singing in a lovely Welsh hymn. I went off to supper afterwards and was not home till 1.30 a.m.

Tuesday 4 April 1978

At the Budget Cabinet the PM apparently lectured them on leaks – the *FT* has been getting everything from the Treasury lately – and they decided not to circulate any Cabinet minutes and to tell nobody.

While Cabinet was meeting, I went to the NEB to discuss the hi-fi industry with the chairman, Lesley Murphy. He is a bit lacking in drive and vision. I don't know if I persuaded him to take a more active interest in our threatened audio industry.

Had lunch upstairs at No. 10. The main topic of discussion is Carter's sudden volte-face decision not to make the neutron bomb, just when Western leaders had gone out on a limb to justify the decision to make it. This adds to the feeling that the Americans are all over the place. The PM said to me yesterday, 'Carter just had not got things together.'

The first PM's Questions to be radio broadcast. The PM was very calm and relaxed and did not tangle with Thatcher at all. She upset people by intervening *three* times, all on statistical questions about comparative unemployment figures. She looked *very* pale and tense and sounded harsh. This was in some ways a trial run for the election, and we came away feeling very confident.

I dashed back to attend the briefing meeting for the EEC summit this weekend. The PM clearly felt on top of the issues and finished things quite early. In a sense this Copenhagen meeting is bound to be low-key because they want to save any *big* decisions and announcements for the World Economic summit in Bonn in July. The PM interestingly raised the question of a European Brookings and said he would fight for it in London, trading off the European Foundation to Paris.

I then went home to listen to *Tosca* on my hi-fi till midnight.

Wednesday 5 April 1978

Helen Liddell came through from Glasgow, Garscadden, where we are in the middle of a by-election. She said that the abortion issue was getting out of hand and the priests were intervening on the doorstep and in the pulpit. She is finding Labour Catholics who say that they can no longer support Labour because of our position on abortion. The PM had asked for a report on my dealings with Shirley Williams and the hierarchy. The PM's feeling was that there was not much that we could do about it. When I saw him later he gave a positive commitment that there would be nothing in the manifesto about freer abortion. I then talked to Bishop Konstant over the phone. He said he had talked to SPUC and warned them not to break the law – they clearly do not know what the law is. On more general abortion issues, I pushed him, but he pointed out that it was not the Church but Labour's extremists who brought abortion on to the political stage. I agreed, but said that the question was not who is to blame, but what to do now. And I felt it was bad for everybody if the priests were intervening against the Labour Party. This would produce a reaction – in the Party and among Labour Protestants. We could have a Belfast situation in Glasgow.

I went out shopping at lunchtime – Carol and the children are still in the country – and snatched a beefburger at the LSE. Came back for the meeting on Brookings in John Hunt's room in the Cabinet Office. We went through the Ford paper for this weekend's Paris meeting. Everybody was remarkably constructive. Treasury is clearly willing to pay several million pounds to get the institute here. When we broke up I felt well briefed.

Will Plowden came in in the evening for a drink. He is desperately keen to leave the Civil Service, being totally bored by the Department of Industry and has applied to be director of the Institute of Public Administration. We were repeatedly interrupted by phone calls – Hayden Phillips from Brussels, Harold Lever on his battles with Joel Barnett over tax relief for small firms, Shirley Williams on abortion, and various friends.

Then I came home at 8.30, buying fish and chips at Tufnell Park and dropping in to the local pub for a pint, and then home to listen to music. I stayed up till 1 a.m.

Thursday 6 April 1978

Cabinet had little on the agenda and was over by midday. I had a chat with Bill Rodgers beforehand – he is gradually relaxing and playing a bigger part in Cabinet.

I worked on papers and then Hal Sonnenfeldt came in from Washington. He said that Americans are getting very depressed by the failure of the Carter administration to pull itself together. He had seen the PM in Washington and said he made a good impression – and that he also praised the Policy Unit. Hal's analysis of the Carter problems is that there is no overall strategy. Everybody is functioning individually and in isolation. Decisions are taken instinctively and in isolation, with no relation to any overall strategy.

I took Shirley Williams to lunch at the Grange in Covent Garden. We had a lovely time: nice food, good chat, some serious talk about education and abortion, but a lot of happy gossip. She is quite delightful, but not single-minded enough to become leader of the Party. We drove straight back from the restaurant to the Commons for Questions. These went well for the PM again. The challenge of broadcasting has lifted him and he is winning each round convincingly.

I did not stay to hear the statement on immigration by Merlyn Rees – which looked terribly negative and wishy-washy to me. Merlyn is very dominated by his Home Office civil servants and recently has great difficulty getting things right politically.

The PM went off to Windsor to spend the night with the Queen. No doubt the problem of Princess Margaret will come up. Ken Stowe was on the phone all day about the Civil List. They seem to have cut down the increase in royal pay a bit.

I am beginning to pursue thoughts about bringing in protection in this country. Since we cannot expand without flooding the country with imports and ruining our balance of payments – in the past seven years production has remained static, but imports have *doubled* – we have to find another way. This does not mean I go all the way with Benn's alternative strategy, but it might mean modified protection. I have talked to David Owen, and he and his adviser, Michael Stewart, are thinking along similar lines. Tony Benn has also put in a paper calling for protection based on multinational negotiations. So it is coming up from several directions. Our 'Buy British' initiative will be a useful vehicle for this.

Home at 9 p.m. to pack for Paris weekend tomorrow.

Monday 10 April 1978

Awoke in Paris and flew back very early – the hour's difference made it a *terribly* early start and I was tired for the rest of the day. Carol came in for lunch – have barely seen one another for two weeks.

Went to the House for the PM's low-key statement on the Copenhagen meeting of the European heads of government. Apparently Copenhagen was not as negative as appeared. At breakfast Giscard put forward his plan for protection *within* the EEC, based on some scheme of protecting *shares* of trade *within* the EEC. Helmut Schmidt has also said that he doesn't mind a bit of protection within the EEC – indeed that he would prefer that Britain had protection for a couple of years rather than that Germany took the risk of reflating.

Back to No. 10 – and then home very early. I was tired, but the children sat up late with me and we played music.

Tuesday 11 April 1978

Budget Day – Healey's thirteenth Budget. It has been carefully designed to offend nobody and should help politically since it gives a little bit to everybody, but overall it is too small to make much difference.

Tom McNally and I watched the Budget on TV. It was a good Healey speech, much shorter than previously and with the proposals integrated into the analysis of the financial indices. I fell asleep in the armchair while watching the TV in the outside room at the Commons. I woke feeling rather ashamed and turned to McNally to apologise, but found him asleep as well!

Went back to No. 10 to clear off papers and discuss with Gavyn Davies our plans to write a paper on possibly bringing in some protection here. I have arranged a meeting with Michael Stewart, David Owen's adviser, and we hope to do a paper to put to the PM at an appropriate time. Nothing can be done till after the election, but we must be well prepared before then. I sense that the PM will not be opposed. Apparently he spoke to Benn after yesterday's Budget Cabinet and said that only three options faced us. In order of preference they are: international action, through the PM's 'Carter Initiative'; protection within the EEC: or protection on a one-country basis. Apparently Benn said he was very interested in protection within the EEC – he had never realised that it might be possible to have protection *within* the EEC.

In the evening I took George Grant and Harry Cowans, two marvellous Labour MPs from the North-East, to dinner at the Reform. They were very pleased with the Budget – and very contemptuous of the left wing for inevitably criticising it. Back to the Strangers Bar at the Commons for a pint and then home at 10.30.

It is still very cold, with snow lying on the Heath and the gardens.

Wednesday 12 April 1978

I started my morning runs again, after a layoff. It is still very wintry, with no sign of spring.

The reaction to the Budget has been fairly favourable. The main strain of *political* criticism has been that it is too cautious. We don't mind that. Once the terrible balance of payments figures are out on Friday, it will be clear that we could not have risked more – because of imports, not because of inflation.

I took David Owen's new private secretary, George Walden*, to lunch at the Reform. Obviously bright and *very* political, probably a Tory. I need to keep that line open, especially now that Owen is pursuing the same cautious 'protection' line as we are.

Back to see Janet Morgan*, who edited *The Crossman Diaries* and is coming to join the CPRS this summer.

The EY Cabinet committee met at 5 to discuss industrial democracy. Great sighs of relief all round. Shirley Williams, Edmund Dell and Albert Booth have reached a sort of compromise, giving trade unions one-third of

board representation and to apply a long timetable. So it is not full Bullock
– but it is progress.

The PM was very pleased. None of us thought it would be possible even
to have a draft White Paper this year. Now we will have a White Paper in
May.

Afterwards I went for supper with Harry Evans. He is very fed up with
the unions at the *Sunday Times* and they are considering issuing notices to
all the staff.

Home at 9 p.m.

Thursday 13 April 1978

Helen Liddell phoned from Garscadden at noon. She was a bit depressed
about the by-election. It was snowing in Glasgow and turnout at midday
was only 8%. She said we had too few workers and no idea of how we had
done at any previous election, as there are no records whatever. Went to
lunch with Joe Haines. He is much happier now he has his regular writing
job, as chief leader writer on the *Mirror* – but they still complain about bad
relations with the No. 10 Press Office.

Back to Commons Questions. Then the PM flew off to the North. Helen
Liddell came back on the phone at teatime, very depressed. The turnout
looked very low – and a blizzard had started. But Bob Worcester – running
an opinion poll from London – told me it looked good, with a forecast
majority of over 10%.

Michael Stewart came in to discuss 'protection'. He has written a good
paper for David Owen suggesting bilateral discussions to restrain imports
and a scheme whereby manufactured imports could only be bought with
foreign exchange earnings from exports. But nothing can actually be *done*
till after the election. Home at 9.

I phoned Garscadden again at 7.30. Our people were still depressed. But
Bob Worcester was jubilant, and certain we would win by about 12%. I
passed this on to the Prime Minister in Huddersfield, where it was given
to him on the platform of a big meeting. (He made a big speech about 'Buy
British'.) Then when I phoned Garscadden at 9.30, they finally realised
Labour was winning – and a late flood of voters pushed the turnout up to
the general-election levels of 70%. So we won by 4,500 – 12%! Worcester
in London knew much more about what was going on than the Party officials
in the constituency. Apparently the Budget had helped quite a bit – and
child benefits were said to have neutralised abortion as an issue among
Catholic women.

I went to bed after midnight feeling rather pleased with life.

Friday 14 April 1978

The PM away all day today in the North. Lunch at the German Economic minister's home. He wants to know from me what his Chancellor Schmidt is up to. The *Financial Times* has reported a German initiative to establish monetary stability in Europe through a modified 'snake'. We have discussed it in No. 10 and are not unsympathetic, providing it is not simply an anti-American move. But the German Embassy knows *nothing* about it. One more example of how the diplomatic corps are redundant in most countries. Serious things now happen at Prime-Minister-to-Prime-Minister level.

Afterwards quickly to the Pig and Whistle in Little Chester Street to discuss the coming Anglo-Irish parliamentary football game with Kevin O'Shea and Jimmy Brazil from the Irish Embassy.

Back to No. 10 to clear my papers and then off to Ascot for a conference to discuss President Carter's first year. I am tired and irritable and won't be much use to them.

Monday 17 April 1978

Another quiet day – things are remarkably calm at present. For some weeks, even months, the amount of paper – reflecting the number of meetings – has definitely declined. The PM has reduced the amount of business that he personally is conducting. Even so, his diary remains quite busy for a man of 66!

I telephoned Archie Kirkwood, who works as personal assistant to David Steel. He made it clear that the Liberals do *not* want a crisis over the Budget. But my old friend John Pardoe has boxed himself into a corner. Having demanded cuts in the standard rate of tax, and not having got them, he feels compelled to make a crisis over it. David Steel doesn't want this, but there is a limit to how far he can control Pardoe. Also Denis Healey has handled Pardoe very badly, bullying him in public. Ken Stowe told me that the PM was complaining about this at the weekend.

Tuesday 18 April 1978

There was a fascinating EY Cabinet committee to discuss a move towards accepting protectionism. It is not that anybody has been converted *away* from free trade. Just that the free traders seem tacitly to accept that at present it no longer works to Britain's advantage.

Afterwards Shirley Williams came to my room for coffee. We had a long chat about abortion (we have arranged another meeting with the Catholic bishops) and protectionism.

Questions ran smoothly again. The Tories have been embarrassed by a story in *The Times* about how they have had a committee reporting on whether they could use troops to break a strike. Naturally we gave this a good run – though the PM was reluctant to in briefing, on the grounds that any responsible government might have to use troops, so it was prudent to examine it in advance. Mrs Thatcher looked embarrassed and I sensed that, particularly after Garscadden, the Tories are getting depressed again.

All the press talk is about whether the Liberals will destroy the Budget by moving amendments to cut income tax, which the Tories would support. But nobody seems to know what they will do. I talked to Archie Kirkwood from David Steel's office, and it was clear that they don't know what John Pardoe is up to. Apparently he was convinced that we would reduce income tax and thought that, by demanding it, he would get credit for it. Now we did not, he feels committed to go on demanding it.

Then Bob Worcester gave a long presentation on elections and voting, with slides, in Tom McNally's room. A lot of outsiders were present. Interesting, but a bit unfocused and very rambling discussion, and the room got hotter and more whisky was consumed.

Home late.

Wednesday 19 April 1978

Nice early morning run over the Heath. Ran into Michael Foot and we had a chat near Kenwood at 7.30 a.m.

Policy Unit meeting at 10 a.m. on protection. We begin to get a more balanced view and decide to look at alternative trade systems.

I attended the lunch for African leader Hastings Banda upstairs in No. 10. Small gathering, very personal and nice. Banda was very emotional in his affection for the PM, who he said was the first British politician ever to invite him to his *home* as opposed to his room at the Commons.

To the Commons for the PM's statement on giving Northern Ireland more seats. We had little alternative since it was a unanimous Speakers Conference decision. But it is not good – part of the drift towards the Prod position of integration with the mainland. It was attacked by Fitt and some Catholic Labour MPs. It will split the Party when it comes. But we have to hold the Ulster Unionists till the election – and the PM was quite clear that there would be no legislation yet. Afterwards both Merlyn Rees and Stan Orme came to me and said how worried they were that Roy Mason had gone totally into the Ulster Protestants' pockets.

Back to No. 10 and then off to Wembley for the Brazil-England football game. Exciting journey, in cavalcade with motorbike escorts. Very good game, with excellent England performance, a bit unlucky only to draw 1–1. Sat at dinner after with Ted and Cathy Croker – our hosts – and the Earl of Harewood.

Thursday 20 April 1978

Very wet so could not go running. I spent the morning dictating letters and reading – though the flow of papers remains low. The workload is still low. Had lunch at No. 10. We discussed Cabinet – which had decided to give the armed forces a 14% pay rise. This breaches the pay policy, and I think it is a mistake. But the PM and nearly everybody else thinks it is the right and only thing to do.

Tom McCaffrey told us that some Civil Service information officers are on strike. They have for long been claiming overtime – at double time – for Sundays because they read newspapers and watch TV on Sundays. Last week one of them claimed eighteen hours = thirty-six hours = about £100 for his Sunday spent reading the papers. This was refused and so they are now 'banning' overtime. Since the ban, the department has found that there is an average of only one call per night or weekend to each of them. Another Civil Service privilege scandal. In their current pay settlement the civil servants have demanded and been given their increments backdated a year. Everybody else is being told – by the civil servants involved – that it is not possible to pay increments until after this round's settlement. Typical of the double standards which operate, with the machine always looking after itself first.

Question Time was again quiet. Mrs Thatcher does not look too happy and has lately been asking very peripheral questions – about engineers' pay today. This probably means they have realised that unemployment, which is an issue on which they have been attacking, actually helps us.

Back at No. 10. There was a briefing in the Cabinet Room preparing for Schmidt's visit next week. I decided not to go to the meeting, but I chatted to Frank Cooper, now at Defence, but formerly at Northern Ireland. He said he 'did not like the smell' of the situation in Ulster. He felt that Roy Mason did not realise that one has to keep working hard to maintain the status quo – and on both sides.

David Bacon, an old friend from the Sports Council in the 1960s, came in in the evening and we chatted about football, business, etc.

During the evening I was in touch with Bob Worcester at the BBC, who was polling in today's Brixton/Lambeth by-election. Bob felt that we were well ahead and doing better as the evening progressed. The swing against us looked like 8½% at 4 p.m., 7% at 7 p.m. and below 5% at 10 o'clock. In fact it was 9% at the end. Clearly some people were telling Bob they were voting Labour – but in fact voted National Front, which came third, ahead of the Liberals. A bit disappointing.

Friday 21 April 1978

The PM was away today in Plymouth and Devonport. We were all a little disappointed with last night's by-election result in Brixton/Lambeth.

We had another very quiet day in the Unit. I did some shopping in the middle of the day and went to the bank – sometimes I often cannot get round to that for weeks on end and anyway have no cash.

Trevor West came in in the late afternoon – he is an Irish senator friend from Dublin. We are trying to arrange a football game between the English and Irish Parliaments.

Then to dinner with Johnny Apple of the *New York Times* at a nice Italian restaurant in Mayfair. Home at midnight.

Monday 24 April 1978

The PM was at Chequers with Schmidt till 4.30. Apparently the talks went well, very friendly, though we did not persuade the Germans to go in for very much expansion. But at least the PM persuaded Schmidt that any solution to the monetary question need not be anti-American, but could be support for the dollar.

I cleared my papers and then had lunch with Robin Butler, who used to be with us in No. 10 and is now back at the Treasury. Afterwards we walked in the Park and discussed the lack of loyalty in the machine – how the moment any civil servant, however good, is under a cloud, his colleagues back off and leave him completely alone.

Back to No. 10 and was there for the arrival of Schmidt and the PM. I did not bother to go into the plenary session, as it was made clear that nothing important would be discussed. The British problem is that we have not discovered what the Germans have in mind. They have talked about a new initiative in the monetary field – but have not told us the details. We have been sceptical, as we want an international, not a European, solution.

I went home early to listen to music.

Tuesday 25 April 1978

Went in early after a lovely dawn run on the Heath – saw Michael Foot up near Kenwood and had a long chat about the political scene.

The PM went off to the Labour Party liaison committee – apparently in a grumpy mood, as he moaned at Tom McNally about the inadequacy of his briefing on these Party occasions.

Had lunch with Jonathan Charkham from the Cabinet Office. We are still trying to make progress on his excellent scheme for opening up public appointments through open advertising for job vacancies. We are having difficulty in getting it on a Cabinet committee agenda. Nobody, political or bureaucratic, seems very interested.

Afterwards I negotiated with the Treasury about Hampden Park football ground, which is falling down. It needs £8 million to repair it and make it, as I want, into a national sports centre for Scotland. But the Treasury refuses to budge. The PM is speaking in Glasgow on Monday night and it would be quite dramatic if he could announce a new Hampden. But I doubt that he will overrule the Treasury on this.

Wednesday 26 April 1978

Again a very quiet morning. Went over to the Commons to have lunch on my own in the Commons cafeteria. Afterwards I ran into the PM in the corridor and we walked back to his room together. He had seen David Steel just before lunch. He still did not know what would happen with the Liberals over the Finance Bill. Steel made it clear that *he* did not want to bring the government down, but apparently he cannot control Pardoe. The PM said, 'We must play this one day to day.' He also gave me the impression that he is pulling back from the precipice of an election even if they do pass an amendment reducing direct tax (by 2p if the Liberals have their way, and 1p according to Tory wishes). We agreed that Healey must stop threatening the Liberals. I left him to work on his file for the 'aircraft' Cabinet committee – and before long he was asleep.

The Cabinet committee on aircraft policy at 4 p.m. was fascinating and very high-level. We had a long and complicated, but good, paper from officials which set out the network of interrelationships between *British Airways*, which wants to buy American planes; and *British Aerospace*, which wants to sell the HS146 and the BAC111 to British Airways; and *politics*, which wants us to (1) buy British and (2) do joint ventures with the *Europeans*; and *Rolls-Royce*, which is closely tied to the American industry, and wants us to do our deals with the US.

I talked to the PM afterwards and he was very pleased with how well it was going. He is treating it the same way as we treated the nuclear energy question – and British Steel – by a series of meetings and full background papers. The PM feels it is more important to get the decision *right* than to get it quick.

Afterwards Carol came to No. 10 with Sir Peter Newsom*, the boss of inner London education. He is very impressive. We discussed the Inner Cities Partnership Scheme – and his feeling that it is not going too well, because the people operating the scheme are the people who have run inner city local government for years. They do not know how to make the inner city work. These are the housing officers who have actually driven employers and jobs *out* of the inner city. All they can think of is spending more on the same.

Home with Carol at 8.30.

Thursday 27 April 1978

A lovely three-mile morning run on the Heath. In early to clear the papers. Cabinet was mainly concerned with finalising the industrial democracy White Paper. I went into Private Office to read the minutes on the PM's meeting with Schmidt. These are being kept very close – the FCO is not being told anything. Schmidt complained bitterly about a story in the *Financial Times* after the PM's last visit to Bonn. So everybody promised to keep it tight.

Schmidt began by resisting the pressures on Germany to reflate. He said it did not work. We no longer knew what 'demand' was and how it worked. The attempt to stimulate economies artificially simply produced inflation and not growth. He then went on to describe his plan for monetary stability based on three factors: a modified 'snake' aligning the European curren- cies with one another; pooling the reserves of each country to protect the currency system; and use of European Units of Account on the designated common currency.

The PM reacted with interest, but scepticism. He said the problem was that it was a way of preventing Germany from appreciating and the pound from depreciating. So it was sad for the weaker countries. The UK would need to enter it at a much lower exchange rate than now – and that meant not until after an election. Schmidt said he understood that. He also said that his scheme would not produce any benefits for five years. He was very critical of American monetary policy since Vietnam for creating our trou- bles. The PM argued strongly that any new reform must *not* be anti- American and anti-dollar, but must be supportive of the dollar. They agreed to pursue the scheme and to try to have something ready for the Bonn summit. Schmidt said it must be kept to Finance ministers and PMs and must be 'kept away from the Brussels bureaucracy'.

He also said that unemployment is now the biggest problem in Germany, not inflation. He accepts that some of Germany's great industries – e.g. shipyards – are going to disappear. The PM said he could not accept this for Britain, which is an island, and he proposed to increase expenditure on military ships in order to preserve a shipbuilding capacity in the UK.

After Cabinet David Owen talked to me about the election. He is very convinced that it must not be this year, but must be delayed till next. There are two by-elections today in safe Tory seats and we don't expect to do very well.

Afterwards to Questions where the PM made his big attack on the Ministry of Defence for leaking the details on Armed Services pay. This made an astonishing impact – it is not often a PM attacks one of his own departments. He later phoned Fred Mulley and told him to get on with the job of finding a culprit. Actually Defence have always been the most leaky department, which is ironic as it contains the most sensitive inform-ation. It also has 170 information officers of course, and I suppose they have to do something. So they leak.

There was a dinner this evening for Muldoon, the New Zealand PM. He is a boring old Tory and the PM was not looking forward to it. The reception started at 7.30, and at 7.25 Private Office had to phone him at the Commons to remind him to come over. I had decided not to go and I went home about 8.30 p.m.

Friday 28 April 1978

Yesterday's by-elections were not too bad for us – swings of around 7% to the Tories, which is the pattern for this year, compared to 20% a year ago. But the Liberal vote has collapsed, which is bad for *us*, as three-quarters of them go to the Tories.

Lunch at Grieveson Grant – whose impressive gilts man argued strongly that interest rates should *not* go up and that if the Bank of England gave a lead on this, we would have no problem funding our borrowing.

A quiet afternoon. Claus Moser came in – he is resigning from the Civil Service this summer and will go to work as deputy chairman of Rothschild's. I shall miss him, as he is a very human being.

Home early to listen to music with Carol, who is tired and depressed with her job – having just been made redundant by Fred Jarvis of the NUT. He has never consulted her or discussed it with her – in fact he behaves in just the way that trade unions complain about capitalist employers.

Tuesday 2 May 1978

Spent the May Day bank holiday Monday in Suffolk. It was wet and grey the whole time – and this morning we had a thunderstorm, with lightning so strong that it cut off the electricity, but we could not see it because of the fog. Even so, the cottage was as cosy as ever.

Drove up early this morning in pouring rain and then went in to No. 10 before lunch. The PM had flown down from Scotland where they have the local elections today.

I went to the briefing for Questions, but then went off to Colchester to give a talk to a graduate seminar at Essex University. Very pleasant and had

a good dinner afterwards with Tony Barker and Ivor Crewe*. Home on a
late train and not back to the house till 12.45.

Wednesday 3 May 1978

Before the meting with the Prime Minister of Guyana I had a long chat
with Ken Couzens, who had been summoned to attend from the Treasury.
Ken was, as always, not very optimistic on the international monetary front,
and does not think much will emerge from the Bonn summit. He thinks
Helmut Schmidt is unbalanced and that his thyroid trouble, which nearly
drove him out of politics in the late 1960s, is affecting him again, giving
him alternate bouts of high activism followed by periods of pessimistic
fatalism. Apparently it was a period of activism which led to the recent
German monetary initiative, but that isn't well thought through and is
running out of steam. The Treasury are against it anyway, because they see
it as a blatant device to hold down the Deutschmark exchange rate and to
prevent the UK, Italy, etc., from devaluing – in other words, it is a form
of protection for Germany, a non-tariff barrier protecting its exports from
becoming uncompetitive and foreign imports from becoming too cheap.

Ken is not at all opposed to more protection for the UK and thinks we
may have to come to that. He is attractive in many ways, not at all the
typical smooth mandarin, talkative, obviously not public school and
humorous. He is small, a perky face like a rabbit, and with distinctly baggy
trousers. I don't know what the foreign bankers make of him, but of course
he is cleverer than any banker.

I chatted to David Owen in the corridor at the Commons. We have arranged
a lunch, with Michael Stewart as well, to discuss our 'protection' schemes.
This is being kept very close, and Owen's civil servants know nothing. David
said it is all becoming more urgent, because he thinks the Bonn summit will
come to nothing, and we then need an alternative economic strategy.

The Cabinet committee on public appointments was disappointing. The
Civil Service Department had come up with a good scheme for advertising
and trawling the regions. Shirley Williams supported this as a way to get
more women and blacks on to our committees. The PM said he was in
favour of democratising the system. But it was strongly opposed by the
DHSS, John Morris and especially by Peter Shore, who made one of his
totally conservative speeches defending the status quo. Peter's whole political philosophy came through, best summed up as 'pluralist corporatist'.
He said that the existing system was perfect, because the main interest
groups were consulted and they put up nominees from within their ranks,
who were then endorsed by him. Thus the status quo of spokesman groups
is totally sustained and perpetuated. As for the wider public, he said he had

'consulted the Consumers Association'. He did not add what we know in No. 10, that on the few occasions when the interest groups do not put forward an approved spokesman, he then appoints a former permanent secretary from the Department of the Environment – as he has done on three occasions in the past six months.

The DHSS supported this approach of keeping the patronage to themselves. As the two departments make the most appointments – about 4,000 a year – that was a problem. Morris added that he knew everybody in Wales who was suitable, so he opposed change. This scuppered it really, as in our government system it is very rare that Cabinet decides to impose something (non-financial) which is unacceptable to the two main departments involved.

Shirley Williams fought very well. She said that the existing system did not work well, because it always threw up 'white Protestant males'. Ian Bancroft, the head of the Civil Service, said that was exactly correct: the CSD had pruned down the list of the great and the good in the past two years from 15,000 to around 5,000 – and 'they are virtually all white Protestant males'.

The irony here is that the Civil Service is actually taking a good and radical line, supported by Shirley from the right and by Tony Benn and Albert Booth from the left. The opposition is from the soggy middle (Ennals and Morris) and the conservative right (Shore). Ironically, Peter wrote a book on 'open government'. He doesn't practise it. Any hope of really democratising the patronage system has been torpedoed – by ministers, not by civil servants.

At 6.30 we had a meeting in Tom McNally's room to discuss arrangements for the next election. Joe and Albert were there, so it was very eerie for me, the old team sitting in Marcia's room. I felt disturbed by it, drank too much whisky and felt 'off' afterwards. In fact they were very good, giving Derek Gladwyn a comprehensive and detailed rundown of the daily routine of an election. Jean Denham from Joe's old Press Office was also good. Tom arrived forty-five minutes late for his own meeting, which irritated Joe enormously.

What is clear is that the great gap in our plans is the lack of anyone to write the PM's speeches – which is the PM's main activity in the campaign.

I went home at 10 o'clock and listened to some Schubert, but felt under the weather.

Thursday 4 May 1976

I went for an early morning run, voting in the local election en route.

David Butler from Nuffield College, Oxford, came in to talk to me about the run-up to the election. I introduced him to Helen Liddell, who had come down from Glasgow, very pleased with the Scottish results, where we hammered the Scot Nats and now look as if we might hold Hamilton in the by-election. She had been over to Labour headquarters at Transport House to have a row. This time they want to put some Transport House people into Hamilton (because it looks as if we will win). She is refusing to have them because 'they are no good'. Political scientists have not yet calculated the 'Transport House Factor' – the extent to which Labour loses votes because of alienation of voters by Transport House incompetents.

I had lunch upstairs and we were debriefed on this morning's Cabinet. They made some changes in the industrial democracy White Paper, but still apparently have not grasped the extent to which non-trade unionists are excluded from their share of the 'democracy'.

There was also a row between the PM and Tony Benn over the bizarre statement by the chief of staff in China last weekend that Russia was our common enemy and Britain and China should unite against Russia. The Tories have supported this line. Benn wanted the chief sacked. The PM resisted this and told Benn off for lining up with the far left and the Russians. He said this lost Labour lots of votes. Actually I have some sympathy for Benn in this. Generals should shut up about international politics, where they always take the same line as the Tories. And in fact the PM was privately annoyed with the chief, thinking the air marshal did it in a silly way. The Russian description of him as 'an intoxicated hare' seemed unusually apt.

Briefing for Questions was quiet – though we now have in there a whip as well as Cledwyn Hughes from the PLP. Usually the whip is lovely Ann Taylor, but today it was Jim Marshall, who is nice, but not so pretty.

At No. 10 we were worried by interest rates. The Bank has decided to lift the MLR by 1% or more this week. Today it gave the market 'a nod and a wink' and rates immediately rose. The PM was not too happy with this and said he would not do it himself, but he told the Chancellor that if he wanted to do it he would not stop him.

The PM had a private meeting with the Chancellor this evening. Apart from the bank rate, they discussed next Monday's vote on the Finance Bill. At present we have a minority of two, so it looks as if we will be beaten, and the Opposition will carry a 1p cut in the standard rate, plus a reduction in the top rates. The PM is now taking a much cooler view of this. He does not really want an election on the issue that 'a vote for the Tories means 1p off your tax'. So he lectured Denis Healey on the need to play it cool and say we would think about it.

So it looks like a reduction in taxes – good politically – but a rise in the PSBR – bad financially and could precipitate a financial crisis. Well, we will see.

I don't mind either way, providing we stop blustering and threatening. Actually a victory for the Liberals might end up being very good for us in an election.

Euen Ferguson, David Owen's energetic ex-private secretary, came in for a drink at 6.30. Afterwards I went to the Festival Hall to hear a lovely concert, James Galway doing a Mozart flute concerto and then Dvorak's 8th symphony. Afterwards we went back to dinner with pretty Susan Peterson from ABC Television. Home at 1a.m. By then the first local election results from England were coming in, and not looking too bad.

Friday 5 May 1978

No run this morning, as I was a little tired and it is still pouring with rain, day after day.

Although the morning papers have headlines about the 'Tories Sweeping to Power', in fact the local elections have been very good for us. We are virtually maintaining our (high) 1974 vote. We lost only about 30 seats and the Tories gained only about 60, whereas they expected a minimum of 300. We are still behind but could easily recover this lost bit.

David Donnison*, my former colleague at the LSE, brought in Maurice Hayes from Northern Ireland. An impressive man, he is very depressed that it is all going sour. There is a total political vacuum in Ulster, and the young people are completely alienated and socialised to violence. I agree totally, and we arrange to set up a small group to study what can be done after the election.

In the afternoon I read a sudden flow of papers – and did not finish them by the time I left, tired, in the pouring rain at 8 o'clock. Suddenly things are moving again. There are plenty of committees and decisions ahead, though little of it on *new* business, as the PM is clearly intervening and initiating much *less* than last year. He is holding a steady course and not taking any risks now things seem to be going well.

Monday 8 May 1978

The PM was in a very grumpy mood today – and took it out on Moshe Dayan* in the afternoon, telling him that the Israelis have to adjust their attitudes or they will have no friends.

I had a nice lunch with Fred Emery* in Kensington.

Really the day was spent waiting for the evening's vote on the Finance Bill. The Tories had down an amendment to knock 1p off the standard rate. The minority parties were supporting the Tories, so we were almost bound to lose – the final blow coming when the Ulster Unionists announced they were against us (apparently they were split by Enoch Powell, who never wants to vote with Thatcher).

I went home in the evening and then back in for the vote – we lost by 8. Afterwards we gathered in the PM's room for a drink and a chat. These meetings are really therapeutic – cheering up the PM. We discussed the need to keep the government moving on and not become a lame duck. The PM also talked about wages – how we must get another agreement – but cannot fix on a number for maximum wage increases until the union conferences are over this summer.

I went home at 12.30.

Tuesday 9 May 1978

I attended the first half of the Cabinet committee on the CPRS report on overseas representation. This was very unsatisfactory and seemed mainly concerned with a haggle over whether home civil servants can have the same high allowances – private boarding schools, etc. – as the Diplomatic Service gets. It is remarkable how the Civil Service can turn any big policy issue into a means of improving their conditions.

Lunch at the White Tower with the television director David Elstein to discuss the Annan Report. He was concerned that we should let the IBA control the fourth channel, otherwise they will fight it and never let it get off the ground. He is a very clever young man.

Back to Parliamentary Questions, which was mainly about last night's defeat on the Finance Bill, the PM attacking Tory irresponsibility and the Tories demanding our resignation.

Jacques Van Ypersele, the Belgian Cabinet secretary, came in from Brussels to discuss Brookings. It is clear that the UK is way ahead of anybody else on this. I took him over to the Commons and then picked up Bishop Konstant and took him to Shirley Williams's room. We discussed relations with the Catholic Church and arranged to have future meetings with ministers present to discuss particular policy issues – nuclear policy, abortion, etc.

The PM saw Denis Howell this evening. Denis wants to issue a public statement about his association with Bryants and to sue *Private Eye*. The PM is not very keen: he believes in keeping quiet and ignoring these things. He said that sensible people know that *Private Eye* is just full of lies.

Wednesday 10 May 1978

At last some fine weather after weeks of rain. A lovely morning run over the Heath. Then in for the Annan meeting on broadcasting. Basically, the

Home Office had decided to capitulate on the fourth channel, giving it to the new Open Broadcasting Authority and not to commercial TV. Having given this one away, the Home Office tried to win on the BBC structure, by having the new management boards appointed by the BBC governors, and so keeping it a rather cosy operation. Several ministers attacked this as too incestuous and the PM finally overruled Rees and decided that the government would appoint the members of the boards.

Had a fascinating lunch with David Owen in his room at the Foreign Office. Michael Stewart and David Stephens, his special advisers, were also there. David is convinced that we will have to turn to protection, so he has asked for work to be done on how we could introduce protection in an EEC context. He is expecting the machine to counter-attack at any time. He also wants the government to begin raising this at the World Economic summit in July. The PM is not so keen on this, but David thinks it will strengthen our bargaining position.

We discussed the electoral prospects. He still prefers to go on until 1979 but thinks we will have to have an election this autumn, in which case he wants it to be announced the moment we get back in September. He would like actually to fight an election campaign on protection, promising to deal with unemployment. The rest of us were more sceptical about this, fearing that it would imply failure of our existing policies and open up too many un answerable questions. But David is now in full flight. We arranged to meet again once the FCO have produced their working papers on methods of protection.

Went to Wembley to see Liverpool win the European Cup – marvellous.

The PM saw Cardinal Hume today about 'moral' issues. The Catholics are certainly beginning to exercise some political weight.

Thursday 11 May 1978

Another beautiful morning run.

Cabinet had an enormously long discussion on educational grants for 16- to 18-year-olds to persuade them to stay at school. This will cost a lot of money, but is desirable. Far too few of our children, especially from working-class families, stay at school. But it won't come into operation until 1979–80 at the earliest. So it will go into the manifesto.

Before lunch yesterday I was phoned by an adviser in Ted Heath's office about last night's vote on the Finance Bill. Heath was in Geneva and thought he was paired with Joan Maynard. But the whips had scrubbed this and left him unpaired. He wanted me to do something about it. It was clear that he had no contact with the Tory whips. The same happened a week ago, when Thatcher wrote asking us to communicate with Heath over the Crown Agents inquiry.

Went to a nice Indian lunch with David Henderson of University College. He is very good on the waste of money in the public sector. He points out that our nuclear energy policy never was costed, and when he went to the Ministry of Defence they did not have anybody to cost the vast military equipment projects that they were proposing.

Back for Questions which went fairly quietly. The PM then went immediately for a big political tour of the North-West. I went to Richmond and did not get home till midnight.

Friday 12 May 1978

In the morning I attended a conference at the London Business School on policies to create employment. Very good actually. I stayed there for lunch. Back to No. 10 to clear papers. Had a drink with Harry Evans at the RAC. Out in the evening to dinner. Am getting tired again.

We have another dinner tomorrow with Jack Ashley and Merlyn Rees. Too much socialising. The PM has also withdrawn a bit from everybody. He is obviously completely absorbed by the big decision – whether to go to the country in the autumn and how to prepare for it.

Monday 15 May 1978

Had a superb football game yesterday – playing against ex-professionals. I marked Johnnie Brooks from Tottenham Hotspur and Denis Bonds from Watford.

Felt shattered this morning, drained. So I took it easy in the morning while the PM first had talks with Ecevit of Turkey and then lunch with Whitlam from Australia. After that he had Kaunda. A terrible day of international flannel, which pleases their egos but rarely achieves anything.

Attended another good committee on the European Brookings – the Civil Service can be very impressive at this kind of briefing, by far the best in the world. If we don't get the European Brookings here to London, it won't be for lack of trying on their part.

Home to bed early and stiff.

Tuesday 16 May 1978

I decided not to attend Gen 130 on aircraft policy. It is fascinating as they examine all the options, but I can read the minutes. As yet there are no committee battles, etc. The Rolls-Royce issue is interesting. The Americans use R-R engines because they can then get huge British orders for Boeing planes. A subtle bribe. So I stayed in the office, caught up on my reading.

I left early to hear Edward Boyle give a lecture on the future of the universities – very lucid and authoritative (and a nice reference to the PM and the Policy Unit). He is such a good man, perhaps wasted at Leeds. The PM tells me that Boyle has written privately to say that he will vote Labour at the next election.

Wednesday 17 May 1978

More foreign visitors and talks – a terrible waste of the PM's time. There are no votes wherever President Khana comes from!

Lunch at Brown's Hotel with the two Toms and the *Daily Mirror* – Joe and Terry Lancaster. We went over the whole field and Joe made his points very forcibly. He is pushing Tom McNally into more systematic planning for the election campaign. Tom is not very systematic by nature, but in reality he cannot go faster than the PM. The PM is taking it slowly and keeping it close to his chest. We are all convinced now that he will call the election in the autumn, which is what we want. But naturally he wants to keep his options open.

He has had a series of meetings with Transport House people and with Derek Gladwyn from the trade unions, and Tom has had separate meetings organising his campaign timetable. It looks very similar to Harold's in 1974, except that Jim is resisting coming back to London every night and wants to spend some blocks of time out of London. Joe thinks that this is a mistake.

We all agreed that the weak point of our position is housing – we have done nothing for the council tenants. Peter Shore is not a great success. His civil servants say that it is impossible to get a decision out of him. He is extremely conservative on every issue – he opposes any innovation in housing policy; on public appointments he opposed change; he is opposing reform of the Official Secrets Act; and he is opposing publishing a survey of reforms in supplementary benefits because he thinks it might upset somebody. Above all he foolishly opposes the sale of council houses on which we had converted Wilson just before he resigned.

When Tom and I got back to No. 10 we agreed to try to resurrect the council tenants charter, which apparently Shore has allowed to get buried.

In the evening Carol and I went to dinner with Professor Nelson Polsby, the Californian political scientist visiting LSE – a huge, funny and fascinating man. I wish there was one teacher in the LSE Politics department with half his imagination.

Thursday 18 May 1978

Came in early for a meeting in the CPRS on National Health Service policy. The DHSS has drafted its PESC application for an increase in health expenditure. The DHSS wants to involve us so that, if we support it, they can argue that they have the backing of the PM and No. 10. We won't be caught in that one – though I do believe that the NHS should come high in our priorities. The problem is that they want the money for staff and not for the patients.

Afterwards I took Shirley Williams to lunch at the Grange in Covent Garden. We had a lovely gossip. After Questions, which Jim regularly dominates, making Thatcher seem shrill, the PM saw Claus Moser. The PM treated Claus very well and Claus phoned later and was very touched by the PM's concern for him. I shall miss Claus from Whitehall.

Friday 19 May 1978

In early for the deputy secretaries meeting at 9.15. Not much came up – except that the PM is spending so much time abroad, and with foreign visitors, in the next two months that there are only six days available for Cabinet committee meetings between now and mid-July. Actually there is not a great deal of business. Most of the legislation is through the Whitehall pipeline and already into Parliament.

Harry Evans phoned to tell me that an NOP poll was showing us 5% ahead. So the politics is beginning to look much brighter. During the past few months we have been on a plateau – 6–9% swing against us in by-elections (compared to 18–24% in early 1977), 5% behind in local elections, 2.5% behind in the opinion polls. Now we have moved dramatically forward – at least level pegging in the opinion polls and a dramatic improvement in Scotland. If we can only produce better results in English by-elections. Presently the right-wing Liberals turning to the Tories is a problem there.

Next week the Liberals will announce the end of the Lib-Lab pact, though it will continue till the end of the session, which is as long as we could expect – and will give the PM an excuse for going to the country in the autumn if he wants.

Went home fairly early. Up at dawn tomorrow to fly to Paris for another Brookings conference. It is tiring, but I enjoy it, especially as we eat superbly. I also love just wandering around the Left Bank, and living in my little hotel – very modest but full of character.

Monday 22 May 1978

Had a nice weekend in Paris – glorious weather, a good conference and a fascinating evening at dinner with Michel Albert, the Commissaire au Plan, and Michel Rocard, the French socialist politician who is pushing up to replace Mitterrand as leader of the French socialists. We met at Albert's flat, just north of the boulevard Saint-Germain, at 8.30 and stayed till nearly 1 o'clock. We spent a lot of time discussing how the French socialists could get into power – and all agreed that the link with the communists had to be broken while still maintaining an appearance of a united front of the left. Rocard has been building up his relations with the non-communist trade unions. Albert, who is very nice, was much more openly 'political' than most British civil servants – not partisan, though he is well known as a supporter of the left radicals, but in his analysis of policy situations he is just less prissy and stuffy than most of our civil servants. Incidentally the whole four-hour discussion – even their private discussions and chat with their wives – was conducted in English!

They both agreed that Mitterrand is too old, not just in years but mentally and psychologically, to take the French Socialist Party into government with 52% of the vote in the 1980s. Apparently he is a bit jealous and wary of Rocard.

The PM was in Scotland making a speech to the Church on the 'family' theme again. This is going to be built up for the election. *Now* he is very pleased we increased child benefits (though he was not too happy at the time). Without that, our 'family' record would have looked a bit thin.

Robert Armstrong took me to the Cariton Club – very Tory territory, though we enjoyed ourselves happily enough. We discussed Annan, where Robert has been playing a much more active part to try to get the Home Office papers more positive. We also gossiped about Jeremy Thorpe, etc. He said that some of the minor characters would be arrested quite soon – the police have been suspiciously slow over this whole business. But he thought that Thorpe would escape the courts, although the publicity will finally finish his political career. Apparently Thorpe's *mother* has been too involved in the business of protecting her beloved Jeremy and has done some silly things.

I spent all afternoon in Dick Ross's room in the Cabinet Office discussing a DHSS paper bidding for 3% p.a. growth from PESC for the Health Service. Four quite good senior officials were there – though one of them lost his temper with me when I said that my fear was that once we increased public spending again, it would all go on the bureaucratic staff and none to the patients. He shouted that it was 'all bloody nonsense' that there had been any excessive growth in NHS bureaucracy. Tessa Blackstone from the CPRS supported me well – she is very impressive, sharp and well informed and always radical. A very good lady.

By the time I got back into No. 10, I barely had time to take a few telephone calls before I had to rush off to the Commons to see Michael Foot. He asked me over to discuss the Official Secrets Act. He is very worried – it is a fairly conservative document and in no way meets our manifesto commitment. Foot sees no point in publishing it, and I agree: there is little to gain, and it will be attacked in all the media. We agree that Foot should see the PM before Cabinet on Thursday, and I will put in a brief. We had a whisky together and a nice chat, and then I went back to No. 10.

Carol came in and we went to a delightful concert, given by children, at Banqueting House in Whitehall. I talked with Keith Joseph, who is always very friendly and interested in new ideas.

I was pretty tired by the end and staggered into bed at 11.30.

Tuesday 23 May 1978

My brother Clem came in at midday to discuss his proposed emigration to France. He is fed up with doing nothing at the Manchester Corporation Works Department – it is ironically called 'Works' because nobody does any. We went to the Reform Club together for a quick lunch. It was a lovely day and St James's Park looked ravishing – sunshine after all the rain.

Went to the Commons for Questions. The PM now oozes confidence. And the Tories looked very subdued. Afterwards he made a statement on the industrial democracy White Paper. It went very well. He did not claim it had all the answers – just a sensible step forward. The Tories asked a lot of very pertinent questions and contributed to an extremely constructive debate.

Permanent Secretary Pat Nairne came in for a cup of tea and a chat about DHSS policy. He admitted that his department was digging its feet in a bit on the 'McElhone' initiative and the 'community' and 'family' themes we are pushing. This is mainly because the DHSS represents the *professionals* – doctors, social workers, etc. – and they do not like any voluntary effort, family, community participation, etc. So I gave him a firm steer to go off and tell them to get their fingers out. He is a nice and straight man, who clearly does not want to get his department too far out of line with the PM's thinking.

The most striking thing about Whitehall departments, and something rarely referred to in the textbooks, is that they become captured by their own client group. The DHSS is divided between the 'administrators' and the 'professional' medics, but it does not move an inch without getting the approval of the BMA, etc. The Home Office is more widespread, but is the spokesman for the police, and on Annan of course it let the BBC and the IBA write its White Paper on broadcasting. Agriculture is in the pocket of the National Farmers' Union. The Department of the Environment is so close to the local authorities that it protects them from all reform and criticism – it does the same with the building societies. Education leaves education to the local authorities and the teachers' unions and just acts as a post office and paymaster between them. Transport was for years a spokesman for the road haulage federation. We saw how the Department of Industry tried to protect the Chartered Engineering institutions at the time of our setting up the engineering inquiry.

So we have a corporate pluralism, or 'pluralist corporatism', in our society, which is reflected in Whitehall – a series of interest groups acting as spokesmen to, and pressing on, the Whitehall departments, and ending up with the departments joining with them to speak to central government on their behalf. In one sense the departments are no longer part of collective central government. Only the Cabinet, the Cabinet Office and No. 10 represent central government.

My close friend Graham Greene came in at 6 p.m. We discussed my future – he offered me a job as managing director of Chatto & Windus. He thought it was too small for me and I wouldn't be interested. In fact I would like something like that.

Wednesday 24 May 1978

In the office in the morning. Then off to a marvellous lunch with Joe Haines at the Gay Hussar. We had a good talk, plenty of laughs, just like old times.

Little going on at No. 10. I saw my accountant. Then off to Wembley with Carol and the Crokers for a marvellous football game, in which England beat Hungary 4–1.

The PM saw David Steel today to discuss the breaking off of the Lib-Lab pact. It will be announced tomorrow, though it will continue till the end of July. This suits us both. It leaves us free to call an autumn election, because we must have a majority. And the Liberals can fight an independent campaign from now on. It has been a fruitful and civilised relationship. A great credit to Steel, though sadly he has not got any political benefits from it – yet. He is hoping that in an election campaign he can sell the Liberals as the party which will tame the extremists of either side. And if we get another 'hung Parliament', he will be able to negotiate tougher terms – possibly proportional representation, or a coalition with seats in a Cabinet.

Thursday 25 May 1978

Michael Foot saw the PM before Cabinet about the Official Secrets Act and persuaded him that it would be a bad thing to publish the present White Paper. The PM said that he could support Foot providing that Cabinet supported Foot. In fact Cabinet did not support Foot. Some did. But Peter Shore especially and others were for taking a hard and reactionary line, offering little on giving greater information to the public and publishing

the White Paper. But it won't be a great political disaster. The press will
hate it, but most people won't care.

Lunch upstairs, where we mainly discussed Cabinet. (They also decided
not to introduce an equalised retirement age for men and women.)

Islington MP Michael O'Halloran came in to see me about the football
game I am arranging between the English and Irish parliaments. We are
arranging a big reception after the game in Islington.

I saw Harry Evans for a drink at the RAC. He showed me the draft of
the piece on the IMF negotiations in 1976. He told me that the Treasury
has been lobbying hard to get its version in – and to minimise the PM's
part.

Tomorrow am off to Suffolk for the spring bank holiday. A few days in
the country will be very welcome.

Friday 2 June 1978

Up at 6.45 and drove with the family up to London. Have had a marvellous time. Glorious sunshine every day and Suffolk looking lovely.

The PM is still in the USA where he has made an impact at the NATO
meeting – both by criticising the Russians for their expansionism in Africa,
and by hinting that the Carter administration is all sixes and sevens.

On Wednesday we had the Hamilton by-election. A tremendous victory
for us, *doubling* our general-election majority. The Scot Nats are now in full
retreat in Scotland – to the point where even the *Tories* might win back
some seats. It adds to the sense of our recovery and that an election in the
autumn is hard to avoid.

Two departmental 'hassles' came up.

Pat Nairne phoned to say that his DHSS officials were taking a 'relaxed'
view of the PM's request that they set up a conference on community and
family themes. This was despite a very sharp minute from No. 10. Pat
confessed that his officials were probably reading into it what they wanted
to find – their own opposition to voluntaryism. I check with Nigel Wicks
and then phoned back to tell Pat that No. 10 wanted some firm action on
this and no more backsliding.

There was also an interesting letter in from the commercial TV companies to the PM complaining about reports that the government had
decided to accept the Annan recommendation for an Open Broadcasting
Authority on the fourth channel. Nigel Forman, the writer, states that the
commercial TV people had several meetings with Home Office officials last
autumn – long before ministers ever discussed it – and they were assured
that the OBA had been rejected. Clearly the officials did not consider that
ministers might have a view. Nobody reading this letter could ever believe

the mythology on ministers deciding and civil servants only advising so recently presented in the CSD's White Paper response to the English committee on the Civil Service. In the event, this time, ministers *did* decide – because the PM became involved and he had political advisers to work on the policy for him.

Home at 8 to go out to dinner.

This weekend the new honours list appeared. Inevitably a *quarter* of the names were civil servants – including a certain deputy secretary at Overseas Development whom Judith Hart tried to refuse to employ at all because he is no good. Cabinet Office and CSD admitted he is not up to it. But still he got his £16,000 p.a. job – and now he gets his honour as well. It is a terrible racket.

Monday 5 June 1978

Felt very fragile this morning; had been ill with food poisoning yesterday after a Saturday-night party.

I cleared papers in the afternoon and went home early, still feeling rough. Clem was staying over his last night before emigrating to France, so I didn't go out to Ron Higgins's party [Ron Higgins first suggested I keep this diary in 1974].

Tuesday 6 June 1978

The PM was very involved this morning with receiving Prime Minister Desai – lovely memories of our Indian visit six months ago. Fortunately the weather was beautiful, almost Indian. The plenary talks with Desai were a complete formality. The PM made a nice opening statement about how the Indians came as friends and members of the same family. Desai responded with a long pause. After several minutes he said, 'Our relations are very good . . . They have always been good . . . I have no problems to raise.'

In the evening I went with Carol to the Desai dinner, which was quite charming – nice company, charming Indians and genuinely affectionate speeches.

As the dinner was breaking up just before 11 p.m. I saw Gavyn Davies outside the reception room door. He had with him a paper – Private Office's summary of the Bank and Treasury's proposals for a crisis package this week: 1% or 2% on interest rates; a 'corset' on bank lending; and recovering the £500 million cost of the Tory/Lib tax amendments to the Finance Bill by raising VAT to 10%.

The PM came across to us and we briefly told him. He said, 'The same old story. They go on for weeks doing nothing. Then they come across at midnight and want action immediately.' He said he was going up to bed and asked us to send our brief upstairs. Gavyn and I went downstairs to discuss it. He already had a draft, as always absolutely on the right lines. We dictated to a sleepy garden-room girl and finished after midnight.

Disgracefully I had forgotten all about Carol, whom I then collected fast asleep, fully clothed, on my office settee. We finally got home just after 1.

Wednesday 7 June 1978

I got up at *5.00 a.m.* to help my brother load his car and go to France.

As I walked in to No. 10 I was told the PM wanted to see Gavyn, Nigel Wicks and me at 10.30. He was in quite a grumpy mood. But he had our Green Paper and took us through it. He clearly agreed with us that we should raise employers' National Insurance and not VAT – mainly because of price inflation consequences. He also agreed with our proposals to do that rise this week and the interest rates next week to dilute the sense of 'crisis'.

The PM had arranged to see Healey and Lever this afternoon at 3 o'clock. He asked for some statistical information on VAT, etc., and Gavyn provided this. At that meeting they agreed with the line we had taken and decided to clear the employers' contribution at Cabinet tomorrow, but to leave the interest rates till next week.

But at 6.30 Healey came back to No. 10 to see the PM and said the Bank wanted to do interest rates as well tomorrow – they wanted a 'package'. They were afraid that if it was spread, in dribs and drabs, it might not make the impact and sell the necessary gilts. So the PM agreed. Who can tell what is the right thing to do tactically in these situations? It is a very fine judgement. The final test will be whether we sell enough gilts as a result to get money supply down and so interest rates will start moving downwards again.

I had lunch at the *Mirror* with Joe Haines, Terry Lancaster and the two Toms. It went very well. Everybody assumed an October election.

Incidentally they decided to do 2½% on the employers' insurance contribution but only 1% on interest rates. Fairly sensible.

In the evening Robin Butler came in from the Treasury and we went out together to dinner with the Canadian commissioner on public expenditure. Quite interesting, but I was getting tired of talking about public expenditure by 10.30. Robin Butler was superb as ever. Staggered to bed.

I forgot to mention this afternoon's meeting of the Cabinet committee on Ireland to discuss our response to an Amnesty International report on violence during interrogating of prisoners in Ulster. Roy Mason was very reactionary in discussion and quite inflexible. The PM tried to persuade him to be a bit more positive and forthcoming in his response and Mason

seemed not to understand. He was definitely taking a liberal line and seems
to have got the message about Mason being totally a 'Prod'.

Thursday 8 June 1978

Another morning run and beginning to get fit for Saturday's football game
against the Irish Parliament.

We had an interesting Unit meeting on protection. Agreed it could not
be done by old-fashioned administrative controls over millions of items.
We did that with licences in the war, but our foreign trade is now infinitely
more extensive. So we believe it is better to fix an amount of foreign exchange
available for imports and auction it.

Cabinet met to discuss the economic package. Apparently little trouble
except Benn also objected, saying it was a banker's ramp.

I walked back into No. 11 with the Chancellor after Cabinet and we both
agreed the package was a reasonable gamble and it could come OK. He
said that we could not raise VAT before an election – 'because prices are
the only thing we have got'. We mustn't be seen pushing up prices.

Question Time was quite tough. Thatcher made a long and angry intervention on the package not being announced to Parliament. The PM was
smooth and avuncular, playing it all down. He got good support from our
own backbenchers – whereas the Tory backbenchers gave little support to
Thatcher, and she could be seen angrily calling for some support from
behind. By the end we all felt fairly content.

The package seems to be working. By 3.30 p.m. we had sold about £500
million gilts. But we heard that the building societies were going for a rise
in mortgage rates of 1½% to 10%, which is bad since it is double figures.

I went home fairly early. It was a lovely summer evening and Carol and
I went for a walk on the Heath before going early to bed – by 11 p.m.

Friday 9 June 1978

A very fast and hot morning run.

Gilts still selling well – another £450 million today, which makes £1
billion since yesterday. But the bizarre situation which emerged was that
the Bank then sold out. It had no more to sell, despite massive demand.
This is ridiculous and typical of the Bank. Having spent so much time and
energy planning and pressing for this package in order to sell gilts, they
fail to have enough gilts ready to sell. It is as if the Royal Navy had spent
the first two years of the First World War preparing for the Battle of Jutland,
the fleet sailed against the Germans, and then after the opening broadside
discovered it had forgotten to bring any more shells!

People at the Treasury sound very embarrassed. The Bank will not have another long gilt ready till next *Thursday,* leaving three days of high demand to pass without sales. This is true amateurism on the grand scale.

In the Unit, Gavyn and I prepared a paper suggesting an independent inquiry into the mechanism for financing the public deficit. We must be able to devise a better way.

I had a sandwich lunch in the office and finally read through my back files of carbons of the PM's correspondence, etc. This took several hours.

Home at 8.30 and to bed early prior to tomorrow's vital football game.

Saturday 10 June 1978

We had a lovely day with the Irish Parliament. We won 4–1. I marked an Irish MP named Bertie Aherne. I was with them at the Tara Hotel till 1.45 a.m. Attended the Irish Embassy for buffet supper after the game. Very odd atmosphere. The ambassador very pompous. His wife seeming drunk. He switched off the lights at 8 p.m. The Irish MPs were furious. We returned to the Tara Hotel to drink in the early hours and the Irish MPs decided the ambassador would 'have to go'. [He did six months later.]

Monday 12 June 1978

On arriving I was told that the PM wanted to see me about our minute on setting up an inquiry into the financing of public debt. Harold Lever was sent for as well.

First of all we had a meeting in the Unit about housing. We all agreed that Shore is being very stodgy, so we suggest that the PM talks to him and we suggested some policy initiatives; a council house tenants' charter; selling life leases on council houses; and breaking the legal monopoly on conveyancing.

David Lipsey and I drafted this, and then Tom McNally and I approved and signed it.

I went up at 11, having first shown Harold Lever our minute to the PM about financing public debt so he would know what it was all about. When we arrived the PM was sounding off about all the pessimists on the economic front. He said that in ten days everybody would have forgotten our last week's economic package and all would be OK. I said I agreed – except that homeowners would be paying a higher interest rate for their mortgages.

He opened by saying that it was time to do something about the problem of selling gilts. The system was not working. Lever said he was afraid of upsetting the Governor of the Bank of England. The PM said he was not.

The Bank was 'not sacrosanct from criticism'. It had failed and must expect to be exposed to criticism, so he inclined to have an external inquiry into financing public debt. 'Let us bring public opinion in.'

The PM asked Nigel Wicks, Lever and me to give him a brief by tonight. Nigel and I went off to draft this, and Lever joined us later. We agreed the lines of the minute and Nigel dictated it – in the form of a brief for the PM to send the Chancellor and set things going.

I had lunch with Lever at his luxurious home in Eaton Square. We ate well and had a nice gossip. We have been working together now for eight years and I like him even more. He will leave Parliament after the election and go to the Lords. I then came back to work on the two briefs – housing and the financial inquiry – and also a letter to Shirley Williams giving support to Frank McElhone and his views on the family and community values, which a committee under Shirley is examining.

Home at 8.30 and pack for my trip to the Orkneys, Shetlands and Hebrides. It should be fabulous.

Tuesday 13–Monday 19 June 1978

Away in the Shetlands, Orkneys, Hebrides, Inverness and Glasgow with Ken Alexander, chairman of the Highlands and Islands Board. A lovely man. A great trip. Island-hopping in a little Piper Aztec plane. Glorious weather. Beautiful scenery. Interesting oil developments and the impact on a traditional fishing and farming community. The Shetlands and Orkneys are quite anti-Scots and very pro-London.

While I was away the government had another crisis. A vote of confidence on the economic package. The Liberals dithered and at one stage looked as if they would vote against. Then they abstained but we still needed some extra votes. In the late afternoon Michael Foot saw the Welsh Nats and promised them that the government would actually campaign for devolution in the referendum. In return they agreed to vote for the government and we won by 5.

Monday 19 June 1978

Returned to London by plane from Glasgow and straight off to lunch with the Mostyn-Owens, Johnny Apple from the *New York Times* and a top Italian communist, Napoletano.

Back to No. 10 for a meeting with the two Toms and D. Lipsey on the Annan Report on Broadcasting. The draft White Paper from the Home Office has attempted to claw back much of what we achieved, and blatantly ignores most of the previous ministerial decisions. It virtually gave the fourth channel to ITV – which is Tory policy. Also the reorganisation of the BBC has been emasculated.

It is an interesting example of how a government department becomes so entrenched in cahoots with the clients it is responsible for that it produces the policies they want rather than the policies which the government wants. The Home Office has repeatedly pre-empted or ignored ministerial decisions on this question. They promised the ITV companies that there would not be a fourth channel OBA. Now that ministers have decided to have one, the officials are trying to give it to ITV through the back door. So we wrote our brief accordingly.

I felt tired and had a terrible headache – partly because of all the aeroplane travel, partly because it was very thundery weather.

I worked on some of the huge backlog of papers and then went home to see the children – dispensing packets of Orkney fudge and early to bed.

Tuesday 20 June 1978

Had a nice morning run. Need it, having put on some fat in the North.

In to the Cabinet committee on Annan. Fascinating. The PM led the attack, from our brief. Tony Benn, Roy Hattersley, Bill Rodgers and Shirley Williams gave support. Poor Merlyn Rees looked very harassed. The PM insisted on great chunks being rewritten – he had clearly read our paper very closely, so we won a number of points. But so did they. By repeatedly ignoring ministerial decisions, eventually some of these decisions are reversed. Although we clawed back 70%, in the end they have won 30% which previously we thought we had won. There is little busy ministers can do against a recalcitrant department where the minister is not dominant.

The economic situation is still dicey. After an initial success in selling over £1 billion gilts the demand has dried up again. Earnings are rising at 15% p.a. Inflation will not fall any more. The PM said again (in briefing before Questions) that he would like to go for a zero norm, but in fact will go for 5%, even if the trade unions don't want it.

Douglas Allen and the Labour MP John Mackintosh came in to discuss a Scottish Brookings. Then Jim Billington from the Smithsonian in Washington to ask if I wanted to go there as a fellow. That would be great – if I did not have a family at school here. Home at 8 p.m.

I feel basically flat. It is time to move on.

Wednesday 21 June 1978

I barely saw the PM at all today since I was so crowded with meetings.

I had a morning run and then went in to try to clear my papers.

A woman from *New Society* came in to interview me about one-parent families – and then took me to a nice lunch at the Charing Cross Hotel.

Back to see a man from the Belgian Embassy who brought a letter with Belgium's formal bid to get the proposed European Brookings for Brussels – which is a sign of how much progress we have made on this. It is hotting up into a battle over location – London v. Brussels v. Maastricht. The continentals always have an advantage, since we are an island and do not appear to be central.

Quentin Morris, from BP, came in – and told me a final story of the Bank of England's incompetence over the BP share issue. The Bank got its numbers wrong and allocated more shares than it had on offer so it had to go into the market and buy shares at 70p premium in order to issue them to the public at a 70p loss. In order that nobody found out, they asked BP to 'wash' the shares so they could not be traced. These people are technically incompetent. It would be hilariously funny if it did not cost the taxpayer so much money.

I went home at 8.30 but then sat up till 1.30 in the morning watching the semi-finals of the World Cup.

Thursday 22 June 1978

Woke rather tired and did not go on a run – anyway a grey and wet morning.

Cabinet went on till very late, mainly discussing top salaries – that is my salary and senior civil servants'. I was not told afterwards what they decided. Lots of top civil servants were animatedly discussing it in No. 10 after Cabinet broke. This was clearly a Very Important Subject.

Joe Haines phoned about yesterday's announcement that Roger Carroll of the *Sun* is to join the PM's election team. This has infuriated the *Mirror* team, who are loyal to the government and see the *Sun* as Tory hacks. It was badly handled. Nobody told the *Mirror*, or Transport House – or me. Not very professional. Tom McNally is busy trying to get a seat. McCaffrey hates the *Mirror*. So it is ballsed up. All the *Mirror* Group editors have protested and asked to see the PM this evening.

Had lunch upstairs. Discussed Cabinet (though no mention of the top salaries decision – that is truly top secret material). Questions again went easily, with the PM winning hands down. Afterwards I had a drink with Margaret Bain the nice Scot Nat about her future when she loses her seat.

Back to No. 10 where the PM had a meeting with Healey and Lever over the inquiry into selling gilts. Healey revealed that he had already got an inquiry under way in the Treasury and this would report in six weeks. The PM had little option but to accept. But it is a defeat. After all it is ludicrous to have a Treasury/Bank inquiry into the failure to sell gilts – by the Bank/Treasury! Still, we will come back to this one. I was not in the meeting, but Lever came and told me all about it afterwards.

Pay policy is buzzing around. Healey has sent the PM a draft White Paper, suggesting a 5% norm. It won't get TUC support. But it is hard to see how we can give up on inflation – have made so much progress – 20% in August 1975, 7½% in June 1978.

I came home early because Carol is away in Wales and I have to feed the children and see them to bed.

Tomorrow off to Paris again. I really enjoy these trips – while it lasts. After the October election, win or lose, I shall leave.

Monday 26 June 1978

The PM was away in Washington receiving the Hubert Humphrey Prize and discussing the future of aeroplane orders with the US air industry.

I spent a lovely weekend in Paris on the Brookings negotiations – we made good progress and London now looks a starter.

Back very late last night. The plane was delayed two and a half hours and I watched the World Cup Final in the lounge of a hotel near Charles de Gaulle Airport. Am terribly tired.

And then had to drive to Northampton and back this afternoon to see my beloved Nannas – one of them has had an eye operation and is nearly blind. Got back at 8.30, exhausted.

Tuesday 27 June 1978

Nice lunch with Hugo Young of the *Sunday Times*, an intelligent commentator and not a hack. Quite a relief not to have PQs. Very favourable reports back from the USA where the Americans are saying all kinds of nice things about the PM.

Went to see Anthony Rawlinson, the second permanent secretary in the Treasury, about public expenditure for 1978–80. Basically there is little headroom for 1979–81 – about £500 million. Rawlinson is not as clever as his predecessors, but is very open and seems straight to me. There are no problems between us – I support him in keeping public expenditure under control. The Treasury has conceded most of the items which last year seemed to me in desperate need of remedy, especially in relation to the family. I do not believe in endless lists of expenditure commitments.

I went from the Treasury back to No. 10 and then quickly off to the Commons for a meeting with six members of the Catholic hierarchy. The main subject was abortion. Shirley Williams and Eric Deakins were there from the government (Ennals was ill and Rees otherwise engaged).

The Catholics were a mixed lot, some very perceptive and worldly; others dogmatic and unable to see why a Labour government should not place the banning of abortion top of its election priorities. Shirley used our 'family' initiatives to show our moral approach. Interesting how useful the Unit's family approach has been – and how few of the politicians appreciated it at first!

I sprinted from the Commons to the Charing Cross pier to get on a boat for a lovely evening arranged by the German Embassy. Plenty of food, wine and dancing. Lots of nice people, including my two favourite Tory MPs – Peter Bottomley* and Barney Hayhoe*, each of whom ought to be in the Labour government.

Back at midnight.

Wednesday 28 June 1978

To lunch with David Jones* from Energy. He has quite a respect for Tony Benn, whom he works with on overseas energy questions. David is a good democratic socialist – and this may be why he was shunted out of the Cabinet Office to Benn. Very bright and a strong social conscience.

Did not see anything of the PM today. He had a very important meeting with David Steel and John Pardoe over the employers' insurance premium. The Liberals insisted on a 1½% increase instead of 2½% and we gave way. This was no problem for us. The shortfall is about £140 million and that will still leave us within our borrowing ceiling of £8.5 billion. Also the PM is keen to give the Liberals a victory. The worse they do in an election, the better for the Tories. Labour needs the Liberals to do well.

The PM also had dinner with the trade unionists on pay policy. We are going to bid for a 4–5% ceiling on pay. The trade unions won't *support* us on this, but we hope that they won't oppose us. The PM is very committed – he would prefer a zero norm. We hope to get some kind of general accord at the TUC, and then go on to an election in *general* agreement, but with nothing specific.

I went home tired to bed.

Thursday 29 June 1978

Had a morning for reading while the Cabinet met. They are still discussing top salaries – where there is an *enormous* award for top people – up to 100%. Very difficult to handle politically at a time when we are trying to impose a 5% norm on working people for the next round.

Lunch at the Athenaeum with John Cole and Bill Keegan from the *Observer*. Decent men. I listened while they talked to me.

Back to Questions. The PM is overwhelmed with business and very tired, so he cancelled the arranged 'seminar' on monetary policy.

Went home early and then on to Brian Knox's party at his stunning modern house overlooking Hampstead Heath. Very pleasant.

Friday 30 June 1978

The weekly deputy secs meeting in the Cabinet Office was heavily concerned with the PM's horrendous programme – civil aircraft, public expenditure, pay, the two summits – all in the next four weeks. Pay policy involved some meeting somewhere nearly every day. I only hope it doesn't kill him. I am twenty years younger and I could not cope.

Lunch at the Gay Hussar with Shirley Williams. Lovely it was. Lots of nice chat and excellent food. I am so fond of her – and of the Gay Hussar.

Back to No. 10 to write a brief on Annan and broadcasting – the Home Office are still resisting, still trying to make the fourth channel an ITV2. It is a scandalous example of officials repeatedly ignoring ministerial decisions.

Karel Reisz, the best British film director, and John Le Carré*, the spy author who was at my old Oxford college, came in at 6 for drinks and then on to a private showing of Karel's latest film – *Who'll Stop the Rain*. Tremendous, but a bit violent for me. Very subtle on character and politics. Dinner – again at the Gay Hussar – afterwards and then to bed, utterly exhausted at 1 p.m. Karel is brilliant and subtle as ever.

Tomorrow drive to the christening of Graham Greene's son in Buckinghamshire. I shall be a godfather for the first time.

Monday 3 July 1978

Very tired today. Another hectic weekend – to Bucks as godfather to Alexander Greene. To Robin and Jill Chapman in Wandsworth on Sunday to see the Nannas, and then to the Palladium in the evening (for a show on fifty years of women's suffrage).

In fact feel generally low. Partly the weather, which is appalling. Partly the way in which the election is being planned in No. 10, in a very ad hoc way, and nobody seems to know what is going on, except Tom McNally (who is having a bad time with his efforts to get a seat. The press is waging a malicious campaign against him). Partly because I again get the feeling that we may lose because of the collapse of the Liberal vote in the marginals. That may not happen of course, and the PM may win the campaign. Really it is because of July – things always look bad in July.

I went to the 'seminar' on monetary policy this morning, in preparation for the Bremen EC summit later this week. Present were Healey, Lever, Owen, Richardson, McMahon, Ken Couzens from the Treasury, Palliser, Hunt and the No. 10 crowd.

There were papers from the Germans and the EEC Finance ministers setting out the proposals for a zone of European monetary stability. Healey and Lever seemed to be for it. The PM quickly pulled them up and said he could see little in it for Britain. He could see benefits for Germany in keeping the Deutschmark down, and for the French in disciplining their inflation since they did not have co-operative trade unions. But he wanted to know how it benefited Britain.

The best answers came from the Bank: that it would mobilise EEC reserves, especially the Germans, to defend any currency under pressure, and that not to go in, to be left out, would leave us isolated and exposed to the first attacks by currency speculators. But nobody had an answer to the PM's point that by forcing the weaker countries to deflate their economies in order to sustain their exchange rates in relation to the stronger currencies, the overall effect would be deflationary. So he thought it was not appropriate in the depressed world of 1978. He was also annoyed that the Germans and French had as usual fixed it up between themselves at the recent German/French summit without involving the Brits.

As the meeting ended and he went upstairs the PM turned to me and said, 'That has torpedoed that load of nonsense.'

Had just a sandwich lunch in No. 10 while I read papers.

In the afternoon we had arranged a garden party in celebration of women's suffrage. In fact the weather was awful so we switched it to the No. 10 reception rooms, packed with women. When I went into the pillared room I was the only man there – frightening. I allowed Edna O'Brien* to take me away into the State Banqueting Room for a quiet chat.

Harold Wilson was there and we exchanged a few words. He looked well. He was telling some ladies that he had given up drinking spirits and now drank only five pints of beer a day. I think I have heard that somewhere before.

Roy Jenkins came in to see the PM about Bremen. He took an EEC communataire line, which the PM gently resisted. They do not get on, though I feel the relationship is not as bad as it was.

Tuesday 4 July 1978

A quiet morning for me. The PM went off to talk to the PLP about top salaries. We have decided to concede the lot. Undersecretaries – i.e. me – to get £16,000 p.a. Far more than many/most production managers or export managers in industry. It is scandalous. But I have not fought this one. The PM is convinced that it has to be done.

Sandwiches for lunch again. Then to Questions. We were all tired at briefing and the PM was less dominant than usual. It is a bad time of year.

Dinner in the evening for Chancellor [Bruno] Kreisky* of Austria. Very modest, just a few small tables in the pillared room. Afterwards the PM asked me to talk to Kreisky about the Brookings Institute. I did so and he agreed to support it for London, dictating a note to his secretary to that effect.

Home at 11.30.

Wednesday 5 July 1978

We had a Policy Unit meeting to discuss our approach to the Bremen summit. Gavyn, David Lipsey and I are in agreement to take a sceptical line and we agree an outline for the brief. As always, Gavyn is brilliantly clear on what to say.

The day rapidly became very hectic as we put in several briefs. On the Bremen meeting, we concluded on balance that the new scheme was not really in Britain's interest – though it would be dangerous to be left out alone and isolated. A brief on public expenditure supporting the Treasury in holding public expenditure growth to 2% p.a. And a paper on 'the family' and 'the community'. Frank McElhone's initiative has run into all kinds of problems. Officials in DHSS resent the intrusions of the family and the community into their 'professional' territory. The DES is not interested.

Had lunch with Edna O'Brien, Neil Ascherson* and Norman Lamont* – a nice and moderate Tory who should do well if the Tories ever get less extreme leadership.

Saw Frank McElhone briefly at the Commons about the problem discussed above and reassured him that we would do all we could. He is the first ever Catholic minister to the Scottish Office and suspects religious prejudice against him – and rightly so in my view. All the Scottish Office officials (and the Northern Ireland officials) I have ever met were on the 'Prod' side.

Home in the evening and then to dinner with the Grahams to meet Mary Warnock, who chaired the committee on special education for handicapped children. It was a good report. She is bright, but very Oxford right wing.

Thursday 6 July 1978

Cabinet approved PESC, the next four years' public expenditure. Apparently there was some arguing and the PM summed up by saying there was 'a majority in favour of the Chancellor', but Nigel Wicks did not think there actually was a majority. This was typical of the PM rightly backing Healey in Cabinet.

They also decided to go ahead and build the HS 146 airliner. The bigger decisions seem to be going the way of Boeing and the USA, which turns our industry into simply subcontractors. Whereas a deal with Europe would make us partners – indeed our industry is bigger than the German and French put together. The trouble is that the French are proving very slow to offer a share in European plane projects.

The PM left straight from the Cabinet for Bremen – though he was going to miss the lunch with Schmidt and Giscard. This may have been inevitable because of Cabinet, but it also reflected his resentment at their excluding him from their recent discussions.

I went to lunch with Joe Haines at the Outer Circle Policy Unit – a Rowntree set-up in a lovely house overlooking Regent's Park and later to dinner with a US Embassy official.

Friday 7 July 1978

This morning's press contained details of the disagreements at Bremen. Schmidt said it was all going well – but the PM told the press he was not very keen on the proposals. I went in late, took things easily, and then to Oxford for a nice college 'gaudy' dinner (till 2 a.m.!) at Nuffield to say farewell to Warden Chester. Some nostalgia – I sat next to a middle-aged lady who had been the friend of a beautiful undergraduate in LMH whom I loved twenty-three years ago. So much sense of Oxford time passed; of lovely things now forgotten; of people so close then and now shadows; of chances missed, roads not taken, of the whole landscape traversed and never to be seen again. That was a marvellous time.

On Saturday Carol came up to join me in Oxford and we went out to Burford to walk around the Cotswolds – across the hills towards Shipton-under-Wychwood where I walked with my fabulous friend Gordon Snell in 1955. This time it was grey and cold. Then it shone sunny and we drank beer all the time.

On Sunday morning I gave my lecture, in Oriel College, had lunch there, then walked all afternoon around Oxford, the Meadow, All Souls, Magdalen (how lovely the chapel is. When I was a student I took it for granted and rarely visited it. Now I would love to go to a service and listen to the choir). Finally to Lincoln [College]. Still lovely and intimate. But no names over doors I recognise.

Drove home in the evening, did some weeding in the garden, listened to music, and then collapsed into bed.

Monday 10 July 1978

Went to the first Cabinet committee on pay policy. The Chancellor had put forward a draft White Paper for the next pay round. No positive support from the TUC or the CBI. Just the government going for 4 or 5%. The PM said he would prefer 4% (or 0%). But the others went for 5%.

The PM said that comparability and pay research for the public sector were totally unjustifiable in the modern conditions of 1978, with unemployment, etc. in the private sector. He was very robust. I was delighted. Curiously I had never heard him take this line before. Even with 5% pay next year, inflation won't come down from the present 8% level. It will simply stop it from going up.

Nigel told me that the PM had asked him what he would do on the EEC monetary scheme if the Germans and French do not make any compromises on our behalf. Nigel said we would have to join in order not to be the solitary member of the EEC outside. The PM said, 'You are assuming that we will be in the EEC.'

I had lunch out and returned in the afternoon simply to read papers. In the evening we had a dinner at No. 10 for the National Enterprise Board and the other development agencies.

Home at 11.45, desperately needing a holiday.

Tuesday 11 July 1978

Spent a quiet morning. Tired and a bit depressed. I now feel that we may well lose the election. The momentum of recovery which we enjoyed earlier has disappeared. And we have no ammunition left in the locker – except the PM in the election campaign, and that is quite a lot. Mainly I am down because it is July again. Everybody is irritable.

There is another point. There is no longer a *team* in No. 10. Tom McNally is away much of the time trying to get a seat in the Commons. Tom McCaffrey works away well enough on press matters but he is a civil servant loner, not a political team man. Private Office is friendly, but does not *offer* anything. Everybody works quietly at his desk, but there is no co-ordinated teamwork.

As for the election planning, that is being kept very close. McNally is working with Derek Gladwyn and Transport House, but nobody else is being consistently informed. Tom and David Lea of the TUC worked out the basic manifesto document for the liaison committee. We were not involved till the last minute, and then put in a note with suggested textual amendments which the PM used in the meeting. It is not that Tom tried to keep other people out. It is just that nothing comes through till the last minute. Clearly the election campaign will be less tightly co-ordinated than under Wilson, though the relations with the TUC and with Transport House will certainly be better.

I had lunch upstairs in the Cabinet Office.

Questions did not go too well. The PM is bored with them. The latest polls show the Tories 4–6% ahead and so they were jubilant.

I have decided to leave this job after the election. If we lose I shall have no choice. If we win I shall tell the PM and quietly slip away. I have no other jobs in line.

Wednesday 12 July 1978

Another quiet day with the PM away at the National Union of Railwaymen Conference laying down the line on pay – and he let slip his 5% limit.

I had a long chat this morning with Archie Kirkwood, David Steel's assistant. A nice lad. He told me that David is very low in morale, and exhausted from carrying the whole burden of the Lib–Lab agreement. We discussed ways of helping the Liberals in the election. I said I would try to get the *Daily Mirror* to campaign for Labour supporters to vote Liberal where that will help keep the Tories out; and I will have a dinner with Steel and Pardoe in September to help plan their election campaign.

Lunch at the *Daily Mirror* with Joe and Terry Lancaster plus Geoffrey Goodman* and Mike Molloy*. Very good discussion over the whole range of policy issues. They are still bitter at exclusion from No. 10 and their hatred of McCaffrey is deep.

There has been a lot of depression after the Bremen summit. The PM is now convinced that the new European monetary and currency system will go ahead – 'it is just a question of whether we are in or out'.

Thursday 13 July 1978

Saw Shirley Williams before Cabinet – very fed up with press, politics, etc. Ready to quit. I tried to cheer her up.

Cabinet discussed pay and decided to go ahead in principle with the 5% limit. Some wanted a higher figure to please the trade unions, some obviously did not want a deal at all. They also cleared the Annan Report on Broadcasting where the Home Office finally accepted virtually all of our (and Bill Rodgers's) suggestions.

Harry Evans told me that he had heard that the price for Jimmy Goldsmith's knighthood was his promise to pursue a *criminal* libel prosecution against *Private Eye* – which had it succeeded would have closed it down. Not a bad idea!

In the evening I went to the CPRS seventh birthday party. Very nice. Foolishly I stayed with them – at a pub and then in somebody's flat – until 1 a.m., and then had to walk home (arrived at 2 a.m.) because no taxis!

Friday 14 July 1978

Went in to the briefing for the World Economic summit in Bonn. Curiously low-key. All our efforts have been expended on Bremen. It all depends on whether President Carter can give enough on energy to push Schmidt to give something on growth. Our role is fairly passive. The PM still thinks the summit will be worthwhile. It is better for leaders to be talking than not talking.

I had lunch in the new Cabinet Office canteen, and then went home to work in the garden and on the car, preparing for the long trip to France. God I need a holiday.

Tuesday 18 July 1978

The PM was back from Bonn, where they hatched up an economic consensus, but with little substance. He worked on the aircraft industry problem this morning.

I went off to BP at lunchtime and addressed a conference in the afternoon. The PM gave his Commons statement on Bonn – which did *not* go very well, with a lot of barracking from the Tories, which seemed apparently to throw him. He is tired.

The TUC came in to discuss the next round of pay policy. They did not agree to the 5% policy – but did not reject it. This had been arranged beforehand. It was a quick meeting with only Len Murray speaking for the TUC.

Wednesday 19 July 1978

The PM saw the CBI this morning. He told them the same story as the TUC – that he could not preside over an increase in inflation, and that meant keeping wage increases to 5–7%. This meant restraining dividends. The CBI opposed this but said they understood the PM's political constraints.

The rest of the day was slack.

Thursday 20 July 1978

Cabinet this morning mainly discussed the parliamentary timetable next week – we will be beaten on the Dock Labour Bill (good) and probably on dividend restraint. But they decided to go ahead because we want to show the TUC that we have tried.

Lunch at Grieveson Grant.

After Questions Harold Wilson came up to me in the corridors and chatted, mainly about the election timing. His advice was to 'keep our options open – decide three and a half weeks beforehand!'.

In the evening I went to a nice dinner party at the French Embassy. Home at midnight.

Friday 21 July 1978

Went to Paris for the Brookings negotiations. It is going well and we may get London as headquarters.

On Sunday I saw the end of the Tour de France. Nostalgia for 1949, when I first saw them speeding through the Burgundy countryside outside Dijon.

Monday 24 July 1978

I dictated letters and briefs in the morning.

Lunch at No. 10 for the *Mirror* team. Very lively. Some discussion of end September for the election (the PM goes to Balmoral 9–19 September).

Tuesday 25 July 1978

Spent the morning clearing off the last of the paper before going away.

At Question Time briefing the PM told us that he had decided to go for Thatcher this afternoon. This is the first time. Previously he has rarely referred to her. Now he calculates it is time to make a big attack to demonstrate his superiority as well as to give Labour backbenchers a morale booster in a week when we expect to suffer some defeats and in what may well be the last serious parliamentary debate before the election.

I heard the beginning of his opening speech in the censure debate and then left for home, listening to the rest of it on the car radio, and to Thatcher's reply. It was a tremendous triumph for the PM. He launched a savage analysis of Thatcher's statements and policies. It was heavy and effective and the excited atmosphere came over the radio. He ranged over the whole policy field in a speech which opened the election campaign. Mrs Thatcher was clearly wrong-footed. Her reply was all economic, full of statistics and completely missed the mood of the House. She sat down to silence.

Thursday 27 July 1978

Driving off the boat in Le Havre on Thursday morning I have the summary of the day's newspapers. They are unanimous – Tories as much as Labour – that it was a victory for the PM and a terrible defeat for the Opposition leader. We also won the vote much more comfortably than expected. It has been a major pre-election triumph for the PM. And people now talk of the government winning Thursday's vote on the bill to continue dividend control. Of course by October this will have been forgotten – but it will affect Tory morale in the short term and make them afraid of any Callaghan-Thatcher confrontations in the campaign.

On a personal note, with the election ahead, it was probably my final Parliamentary Questions briefing. A curious ritual. The PM dislikes it but has become very adept and does not really need any help at all.

IV

Things Begin to Fall Apart
(September–December 1978)

Friday 1 September 1978

Back last night from a marvellous holiday at Ceret in France and a happy time with the family. It seems ridiculous to return to the low level of the Whitehall jungle.

The PM was in when I arrived but I did not see him before he left for the farm. He has a big speech at the TUC next Tuesday when he is expected to announce an election. Curiously, he has forbidden the 'entourage' to go with him to Brighton. He wants to be personal, accessible, a former trade union official and not a Prime Minister surrounded by aides and civil servants.

Tom McNally was not around, as he is wholly devoted to getting and keeping the nomination at Stockport. So David Lipsey, who used to be Crosland's aide and is now in my Policy Unit, is helping to run the Political Office. The new speech-writer from the *Sun*, Roger Carroll, is in that office as well, preparing speeches. The fact that he has taken the job now seems to indicate the election will be in October – otherwise what is the point of his coming? I went for a walk with him after lunch and we discussed themes for the election campaign. It is easy to find 'fear' themes – that the Tories will create wage anarchy, industrial confrontation, more unemployment, etc. The problem is to find *positive* themes – what a new Labour government will actually do!

Private Office were discussing the problem of the PM's new car. For about a year now there has been discussion to replace the marvellous old black Rovers, which were roomy, comfortable and powerful. But they are now getting old and have done over 200,000 miles. The PM must have a British car, but not an ostentatious one like a Rolls. So they finally decided on a new Rover 3.5, even though it is less comfortable than the old ones. Two cars were ordered specially from British Leyland. They took a long time to arrive. When they finally came in July they were found to have *thirty-four* mechanical faults and had to be sent back to the garage to be repaired and made safe. Then in August they were sent to be converted to the PM's special safety needs – bombproof, bullet-proof, special radio system, etc. This all cost a vast sum of money. When they returned the PM went on a trip in one. He decided to open the window for some fresh air and pressed the button which does this electronically. The result was that the window immediately fell in on his lap.

The PM has now said that he does not wish to see the new cars again and Ken Stowe has the problem of what to do with two large expensive cars with a quarter of a million pounds' worth of security extras.

The main policy issues around were aircraft and the Rhodesian oil blockade scandal. The aircraft business has gone well and decisions have been taken on the main issues that were identified on his visit to Washington: building the HS1 46 and buying Boeing's 757 for British Airways.

The Rhodesian thing looks much less healthy. The Bingham Report makes it clear that Shell and BP were breaking the boycott and supplying Rhodesia with oil via South Africa, and knew they were. It seems that the Foreign Office and the Department of Energy knew this was happening, so some ministers and civil servants may be involved and may be prosecuted. It has been sent to the Director of Public Prosecutions, and the Law Officers' personal view is that some people will be charged. The discussion in Cabinet was over whether to publish the report: David Owen was strongly for this and it was agreed. It is a major crisis and scandal. But it looks as if nothing will happen in the courts till after the election (ditto the Jeremy Thorpe scandal).

Cabinet also had a brief discussion about election timing. Michael Foot is against the autumn and wants to wait till February and the new register. David Owen has always had doubts about the autumn. Healey has been ambivalent, telling the PM that next spring is as good, economically, as now. But the majority are for going now.

The PM has been saying this week that he 'has made up his mind', but without telling anybody in which direction. The assumption is that it is for polling on 5 October. The *Daily Mirror* believes that it has firm evidence that the date is the 5th. Ron Hayward came in early this morning to see the PM. Presumably they were finalising election arrangements. I have also been told that Hayward wants to give up as general secretary of the Labour Party and become secretary of some European assembly. This will be very good for the Labour Party, as he has been a disaster and a major electoral liability, but bad for Europe. He is also rumoured to have had some embarrassing financial relations with Eric Miller and Rudi Sternberg.

Geoffrey Goodman of the *Mirror* has been approached to see if he wants Hayward's job. But there might be problems, as Goodman was never given security clearance in Whitehall when running the counter-inflation unit, which is all on file and would be used against him by the Tory press if he ran the Labour Party.

The best solution would be to have Derek Gladwyn of the General and Municipal Workers Union as general secretary replacing Hayward, Goodman as press secretary replacing Percy Clarke, and Helen Liddell as national agent replacing Reg Underhill. It is curious that we are approaching the election with our three senior Party officers all due to retire next year. Hardly a vigorous team.

On a more personal note, I discovered that the Civil Service has decided *not* to pay the senior special advisers, including me, the recent Boyle pay increase. All the Civil Service undersecretaries have been paid their increases. But they try to exclude equivalent special advisers. I shall deal with the bastards next week.

Monday 4 September 1978

The PM was away at the farm all day today preparing for tomorrow's big speech at the Brighton TUC. I spent much of the day reading through back papers and finally cleared my holiday backlog by the end of the day.

The news was dominated by Harold Wilson's announcement that he knew nothing about British oil companies evading sanctions to supply oil to Rhodesia. This depressed me. One of my golden rules about Harold Wilson is that 'Harold only bothers to deny that which is true'. (If an accusation is untrue, he doesn't bother to deny it.) So I now assume that he did know. Bizarrely, a friend on *The Times* told me that Harold walked un-invited into *The Times* and offered them this exclusive story. So they ran it on their front page. He sadly cannot resist a chance of getting into the news.

I had lunch with Graham Greene in Manzi's. I enjoy seeing Graham more than almost anybody else in London. We discussed the possibility of my joining Guinness Mahon as chairman of the bank. (Graham, as trustee, is a very large shareholder for the Guinness side.) I have always been reluctant to go into the City, but it now looks as if I have little alternative. Universities are reluctant to employ anybody who has been into the real world and has learned what actually happens in the fields they teach, such as me teaching politics at the LSE.

In morale terms I feel little different from before the holiday – very ready to leave and hoping there is an election immediately, so that I can have a fresh challenge somewhere else. It is a marvellous job in No. 10, but not one that one can do for ever. Five years is the practical limit.

The Political Office is full of activity preparing for the expected election. Tom McNally's room (Marcia's old room) is crammed full – McNally, Roger Carroll working on speeches and David Lipsey who has effectively moved across from my Unit to the Political Office and is busily handling all kinds of nuts and bolts. I, of course, do not know anything about the election date. I know that the PM won't announce it to the TUC tomorrow but will make an announcement on Thursday. The *Daily Mirror* is convinced that he will announce 5 October. (Joe tells me that their source is Tom McNally!)

In the afternoon the PM phoned me to ask who used to sing the music-hall song 'Waiting at the Church'. I found out from Joe Haines that it was Vesta Victoria, and passed this on. Later I was phoned at home to get more details of the song and of Vesta Victoria. Apparently the PM is going to sing the song to the TUC!

The PM has vetoed any of his personal staff going to Brighton. This was inconvenient for me, as I had arranged to go to the *Mirror* party. Tom McNally had a flaming row with the PM over the phone and decided to go regardless. It is one of Tom's many merits that he is fearless and is perfectly willing to oppose the PM. However, it is one of his few faults that he is unpunctual so he was late to the station, missed the train and so he did not actually reach Brighton in time.

Tuesday 5 September 1978

Saw the draft of the PM's speech. Pretty heavy stuff on incomes policy. He is singing the song, but has been advised by his civil servants with him to ascribe it to Marie Lloyd, not Vesta Victoria, as more people have heard of Marie Lloyd. That may be true, but, as I protested, it was Vesta Victoria who sang the song!

Lunch with Geoffrey Smith, a very fat man from *The Times*. Then back to watch the PM's Brighton speech on TV. He changed the order from our final office draft. On delivery he put the hard union inflation stuff first and finished with the fun, the song and the political uplift. Absolutely right. On the election, he clearly sang that he would not be 'at the church' in October. We wondered if he now means 28 September for the poll. But most people assumed he was playing cat and mouse with the press. Apparently the *Mirror* checked back with Tom McNally but he assured them that it was still all set for 5 October.

Wednesday 6 September 1978

A very quiet day. Tremendous press for the PM. Everybody agrees that it was courageous and statesmanlike. Great send-off for an election campaign – assuming there is one.

No. 10 has a curious atmosphere. No papers coming through. The civil servants in Private Office sitting there reading novels or newspapers. People wandering around reading the tickertapes or gossiping. The Political Office has its door closed and gives an impression of the Allies' military headquarters on the eve of D-Day, 5 June 1944. I feel very detached, uninvolved and waiting to get it over. But I don't like doing nothing. It will be nice to get thoroughly involved in something else.

Had lunch with Peter Gibbings, chairman of the *Guardian*, a very decent man. We talked on the assumption that an election would be announced tomorrow, but I did not pretend to know. He also told me that the Newspaper Proprietors Association is completely fed up with Dick Marsh as chairman – 'hopeless and idle'.

No 10. virtually closed down at 6 o'clock and we all went home. The PM returned just before lunch and spent the rest of the day upstairs. He passed on to me his regret about Vesta Victoria! (Today's press slates him for his mistake.)

Thursday 7 September 1978

This was the Big Election Announcement day. And what a day!

Cabinet was at 10.30. Foot, Rees and Healey are the only ministers he has talked to before the Cabinet. None supports this October.

Outside the Cabinet Room I talked to Shirley Williams and Bill Rodgers, each of whom wanted the election over quickly. But Harold Lever came up and said he wants delay – and has written to the PM on those lines. They went in for the 'political discussion' – civil servants were excluded, with John Hunt and other secretaries sitting outside at the round table. This went on for twenty-five minutes, and then at 10.55 the doors were opened and the officials called in.

While waiting outside I talked to Attorney Sam Silkin who said the Rhodesia sanctions business is getting very tricky. The minutes of the Overseas Defence committee in 1967–68 (and especially March 1968 and December 1967) show that ministers – and especially H. Wilson in the chair – were completely aware that the British oil companies were evading sanctions by supplying oil to Rhodesia, both through South Africa and Portuguese Mozambique. In March 1968 the committee discussed this and decided nothing could be done about it. The committee acknowledged that it was a constraint on our putting pressure on foreign sanctions-breakers that our companies were doing it as well. There are also telegrams to the Foreign Office stating this, including one from Lord Caradon in New York, which I have seen, so clearly the FCO was aware at several levels.

David Owen is pressing the PM to agree to publish *all* the minutes and papers. I heard John Hunt and Ken Stowe discussing that this must be resisted at all costs. The irony here is that when Bingham was doing his sanctions inquiry he was accidentally shown FCO files that included these minutes which the machine intended not to disclose to him. A paper for today's Cabinet states that, by mistake, these files were included in the official submission and so 'unfortunately' Bingham did receive 'a full picture'. (Clearly he was not intended to.) It reported that Bingham had been approached subsequently and had agreed not to make any reference to these dynamite papers, though of course they must have influenced his thinking and writing.

Later in the day Harold Wilson issued a statement now admitting that he did in fact know of the sanctions evasions. He made little reference to the Cabinet committees and none to the fact that these showed him (1) fully aware, (2) deciding what to do, and (3) deciding in December that nothing could be done and that sanctions should not be pursued so rigorously. Worst of all HW referred to Callaghan as being involved and said that Jim had admitted this. In fact the PM has not said a word.

The silly thing about this is that Harold has nothing to be ashamed of or to lie about. He is a fool to have denied he knew anything about it, because there are living witnesses and accessible documents (I have now seen these) that are bound to prove him wrong. Anyway Prime Ministers are expected to know what is going on. He should simply have said that we did what we could, and could not succeed without confronting South Africa and Portugal, which we were not prepared to do – as the British public did not want us to do it. And the minutes show that the Cabinet committee discussed it all responsibly, and reluctantly decided nothing could be done. There is nothing dishonourable in that.

The trouble with Harold is that he has to be Simon Pure on everything, must self-justify. He is like a little schoolboy, caught with the half-eaten stolen apples in his pocket, always saying, 'Please, sir, it wasn't me.'

The 'election' Cabinet broke at 1.10 p.m. They all look uncomfortable. Bill Rodgers said to me, 'That is the most depressing Cabinet I have ever attended.' I walked out with David Owen, who said, 'Of course you are pleased. No wonder you are smiling.' I was puzzled, but did not have time to ask what he meant.

The PM stayed in the Cabinet afterwards and sent for Ruth Sharpe to dictate something. I presumed this was the script for his television broadcast, which has been announced for 6 o'clock this evening.

When I got back from lunch at the White Tower the house was full of television engineers setting up the equipment for his broadcast that evening. Then Terry Lancaster of the *Mirror* came in at 3.30 p.m. He asked me the election date. I could not tell him because I did not know! Then Tom McNally rushed up and handed Terry a piece of paper with '1979' scribbled on it. I could not believe it. No election now! Terry said he thought it was a mistake – and that was my first reaction. I wanted to phone and tell Joe, but Terry asked me to wait until he reached the *Mirror* and was able to tell them all. Joe phoned shortly after, absolutely furious. The *Mirror* looks a fool in Fleet Street. They blame McNally who assured them even yesterday that it was 5 October. Like me, Tom did not actually know the date.

I felt terribly disappointed. At first I thought the PM was mad and badly wrong. In time I realised that it is a balanced decision. If he thinks that we are not in the lead and will at best get back only with a minority, why not wait and hope to do better later. Of course he might then lose more decisively than now. But he clearly believes we won't win decisively now. In fact my basic reaction was subjective disappointment rather than objective disagreement, because I want to leave No. 10.

I went along to the Political Office where Roger Carroll and David Lipsey were nervously drinking large whiskies and clearly still did not know. They suffer most from the decision. Carroll will have to go back, humiliated, to the *Sun*. David has looked forward to moving into Tom McNally's job. Now it is back to square one, and they have done a lot of work to no (immediate) purpose.

We all went along to the Press Office to watch the television. It was a superb performance by the PM. Most of the watchers were astonished by the news of no election. Carroll and Lipsey were totally speechless. Tom McNally simply said, 'Either he is a great political genius or he has just missed the boat.' It is hard on Tom, who was looking forward to being in the Commons next month.

Another 'official' gathering was watching the TV in Private Office – all the secretaries and John Hunt, who came through from the Cabinet Office to watch. He showed no sign of knowing what the decision was when I talked to him on the way in.

My Unit was flabbergasted. I left then at 6.30 and went to the Reform with Lord Kissin, who offered me £30,000 p.a. to join the board of Guinness Mahon. I said I would tell him within six months.

Home at 9.30 to watch the TV commentators, who are still astonished and clearly furious with the PM for depriving them of the election they had announced in advance. I went to bed, also feeling deprived.

But why did he do it, and when did he decide?

On why, I think it really is because he wants to win decisively and thinks that will not happen yet. He has said several times that people need to have extra prosperity for at least six months before they appreciate it. I also remember that evening, late, in his room after winning a big vote, when he talked of the advantages of going into the next Parliament and asked Tom McNally and me to start preparing a political Queen's Speech. And again, in July, he said to me in No. 10 one day, 'Don't worry, Bernard, I have been having some talks and it looks OK.' I presumed that meant that the Scot Nats had agreed to support us next session, providing they got the devolution referendum. So he probably has always kept open the option of soldiering on if it looked as if we could not win decisively. Hence Michael Foot has had talks with the Nationalists and with the Unionists.

But when did he decide to go for that option? Because he certainly kept open the option of holding an election now if that looked either promising or unavoidable. He claims that he decided on 17 August, on holiday. And he asked John Hunt to prepare a working government programme for the autumn. But equally he did not discourage the Party from getting ready and he did not tell anybody that he had decided against until the very last moment.

I think that he kept *both* options open until nearly the last moment. But in August he began to feel against, and increasingly inclined that way. But he waited until by the time of the TUC he was firmly decided – and he did not tell anybody because he wanted to make fools of the hated press, which he did.

Friday 8 September 1978

Today is my 44th birthday, and I did feel older on my dawn run! Nobody remembered my birthday at home except Katie.

I went in to the meeting of deputy secs in John Hunt's room. They were desperately digging around for business to engage the machine in the weeks ahead. John Hunt quite rightly said that it was crucial to re-engage ministers as soon as possible. They have geared themselves up to an election and psychologically have stopped thinking about government business.

I saw the two Toms who have both been bruised by the decision.

The PM sent for us later – the two Toms, Ken Stowe and me. He asked me if I was surprised. I said yes – because I had come to believe what I read in the press. He said he made up his mind some time ago, and that there were plenty of clues to show which way his decision would go. That is true. But he did not explain why he did nothing to dampen down the speculation.

Then we got down to business. He said he wanted the Policy Unit revitalised and to feed in more ideas – 'like the Great Education Debate'. He also told Ken Stowe that he wants the official side to work more closely with the Political Office and with us. We discussed possible 'themes' and agreed that unemployment must be one, and that reviving the NHS might be another.

I went back to the Unit, discussed it with Gavyn, and then drew up a crash programme of meetings for next week, using outsiders as well, to discuss ideas and themes. It will be a pleasure to get cracking again – though honestly it is not easy to mobilise oneself again. I was psychologically retired from No. 10, and just going through the motions of coming into work. My appetite has gone and it will take a little while to sharpen it up again.

Had lunch with Johnny Apple of the *New York Times* at the Tate at 2 o'clock and was not back till 3.30. Then I continued to work in the office until quite late.

Quite a week. France seems a long way away.

Monday 11 September 1978

The PM didn't get back from seeing the Queen at Balmoral till lunchtime.

I began a week of meetings in the Unit, with selected outsiders, designed to reactivate us. We are meeting every day to discuss a separate policy theme. It will get us back in the mainstream of policy thinking. In fact we were all psychologically withdrawn, expecting an election, and perhaps expecting to leave after that. Today we discussed the general themes that interest us – unemployment, the NHS and law and order.

Went to lunch with John Lippitt from the Department of Industry at the Gay Hussar. He is always lively. He said that Eric Varley is clapped-out as Minister of Industry and seems to be ambivalent whether to be in politics at all. The department is a bit depressed by his lack of leadership. Went back to No. 10 and had tea with Lionel Robbins*, discussing the LSE, Brookings and the world in general.

Some of the rumours going round about the Jeremy Thorpe case are horrendous. If true, that was a nasty world.

Tuesday 12 September 1978

Today's Unit meeting was on the NHS. Tessa Blackstone joined us and was particularly imaginative and constructive and fed in a lot of good ideas.

PM came to No. 10 lunch upstairs, in top form, still delighted with himself for not calling an election, and so making a fool of all the commentators. He talked quite a lot about the television he watches and likes. He was immensely knowledgeable, knowing all the main actors. He discussed programmes I had never seen, mainly drama series and light comedy. After lunch he took me to his study and we discussed building society mortgage rates – he is insistent that they should not rise, and he very much agreed with the note which Gavyn did last week, opposing any increase in the *levels* of lending, which itself would have led to pressure for an increase in rates.

Later in the afternoon I dictated a paper on 'Themes and Initiatives'. The PM has already asked that Thursday's Cabinet be devoted to this, with everybody making suggestions for themes for the coming year. So I put in a paper with some suggestions.

Home late because I go by public transport now. Carol has the car to go to her new job at the Open University – and after 8 p.m. there simply is *no* public transport.

Wednesday 13 September 1978

The PM has sent back my Green Paper on 'Themes and Initiatives' full of marks of approval. He has asked for it to be converted into a speaking note for tomorrow's Cabinet.

We had another Unit meeting with Home Office people to discuss law and order. They were clearly not very happy about the PM intervening again in their territory and could see no scope whatsoever for anybody to do anything more than they were doing already. Typical Home Office conservatism. But I do not want law and order to be his main theme. The NHS is much better.

At the end of all this I was pretty exhausted.

The PM had King Hussein in to tea, and the area was covered in security guards. One interesting bit of information arose from this: the government hospitality service charges £9 a head to serve tea! So the parsimonious PM arranged for our cook Sarah to do it.

Thursday 14 September 1978

I went down to the foyer before Cabinet and chatted with Michael Foot – who was in very high spirits about the decision to postpone the election. The older ministers – Foot, Rees, Lever – support a delay because it extends their last time in government. The young, except Owen, wanted an early election partly to clear out the old generation and leave space for their promotion. And chatted with Bill Rodgers about the proposed Channel

Tunnel. Bill is pursuing the latter through European channels. It may provoke a coronary in Peter Shore, but is an exciting thought.

Today's Unit meeting was on housing. Tessa Jowell came in and spoke brilliantly, very clear and with a tremendous grasp of the detail. We were all immensely impressed – and immediately began to draft a speech accordingly.

The PM came to our lunch upstairs again. He told us about Cabinet. The discussion on 'Themes and Initiatives' was clearly very good. He was particularly pleased that they did not just talk about economics. He said this was quite different from ten years ago when the Cabinet would have concentrated on economic solutions. Now they realise it goes wider into the social field. He said he wanted to get going on the NHS for his own theme.

He talked a lot about British Leyland. He said that we must be prepared to break it up, and close parts of it down and this should be done regardless of an election. He suspected that the British were just no good at large-scale assembly operations. We could make engines, work in small plants, but we could not work in large assembly plants. He said he had firmly told Eric Varley to proceed on that basis, and he would support him.

He then switched to TV and the question of nudity. He said that he was embarrassed by nudity, on TV or on the stage, and he asked us in turn how we felt. He said he felt embarrassed in the company of his children – even though they were now in middle age and had children themselves.

He also asked me to fix a big meeting to discuss our paper on 'Themes and Initiatives', which he liked.

George Jones came in during the evening, and told me sad stories about how dead and reactionary the LSE is now.

Went home for supper with Tom Read, whose lovely wife Celia is in hospital.

Friday 15 September 1978

The PM was away all day today. I went in late, read the papers, had a sandwich lunch in the office and then finished the week's dictation. Little was going on around No. 10. The private secretaries are bored reading novels. Tom McNally is away in his [prospective] Stockport constituency much of the time. So the whole house is fairly quiet.

Home at 7.30, and off to the cottage tomorrow, where Robin Butler and family will come to join us.

Monday 18 September 1978

Robin Butler told me at the weekend in Suffolk that he had recently seen Margaret Jay/Callaghan, who is an old friend. She claimed to have been very surprised by the PM's election decision. She had spent the weekend before the decision with her father and he had left her with the impression that he was going to have an election. But he seemed pessimistic about the outcome, and was talking – almost with pleasure – about retiring soon to the farm. Robin is convinced that the PM made up, or changed, his mind at the last minute. And he thinks it was a mistake, because like me, he thinks we would have won now.

The PM didn't come up from Chequers till very late. We worked on a brief for tomorrow's meeting with him about 'Themes and Initiatives', which I didn't finish till quite late.

Tuesday 19 September 1978

Swinging back into business. I went to the EY Cabinet committee at 10.30 for a very good discussion on abolishing vehicle excise duty. Actually Cabinet decided in 1976 to abolish VED, but the Treasury and industry combined to make sure that it never happened. So they went round the course again. I did not stay for the discussion of the industrial strategy which promised to be wide and waffly.

I went to the Garrick for lunch with Claus Moser, but he did not arrive, being ill in bed apparently. Back for the meeting with the PM – the two Toms, Roger Carroll, the Unit and me. The PM asked me to speak first, and referred often to our brief. He said that he wanted to make a philosophical speech at Party Conference, reinterpreting the Labour Party's philosophy, what we stand for rather than against. He wanted 'more vision'. So we had a discussion about that. Then we went more widely on to other themes and topics that he might use – the NHS, law and order, housing, jobs. He responded positively to Gavyn's suggestion that we should make a guarantee of jobs to all the long-term unemployed – and withdraw their social security if they don't take a job: we shall follow that up. But finally he came round again to themes and philosophy, saying he wanted to include more on responsibilities as well as rights, community involvement, traditional values, etc. He accepted law and order, but said, 'I won't go into police stations to talk to policemen.' (From his time at the Home Office he actually dislikes the police, thinks them often incompetent and corrupt.)

He digressed to attack the public sector interest groups and trade unions, saying they are privileged and pampered. He has taken our message that they have been too protected from the recession. He brought everybody in, and told Tom McNally that he must include us all in drafting his conference speech. The Unit members were very pleased and morale was high.

Afterwards I went to play five-a-side football with Gavyn – and scored two goals. We went to a nice pub afterwards. Then I came home very merry and played music loudly till after midnight.

Wednesday 20 September 1978

To Northampton to visit Nene College, where I have been made a governor. One member of staff told me that he was up at Jesus College with Harold Wilson before the war. He said he liked Harold, as a fellow Yorkshireman. He worked very hard, a bit of a swot. Then when he got his first he changed and became terribly boastful and conceited. He said Harold was completely middle class – his family had moved 'up' from Huddersfield to Cheshire – and was then an active Liberal, with no Labour inclinations. He remembered that in spring 1939 Harold went to a college society meeting and gave a learned talk on why – for mainly economic reasons – Hitler could and would never start a war!

Thursday 21 September 1978

Cabinet discussed Bingham and Rhodesian sanctions this morning, mainly opposing an inquiry into the scandal of breaking sanctions. At lunch discussing it with the PM it was clear that Ken Stowe and the Civil Service is very anxious *not* to have an inquiry. Every suggestion I put up was quickly opposed by Ken. The PM said that the basic point was that it was now a political problem. The technical details of sanctions-busting had been sorted out by Bingham. All the remained was political responsibility. But only Parliament, he thought, could decide that. So he inclined towards a four-day debate. Obviously Ken and John Hunt had suggested this. I saw them stay on in the Cabinet Room with the PM after Cabinet this morning. The Civil Service is automatically filled with horror at the thought of any of their proceedings appearing in public, good or bad. Ken looked worried at the end, because I had reopened the question that he clearly thought was closed. But in fact I doubt if I made any difference. The PM will follow their line of resisting an inquiry as long as possible – and then Parliament will force it on us with the maximum humiliation.

In the afternoon finished reading various papers, and then went home quite early to listen to some new records.

Friday 22 September 1978

In to the deputy secs meeting. Still not much business ahead. The PM has gone off, leaving No. 10 at 7.20 a.m. to see Begin of Israel at London Airport on his way back from Camp David; and go to Kano in Nigeria to meet Kaunda, to discuss the future of our Rhodesian policy.

Had a meeting with some people from the Department of Employment and the Manpower Services Commission on Gavyn Davies's idea for a guarantee of jobs or training for the long-term unemployed. They were helpful and we will try to take it forward, though it is much more difficult than our proposed guarantee for the youth unemployed.

I read till quite late at the office, then home.

News on the industrial front is bad, with Ford workers walking out in protest against the 5% offer. We shall have the most difficult time yet on pay this winter, and I suspect we will often look back and regret not having taken an election during this beautiful sunny September.

The reason the PM did not go is clearly that he thought the result would not be a *clear* majority. It might not be a defeat, it might be a repeat of the present situation, but then, as in 1951, the government would slowly crumble. He is waiting for a time when things have changed so much that we will go back with a majority and new authority. But the risk is that we may get a big defeat – which I am convinced would not have happened this autumn.

Monday 25 September 1978

A quiet day. The PM stayed at the farm all day (his trip to Nigeria to see Kaunda worked very well). Lunch at the Reform with John Torode of the *Guardian*, who is writing about long-term unemployment, which also interests us in the Unit.

Back in the afternoon to clear papers. Then I left early for home. Not much is going on. Even so the weather is beautiful, people feel better off, and I feel in my bones that this would be the time to hold an election. We could have won now. Later it may be difficult – the car workers are all going on strike against the 5% policy. It will be very difficult to hold it. I do not think we should be too rigid in the private sector. For me it should be a public sector pay policy.

Tuesday 26 September 1978

The PM went to the lunch upstairs, but unfortunately I was out, having lunch at the Gay Hussar with John Campbell of the Irish Embassy. We discussed policy towards Northern Ireland. I predicted a shift in British opinion towards withdrawal, but not enough to change policy, and suggested that the Republic should stay quiet and responsible.

In the afternoon Al Bakash, my Iranian friend from Harvard days, came in and told me all about the Shah's problems in Iran.

I went to play football in the evening and came home at 9.30, rather stiff.

Wednesday 27 September 1978

My bank manager came in to reassure me about my enormous overdraft. Then I cleared papers and looked at the third draft of the PM's conference speech, which has been put together by McNally and Carroll, though including three large chunks by the Unit – on microprocessors, the NHS and housing.

Went to a Cabinet committee (Gen 140) with Michael Foot in the chair considering 'Themes and Initiatives' for the government in the period ahead. Benn made a sweeping demand for reopening the whole issue of the alternative 'siege economy' economic strategy, as well as to give away free coal and free TV licences before the election. Michael Foot was very funny in hosing down Benn.

I dashed off from it to lunch with Joe Haines at the Gay Hussar. He was very depressed by news that Wilson is to appear as the special star on the Morecambe and Wise Christmas show. Like some political Archie Rice in *The Entertainer* doing a song and dance for a few miserable pounds.

Back to a quiet afternoon reading.

Then to dinner with David Webster of the BBC. He had spent three hours this afternoon with the Home Office trying to persuade them not to implement the White Paper section on reorganising the BBC management. He knew all the details of ministerial dealings on this having been shown the secret Cabinet papers by officials. The civil servants get closer to their client groups than to the government.

Thursday 28 September 1978

The fine spell has broken and it has started to rain.

Cabinet went on till nearly 2 o'clock. They spent ages on the Queen's Speech – and agreed the point we put to the PM about getting Annan into the Queen's Speech. So they did not get round to Bingham till 12.50. A private secretary told me that this was a deliberate tactic to avoid taking a decision on having an inquiry. The tactic is to delay, play it long and hope that the steam will have gone out of it. They agreed the policy that the

PM and Ken had been advocating last week at lunch – to have a full two-day debate on the Bingham Report in the Queen's Speech. They hope that that will satisfy people and then there will be no need for an inquiry. The government will take an 'open mind' position, listen during the debate and then announce its position on an inquiry.

We had lunch upstairs with the PM. It was after 2 o'clock and we were all famished. During lunch we kept being interrupted by the telephone with messages from the big Ford strike. The management is being a bit difficult, talking of insisting on a full return to work before reopening negotiations. But it still looks more promising. The PM is resisting pressures to be drawn into the 'beer and sandwiches at No. 10' syndrome. He clearly wants to run it differently from Wilson.

The PM said he was also enjoying life, but he wished that all the problems did not come together. 'I like to take issues one at a time,' he said. He also said, 'I don't like too much pressure.'

Incidentally, I saw the transcript of the PM's telephone call to Wilson in the USA, about Bingham. Harold was giving a talk at some American college. HW said he was happy to have a debate, in which he would speak, and he was also happy to have an inquiry. He claimed he had written this in his draft statement about sanctions the other week, but John Hunt persuaded him to take it out (to reduce the pressure for an inquiry, which the machine does not want). Harold was very open and did not seem at all worried.

Friday 29 September 1978

The PM went to Blackpool for the Party Conference last night. I went for a lovely run this morning. Am at last feeling fitter. But shocked by the sudden death of the new Pope. He seemed a promisingly good and simple man.

Lunch with Grieveson Grant discussing monetary policy.

In the evening to journalist Fred Emery's home for a nice buffet supper.

Next week another Labour Conference, shabby Blackpool again. I had hoped I would never see the Imperial again! It threatens to be an ill-tempered conference, with people curiously feeling cheated of an election. But I do not feel as depressed by the prospect as in previous years. I treat it as a bit of a joke now. Though it is also a serious opportunity to help the PM give a good speech.

Saturday 30 September 1978

I went up on the train to Blackpool with Joe Haines, arrived about 8 o'clock and then had dinner with the No. 10 party in the Imperial Louis

Seize restaurant. The speech is still in the same basic form it was in on Thursday.

Sunday 1 October 1978

I walked to church with Shirley Williams. She, though Catholic, was reading the lesson with the PM at the Anglican church. We walked down the aisle together – and Tom McNally said we would make a good wedding pair. Afterwards we came back to the Imperial together.

Shirley told me that efforts were being made to put pressure on the unions to switch their votes on the pay policy motion tomorrow. There is no hope from the barmy T&G, but the Engineers ought to do better, with moderates John Boyd and Terry Duffy running it, though Duffy is reported to be a very confused man. We also discussed the NEC elections. Although Boyd had promised to switch the Engineers' vote away from some of the left-wing women to Shirley Summerskill* and Betty Boothroyd, in fact he failed, and they are still voting for Joan Maynard and all the other 'Stalin's grannies' gang.

The PM asked me to go and see David Basnett to try to get some pressure put on the unions to vote for moderate Danny Crawford for the trade union section. I went to his hotel and we had a friendly chat. I reported back to the PM when I had lunch with him in the hotel. Spent the evening in the Imperial, drinking and chatting in the usual excited atmosphere. These days I can enjoy conference. I feel less pressure. I also went up the Tower today, for the first time in thirty years – 1948 was the last time with my dad and brother Clem.

Monday 2 October 1978

Had a lovely early morning run on the Blackpool sands, towards Fleetwood, with the tide out. There was a great deal of toing and froing on the pay policy vote for this afternoon. Shirley Williams was organising hard and they had persuaded the AEUW to reconvene at lunchtime to reconsider its vote – if it switches, we will win by a whisker.

The PM had recovered a bit from yesterday's NEC, which went on for five and a half hours in the afternoon! He persuaded them by 15–13 to support a motion to remit this afternoon's pay policy motion. Then afterwards Moss Evans told a press conference that he would still vote against – and the PM began to talk about resigning. He stormed back to his room last night, sent for Healey and Varley and asked them to get to work on Boyd and others. Late last night he had Moss Evans, David Basnett and John Boyd in his room, but Evans was truculent and the PM was very rough with them. The NEC reconvened at 11 o'clock, but the PM did not go. He was reported to be in a black mood. But this morning he seemed better.

We went back after lunch a little more hopeful but then the news from the AEUW was bad. They had refused to change their decision – and Terry Duffy, the general secretary, had not even bothered to turn up. The debate was actually terrific. Good speeches on both sides – especially Sid Weighell of the Railwaymen, who was tremendous. But the vote was massively against us, and all the press were saying this meant the end of the government. Afterwards the PM called us into his room and asked me what we should do on pay policy. I said use tighter money supply, cash limits and maintain the exchange rate. Healey then came in and said the same – plus increased taxes, which we opposed. Then we pressed the PM to take a positive line tomorrow – firm on pay, but generous to conference.

Had dinner with the *Mirror* people. Riotous. David Owen joined us for coffee afterwards.

Tuesday 3 October 1978

The great conference speech day. This morning's press was terrible, writing us off as finished. The PM this morning still had not written the central bit on pay policy and he told Roger Carroll that he was going to ad-lib it. And so he did – brilliantly. He chopped and changed the rest of the speech, dropping whole chunks on foreign policy, though he kept in our piece on housing, which went down very well. It was a brilliant performance and received a standing ovation. It completely changed the atmosphere of conference, unifying but no trimming. Tony Benn passed him a note which said it was the best conference speech he had ever heard. We all felt proud. Afterwards Mrs Callaghan came in and gave him a hug and they were very happy together, sharing the joy of his success.

We went back early to the hotel and had lunch with the PM in the *Daily Mirror* room. It was very jokey and good-humoured – though the *Mirror* people told him they thought he ought to have held his election in October.

Dinner in the evening with Joe and Helen Liddell. Bed at 3 a.m.

Wednesday 4 October 1978

I did not go for a run because the evil *Daily Mail* had a photographer waiting for the morning 'joggers'. So I walked down to conference which was much calmer, and still full of the PM's triumph yesterday – as was all this morning's press. Certainly his best-ever speech.

The PM had a private lunch with his economic ministers to discuss pay, in his room. I ate with the No. 10 group in the Imperial and then went out on the tram beyond Fleetwood with Helen Liddell, discussing how to get the Party machine in shape for an election. It is very depressing. Hayward is the worst general secretary in history. On top of that we have only 77 constituency agents (the Tories have 300). So effectively there is no Party machine at all.

Embarked on an evening of pleasure: the *Daily Mirror* party at 6 p.m.; to dinner (where Ken Stowe revealed openly that H. Wilson had 'heart attacks' in 1975–76); then to the ITV party from 10.30 to 2 a.m. I enjoyed myself immensely, gossiping with an endless flow of ministers, trade unionists and even with journalists. It is clear that I no longer dislike conference so much. I am more detached, less hurt by the lunatic antics of the Party activists. It is all a game to be enjoyed and judged by the lowest and most tolerant standards.

Even so, I think this conference has damaged our election chances. We might have won an election last week. Now we will certainly slip in the polls – and we will find it difficult to recover now that we have lost the unions on wages.

Thursday 5 October 1978

Awoke surprisingly bright and perky and had a refreshing run on the sands at 7.15. Had breakfast in my room and then walked down to conference. They had a ragbag of topics for discussion today, and the atmosphere was fairly subdued. I wandered around the hall chatting to various friends.

Back to the Imperial for lunch with the PM and Mrs Callaghan. We discussed public service pay. I said that I favoured a big agency to survey the whole of public service pay, because the individual review bodies and the ad hoc review committees get too close to their clients. He agreed and we decided to make a push on this. He said, 'We might as well be hung for a sheep as a lamb.'

He went off for his usual nap after lunch. I took a long walk to the South Pier in a gale, then for a final visit to conference. Back to the Imperial for tea with Roy Mason – he is very pleased with his 'low profile' policy on Ireland. Then off on the train home with Joe Haines.

Home at 11.30 p.m.

Monday 9 October 1978

Went in early to show my pretty nieces, Tanya and Nadia, around No. 10. Spent the rest of the morning clearing off last week's papers – and the flow is greatly increased.

Trevor West came in from Dublin for a sandwich lunch. We discussed another football game with the Irish. Also a suggestion that he might be able to negotiate with me an end to the strike for political rights by prisoners in Long Kesh and the Ulster detention camps (with Mick Mullen, secretary of the Irish TGWU, as mediator). This has to be handled carefully, but he will come back on it.

In the afternoon Gavyn and I finished our paper on the European Monetary System (EMS), ready for tomorrow's 'seminar' meeting. We marginally incline to go in in December, for the short-run political and financial advantages, but can see no long-term advantages.

The PM had a meeting with the economic ministers to discuss the pay situation. Apparently they still could not see a way through. Certainly we have little power over Ford or British Oxygen. But it could still work out OK. If the profitable private firms such as Ford get 10%, other private firms get 8%, and the public services get 5%, with public industries spread around, we could end up with single figures.

Tuesday 10 October 1978

In at 9 a.m. to read papers before going to the Gen 136 Cabinet committee on the European Monetary System. It was a good discussion with Owen excellent, advising the PM not to take too hard a line with Schmidt next week, but to say that, *as it stands*, the EMS scheme has no attractions for us and so we won't join, but we will if it is amended. Healey said the EMS would collapse in six months, with the French and Italians pulling out. The PM gave a firm steer against throughout, clearly influenced by the Party politics – he does not want a Cabinet split over something which won't last anyway.

I felt depressed after the meeting, because of this country's inability to find any international situation which does not seem to be a threat to it. Afterwards I worked on papers, including a very bad draft White Paper on Bingham.

Then to Covent Garden for a lunch alone. I have found an excellent place to eat – Johnny's Café – with a good two-course meal for 90p, surrounded by opera and ballet people, no politicians at all.

Football in the evening. Home at 10 p.m. and listened to Mozart till after 11.

Wednesday 11 October 1978

The PM called a meeting this morning to discuss the strategy for his big speeches ahead – the Queen's Speech debate and the Lord Mayor's speech. The PM said he wanted the latter to contain a big attack on the EEC budget, where the UK contribution goes up by another £250 million next year. The PM talked about his time at the Home Office, and how in an alcove behind his room was a special calendar which ticked off the days to a condemned man's hanging. He has told me this story before. It clearly appalled him and he visibly shuddered as he told it. On the speeches he said we must prepare the way for our not joining the EMS.

On the way home I dropped in on my old friend, the playwright Alan Bennett, and we chatted about his writing. He is doing a screenplay on the gruesome Joe Orton murder. He is very special.

Home at 9.30 pm.

Thursday 12 October 1978

A quiet morning. Cabinet dealt with the handling of Bingham and the Xmas bonus for pensioners. The PM also promised them a proper run over the European Monetary System.

I had a quick chat with David Owen beforehand – we went into the toilet for a pee and a chat. He accepts that we now won't go into the EMS (he has always been agnostic on it), but he is worried that we are fighting the EEC on virtually everything – fishing, EMS, CAP. Tactically he is right, that we cannot fight on every front. However, this simply reveals how often the EEC is contrary to our basic national interest.

Walked up to Covent Garden for lunch again in my favourite Johnny's Café in Floral Street. The glorious autumn weather continues; the temperature has been in the seventies all week.

I went to the ministerial committee on official information and open government. It had been meant to discuss whether to include reform of section two of the Official Secrets Act in the Queen's Speech and what else could be done to open up government. But this had been held up by the PM. The fact is that the whole equilibrium of this open government issue has shifted to the 'left'. Quite right too. But it would have been much better if the government had recognised it earlier and taken some credit, instead of finally capitulating to outside pressure.

On the way back from the Cabinet Office, I walked through to No. 10 with Denis Healey, who was in very jovial mood. He said that he could not understand what all the fuss was about with open government. He had always practised open government. 'I have always told everybody what was going to be in the Budget months in advance,' he said, roaring with laughter.

I then went off to the Treasury to talk with Sir Anthony Rawlinson about the Treasury's public expenditure proposals. He is not a subtle man, but friendly and straight. Curiously, he did not know of the PM's initiative on the long-term unemployed.

In the evening I took Carol and Rachel to the Arts Theatre to see *Dirty Linen* by Tom Stoppard. A bit slight, but enjoyable, and with a brilliant performance by old Richard Goulden.

Friday 13 October 1978

A relaxed day, in more lovely sunshine after initial fog.

Went in to John Hunt's deputy secs meeting. One nice comment by John Hunt: he said he feared that they 'might have to have an inquiry into Bingham: the policy of hoping it would just go away doesn't seem to be working'.

The PM went to Kensington Gardens to see the Henry Moore sculptures, and then had Moore in for lunch.

I went to the launch party for Arianna Stassinopoulos's new book. She used to be my student at the LSE. Plenty of flowers and champagne. I chatted to Sam Brittan* about the EMS. He is against – but assumes we will go in. I did not give him any clues.

Back to No. 10 to clear off papers – the flow has greatly increased – including a very good paper from the Department of Industry on microprocessors.

Home quite early feeling fairly relaxed and fit.

Monday 16 October 1978

A quiet morning. The PM at Chequers.

Harold Lever was summoned by the PM at 2.30 to discuss the EMS. Partly the PM was trying to win Lever over to a more sceptical attitude; partly he was using him as a trial run for his meeting with Schmidt, testing out his own arguments against an intelligent supporter of the EMS.

Gen 130 met to discuss the situation on the European Airbus and our aircraft industry. The report was bleak, with the French as always blocking our participation because they know our engines are better than theirs and the Germans clinging to the French tail. The PM seemed content for us to withdraw and work with the Americans. He said that British Aerospace was not much good anyway and we must look after Rolls-Royce and British Airways.

I chatted to Pat Nairne and David Ennals before their meeting with the PM to discuss the NHS and told them that we might be able to get a little more money for the NHS since Audrey has been pressing for it. Joel Barnett and the Treasury had told me that there was a little elbow room in the Contingency Reserve. But they don't want the whole thing reopened for all spending ministers. I briefed the PM on this later for tomorrow's Cabinet on public expenditure. Incidentally, in his meeting with Ennals and Nairne, the PM said he was not happy with the present method of settling public sector pay and that he was 'pleased that pay was coming to a crunch early on'. He did not propose to yield.

I went home fairly early.

Tuesday 17 October 1978

Nice early morning run. Cabinet dealt with Namibia, public expenditure, and the problem that our short-time unemployment scheme has run into difficulties through total opposition from the CBI and so will have to be dropped. They are now scrabbling around to find ways to create substitute jobs.

I went to lunch at Guinness Mahon bank, where I may work later. Returned to No. 10 in time to attend the Bonn briefing. (Interestingly, the Bank of England had not been invited.) The Chancellor opened by reporting on yesterday's Finance ministers' meeting on the EMS in Luxembourg, which had apparently produced an astonishing turnaround. The Irish and the Italians both deserted the Germans and said that now the proposed system was just the old snake they were less interested. Only the Dutch fully supported the Germans. This is partly due to successful lobbying on our part but basically it is because the original impulse was to a *new* European Monetary System. Now we just have the existing currency 'snake', with the parity *grid* system, not the 'basket', and with only £15 million of credit reserves to support it, not £50 million as originally discussed. So Ireland, Italy and even France find little new incentive to go in (except for Giscard's political will).

The PM then announced what he was going to say to Schmidt in Bonn. He said he would put a series of questions to Schmidt about the fundamentals of the EMS and what it is supposed to achieve. He would then tell him about the British situation – that we intended to stick to tight monetary control in or out of the EMS; and that in fact the EMS would hinder rather than help us – it would be 'a diversion' from the running battle against inflation. There might be a majority against in the Commons. It would divide our politics without helping in the main battle against inflation. So he would press Schmidt to defer it, and would promise that the UK would join when the other changes are made and conditions met. 'I don't think that I could recommend the Cabinet to join at this moment.'

Kit McMahon came in to see me and was a bit peeved that the Bank had been excluded from the EMS briefing. But he had mainly come to argue for a stiff autumn Budget package. He said that he expected the pound to come under pressure once it was known that we were not going into the EMS. And because of the collapse of pay policy we would not sell any more gilts, so we would not be able to control the money supply. He wanted a hike of 2% in interest rates. We discussed around it, and I made the case against, but he was fairly firm. So I will brief the PM to see if we can find a way out. Kit kindly drove me home.

Then Carol and I went out to dinner with Brian MacArthur, deputy editor of the *Evening Standard* and an old friend. Very pleasant, though not home to bed till 1.15.

Wednesday 18 October 1978

I came in quite late, and did not see the PM before he set off for Bonn.

Trevor West came in from Dublin. He has become involved with the IRA as a mediator on the problem of the IRA prisoners in Long Kesh prison, who are on strike and refusing to wear prison uniforms, claiming the right to be treated as political prisoners. They want to get off the hook. The chief linkman is Mick Mullen, secretary of the Irish T&G, who is using Trevor to link to me. I have arranged to see Brian Cubbon* at the Northern Ireland Office tomorrow to see if we can find a way through, as the British government needs to find a way out as well. The situation in Long Kesh is appalling.

David Hill, Roy Hattersley's special adviser, came in to talk about Roy's scheme for dealing with pay policy through price controls on firms who exceed the limits.

Then I went home early, feeling tired, and fell asleep listening to a lovely requiem mass.

Thursday 19 October 1978

Went in to see Brian Cubbon, permanent secretary of the Northern Ireland Office. I put it to him that I had been approached by Irish friends to try to reach a compromise over the prisoners in Long Kesh who are striking for political status. He immediately looked frightened. He said that the government's policy was never to talk to the IRA and never to talk to inter-mediaries.

When I said that the proposal to allow trade union teachers in to give seminars to the prisoners looked attractive, he said it was unacceptable, because the prisoners might receive the tutors 'on the blanket' (i.e. still refusing to wear prison uniforms) and that would be a terrible defeat for the government. It would also upset the Protestants and the warders. I tried several probing approaches but got nowhere. Any concession would be seen as a defeat, therefore we must make no concessions, even if the IRA were offering concessions.

As we parted outside, I told him that he was on a totally sterile course. He said that our policy had been 'enormously successful', because it had reduced the amount of overt violence. I replied that I was more worried by the political vacuum in Ulster and the way that Northern Irish youth was being socialised to anarchy. He did not respond to that.

I understand his personal position: Cubbon is a very nice and able man who was blown up by the IRA barbarians in the incident when our Dublin ambassador was killed. I cannot see how he can handle that job sanely. But his course and his attitude point straight to the political desert, and disaster lies at the end of it.

I had sandwiches for lunch, then went shopping.

Returned to clear my papers, then out to a very tasty dinner at the Café Royal with Ian Trethowan and David Webster of the BBC. They are still lobbying hard to get the government to change the broadcasting White Paper policies. They made some reasonable points.

Friday 20 October 1978

The PM was away in Wales all day.

I went to John Hunt's meeting of deputy secs. Various looming industrial crises were discussed in the nuclear, power plant and motor car industries. It looks like a winter of pay and industrial collapse.

Gavyn and I worked for the rest of the day on a paper on tightening the money supply. On the pay front, the union leaders are pressing for a price control policy which will get them off the pay hook. This may coincide with Hattersley's approach, but it still looks very vague. There is another meeting between the TUC Six and ministers, with Healey in the chair, next Tuesday at 3 p.m.

Home early, at 7.45 p.m.

Monday 23 October 1978

Went to the Motor Show at the new Exhibition Centre at Birmingham. Sat at lunch next to Hartley Shawcross, who was in the 1945 Labour government and gossiped hostilely about Harold Wilson.

Tuesday 24 October 1978

Finally got hold of all the pay policy material – a mass of papers which had *not* been copied to us by Private Office. It looks as if no union agreement is possible. The unions have agreed on a common target of single figure inflation, but want to be left to free collective bargaining to achieve that. The one possibility is a mechanism of linking pay to prices – allowing employees to fix their own pay rises with the unions, but not allowing the employers to raise prices if they go above 5% on pay. So they can pay more out of productivity or profits. But if they pay too much they couldn't recoup it by inflationary price rises. This approach has been pushed by Hattersley from the government side and by Moss Evans and other unionists. However, it is clear that the Treasury do not want this. Because they think it would be used by the unions as an excuse to bury the 5%, and then they would get around the price controls. The Treasury also fears that it would damage industry's profits and would offend the CBI.

The trade union leaders are meeting the Chancellor and ministers this afternoon for a long session. They will have before them a draft statement, which if agreed will go before the general council tomorrow, which declares their agreement on the common target of defeating inflation, but then as good as says we agree to differ. This does not make much sense to me. It will simply publicise again that we are in disagreement with the unions. I think it is much better to go on talking until the election.

Went to lunch with Edward Boyle. He was charming as ever, but I felt he was very low – older, as if he had been ill. Back to No. 10 to clear more papers.

Had a rather pompous reply from Brian Cubbon rejecting all mediation on the issue of the IRA Maze prisoners – 'We are not in the business of doing business with the Provisionals, directly or indirectly.' There was not the least sense of how we shall actually make any progress on this. The Northern Ireland Office has no ideas at all on how to make progress in Ulster. They are proud that they will not negotiate and will not accept mediation. But beyond that, they have nothing. I understand why Cubbon hates the IRA. But somebody has to deal with these hateful people other than on a basis of hatred. I wrote back a suitably sharp reply. Now we wait while it all gets slowly worse – politically if not militarily.

Later I played football and came home feeling relaxed.

Wednesday 25 October 1978

Carol and the children went off to the country this morning for half-term. As I reached No. 10, the PM was setting off for Transport House, where he had an NEC meeting.

Tom McNally is still around in No. 10 although now a candidate for Stockport – the GMWU and the Electricians have jointly provided the money to employ him.

I spent the whole morning reading papers. Then to lunch with Joe Haines at the Gay Hussar. John Torode was there as well. The two of them discussed Marcia – John was Sue Lewis's girlfriend in the late 1960s when Sue worked for Marcia, and saw a lot of chaos then. He explained the background to Joe's story about the time when, at a Blackpool Party Conference, Marcia made Sue go back to London each night on the train, taking some papers, and then return next day. John claimed that this was to prevent Sue spending the night with him.

John said that Kagan also used to frighten people on behalf of his political friends. He threatened Sue Lewis's father and warned him that he 'would be found in a ditch'.

I dashed back early to attend an EY Cabinet committee on the future of the motor industry. It was very gloomy: output way down compared to ten years ago. Leyland producing fewer cars from more men than in 1972; 15% of the UK's strikes occur in the motor industry, which has only 2% of the national workforce; there has been £800 million government aid to Leyland, but still not a single new model.

Most ministers took a gloomy view. The PM said they should not assume that there would be a motor assembly industry here in the future. But they all agreed that nobody in the industry would ever believe anything bad would happen. They all assume that the government will always bail them out.

Benn was the exception. He said that it was all management's fault. He said that the strike situation would be solved if only the workers were given industrial democracy and planning agreements, etc. (Varley pointed out that the Leyland workers had been offered these things but had refused them.) He also recommended protection, or else we will suffer another massive dose of de-industrialisation. He was more wild and less convincing than usual.

I then had an indecisive Unit meeting on pay policy. Yesterday's meeting between ministers and the TUC Six did not get very far. Fortunately they rejected the suggested draft declaration, which simply announced that our marriage with the unions was over. But the rest was not too helpful. They mainly pursued the 'prices' approach. The trouble here was, as Roy Hattersley told me before EY today, that different people understood different things by a 'price-wage policy'. To him (and me) it is a way of tying pay increases to real increases of a maximum of 5% in real unit costs.

But to Moss Evans and the unions it is a cosmetic formula allowing free collective bargaining. They want to leave it to the local unions and management to agree that big price increases won't result from the wage settlement. This would leave terrible scope for deception and misplaced hope.

Finished the day at a nice party in the state dining room, given to say goodbye to various duty clerks. These have been a good lot and helpful to us in the Unit. One of them, Larry, told me that when we special advisers came in to No. 10 he 'shared the general Civil Service scepticism'. But after a few months reading our briefs he was 'totally converted'.

Came home around 9, listened to the radio, read a book, and then to bed.

Incidentally, Tom McNally approached me recently, on behalf of the Prime Minister, to ask if I would like a peerage. Labour is very short of young spokesmen in the Lords. I declined. I want to see this job through to the end and I do not want any rewards other than the satisfaction of doing it.

Thursday 26 October 1978

I went in a bit late because the kitchen plumbing burst and there was water everywhere. When I arrived, Cabinet had already begun with a huge agenda on public expenditure.

I worked in the office, and began preparing tomorrow's talk to the Anglo-French seminar at Nuffield.

The PM came to join us for lunch. He was in tremendous form. He came in rubbing his hands and saying, 'What an interesting day. It's all marvellously interesting.' We discussed the philosophical basis of the Car Seat Belts Bill, agreed this morning – i.e. on what basis should one force people to save their lives? The PM said it was simply a question of saving medical costs. He went on to reminisce about how as a child he had always dreamed of owning a pedal bicycle, and had saved up, but had never had the necessary £3.50. So he never had one. He again said British Leyland should be closed down, but recognised that it would be difficult to get ministerial support.

Today's Gallup poll shows us in the lead by 5% (compared to 7% *behind* last time). It also shows a massive support for incomes policy, particularly among trade unionists! Once again the Party and union militants are shown to be completely out of touch with their memberships. The PM was very bucked by all of this. (Tom McNally later told me that at Blackpool the PM had predicted this, saying that the polls would come his way at the beginning of November.) But it leaves an odd question mark over whether we should have had an October election.

We finished with a long discussion on the collapsing dollar. The PM is very keen to help the Americans. His basic instincts are still to go for a new world reserve currency – SDRs – and e.g. begin by designating oil prices in them.

Helen Liddell phoned from Berwick and East Lothian, where we have a by-election today. She felt we might just win – and she is usually pessimistic.

The Cabinet committee on Ireland took place at 4.30. The PM was very good, quizzing Mason about 'the negativeness' of our position in the North: 'Where is it leading, Roy?' He asked whether we should take an initiative in Northern Ireland, like Carter on the Middle East at Camp David. He said that the present quiet 'won't last. We will start to get a ferment again.' But other ministers were worried about opening up the Irish issue again before the election. He told me after that he 'just wanted to stir up the Northern Ireland Office into thinking ahead'.

The PM went to see Sammy Davis at the Palladium this evening. This is his third visit to the theatre in a month. He is relaxing and enjoying himself before Parliament meets.

I went home fairly early and watched Bogart and Bergman in *Casablanca* for the twelfth time. It still made me weep at the sad end.

Friday 27 October 1978

To Nuffield College, Oxford, to give a talk. It went well and I had an enjoyable day – not home till after midnight.

We won the by-election at Berwick – with an increased majority! The first swing to a Labour government since Hull in 1966! So it still looks open and interesting and suggests we might have won an election now.

Monday 30 October 1978

Did not see the PM today. Found a lot of paper waiting since Friday and I worked hectically to clear it.

Off to lunch at Lloyd's Bank in the City. They had gathered a group of experts to discuss control of public expenditure. Quite interesting. But they failed to see that ministers will never agree to *cuts* in public expenditure, as they are nearly all spenders and stand together, supporting one another's bids. The Treasury is alone resisting. And departmental officials press their ministers, feeling it is a defeat for their department if it suffers cuts. Nobody involved in the top decision-making process, except the Treasury, has an interest or incentive in making cuts.

After lunch returned to work on papers and make a series of phone calls: Jean-Claude Morel in Brussels told me that the commission has cleared progress on the European Brookings; Helen Liddell phoned from Scotland, delighted with the Berwick by-election result and also that she is now expecting a baby. This latter is lovely news, but will interfere with our general election plans: she is the only person in the Labour Party who knows how to organise.

Then had a Unit meeting on low pay, and came home early to look after the children while Carol was out.

Tuesday 31 October 1978

Very quiet day. The PM was working on his speech for the opening of Parliament. He also saw the various ministers concerned with devolution early in the morning in the Cabinet Room, to decide the date of the referendums in Wales and Scotland. They were in there when I arrived.

Went to lunch with Ed Streeter, minister at the American Embassy. He had been very impressed by his visit to the Cabinet Room last Thursday to discuss the monetary situation.

Read papers in the afternoon and then went home early to play football this evening. Home at 11.30 after a couple of pints.

Wednesday 1 November 1978

Had a terrible journey in this morning, with the traffic at a total standstill, probably because of the State Opening of Parliament. Not very much to do in the office. The work for the Queen's Speech is over and we have not yet moved into the next phase. But there is a lot of rumbling on the monetary front. The Americans are taking some tough measures, including higher interest rates, which will hit us. The Bank still thinks we need a package to sell gilts and fund our deficit.

Out to lunch with Joe Haines at the San Martino. Very good company as ever. Then to the Commons for the opening of the debate on the Address. Mrs Thatcher was a bit tortured on incomes policy, reflecting the divisions in the Tory Party, but apart from that, I thought she was quite effective.

The PM went through his speech rather hurriedly. Not a very inspiring text.

Thursday 2 November 1978

Cabinet discussed the EMS, and a clear majority spoke against. Only Shirley Williams was really passionately in favour. On Bingham and Rhodesia they agreed to wait to see how the debate goes. Officials are still hoping to avoid an inquiry.

At lunch upstairs, we discussed the various Cabinet items. People were also worried about the PM's Christmas vacation plans. He is talking of going to the West Indies on Boxing Day. His staff don't want to go, and McNally and Stott say they are definitely not going.

In the afternoon Harold Wilson made a striking speech on Rhodesian sanctions, saying that he thought that all the Bingham papers, including the Cabinet papers on sanctions, should be published. Ken Stowe was complaining bitterly about this at the farewell dinner for Nigel Wicks in the evening. He said that HW did not know what he was doing.

It was a lovely dinner. We all served one another, with the PM joining in handing out the plates. He and Nigel made nice speeches. It is clear that the PM is very fond of him. Certainly Nigel is one of the nicest people to have worked in No. 10's Private Office.

The wine was superb, a 1955 claret, and so Carol had to drive home.

Friday 3 November 1978

Straight in to John Hunt's meeting of deputy secs. Hunt was very agitated about Harold Wilson, who had apparently said that he had seen *all* the Cabinet papers on Bingham and sanctions. In fact he had seen only those for his own administration. Hunt said, 'The others were not even in the same room.' He was obviously worried that Heath and Callaghan would think that the Cabinet Office had been revealing *their* papers. He ordered Ken Stowe to tell McCaffrey to start briefing the press accordingly.

I went back to the office and worked till lunchtime. I put in a brief on poverty and low pay. Liz Arnott has produced some fascinating figures showing that the low paid are nearly all youths and single women, and that the poorest families are rarely those on the lowest wages.

Went out to lunch and back to clear more papers. Home early to start fixing up my bedroom Quad valve hi-fi system. I now love these practical things, a marvellous escape from economics.

Monday 6 November 1978

Saw the PM before lunch. He was very pleased with our paper on low pay and the lack of relationship between it and family poverty. He said, 'I keep reading that our 5% is finished. But nobody has told me a better way to fight inflation. Of course we shall lose some. But I mean to stick to it. I am not going to give up now.' He had talked to the Chancellor over the telephone on Friday and told him not to give away too much to the trade unions, when really they are offering little in return.

The PM was very angry with Brian Sedgemoor, Tony Benn's PPS, who read out a secret Treasury paper at a select committee session with Denis Healey. It is not clear where he got it from. But the PM said he was going to sack him. I tried to defend Sedgemoor, whom I actually like, but the PM was very strong and described him as 'vulgar. He will have to go.' Brian has certainly become sillier while working for Benn.

I went out to lunch with Gavyn Davies at my favourite little café in Floral Street and also bought a bargain copy of Mozart's *Requiem*. But basically we went to discuss monetary policy and our brief to put in to the PM on monetary policy for tomorrow's seminar.

At 5 I attended the meeting with Arnold Weinstock* and two colleagues from GEC discussing very technical questions about turbine generation, where GEC is pushing a 'four-flow' system and Parsons is pushing a 'six-flow' system. Weinstock wants the electricity board to buy his system, which is the only one with export potential. But it soon became a real punch-up. Weinstock was brilliant but very provocative, exaggerating, giving only one side of a case and interrupting ministers. The PM began to treat him fairly roughly and Arnold began to sulk. He was very harsh on Tony Benn, saying he was personally preventing the pressurised water nuclear system from getting started.

The meeting broke up in a rather tense atmosphere. Yet afterwards the PM said he was sympathetic to the GEC case – it was the only system with a hope of selling in the export market. But he always followed the principle of not interfering with a nationalised industry in its purchasing policy.

I went back to finish papers, and then out to dinner in the evening with Paul Fox of Yorkshire TV. He was pressing me hard on Annan against creating an Open Broadcasting Authority but instead putting the fourth channel under a revamped IBA. The trouble is that the IBA may not get revamped. The ITV don't really want a *different* fourth channel under a *different* IBA. They just want an ITV2 which is a mirror image of ITV1. They are still hoping simply to double the amount of pap and crap they push out. We had a good meal and I did not get home till after 11.30 p.m.

Tuesday 7 November 1978

Began by reading the Treasury and Bank papers for tomorrow's seminar. They want interest rates up a crippling 2–3% and no changes in the method of handling gilts. The papers were thick and rambling. Afterwards I had a long talk with Gavyn and we agreed our approach in our paper to the PM.

To lunch with Paul Neild of Phillips & Drew, a very clever young man. I might try to employ him some day. He thinks we will have to do a monetary package, with higher interest rates and higher VAT. Because the City expects it, therefore it won't buy gilts, therefore we have to raise rates in order to sell gilts. These City expectations become self-fulfilling.

To the Commons for the first PM's Questions of the session. The PM was a bit edgy, as always at the beginning. He was very concerned with Sedgemoor, who had at first agreed to resign quickly, but then was persuaded by his minister Tony Benn not to. So the PM is going to sack him. The actual Questions went OK, surprisingly low-key, which certainly means that the Tories accept they won't win for some time.

I came straight back to Downing Street to have a meeting with Kit McMahon from the Bank of England. He put to me his ideas for handling EMS and our staying out. He said that we must separate the particular *intervention mechanism* from the wider question of getting greater monetary stability in Europe. In fact Schmidt has picked on the intervention mechanism to push first, but it is the most difficult part and should come last. We should begin with the European Monetary *Fund* and the mechanics of credit, and get ahead with negotiating that. On these, the British could participate and take a very positive line. Then we could say that it is only the intervention mechanism which we are staying out of and that that should wait anyway, until the EEC economies have converged, when the mechanism is more likely to survive. This all seems to me very constructive thinking and we will support it to the PM.

We put in our own paper for tomorrow's seminar. Then I went off to play six-a-side football and home to listen to my new Mozart *Requiem*.

Wednesday 8 November 1978

Went straight in to the seminar, which was fascinating. The PM was clearly not impressed by the Governor's arguments for a rise in interest rates and complained about the Duke of York system, whereby every few months the City was led up the hill of rising interest rates and then they came down again, buying gilts on the way. Harold Lever strongly supported him, convincingly demolishing the Governor's arguments. But in the end the PM was not prepared to overrule the Chancellor and the Governor when they were in agreement. We of course had greater doubts, but these decisions are often finely balanced, and one has to accept that once a government has established itself as monetarist, it has to follow the monetarist mumbo-jumbo. The seminar continued till 12.30 and I then went off to lunch with Joe Haines at the Gay Hussar.

In the evening I went to see Harry Evans at the RAC. Have not seen much of Harry lately. He was a bit depressed by events at the *Sunday Times*. There are a lot of journalist rats on his staff anyway, but under the pressure of the threat of closure they are behaving even worse than usual. He obviously thinks that they really will close down. Home at 9 o'clock.

Thursday 9 November 1978

Cabinet discussed Bingham and Rhodesia again this morning. Ministers apparently accepted that there would probably have to be an inquiry – even Shore and Healey, who have been strongest against. But they came up with a clever device – suggested by the Cabinet Office. This was to set up a parliamentary inquiry of privy councillors by special statute empowering them to send for papers. This had the attraction to officials that it would take some time to set up, Parliament might delay or defeat the bill, and then it would have to be redone for the next Parliament and might never happen. A committee under the Lord Chancellor was set up to examine this.

They also discussed the TUC talks on pay. The draft agreement looks pretty bad to me – all concessions to the TUC on low pay, on comparability in the public sector and on prices, but very little in return to us, not even to be able to mention 5% specifically in the paper. Clearly the TUC have outnegotiated Healey, Booth and the other ministers so far. It does not look worth having to me. But the PM has already warned Healey to be tougher, and they may claw something back.

At lunch upstairs I attacked the civil servants because the Unit has not been receiving these pay papers. They apologised and promised to send them up – and in the afternoon they flooded up.

The Bank has announced a lending rate of 12½% – up 2½%. My friends in the City say this is 'overkill', unnecessarily high, giving an impression of panic and crisis. But it will sell a lot of gilts. (It will also push up the RPI, public borrowing costs and mortgage rates: we will pay for that later, while the City is chuckling over its gilts profits.) At Question Time the PM took the opportunity to explain it as part of our unwavering dedication to defeating inflation. He looked very honest, given that there is a big vote of confidence tonight. Nobody can say that he delayed it until that is out of the way.

I went back briefly to No. 10 and then on to the LSE to hear Michael Zander's excellent inaugural lecture on 'Change and the Law'. He paid a nice compliment to me for helping to get the Royal Commission set up. A good, clear lecture and a big audience.

Afterwards we had dinner in the director's room – journalist Hugo Young and lawyers Geoffrey Bindman, Jeffrey Jowell and Ronald Dworkin.

A good meal and a very good discussion afterwards. Michael really has made a big and radical contribution to our society, forcing change on one of the key professions – who are of course the bastions of reaction in this country, much worse than the few remaining beleaguered capitalist entrepreneurs. I enjoyed it enormously, drank too much good wine and then was driven home by Geoffrey Bindman in time to hear that we had won the confidence vote comfortably by 12. This won't be good for Thatcher. Nor will the latest *Express* poll which shows that the Tories are 3% ahead of us – but would be 14% ahead if Heath were leader. She sacked Winston Churchill yesterday over the rebellion against Rhodesian sanctions. That is to her credit; he is a stupid man.

The PM has also finally sacked Sedgemoor as Benn's PPS. Once quite a nice man, he has deteriorated politically under the influence of Tony Benn. The PM was obviously peeved with Benn for refusing to rebuke Sedgemoor for reading out a secret paper in public. One day he may get Tony – though the latter is still fairly shrewd and always capitulates when he is confronted by the Prime Minister.

Friday 10 November 1978

At the deputy secs meeting in John Hunt's office they discussed Rhodesian sanctions and the proposed committee of inquiry. They were hoping that nobody realised that the really explosive papers are not the Cabinet papers at all but the papers on the *No. 10 files*, and also the Parliamentary Questions files – which contain lots of background briefing on the way to evade awkward questions on sanctions. (NB: the George Brown answer in the Lords to Brockway, which was deliberately phrased to avoid the truth.)

I went back, called a meeting with Gavyn Davies and David Lipsey and we began to draft a brief for the PM on the TUC agreement on pay. They disagreed with me and most officials in thinking that the agreement was worth having, almost at any price, so we argued out a compromise. In the end I conceded to them that it would be very damaging to break with the TUC now, and they agreed to set out the concessions we had made in a realistic (pessimistic) light.

I went for a fascinating lunch at GEC with Arnold Weinstock and Lord Aldington. Weinstock behaved quixotically, making wild and exaggerated statements against politicians, politics and various other general matters, but was then quite brilliant discussing the future of the nuclear industry. He was savage about the Central Electricity Board and about Benn allegedly trying to destroy our nuclear industry.

Came back to finish off the TUC brief. Then cleared a lot more paper. Made telephone calls to Brussels, New York, etc. about the European

Brookings (which is making quite good progress through the EEC Commission) and then came home early to go out to drinks with our friends the Grahams.

Quite a good week. But today's news was dominated by the increase of 2% in mortgage rates – this will hit us badly politically. It was bad for Peter Shore too, who had assured yesterday's Cabinet that the increase in MLR would *not* lead to an increase in mortgage rates this year.

Monday 13 November 1978

Worked in the office in the morning. Still not a great deal of paper. Compared to the flood days of 1974–76, the government is clearly working at a much lower tempo, over the whole of Whitehall as well as in No. 10. Went to lunch at my Covent Garden café with Gavyn. It is now such a lovely and lively area. Would like to buy a flat here if I had any money.

Back to the EY Cabinet committee on the joint pay agreement with the TUC. Every minister, including the PM, took the same line: it was worth having, because it kept the special relationship with the TUC and meant that we could take on an individual rogue union without taking on the whole TUC. Most important is that it provides the basis on which the TUC can stay in contact with the government over pay/prices, enabling it not to support individual unions in conflict with the government and committing it to further talks on long-term incomes policy.

The PM went off to give his Guildhall speech which contains quite an attack on the EEC budgetary system. There is no prospect of the Europeans at present changing the system, and in its present form it is increasingly costly to us, with very few benefits.

Carol came in and we went out to the Powells to a marvellous party. Italian Carla is a great life force. Charles is more sedate and less bright than her. I enjoyed myself immensely and we came home at 1.30 a.m.

Tuesday 14 November 1978

Woke feeling tired and jaded, but no regrets. A cup of tea and aspirins put me right, but I did not venture out for a run.

Did not attend the EY Cabinet committee on nuclear power, even though we had put in a minute last night. It is a highly technical issue, in an industry full of prima donnas, with the government side led by Tony Benn, who totally ignores Cabinet decisions. Apparently the PM ticked him off and read out the last Cabinet committee minutes to him.

I worked rather lethargically. Had a quick lunch with Gavyn in the CSD.

Then to briefing for Parliamentary Questions. The PM seemed a bit tired and flat.

Back at No. 10, Joe Haines phoned to say that Tom McCaffrey had been briefing today's lobby to say that the pay agreement with the TUC (which went through the Economic committee this morning and to the general council of the TUC this afternoon) was hardly worth having. The *Mirror* was puzzled and wondered if this was the PM's line. It is not.

Then at 5 p.m. we heard the devastating news that the TUC had rejected the pay agreement. Nobody had expected this, once it was accepted by the Economic committee this morning – without a single vote against. Now that we had lost it, we all realised how much we wanted the agreement. I saw McCaffrey near the tapes and he said, 'Perhaps there was something in it for us, if they wouldn't have it.' This is a real setback. We shall have to see how the markets react tomorrow. A pity, as we were selling gilts well again today and the balance of payments figures today were good – £200 million in the black.

Incidentally, Edmund Dell resigned from the Cabinet on Saturday to earn money in the City and was replaced by John Smith. I was sorry to see Dell go – a sane man, though with little political imagination and deeply negative. But John Smith's promotion gave me great pleasure. He is the last of my April 1976 suggestions to the Prime Minister for promotion from Minister of State – Dell, Owen, Orme, Booth, Rodgers, Hattersley and Smith. An excellent man who strengthens the band of young moderates.

Shirley Williams is talking of resigning if she does not make any progress with her educational maintenance allowances at Cabinet this week. She also has a bad wisdom tooth, which cannot help her state of happiness. I talked to her yesterday and promised to take her out to lunch (but not until the tooth is out!).

Wednesday 15 November 1978

The PM spent the morning in his study reading a biography of the Duke of Wellington in preparation for today's visit by the Portuguese Prime Minister.

I saw the PM and he took me into the cloakroom opposite and said he knew that we were all very pessimistic because of the failure of the talks with the TUC, but he was philosophical. He thought that the wage outcome would be much better than most people expected, though he saw the 'political' point about keeping alongside the trade unions. Then he met President [Antonio] Eanes, brought him to introduce him to me and took him off upstairs for talks.

We all went up for a big Portuguese lunch at 1 o'clock. I chatted to David Steel beforehand, and we agreed to make a fresh arrangement for a dinner soon. The speeches were rather good. The President spoke very emotionally about how the Portuguese had to struggle for their democratic freedom from fascism and how the British – and Mr Callaghan particularly – had stood by them in their hour of need. He revealed that we had promised them military support, which has never been said in public.

In the evening I took John Lyons, of the Power Workers Union, to supper. We discussed trade union politics in general and the opportunism of several of the trade union leaders. He was as usual very critical of Tony Benn, saying how disloyal he is to this government in private and how he is refusing to produce a new bill to reorganise the electricity industry along the agreed lines. In particular we discussed pay. His union, as always, wish to increase differentials with Frank Chapple's electricians. So they are going to wait to see what the electricians get and then go for something on top of that.

Home at 10 o'clock, feeling physically drained.

Thursday 16 November 1978

The Cabinet had its photograph taken in the pillared room. I worked in the office during the morning. At lunch upstairs we had a full report on Cabinet. They actually approved Shirley's revised pilot scheme to introduce educational maintainance allowances in a few selected areas. The PM resisted it to the end, supported by Peter Shore, but the rest backed Shirley, who had lobbied colleagues effectively.

The PM was a bit tetchy at briefing at Questions. Mrs Thatcher scored some points off him over pay policy and he showed that he was not on top of things. I don't know what is wrong.

I went back to No. 10 feeling a bit low, as if sickening for a cold. So I went home early and had a rest before going out to a nice party at David Sainsbury's home in Notting Hill Gate. Home at midnight.

Friday 17 November 1978

Quite a busy day. In early to clear papers and then to John Hunt's meeting of deputy secs. Some chat about problems on the pay front.

To lunch with Geoffrey Smith at the Gay Hussar, then back to work on a couple of briefs. We are worried that Healey will give away too much to the idle local authority manual workers. So we put in a brief telling the PM to hold firm – and also supporting a very good paper from Nuffield's Bill McCarthy* and Hugh Clegg* suggesting a new body for settling public sector pay. This is in line with the PEP pamphlet I published in 1962. So we give it a push.

In the evening French President Giscard d'Estaing phoned. The PM was at the farm, but the call was monitored in Private Office. Apparently Giscard was being very friendly and trying to establish a warm atmosphere, inviting the PM to stay overnight, but the PM was fairly cool in response. This is typical of him. The French have been fairly unhelpful to us lately, e.g. on the Airbus and the EMS, so the PM does not pretend a few warm words can win him over. Even so, I think he should have been a little more responsive.

I went home and then straight on, without supper, to see a nice film about Stevie Smith, the poet. Met poet Dannie Abse at the cinema and we went off for a drink afterwards. I first met him when I was president of the Oxford Poetry Society twenty-four years ago.

Incidentally the whole 'secrets' case saga – which started with Agee and Hosenball and then proceeded to the trial of Berry and Aubrey – collapsed today. It was a ludicrous farce and a waste of money. Our security services and Home Office are incompetent and paranoid – perhaps you have to be to be in that business. It is over a year since I had Robert Armstrong over to my office from the Home Office to quiz him on whether they really knew what they were doing. He said yes, it was crucial to the safety of the troops in Northern Ireland. Yet the prosecution never mentioned Northern Ireland throughout the case!

Monday 20 November 1978

The Italian ambassador, Ducci, came to talk to me in advance of Prime Minister Andreotti's visit on Wednesday. We discussed the European Monetary System. He said that the Italians still had some doubts. But I still feel that the Italians will go in.

Prince Charles came in for lunch with the PM. I went out for a quick lunch with Richard Faulkner at the White Tower. He told me he operates as a PR man for an enormous number of organisations.

Dashed back to see Dick Cooper from the US Treasury. We mainly talked about the EMS. But he was also fairly bullish about the battered dollar – he said there had been little support in recent days and it seemed to have stabilised, though he expected fresh pressures in the new year.

I then got a message that the PM wanted to talk about public sector pay. He agreed with our paper saying that he liked the idea of an umbrella body to cover the whole of public sector pay. He was encouraged by the latest polls: we are running neck and neck with the Tories, and Thatcher is a long way behind the PM, and even running behind Heath.

I went out in the evening to a lovely birthday supper with Johnny Apple at Ma Cuisine, a tremendous French restaurant in Knightsbridge. Home just after midnight.

Tuesday 21 November 1978

Went in to EY to discuss a CPRS paper on the economic and social consequences of the microprocessor revolution and agreed to publish it. When Tony Benn said he did not agree with it, the PM said, 'Tony, I sometimes wonder what you would support done by this government.'

In his conclusions the PM said that, 'Microprocessors are not something to be feared, but offered great potential if used to our benefit.' He asked Varley to organise a conference of trade unions to help 'educate' them.

Lunch with Jacques Van Ypersele from Brussels. We discussed the European Brookings, which he is quite optimistic will go through the Foreign Ministers Council in December. Mainly we discussed the EMS – he is the chairman of the European Monetary System committee. He is clearly sad that we won't go in. Says that the Europeans will say it is typical of the British – always talk of the disadvantages of things, then wait and see if it works before joining. Back to the briefings for Andreotti's visit and the PM's visit to Giscard. Healey reported on yesterday's Finance ministers' meeting in Brussels – where basically we made no progress. 'We got a dusty answer.' They ranged over a lot of other things and the PM called on me to talk on the Brookings. He said he was not sure he yet had the feel for that.

In the evening I went to play football – and scored two goals.

Wednesday 22 November 1978

I worked in the office right through the morning. I went out to Johnny's Café in Covent Garden for lunch, and then wandered around that area and visited some gramophone record shops. On return, I decided not to go into the Andreotti talks which I later gathered were dreary. The only important moment was when the PM said about our EMS position that it was 'not a question of "Yes, but", but of "No, unless".' Andreotti indicated that Italy will go in, as we all really expected, as in the last resort they never ever go against the EEC line, and anyway they are German pensioners.

In the evening Carol came in and we went to Lionel Robbins's 80th birthday dinner. It was a glamorous occasion at the Skinners Hall in the City, with the entire intellectual Establishment there. I sat opposite a row of three Nobel prizewinner economists – Hayek, Hicks and Meade – and between the Governor of the Bank of England and the editor of the *Financial Times*. Ralf Dahrendorf made a brilliant speech about Lionel, while Lionel went on at some length in a rather Lionel fashion. There were lots of old LSE friends there and I enjoyed it enormously, staying till nearly midnight.

Thursday 23 November 1978

Cabinet this morning discussed the EMS Green Paper. Beforehand I talked to Shirley Williams and Harold Lever who are the only two in the Cabinet keen to go in. Shirley looks much happier now that she has received approval for her limited schemes for educational maintenance allowances and has had her wisdom tooth out. The EMS paper went through with little discussion of the general principle (that is next week). I thought it was quite good and said so to the PM later, but he disagreed and said it was 'too technical and not political enough'.

Parliamentary Questions were mainly about Ford and sanctions to support the pay limit, which the PM was able to bat back fairly comfortably.

We had a quick deputy secs meeting, where the business timetable till Xmas was fixed. The PM has quite a lot of overseas work. Then out to a lively party at the Italian Embassy and I was able to have long chats with Ken Couzens from the Treasury and Kit McMahon from the Bank. Ken is really against the EMS – and indeed against all grand visions – psychologically. He is a deeply sceptical Whitehall professional, with a profound contempt for all ministers and all ideas. The heart of his and the Chancellor's opposition to going into EMS is that if we were in, and there was a huge dollar crisis, with massive funds switching into the Deutschmark, we would have to intervene massively to hold the grid parities and keep the German mark down. It would cost us a fortune, whereas at least if we were outside, we would only have to intervene to defend our own rate, not the Germans'. Kit McMahon agreed with this, saying also that if we went in and then wanted to drop out, 'the exit ticket will be very expensive'. So I was interested to learn that the Bank of England want us to join the fund credit arrangements and get alongside in every other way, but not to join the exchange mechanism now. So we have a position where the *PM* is against for domestic political reasons, the *Treasury* is against temperamentally and psychologically, and the *Bank* is against because they actually think it will be too expensive in the short run.

In these circumstances it is not surprising that the decision is going negatively the way it is. For myself, I am finally 51–49 for going in. I think we should take a chance, risk the disadvantages for the European advantages and go in to try to make it work. But I am only 51–49 – and it won't happen.

Home at 11 p.m.

Friday 24 November 1978

The PM was away in Paris seeing Giscard today. I spent the morning with David Cook, Lord Mayor of Belfast, mainly discussing the implications for Ireland if the Republic goes into EMS and we don't – with all that that means for separating our monetary systems.

Went shopping over lunch and bought some lovely records – Mozart operas and some Schubert. Back to No. 10 and wrote a brief on Ireland and the EMS for Irish PM Lynch's visit next Monday. Then had a lovely picnic in No. 10 with the Butlers and Carol, and after went to the Lyric Theatre to see *Filomena* – a joyous and uncomplicated evening.

Reports from Paris are very encouraging: the PM has been positive about the EMS and Giscard has been understanding about our staying out of the Exchange Rate Mechanism – the French deep down would prefer us out of Europe altogether.

Monday 27 November 1978

A beautiful morning, sunny and very cold. I worked in the office all morning, except when Mrs Callaghan phoned up to ask me upstairs for coffee. We had a nice gossip. She is a very lovely lady. The flat also looks much more comfortable than in the old days.

Had lunch with the Irish officials who had accompanied Prime Minister Lynch (he, plus the Finance minister Colley and senior civil servant Dermot Nally were at lunch with the PM and Healey). I sat with Ken Couzens and we quizzed their finance officials. What struck us was their innocence. They thought it was all so simple. They would go into the currency 'snake' – but if it got too hot they would just come out. They thought they might be able to spend £100 million in a currency crisis – with no awareness that sometimes one loses £500 million in a morning. And they assumed that if the Germans and French promised them £650 million from *EEC* funds, there would be no problem with other member countries (including us!) approving this.

The real attraction for them is the prospect of finally completing Irish independence from the UK. I understand that. The PM later told me that he felt that Lynch was beginning to see the difficulties but if they got their £650 million grant bribe they would go in.

Later in the afternoon we heard that a meeting of the NEC international committee had passed a resolution insisting we stay out of the EMS. Benn was in the chair. I said to the PM (in the car en route for dinner with the committee on invisible exports) that Benn was 'courting martyrdom'. He agreed, and added, 'He won't have to wait long to get it.' Perhaps.

The dinner went very well, just the top men from the City, and there was a good discussion. William Armstrong, who ran the Civil Service for Ted Heath, came and had a discussion with me beforehand – a strangely excitable man.

Came home at 11 o'clock. Brought with me some lovely Schubert records for Carol – it is our nineteenth wedding anniversary.

Tuesday 28 November 1978

Went in to an EY committee on the crisis in the shipbuilding industry. Clever but reptilian Gerald Kaufman presented a crafty plan for some 'step by step' reduction in the labour force. But the cost of keeping the bulk of the industry going over the next five years was appalling – £1 billion. The PM was clearly shocked by this and argued that it would be better to spend that amount of money on creating jobs in new industries. The PM was keen that there should be more orders of military ships to keep some yards going. 'We are an island and we must have a navy,' he said.

Afterwards I went to lunch at the Commons with Jim's PPS Roger Stott. Then Gerry Fowler came to sit with me. He was savage about the NUT behaviour when he was minister at Education.

Parliamentary Questions was mainly about the sanctions against Ford for their breach of the pay policy. Afterwards the PM held a meeting with ministers about the devolution referenda. He was obviously reluctant to take part in the referenda campaigns. He said he thought that once the government had 'seen the legislation through and arranged the referenda, it had done its job'.

Michael Foot stayed behind and persuaded the PM to intervene in *The Times* dispute. So he talked to Albert Booth and suggested he ask the management to call off the lockout, providing the unions agreed to go back without disruption – but with no reforms of labour practices. I was furious, as this confrontation is the only hope of sorting out Fleet Street, and once the management is forced to compromise, they will capitulate.

I went out to play football in the evening. Very cold – below freezing. Today we had the first snow of this winter.

Wednesday 29 November 1978

A very quiet day. Work on my papers for my visit to Berlin tomorrow – a great wodge of material which took me through till 6.30. I did a quick note on pay, where Booth and Healey seem to be giving way all along the line in the public sector. Then off to a dinner for James Schlesinger, the American Energy secretary, and a party at Cape, the publishers, till 1.30 in the morning. Very tired.

Thursday 30 November 1978

Left for Berlin at 11.30 a.m., so only had a couple of hours in the office, but I did a memo on pay policy. We are very worried that ministers – especially Healey, Varley, Shore and Booth – are giving way too much. On local authority workers, on British Leyland, all the signs of surrender are there. We suggest to the PM that he bring them together and tighten things up.

It was a lovely sunny day when we took off for Germany. But Berlin was grey and wet. However, it was very exciting to be in Berlin at last.

Friday 1 December 1978

We worked very hard at the meeting at the Environmental Institute. Then I had a *very* late night out drinking in the Berlin beer cellars.

Saturday 2 December 1978

First half of the morning touring East Berlin with a military escort carrying Sten guns in an army jeep – very exciting and appealed to all my boyish instincts. The old city of East Berlin is quite impressive, but the rest of East Germany is just as dreary as our propaganda claims, with the air clogged with orange coal smoke.

Came back for a meeting with [Dietrich] Stobbe, the young Lord Mayor of Berlin. He gave me as a present all the Karajan records of the Beethoven symphonies – signed by the Great Conductor – and ex-Nazi – himself. Afterwards a three-hour tour of West Berlin so I saw a great deal and next time will be able to be more selective.

Stobbe invited me to stay for the evening and have dinner at the Charlottenberg Palace, where a big reception was being given for Henry Kissinger. But I have to play football on Sunday morning in Barnet in a charity game against a Jimmy Greaves XI. That I cannot miss, as they include lots of ex-professional footballers. We lost 8–4, but very exciting. I tried to mark Greaves, who was drinking a whole bottle of whisky at half time, but I never laid a foot on him. He controlled and laid off the ball before I got to him.

Monday 4 December 1978

The PM was away in Brussels today at the EEC summit, negotiating the new EMS. A vast amount of paper had accumulated since last Thursday. Also the PM had reacted very positively to our paper on pay last week. He completely agreed about the danger of 'slippage' and asked me to talk to the Chancellor. Healey was at home in Sussex, so I wrote him a letter and arranged to talk to him tomorrow on the phone.

After rowing about some nonsense with McCaffrey and his silly Press Office wanting to sit in on my meetings, I felt ill and irritated in the evening. And in Brussels the going was apparently very tough, with the talks going on till nearly 3 in the morning.

Tuesday 5 December 1978

The PM was away in Brussels all day at the European Council. The talks on the EMS got into great difficulties. Apparently the Irish and Italians began to get cold feet about joining the EMS, especially as it became clear that they were not going to be given their huge financial bribes in return. When it was suggested that the Regional Fund be increased to help the Italians and the Irish the French brutally vetoed it. Giscard had secured what he mainly wanted – German marks to back the franc in the 'snake'. Then he did not care whether the Italians or Irish came or not.

But the collapse of the EMS initiative was a bad blow for Schmidt, who had invested a lot of personal prestige in it. The PM emerged very well. Instead of isolated and obstinate, his arguments were shared by other EEC members. So now all we have is a larger 'snake', with the French in. But I still hope that we can create and join a bigger European system one day.

I phoned Denis Healey first thing in the morning to talk about pay policy. I conveyed to him the PM's worries about conceding comparability in the public sector, which Healey had suggested in his paper for this week's Cabinet. I also told him that I did not like the tone of the officials' papers on pay, where there was a strong smell of defeatist 'Petainism'. He responded in a very friendly way and said he agreed with every word in my letter last night. He said it would be 'fatal to give away comparability on an ad hoc basis'. He was also attracted by the suggestion of a big body for pay in the whole of the public sector.

I was feeling pretty low, with a cold and temperature, so in mid-afternoon I went home to bed for a couple of hours. Then to dinner with Robin Butler in Dulwich in the evening. I left Gavyn and Jim Corr in the office to write a paper on British Leyland pay, which looks like going badly wrong.

Wednesday 6 December 1978

We had a Unit meeting to discuss pay policy prior to putting in a brief for Cabinet tomorrow.

Had lunch with Joe at the Gay Hussar. I dashed back early to an official meeting in the Cabinet Office to prepare my briefs for the European Brookings meeting in Brussels this weekend. Then I nipped over to the Commons for the PM's statement on the breakdown of the EEC talks on the EMS. He was clearly in a strong position, appearing as the defender of the national interest. He received support from both sides of the House.

I talked to Giselle Hammers in the Bonn Chancery and she said that the EMS collapse was seen as a big blow to Schmidt. (We shall have to do something to help Schmidt.)

Thursday 7 December 1978

Went to a special advisers meeting in the CSD to consider our own pay: the CSD is pressing us to take our 5% quickly and in advance of the Civil Service settlement, while in the past they have always pressed us to wait until *after* the civil servants settle. We all assume that the CSD hopes for a *bigger* settlement for civil servants and is trying to persuade us to settle for less in advance.

At lunch upstairs we discussed 'sanctions' against employers to back up pay policy. It looked as if we were going to lose the vote in the Commons tonight on this and apparently the PM was considering resigning. He told Michael Foot yesterday that, if defeated, *he* would resign, but not the government.

At Cabinet this morning the main item was pay in general, and the PM laid down the hard line. Bill Rodgers questioned whether it was worth sticking to 5% if it was going to be breached quite often. The PM slapped him down and said (1) we stick to 5% and (2) we openly admit it if particular settlements are in breach.

On Bingham and Rhodesia Michael Foot now wants a free vote in the Commons on the type of inquiry. This worries the machine, as they had carefully sewn up the package so that the proposed commission would have access to selected Cabinet documents only on the advice of the chairman. Now it is possible that it will all be opened up. The civil servants are blaming Foot.

At Questions the PM was clearly mainly concerned with tonight's crucial vote on pay sanctions. The whips reported that we still had about 23 Labour abstentions and so would lose by about 10. The PM seemed very cool and calm, and said, 'Well, they must take the consequences.' He had in his hand three pages of handwritten script for his talk to the PLP at 6 this evening. We all got the impression that he was going to say that, if we lost, he would go. As he got up to leave for the chamber he sang us a hymn – I think it was 'We'll meet again with the Lord'. It was completely unaffected and not embarrassing. But I have noticed before that he sings hymns at times of stress and crisis.

After Questions the PM was having a very heavy programme – Thatcher on Bingham and Michael Foot on planning what to do about tonight's vote; the Egyptian Prime Minister; then his statement to the PLP (in which he did *not* actually threaten to resign); the dinner with Pierre Trudeau.

I went home for a quick supper, intending to travel back into the Commons for the final vote and to have discussions if we lost. But on the 9 o'clock news I learned that there had been chaos in the Commons – and no vote. The left wing had disrupted the debate for four hours and finally somebody in the gallery threw a pot of red paint, so the Speaker suspended the session. This helps us to escape for a few days until the debate is taken next week.

So I did not have to go back into work. I played more Schubert instead.

Friday 8–Saturday 9 December 1978

I went to Brussels to negotiate the European Brookings. We had a lovely dinner at the home of Jacques Van Ypersele, who is secretary to the Belgian Cabinet, on Friday evening. Then we met all Saturday morning, from 9 to 1.45 in the Cabinet Room in the Prime Minister's office. I emerged less optimistic – the whole scheme is bogged down in EEC bureaucracy and I doubt if anything worthwhile can emerge alive from that.

Incidentally, the other participants were immensely impressed with Mr Callaghan's performance at the Brussels summit. They were not *pleased* with it, but they felt that he had dominated the whole proceedings, even when silent – as he often was.

Monday 11 December 1978

Went on an early run over Hampstead Heath to Kenwood House on a lovely wintry morning. Then drove into the office. The PM was away visiting the army in Dorset until the evening. I sat in the office reading a great deal of stuff on pay questions – including preparations for a state of emergency in the New Year when we expect strikes by the oil tanker drivers, the water and sewerage workers, the other local authority manuals, and so many essential public services will come to a halt. We are planning to bring in the army. It will be the crunch for the government – on the fifth anniversary of Heath's confrontation with the miners! If we lose it, we lose the battle against inflation – and the election. I am quite looking forward to it.

I had a quick lunch at the Reform, talking with Hans Liesners from Industry. He (and his permanent secretary Plietzky) are very against the EMS.

In the afternoon Trevor West from Dublin came in and we chatted about the EMS. He said that in Dublin they felt that Mr Callaghan had emerged the winner and they had lost badly. In the evening we had a party for 'disabled' pressure groups. The PM gave a very nice speech. I was late home.

Tuesday 12 December 1978

I stayed home this morning to go to the Christmas play at my twin boys' local primary school. Lovely. I do regret having not spent more time with them, instead of all this political fantasy stuff.

Then in to lunch with Shirley Williams at Manzi's. I promised to come to her cottage and fix her hi-fi system, which is old and left over from her marriage to philosopher Bernard Williams. Unfortunately we had to dash away early because she was answering questions in the Commons.

To Questions – which was uneventful. Back to No. 10 to clear papers and then I went off to the Irish Embassy for a party. Enormously enjoyable. Lots of old friends were there – Gordon Snell, Willie White, Eileen Fitt. So I did not go to play football but just stayed and drank a great deal of Irish whiskey instead. The new Irish ambassador, Eamonn Kennedy, seems a great improvement on his dismal predecessor.

Home after 11.

Wednesday 13 December 1978

Today was a dramatic and eventful day, culminating in our being defeated on a major plank of our pay policy, over sanctions on employers who breach it.

The PM was very angry with our rebels. He had woken up this morning 'at the end of his tether'. He said that tonight's vote might not be a vote of confidence but 'this is it'. At the House he had a long meeting with six of the left-wing Tribune Group MPs. The Tribune people would not give way, nor would he. So he told them this was 'the effective end of the government'.

He came back to No. 10 for a Defence meeting but they began to discuss the political situation and after a few minutes the PM cancelled his arms meeting and sent the officials out of the Cabinet Room. This political meeting then went on till lunch, when he broke to eat with the chiefs of staff. But afterwards the ministers resumed – with Michael Foot plus Hattersley and Barnett as the two ministers taking part in the sanctions debate. News was filtering out that the Ulster Unionists and Scot Nats were going to vote against us, so we would certainly lose.

At No. 10 reception I had a long chat with Harold Wilson, who was just back from Israel. He did not mention that while there he had met with Lord Kagan – who was today charged with criminal currency offences. Peter Jenkins also told me a story about Kagan using Harold when president of the Board of Trade to change the regulation on the import of *blue dye*, to help his denim company. Peter knew him when Kagan was trying to get him to procure some young woman for his personal use.

To the Commons for the sanctions vote. I stood in the corridor behind the Speaker's Chair and watched the MPs file in and out of the lobbies. There was a buzz of excitement. Our people seemed at last to grasp that we were going to lose (when I came over to the House for lunch and talked to several Labour MPs, none of them seemed aware of the danger). Four left-wingers abstained in the chamber, each one a mediocre nitwit. Ironically, the 'hard' left finally decided to vote for the government and tried to whip in the others. But Arthur Latham hid at home, allegedly refusing to answer the phone. It confirms something I have often observed: those who most loudly preach socialism also most often practise disloyalty to Labour and give comfort to the Tories. I went up to some Tribune MPs and informed them that Mrs Thatcher was going to put them in her first honours list 'for services to the Conservative Party'. This nearly led to a fight between Martin Flannery and me.

So with the left abstaining, the two Irish Catholics staying away because of our Northern Ireland Representation Bill and the Ulster Unionists voting against *despite* our giving them this bill, we ended up losing the amendment by six and the substantive motion by two.

The PM rose after the vote and immediately announced that we would put down a motion of confidence for tomorrow. When he came back to his room, we all joined him to discuss tomorrow's speech. Philip Wood from Private Office had already done a provisional draft which was very helpful and cheered up the PM enormously – he likes to know that the next job is already under way. But he said he needed more politics in it. He did not want much about sanctions or pay policy – that was today. But it was also clear that we would still stick unyieldingly to the 5%.

However, pay sanctions are finished because of the vote. The Treasury had sent a draft statement for the PM to make which was completely capitulatory. We squashed that as too craven, and the PM sent for Healey. Denis came in and said that he did not really agree with the Treasury draft either. However, *something* would have to be said about giving up sanctions, so the PM asked Healey to produce a draft for tomorrow's Cabinet. The PM and the Chancellor began to misunderstand one another and get irritated. So the PM said, 'It is getting late,' and brought it to an end.

Really it has been a bad day. An important plank of our pay policy has gone. It is hard to see how we have the authority to deal with the big pay clashes looming up in the New Year. I said this to the PM. He is confident that we will win tomorrow's vote because the Ulster Unionists will abstain. But I said this will not take us back to square one. It makes it very difficult for us to delay the election beyond March, and there will be a 'lame duck' atmosphere till then.

Thursday 14 December 1978

The PM worked on this afternoon's speech upstairs before Cabinet, but nobody had seen what changes he had made. I went down before Cabinet and chatted to Roy Hattersley, who had a bad day in the Commons yesterday, giving a poor speech.

Cabinet went quite quickly. It was agreed to make a statement tomorrow announcing the inquiry into Rhodesian sanctions. The main talk was on pay, where ministers were encouragingly robust. So the PM got full backing for his line this afternoon.

I went off to lunch at Grieveson Grant in the City and came back for the big debate. The PM opened and was extremely good. He has this ability to engage the House in a dialogue. He draws in the Opposition, responds to their interruptions, plays them off one against the other, and overall makes it a living performance, with a touch of showbiz. Mrs Thatcher, by contrast, rattled off her paragraphs and statistics at such a pace that they became a gabble. She sped on as if nobody else was in the House, and very soon people were chatting on the back benches or leaving for tea – because she does not *involve* them. It was clearly a disappointment to the Tories, and the morale on the Labour benches visibly rose.

Afterwards I went back to No. 10 to clear papers and then to LSE for a reception. Carol joined me there. We went back to No. 10 to clear up, and then on to the Commons for tonight's vote. We had drinks beforehand in the bar with Bob Mellish, Gerry Fitt and my local MP Jock Stallard.

Then a quick bite in the cafeteria – where Harold Wilson's driver Bill Housden joined us. He was very disparaging about HW. He said he still drinks much too much, and that his memory is completely going – he cannot remember where he is going in the evening, even though Bill keeps reminding him. Harold apparently sits most of the day in his room in the Norman Shaw building finishing his book on the 1974–76 government. Bill says that nobody visits him and he has no friends: 'It is very sad.' As for Marcia, she is 'leading an incredible life, mixing in very right-wing circles'. Bill said that 'they like the way she denounces Callaghan and the Labour government'.

He said that Kagan was a real crook. He remembered how once – he thought at the Paris Embassy – Judy Innes (whom Bill claims Kagan stole from her husband and abused terribly) had told Bill and Wilson terrible stories about Kagan, about his violence, promiscuity and financial corruption. They shut the door and left Michael Halls sitting outside. Bill said that till then HW did not know how dreadful Kagan was.

Bill also said that few people had got on to the fact that 'the original Godfather to them all was Camden Council leader Sammy Fisher'. He said that Sammy had introduced all these Jewish businessmen to Harold and Marcia long, long ago. Bill thought it was curious how Sammy had escaped investigation.

Carol and I went upstairs for the vote, and again stood behind the chair, watching them vote. This time we knew we would win – actually by ten. Our people looked much more cheerful. I walked along with the PM to his room after the vote. He was cheered by the result, but we again agreed that it still did not put everything right. The PM said that Thatcher had failed to realise that these were showbiz occasions and people expected 'a performance'. He thought she was good when provoked. But left to herself she failed on all the big occasions. But we warned him that the press would say that the government was effectively finished.

And I asked him how long he expected the support of the Ulster Unionists, because we have foolishly scheduled the Northern Ireland Bill for extra seats to go through all its final stages on the first day after the recess. (He said, 'Perhaps that is how we got them to abstain today.') This means they won't have an incentive to support us much longer – and we have lost the Irish Catholics Fitt and Maguire because of it. He agreed and said we must do something to slow it down in the Lords.

Then we all drifted off to bed. We all know that the government took a big step towards its end this week.

Friday 15 December 1978

I took most of the day off. Home in the morning then to Oxford in the afternoon for a 'Gaudy' dinner at Lincoln College – it is twenty-five years since I went up as an undergraduate. Yet I can remember almost every day of that wonderful first term with my lovely rooms overlooking the chapel quad almost as if it were yesterday.

Monday 18 December 1978

On Friday, after I went to Oxford, Gavyn Davies and David Piachaud put in an excellent paper on strengthening the powers of the Price Commission and using this as a replacement for 'sanctions'. The PM responded favourably, but not very strongly. A message was sent to the Chancellor and to ministers on EY(P), the Cabinet committee on prices, urging them to look closely at amending the price legislation accordingly. The Treasury doesn't seem too keen on this, as it will offend the CBI. But it is the only way to restore a credible pay policy in the private sector.

The PM seems to have been a bit knocked off course by last week's defeats. Without doubt his and the government's authority have been weakened.

I went for lunch with Robert Armstrong at the Reform Club. We chatted about the problems of his Home Office. He admitted that it is a very introverted place. It is not really a part of the collective government. I still like seeing Robert. He has a breadth of view and a humour which is rare among the top mandarins. So I expect that the machine will try to shut him out from the top.

I worked on papers in the afternoon and then went home early because my brother Clem had arrived from France. It was bitterly cold outside.

Today we had the annual Xmas party for mentally handicapped children. I looked in only briefly. This is my fifth and last Christmas here.

Tuesday 19 December 1978

Before Cabinet I talked to Bill Rodgers and Harold Lever. The PM also wandered among his ministers outside the Cabinet Room, talking to each one and encouraging them. But they all seem a bit tired and dispirited. Cabinet mainly dealt with the impending tanker driver's strike. This could paralyse the nation very rapidly. The government is preparing a state of emergency, to be announced either just before or just after Christmas. This could produce a major confrontation, with troops on the streets. It won't look good politically.

January is going to be a very difficult month, with pay disputes for the tanker drivers, the water and sewerage men, the other local authority and NHS workers, and the coal and electricity workers looming. If we get through this lot with the counter-inflation policy intact, we shall finally be winning. But if not, and I suspect not, the government is finished – and inflation will rocket again, which will destroy the next government.

My brother Clem came in for a talk and then I went off to lunch with Joe Haines at the Gay Hussar – which is now very much my favourite restaurant in London. Came back to have a quick meeting with the two Toms on the BBC. Little is happening on the White Paper on broadcasting.

I went home early again to have dinner with our friends the Reads, celebrating Tom's and (my) Carol's birthday. London was fairly empty because the IRA have started bombing again.

David Basnett came to see the PM this afternoon and suggested a specially favourable deal for the local authority unions. Afterwards the PM claimed to have 'sent him away with a flea in his ear'.

Wednesday 20 December 1978

In to the office to finish off our Christmas briefing – on the dollar, on pay policy. It was still very cold and filthy with snow and sleet.

The PM went to the Party NEC. He had another clash with Tony Benn about obeying Cabinet collective responsibility.

I finished the day at the *Daily Mirror* Xmas party. Had a nice evening with Joe, Terry Lancaster and Mike Molloy, the excellent editor. They are depressed by all the industrial troubles in Fleet Street.

Thursday 21 December 1978

A very mixed and none too satisfying day. Went to the dentist in the late morning – a bit painful, two fillings without anaesthetic since it upsets me. Right up in North London, so I did not get back to the office till mid-afternoon and then had my flu jab.

The No. 10 Xmas party in the evening. I was feeling a bit down, surrounded by people, *all* of whom had arrived at No. 10 after me, and by ghosts from the earlier years, some of whom I hate, but most I miss.

The party was actually excellent. The PM led everybody in singing hymns in the pillared room (Private Office with customary efficiency had prepared hymn sheets). Everybody sang their heads off (except me, as I cannot sing!) and it was very jolly. The PM then made a nice speech, which I felt had a touch of suspicion that it might be his last Christmas in No. 10.

Then he went off to some royal dinner. We turned on the hi-fi and began dancing in the Blue Room. It is not often that the state rooms at No. 10 have shaken to such loud rock music.

As usual I became a bit nostalgic and maudlin. I know I won't be here again, and in one sense don't mind at all, yet in another am sorry. It could be all downhill from here onwards. I sat in the window seat of the Blue Room and looked out over Horse Guards Parade. It was a cold and foggy night, not too much traffic because people have been scared off by the IRA bombing. No. 10 is a comfortable and interesting place. But I need to move on – the problem is that I don't know where. Where does one go after No. 10?

I went home by bus and to bed at about 11.30.

Friday 22 December 1978

The PM had a meeting with his public service ministers this morning – Shore, Ennals and Booth (all second division) and Healey (definitely first division). I was delayed in the traffic and missed it. They had before them figures which proved that contrary to all the bleating from the appalling public sector unions, their earnings are 98% of the average national earnings, and are actually higher than they were in 1974. That is apart from all the benefits of job security, inflation-proofed pensions, etc., that they have.

Later in the morning there was a meeting of the Gen ministerial group which is handling the tanker drivers' dispute. There is a glimmer of hope, because the Esso unions have recommended a settlement, which will break the solidarity. But we are still planning to announce a state of emergency on 29 December – which will mean *no* petrol for private driving, just for emergency purposes. Hundreds of troops are being specially trained to move in early in the New Year. This will be quite dramatic. Having troops on the streets strike breaking will take us beyond Ted Heath in 1974! It will also look bad and is not a good way to prepare for an election. Also it won't work: distributing petrol is a complicated matter.

The PM had a sandwich lunch in the flat and set off to Chequers with Audrey around 2.45. I walked to the door with him. We discussed pay. He was a bit more optimistic, about both the tanker drivers and the local authorities, after this morning's meetings. But I thought he looked tired and a bit flat.

I told him that I was putting in a paper on pay which I hoped would show a way forward. In fact I didn't start on it till late morning, and then I worked right through lunchtime on it. I slipped out for a quiet bite in St Stephen's Tavern while it was being typed. Gavyn was also doing a paper on the dollar, which he was still writing when I left at 4 o'clock. Officially the Civil Service broke up for Xmas at noon. No. 10 was fairly quiet. Private Office was clearing up.

Ken Stowe fervently agreed with me that he hoped this was his last Xmas at No. 10. Ken has done a very good job. He is absolutely right for *this* PM, who likes his civil servants to be properly bureaucratic – calm, efficient and reticent. A more flamboyant – and more intellectual – character as principal private secretary would suit him less well. Jim likes the work output to come quite uncoloured by personality.

I went shopping on the way home to get 'small' things for the kids' stockings: in fact it cost over £50. Families don't make economic sense! Still I am looking forward to Christmas at our Suffolk cottage. We shall be eight – the four children and my brother Clem and his French girl-friend and the two of us. Quite a crowd in a tiny cottage. But the children love it. And both Clem and I enjoy sharing together what we never had as children – a warm family Christmas.

It is Carol's birthday and we had thought of going to the cinema tonight. But instead we sat with the girls, talking till 10 o'clock. Carol dozed in front of the fire. Then I woke her and we walked to the local pub for a pint. It was warm and friendly in there, with several Irishmen sitting quietly singing into their Guinness glasses.

Tomorrow we do the final shopping and cooking. Then off to the cottage on Sunday morning. We shall stay there till the New Year: no telephone, no television. A lovely week's rest. Not because I am exhausted from overwork. Really there have often been periods of slackness this autumn. The government is doing little except hanging on to fight inflation. There is no question of having long-term policies. So in the Unit all we can do is react to events. The pity is that for the past year there has been an atmosphere of always expecting an election within three months. We have spent a very long time expecting to have only a short time. It does affect one's approach to government – and the approach of most ministers, I suspect.

Both Tom McCaffrey and David Lipsey have spoken to me in very pessimistic terms in the last forty-eight hours. The pay front is bad. We are faced with possible big confrontations in the public and private sector. Inflation is turning up. There is no scope for any further tax cuts. Unemployment will probably start turning up again soon. These are all the reasons that we set out in our Green Paper last spring for having the election this past autumn (we preferred November to October) rather than waiting till 1979. McCaffrey and Lipsey – and Joe Haines – now think that was Jim's big mistake. That might be right. This autumn was a 'window' when everything was temporarily going right. Still, we will see. Nobody will know till we have fought the election. Then Thatcher will find Jim hard to beat.

Whatever happens, 1979 will see a new start for me. Who knows where to?

V

Nemesis: The Winter of Discontent
(January–May 1979)

Tuesday 2 January 1979

I came back from Suffolk yesterday afternoon, after a lovely Christmas at the cottage. We had a marvellous time with the children, probably closer and happier than ever before. This matters to me more and more – other more worldly successes matter less and less. My brother Clem and his girl-friend Agnes also stayed on Christmas and Boxing Day, so we had a big family time.

It did not matter that the weather was less good than usual – it rained over Christmas, then turned bitterly cold and finally we had a blizzard on 30 December which froze up everything – pipes, car, the lot. So New Year came with everything snowed up. We drove back to London in glorious sunshine, but so cold that the car windows kept on icing up on the *inside*. It was a nightmare drive. I had to stop frequently to clear the windscreen. Even on the motorway there was only one lane free of snow. The local authorities had made no attempt to clear the roads – still more evidence, if more were needed, that our local government provides *no* services at all now and that local government employees are the worst 'scroungers on the welfare state'.

This morning I went in to No. 10, but did not go into the briefing meeting for Guadeloupe, as I am not going there. We had lunch in a small anteroom on the second floor, with only a few people present. Ken Stowe has flu and Tim Lankester* [home affairs private secretary] is snowed in in Norfolk.

At the subsequent seminar on the dollar, Harold Lever made savage attacks on the negativism of the Treasury. Healey then became very personal and offensive. It began when the PM said, 'Harold understands more about money than you do, Denis.' Healey said, 'Well, he has made more money than me, but that is because he has spent more time thinking about making money. If I had spent as much time on it, I would have made more.' 'I agree you would have made more,' said Lever, 'because you would not have been inhibited as I have, by sentimentality.' 'It is not a question of sentimentality,' said Healey. 'You care more about making money than I do.'

It was an insensitive thing to say and Lever looked very upset. His hands shook, and he lit a cigarette, which he rarely does. What worried me was that he looked as tense as he did at the time of his stroke. I hope he will not have another.

Incidentally, the Governor of the Bank was very sensible. His style in dealing with the politicians is excellent – gentle, modest, leaving the politics to them. He grows on one.

Afterwards I chatted briefly to the PM about Christmas and such things, and then went to my room to clear papers. Tom McNally came up for a drink and a chat. He told me, in relation to the September decision not to hold an election, that the PM had revealed that he was influenced by Bob Worcester's July survey of Labour marginal seats. He had taken them to the farm, together with *The Times* election books for 1970 and 1974, and gone through them, constituency by constituency. He had come to the conclusion that the best we could achieve was 325 seats, and we might easily be as low as 305. As we already had 310, he did not see the point of holding an election.

The weakness of this analysis is that it makes no allowance for the difference that would be made by the campaign, especially by the PM versus Mrs Thatcher.

Tom also thought that, on a more personal level, the PM probably was attracted by getting through to 1979 and achieving three years as PM, which sounds so much more susbstantial than two years.

I then went home quite early. It was freezing very hard and we snuggled around the fire to keep warm.

Wednesday 3 January 1979

I stayed at home in the morning, wrote up the previous day's diary and then took Paul sledging on the Heath. It was lovely, very cold and sunny, and the hillside was covered with children.

I then went in at lunchtime. It was the PM's last afternoon at No. 10 before going off to the Caribbean for a week and I thought I had better be there, in case he wanted a chat. This proved prudent. At around 4 o'clock I was on the phone talking to Arnold Weinstock when we were interrupted by the switchboard to say that the PM wanted to see me immediately in the study. I went up and he was sitting reading his last few papers (he had cleared most of his work on Christmas Eve and it all came back last week. He kept back a few papers on pay problems – on the BBC, where he scribbled 'another defeat', on the road haulage drivers, the oil tankers and the local authorities).

He also had my Green Paper on pay, which he handed back saying he liked it. He had written on it that he would talk to the Chancellor of the Exchequer about it. But he began by adding that he was very worried about the way things were drifting, and that he felt I had been 'too optimistic'. It was 'all falling apart'. He was particularly agitated about the transport drivers, who had rejected 15% and had been told by their employers to come back for more. He said, 'What is going on? This doesn't look good. There is an ominous calm. Everything is quiet here in government. Denis has gone away to the country. But I don't like the smell of it. We shall wake up in a few weeks' time and find that it is too late, everybody is settling for 20%. I have never believed very much in incomes policy: it doesn't make a great deal of difference – except when people start settling for 20%. If they were "responsible" and settled for 8%, it wouldn't matter. But this does not look good. It will destroy our competitiveness, inflation will roar and we shall have more unemployment.'

He then asked me to look into the road haulage dispute. 'You have a lot of contacts,' he said. 'Find out what is going on.' It was clear that he did not trust the machine to tell him the truth. He said that ministers and departments were selling out or fudging. Maybe he, or Bill Rodgers, should have the employers in and read them a lesson. This could be the domino issue, where, if it falls, everything else will go with it.

He then paused and we considered what he could threaten the employers with, now that we don't have sanctions. I said it came back to my paper, and the section on prices. With price sanctions, we could make the employers afraid of settling too high because they would not be able to recoup the costs of the higher pay from higher prices. He agreed and said, yes, we must have the prices legislation.

I then said that I was interested in more than just having a sanction. It was part of having an election platform, with a viable pay policy: prices for the private sector and the Comparability Unit for the public sector. And he needed that soon, in case we had an early election.

He immediately sprung into action. He said he entirely agreed and he must talk to Denis, so he asked for the Chancellor on the phone. Denis was in Sussex, so while we waited, he went over the points he would make to him. In particular we discussed the Clegg/McCarthy proposal for a public service pay body and its relation to the local authorities. The Treasury is proposing to respond to the local authorities' strike on 26 January by offering to set up this comparability body to deal with them. The PM felt that this ran the risk of messing up the big long-term scheme by hurrying it in. He wanted it for all the public service groups, not as a short-term way out of the local authority problem.

So he phoned Healey and discussed all these points (which he had written on a piece of paper). He told him not to mess up the *public service comparability* body. Anything set up for the local authorities must be suitable for a wider purpose. To take a firm line with road haulage. To get some legislation on *prices*. He said, 'I wouldn't mind being beaten on that. It is a good issue to go to the country on.' He also asked Denis to talk to Len Murray about a new election platform with the TUC – based on our paper's proposals for a diminishing rate of inflation, for a prices policy, and for public sector comparability.

Healey was clearly a bit sluggish in his response, so the PM told him to get on with it. He also told Denis that he had asked me to get working on these issues, which will help me in dealing with the Treasury.

We then had a long chat about the 'diminishing targets' for inflation, where he said he would prefer to go for 'below 5% by 1982' – that was 'credible and possible'. On the election date, he said that he was keeping his options open and leaving people guessing between spring and autumn. It was clear that he had not made up his mind. But I said that (1) he could not get a Finance Bill through, and (2) to hold on till the autumn *without doing anything* would look very bad. He agreed – and began to talk about March as the election time. He again said that was why it was urgent to get a platform with the TUC – 'though we must not give anything away to them: they are very unpopular'. And that the prices legislation would fit in to that timetable.

I then raised with him the question of how long he would go on as Prime Minister. I said that many people wanted to vote for him, but were worried about who would lead the Party after him. So it would be helpful if, very obliquely and discreetly, he could indicate that he would stay on for some time. His commitment to a three-year anti-inflation programme was a way of giving an assurance that he could personally go on for some time. He smiled and wrote something down on a pad of paper.

He asked me about various ministers and their commitment to anti-inflation. He said he was relieved that it was not Peter Shore who was taking the lead on the local authorities. He asked if Hattersley was sound. I said, 'Yes, probably,' though at first I had worried that he was 'a bit flash', like a journalist. He said, 'Yes, he is a bit flash and like a journalist, but all young men are flash.'

He said that Alan Fisher* was 'a windbag'. We discussed the local author-ities and I said that we had no need to fear them – apart from the water and sewerage people, we could take them on and beat them. He agreed. He told me that he received vast numbers of Christmas cards. The two biggest categories were (1) 'Thanks for the £10 pensioners' bonus', and (2) 'Stick at it against inflation.'

We finished at about 5.30 and I went down, summoned a Unit meeting, and we began our work. We started work on the road haulage strike. And

I phoned Hattersley – in a Bath hotel recovering from pleurisy – to get things moving on prices. He was delighted to know that something *might* happen. But I warned him that, without converting the Treasury, we would get nowhere.

Got home at 9.15 p.m.

Thursday 4 January 1979

When I arrived at No. 10, the hall was full of cases as the party prepared to leave for Guadeloupe. I was a bit envious, as it was bitterly cold here and it would be nice to lie in the Caribbean sunshine. However, I don't envy them twelve hours in a plane, even the VC10. Actually Heathrow was blocked by frozen snow, so the PM's plane was delayed for an hour while it was dug out.

The PM came up to chat to me. We went over yesterday's ground on prices and especially on the road haulage strike. He also asked me to do some work on the polls – today the *Mail* published a NOP showing Labour 3% ahead. But the PM said he was not complacent. He remembered that 'Harold was ahead of his Party and of the Tories in 1970, and still he lost'.

We were very busy in the Unit. On price controls, I talked to Hattersley again in Bath. In particular I warned him not to repeat what I had told him yesterday, that the PM had said he 'would not mind being defeated on prices legislation' as a trigger to an election. This morning the PM told a private secretary that this was between him and the Chancellor and he 'did not want it all round Whitehall'. Three of Hattersley's officials came round to discuss the options for action on prices and we worked on till lunchtime.

I had lunch of sandwiches in my room. Then the children came in and I took them to a magicians show at the ICA. Afterwards they came back to No. 10 and sat reading and drawing for an hour while I worked on clearing my papers and sent off a telex to Guadeloupe giving the PM the latest picture.

Drove home in freezing weather, with solid ice everywhere. Then went out in the evening to dinner with Graham Greene. Home at 1.15. It would be nice to be in the Caribbean.

Friday 5 January 1979

Spent the day on strike news. The situation is building up into the most serious industrial relations crisis since Labour came into power. The Texaco oil tanker drivers have decided to strike – the others will decide on Monday and Tuesday. The road haulage strike is also spreading quickly and food is in short supply in some areas.

Actually it presents an 'image' problem to the PM. Pictures of him basking in the Caribbean sun do not look good when Britain is frozen in and coming to a halt. He may have to return early. Deeper than that is the confrontation with the unions over pay policy. Both groups of drivers are threatening to reject offers of around 15%. If it goes on like this, we shall be back on the inflation escalator.

The PM phoned Private Office just before lunch. [Tim] Lankester took it but I was there and listened in. He was very concerned with the industrial front and was reacting to our telegram last night. He wanted us to continue to keep an eye on it. We also told him about Bill Rodgers's tough speech last night, in which he took a firm stand on the 5% policy.

I had a quick lunch in the Cabinet Office and continued to work in the afternoon in the office. Then my daughter Rachel and a friend came in and we went off to the theatre to see Alan Ayckbourn's *Ten Times Table*. It was bitterly cold and the theatre was only half full.

The irony is that there is a smell in the air reminiscent of January 1974, and the PM's posture, though much less rigid, has much in common with that of Heath. And this is not wrong. It would be better to take a stand and lose than to capitulate to inflation and have a new 1974–75 crisis.

Saturday 6 January 1979

A lovely evening at Covent Garden, seeing *Un ballo in maschera* with Harold Lever.

Monday 8 January 1979

I went in early to see how the strike situation was developing. The outlook has worsened considerably. The road haulage dispute is now affecting twice as many men as last Friday, mainly because of picketing. There is a threat of a rail strike this week and next. And we are waiting for the results of the oil tanker drivers' ballots today and tomorrow. In this context the newspaper pictures of the PM lazing in the Caribbean sun do not look good. Although he very much deserves a few days in the sun, it causes resentment when Britain is freezing and paralysed by strikes.

The PM has sent a long telegram asking about twenty detailed questions about the strikes. When I arrived at 9.30, Tim Lankester was already through in the Cabinet Office arranging for departments to handle the answers. I cleared my papers – there were not very many – and then we had a long Unit meeting on the strikes and on the possibilities of prices legislation.

I went to lunch with Joe Haines. He thought that the PM should come back early. In fact he had stopped the *Mirror* running a front page demanding this, as he knew it would be read as critical of the PM. Joe also told me that the main prosecution witness in the Kagan case has been talking to the *Daily Mirror*. He says that Kagan has smuggled out about £1 million – he used as a vehicle a special fund set up to help Jewish refugees to Israel – but in fact he was the sole beneficiary. He said that Kagan gave £50,000 a year to the HW Political Office. Large expenses were paid to Douglas Houghton (Kagan's Labour friend). Joe also told me a story about Kagan being sent to threaten Milhench, the 'land deals' man, who went to jail over the 'land deals' forgery.

I dashed back to attend the two Cabinet committees dealing with strikes: (1) the Gen 158 (Rees in the chair) which deals with 'contingencies', and (2) EY(prices) which is the main committee dealing with pay under Healey. Afterwards, Healey came to my room and we had a long talk. I put to him the case for action on prices. He did not disagree, but was wary. He said that he would only do it on two conditions: that the legislation should be effective, not symbolic; and providing there was 'balancing legislation' restraining some excesses of union power. He said that we had 'buggered around with industry more than any country in the world'. So he would only use the prices weapon against them if we could offer them a compensatory restraint on the unions. He had drunk a couple of whiskies with Michael Foot before coming to see me and was a bit belligerent at times.

The PM had arranged to talk to Healey at 8 p.m. (4 p.m. in the Caribbean), but he was obviously enjoying himself in the sun and was not in his room at 8. Healey went back to No. 10 to wait. The call finally came through at 9.30 and I listened in, sitting at a desk in Private Office. The Chancellor reported at great length. The main interest was that they both agreed that something tough would have to be done about the unions. But when? Ever by Labour?

I finally got home at 10.30 p.m.

Tuesday 9 January 1979

The general situation feels much worse, even though the oil tanker drivers are going to settle. The road haulage strike is deteriorating, and the railways are going to strike. Suddenly there is a madness in the air, with unions threatening strikes long before the negotiating procedures have been completed. This looks very bad for the big claims that lie ahead – coal, gas, electricity, the local authorities and the Civil Service, as well as road haulage, all within the next seven weeks. We cannot take them all on at once. So they could sweep our counter-inflation policy away – and we don't have much else.

I went off to Gen 158 – the 'emergency' ministerial committee, with Merlyn Rees in the chair. They went through the oil tanker and road haulage situation and updated the army's readiness to intervene if we have a state of emergency – though that possibility is receding now. We then moved on to another conference room in the Cabinet Office for a meeting of EY(prices) under Denis Healey. Really these committees merge into one another, with similar agendas and overlapping membership.

I returned to my room at 5 for a meeting with Geoff Littler and Jeremiah from the Treasury. Gavyn and David Lipsey were there and we went over the possibilities of action on the prices front. They are not too pessimistic on the pay situation so far, but sense that it has begun to slip badly since the loss of sanctions. They are also very worried about any fresh attempts to negotiate new agreements with the TUC, as we get nothing back.

I have urged since Monday, in the Unit and in Private Office, that the PM should come back early (and Joe has been pressing this view). But I decided not to telephone them in the West Indies and say so. Mainly because they would have thought it was just sour grapes on my part, jealous of them being out there. Well, I am jealous, but I think they are mistaken to sit out there in the sun, with photographs of them lazing on beaches surrounded by topless women, while this country is increasingly paralysed. There will be a backlash and it won't help the PM's authority when he comes to tell the unions that they must take a more puritanical line.

Went home at 9 o'clock and listened to some music.

Wednesday 10 January 1979

I left late, having mended the electrical circuit in our house.

We had a meeting in the Unit on ways of limiting social security benefits to strikers. Liz Arnott has done quite a good paper on this.

The PM returned at 12.15. I went downstairs and he was in Private Office chatting. He looked very well and was stressing that he was not panicking. He had told the press at the airport that he was completely in touch with what was going on. But the danger is that the 'unflappable' image will look very complacent.

He went upstairs and I dictated a quick note telling him what we have been up to and steering him towards a prices policy.

I saw Denis Healey after a meeting on pay in the Cabinet Office and praised him for trying to hold the line at the committee. He said that Booth was very soft and that Michael Foot was 'totally unrealistic'. He thought we would have to give way a bit on the public services but that should be done at the last minute to get a settlement, not from the beginning. He again said that arbitrary trade union power would be the main issue in the election.

I came home at 9 p.m. to dinner with Celia Read and we listened to the *Marriage of Figaro*, in preparation for our visit to the opera on Friday.

Thursday 11 January 1979

Quite a dramatic day!

Before the meeting on public service pay at 10 o'clock I chatted with Roy Hattersley and Shirley Williams. They asked me what I thought. I said that I was a hawk and that if we are going to be beaten it is better to be beaten on a policy one believes in, than to trim and end up finding one is beaten by steady erosion. Roy agreed, though Shirley was afraid that if we are too rigid we may be broken quickly.

The meeting was very tense. Ennals led with his bid to abandon the 5% increase on pay for the Health Service. This man has no balls. His bottle has completely gone. Last November he was all for others taking sanctions to force the Ford management to take on their strike. Now he is facing the crunch in the NHS, where he is the minister responsible, his nerve has gone, he wants to run, and even to argue that the whole government should run as well, as cover for his own cowardice.

I went off to EY(prices) in the Cabinet Office at 5.45. In fact we didn't start till 6.30, because we waited for Healey to arrive from Neddy and his talks with the TUC afterwards. Booth and Foot were also late, after a totally unrewarding talk with Moss Evans of the transport union. While waiting, I had a talk with Peter Shore. He came over much more human than usual. We found we shared a love for India and for Paul Scott's novel. He told me that he had been to India in the army in 1946–47 and this had clearly been a formative time for him.

The committee meeting itself was very worrying. A strong whiff of Pétainism in the air – with Ennals especially wanting to abandon the pay policy. He has no balls at all. Healey did well in defending responsibility, but Ennals, Foot and Booth were retreating out of sight. I sat next to Hattersley, who was very silent. He thinks we lost the election when we decided to soldier on last October. It certainly feels as if we are losing it this week. We have slipped badly, seeming out of touch, and helpless before the irresponsible power of the trade unions. I think of poor Ted Heath!

The committee finished at 8 o'clock. I went back to No. 10 and dictated a note to the PM telling him that he must whip his ministers into line on public sector pay. Everybody had gone home from No. 10, except Gavyn. Private Office was closed. The Press Office and Political Office were empty.

The PM was having supper in the flat. It didn't feel like a very impressive command headquarters as we go into the last battle.

In the committee all the time they kept swinging from fine details about the local authority situation to the general anti-inflationary problem. But they rarely faced up to the key issue, until Bruce Millan asked the blunt question – 'Do we or don't we stick to 5% in the public sector?' Nobody answered this, until Hattersley intervened and said, 'Yes.' Nobody else supported this position, except the PM. Then the PM, who had been looking tired and grey, sitting there grunting and rumbling away, sat up in his chair rubbing his hands together, and summed it all up! 'We have an election ahead in March. We must have a credible counter-inflation policy. That means we must have some new policies. We must also stick to 5% wherever we can.' So that was that.

Incidentally, the PM also quoted the sentence about 'inflation going from 13% to 30% in 1975', which was in my paper last night. He obviously liked it – and used it again with the T&G today and on the phone to Moss Evans last night. In fact it was a good bit over 13% at the beginning of 1975. I used that because I thought he would like the alliteration! He obviously did! We finished after 11.30, and the rest of Cabinet ministers were waiting outside for Cabinet to begin. So the two meetings really merged. I talked to David Owen as he went in. He said that he was against an early election and thought 'we may have to sit all this out till the autumn'.

We had lunch upstairs and heard about Cabinet, where apparently they went over the same ground and again decided to stick to the 5%. The newspapers are demanding a declaration of a state of emergency, but in fact this would be quite irrelevant. There are only about 5,000 soldiers and lorries available. They were training to intervene in the oil tankers strike and would then have carried about 30% of normal supplies – because it is a centralised operation based on about five big oil companies. But road haulage involves half a million drivers, half of whom are going on strike, and a mass of distribution networks. So the army's intervention would be just a drop in the ocean.

The PM saw the Transport & General Workers Union, asking them not to make the road haulage strike official. They refused. The PM laid it on the line and told them that the government would have to fight them.

I went off to a pay meeting in the Cabinet Office at 3.30 p.m. Healey from the chair declared his own strong support for the price policy in Hattersley's paper and even argued for a 'tougher' option than Varley and Hattersley were agreeing on, so Hattersley gratefully accepted and I felt we have made a big leap forward towards a new prices policy. The Unit has done quite a lot here – briefing the PM, lobbying the Chancellor and the Treasury, encouraging Hattersley, nobbling Varley. But the policy still may fall at the last hurdle of next Monday's Cabinet, opposed by officials in industry and in the industrial side of the Treasury, and by public sector ministers who are afraid that it may put them in conflict with their sponsor industries.

I then dashed back from the Cabinet Office to a Unit meeting on our paper covering new policy measures to fight inflation. Each Unit member is doing a section – Gavyn on prices, David Lipsey on low pay and comparability, Jim Corr on unions, Liz on taxing social security benefits. We are going to sew it together into a big policy paper, as a prelude for Cabinet on Monday and the big parliamentary debate on Tuesday.

Just as we were finishing, Ken Stowe came in to say that the PM had asked us to do a draft of his speech for next week. Tim Lankester has fallen sick and Tom McNally seems to be away a lot. So we have to fill in. Some of the Unit were reluctant to take it on, as there are never any medals for speech-writing. But I, for the first time, was keen to do it, partly because I think I can do it; partly because it may be a historic debate – it may be the PM's last in Parliament, if we are beaten! Also because we are up against it, everybody is writing us off, so this is the time to pile in. We rapidly sketched out a work programme – tomorrow will be incredibly hectic, with both a policy paper and a speech.

Then I dashed off to the Belfry Club, off Belgrave Square, to have dinner with the German Embassy, whose guest was the chief finance civil servant from Bonn – Obert. Several of the British Treasury colonels were there as well – Rawlinson, Robin Butler, Alan Bailey (who I find stuffy) and Hans Liesners (now at Trade and Industry). It was a lively dinner – the German economic minister, George Massion, is a very good man.

We broke at 10.30 and I drove home, tired, but excited and with the adrenaline flowing. Really I am only happy when things are buzzing and there is work to do.

Friday 12 January 1979

This is the big day. When I got in the Unit was working on our policy paper – which really meant Gavyn, as he was doing the main work. The PM was upstairs in the flat. Not much was happening in Private Office. None of the departmental briefs for the speech had arrived. So I decided to sit down and write the speech.

I scribbled from 10 till 12, then sent for a garden-room girl and dictated the first ten pages. Then Gavyn brought in the draft of the policy paper. It was brilliant, word perfect. I read it while the others were out for lunch. So I went straight downstairs to photostat it and I then took the top copy upstairs to the PM. He was sitting in the lounge of the flat, in front of an electric fire, reading *The Economist*. I handed him the paper. He asked me to sit down and we discussed it as he read it. He agreed most of it, but would not go along with taxing social security benefits and limiting benefits to strikers. He felt that the politics of that were not yet quite right (that will come). But he was clearly very pleased with the paper.

We chatted in general. He said that it was clear that we had to stick to 5%, even though we might have to fiddle some of them to get a particular settlement. We must not surrender the broad approach. He finished by saying that he was still absolutely convinced that we would win the election.

He is staying at the flat this weekend. I think they admit now that it was a mistake to stay so long in the West Indies. And the disastrous press conference at London Airport, producing 'Crisis, what Crisis' headlines, broke Harold Wilson's golden rule of politics: never give an interview about the domestic situation when just returning from abroad, as one is bound to be out of touch with the home scene – as the PM clearly was.

I returned downstairs and began working on the speech again, after debriefing the Unit on the PM's reactions. Gavyn did a piece based on the policy paper and I did the rest. So in the end I had done 90% and Gavyn 10% (often it is the other way round). I began to get desperate when still dictating after 6 o'clock – I was due to join Carol at 7 p.m. at the Coliseum for the *Marriage of Figaro*. I was running up and down stairs to the secretaries and the photocopying machine. I finally had a complete version at 6.50 and sprinted up to the flat to give it to the PM, who was sitting there working through a big box of official documents. I pointed out that the draft contained nothing on the actual strike situation, as we have to wait to see what it looks like on Monday. But he was very pleased. I was quite satisfied, as we have done a lot today.

Then I ran down the stairs from the flat and leapt into an official car, which got me to the Coliseum just after the curtain rose – so I had to stand for the first act. It was lovely, marvellous, and I felt in very high spirits.

We went home to dinner with our friend Celia Read. We were held up by finding a youth drunk and unable to move on the doorstep. I looked after him for half an hour, revived him with coffee and then half-carried him home to the council flats up the hill. He was actually touchingly apologetic. He told me that he could not read or write.

We finally got home at 1.30 a.m. Very tired. A bit drunk. But with the adrenaline still flowing.

Monday 15 January 1979

The PM was upstairs in the flat working on his big speech for tomorrow. He had worked in No. 10 all weekend on his speech and now has a thick wad of pieces of paper on which he will scribble his notes. So far he does not intend to have a long typewritten formal speech. But he will do one of his 'card-shuffling' acts. He was reported to be in robust and buoyant mood.

Cabinet met at 11.30 and apparently supported the PM's anti-inflation programme. It also discussed more 'stratospheric' questions. Most interesting, Eric Varley floated the thought that now that we have a completely irresponsible trade union movement, there was no alternative to a statutory incomes policy. Nobody rejected this. Rodgers, Williams, Hattersley and Healey all supported it.

Benn said virtually nothing throughout. Once he intervened to say that we must strengthen the TUC. The PM interrupted to say he agreed, but that it was irrelevant to the present problems, and asked him about what we should do *now*. Benn did not reply.

Tom McNally and Roger Stott have both returned from their constituencies in the North-West very chastened! They now really realise that staying on in Barbados was a mistake, that the PM's press conference was a mistake and that they completely misread the situation at home. They met a lot of hostility in the Manchester area, which has had a very tough time and pictures of them bathing in the Caribbean sun were not much appreciated.

I went out to lunch with Harry Evans at his new house in Pimlico. He is very depressed by *The Times/Sunday Times* closure. He also had lots of sad stories about the cowardice of his journalist colleagues. It is the old story – any crisis reveals that most people have no vertebrae.

We had a long and depressing talk in the Unit. People are very depressed – not about the government, but about the country. It really does seem as if the British people now lack the ability to reach greatness again. The assumption that everybody can have a big *real* increase in wages while the nation as a whole produces *no* extra real resources is quite bizarre. Recent experience has finally convinced Gavyn (and, he says, many other economists) that institutionalised trade union power really does cause inflation. We hung around till quite late. Reports and briefs were flowing in from departments. I got home around 9 o'clock.

Tuesday 16 January 1979

The general situation is pretty awful today. The road haulage strike is progressively bringing industry to a halt. Now there is a rail strike. This is all creating a strong public reaction – against the unions, and against us. So this crisis is the worst for us in the past five years. The Tories have never been able to really hurt us. But our strongest card has been that we have seemed able best to deal with the unions. Now that card looks very weak. The next opinion poll is bound to show us slipping behind.

I walked in most of the way to work because the whole transport system has been damaged by the rail strike.

The PM stayed upstairs all morning working on his speech. We had lunch upstairs. People felt more tense than usual. Everybody now senses our weakness.

Mrs Callaghan travelled over for Questions with the PM in the car, as usual on a day of crisis. Mrs Thatcher's speech opening the debate was extremely effective, passionate and with a slashing attack on the excesses of union power. Typical of her at her best, articulating popular resentment and prejudices. But also showed her weaknesses, narrow and concentrating wholly on tightening the law against picketing. She did not talk at all about inflation. But the strength of her conviction shone through and her supporters were immensely cheered. If she comes to power it will be wholly because of the trade unions. They have given her the only platform on which she is impressive and we are weak. Moss Evans and his T&G have acted as her storm troopers.

The PM made a statesmanlike speech, factually reporting on the strike crisis and arguing coolly on secondary picketing. He finished with a strong appeal on the inflation threat. It was good but inevitably did not make the strong impact which Thatcher certainly did.

Afterwards I discussed the debate with Jim. He was impressed by Thatcher. He was clearly tired. He must be daunted. There is no way he can win if the unions continue to behave like second-rate thugs. But if we can get that issue off the stage, we stand a chance again. Then I chatted in his room with Healey, preparing to wind up the debate. I floated with him the taxing of short-term social security benefits and he said he would look at it after the next Budget. He also said it would be necessary soon to have a statutory incomes policy.

I did not wait for the vote since the nationalists were voting for us – we got a majority of over twenty. But the issue is not now about constructing parliamentary majorities. The point is whether we lose public opinion over the trade unions.

Wednesday 17 January 1979

The PM had an emergency meeting on the water strike with Rees, Healey and Shore. The situation here is deteriorating fast – some parts of the North-West have had no fresh water for ten days. This is an area which we would lose totally in any quick election. They have had freeze-ups, oil starvation, rail strikes and water shortages since the New Year, and must be completely fed up.

Tom McCaffrey put up a paper, rather hysterical in tone, suggesting that the PM call together a conference of the TUC and CBI to sort it all out, and then make a TV appeal to the nation. McCaffrey has panicked and thinks that 'we are near the end' and advised us to start finding another job. His bottle has gone. So in the Unit we worked on a reply to McCaffrey and put in a note suggesting that the PM takes things coolly and thinks carefully before making some big empty gesture.

An emergency meeting of the Cabinet was called at 6 o'clock, mainly discussing whether to call a state of emergency. The PM had come to the conclusion that we should now have an emergency. But his Cabinet ministers did not agree and he could not get full support. J. Silkin in particular is against – not least because he is a T&G MP and is also trying to get the support of the left in any Party leadership battle.

The PM called in Len Murray and Moss Evans at 7. Originally this was intended to tell them about the state of emergency. Instead, the PM took them over the strike ground again, and Evans agreed to try to implement a code of conduct on secondary picketing.

I had a chat with the two Toms. McCaffrey was completely desperate, McNally was different and much better. He thought the situation was bad, but was not talking about bailing out.

The situation is not good. Tory morale is high. The Tory press is whipping up a frenzy. The strikes are bringing the economy to a halt – tomorrow is another rail strike. Our authority has slipped badly. But all is not lost. It need not be the end. We can still fight our way through, softening on some strikes, taking a hard line on others, keeping our nerve until this fever has passed. It all depends on the PM. If his nerve goes, then we are lost.

I went with Roger Stott to the Strangers Bar for a pint. He admitted he was more pessimistic than ever before. I said I still feel that it is all to play for in the campaign. But it is clear that morale in the PLP is low.

Thursday 18 January 1979

I had to go to the dentist in the morning, sitting in the chair for over an hour. It was snowing outside, and it was a pretty painful and miserable start to the day.

When I reached No. 10, Cabinet was already in session. They decided not to announce an emergency yet. But there was little discussion of general pay policy. The assumption was that pay policy had been destroyed, but nobody made any suggestions about how to replace it or what to do in this situation. Afterwards the PM said to McCaffrey with a straight face: 'How do you announce that the government's pay policy has completely collapsed? I don't want an answer now. Just think about it.' The PM also said to McCaffrey, 'Well, it will all be over in eleven weeks.'

Incidentally, the flow of papers has completely stopped. The PM's trays in Private Office have been empty all day. Ken Stowe says this is just like 1974: Whitehall has come to a total halt while they wait to see which way the cat will jump politically.

The strike situation is even worse, with lots of secondary picketing. Last night Moss Evans agreed to issue a code of conduct that would order his members to cease picketing. Apparently the PM was very tough with Evans and Len Murray. He told them that they had no more than six weeks, by when any government would have to legislate. Len Murray asked not to be rushed!

Ken Stowe made the sound point at lunch that we are in such concentrated trouble because all the negotiations have snarled up together. They have taken too long. Each wage negotiation is trapped in EY(prices). The water workers have been there two months. 'That bloody elaborate machinery in the Cabinet Office delays everything while it monitors every 10p offer. We should just set out broad guidelines and let the negotiators get on with it.'

Going over to Questions, the PM went to the front door with me and thanked me for last night's Green Paper on the strike situation. I said to him, 'I hope none of your colleagues are losing their nerve.' He replied with an understanding smile, 'No, I am not losing my nerve, Bernard.'

Questions was fairly sombre. The Tories are in high spirits. Our troops look very low. Even the left wing had finally realised the damage that was being done and began to ask helpful questions – a sign that they realise that they have nearly succeeded in bringing Mrs Thatcher to power.

After Questions the PM made a statement about the strike situation. He announced the new voluntary code of conduct for picketing. It didn't go well. Most people don't want to know what Moss Evans will do. They want to know what the government will do. We shall have to make some demonstration of authority soon – which is what I put in my paper last night. People also want a state of emergency, even though it will make things worse. We have explained to the press time and again that an emergency would do nothing to move any goods and might harden the strike. But they won't publish these arguments, as they are interested only in embarrassing a Labour Prime Minister, not in facts.

Afterwards the PM came back to No. 10 and sent for Ken Stowe. He said we would have to bring the strike to an end – by effectively giving in. He feels that every day it goes on, the Tories will have a field day and the government will be demoralised. This is a sign of our weakness. There is no point in fighting for a pay policy which has disappeared. He asked Ken Stowe to summon Albert Booth so that the PM can tell him to bring it to an end.

Ken Stowe called a meeting with Tom McNally, McCaffrey and myself in McNally's room. Ken said that no ideas were coming up from ministers or the Civil Service. The government was simply 'staggering'. The Treasury had made its inevitable reflex response – it has taken down from the shelf its folder on a statutory wages freeze. Ken said that at this very moment Douglas Wass was with John Hunt explaining the new machinery that the Treasury wanted to carry out the freeze. Ken had told the PM that the Treasury paper would be on its way soon. The PM had ordered, 'Tell them not to bother to send it.'

In the Unit we ask whether the voluntary norm of 5% has been destroyed. Statutory freeze? Fighting selected settlements, especially in the public sector? Surrender on all fronts and then hold a quick election and bring in a tough new policy? Rely on rigid monetarism? How to survive while it slowly works? We don't have the answers yet.

I was home by 8.30 to eat with the children and play some music – a lovely old record of Solomon playing a Schumann piano concerto.

Friday 19 January 1979

The end of the worst week – worst, politically, that is – since I came to No. 10. The depth of the crisis is reflected in the fact that it is *not* hectic and fraught, with people dashing around desperately trying to rescue the situation. It is all very quiet. There are no papers coming through. Ministers meet regularly to receive reports, but don't seem to have any ideas. The atmosphere is one of quiet despair.

This is a pity because I think we can win through. The transport strike will end. The water workers settled today for 13½% – far better than we expected: the Cabinet had decided to buy them off at any price. This means that the local authority workers have lost their most effective squadron. We can get through. But it will be at a much higher – disastrously higher, in my view – level of inflation. Some bad decisions have been taken this week: to finance the offer of 9% to the local authority manuals from an increased rate support grant; not to apply the price controls to the road hauliers, which means that nobody will take the threat seriously in the future; and to give the nod and wink to the hauliers to settle.

After lunch at the Commons, the PM came back and summoned Ken Stowe, Tom McNally, Tom McCaffrey, Ron Hayward and myself to discuss what we should do. He said we should assume an election in March/April. Hayward said we would be 'decimated' at present. McCaffrey and Hayward said the only thing was to go back to the TUC for a new agreement. I said the problem was that the TUC could not deliver anything. And that the country did not want to see evidence that we could persuade the TUC to help run the country, but evidence that *we* could run the country.

The PM took down notes but said little. He did say, however, that we had been 'gravely politically damaged' this week. And he thought the government looked weak in the country – 'soft-centred'. We broke at 3.45 and I went to the Unit, where we discussed a paper setting out the options, but did not manage to sort it out.

The PM stayed on his own, resting and reading in the study till 5 o'clock, when ministers came in for another informal Cabinet. They decided to announce that we would not impose price controls on the haulage contractors.

I came home at 8 o'clock to look after the children, as Carol is away for the night in Edinburgh.

Joe told me that he had lunch with Candler, who was an accountant in HW's Political Office a decade ago and now works for the GLC. Candler said he had kept papers that showed the passing of money and when the sale of political honours was mentioned, he looked very agitated.

The PM spoke to Booth last night about getting the road haulage capitulation moving. He also saw Transport minister Bill Rodgers to soothe him – because they are pulling the rug from beneath Bill's tough line.

Monday 22 January 1979

I had a very long night's sleep and woke feeling fresh and ready to do battle. This may be necessary, as the political situation feels much worse. The weekend press has been bad. Full of the collapse of our pay policy – and of the government with it.

Now today we have the 'Day of Action', a national strike by 1.5 million public service workers. For many of them, this will be the first action they have ever seen, as they certainly never do a day's work for whichever local authority overpays them. But it will add to the nuisance. Tomorrow we have a national rail strike. Apparently the British, never very keen on hard work, have decided on permanent inactivity.

The effect on confidence in – and within – the government is devastating. The PM is clearly, if hopefully temporarily, undermined. The Chancellor has gone silent. Other ministers are bewildered. The left has inevitably begun plotting again. Ken Stowe learned through the private secretary network that last night there was a dinner of left-wing ministers at Judith Hart's house. Present were Foot, Silkin, Shore, etc. (These dinners usually take place regularly on Sunday evenings at Michael Foot's.) They had agreed that the government should abandon the 5% policy; reach a new agreement with the TUC; and issue a White Paper and then immediately fight the election on it. This White Paper would contain nothing specific on pay policy or inflation. It would just be a general statement on working together.

Ken Stowe was complaining bitterly that his ministers are letting the PM down. But he admits that the PM himself has lost his direction and is still unclear what to do. Clearly this onslaught from the trade union movement against a Labour government has stunned him. He has always said that he would not fight the trade unions. Now his dilemma is that unless he fights the unions, he will look weak and will lose public opinion. Really what is happening is the result of years of zero growth. This means that there is no surplus to redistribute. So the unions are fighting one another to grab a bigger share of a static cake – the 'zero sum' game.

I went through to the CPRS for a meeting with Ken Berrill and Gordon Downey at 11.15. The CPRS has been asked to do a paper on the future of counter-inflation policy. The PM has asked the Unit to work alongside it. We had a preliminary run around the course. Berrill is against a 'freeze', which the Treasury is now working on. It would need legislation, and he thinks we would never get it through the House. That is probably true, especially a twelve-month freeze, which the Treasury favours. But we think we might get a three-month freeze to stabilise things while we work out a longer-term policy (a prices and incomes board, comparability, low pay, prices legislation, monetary targets, etc.). Gavyn came with me and we concluded that, although the CPRS work is useful, we may have to produce something quicker and more political. The PM needs to be shown a way through very soon.

I went out for lunch at my Floral Street café and did a bit of shopping. Back at No. 10 I cleared such papers as were coming through and did some phoning to Brussels about the European Brookings, which still progresses slowly.

The Chancellor has written to the PM about the monetary situation. The decision by last week's Cabinet to finance the increased offer to the local authority manuals, by raising the RSG, was catastrophic. It is no good the PM talking about applying strict monetary targets when in each case we decide to finance increased public sector wages.

We had long talks in the Unit. I would like us to put in a decisive paper, giving the PM a positive steer. But we are still not clear that there are any rabbits left in the hat.

Joe phoned. The *Daily Mirror* is working closely with Customs and Excise on the Kagan scandal. They now believe that Jack Cohen of Tesco paid the Political Office £50,000 for his peerage through Kagan. But they cannot find the paper documentation. The name of the businessman 'broker' for the sale of honours in the Liberal Party has emerged. So the murky side continues to bubble.

I went to bed early and started reading Evelyn Waugh's *Brideshead Revisited*. I dislike him intensely, but appreciate the brilliant writing.

Tuesday 23 January 1979

The railway strike was accompanied by an overnight blizzard, so road traffic came to a halt. London Airport was closed. And no trains. It is a terrible situation. The Anglo-Saxons are normally very sensible, but when they go mad they go completely barmy.

I walked in most of the way to work, slithering through snow and slush. No gritting had been done because the local authority workers were on strike yesterday – though they might not have done it anyway, as they generally refuse to come out to grit the roads in bad weather and are not needed in good weather.

I saw the PM before he left for the Industrial Strategy Conference. He came up to me near the tapes and threw several mock punches. He said he was feeling cheerful. He had woken up feeling he could see the way through, he said, 'and I now think we will get through'. Interestingly, the whole spirit in No. 10 rose. We – and the Cabinet – take our mood from the top. If he is depressed, so are we. If he is pessimistic, we all give up. But when he cheers up and is optimistic, we all start fighting again. Gavyn, David and Jim were delayed by the weather and did not get in till around noon.

Ken Stowe showed me his note on last night's ministerial dinner (this note is going to the Treasury, with no copies). They moved towards trying to negotiate a three-year agreement with the trade unions, after the PM had stamped on the left's more vapid proposals, especially Foot's move to abandon the 5% target. He said oppose all high public sector wage claims and play the private sector as best we can – basically my Unit's policy. But it is clear that they have not resolved how to get modest settlements in *this* pay round, when the going rate is 15–20%. The PM said that the country is not yet ready for a statutory wage freeze.

The PM returned for the ministerial meeting to discuss the very difficult situation in the pharmaceutical and medical supply industries. They decided to negotiate with Moss Evans to try to open the local pharmaceutical factory at Runcorn, but to send in the troops if Evans, as usual, failed to deliver.

Question Time briefing was mainly devoted to discussing our attitude to the trade unions and picketing. Tom McNally and Ann Taylor, the young Labour whip from the North who sometimes helpfully sits in with us, wanted the PM to stay out of this area. But Cledwyn Hughes was all for a tough stand, and the PM said that we would have to come round to legislating to restrain the unions in the end.

The PM effectively said this in the House. He also told people who wanted to work to cross the picket lines. The Tories cheered and our side looked very uncomfortable. Afterwards he said to me that he should have said it was *secondary* picket lines which people should cross. But by then all the media was excited by what he said.

I came home at 8 o'clock, again by the same method of walking and hopping on buses.

The PM may be right that the worst is now over and we will begin to fight our way back. But it will be a hard climb. Certainly God and the weather seem to be on the Tories' side.

Wednesday 24 January 1979

Things are buzzing in No. 10 as arrangements were made for the big meeting with the TUC on Monday. This was decided at the dinner with the Neddy Six trade unionists at No. 11 last night. They agreed to get the general council to ask for the meeting.

But little else of value emerged. Michael Foot argued passionately for a new pay 'norm' – 10% – which the TUC would endorse at a special congress. Terry Duffy and Moss Evans (yes!) supported this. But others pointed out that this was because Evans had already got 20% for his members, so he could naturally support 10% for other people's members. Basnett and Geoffrey Drain (local government) said that they would not support a 10% policy, wanting more. The final clear view was the TUC could do nothing on pay in the current round. All the discussions for a new agreement would be about other things: pay over the following three years, picketing and union power, industrial democracy, etc.

Incidentally, on industrial democracy, the PM has said that we can no longer support the TUC position of 'single channel' representation.

I returned to go to the CPRS for a talk about pay policy. They were very vague and talked wholly about picketing. Gavyn thought that they were preparing for a Tory government and therefore wanted to keep at arm's length from this Labour government. Certainly the machine has withdrawn. Few papers are coming through. Legislative proposals have come to a halt. Merlyn Rees was complaining yesterday that when he was making a big statement on the present crisis, there were no Home Office civil servants in his box. They had deserted him and gone home. Whitehall has decided this government is already beaten.

It is very depressing to see how some ministers have given up. Cabinet seems to have very little fight. And the total lack of understanding about inflation is appalling. Several of them – Ennals, Foot, Silkin, Orme – seem to believe that all we have to do is to 'give them the money'. They surrender at the first sign of union militancy. They totally fail to understand the union bargaining process. They think that if you wave white flags and offer to surrender, the unions will take a moderate settlement. They don't realise that it is the nature of the bargainer to get as much as he can. By refusing to fight for 5, 8 or 10% these people guarantee that the unions will insist on 15, 20 or 25%. They refuse to admit that there may have to be compensating cuts in public spending. It is all self-deception: my 'Waterloo Bridge' principle – the belief that it is possible to jump off Waterloo Bridge and somehow avoid the consequences of getting wet. Not all ministers are guilty. Bill Rodgers and Roy Hattersley are emerging with credit and honour. The PM has praised Bill strongly to us in No. 10.

Agriculture minister Silkin is playing a very devious game. He is refusing to agree to the use of troops to open up food and agricultural supplies; he has told his officials not to co-operate with any such scheme. This is because he does not want to upset his sponsoring union, the TGWU, and wants the support of T&G members in any leadership battle. Presumably Shore and Benn are doing the same.

Watching this happen, it strikes me how governments are beaten – from *within* and not without. The Tories have never done us this kind of damage. Nor did the IMF. The present demoralisation arises from within, from within the Labour movement and from within the Cabinet itself.

The TUC has also clearly written us off. Len Murray said at last night's dinner that perhaps the TUC will have to accept some 'short-term discomfort' (i.e. a Tory government). The delusion here is to believe that the discomforts would be short term. The Tory government under Thatcher would bash the unions on the whole social wage area. The unions have benefited much more from what this Labour government has given them in social legislation than they can ever hope to gain from free collective bargaining.

In the evening I began working on a paper for the PM, setting out options for dealing with wages in the current round over the short term – basically through the next ten weeks till the election. We will continue to work on this tomorrow morning. I go to Berlin at noon, but I will leave it to the boys – Gavyn and David – to complete this.

There was a meeting of ministers at 4.15. The PM put to them his plans to go back to the TUC for a new agreement. But there was little reaction. The PM is still optimistic, but whether this will survive the present lack of progress remains to be seen.

I came home at 9 o'clock. I don't feel depressed – just angry that the government has so little fight. I don't mind being beaten, but I cannot bear going down with so little fight.

Thursday 25 January 1979

I went in early and dictated a three-page paper on how to handle short-term pay policy over the next ten weeks till the election. Discussed it with David Lipsey and Gavyn Davies, and left them to finish it off.

I left for Berlin with Carol at midday. The Aspen Institute had invited me to give advice to the Germans on founding a new Institute of Advanced Studies in Berlin. It was not the ideal time to leave the country. But I had promised to go, and there is little else to do here until the PM meets the TUC on Monday afternoon at No. 10. Berlin was covered by very thick snow. Yet somehow the Germans overcome these problems, whereas in Britain any minor disruption seems to bring the country to a halt. Really it all depends on whether the people are looking for an excuse not to work.

Friday 26–Saturday 27 January 1979

Friday and Saturday were very exciting. Carol and I went to the opera – *The Magic Flute* – on Thursday and, best of all, to the Philharmonic on Saturday. It was Karajan's fiftieth anniversary of concert performances. The BPO played Schumann's Fourth Symphony incredibly. An astonishing performance.

Back on Sunday morning to the gloom!

Monday 29 January 1979

I went in early and spent the morning in my room, clearing the backlog of papers and making some phone calls.

Ken Stowe suggested we had lunch together, so we went upstairs into the new Cabinet Office canteen. He was worried about the PM's frame of mind and felt it was time for a political input. He was worried that the PM would stake everything on reaching this new agreement with the TUC. And then would incline to resign if we did not get all we wanted from the TUC. He felt it was more likely that we would get some things but not everything. Above all he felt we must devise a way for the PM to appeal over the heads of the normal union hierarchy and get through to the rank and file. He believes that it is no good going through the old boy network at the top of the hierarchy. We will think along these lines in the Unit and see if there is anything we can write.

We came back and went straight to the meeting of ministers in the Cabinet Room. This was to prepare the line for the coming meeting with the TUC. The atmosphere was fairly gloomy. Michael Foot and Stan Orme launched another bid to 'do something for the low paid'. The PM and Healey were fairly sharp in pointing out that we had already done the £3.50

underpinning for the low paid, and it had made no difference whatsoever. The unions had just pocketed it and continued greedily as before.

We then went upstairs where the TUC general council were already sitting in the big dining room. They had been meeting during the previous hour and had decided that only four of them would speak: Murray, Urwin*, Allen* and Basnett. Then the PM would sum up.

The PM struck me as more than usually nervous at the beginning. He put the line firmly, made the options clear, denounced some aspects of current trade union behaviour, and said we had only two weeks.

Their reactions were mainly bland 'reporting'. They all said they wanted an agreement but didn't want any legislation, and could not deliver a new pay norm. The forty-odd TUC people were very quiet. Some were shaking their heads in disagreement with the PM. It all ended within an hour – which worried Tom McCaffrey, who had foolishly hoped this would be the big rescue act. I never shared that naive view.

Soon they were all streaming out. I met Frank Chapple coming down the stairs, and he asked me for a cup of tea and suggested that Sid Weighell of the NUR came along as well. I agreed. So we went to my room.

Frank was voluble and funny as ever. He was very critical of the TUC for not giving a lead. He said, 'We keep sitting there nodding our heads, agreeing that we want to help the government, but nobody makes us an offer, nobody puts a specific suggestion on the table.' He said, 'I don't support a fucking incomes policy, but I will support one now if it will help this government.' Sid Weighell said that Joe Gormley had said that he 'was not in the business of saving a dead government'. But he said, 'I am in that business.' However, all they could do specifically was to delay their own settlements until the summer, then if we have got the going rate down again, they would follow it.

They both said it was crucial for us to take a tough line with the public service workers. They spoke with contempt of Alan Fisher of NUPE and said that most of his members 'have never done a hard day's work in their lives'. Chapple said his members would insist on 'fucking Fisher times two'. He added that if the government thought that the public service workers had power, we should wait until the real power workers pulled the switches. But if we could get the public services to settle for a low figure, they would lower their demands.

David Owen and I later had a long talk about the present crisis. He was insistent that we must not hold an election in March/April because 'we would be massacred'. On pay he thought we should fight a few and concede a few, but not start giving way all round. He then thought that with low pay comparability and a long-term programme we would have a reasonable election platform. He was very critical of David Ennals for weakness and said, 'He is a cretin who should be sacked.' I agreed but Jim seems unwilling to take radical action with the weak members of his government, trying to preserve the left-right balance regardless of ability.

I went back into a reception and David Steel took me on one side. He is very worried about the Thorpe trial, which is scheduled for May. Therefore, he wants the election before it – in April/May. However, if we were to try to go for 7 June, he wants the trial delayed until July. He suggested a dinner and I will arrange that.

I ran into Shirley Williams who was less depressed than last week. I told her that I thought we should take on the teachers, who have claimed 35%, and they must start to deliver the Houghton condition of 'professional' behaviour. She looked a bit worried.

I finally got away, and home rather late.

Tuesday 30 January 1979

In Cabinet they took no pay decisions and basically decided just to have another discussion on Thursday. But Shore made a bid to get agreed a new higher pay norm. All the craven spending ministers – who are terrified of the looming strikes in their own sectors – supported this. The PM and Healey firmly rejected it. The PM said that 'in reality the new norm was a rising going rate'. Benn argued ludicrously that they should announce that it was all the fault of the Cabinet. Shore dismissed this with a contemptuous sweep of the arm.

I went out to lunch with sensible David McKie of the *Guardian*. He said that most of the *Guardian*'s staff believe that the answer is to turn industry into a mass of small co-operatives, overnight!! Thank God journalists don't run anything!

The PM went to the *Evening Standard* drama awards and returned to the Commons very happy. He said he had enjoyed it enormously. He had seen all the plays that won awards. At briefing he was very subdued and said how ludicrous it was that he had to go through this Questions farce twice a week. But he actually did very well, ebullient and funny. Somehow the conversation moved from the theatre and the drama awards to homosexuality. He said he was completely unaware of homosexuality until well into adult life – it was the notorious behaviour of the Labour queer Tom Driberg that brought it to his knowledge. He said, 'They say we are all suppressed homosexuals. But it all puzzles me. There have always been so many attractive girls.' He seemed surprised when we pointed out that there were a number of well-known homosexuals in the present House. He obviously knows nothing of those in his government.

Roger Stott then did a hilarious imitation of a homosexual cook who had served on ship with him when he was in the navy. The PM looked very shocked and said he 'never came across anything like that' when he was in the navy.

Afterwards Tom McNally told me that when they had a similarly bawdy discussion in Guadeloupe, the PM had said to him, 'You won't tell those stories in front of Audrey, will you? She would be very shocked.'

Later in Tom McNally's room with David Lipsey we discussed the dreadful behaviour of NUPE in taking action that is bound to kill people in hospitals and leave the dead unburied. I suggested a new TUC Charter of Trade Unionism and Human Rights, which the TUC could introduce as a guide to its members. Unlikely in the present climate of anarchy.

I then went home about 8 o'clock. The weather is still appalling, sleet, but it is forecast to improve by the end of the week. And the road haulage strike is ending – a terrible settlement of 20%, but it will ease some of the pressure on us, and enable us to try to restore some pay sanity, providing we have the will. The trouble is that there are too many marshmallows in the Cabinet.

Wednesday 31 January 1979

I went in early. My secretary was off sick again. I cleared papers, made some telephone calls abroad about Brookings.

The PM stayed upstairs this morning. He had a meeting with Charles Donnett of the GMWU about the health and local authorities strike. Donnett was very pessimistic and said they wouldn't settle for much less than 15%. This is ridiculous. The average private sector settlement now is 10–11%. But the public services want as much as the highest private sector people, Ford and the lorry drivers.

In the afternoon I wrote a minute to the PM suggesting a TUC Charter of Trade Unionism and Human Rights – which would reaffirm the best side of trade unionism, but also set out some constraints on the present bad behaviour by the NUPE pigs.

The PM stayed over at the Commons all afternoon and evening, voting on the Prices Bill, which went through all its committee stages.

I came home early and listened to Beethoven. I begin to feel tired and pessimistic.

Thursday 1 February 1979

I worked in the office in the morning. Cabinet apparently had endless discussion on pay and on the trade unions. At the beginning the PM went round the table asking each person for their views on what line to take with the trade unions. He was inclined to go on television and both appeal to decency and attack terrible trade union behaviour. On balance, ministers were against. It was a discussion full of agony and angst.

On pay they decided to make one last big step to try to get a new norm. The government will announce that it will finance up to *10%* in the public sector, but not an inch more. I was shocked when I heard this, because it is a dreadful weakening. But I was told afterwards that this was seen as a *tough* line. The marshmallows – Ennals, etc. – wanted 15% or 16%.

The trouble is that every week we have a 'positively last concession'. At first it was not a penny above 5%. Then it was 8.8%; now it is 10%. If I was a trade unionist, I would just sit and wait for further concessions. This is the consequence of having people in the Cabinet – Ennals, Shore, Foot, Orme – who are weak and, in the last analysis, never prepared to stand and fight. They would be perfectly capable, in three weeks, of arguing that 30% is not enough and not fair to the low paid, so we ought to offer 100%.

The enigma for us is – what does the PM really believe? He talks toughly. But maybe he has decided on a policy of calculated capitulation in order to limit the strike situation up to the election. If so, I think he is wrong. Cabinet did not end till 1.30 p.m.

I went to lunch with David Watt of the *FT* at the Travellers Club. We discussed research institutes. Back to Question Time. The PM was in a very anti-trade union mood. He is clearly completely fed up with them. But Question Time did not go too well. The PM was less ebullient than on Tuesday. The Tories are an unbeatable horse. Thatcher simply asked whether the PM supported the use of volunteers. The PM tried to duck it so as not to appear to be 'blacklegging', but he just looked weak.

Afterwards Ennals made a statement on the terrible situation in the Health Service, where NUPE is on strike and leaving people to die. Ennals was absolutely terrible and the Tories howled him down. I now understand what my father used to mean by his expression 'farting into the wind'. Ennals is a human fart.

I went back to No. 10, cleared papers and then went to the Royal Institute for Public Administration. Will Plowden has become the new director. We had a celebration drink. He also had there Adam Ridley*, the Tory adviser, who will probably head Thatcher's Policy Unit if she wins the election. We discussed the organisation of No. 10, talking as two professionals with a common interest in getting Prime Ministers better advised.

The PM saw the leaders of the four public service unions involved in the present disputes. He lectured them, but I gathered that little progress was made. They simply cannot control their own members. And the Trots have virtually taken over NUPE. Today in Cabinet the PM said ruefully, 'NUPE used to be a reasonable union when Alan Fisher was alive.'

I came home at 9 o'clock, watched the *Mask of Demetrius* with marvellous Sidney Greenstreet and Peter Lorre, read some Evelyn Waugh, and then went to sleep quite early.

Friday 2 February 1979

In deputy secs Ken Stowe reported that last night's meeting with the local authority union leaders went badly. The ministers were completely outmanoeuvred by the trade union leaders, who first broke through on behalf of the NHS and then insisted that the local authority manuals be linked to the NHS. Ken said he felt that the union leaders went away convinced that they had broken through towards 15%.

We were also told that Ennals has encouraged the area health authorities actually to *pay* the strikers, even when they are on strike. This is truly cretinous behaviour. We are going to pay a high price for having shallow cowards in charge. The terrible thing is that it was only yesterday that Cabinet decided to abandon 5% for 10% and this was to be absolutely final. Already it looks as if Ennals and Shore have abandoned 10% for 15%.

John Hunt said that it was essential that there be *no* more meetings between ministers and trade unionists. It is a case of men and boys, professionals and amateurs. The trade unionists outmanoeuvre them every time. I said that if it happens again, we should call in the RSPCC.

The PM had gone north to make his big speech to the local authority conference. Here he announced that government will finance settlements higher than 5%, but not above single figures. That is this week!

I went to lunch at the *Mirror* with Tony Miles, Terry Lancaster, Mike Molloy, Geoffrey Goodman and Joe. They are all very depressed. Terry thinks we have no chance whatsoever in an election. But they will fight for us.

I was late back from the *Mirror* and then out to dinner with Brian MacArthur. He says that working on the *Standard* is now terrible. They are instructed to get pictures of pickets with beards, but that is all. No analysis.

At my meeting on Monday with Sid Weighell and Frank Chapple, Sid asked Frank if he had signed the helpful document published this week by a dozen moderate trade unionists. 'Yes,' said Frank. Then added, 'Well, I ain't exactly fucking signed it. In fact I ain't exactly fucking seen it. They just phoned me up and said there was this document, supporting moderation and an incomes policy. Well, you know, I don't exactly fucking agree with it, as I don't go along with incomes policies, for other reasons. But, yes, in that sense I fucking signed it. I thought I would help the government.'

I need Frank Chapple to cheer me up – though his chilling warning that his members will want 'fucking Fisher times two' is close to reality.

Looking back, it has been a depressing week. They are making progress in the talks with the TUC, but down on the ground it is terrible. These pickets are letting the sick die and preventing the dead from being buried. This has nothing to do with trade unionism. It is hard-faced, grab-what-you-can capitalism with a union card.

The government has not come out of it well. They no sooner retreat and decide to make a stand, than they start retreating again. The PM has been tough in his general statements, but weak in particular decisions. I do not believe he is capable of fighting against the trade unions. He always said that he would not fight the unions: he would resign and go to the farm. He is neither fighting nor resigning. He is holding on in No. 10 and surrendering yard by yard.

Denis Healey has been curiously subdued. Bill Rodgers has come out of it best, standing up and speaking out loud and clear. Hattersley has also done quite well, as has David Owen. The new young right is actually much *tougher* than were the Jenkins/Crosland generation.

As for the rest, some like Orme and Morris are paralysed; some, e.g. Rees, are permanently puzzled; and some, e.g. Shore, are enigmatic; some, e.g. Benn and Silkin, are cynically and blatantly playing the left-wing union card for the leadership; some, especially Ennals, are just cowards, small farts in a storm.

Unless the PM pulls them together next week, it could be beyond saving. Of course, in the election campaign, I still think that the PM can pick up 7–10% on Thatcher: it just depends how far behind we are when we begin the campaign. All this points to soldiering on until the summer and hoping for calmer waters, which is what David Owen advocates. But the danger is that the longer we go on, the worse it might get.

This is really the end of the old Labour movement as a potential government. Labour needs a new social democratic way, without the old dependence on the unions and on Benn's lunatic Marxist left.

Monday 5 February 1979

I had a haircut before going into Downing Street – a 'prison' crewcut, because that was how I felt – brutal and ready for a fight.

The PM had made a speech at the weekend, at the local government conference in Newcastle. He had written it himself, without showing it to anybody. He had not told the Press Office what was in it. In fact it was a confusing speech: it mentioned both 8.8% and 'single figures' (i.e. 9.9%) as the sticking points. So everybody is bewildered and he got a very bad press. There is a feeling that we are surrendering to every pressure. I suspect that we are. There is no consistency in our position. The PM makes excellent, tough, *general* statements. But in specific situations he always retreats. He has been so good for two and a half years. But the recent evidence is not good. And he is not discussing his strategy with anybody. Nobody knows what he really wants.

Ministers are clearly confused. Hattersley took a hard line for 8.8% on Friday – and in less than twenty-four hours the PM had abandoned him. Hattersley thought he was defending Thursday's Cabinet decision. But with a moving position, who knows what is right?

I had lunch with Joe Haines. He is very depressed. The *Mirror* is losing faith in us. They want to know where we are going.

Yesterday Douglas Hurd printed his memoirs of the end of Heath's government in February 1974 in the *Observer*. He said that the Civil Service failed to give any advice then. It is equally quiet now. Nothing from the Treasury. It is all standing off, waiting to see if the government falls.

I came back for a meeting with Tom McNally at 3.30. Roger Stott came in, with Gavyn Davies and David Lipsey. I asked straight away, 'Where are we at?' Tom said his basic position is that we should sell out, give them the money and hold the election when all is quiet and people feel well off. This may work. But it may not. Once it is clear that we are capitulating like this, the roof may fall in before we can hold the election. Tom got a bit annoyed when I said this. Really my problem is that I can see that he may be right *politically*. But I simply hate the policy of capitulation. It is cowardly and deceitful. It also assumes that people are mugs.

I dashed from this meeting to the airport to go to a Brookings meeting in Brussels – which will take all Tuesday. So I will miss a crucial crisis day. Pity, but I cannot help it.

Before leaving, Private Office told me about the TUC meeting happening upstairs. Clearly there *will* be a *joint* statement. But whether it will add up to much remains in doubt. Healey pressed the crucial point of current pay. The unions ducked it and Len Murray said he did not think they could help on that. That is the big issue. Nothing else matters.

Tuesday 6 February 1979

Had a fascinating day in Brussels. The 'European Brookings' venture has now gone into the official EEC machine. It was taken yesterday at an economic committee, where we got through most of the commission paper. I led the British negotiation team of three – the others were Richard Cardon from the Treasury and Brian Crowe from the FCO in Brussels, both very able. I was a bit uncertain at first, but soon got the feel of it! Actually I enjoy negotiating very much.

This morning's *Daily Express* carried a poll which shows the Tories 19% ahead! That suggests we would be massacred in an early spring election. I was not surprised. We have given an impression of weakness and vacillation. So we lose our friends who want firm government, but we don't gain anybody. By refusing to capitulate immediately, we ensure that the streets are full of garbage, but by making concessions every few days, we look weak and in fact sell out on inflation. We should either surrender straight away, or stand and fight properly.

The PM has suffered a catastrophic decline in personal popularity. He has not got it right. And he still has not shown his face on television. The Tory press certainly think they have him on the run.

Went out with Graham Greene to dinner. Not home till 1.15 (2.15 Brussels time!).

Wednesday 7 February 1979

I drove in early, rather tired after that very late night. There was quite a bit of paper – though mainly committee reports on individual pay settlements. We should not be trying to monitor every deal. Had lunch with Harold Lever who thinks we will be out of power for ten years – mainly because of the wild men taking over the Party. He also said he had never seen the PM as rattled before, as recently he has.

Frank Chapple phoned this morning. He said that the concessions in the public services were making it impossible for him to hold his electricians back. His men in the steel industry had refused to go on strike and were willing to take a moderate pay settlement in single figures. But now that the public services were getting double figures, he could not hold them back. Frank described how tough it had been leading the Electricians Union over the past twenty years. He said, 'My executive are enemies of mine, and they are a fucking horrible lot. In fact my supporters are a fucking horrible lot.'

Went to Wembley for England v. Northern Ireland. Frivolous escapism. But at least the footballers turn up to play!

Thursday 8 February 1979

The PM had a meeting to discuss interest rates with Healey, Lever and Shore. Lending rate went up to 14% today.

Cabinet discussed the draft of the TUC 'concordat'. They will agree it, though it is not worth a lot as there is nothing in it on *current* pay. But we cannot afford *not* to have it.

At briefing for Question Time, the PM was still fairly subdued. When we discussed his broadcast tonight, I said that the crucial point was to give an impression of control, because it was the sense of dithering that was damaging us. He said he agreed – 'but we could not successfully give an image of control, because we don't know what to do, do we?'

After Questions I went to the airport and flew to Berlin. Arrived late, in cold high winds. Then out to dinner till 1 in the morning.

Friday 9 February 1979

A very heavy day in Berlin discussing research institutes. The meeting lasted from 9 till 6.30, then I went straight to the opera to see *Don Giovanni*. Afterwards Meinolf Dierkes took me out to dinner, and I did not get to bed till 3 o'clock.

In the day I phoned London and learned that Healey came to see the PM this morning bringing a crisis package, including some tax proposals and public expenditure cuts. The PM threw them all out. I was told that he thought it was not politically possible. And relations between him and the Chancellor appeared less good than usual.

Came back very tired on Saturday afternoon and went straight to bed.

Monday 12 February 1979

The PM went off to Scotland today to make a big speech opening the devolution campaign in Glasgow. Helen Liddell phoned me and said that the PM went over well in public, but in private was fairly sombre. He had led her to expect a March election.

I played football at lunchtime for the Commons against the Press Gallery. It was played in a blizzard and my boots were frozen on, with packed ice over the laces. I had to thaw them out before I could get the boots off. (I scored our first goal and happily managed to scar a few cowardly journalists, but we lost 5–4.)

I learned more about last week's pay negotiations. On Thursday night when he came back from the American Embassy, the PM sent for Len Murray and they talked till after midnight. This was in preparation for Friday's meeting with the local authority union leaders, which also went on till after midnight. Afterwards everybody was fairly optimistic that they had a deal: 9% on pay now; and comparability, with the first stage paid in August. Ministers were very pleased and hoped to have this at about the same time as the TUC/government concordat is announced next Wednesday.

In the evening Carol and I went to a lovely concert at the Goldsmiths Hall, with Isaac Stern, Pinchas Zukerman and the English Chamber

Orchestra. It was put on by Rothschild's. We did not get back till nearly 1 o'clock.

Tuesday 13 February 1979

I went in early. Apparently the pay deal with the local authority manuals and the NHS ancillaries is fading. Alan Fisher, the appalling leader of NUPE, has reneged on his agreement last week and now says that he wants the comparability now, not in August. I was worried that the PM might give in to this, in order to have the settlement. But apparently he is holding firm. David Ennals came to see him before Question Time, pressing him to give way, but the PM sent him away with a flea in his ear. However, I am not sure he will hold firm to the end. He clearly would like to get this strike out of the way, especially if he is to hold an early election.

Prince Charles came in to spend a day including lunch at No. 10. He arrived at 10, was with the PM in the study for an hour and then came down to sit in on the EY Cabinet committee. The PM opened by saying it was a long time since a member of the Royal Family had sat in at a Cabinet meeting – and guessed it must be the first time since George III. He asked Charles how he thought it had changed since then. Charles said with a wry smile, 'Well, then I would have been in your chair.' He sat in for briefing for Questions. It was a bit stilted.

Questions went as usual, with the PM under a lot of pressure over the trade union question.

Afterwards I went back to No. 10 with Ken Stowe in the car. We discussed the proposed concordat with the TUC, which will be announced tomorrow. The bizarre fact is that none of these papers relating to this have been circulated to the political side – Tom McNally or me. They have been kept very close by the Civil Service. It is mad that something as political as this should be kept hidden from the political advisers. In fact I have got hold of and read everything, but by the usual devious means. This is all such a ridiculous bore.

I cleared my papers, and then the head of MI6, Dickie Franks, came in for a drink. He is a pleasant and gentle person, who has been kind to my 9-year-old son Stephen, who wrote to him about his own plan to train spies at the bottom of our garden.

Afterwards out for dinner with Johnny Apple of the *New York Times* at the Gay Hussar and I did not get home till 1.30 a.m. I am feeling tired, with an incipient cold. Also I am not enjoying the way the government is just hanging on. We are not actually doing any governing, in the widest sense: just fighting the pay battle, and that in a sporadic way. It may all work out. But it is not something one feels particularly proud of.

Incidentally, the PM sent for Tony Benn at 6 p.m. and saw him for an hour and a half. Benn had voted *against* the government at the NEC over the question of the sale of Harriers to China (all the communists, fellow travellers and Soviet mouthpieces have been opposing this, and presumably Benn was courting this vote). Nobody was with them, so we don't know what was said. But the PM did not sack him, which is a pity, but understandable in the present political troubles.

Wednesday 14 February 1979

There was another blizzard last night, and the country was paralysed again this morning. It took me two hours to get to work, walking much of the way through beleagured London. There was *no* train on the Barnet to Charing Cross line till after 11 o'clock. I sat at Kentish Town Tube station for over an hour without any trains. It was a nightmare.

When I reached No. 10, the trade unionists were already there upstairs, discussing the concordat joint statement. Len Murray had told Ken Stowe that it would only take fifteen minutes and that ministers should be ready to join them shortly after 10. In fact the union discussions went on till after midday. The ministers had sat in the Cabinet Room, talking and waiting to be summoned. But in the end, when David Lea came down to say it was all agreed, he said that the general council did not want a meeting with the ministers, so they began to break up straight away.

After lunch I went over to the Commons to hear the PM announce the new concordat with the TUC. I must admit that it is better than I had expected. There is still nothing on *current* pay, but quite big concessions on union behaviour, and it is a fairly firm commitment to get inflation down to 5% over three years. The PM was in great form. It is clear that he is much revived – because he has a policy platform. However imperfect, any policy is better than none to him. He does not, as Wilson did, like flying on the seat of his pants. The Tories looked surprisingly subdued. They realise that our breach with the unions is what has revived them; and any new alliance is a threat to them.

Ronald Taylor, my bookseller, came in with some lovely first editions for me to give to my godson, Alexander Greene. I pick John Masefield's sonnets, signed by him – my kind of poet, though not currently fashionable. Then home in the bitter cold. The roads were treacherously icy. Carol is in bed with a bad cold. So it is a very hard winter. But we all have a feeling that things have bottomed out, are not getting any worse. We wait to see if recovery is possible. There is a long way to go – the latest Gallup poll tomorrow shows us 20% behind. That means quite a long hard pull.

Thursday 15 February 1979

More blizzards overnight. So I drove in early and took the girls to school.

In Cabinet they spent hours on cash limits. They rejected Joel Barnett's paper as inadequate. But the PM and others put the same point as we put to him – that the staff cuts must be higher if the pay awards are higher, a kind of graduated scale. The only real decision taken was to stick to the borrowing limits and to announce the cash limits soon.

I read papers all morning and then went to lunch upstairs. We then learned that the NHS and local authority pay settlement was really going wrong. Not only Alan Fisher's NUPE, but also the GMW union are backing off. They all say that they need *double*-figure increases for presentational reasons – and we need them *not* to have double figures for similar reasons.

Afterwards I came back to No. 10. Then I went home very early – at 5.30 p.m. – because I have a bad cold and the weather is terrible. It was bitterly cold, with heavy snow and sharp winds. It took one and a half hours to get home. The roads were so slippery that the traffic could only crawl along. The weather is now as bad as in 1947.

Friday 16 February 1979

Awoke with a terrible cold, headache and eyes streaming, but I went into work.

Ken Stowe told me about Len Murray's visit to the PM last evening. Len put forward a new compromise proposal on local authority pay: on top of the 9% on basic pay there would be a productivity payment immediately, as well as the comparability payment in August. This is a way to get their immediate increase up into double figures, and also means that the final total increase will be about 16% – disastrous!

The PM told Len he would not have it and refused to see the union secretaries. As he left, Murray made it clear to Ken Stowe that it was right to stand firm and that we must tell the local authority employers not to concede the productivity deal because everybody knows it is phoney. The union leaders make it absolutely clear that they have no intention of delivering any extra productivity. To them 'productivity' is just a device to get an extra payment. There have *never* been any productivity improvements either in the Health Service or in the local authorities. Len Murray knows this, and having done his official job of trying to get the PM to give way, he then conceded that it would have been quite wrong to do so.

The pity is that we shall give way in the end. The employers and the unions will combine to put pressure on the government. Ministers will then combine to put pressure on the PM. And he will have to give way. Everybody prefers a quiet life in the short term. Nobody understands that unless we have more productivity and print less money, we shall be finished as a nation. In fact the decline will continue, and probably accelerate, simply because nobody is prepared to take the hard way to recovery. Sadly the unions are at the heart of the problem – because they won't accept that extra productivity is essential, but continue to act as though all that is needed is to use their strength to redistribute resources in their favour – when all that happens is that paper money is distributed in all directions, inflation rises and real living standards stagnate.

At the deputy secs meeting, John Hunt was fuming with anger at Robert Armstrong. It was something to do with the 'open government' exercise. The Home Office had failed to produce the required draftings for the proposed White Paper. It is now five months since the PM asked for a White Paper. Since then they have been going round in circles. Hunt had had a row with Robert and was obviously thinking of taking over the operation in the Cabinet Office.

I went straight home to bed in the late afternoon feeling unwell. In the evening papers was a sad report of an interview given by Harold Wilson – attacking the PM for his conduct of the crisis and suggesting he would have done it better. This is HW at his worst.

The flow of papers is still very small. Government is nearly at a halt except on the pay and strikes fronts, which were very active. This crisis is *stressful*, because it is going so badly, but it is not tiring in terms of work.

I put into the PM a Gallup poll which shows that people think we should have a *tougher* pay policy. I think that is true – but the respondents want us to be tougher with *other* people's pay, not their own.

Monday 19 February 1979

The weather is still horrible, very cold and still a lot of snow and ice around.

My secretary is still away with flu – this is the fourth week! So I have to write everything by hand. While dealing with it, I was told of a Civil Service practice called 'taking your Whitleys' or 'your sickies'. Apparently the Civil Service unions have negotiated two weeks' 'uncertified sick leave'. This means that they can take two weeks' sickness leave without needing a doctor's certificate. As a result, every civil servant except the senior ones takes the maximum sick leave and they all treat it as holiday. Just one more example of the privileges of the public service sector. But my secretary is a different case and is genuinely sick.

The PM saw Peter Shore at the weekend. Shore pressed a solution for the local authorities strike – to give them an extra 1% for so-called 'productivity', which would give them more than 10% in total. The PM still said no.

We had very little to do. The only papers coming through concern the strike situation. There are dozens of papers from the Civil Contingencies Unit, reporting on schools and hospitals closed, rubbish uncollected, etc. There are also a few papers on open government and British shipbuilders' problems, but not much else. I cannot think what some ministers are actually doing.

Tuesday 20 February 1979

The PM was upstairs in the study all morning. He dealt with papers and, according to Ken Stowe, 'fiddled around with this and that'. He was very annoyed with Ennals and Shore for giving so much away in negotiations. The unions, having failed to get a productivity payment *without* productivity, now want a £1 a week comparability payment immediately in advance of the comparability studies this summer. This is a farce, as many of these public employees are actually paid *more* than comparable people in the private sector. Even so, Shore and Ennals welcomed the proposals – because they want peace more than they want to defeat inflation. Tom McNally told me that the PM had said, 'Shore did himself out of the chancellorship by his weakness this weekend.' Tom also said that 'Ennals is finished, busted'. I suggested a reshuffle.

Incidentally, the PM has said that he cannot sack Tony Benn ahead of the election. He actually told Benn, when he saw him at No. 10 last week, that, but for the election, he would sack him. He has told McCaffrey that he will drop Benn after the election if we win. I wonder.

The PM sent for Denis Healey just before noon and told him, 'You will have to give way to the local authority and health workers in the end.' So once more, after a lot of tough talk, we give way to all the union demands and get nothing back in return. Everybody at EY(prices) agreed to settle. It will be around 10% on basic pay, plus £1 on comparability now, and much more in August and again next spring. In the end it will cost about 15%. So this will be the basic rate for the others to try to beat.

These negotiations have shown how appallingly cynical the pay negotiating process is. First the public service unions were offered comparability with the private sector, but rejected it because they knew they would not get much from *strict* comparability. So they went for 'phoney' productivity deals, but withdrew from that when it looked like being *strict* productivity, which is alien to them. So they went back to comparability and got a comparability payment before any comparability study has even been done. To them it is just a game of con.

The PM said at Questions briefing that his favourite story about Tory minister Reggie Maudling concerned when Ted Heath was abroad and Maudling was left as Deputy Prime Minister. He went out for a very long lunch and came back abound 4 p.m. to tell his secretary that he needed legal advice. 'Yes?' queried the secretary. 'What is the maximum penalty for being drunk in charge of a government?'

Afterwards we went off for the PM to open the new Institute of Policy Studies. This is a remodelling of the old PEP, where I worked eighteen years ago. My old colleague Keith Hindell was there, together with a vast gathering of the Establishment. The PM scrapped his official speech and mainly used some ideas I gave him after Questions. He put them together into an excellent speech.

The PM drove back to the Commons. I cleared my papers in No. 10 and then went home. Really not much is going on apart from the pay battle.

Wednesday 21 February 1979

The political scene feels dreary and flat. The local authority pay deal will be announced today. We will try to make the 9% part look good, but the £1 on advance for comparability will look what it is – a con, which takes the settlement well into double figures.

I did not bother to attend the Gen on the Rhodesian sanctions report. John Hunt has put in a long minute to the PM suggesting that we now can drop the idea of another inquiry (the House of Lords defeated our first proposal for a commission of the two Houses). The machine now sees a good chance of escaping any investigation.

Had lunch at the Neal Street Restaurant with Frances Cairncross – a very bright girl. She shares my views on the public sector slowly stifling the private sector.

In the evening I went to an appalling lecture at the IBA given by Lord Fulton. Rambling and incoherent and a complete waste of an evening.

Home feeling very depressed indeed. Ken Stowe has told me the latest strategy evolved by the PM and the Chancellor at this morning's meeting. If we lose a vote of confidence after the devolution referendum, we have an election on 5 April. If we win the vote, we go for a big Budget on 3 April, including all the necessary tough measures. This will be on the assumption of an October election. If Parliament rejects the Budget, then an election will be held on that issue – presumably on 7 June.

So we may survive, stumbling on possibly till the autumn, often humiliated but never brought down, achieving little in policy terms, just surviving, until, with our credibility and self-respect eroded, with our ministers tired, with no platform and few friends, we are finally beaten in October. Hanging on until we are hung.

It may not be as bad as that. If pay inflation goes no higher, we have a fine summer and peace on the industrial front, the PM may be too shrewd for Thatcher in a long election campaign and then we win. But that looks a long way away.

Thursday 22 February 1979

Talked to Roy Hattersley about a reshuffle – he naturally agrees it would be a good idea, hoping to benefit. Later on I put this to Tom McNally, and he says he will put it to the PM on Saturday when he addresses the meeting of parliamentary candidates.

Cabinet had a long agenda. Most important was cash limits, and they took a fairly tough stand on that, agreeing to stick to the borrowing target of £8.5 billion.

I went to Grieveson Grant for lunch. Today the two new gilt issues were massively oversubscribed, so we have funded the deficit for the rest of the fiscal year.

At Questions briefing the PM talked a bit about Parliament – 'Always be accurate,' he said, 'always understate, never exaggerate. There is always somebody who knows better than you do.'

I came home early to watch hilarious Buster Keaton in *The General*. I first saw it twenty-five years ago in Oxford.

Friday 23 February 1979

A very quiet day. I did not bother to go to the EY Cabinet committee dealing with the energy crisis arising from the Iran revolution.

After the EY the PM kept the Chancellor and Shore behind and they discussed how to deal with the NHS and local authorities now that the NUPE executive have rejected the 11% pay deal which the general secretaries agreed. So the strikes, etc. will drag on. Some of the Civil Service – but nobody from No. 10 – went on strike today. This was in support of their pay claim which is not yet on the table. What an example they set from the centre.

The Treasury paper on cash limits suggested that the government should pay all of any public service pay claim except for the last 2%, which should be taken as staff cuts. Some people assume that this is tough with 2% sackings. In fact, I am told by officials, it is wholly geared to let the Civil Service through. Their claim will be for about 26%. The CSD has worked out that they can organise 2% staff reductions through natural wastage, without a single sacking. So they will have 24% on pay and 2% wastage – no pain at all. So the government's whole policy, drafted by civil servants, is geared to suit the convenience of Civil Service pay.

I went to Johnny's Café in Covent Garden for lunch and looked in the bookshops and my favourite record shops. Cleared my papers and then went home early and looked after the children. Then in the evening Carol and I went to see Shaw's *Philanderer*. Very enjoyable.

The PM went to Chequers before lunch. He was beginning to show signs of a cold.

Monday 26 February 1979

It was such a pleasure to see some sunshine at last. The weekend and today have been the first fine weather this year.

Immediately on arrival the PM sent for me. He was in the study, making notes for his television appearance tonight. He had been in bed over the weekend since his speech to Labour candidates on Saturday. The doctor came on Saturday afternoon and pronounced that he had laryngitis. Certainly he was complaining and spluttering very badly. He told me that yesterday his voice had totally disappeared. He asked what he should say on TV. I said he must be positive, show he is in control, and try to suggest that the government has good reason for going on – because it has a job to do. We then discussed long-term pay policy. He was very critical of Ennals and Shore as negotiating ministers (so why doesn't he sack them?). He said he would 'like to recruit two or three trade unionists, pay them £20,000 a year and get them to negotiate with the unions on behalf of the government'.

At the end he asked what demeanour he should adopt on TV. I said 'Be yourself. Be natural.' He said, 'Yes, that is the only thing to do. There is no point in trying to adopt a style.'

I went back downstairs and cleared papers before going out to lunch with my footballing friend Kevin O'Shea and a Catholic priest from Fulham at the Pig and Whistle.

On return I phoned Berlin to cancel my visit to the Aspen Conference on Germany. I am sorry about this because Helmut Schmidt will be there. It would have been exciting. But the situation here is very fragile. Devolution is going badly and in one poll there is only a 3% majority for devolution even in Scotland. Certainly we will not get the necessary 40% of the voters. With the PM ill as well, I had better stay around.

I read papers until nearly 8 o'clock and then went home.

Tuesday 27 February 1979

The PM was away all day visiting the Midlands. So I came in late, and there was little to do all day.

We had lunch at No. 10 and discussed a possible reshuffle. Tom McNally said that the PM is resisting it, but sees the advantages. He worried us by mentioning John Silkin as a possible Chancellor! A disastrous choice. Ken Stowe said that the reshuffle would be a chance to reorganise the machinery of government, especially to deal with the problem of the Civil Service Department, which is inefficient and overstaffed. But will Jim in his present mood ever get round to biting the bullet of a reshuffle?

I went out shopping after lunch, and dropped into the handsome Catholic Cathedral, Westminster, to sit and reflect. I feel comfortable there.

Andrew Graham, who was so good in my Unit from 1974–76, came in for a chat, which was nicely nostalgic. He told us that Harold Wilson is an awful chairman of the City Royal Commission (Andrew is on it), very rambling, and often referring matters to subcommittees which don't exist!

I came home early and had pancakes with the children. Then to bed – have nearly finished Waugh's *Brideshead Revisited*, which is a much more serious and melancholic book than I had remembered.

Wednesday 28 February 1979

Five years since winning the 1974 election. What tumultuous times! How much has happened to me! But today was a very quiet anniversary. I spent the morning in my room reading and telephoning. Outside it was cold and rainy, and I wished I had gone to Berlin after all.

Went to lunch with Harold Lever. He is very depressed by the whole economic situation. He says that the government simply is not interested in helping the wealth-creating private sector. He is also very worried about his constituency, where the Trotskyites are doing a takeover.

I talked to Joe about this, and he mentioned that the *Guardian* had evidence of a link between de Chabris, the crook who ripped off the National Liberal Club, and Wilson's office.

In the afternoon I did a lot of telephoning about the European Brookings operation – to Dermot Nally in Dublin, Jacques Van Ypersele in Brussels and Giselle Hammers in Bonn. We are making a last big push next week to get the institute before our election.

Thursday 1 March 1979

Denis Healey told Cabinet that he would have to find cuts of £1 billion, partly from VAT and excise duties. Benn was the only one who spoke for higher direct income tax. The PM said this was not the year to clobber anybody. Really it was a decision for a 'soft' Budget – though they agreed to put out the word that it would be 'tough'.

I went to a meeting of special advisers, where Bob Worcester gave a presentation on the state of the opinion polls. It all looks bad! One interesting poll showed that 94% of *trade unionists* support the Thatcher policy of a compulsory ballot before a strike.

The EY(prices) Cabinet committee last night agreed to give the civil servants the whole of their pay claim – about 24% in two stages by next April. The PM at first rejected this, but the Chancellor complained that the PM should not overthrow Cabinet decisions: he should either chair them to get the decision he wants, or accept them. So the PM gave way. Once again the Civil Service gets privileged treatment.

The PM gave a lunch for the *Daily Mirror*. It was very good, with plenty of serious discussion. He told them that he would try to go through till October if he could. The PM talked about pay. He was very critical of Ennals and Shore for their handling of pay. They asked him for his assessment of President Jimmy Carter. He said that he is very good, face to face, in persuading people to accept his position, and learns quickly, but he is inexperienced and is dealing with too many things for the first time. This, the PM said, was a criticism of the American system, which catapults a man from Georgia into the White House. He tried to go over the heads of Congress to the state government – and this upset Congress. The PM had told him that he would have to work with Congress.

Afterwards the PM said he enjoyed it and asked us to fix another one soon. Terry Lancaster said, 'You can tell that an election is imminent – the PM wants to see the *Mirror*.'

Robin Butler came in from the Treasury for tea and we discussed public expenditure. He thought that the Treasury forecasters were being silly in refusing to take the Chancellor's orders to massage the forecasts: 'We are all prostitutes here; if they want to be pure they should go elsewhere.' Robin is still an immensely impressive administrator and ought to be made boss of the Treasury now.

Helen Liddell phoned from Glasgow. Obviously devolution has been a strange campaign – with no candidates, just arguments. She thinks it will be close, but we will win, though with only about 36% turnout. She ought to be made head of the Labour Party. It is the same as with the Treasury. There are able people, being held back because they are said to be too young. (Robin is 40 – what a criticism of this country.)

Came back home quite early.

Friday 2 March 1979

At the deputy secs meeting in John Hunt's room, Hunt revealed that last evening he had a meeting with the PM to discuss the machinery for pay negotiations now that the government is so deeply involved. After the disastrous performances of Ennals and Shore it was recognised that departmental ministers could not be left to do this job. So Hattersley is to be put in charge, and will sit alongside each departmental minister. Hunt told it as a great state secret and particularly asked me not to tell anybody in No. 10. In fact we have been discussing this for days in No. 10, and Ken Stowe put in a paper along these lines to the PM.

In the Unit we switched on the television and began to watch the devolution results. They were disastrous. At one time it looked as it the No's might win! In the end we scraped by with 33% to 31%. But it was a poor result, and nowhere near the minimum 40% required in the Act. As Tom McNally said, the Scots might have told us during the past five years that they did not really want devolution.

This puts the government in a terrible mess. Pressing ahead with devolution means asking our Party and others to vote to override the 40% clause. But if we don't, the Scot Nats will say they cannot support us on a confidence vote. And the Liberals say they won't anyway. We get more and more boxed in. The PM seems mainly concerned to try to survive till October. We are doing little else. If we fail in that, it will look very bad.

I wonder if he would now like to replay last autumn's 'non-election'?

The next ten days will be vital. There will be a confidence vote some time and, if we are beaten, that means an early election.

In the evening I took my Katie and Paul to *Carmen* at the Coliseum. A nice escape.

It is terrible that devolution has ended in this mess. We have worked at it for the whole five years, with the Scots always, in general, saying they wanted it. Most of us in London, including the PM, did not. The polls have shown 2–1 in favour of our middle-of-the-road proposals. So we have worked to convert many sceptics in our own Party, in the Cabinet and in Parliament. We have had to mollify the English regions. We have lost one bill and fought it through the House a second time. Then suddenly the Scots change their minds. And we are left holding the baby.

Actually I think it shows a terrible dependence and lack of confidence that the Scots and Welsh want to stick to Whitehall. I fear it is our subsidies and handouts to the Scots that have corrupted them. Now the government will have to decide what to do. Perhaps we should promise them another referendum in twelve months' time. But really we need a government in London with the authority of a new election mandate.

Monday 5 March 1979

This is the fifth anniversary since we came into office in No. 10 (it is misleading to say 'into power') in 1974. What hopes, what excitements, what boredoms and disappointments I have experienced. My main feelings now are of our impotence to move such a complex society in the right direction when the whole national personality is clearly deteriorating; and that this government is without motivation or impetus. But for the belief that it will do less badly in the autumn than now, it would not be trying so desperately to hang on.

There was definitely an air of crisis around the house. The PM stayed upstairs most of the time. I saw him at the tapes outside Private Office, but he didn't speak to anybody and looked pretty grumpy.

We had a Unit meeting to discuss the post-devolution situation. The general view was that we should play it long – take our time, perhaps fix a debate for two weeks' time, not having to table the parliamentary order to repeal the Devolution Act, and hold all-party talks to discuss the way forward. The further away we get from the referendum, the less embarrassing it will be. I talked to officials in Private Office and this was their view too, especially Philip Wood, who is the parliamentary expert and the shrewdest of the present team.

A ministerial meeting was planned for this evening to discuss what to do after devolution, and it is expected that they will take this 'long' line. But I wasn't here for it, as I flew to Brussels after tea.

Tuesday 6 March 1979

It was a lovely sunny day in Brussels, though I still find it a boring town. I went across to the commission building for the 10 o'clock start. We had a dreadful and desultory morning. The commission secretariat had failed to distribute papers. Discussion wandered all over the place. The Germans were garrulous and irrelevant. After a long lunch we rambled on again till 3.30 p.m., and then it all rambled again. Very disappointing. I could see the European Brookings going down the drain.

I don't like what I see of the EEC process. There is no sense of urgency. My doubts about the EEC increase!

Back in the evening, tired by travel and a noisy hotel. It was good to see the family again – the only place where people are happy and constructive and developing. Went to bed early and started to read Isherwood's *Mr Norris Changes Trains*, part of my interest in Berlin.

Wednesday 7 March 1979

The PM seemed tired and a bit grumpy. At one point he came into Private Office and, referring to David Ennals's latest statement (from his hospital bed), said to Tim Lankester: 'Phone Ennals's private secretary. Tell him to get on to the hospital and ask them to take the plaster off his leg and put it over his mouth.'

In the file of carbons was a minute from the PM to Ian Bancroft about the machinery for handling pay problems. It said the PM was dissatisfied with how departments were handling pay and was therefore appointing Roy Hattersley to sit in on all discussions. This is quite a rebuke for more senior ministers, such as Ennals and Shore already, and Peart and Benn, whose negotiations lie ahead. On machinery of government, the PM said he could not do anything *before* an election, but he would 'in due course wish to consider some fundamental changes involving not only the central departments of the Treasury and CSD but also the departments who might be concerned with the central direction of pay and prices policy'.

I went to lunch at Johnny's Café in Covent Garden and had my favourite meatballs. I also bought a Chopin record. I returned intending to go over to the Commons to hear the PM announce the new public sector pay Comparability Commission, but some people from the American Embassy came in to see me, so I did not go.

I came home early to dinner with David Steel and John Pardoe. Just us and Carol. We talked till after 1 o'clock. David had seen the PM last night in the Commons, but that had apparently not been very satisfactory. David complained that Ken Stowe had been there and he found this inhibiting. The main position, which they emphasised again and again, was that they did not want to go on until October. They would prefer an election now, before the Jeremy Thorpe trial starts in May. But the real problem for them is the European elections on 7 June. They will lose every seat and this will be demoralising. So the very latest time for them is 7 June. So they will be voting against us on confidence motions and on the Budget.

Interestingly, they told me that they ended the Lib–Lab pact only because they assumed an election last autumn and the PM never guided them otherwise. If he had told them that he was going on till 1979, they would have continued the Lib–Lab pact!

They talked a lot about their previous leader Jeremy Thorpe. They had known nothing of his homosexuality until the case blew up.

It was an interesting relationship between Pardoe and Steel, the former attractively ebullient and imaginative and always exaggerating (with just a touch of Reggie Maudling about his love of the good life); and the latter, a true son of the Scottish kirk, prim and boyish, easily embarrassed, cautious in his statements, a bit short on political imagination, but sensible and realistic in all his attitudes, and clearly an attractive and deeply honourable man. It is sad that such people get lost in the pathetic Liberal Party and do not get near to power. They have so much more to give than so many of our clapped-out middle-rank ministers.

It was very successful as an evening, relaxed and amusing, but with a continuing thread of serious political exploration.

Incidentally, earlier today Harry Evans phoned me to say that there was a possibility of a compromise settlement at *The Times*. Employment minister Albert Booth has worked out a formula which is acceptable to management. Everything would depend on the unions' reaction. The problem is that Tony Benn has agreed to address a mass meeting of *Times* workers tomorrow. He had not informed Booth or consulted the PM. And so far Benn has been working *against* a settlement, aiming to get *The Times* nationalised. So I told the PM and he started putting the squeeze on Benn, instructing him not to attend *The Times* meeting.

Thursday 8 March 1979

Cabinet spent most of its time discussing the consequences of devolution. There was little disagreement with the PM's line of delaying for at least another week and trying to negotiate a compromise. It was agreed that there was little hope of getting a majority to push devolution through. Towards the end the PM asked John Hunt and the officials to leave while ministers discussed the election strategy. According to John Smith later, they did not have much to say and the mood was very subdued.

I spent the morning in talks with the Unit. Then had lunch at No. 10. Little emerged.

The PM was in better mood at PQ briefing. He said, 'It is time to go on the counter-attack.' And he was very forceful in replies and helped lift the morale of our people. Even so I can sense that most of his staff believe that he cannot now win and that last September's decision not to hold an election was a grave error.

Joe Haines phoned me with fresh news on the curious 'Defence minister's scandal'. The blonde lady involved has allegedly fled the country to Los Angeles. I have learned that there is a large security file on her, as she has led a 'full' life, consorting with lots of MPs and some East Europeans. (But she is not believed to be a security risk, Private Office told me, just a good-time girl and a gossip.) The press still think they have a Profumo scandal here, but it seems they may be exaggerating.

I went over to the Commons again in the late afternoon for a meeting with John Smith. He is a bit depressed by the devolution result and admits that we made a mistake in fighting the devolution campaign as a party battle. That meant that devolution suffered from Labour's unpopularity. On reflection, it would have been better to form an umbrella 'all party' organisation.

Friday 9 March 1979

Went in to John Hunt's weekly meeting of the Cabinet Office deputy secretaries. Not much came up, except concern over British shipbuilders, who are apparently bankrupt. Also learned a Treasury messenger this week was taking the top secret Budget papers in a briefcase to the Bank of England by Underground. She left the case on the Tube! Fortunately it was put into lost property and recovered unopened.

Had lunch with Michael Cudlipp, who is now with Thomson and involved in the negotiations to restart *The Times*. The unions have not agreed any changes yet to improve productivity. They have just agreed to resume talks.

Home very tired. I wish there was more purpose to the government, so that one could end the week feeling that a job of work had been done.

Monday 12 March 1979

The PM was in Paris today for the EEC heads of government meeting – mainly attacking the EEC budget and the Agricultural Policy.

I stayed at home in the morning and wrote my talk in the evening to the LSE Government department, which went quite well.

Tuesday 13 March 1979

Spent the morning reading papers, telephoning and making arrangements for my various overseas visits that lie ahead. Lunch in the Cabinet Office canteen with Gavyn and David Lipsey. We planned a brief on changing the tax law to allow unit trusts to buy gilt-edged stocks. I have been pushing this at the Treasury for years.

Saw the PM, back from Paris. He said, 'It went much better than I expected.'

The PM saw the Scot Nats leader Donald Stewart, at the latter's request, about devolution. The Scot Nats are threatening a motion of censure if we do not move to implement devolution. The Liberals and Tories will support them. This is the first crunch and will depend on Enoch Powell and the Ulster Unionists. But it won't come till just before the Budget at the beginning of April, so it would not mean an election till May even if we lost.

Graham Greene came in at 6 o'clock, and we discussed my job possibilities for the future. Afterwards I went with Carol to dinner with George Massion, the admirable economic attaché at the German Embassy. Donald MacDougal the Oxford economist was there and he thinks it is disastrous that sterling has risen 15% in the last few months.

Home at midnight. Feel rather depressed about work. There is nothing constructive to do. We help Private Office on bits and bobs of briefing. But there is no real policy development. The PM cannot go on like this for six more months. We all want less 'government', but this is just a vacuum.

Wednesday 14 March 1979

The PM saw the Chancellor this morning before the EY Cabinet committee. Healey took him through his plans for the Budget – basically VAT, excise duties and tax allowances up substantially to pay for reduced income tax. This makes sense. Unfortunately it means that indirect taxes and prices will go up immediately, but the tax reliefs on pay will not come through till the summer. And if the election comes early, it will be held after the Budget prices pain but before the pleasure of lower income tax.

At EY it was clear that the PM's mind was not on the agenda (Tim Lankester said the same was true of his meeting with the Chancellor). Really he was thinking about the election, following his meeting with Donald Stewart of the Scot Nats last night. We do know now that both the Liberals and the Scot Nats will certainly vote against us.

The main item at EY was nuclear policy. Tony Benn had done absolutely nothing about the instruction from EY four months ago that he should make progress on management changes in the industry. He had done nothing about restructuring either, nor about fast-breeder reactors. In fact Benn has done nothing in his department for a year and rarely goes in there. He spends all his time on Party activities. So we do not have an energy policy at all. The PM told him off quite sternly, like talking to a naughty boy. The PM then said he wanted to talk politics and he asked officials to leave. So out I went with John Hunt.

I took Bill Rodgers to lunch at the Reform. He told me that at EY the PM had said that he was fed up with living from week to week, with his authority slipping away, so he no longer wanted to aim for October. He anticipated a May election! Either we would be beaten on a confidence vote at the beginning of April and be forced into a May election, or we would win and might choose to go then anyway, possibly to coincide with the local elections.

We had a Policy Unit meeting to discuss policy themes that the PM might pursue to give him some kind of policy platform. Some of this will be used for election speeches too. David Lipsey said that he does not think that the PM has given much thought to election planning since last September. The election 'team' has remained in existence, but the PM has had little contact with them.

The PM saw Tony Benn this afternoon about the activities of his special adviser, Frances Morrell. She has been openly organising political groups that attack the government. So the PM is going to say desist or be sacked.

I put in a brief on nurses' pay and then went to Tom McNally's room and had a drink with him and Tom McCaffrey. The PM had told them of his plans for a May election and said that he was 'fed up with waking up every morning feeling that he had no authority'. They were both a bit low and critical of the PM, especially for being completely in the hands of the Civil Service. Tom McNally said it was interesting how Heath had been run by the head of the Civil Service (William Armstrong), Wilson by the Cabinet secretary (Hunt) and Callaghan by his private secretary (Stowe). The offices varied, but the control was the same. Both Toms said that he rarely discussed his intentions with them. It is curious. Jim is incredibly close, and the more difficult a situation gets, the less he talks about it, the more he retreats into his isolation upstairs.

Joe told me of further developments in the Defence Ministry scandal. It has emerged that the blonde lady was once engaged to an arms dealer with three passports considered a security risk by the Ministry of Defence. It has added to Fleet Street interest in her and her alleged relations with a junior minister.

Came home at 9 o'clock and joined in Katie's 12th birthday supper party. Then she sat on my lap for an hour in front of the fire while we listened to her records.

Thursday 15 March 1979

Cabinet dealt at length with our electoral outlook after devolution. On the problem of nurses' pay Cabinet decided to pay them £2.50 in advance of comparability, which will set a new target for other unions to go for.

I had lunch with Shirley Williams at an Italian restaurant in Pimlico which she seemed to know very well. We had a nice gossip. She was also complaining bitterly about the situation on civil servants' pay. They had been offered rises of up to 49%! To be paid over the next twelve months. Shirley said this would make it much harder to screw down the teachers. It would also mean that her assistant secretaries are paid more than she is.

Back for Question Time. The PM was in an aggressive mood and in fact did well. Mrs Thatcher was very subdued, waiting for her chance to make a decisive killing.

I went off to a lively (and premature) St Patrick's Day reception at the Irish Embassy and then home to give a late dinner to some friends from Berlin.

Before going I heard about the PM's meeting with David Steel. David is going to give a big speech in Scotland this weekend and will say he sees no prospect of moving forward to devolution in the present parliamentary situation and supports all-party talks. This suits us, as that is how we see the situation.

I took the Berliners home to their hotel after midnight.

Friday 16 March 1979

At deputy secs meeting heard a fascinating discussion about Civil Service pay (up to assistant secretaries like me). They were considering how to manoeuvre the decision on their increase through Cabinet next week. They felt it would be better if ministers did not know the actual figures – up to 49.6%. So the papers for Cabinet would not quote the figures. They decided instead to have a short 'fact sheet', which would set out how there were 'more low paid in the Civil Service than in local government'. However, they said that they 'could not trust the Prime Minister to circulate this paper', as he was 'prejudiced against them' on this issue. So they would give the paper to Peart and tell him to circulate it at Cabinet itself, without warning. A lot of Civil Service time, experience and skill was being devoted to handling their own salaries. As always, they are very impressive on this.

I said nothing, and only spoke at the end to suggest that perhaps a Cabinet committee should consider Ireland. A lot is happening there, with fresh scandals about police violence against prisoners. Yet the government has not considered Ireland at all in 1979! John Hunt took the point and will try to arrange something.

We worked on a Unit paper in the afternoon – on public service pay, which is going through the roof – and then I went to another St Patrick's Eve party at the Irish Export Board. Home late and carrying a lot of Irish whiskey!

Monday 19 March 1979

The PM had come up last night from Chequers, which was virtually cut off by snow. The weather has been appalling again, very cold, whole areas of the North are cut off, with drifts up to twenty feet.

I had a unit meeting on our planned input for the election.

Then to lunch at the Gay Hussar with Joe. He told me that David Seligman, who is a close friend of the PM from Cardiff, told him that last summer the PM told his constituency agent to print his election literature for an October election. He is convinced that the PM changed his mind and backed off from an election at the last minute.

A Cabinet committee to discuss devolution decided the PM would make a statement on Thursday announcing all-party talks. The intention is to try to delay a debate on devolution until after Easter – and it may never take place. But the vote of confidence is still expected next week.

In the evening I went to the Commonwealth parliamentary reception upstairs in the state rooms. The general view was that we should go on as long as possible, through a crude deal with the Ulster Unionists if need be. Enoch Powell has stated his demands for a return to local rule in Ulster and this afternoon was letting the press know that he had a deal. In fact no deal has yet been done. Michael Foot has talked to him. And this morning Roy Mason came through to No. 10 for permission to talk to Powell and Harry West (the Protestant leader in Belfast who has flown to London). But Ken Stowe told me that the PM vetoed this. Apparently the PM is feeling pretty annoyed at accusations of being a 'wheeler-dealer'.

Even so, it looks as if it will all depend on the Ulster Unionists. The question is: can we rely on Enoch and his friends to support us anyway without concessions? I do not want us to do bad things in Ulster just to buy a few more weeks of staggering on here.

I did not feel like too much drink and company. I was at the Professional Footballers dinner till after 1 a.m. last night, sitting at dinner next to my old footballing hero, Tom Finney, and then having drinks later with Joe Mercer and Denis Howell. So I went home early and to bed to read Isherwood.

Tuesday 20 March 1979

Work is at a near halt in Downing Street. The only papers coming through are on industrial democracy (where Booth is still pushing for a single trade union channel, but Shirley Williams is resisting), open government and a smattering of pay policy papers. In Private Office the secretaries sit there, with their feet on the desks, reading magazines. Ken Stowe said that most people seemed to be assuming there would be a change of government.

There seems to be no follow-up to the TUC concordat. It is hard to discover what is going on about the 'joint economic assessment' between the TUC and the government.

The PM sat upstairs all morning 'thinking about the election'. He had Denis Healey in at 11.15 to discuss a 'standstill' Budget in case an election is *announced* before the Budget, but to be held after. Then it is needed to have authority to raise revenue after 5 April.

We are all expecting a vote of censure next week. But curiously there has been no word of this through 'the usual channels'. Presumably the Tories are waiting to be absolutely certain of the result – which means waiting to be certain how the Ulster Unionists will vote – before they commit themselves. They do not want to lose. They know they only have to wait and the prize will eventually fall in their lap. Our information is not very clear, but it looks as if we could lose by about three votes.

Question Time briefing was as usual these days fairly subdued. A very flat atmosphere. The PM goes through the preparation process very thoroughly, but there is a lack of excitement or hunger for victory. It is as if this administration is just petering out, not with a bang but with a whimper. There is a sense, in fact, that the government has already ended. We are just going through the final motions.

Ralf Dahrendorf came in to talk about our futures. He is almost certainly going to go back to Germany to direct the Max Planck Institute in Munich. He has done six years as director at the LSE and does not think there is much else he can do there. He begged me not to go into the City but to stay in 'public' life. He said that he would recommend me for the Open University as vice chancellor.

I stayed late to clear papers and then drove home. Things are drawing in. The walls of the boxes get closer. It is hard to see a way through. If the Unit could, would anybody be interested?

Wednesday 21 March 1979

I did not bother to go to EY at 9.30. which was on energy and the consequences of the crisis in Iran. Instead I worked in the office, clearing all my papers.

Had lunch with Alan Otten of the *Wall Street Journal* at the Gay Hussar – which is now a very friendly Labour club: Joe was there, and lovely, just-married Tessa Jowell, and Michael Foot's special adviser Elizabeth (who told me that Foot prefers 3 May as an election date, to coincide with the local elections) and Percy Clarke from Transport House, etc. Back to a Cabinet Office meeting on the European Brookings briefing for my Friday visit to Brussels.

Coming back from the Cabinet Office, I found Gavyn in a high temper. He had asked Private Office for the papers for tomorrow's Cabinet on civil servants' and teachers' pay. He was refused. They said that the papers were not being distributed. Gavyn had blown up, pointing out that we saw Budget papers, exchange rate papers, interest rate papers, the most sensitive and dangerous. But the line was drawn at civil servants' pay. He asked who was supposed to brief the PM and other ministers on civil servants' pay. They were quite honest – only civil servants with a self-interest could do this.

After a long row they finally handed over the papers. Inevitably these contained very little. They did not even contain any financial numbers of the proposed civil servants' increases (in fact ranging to over 45% and averaging 26%). There was no mention of counter-inflation. And the enormous cost of the Civil Service settlement – £550 million – which is 2p on income tax, is only referred to in the footnote to an annex to Roy Hattersley's paper. The CSD paper is wholly devoted to the justice of the Civil Service claim.

Gavyn Davies and I started to prepare a paper. Ken Stowe came up to see us looking very jumpy and asking if we were going to brief. I said yes. He said that it would have to be quick, because he was putting these papers in to the PM early and in a sealed envelope. He then said that we might like to think carefully before taking on the Civil Service. He said that the Civil Service Department had realised that under the Health and Safety at Work Act the temperature in offices had to be maintained at a certain level. If we did not give the civil servants their pay, they would pull out the boilermen, switch off the central heating and 'government will come to a halt'. I refused to be terrified at this prospect and replied, 'Well, government is doing bugger all anyway, so it won't make any difference.' He left looking worried.

Then Derek Scott, the Chancellor's special adviser, arrived. He had been refused the papers by the Treasury Private Office. He said, 'I am a simple, trusting man and have never believed in conspiracies, but now I begin to wonder.'

Gavyn and I wrote our quick brief and included a cross section of advertisements from this morning's papers, which show that senior electrical engineering managers in industry earn less than young No. 10 duty clerks and managing directors of large export companies earn less than Whitehall assistant secretaries.

When I went down to hand over the brief in Private Office, I saw the PM at the tapes. I mentioned Civil Service pay to him. He said he would read our brief. But he was not encouraging. 'How do you take these people on, Bernard?' he asked. 'It is very difficult to beat them,' he added. This is sadly only too true. But I was struck by the PM's lack of fight. It seemed that all the drive had disappeared from him.

I went to discuss it with Tom McNally, but he did not seem to have any time. Interestingly, he has arranged for his election address to be printed. There really does not seem any point in going on.

I went to a meeting in Regent's Park with Claus Moser and others on the way home. A local music group, the Divertimenti, is trying to build itself up into a string orchestra and we are forming an advisory council to help them. My spirits lift at this. Music is a very attractive alternative to politics. So I went home to play some Mahler on my great turntable.

Thursday 22 March 1979

I lobbied quite a few ministers before Cabinet about civil servants' and teachers' pay. But it is clearly too late. The commitments have been made. The main point is that ministers are thinking of other things.

Afterwards it was difficult to discover what had happened: people were being very tight. But one civil servant from the Cabinet Office was grinning and gloating about it being 'all right'. I told him sharply that it would not be all right in twelve months' time when the second staging of these public service awards became due – inflation next year is now bound to be worse than this. At lunch Stowe and Tim Lankester were very cagey. Tom McCaffrey had been told nothing. I remarked that it was unthinkable under Wilson that the press secretary to the PM would not be told about a major item on the Cabinet agenda.

The PM saw David Steel last night and David told him that it was not certain that all the Liberals will vote against us. He said that not all of them feel the same about devolution. Ken Stowe also hinted to me that there may be an attempt to win over Liberal Cyril Smith with a peerage. 'We will have a word with Cyril's mum,' he said. Presumably they won't, as under Wilson and Thorpe, have to pay for it.

Cabinet was mainly concerned with the PM's statement to the Commons today on devolution. The main argument was about whether to include a commitment to have a Commons debate by a particular early date. Our whips have told us that, *without* that, the Scot Nats will not support us. The PM resisted this in Cabinet. He does not wish to give promises in return for votes. He keeps mumbling about 1969 and accusations that he then 'gerrymandered' by delaying the redistribution of seats. He says he is fed up with being accused of wheeling and dealing. Cabinet amended the statement so that it gave a commitment to an urgent Commons debate and vote. But the PM phoned Philip Wood during lunch, when we were upstairs in the small dining room, and said that he did not want the commitment in, so out came the reference to an early debate and we lost the Scot Nat support.

At this news, people round the table looked downcast. McCaffrey said, 'Those whose jobs depend on the PM should start to pack their bags.' I replied, looking around the table at the civil servants, 'Why use the plural? "Those" are just me.'

We went over to Questions and the PM was in a tense mood. He soon had a row with Roger Stott about offering the Scot Nats their date. The PM got very angry and said he was near the end of his tether. He had had enough of wheeler-dealing. He still remembered 1969. He had compromised in many areas to achieve majorities for the government. He had done many things he did not believe in. Now he had had enough. And if there was an election, so be it.

Nobody was brave enough to speak up in support of Stott, who was right politically. Jim's team have had no opportunity to discuss with him the pros and cons of including a firm commitment on a date in his statement. And there has been no collective discussion with him of his television script. I saw this before lunch. McCaffrey and a private secretary had done some paragraphs and the PM had revised it several times. It was terrible! Very technical! Full of sentences about 'laying orders', etc. The British public understand what it was all about. It should have started by stating simply that he was 'going to explain why he was going to hold all-party talks about the future of Scotland'. But ordinary listeners won't have guessed that. And it gives Mrs Thatcher a marvellous opportunity tomorrow night to make a wide-ranging statement on TV, effectively launching her election campaign.

Yet there has been no obvious channel to feed in these points. Harold Wilson would have held a meeting in the study. That never happens now. It is all handled by a single civil servant. If it is Philip Wood, it is OK, because he is very skilful. Otherwise it is bound to be sensible but lacking in politics.

Question Time went off OK, with the House in a frivolous mood. The Tories are jubilant and clearly expecting to be in government soon. The real drama was reserved for the PM's statement. It was quickly clear that it was not enough for the Scots. Before he had finished, the Scot Nats were shaking their heads and waving their order papers dismissively.

Thatcher responded curiously passively. She made some criticisms, but did not say anything about a motion of censure. Clearly the Tories are uncertain what to do. They don't want to lose, so they are waiting to see how the minority parties will vote.

I went back to the PM's room in the House, where Walter Harrison, the deputy whip, arrived with a copy of the motion of censure signed by the Scot Nats. Walter was clearly unhappy, saying that it could have been avoided if we had offered them a date for the debate. The PM returned and sat slumped in his chair. He argued that the vote of censure would have happened anyway. He arranged for Ken Stowe to send off letters to the other parties calling for talks on devolution. He did not seem too depressed, though a bit edgy. He said to Tom McCaffrey that he hoped that Tom's idea of a TV broadcast proved right. I have my doubts, as the script is so awful! We all left him in his room to rest and have a last look at his script before doing his recording.

I went back to No. 10 and rushed through my remaining work before setting off for London Airport and Brussels. I listened on the car radio to the PM's statement. It was as bad as I feared, technical and incomprehensible to the average voter. But there was some good news – the Welsh Nats have implied that they may vote for us in return for the bill giving compensation for Welsh sufferers from pneumoconiosis. That will help. But with the Liberals, Scot Nats and Ulstermen against us, it won't be enough.

I found the entire first class of the aircraft to Brussels full of civil servants (including me!). We all went out for a drink later, and I had a row with them about Civil Service pay. It depresses me so much that we are paying our public service more than manufacturing industry. That is a formula for national bankruptcy. However, I successfully lobbied the key Treasury official on making it tax effective for unit trusts to invest in gilt-edged stock, helping us to sell more without raising interest rates.

Friday 23 March 1979

I was in Brussels all day negotiating about the European Brookings. We made much more progress than last time. But time is running out. The European Parliament will soon rise for elections. I won't be here. It will all string out and may run into the sand.

I flew back in the evening, and my driver home told me that the news had reported that Powell and the Ulster Unionists (except perhaps for Carson) would vote against us in the confidence vote. If so, we are sunk. The news was full of Thatcher's TV broadcast, which was clearly very effective. We have given her a party political free.

At London Airport I saw Douglas Hurd and we had a friendly chat. He said that he is a strong supporter of having a Policy Unit. His impression is that Thatcher will merge the Policy Unit and the CPRS. Well, that should be interesting.

The papers are full of election fever. I feel completely detached. I really do believe that our side has run out of steam. The PM has lost his drive. He is doing nothing to win back the initiative. If he had done a reshuffle, at least ministers would be buzzing around making a mark in their new departments. He should have dropped Ennals, Shore and Varley, promoting Smith, Rodgers and Howell. But nothing is happening. No policy ideas.

No meetings to try to examine how to restart our political momentum. I get the feeling that most ministers have already conceded defeat. They may be wrong of course – once the election begins, the adrenaline will start flowing and we should be able to exploit our advantages in having superior people, from the top down. But probably not.

Monday 26 March 1979

The political atmosphere was electric today. All the conversation, every newspaper, is full of discussion about this week's big confidence vote. The arithmetic shows us losing by two or three. The Prime Minister has – possibly wrongly in my view – forbidden his ministers and whips from doing any wheeler-dealing to gain those key couple of votes. (And Mrs Smith is apparently not interested in her son becoming Lord Cyril!) So at the moment it looks like being the first time a government has been thrown out in Parliament for over fifty years (since 1924). That means an election, starting with a big defeat, which would be bad psychologically.

The PM had his 'party political' office team – McNally, Roger Carroll from the *Sun* and Lipsey – at Chequers yesterday, working on the election manifesto and on Wednesday's speech. I am happy to be considered 'policy' not 'political' and worked in the office in the morning and went to lunch in the City, where the assumption was that the Tories were about to come in.

The PM had lunch at the Commons. Ken Stowe said that meant that Michael Foot would 'bend his ear to do some deals for Wednesday'. This is quite ironical. Foot has been doing the crudest deals – and is keen to do more. The PM finds this distasteful. Yet Michael's reputation remains that of the unworldly man of pure socialist principle and the PM's is that of the typical Tammany Hall wheeler-dealer. Tom McNally told me that the PM was complaining about this at the weekend. He is clearly very upset about this reputation as a 'fixer' – and especially references to the 1969 gerrymandering of boundaries. Personally I think this vote needs fixing.

Sam Beer, the famous American professor of political science, came in to see me for tea, to discuss changes in our political system. Many conventions and constitutional traditions have changed in the past five years of minority government, which has put Parliament back at the centre of the system.

Tuesday 27 March 1979

The PM stayed upstairs all morning working on his speech. Tom McNally did a first draft, but this seems to have been dropped. The PM has taken the draft of Healey's proposed Budget speech as the basis for the economic first half of his speech. And he has asked Philip Wood and Nick Sanders from Private Office to write the other 'political' half. Of course the PM does an enormous amount of work on it himself. Even so it is odd that he leaves the most important political speech of his life to two civil servant assistant secretaries. It reflects the grip the machine now has on him.

Had lunch in No. 10. Nobody seemed to know anything new. Ken Stowe said he still felt that we could win if the whips were really to try, but that the PM was still forbidding any such activity. He has told Roy Mason not to negotiate with the Ulster Unionists. The general atmosphere was still one of resigned defeat. There was much talk of what the Tories would do if they came in to No. 10. Ken Stowe said that the Tories had been in regular touch with him through John Stanley MP, who phones Ken on first-name terms to discuss procedures for the Tories to take over. The civil servants have to co-operate in all this, quite properly, but it must affect how they view the present administration. They must begin to write us off mentally.

At briefing for PQs the PM said, 'The funny thing is that we are going to win the election: we will surprise everybody.' Maybe.

In Questions he lost his temper over the question of the bill to help the Welsh quarry workers who suffer from lung disease. Everybody is denouncing this as a bribe. But in fact it was in the Queen's Speech, was progressing anyway, and Jim has long supported it passionately. It came to ministers in January, when ministers approved it, but decided to add some other groups – iron ore workers, etc. The trashy press know this but refuse to publish it, instead insisting that the bill was produced only to bribe the Welsh Nationalists. The PM lashed into the newspapers for this. It won't make any difference. They are not in the truth business.

After Questions the PM came back to his room and we all chatted a bit about the iniquities of the press – which the PM now hates as passionately as Wilson ever did. Then he sent for the chief whip to get the latest reports.

We sat in the outer office – Tom McNally, Tom McCaffrey, Roger Stott and myself. After about ten minutes Michael Cocks the chief whip left, looking glum, and the PM came out and sat with us, first shutting the door. He said, 'Well, we are still set to lose.' He then began to talk about the coming election, clearly looking forward to it. He said, 'I am going to enjoy myself. Once the adrenaline starts flowing it will be fine. I think we will win. We should all believe we are going to win. Then we will wake up on the morning after and then we will find out.' Tom McNally asked him straight to his face, 'Are you sure you really want to win?' The PM said yes, but I thought it was a good and brave question. Tom then began to tease the PM about his unwillingness to do any deals in order to get an extra couple of votes for tomorrow. The PM bridled and said he was just not going to do it – he admitted it was 'personal priggishness on my part'.

Both Toms and I began to pile into him. Without any prior planning, and in quite different styles, with different arguments, we told the PM that he was wrong. Because it is very important for the government to win the division tomorrow. If we do not, several bad consequences will follow: the Labour Party will be demoralised; the general public will see the government as finished; the Tories will have rising morale and Mrs Thatcher will look more and more a winner; and our voters probably won't turn out in the Edge Hill by-election on Thursday, so the cycle of demoralisation will continue. Alternatively if we win on Thursday, our troops will be uplifted. Then we may win the by-election and go into the election on a rising tide. All this assumed that we would have an election almost immediately, whatever the result.

I said that it was worth two dukedoms for the Liberals if we could win. The PM sharply rejected this. I said that I understood his personal feelings of distaste, but the majority of our people in the country expected politicians to try to win – and 'there is no substitute for winning'. I said that the government's past record was a winner. But the problem was whether we could persuade people that we had enough to do in the *future*. He later referred back to this and agreed: 'That is the problem – how to persuade them to give us another five years on the basis of our future programme.' He asked me what policies would achieve that. I replied that a convincing incomes policy and guarantees for the long-term unemployed would make the start of a platform, but we needed more than that.

We came back to tomorrow's vote and again made our point about the importance of winning. When we broke up he had not conceded anything, but I sensed that the point had gone home. Later on, back at No. 10, I learned that the PM had telephoned the chief whip and said, 'I want those two votes.' So we did have an effect.

My old Oxford friend John Hale, chairman of the National Gallery, came in to see me about appointing new trustees. He was thinking of John Hunt and former ambassador Nicholas Henderson. I supported them both.

I went upstairs at 7 o'clock to the state reception rooms, where there was a surprise 67th birthday party for the PM. Audrey had organised it, with Roger Stott. Present were his personal team plus his son Michael Callaghan and his wife, Monty his doctor, Merlyn Rees, John Cunningham, Roland Moyle (his PPSs), plus wives. While we were drinking, we heard that the PM had received a message from the chief whip that we 'would win'. Apparently Roy Hattersley had told Gerry Fitt that he, not Roy Mason, would be Northern Ireland secretary after the election, and this had swung Fitt to our side.

But our MP Broughton is very ill and may not be able to get there. So it still looks very close and may end in a tie, with the Speaker's vote keeping the government in. My instinctive feeling is that we will win by one.

We adjourned for dinner in the small dining room. It was a very relaxed and cheerful occasion, with plenty of drink and laughter. I sat between Shelagh Moyle, who is very attractive, and Colleen Rees, who is one of my favourite ladies, quite a lovely person. Curiously both of them are of Irish/Welsh mix, from Irish families married to Welshmen. And the PM has a kind of Irish/Welsh mix. McNally is of Irish descent, with Catholic parents, and McCaffrey is presumably a Scots Celt, though with little of the humour and flair. The PM is surrounded by Celts, although he is not really a Celt in style or temperament.

I had a long talk with Tom McCaffrey afterwards. He was quite critical of the way the PM runs things. He said that if we won the election, he would only come back on quite different terms – more access to papers, a car home, etc. In fact I won't come back on any terms.

I got home, by taxi, at 11.45. Am looking forward to tomorrow's big vote with great interest and anticipation.

Wednesday 28 March 1979

Day of the big confidence vote. The PM did not go to the appalling Party National Executive. I had a Unit meeting, preparing a summary of our policy in each particular area. We hope this will be of use to the PM in the election campaign.

I went out to lunch at L'Escargot (now a shabby restaurant on the way down) with Johnny Campbell from the Irish Embassy. I found it hard to concentrate on anything except tonight's big vote. We discussed the role of the Irish in this – because Fitt and Maguire will be crucial tonight. It is an irony that our fate should be decided by the Irish – those two from the Catholic side and any from the Unionist side. The basic position is that Roy Mason's policies have been completely pro-Unionist. This has alienated Catholic Fitt and Maguire. But tonight we won't have the Unionists either. So we pay the price for Mason's policy without getting any return for it. Campbell said that the Dublin government were very nervous about a Conservative government.

Back at No. 10 we waited for the PM to come downstairs. He was sleeping after lunch and before going across for the speeches. Members of staff from all parts of the house gathered to give him a cheering send-off. Outside were hordes of television cameramen. We all streamed into our cars and zoomed off to the House.

Reports from the Whips Office at this stage were not discouraging.

We were hopeful of getting McCusker from the Unionists – most people still assumed that Fitt and Maguire would be with us. The sums showed us around even. That was OK, as the Speaker would have to cast his vote for the government.

We all went in to the box at just after 3.30 p.m. The House was absolutely packed. The Tories looked surprisingly glum as Thatcher made her speech. Our side had been told not to interrupt her since on previous occasions silly interruptions had given her the chance to score points and raised her side's spirits. The silence was effective and clearly unnerved her. She made a bad, flat speech and sat down to a disappointed reception from her side.

The PM was quite superb. He had some flat bits in the middle when he was listing the government's achievements – this was a rehearsal for the election campaign. But the beginning and the end were excellent and he was given a standing ovation that went on so long that the Speaker had to intervene. He sat in the chamber afterwards and listened to some other speeches. So did I. During a speech by Joan Lestor the PM was passed a letter from Mike Noble, one of the whips. His face dropped. I knew it was bad news. He rose and left the chamber with Roger Stott. I followed from the box. As we walked down the corridor, the PM said, 'They cannot get Doc Broughton here. He is too ill. We will lose. Please go and get Audrey. She should know this as soon as possible.' (Would Wilson have thought of Mary at such a time?)

I said to him that he had made an excellent speech. He said, 'I'm sorry, but speeches don't make any difference. We won't get the votes and that's what matters.'

Audrey arrived and then they went back to No. 10. The large crowd of officials slowly drifted away. I went for a walk around the Commons, which was very dead because the catering staff had gone on strike and all the bars and tea rooms had closed.

I went back to No. 10 to make some phone calls and I dropped in upstairs on the farewell party for Doris Knight, a nice lady from the Press Office, who had worked there ever since Clem Attlee's days. I then nipped off to a party of the Publishers Association at the Fishmongers Hall. When I returned Tom McCaffrey told me that the situation on the vote was 'either evens or down by one'.

While I was in Private Office the PM came in and again said, 'We will lose tonight.' He then went back to the Commons for the winding-up speeches. I called in at St Stephen's Tavern to have a drink with Joe Haines, and then we went to the Commons and sat in the box for Michael Foot's winding-up speech, which was marvellous, all of his rhetoric and humour. The Tories looked down and seemed to expect to lose. One of them who is a friend signalled to me with a thumbs-down.

The count seemed to take an age. Members filed back into the chamber and reported news of the voting. Private Office's final estimate was that we would either draw or win by one. They seemed to assume that Liberal Clement Freud would not vote, because of his desire to get through his own Freedom of Information Private Member's Bill. I was not so sure. It was reported back that McCusker had voted for us. Spirits rose. But then we saw that both Fitt and Maguire had abstained. So nobody knew any more.

The Tory chief whip walked in and reported what was presumably the Tory total to Thatcher and Whitelaw. Then looked disappointed, even angry. Then our teller came in waving his paper gleefully. Our side began to cheer. But when the tellers all came in, it was clear from the grins on the Tory faces and the gloom on ours that we had lost – by one vote. (Our chief teller had thought we would win when he saw their total of 311. He thought we had 312, but had forgotten to subtract the two tellers!)

The Tories leapt to their feet and cheered. Our side looked stunned.

So many ifs! If only we did not have two pending by-elections – at Edge Hill and Derbyshire. If only Broughton was not too ill to come in. If only Roy Mason had not completely alienated Fitt. But it was too late for ifs.

The PM made a brief response, saying he would announce the decision about dissolution, etc. tomorrow. Then he left the chamber, with our Tribunites singing the 'Red Flag'. He went back to his room, sent for Rees, Healey, Foot and the chief whip. The rest of us stood around outside, a gang of sad-faced advisers and officials. The triumphant Tories walked down the corridor outside to a Shadow Cabinet meeting.

Audrey Callaghan arrived with Merlyn Rees. The PM asked Audrey to go in. They were discussing their plans – and election dates. Roger Stott told me it would be 3 May. No other date was treated seriously. There was a ceaseless coming and going. Then at about 11.15 the PM went back to No. 10 and everybody else drifted off.

I went upstairs to the ministerial corridor. I saw Stan Orme, who told me that he had done everything to get Fitt and Maguire into the lobbies, but nothing would move them. Maguire's wife had come with him – along with two sinister Republican 'heavies' – and they forbade him to vote. Stan said Maguire was nearly in tears.

I went into John Smith's room for a quick drink and then into Roy Hattersley's, where Mike Noble, lovely Ann Taylor, David Hill and a few others were drinking. They told me how McClusker had been in that room for the previous twenty-four hours while they guaranteed him a Price Commission Inquiry into prices in Northern Ireland. This is what secured his vote.

We all drifted down to the Whips Office, where a very subdued party was taking place. The whips clearly felt they had failed in some way. They started attacking me – basically because the PM had forbidden them to work to get the necessary votes until yesterday, which was too late. They had got the two Ulster Unionists, but had time for nothing else. The chief whip Cocks told me that he could have persuaded the Tory Glyn to abstain for the price of a peerage. He complained about John Silkin as chief whip under Wilson giving away the 'patronage money' to No. 10 in 1966, which meant that the whips had no way to buy votes any more.

Deputy chief whip Walter Harrison, who is a marvellous man, gave us a long explanation of why they had decided not to bring in Broughton in an ambulance and get him nodded through. It was a bit emotional. Later some other junior whips – Ann Taylor and Jim Marshall – said this had been a big mistake. Broughton was willing to come. But they left the organisation of the ambulance till too late. And that was the crucial vote.

It became a very unsatisfactory party and Peter Snape became quite aggressive with me. Slowly people left. I should have done, but in fact stayed till the end, drinking more and more whisky, but getting more and more sober. And deeply angry that we had lost. It was unnecessary, a self-inflicted wound. The PM was too priggish about doing deals for votes. The whips squeamish about bringing in Broughton to vote. The alienation of Irish *socialist* votes, Fitt and Maguire, was crazy. The recent deaths of our MPs Tom Swain and Sidney Irving were bad luck. It could have been different. But now we have another election campaign – my third – and then all of this will come to an end.

I got home at 3.30 a.m. and was woken at 6.45 by the alarm to start writing this. Tonight I go to Paris to a conference. A strange time to be going away perhaps, but really this is an interlude between two battles – the one we have lost in Parliament and the one that starts next week in the country.

Thursday 29 March 1979

I awoke very tired – and still angry that we had lost a vote that might have been won.

Cabinet met this morning to agree on 3 May as the election date. They seemed subdued, but in no way depressed. The Tories were pressing for 26 April, but they ignored this. Cabinet broke at about 11.30 and the PM went off to the Palace. Ken Stowe told us later that the Queen had given him a birthday present – a paperknife – on Tuesday and said she hoped *not* to see him today. Apparently she was very nice to him today.

In the Unit we were putting together a handbook of policies – just one page for each policy, and a selection of the dozen most important policy areas. This should be useful for the PM when travelling in the campaign.

He returned from the Palace shortly after midday and went upstairs to the study. We all had lunch upstairs in No. 10, recognising that there may not be many more of these. It seems so long since I set up these lunches and had those silly battles with Marcia.

Question Time went off easily. The Tories were in a slightly hysterical mood. I went back promptly to No. 10 afterwards to see the policy handbook through. Then I left for Paris at 6 o'clock, having first watched the PM's statement on television. It was a straight appeal to conservatism – warning the public against taking the sudden lurches into radical new policies that Thatcher would involve (some of which I personally sympathise with). We really are the party of caution and conservatism now! Even so, he was quite good.

Friday 30 March 1979

I woke next morning with that lovely Paris feeling – a mixture of the smells of coffee and croissants, that curious French floor polish with its aroma of pepper and the sight of those orange Parisian roofs from my garret room. I went downstairs, had breakfast and phoned London to catch up on the news. It was pretty shattering. The Liberals had won the Edge Hill election with a massive swing of 32%. I went to the conference at the Political Science Institute and enjoyed that. But in the late afternoon we heard of the assassination of Tory MP and aide to Thatcher, Airey Neave, killed by an IRA car bomb in the precincts of the Commons. This is terrible.

I had a lovely evening out in Paris with 'M' from Michel Rocard's office. A marvellous piece of fantasy and preparation for the harsh realities of the five weeks ahead.

Saturday 31 March 1979

Flew back at lunchtime to watch the Grand National on TV.

Sunday 1 April 1979

Played in a marvellous charity football game at Wimbledon FC ground. We were winning 3–2 until the last seconds – then I inevitably gave away a penalty with a savage tackle and Martin Hinchelwood of Crystal Palace scored with the last kick of the game.

Monday 2 April 1979

The PM went off to the NEC this morning. In the car he told Tom McNally to arrange for the Unit to brief him regularly in the campaign. We shall probably give him a strategic brief each evening.

The Political Office has been working on a 'secret' draft manifesto for weeks. This is to be 'sprung' at Friday's formal meeting of the Cabinet/NEC/TUC, so that the PM can have the manifesto he wants and not the Transport House document, which is full of lunatic left-wing policy proposals that would alienate the entire electorate. Unfortunately, the Political Office also circulated it to today's meeting of the Campaign committee – including Benn and the left. So the plot is revealed. Political Office were embarrassed and the PM allegedly 'livid'. This is a very inexperienced election team, so it will make mistakes.

I went to a nice lunch with Alastair Burnet of ITV at the Savoy. Discussed politics and racing. He thinks the Tories will win narrowly, but says that his Heathite friends will prove difficult for Mrs Thatcher whom they 'hate'.

I came home early, under-involved.

Tuesday 3 April 1979

I cleared a few bits of paper in the Unit and then went with the others to the meeting of special advisers. Some of the contributions were not too good and the contributions by the PR/advertising man were worryingly banal.

Back at lunch upstairs the civil servants discussed the election arrangements. They were all very critical and repeatedly accused the Political Office of incompetence and inefficiency – apparently there have been some unfortunate incidents which I did not know about. Ken Stowe said he was worried that the campaign would collapse in chaos when pressure was put on a very inexperienced election team and that the PM would then turn to his regular civil servants. 'There is no way we officials are getting involved in picking up the pieces,' said Ken. The election team does not look strong without McNally. David Lipsey is to be in charge at Transport House. He has great intelligence and excellent political judgement, but is young and already overwhelmed physically by the enormous workload that has been put on him. The Political Office in No. 10 will be run by Lord Terry Boston – 'Bless my soul Boston' from 1974. A very charming fellow who most importantly will keep the staff happy, but does not claim to be a political heavyweight. Then there will be Roger Carroll from the *Sun*, who is fertile with ideas but like all the others he has never served in an election campaign before. The general air is of bemused inexperience. But David and Roger are both capable and may well learn quickly and gain strength throughout the campaign. The danger is that if things start going wrong, they will lack the experience to react quickly and coolly. I am less worried about the entourage which will travel around with the PM. Derek Gladwyn is first class and Jean Denham is excellent and very experienced.

The real trouble so far is that nobody seems to know what is going on. David Lipsey came to see me and told me that he had only learned of the election arrangements by listening to a string of telephone calls by Tom McNally, putting together the little bits of information overheard and finally fitting the jigsaw together. This is one of the less admirable aspects of this regime. Nobody tells anybody anything. People operate in separate little cells. At first we all assumed – and resented – that somebody else was being told everything and we were being shut out. At first I thought that of David [Lipsey]. Now we realise that nobody is 'in'; everybody is 'out'. Tom McNally knows more than anybody and is the closest confidant. But even he is often not told things, and when he is he does not instinctively communicate to others. And anyway he is going away to campaign in his Stockport constituency. The secretive style is set from the top. So there is no 'team' in the sense that Wilson tried to maintain. This must make it terribly hard for David and Roger, trying to get the election under way.

Question Time was fairly frivolous. The parliamentary battle is over. People's minds are on the hustings. The PM was quite good, but he already looks tired. It was quite sentimental for me. Almost certainly my last Parliamentary Questions, after five years.

In the car coming back to No. 10 the PM apparently told Brian Cartledge that he was very worried about how he was going to write all those speeches in the campaign. I said that the point is that he should not write *any* speeches. That should be done for him. Joe and I learned that in 1974. I hope this will all be worked out satisfactorily by next week!

In the evening we had a farewell party for Philip Wood, who is handing over to Nick Sanders as parliamentary secretary. Philip has been a superb adviser, giving the PM tremendous backing in the parliamentary battles. We drank a lot, and finished up at midnight in the Whips Office in No. 12. It was a delightfully disreputable party, with all kinds of relationships developing among the duty clerks and the garden-room girls. I felt old and ready to move on. Too many people have come and gone; too much has been seen before; and the outlook is not brilliant, with a Tory lead of 13% in tomorrow's papers.

Home at 1 o'clock.

Wednesday 4 April 1979

The PM did not arrive from Windsor till late morning, a bit grumpy. Either he was bored by the royal conversation last night or this morning's poll with Labour's 13% deficit depressed him.

I had an excellent Unit meeting to discuss themes and strategy for the election. David Piachaud came in with a lively paper and set us thinking. Kay Carmichael also dropped in, so it was a lovely reassembly of the old team from 1974. Whether we will be able to recreate the victories of 1974 is another matter.

I went out for lunch with Joe at the Gay Hussar and we discussed ways in which the *Mirror* can help the Labour Party. I came back to No. 10 for more meetings planning the election strategy and daily routine. At present it is intended to start the day at 7 o'clock with a meeting among ourselves, prior to meeting the PM for breakfast at 7.30 a.m. We are also planning to have Unit meetings late at night.

The Neddy Six trade unionists came in this afternoon to talk to the PM – among other things about what he could say about curbing trade union power. I met Len Murray and David Basnett coming in via the Cabinet Office and told them that the unions had destroyed the Labour government and they would not enjoy life under Thatcher.

In the evening the PM gave a big reception for ministers and their wives. It was a very cheerful occasion, no sense of '*fin de regime*'. I chatted with lots of old friends. I also had long political talks with David Owen (about the manifesto) and with Shirley Williams (about planning the television coverage in the election).

The PM stood on a chair and gave a rousing speech to send them off to the hustings in the right spirit. He said that the problem with being a long time in government was that ministers became too bureaucratic and ceased to be political. He said that they must fight on traditional Labour themes – 'need, not greed'. He seemed full of vigour and very keen to get cracking. He is very pleased that Thatcher has declined to go on television against him – a relief to us all, since I think she would have done well. She is much more effective than most of our people – or her advisers apparently – seem to realise.

After the party, Harold Lever and Diane came to my room for a chat. Then we all went home. Parliament has ended. The Cabinet meets for the last time tomorrow. Things draw to an end.

I went out to a lovely dinner with our local friends the Reads and came home at 11.15. It is still very cold, and there have been more snowstorms in Kent. We need the spring soon.

Thursday 5 April 1979

I worked on revising our Unit document summarising the government's achievements. Then I went downstairs to see the Cabinet assemble for their final meeting. I talked with Bill Rodgers, Shirley Williams, John Smith and Roy Hattersley. It is clear that they all think we have a chance in the election, though everybody realises that the odds must be against. There was no agenda for Cabinet. The PM encouraged them all to talk in general about politics and about their departmental problems.

The PM came to have lunch with us upstairs in the small dining room. He talked about the problems that lie ahead for whichever government comes into power. He said there will have to be big public expenditure cuts and also a wage freeze. He was particularly worried about the vast increases conceded and proposed for the public services on pay.

The PM discussed arrangements for the election. He said he wanted a daily working breakfast with me, Tom McCaffrey, Derek Gladwyn, Roger Carroll and David Lipsey. He also stressed to me that we must make sure that the Policy Unit members were involved. He said that David Lipsey would be the central communications anchorman in Transport House, receiving and passing all messages. Apparently this was in response to something Ken Stowe had said to him about the inexperience and generally shambolic appearance of the election team.

I suggested to the PM that he should have the grandchildren with him for Easter. The media won't want any serious politics over the holiday, but they will use some nice pictures of him with his grandchildren. He resisted it, saying grumpily that 'they are decent people' and he did not see 'why they should be involved with our awful media'.

He left to have a sleep. 'To quote my old skipper,' he said, 'I am going to examine the rivets in the ceiling.'

Ken Stowe then told us that Mrs Thatcher had summoned John Hunt to see her at 5.30 today. She saw Ian Bancroft last week – and apparently he 'could not get a word in edgeways'. She has forbidden any other of her Shadow ministers from seeing their potential permanent secretaries – except Geoffrey Howe who has seen Douglas Wass. Ken says that she gives the impression of wanting to run the whole show herself. It is clear that all the Civil Service is viewing the prospect of her arriving with some dismay.

The PM met with the subcommittee who are working on the draft manifesto. Tony Benn wanted a commitment to make civil servants 'accountable'. The PM resisted this. He said that 'if the permanent secretaries were summoned before Commons committees, they would convert the committees to their views just as they convert ministers'. There was also a battle about abolishing the House of Lords, which Benn wants but the PM opposed successfully.

We had a farewell dinner for Philip Wood in the evening. A nice occasion. The PM and Philip made good little speeches. The PM pointed out how many ex-private secretaries he had had in total and how half a dozen of them were now permanent secretaries.

Except for Colin Peterson (who deals with church appointments), nobody there was at my first farewell dinner for Lord Tom Bridges in 1974. Three of the private secretaries were fairly new – Tim Lankester, Nick Sanders and Mike Patterson. They are all very bright. Lankester is especially good.

Ken Stowe looks much older after his four-year battering at No. 10. He has served both PMs extraordinarily well, with exactly the right quiet style. He told me that he is going to the Northern Ireland Office shortly after the election. He will start as deputy sec, and will then replace Brian Cubbon as permanent secretary in the autumn. Cubbon is apparently lined up to replace John Hunt as Cabinet secretary – so the machine has managed to block Robert Armstrong! I am sorry about that. Ken told me that the PM did *not* want Michael Palliser and that everybody agreed that somebody from the Diplomatic Service could not do it. Has to be from the central machine.

We broke up at 11 o'clock. I am *starting* the campaign pretty tired. God knows what I shall feel like in a month's time. I hope the PM can survive. He said to me a week ago that his only worry about the campaign was 'whether I have the stamina'. To me, it is incredible that a man of 67 can do what he does – the manifesto meeting earlier this week went on till 3 o'clock in the morning.

Friday 6 April 1979

The Cabinet and NEC were upstairs all day working on the manifesto. As pages were agreed, the final text came downstairs and my helpful secretary Linda (a regular civil servant!) typed out the final version. When it was all over, at around 5.30, I saw Harold Lever and Shirley Williams leaving. They were both a bit depressed – Shirley especially so. Apparently the argument about the EEC was very heavy and Shirley came close to resignation.

I spent the morning and afternoon in a succession of meetings – with Roger Carroll about the PM's Monday Glasgow speech, then with McCaffrey and Booth-Clibborn, our PR adviser, about the first television script. I was also working on a tactics paper for the PM, which I finalised in the early evening. My main point was to try to get him to use a 'repeated questions to Thatcher' technique every night about the damage her policies will do to prices, jobs and public services.

The polls are still terrible – 21% behind in the *Observer* on Sunday. But I still think it will be close. And, curiously, I am beginning to enjoy it – certainly much more than in October 1974. It is a challenge to come from behind. And nice not to have to see that fool Ron Hayward from Transport House every day.

Sunday 8 April 1979

I travelled in by bus on Sunday evening. It had rained all day and was grey and there are floods in the West Country. When I arrived, a meeting was already taking place in the Press Office, discussing the draft for the first party election broadcast. Actually it was encouraging – sharp and lively. They want contributions from Gavyn and me to the factual/policy parts. Gavyn is contributing marvellously, as always.

The PM arrived shortly after 8 and came in to join us, full of good spirits, and immediately said how much he liked our Unit weekend paper, and then invited his team upstairs to his study – Carroll, Gladwyn, McCaffrey, Jean Denham, Gavyn, David Lipsey and myself. The PM said we were going to win and that he was going to 'adopt Bernard's approach' – attack from the beginning and keep on putting the unanswerable questions to Thatcher on the implications of her policies for prices, jobs and public services. He wants his speeches tougher – 'I want it jagged. I want a broken bottle in each fist,' he said.

He broke up at about 9.20 p.m. and the others went downstairs. He called me back in and said he was confident and was enjoying it enormously. 'I have nothing to lose,' he said. 'I have pleasure if we win and consolations if we lose. I am not eaten up with ambition to get here, like she is.' He then went on to discuss Thatcher, and said that 'she is the dominant personality of the campaign. If we win, it will be because people cannot take her.'

He also said that he did not want trouble with Transport House, where Ron Hayward and Percy Clarke have as usual been creating terrible difficulties. They have been refusing to co-operate with our PR and television team. There have been rows and even tears. Percy has threatened to resign yet again, and has ordered PR man Booth-Clibborn – who was Percy's personal choice for that job – not to enter Transport House. On Friday, for the great press conference to announce the manifesto, they had forgotten to put any chairs on the platform. The PM had to go and look for his own chair from a side room!

But morale in No. 10 is high. The team is beginning to settle down together. The PM is clearly in fighting spirit. When he went up to the flat and I walked downstairs to join the others, I felt reinvigorated.

Carol came in to collect me at 10 p.m. and we went to the Mostyn-Owens for dinner with Claudio Abbado, who is taking over the London Symphony Orchestra. It was delightful, full of musical people and a nice break from elections.

We left at 12.30 a.m. – and I had to get up at 6 a.m. to go to my morning meeting at 7.15! By the end of four weeks of this I shall be knackered!

Monday 9 April 1979

I awoke at 6 a.m. and drove in for our first morning of the campaign proper. It was wet and grey, with still no sign of spring.

We had an initial meeting in the Political Office – McCaffrey, Carroll, Booth-Clibborn and myself. Then we went upstairs to the small dining room. The PM was already there, with Mrs Callaghan and their son Michael who is a good organisation manager. The PM looked at the newspapers while he ate his egg and sausages. It was not cheerful reading. Most of the papers have become total propaganda sheets. The *Daily Mail* might as well be published in Tory Central Office – except that even they, employing some decent people, might find its malicious lies embarrassing. They are just political propaganda hacks. Editor David English is bound to get a knighthood from Thatcher as reward for services to the Tory Party. [He did.]

We finished just before 8.30 and the PM went off to Transport House with Derek Gladwyn and Roger Carroll. I learned later that almost nobody turned up for the Campaign committee and the PM asked Hayward for the list of invitees, which was very small. Hayward's ego is so sick that he really wants to exclude everybody except himself from everything. After that they had the press conference, which seems to have gone fairly well, with Peter Shore supporting the PM on housing policy. The Tories have adopted the Unit's policy of selling council houses to tenants, with great benefits in the opinion polls. Shore foolishly dropped it.

Staff drifted in to No. 10, and for a while all hell broke loose. Telephones were ringing. People were asking for facts, paragraphs, etc. So the morning flew by. The PM came back at midday, had lunch, and then left at 1 o'clock for Glasgow.

David Owen's special adviser told me that Ron Hayward had been to see Owen personally to ask for a colonial governorship with a cocked hat for when he retires. There are not many of those left. I said that a very malarial island might be appropriate.

I spent the whole afternoon with Edward Booth-Clibborn working on the script for the first television broadcast. Then to supper with Ted Croker of the Football Association at the Reform. I returned at 9 o'clock and watched television with the Unit team. There was not much on – the Tories do not want the election to begin yet, so the BBC obeys the Tories as always. ITN was much better. Was very tired by 11 o'clock, so I drove home. At least tomorrow morning the PM will be in Manchester, so I don't have to get up at dawn.

Tuesday 10 April 1979

Much quieter in the office today. I went through my drawers, clearing out old papers – and I even found a couple of poems I wrote in here. I want to get the room cleared by 3 May, so that I can depart with dignity and without rush.

The press has been appalling. It ignores what the PM says and just picks up stories to embarrass him. The same Tory 'lines' also crop up each day in the *Telegraph, Sun, Mail* and *Express*. They are all written in Tory Central Office. I went to lunch with Hugo Young of the *Sunday Times* at L'Escargot. He is a Tory but says that he is ashamed of the daily newspapers – not newspapers at all, really, just political propaganda sheets.

Back at No. 10 we had another meeting on the party political broadcast TV script. Then my French friend Michel Albert came in to discuss 'planning'. He is director of the Commissariat au Plan in Paris and an extremely intelligent and nice man.

In the evening I went home early for Rachel's 14th birthday supper.

There are encouraging signs that our tactics are working. People are beginning to talk about how many jobs the Tories will cut. The PM is putting my three questions every day – and journalists are beginning to pick them up. With a little more persistence and luck, we shall get them fighting on *our* ground, on *our* issues.

I fell asleep at 10.30, very tired.

Wednesday 11 April 1979

In at 7 o'clock this morning, driving through nearly empty streets. For the first time it was neither snowing nor raining.

At breakfast in the small state dining room the PM looked tired, but he was obviously pleased with his visit to the North. The feedback on unemployment is quite striking. Today the Tories launch their manifesto, so he will say *in advance* that he will be looking for the answer to the questions on jobs, prices and public services.

Breakfast is quite pleasant really. A nice aroma of bacon and coffee. Plenty of hot toast and marmalade. I usually sit next to Mrs Callaghan. She moves around quietly and looks after the PM. She is marvellous and very important to him.

He dismisses the polls, though he actually reads them quite carefully. The Tory lead has now settled down at around 10%. He says it will be only 7% this time next week. He also observed that I had not been present at Monday's press conference, so I decided to go from now on. Walking over to Transport House at 9.20 a.m. in the drizzle it was quite nostalgic, walking up Lord North Street again as in 1974 with Joe. Afterwards I returned to No. 10 and we had yet another meeting on the TV script. The TV man – Booth-Clibborn – was complaining bitterly about Transport House, who are trying to obstruct his work. At Monday morning's press conference the microphones again did not work. Today Private Office told me that Transport House had told them to stop doing a daily diary for the PM, as that was TH's job during the election. Private Office stopped, but TH have not done one, so Private Office is to start again.

I took my daughters, Rachel and Kate, out for a delightful lunch at Johnny's Café in Covent Garden – £3.25 for the three!

We spent all afternoon recording the PM's part of the first television party broadcast. He then went off to Ilford and Upminster. I went to a dinner at the American Embassy for Hal Sonnenfeldt, who used to work with Henry Kissinger. It was quite a distinguished gathering – Harold Lever, Harry Evans, Michael Palliser, Anthony Parsons (ex-ambassador to Iran), etc.

When I returned to No. 10 at 9.30 the PM was already back and had gone up to the flat. The rest of us in the team then had a long discussion about tactics for tomorrow. Roger wanted to hit the Tories very hard on raising prices through increased VAT and excise duties. He has a specific list of price rises which would result from 17½% VAT. But the PM had said that he did not want to mention specific prices. He felt it was not really him – 'not responsible'. He preferred to keep it general. We had a long argument. We knew that Private Office had got at the PM not to go hard on VAT (because if we won, we might increase it anyway). In the end we agreed a compromise.

I finally went home at 11.30.

Thursday 12 April 1979

In again at 7. The weather much improved, even a sign of the sun, though I have forgotten what it looks like.

I went to the press conference where the PM spoke about tax rises in a very general way, leaving the specifics to John Silkin. He is clearly intent on being 'responsible'. In the car going back to No. 10 he agreed that the campaign had gone well *tactically*. In fact the 39–40% we were getting now in the polls is as much as we finally secured in votes in both 1974 elections. So we are getting the *Labour* vote. The problem is that the Tories are polling very high – 49–50%. The PM said he was quite optimistic that we would win, 'unless there has been one of those sea changes in public opinion towards Thatcher. If people have really decided they want a change of government, there is nothing you can do.'

I had lunch with Michel Albert, his wife and Carol at L'Escargot. I had to pay, and it cost £32! And the food was nowhere as good as you could get in France for that much money. After lunch I did a couple of briefs to the PM and then came home quite early.

Tomorrow is Good Friday and we will have that off.

Friday. Sunshine! I tape-recorded *Tosca*, with Callas. Then dug the garden. And in the evening went to dinner with Bill and Silvia Rodgers.

Saturday 14 April 1979

Came in for breakfast on a lovely spring morning, all sunshine and warm haze. The PM was grumpy this morning. He told me off for pushing him to attack the Tories over our suggestion that they will greatly increase VAT and over their threats to cut government staff. He said he would have to answer Commons Questions on these over the next five years and he did not want to be 'irresponsible'. I said he must first make sure that he is there for the next five years. He kept criticising Roger Carroll's drafts for the press conference and for tonight's speech. In fact I thought they were good – the best yet. It is just that he is edgy, a bit tired from a week's campaigning and probably resentful that he has to work on such a glorious day.

The press conference was particularly good. There were not many journalists there – just the TV and the Sundays – but it will ensure that we get some coverage tomorrow. We came back from TH in a cavalcade of three cars. The PM stayed about half an hour and then left for Portsmouth and Southampton. The rest of the staff quickly left No. 10 to enjoy the sunshine. I waited a bit until my French friends, the Leger family from Orleans, arrived. I showed them around No. 10 and then we drove off together to Suffolk. We got to the cottage at 2.30.

It was a glorious Easter break. I was annoyed that I had to come back to London for the Monday morning meeting, so I came by train from Cambridge on Sunday evening, finally getting home at midnight and feeling sad to have just Pushkin the cat and me in the house alone. And I have another bad cold starting.

Monday 16 April 1979

Easter Monday. I awoke to Pushkin scratching at the door at 6.30 a.m. Another glorious morning. I showered and then set off to walk to Camden Town and took a bus to Downing Street from there.

When I arrived at 7.25 the morning meeting had already started. The PM was grumpy again. He had done his own speech on the unions and industrial relations. It was good. He said he felt that the speeches so far were a bit thin and he wanted more substance to them. He said that we could win by getting out our maximum vote and said that it was twelve million in 1966. There was a discussion about his style. Somebody had said he was too complacent. He said, 'Well, there is nothing I can do about that. I can only be myself.'

He left for Leicester at 11 a.m. I summoned Jim Corr from home and Gavyn from Southampton to work on various briefs the PM has asked for. We spent the rest of the day on them, and on planning the week's strategy. We want to hit prices and jobs again. But we will also take up the EEC – that is a subject for a more serious substantive speech.

My cold was becoming very bad. I went home at 8.30.

Tuesday 17 April 1979

I went in for the early breakfast feeling unwell, with a sore throat and heavy eyes. I can do without any illness at this time.

The PM was particularly grumpy. He said he did not like the drafts he had been given overnight – the press conference statement and the speech. He said he wanted something with more thought in it, more substance, 'less flip sentences'. This was really a direct attack on Roger Carroll, as his *Sun* style is very distinctive, with its snappy aphorisms. The PM is finding that he simply cannot enunciate these speeches naturally. So he is reacting against the whole speech-writing process.

He appeared to attack me personally for the badness of the press conference statement, reading it out to me and saying that he 'did not know what Bernard was up to, producing stuff like that'. I sat silent, not pointing out that I had not seen the statement, let alone written it. He then drew a paper out of his file, saying that this was the kind of thing he wanted. I also declined to point out that this was the draft that I had put in last night.

Clearly things are not going right in the team. The PM is not satisfied with Roger's drafts. The Unit is producing alternative drafts, containing more argument and facts, but these have to go to Roger – who ignores them for his own speeches and puts them in the waste-paper basket. So we are working to no purpose. And the PM is growing more and more disgruntled.

Thatcher's speech last night in Cardiff was full of right-wing philosophy, extreme language and few facts or policies. The PM had said at breakfast that this would do her harm. It was 'too extremist and reactionary. The British people don't want a reactionary.' He said he also wanted 'a philosophical speech' in reply to it. So he asked me to do it. 'Put a towel round

your head, Bernard,' he said, and asked for my paper by the time he got
to his hotel. So I went back to No. 10, called a quick Unit meeting and
then sat down to write. I had it done by 3 o'clock. I was quite pleased with
it and was told later that he liked it.

Actually I needed the towel around my head, because my cold was worse
and my temperature higher. So I went home early – and straight to bed.

I am a bit worried about the whole election team situation. It is not running
smoothly. Too many chiefs – Derek Gladwyn, David Lipsey and Mike
Callaghan are all doing overlapping functions on the organisation side, but
on the speech side there is only Roger, who is not pleasing the PM, while
not allowing others a look-in. Already there have been rows, and Gavyn has
said he simply will not write any more drafts if they simply end up in Roger's
waste basket. He will either write parts of actual speeches or nothing at all.

This morning the PM sent for just Roger and Derek and told them that
he wanted a different speech system, with more substance and more advance
discussion. To make things worse, this evening's party political broadcast
was a disaster. The lighting was horrific, making the PM and Healey look
like Dracula.

Not a good day. If the speech-writing function and the TV function are
failing, the campaign cannot be a success. This is the problem with using
inexperienced people. Their enthusiasm is valuable, but if they don't produce
what the PM needs, we are left up the creek. And Bob Worcester's polls
all look bad.

Wednesday 18 April 1979

I had a very bad night – sore throat, temperature and little sleep. I could
barely totter out of bed, so I did not go in to the office. I telephoned a
couple of times. Was told that the PM had reorganised the speech system.
He had asked for drafts of substance from the Policy Unit. These would
go to Roger Carroll for 'spicing up'. Then David Lipsey would produce a
final draft, making sure that we did not lose any of the 'substance'.

I heard that tomorrow's MORI poll will show us still 12% behind.
Depressing.

I slept much of the day, the antibiotics making me very sleepy. I only
hope I have not given the PM this infection!

Thursday 19 April 1979

Another bad night, with little sleep because of the pain in my throat, ears
and chest. But during the morning I felt a little better. So I spent a lot of
time on the phone to No. 10 getting reports on progress.

Gavyn had been to the early morning breakfast and was not wholly happy. The PM spent a lot of time complaining about trivial matters and they had very little discussion of broad strategy. They did agree to switch our attack to taxation and the link with prices. To undermine the Tory case on cutting taxes by demonstrating how it would involve large increases in prices because of the consequential increases in VAT and excise duties. However, at the press conference, to the dismay of his team, the PM took a quite different line on tax. He said he broadly agreed with the Tory wish to cut direct taxes, and he too would raise VAT and excise duties if that is what people want. So Gavyn was very perplexed. He has to write the main speech draft on tax and prices, and doesn't know whether to take the attacking line from breakfast or the 'responsible' line from the press conference.

The PM went off this morning to Cardiff and will go to Liverpool tomorrow and Saturday, so we won't see him back at No. 10 till Sunday night. It gives us time to think about things and perhaps to introduce some changes in strategy.

Bob Worcester phoned in the afternoon. He is depressed by the poll results. His private poll for the Party today was 52% to 40%. We have shown some progress – in the lead on NHS and eliminating our deficits on prices and jobs. But the Tories are still miles ahead on tax and on unions and strikes. It really does look as if we are 10–12% behind. We are winning the tactical campaign, but so far the campaign is not having any effect on votes. I believe it may in the end, providing we have the time.

Friday 20 April 1979

I was home all day again, still with a viciously sore throat, earache, heavy cold, etc. Despite filling myself with antibiotics, vitamin C, etc., I was not fit to go to work. So I lay in bed and fumed.

I phoned No. 10 regularly. The speech arrangements are now quite different. Gavyn is doing substantial chunks, which Roger Carroll keeps in, weaving his own sharp jabs into it. But the PM is altering the speeches at the last stage, so nobody is quite sure what will be said.

It has been decided to concentrate on taxation (and its relation to prices) from now on for a while. The Tory campaign – and support in the polls – is based wholly on pledges to cut taxes. If we can undermine that, Thatcher's campaign will fall apart. But it won't be easy, as it is so difficult to get media coverage. We can decide tactical moves, such as exposing the cost of her taxation policies, while sitting in No. 10. But if nobody outside the hall knows what the PM has said, it doesn't have much effect.

The latest poll shows us 8% behind – not bad, improved by 4%. We can make that up. But if we lose, I am more and more convinced that we will lose in London. Labour local authorities have been appallingly inefficient. They deserve to be thrown out. The problem is that the government may get thrown out with them.

Harry Evans phoned about the *Sunday Times*. They are very depressed. The unions won't compromise an inch. I suggested that they should leave Fleet Street and start again in a greenfield site like Milton Keynes. [Murdoch did that, to Wapping, later.]

Saturday 21 April 1979

I felt a bit better today and spent the morning shopping with my daughter Katie. We had lunch together at Johnny's Café and then I went in to No. 10.

Members of the Unit were already working on papers on various subjects for the PM. I had also asked Tessa Blackstone to come in: she drafted a good speech outline on education. By late afternoon there was a lot of activity. But the ridiculous thing was that no typing was provided over the weekend. The Labour Party and the Political Office have each provided typists only for normal union working hours – 10.00 to 6 p.m. on Monday to Friday. Unfortunately, the election does not coincide with normal working hours. So we had to make use of one lone garden-room girl for our election work – which she should not have been doing anyway, as it is 'political'.

In the afternoon Bob Edwards phoned from the *Sunday Mirror* to say that they would have to go to press with no reference to the PM's speech in Huddersfield, because they had not received a press release from Transport House. This is not the first time this has happened. After all the work on the speeches, it is a terrible waste.

I put a note in to the PM – 'midterm thoughts' – saying this week our campaign has had no pattern, no strategy. The PM has proceeded on daily 'ad hoc-ery'. The Tories are not even fighting an election campaign: they are just gliding Thatcher through a series of PR soft situations that make nice pictures for their captive media. So we are in the ring, but cannot find an opponent. Morever, Jim also seems very unhappy talking about the taxation/prices syndrome. Our suspicion is that he actually thinks the Tories are right in their big switch from direct to indirect tax. So he finds it difficult to attack Thatcher and keeps changing speeches and talking about jobs, where he feels happier.

I finished about 9.15 p.m. and went home, still feeling tired and weak from my illness.

Sunday 22 April 1979

The polls are all over the place: 20% behind in the *Observer*, 5½% in the *Sunday Telegraph*; and 9% (unpublished) in the *Sunday Times* (probably closest).

It looks as if we are making very little impact on overall voting intentions. It is as if people have made up their minds: they are fed up with the unions and our craven attitude towards them; they want tax cuts even if it means price rises; they want a gamble on a new face; and no rational argument in the campaign will change this. That is our basic situation.

This afternoon Roger Carroll phoned from Chequers. They – Hayward, Carroll, McCaffrey (what a team advising him!) – had a meeting today with the PM. They decided to go heavily for prices and wanted the Unit to work tonight on a series of papers for tomorrow morning. As usual, the Unit will have to do the hard graft on the drafts. There are lots of generals in this campaign, but the Unit is the only place with experienced troops who know what ammunition to use. Nobody else knows the facts and figures. It is simply a question of professionalism. My lot are real professionals.

Monday 23 April 1979

Carol drove me in early in the morning to get to No. 10 in time for the breakfast meeting.

The PM was grumpy again. He had my note on keeping down domestic energy prices, which he said was useful, but he would leave the detailed comments to Benn and Shore. He was reluctant to say anything on the Price Commission keeping down domestic energy prices, but he is still reluctant to mention detailed price rises that would happen under the Tories. He still feels that is not 'prime ministerial', though he accepts the argument of all his team that he must attack the Tories on the price consequences of their tax change proposals, in order to undermine their tax cuts platform, which is still their most attractive policy.

I went to the press conference. OK, but fairly tame. Energy is not a political issue, so it seemed a bit of a waste of the first day of the final full week. Afterwards we had a meeting in the Transport House room to hear the report on the Tory press conference. We had a tape recording of Thatcher. It was clear that our strategy of questions on prices and jobs was beginning to work. The journalists were beginning to press them, and the Tories were dodging the answers. We were encouraged by this. But it may be too late.

Went up to the *Daily Mirror* lunch. The usual team came from the *Mirror*. They offered their advice, some a bit sycophantic, but Joe and Terry Lancaster and Victor Knight were all helpful and tough. Joe said that we were in a logjam, and we had to move it and get the political situation shifted, or the Tories would coast down the tramline to victory. I wish Joe was here all the time.

The PM said that Mrs Thatcher was, in his own view, the dominant character of the campaign. For good or ill, she was what the campaign was about and what people were talking about. He also said that he would not himself attack her personally.

The lunch ended quite early so that the PM could set off for a walk-about in Uxbridge. As we left the large state dining room the PM paused and sang a verse from the 'Red Flag'. It was just like a hymn and sounded very nice. He can do that quite unpretentiously.

I worked on various bits of paper and had a quick supper of McDonald's hamburger. Then the PM came back at 9 o'clock and I went down to watch the TV news with him. He was not too pleased with his meeting in Wandsworth. He said that the audience was flat. And he had clearly been put off by the Irish hecklers.

Much more worrying were the race riots in Southall this evening. The National Front held a meeting there and there were terrible clashes with the Asian community and the police – 300 people arrested and 100 injured. This is bad for us. It dominated the press and pushed the election campaign to a low priority. This suits the Tories, as they are ahead and don't want people to think about the election. It also suits them to have riots on the streets just as they are about to launch their 'law and order' campaign. There was very little mention of the PM's speech.

He went up to the study and asked a few of us to come up with him. We first agreed on his statement for tomorrow about the Southall race riots. He would only give this if pressed – as we don't want all the attention diverted from prices and our 'Tory Budget'. We then had a discussion about future speeches. I suggested the 'Two Nations' theme – the Tories were going to create two nations in Britain, rejecting the Heath-Disraeli tradition of One Nation. He liked that and asked me to work it up into a speech.

By the time we finally broke up to go home it was nearly midnight. And I had to travel back to Kentish Town, have a few hours' sleep and come back in at dawn. It was worse for Gavyn. He was still working on the 'Budget' tables when I left.

Tuesday 24 April 1979

Once again Carol drove me in at 7 o'clock in the morning. Afterwards she was going to take the children to the Suffolk cottage for a few days.

At breakfast we briefly discussed the 'Tory Budget' for the press confer-ence. The PM backed off a bit and said he would leave all the tax detail to

Joel Barnett. Again the PM is reluctant to get involved in too much hard detail.

We then discussed the Southall riots, which this morning look much worse than last night. So the PM strengthened his statement a bit. But he refused to say anything 'pro-police' or to get involved with the police over it. Really he does not like the police.

The press conference went surprisingly well. Although the race riots came up, the press was interested in the 'Budget' we presented, and this will help us to keep up the campaign on the Tories about the price consequences of their tax proposals. Incidentally, Transport House had forgotten to produce the table of figures for the 'Budget' and Gavyn had to go and do it himself. Afterwards the PM again expressed interest in the Two Nations theme.

I went upstairs for lunch. Only McCaffrey and two private secretaries, Tim Lankester and Patterson, were there. Tim said he was personally pleased that the Policy Unit was now so heavily engaged in the battle. He said he thought that in the first few days the Political Office was running it as 'a total shambles'.

The PM headed off for Coventry. I stayed late, working on the Two Nations theme. It was 1.30 a.m. when I finished, so I decided not to try to go home. Instead I went upstairs, took off all my clothes and slept in a spare bed. 10 Downing Street is now like a familiar old boarding house to me – though with a better breakfast.

Wednesday 25 April 1979

Woke at 7 and got up to shave and shower. But I had to put on yesterday's clothes because I had not brought anything clean and fresh with me, not expecting to sleep in No. 10.

The PM spent the day in the Midlands. I dictated the Two Nations speech and then worked in the Unit. At 11.30 I went home in a car to change into clean clothes. Then I went on into the City to have lunch with Paul Neild of Phillips & Drew. He does not believe that the Tories' sums add up, but still expects them to win.

The tide may be turning. Gallup in the *Telegraph* showed us only 5% behind – and the MORI deficit in the *Express* is down from 12% to 6%. This gave us all a boost. It got better in the evening when Bob Worcester told me that our private polls are going the same direction. We have now had four polls since last Friday showing a narrowing swing against us in the marginals. This is a very encouraging trend – with echoes of February 1974 – though there is still a long way to go.

Before dinner I had drafted a long letter to the Catholic Archbishop of

Cardiff, reassuring him about our position on abortion. The PM arrived back at around 11 p.m. He came into Political Office and asked us all in turn what we thought. I told him it was moving well. We had begun to demolish the Tory position on tax. But from now on we had to be more positive – stressing what Labour stands for. He seemed to agree. After he went to bed I took a taxi home – arriving at about 12.30 a.m.

It has been a good two days. Perhaps the logjam is moving. Whether we can move it enough to win still seems doubtful.

Thursday 26 April 1979

Breakfast was a fairly cheerful occasion today. The PM was clearly boosted by the polls.

We discussed capital punishment – Thatcher has come out in favour of the restoration of hanging. Jim will do a big TV interview this morning and expects to be asked. He said that he had always been against. And it would just create martyrs in Northern Ireland.

He asked Derek Gladwyn to talk to Shirley Williams and tell her to stand firm over teachers' pay. It looks as if a terribly big pay rise is coming up for them. So the PM put his foot down – which may cause trouble before the election.

The PM asked me to prepare some notes on one-parent families, so I took over a page of information to Transport House. Actually the press conference went very well indeed. Two attractive lady candidates, Pat Hollis from Yarmouth and Anne Davies from Bromsgrove, were on the platform and they did very well. The PM was also strong. He squashed the appalling Paul Johnson, who asked some gutter-level question. He also defended one-parent families, pointing out that his own father died when he was 8. He read out my list of government achievements in helping one-parent families. Labour morale is rising.

The PM left at midday to go to the North. I went off for lunch with Harold Lever in Eaton Square. He really thinks we will lose, and lose quite heavily. But he is looking forward to plenty of activity afterwards. He told me how all his family businesses were thriving. Back to No. 10, where I cleared various papers and then I went home in the late afternoon. Had a sleep, made some phone calls, fed my beloved Pushkin the cat, and wrote up Wednesday's diary.

Back in No. 10 at midnight I learned that the Marplan poll in the *Sun* shows a Tory lead of 7% – down from 10%. In the right direction, but not enough really.

If we lose it will be for four reasons. Two self-inflicted: the winter strikes and the excesses of various Labour local authorities. One positive Tory feature, their tax cut policies. And a deeper secular trend of people 'wanting a change'. Jim's 'sea change to Thatcher'. This will help the Tories whatever the logical arguments on particular questions.

Friday 27 April 1979

Relieved I did not have to go in at dawn today. I stayed in bed and wrote up yesterday's diary, waking at 6.30 a.m. as usual, and then went in at 9 o'clock. There was not a lot going on. Various journalists phoned in to say that Mrs Thatcher had been very tense and shrill at their press conference. We assumed that she is beginning to get bad news from her opinion polls and is getting jumpy. The increasing hysteria in the *Daily Mail* and the *Sun* tend to confirm this interpretation.

I went to lunch with Gavyn at the Reform to discuss our future prospects if we lose – or indeed if we win, as we both propose to leave, whatever happens in the election. Immediately on return to No. 10 I received a call from Michael Callaghan who was in the North with the PM. This afternoon the PM has a long interview on the *Nationwide* programme, and I had to get the Unit to do research on various factual matters.

I then heard that the later *Express* MORI poll showed the Tory lead cut to only 3% – down from 6% earlier in the week – and the PM's lead over Thatcher as 'best PM' has risen to 19%. We were all very excited at this.

The PM scrapped Roger Carroll's proposed speech on prices. Instead, he had decided to do the speech I had done – based on Tessa Blackstone's new material on the Two Nations. Apparently he liked it a lot. And later the TV gave a good extract from it.

Trevor West came in from Dublin at teatime. We discussed the Irish problem and agreed to keep working at this whatever happened in the election.

More irritating is a story in the *Daily Mail* of an interview with Harold Wilson, saying that Mary Wilson might vote for Thatcher. It is very silly of Harold. Partly it reflects his own subconscious wish that Jim will lose. Harold is jealous and wants to be the [only] Labour leader who won elections.

I went in the evening to the Coliseum to see a marvellous production of *Manon*. Gorgeous sets, ravishing costumes and lovely singing by Valerie Masterton. A welcome relaxation. Afterwards we went back to supper with our friends the Grahams and I did not get to bed till 1.15 a.m. I am tired but the adrenaline of battle – and the possibility that we may just avoid defeat – keeps me going.

Saturday 28 April 1979

I went in at 9 o'clock to Transport House to hear the press conference. It was a dreary and wet morning and there were not many journalists there – just a scattering of the Sundays and some Transport House people. Not much interest in John Silkin and Lena Jeger, our second division spokesmen.

I chatted to Bob Worcester, who is still cheerful. His *Sunday Times* 'panel' recall shows the Tory lead down to 5% from 9%. But the Gallup poll is a bit worse – out towards 6%. Also talked to Adam Raphael of the *Observer*. He described our campaign as 'brilliant'. But he was properly sceptical about whether we could close the final gap.

I went back to No. 10 and phoned Cardiff, but the PM and everyone else were out on a walkabout. Little was going on here.

Sunday 29 April 1979

I took the boys out in the morning to Hendon Air Force Museum to look at the old planes. Many I remember seeing in the sky in the war. Then I received calls from Chequers asking for contributions to the final party political broadcast. My pretty nieces Tania and Nadia arrived at home to see us, but I had to leave to go into No. 10 where I drafted an election strategy paper – I have done one each weekend. I also did a draft piece on the trade unions and then a longer piece which could be used for a speech next week, when we shall have terrible pressure for speeches, media interviews, etc.

The PM came in at about 9 p.m. to the Political Office, where we were gathered. He went through my note – and immediately agreed my suggestion for an eve-of-poll message to the electorate. I feel I am contributing more and more as the campaign progresses. The PM went upstairs to work on the final party political broadcast on Tuesday, the most important event to come in the election. I have pressed him to do the script himself, and that is what he is doing.

We all went off to the St Ermin's Hotel for a late supper in Derek Gladwyn's room. Bob Worcester came to join us and said his polls were not very encouraging. They showed us behind on nearly every issue – including jobs – and I find it hard to believe things are this bad.

I finally left for home at around 1 o'clock.

Monday 30 April 1979

At breakfast we discussed the proposed press conference statement on public expenditure cuts and the damage to the public services that would result.

The PM was not enthusiastic; as usual reluctant to accuse the Tories of things that he said were 'not credible'. In the end he decided to let Denis Healey make the particular points with the hypothetical cuts. The press conference went quite well.

We had a sandwich lunch in No. 10 with the television team, including John Birt, who is helping to produce this last broadcast. We finally decided not to have any film or any gimmicks – just the PM straight face to camera.

I decided to travel with the PM to hear his evening speech at Chatham. In three general election campaigns over five years I have never heard either Harold Wilson or this PM make an election speech, although I wrote parts of many of them. The hall was completely packed and the meeting went very well. Although there were Irish 'Troops Out' demonstrators in the hall, they did not interrupt. This was lucky, as the microphones, inevitably for any party meeting, did not work!

We got back just before 10 and went with the PM to watch a playback of the Tory party political on a video recorder. It was extraordinary – completely artificial, all sugary, an attempt by Mrs Thatcher to imitate the Queen's Christmas broadcast. The PM reacted by saying that by contrast he would give a straight and tough broadcast tomorrow, with no soft sell at all.

We were just about to set off to St Ermin's for late supper when the TV news flashed an incredible headline – Labour was ½% ahead in the latest NOP poll. Everybody was elated. I phoned Bob Worcester and he checked details – we were 2½% behind on the first question, but moved into the lead when the 'don't knows' were probed. That is not so good, because I don't believe the 'don't knows' will vote. Still it is very encouraging, will make the Tories jumpy and will give a great lift to our activists.

The PM phoned down and asked me to take up a book. I found him already in bed. We discussed the campaign and I said how much I had enjoyed it – especially because Derek Gladwyn and Michael Callaghan had been so good to work with. He said, 'Yes, it must be better with no Marcia.' He was reluctant to be too encouraged by the polls. He said, 'Now it is just a question of whether we have enough time. Thank goodness we had a long campaign.'

I went down, joined the others and we went across to St Ermin's for supper. There was a generally euphoric mood, compounded by alcohol and exhaustion. We had a bit of a row over Transport House, with David Lipsey defending it and Derek Gladwyn saying it was the most incompetent organisation he had come across. That, in my experience, is an understatement. Derek said that after the election the unions will have to sort it out.

We finally finished eating at around 1 o'clock. Afterwards I walked back to No. 10, down Queen Anne's Gate and across the Park. Outside the

Foreign Office I met dear David Piachaud, who had been working in No. 10 helping to improve the draft of a speech I had dictated in fifteen minutes this afternoon for the PM's final eve-of-poll rally in Cardiff. It always cheers me to see him, a truly good man.

When I got to No. 10, where I was sleeping the night, there were no empty rooms. So I had to share a room with Tom McCaffrey, who was already snoring. I have not shared a bedroom with any man since with my dad in a scruffy Blackpool boarding-house bedroom in 1947. I did not get to sleep till 1.45 – and was woken at 6 o'clock by Tom's alarm clock.

Tuesday 1 May 1979

At breakfast the PM was full of drive, handing out work in all directions. He also decided to give the three questions with which we started the campaign – and show how the Tories had still not answered them. So we completed the circle of strategy that I had started in my initial strategy paper.

We worked in the Unit on trying to get our own answers to these questions – how much prices would go up under the Tories, how many jobs would be lost, etc. The PM was upstairs doing a radio programme with tough but fair BBC interviewer Robin Day. We barely had the press conference material ready for him in time for today's press conference.

The press conference went marvellously. The PM was sparkling with humour and confidence. The conference rocked with humour and once burst out with applause. The journalists clearly sensed the confidence and good mood in the Labour camp – not because we are confident we will win, but because we feel we have fought a good fight and have won the actual campaign. So that is satisfying. As for the actual result, I still find it hard to believe we will win, because we are doing so badly in London and the West Midlands, where so many marginals are. But it looks as if Thatcher will have difficulty in getting a satisfactory majority.

On return, the PM set about writing his script upstairs.

I had lunch in the dining room with a few of the private secretaries. I raised with Ken Stowe the question of what would happen if the election was a 'close loss'. I said it was important that the PM should not make any melodramatic resignation dashes to the Palace. I said he must take it slow and calm. And if it is a hung Parliament, he should talk to David Steel and the small parties.

Ken Stowe agreed and said he had already warned the Palace not to expect any rapid action. He had told the PM that it was for *him* to try to create a new government, coalition, etc. He should take his solution to the

Queen, not leave her to find a solution. He was also arranging for an aeroplane to stand by to fly David Steel down from Scotland. We all agreed that there should be a lunch with the PM on Friday after polling day before taking any final decisions.

I also said that we must end the barbaric system of throwing governments out of No. 10 within hours of defeat. Wilson always complained about the way he was bundled out in June 1970, and I know that the Homes were deeply hurt by the way they were thrown out by HW in October 1964. So we agreed to try to establish a new tradition of civilised transfer of power.

The PM did not have his draft TV script ready till 3.30 p.m. He sent for some of us – Lipsey, John Birt and myself – to discuss it. I made several suggestions for amendments which he accepted. He finally sat down to record it at around 5 p.m. The first three takes were terrible – one gabbled so fast that it took only five minutes out of the ten minutes available. But then he did it properly with some ad-libbing, often departing completely from the autocue script. He had more authority and conviction. Then he left for Ealing with Audrey. After Ealing, he went straight to Cardiff. He won't return till Friday lunchtime. By then we will know his fate. So that is really the end of this government. Next time he comes in it will all be different, either way, whatever the result. Well, he has fought a good fight and has been an honourable Prime Minister.

It is really the end of a chapter for me too. I wonder what will come up next?

Wednesday 2 May 1979

The last day before the poll. And the weather is appalling – freezing cold, rain, hail and snow. In May! God really is a Tory. The forecast is bad for tomorrow as well.

The PM is in Cardiff so I did not have to go in early. I felt tired and a bit flat. My fingertips told me that we had not been able to make the final push. Gavyn said he felt exactly the same. Later in the day we began to hear rumours that the opinion polls were bad – Marplan at 7%, NOP 6%, Bob Worcester's MORI at 5½%, and Gallup 2%. They may be wrong, but it does not feel wrong. Basically people want a change and they hate the trade unions. All the other arguments are at the margin.

No. 10 was very quiet. People sat around doing very little. I was quietly packing to leave. Nobody seemed to have any energy. Certainly I felt completely drained. Private Office also exuded depression. Most of the private secretaries have made it absolutely clear that they personally wanted Mr Callaghan to win. They have briefs, prepared by the Cabinet Office, getting them ready for the new Thatcher administration, but they could not bring themselves to read them yet.

In the background I could hear Ken Stowe on the telephone discussing whether Adam Ridley and Caroline Stevens of Mrs Thatcher's personal staff (both friendly acquaintances of mine) had been positively vetted. In the afternoon Ken showed round her political adviser, a bright young man named Richard Ryder [future Tory chief whip].

We spent the afternoon making arrangements for Thursday's Policy Unit farewell party – I arranged this a week ago on the assumption that it would be farewell. Then in the evening I went off to the *Daily Mirror* and had drinks in the editor's room with Mike Molloy, Terry Lancaster, Keith Waterhouse and Joe. Loyal Mike Molloy still felt we would win. But the others were obviously gloomy. I telephoned the bookmaker to back Labour to hold Frank White's seat at Bury. [He won and I won £250.]

Joe and I walked back along Fleet Street to Charing Cross. It was a cold and miserable evening, not one to encourage our canvassers. We discussed the future. Joe is very keen that I should not go into the City. But I pointed out that all depended on the choices I had. I did not particularly want to go to the City, but I do need a job to feed four young children.

The PM is apparently intending to continue to lead the Party into the autumn and will then give up, probably after the Party Conference. He has asked McCaffrey to run his office during that time. He has not talked to anybody else about the future.

Joe says that the *Mirror* will be quite tough in laying the blame, if Labour loses. They will name the 'guilty men' – union leaders Moss Evans and Alan Fisher. The union question is made even worse by the appalling National Union of Teachers deliberately coming out on strike this election week. I am consoled to think how they will pay for their irresponsibility when Thatcher gets in and rightly bashes them.

I came home at 11 o'clock. Feeling impotent. As Montgomery said at the battle of El Alamein, there is now nothing else I can do, so I will go to bed.

Thursday 3 May 1979

This is the fatal polling day. On the way into town I called in at our local polling station. It seemed very quiet, just a trickle of old ladies. I could tell from the determined look in their eyes that they had not come to vote FOR anybody. They had come to vote AGAINST Alan Fisher, Moss Evans and every trade union thug who stood in a picket line barring the way to the hospital or the graveyard that they feared might be their destination tomorrow. And against every Labour local authority which had left piles of rubbish in the way of their shopping. And against every union leader who had stared at them on the TV screen and said, 'To hell with the public, my members want as much as they can grab.' It was all very well for Labour – for us in the PM's speeches – to argue that Mrs Thatcher and the Tories preached the harsh doctrine of 'weakest to the wall'. As far as these weak old ladies were concerned, Labour and the unions practised it.

Little was happening at No. 10 when I arrived. The PM was in Cardiff, touring ward committee rooms and giving interviews. I went to lunch again with Alastair Burnet of ITN at the Savoy Grill. On the way I called in at the British Council and dropped in my application for the job as Director General. I won't get it, since they will fix it for some ex-civil servant, but it gives me the feeling I am doing something about the future.

Alastair was in sparkling good humour, as usual. We mainly discussed the election, which looks lost, and our shared love of horse racing. If there is a last minute turn-up for us, it will be because of people hesitating before the radicalism of Thatcher herself. But pulling the other way are 'time for a change' and revulsion against the unions.

At 3 o'clock one of the private secretaries came in to the Unit to tell me that the PM had been on the phone from Cardiff. 'He said we had lost. Mrs Thatcher would be in No. 10 as Prime Minister tomorrow. So we must be out by 3.30 p.m.'

We had a farewell Policy Unit party at 5.30 p.m. About eighty people came and it went with a swing. All my old members of the Unit and ex-members of Private Office came – Robert Armstrong, Robin Butler, Nick Stuart. It was very pleasant. John Hunt came in for an hour, and was clearly enjoying the excitement of a change of government. He admitted that he had advised the PM not to hold the election last year but to continue through into 1979, but said he wanted right through till October, so that he could retire before the election. Pity we didn't make it.

The party broke up about 8 o'clock. A few of us then went upstairs to a farewell supper party given by the Political Office. Joe Haines attacked their 'amateurism'. I suspect that the PM's compulsive secretiveness and the pressures from Ron Hayward that he should be the only person involved while at the same time contributing nothing have made the Political Office a very difficult shop to run. Everybody thought somebody else was 'on the inside', but in reality only Jim was.

After washing up our dinner plates, we all broke up. I went down to my room to watch TV. The first results were from Scotland and they seemed quite good: definitely a swing to us. It seems that my prediction yesterday to Ian Aitken of the *Guardian* that there would be a 'political Hadrian's Wall' with Labour to the north of it would be correct. The early results from England were discouraging.

Gavyn and Jim Corr came back shortly before midnight to watch the TV. I felt that I did not want to share our defeat with anybody I had worked with. So I decided not to go to the *Mirror* party with Joe. I left for ITN. They had a party in two rooms. One was for top people, the other for junior employees. I sat in the latter, known by nobody and knowing nobody, painfully watching the results streaming in. It was particularly bad in East and North-East London, where the rail strikes and the rubbish situation have been particularly awful. It was sad to see Bryan Davies and Tessa Jowell both swamped by the remorseless swing.

I finally moved into the other room. Shirley Williams was just leaving, looking very tired. I sat next to a jubilant Michael Heseltine, who was at Oxford when I was up.

I stayed on and on, ticking off the losses on my checklist of 'marginals'. Some of the losses were in safe seats with a 20% Labour lead previously – such as dear Cledwyn Hughes's former seat of Anglesey. The West Midlands did not come in till late, and then was nearly as bad as London. Those British Leyland workers, whose jobs we saved, had apparently voted Tory for a tax cut as well. By 4.45 a.m. when the programme stopped, I was the only person left in the party room. I waited till Alastair Burnet came up from the studio and I said thanks and cheerio.

Walking along Wells Street and past Middlesex Hospital it was already light. I drove slowly home, making the final mental and emotional adjustments. Although the Tories had not yet won the necessary 318 seats, that was only a question of time. We had lost. Mr Callaghan would have to resign as Prime Minister tomorrow morning. I was unemployed.

Although it was not a surprise, I felt completely numbed. Not tired – I did not feel sleepy. Not bitterly disappointed – I never really thought we would win, apart from the brief euphoria over the NOP poll last Monday. Just flat and numb. As if bereaved, as if somebody close to me had died, predictably but still a sad loss, leaving a void.

Home, I walked upstairs in the morning light to my bed. Carol was awake and we exchanged a few words. I lay awake for some time. The birds were singing in the garden. It must have been 6 o'clock before I fell lightly to sleep.

Friday 4 May 1979

I awoke shortly after 8 o'clock, having had less than three hours' sleep. The children buzzed in and out of my bedroom, on their way to school. I could hear excited discussions about what would happen 'now Daddy has got the sack'. Stephen, aged 9, was clearly delighted, saying that now that I would be at home in the day I could cook his lunch and he 'would not have to

stay to school dinner', which is one of the main burdens of his always fastidi-
ous life.

I lay in bed a while. I vaguely listened to the radio discussion of the election results. It was clear that nobody had believed, even to the end, that we
would do as badly as we did. The polls were right. On the final day every
poll but Gallup showed within 1% of the final result – a 5% swing, giving
the Tories a 7% lead.

Overnight there were still about a hundred results to come in, but the
outcome was clear by the time I got up at 9 o'clock: the Tories were about
seventy ahead of us with an overall majority of around forty – easily enough
to take them five years, especially with Ulster Unionist support.

I showered and drove in to No. 10, walking in through that lovely black
door for the last time at about 10 o'clock. The atmosphere was subdued. I
went into Private Office and the private secretaries seemed nervous. They
had on their desks their briefs for the new administration.

One of the secretaries told me there was not much in the briefs. There
was apparently no 'general brief' as such, just half a dozen separate briefs
on particular policy problem areas. I saw one on pay policy, from the Cabinet
Office. Basically it said sensibly that, as the Tories would have no pay policy
for the private sector, there would be no need to have all the bother of
monitoring pay settlements there. So the question was simply: what did
they do about the public sector? As yet there was nothing on public expenditure cuts. This had been asked for, but nothing had shown up yet.

I went to my office and the others soon arrived. We sat down to finish
our clearing up. I had removed most of my stuff a week ago, knowing I was
going to depart. But there were still my personal letters, which needed
careful scrutiny. I threw most of them away – some were nostalgic echoes
of those curious days in 1974 – but kept a few which had useful addresses,
etc.

By the time I had finished I had two great waste-paper bins full of paper.
This was nothing to what was going on in the other rooms. All our Unit
files and papers – including all the Cabinet and Cabinet committee papers
– were being shredded. Four garden-room girls sat on the floor and tore
them up, file by file, and put the shreds in great plastic bags. There was
masses of it, all those arguments about pay policy, the industrial strategy,
the Health Service, the Price Commission, renegotiating the EEC terms of
entry, down to saving the 'pint' measurement, all into black plastic bags.
Thus go governments.

All that was left were the Policy Unit memos to the Prime Minister.
These go into the archives for historians of a later generation. I hope they
stand up to the scrutiny of time. My secretary kindly offered me copies of
my personal files, many of them confidential.

The PM had come straight up from Cardiff last night, leaving around 5 a.m., having said goodbye to his constituency workers and then packed. He arrived at 7 o'clock and went to the flat for a sleep. He then did a final tour of the house, saying goodbye to all his staff. So I slipped up to my room and we cleared away some of the sacks so that the place was presentable.

He arrived with Audrey at about 12.30 p.m. He shook my hands and said, 'Thank you, dear Bernard, for everything.' He then asked what I was going to do. I said I did not know. He said he would do what he could and asked me to come to see him in the House of Commons next week. [For some reason I did not.] He then shook hands with the others, Gavyn and Jim, and left.

A bit later I went down to Private Office. The PM was sitting with the private secretaries watching the television. Occasional results came through, but it was mainly talking heads. The one good result for me was Bury and Radcliffe. I had placed a bet of £50 with Coral bookmakers that we would hold Bury – our *third* smallest majority marginal, needing a swing of only ⅓% to lose it. Despite a swing of 5% nationally, we held Bury, so I get a consolation of £250! I thought Frank White, a Catholic, a football referee, and an exceptionally diligent constituency member, might just hold it and he did.

At around 1 o'clock the PM said, 'Let's have lunch.' So we all went upstairs for our farewell meal together – 'the last supper' as the PM called it. It was cottage pie.

We were all sad of course. Sad at having lost. Sad at having to leave No. 10. Sad that it was the end of Jim Callaghan's ministerial career, and he deserved better. Everybody agrees he fought a brave, honourable and honest campaign. He has lived up to the office of Prime Minister, and history will write well of him.

But it was not a gloomy occasion. Most of us had been resigned to defeat since Wednesday, so the emotional and psychological adjustment had taken place. There was a buzz of conversation, some jokes and calm discussion about future plans.

Present were the PM, Audrey, Michael and his wife and Margaret [Jay] who had flown over from Washington on Tuesday. She told me that Peter would resign immediately as ambassador in order not to give the Tories the pleasure of sacking him.

The private secretaries were all there – Ken Stowe sitting beside the PM, Brian Cartledge, Tim Lankester, Nick Sanders, Mike Patterson, Colin Peterson and dear David Holt, who has been the PM's loyal diary secretary since 1974. From his personal staff were Tom McCaffrey and myself.

We all served ourselves and chatted away. No formalities, no speeches, just a nice friendly farewell lunch. The PM spoke briefly about the problems that faced Thatcher, clearly passing on the list of priorities that he had drawn up for himself. 'There is Ireland,' he said, 'there is pay.' But then he dried up.

I reminded him of the problems that she *won't* have, because we have bequeathed to them a far better situation than they left to us in 1974. Balance of payments in surplus; nearly self-sufficient in energy; inflation below what it was when they left office in 1974; official reserves at over £20 billion; many debts, including the IMF, paid off; unemployment steady. Not a bad record. The PM said he would mention that in his farewell press conference. I did not mention the trade unions, with whom Thatcher is best placed to deal severely.

He reminisced on the campaign a bit. He said he did not think there was much else we could do. 'The people wanted a change.' I recalled that he had said that in the car coming back from Transport House a couple of weeks ago about 'the sea change to Thatcher'. Finally he said it – 'The unions did it: people could not forget and would not forgive what they had to suffer from the unions last winter.' Here I mentioned my joke about Thatcher giving Moss Evans and Alan Fisher a life peerage each 'for services to the Conservative Party'. He laughed easily and with pleasure.

Then we all rose and drifted out.

The PM went to the flat for his final packing and preparation to leave for the Palace – at 2.25 p.m., in about a quarter of an hour. I talked briefly to Margaret Callaghan about the Jays' future plans. Then I went down and took my bag of possessions out to my car. Downing Street was packed with cameramen and onlookers. As I returned, Joe, the PM's driver, was packing his cases in the back of the black Rover.

We all lined up in the hall and the entrance. The PM approached from the Cabinet Room direction. (Incidentally, before lunch he went for a final walk in the garden of No. 10.) He walked slowly between the lines of staff, who were clapping and cheering. There were clearly tears in the PM's eyes, and some of the staff, including David Lipsey, were openly weeping. He paused to clasp the hands of one of the messengers, who is always cheery and we know to be a good Labour supporter. Then he walked out through the front door. I moved to the doorway as he climbed into the car. As the car turned to drive away the PM – and this was the last time we would see him as Prime Minister – turned to wave to us.

We all went back to our offices, said quick goodbyes and left for the last time. In fact I had to sprint back in because I had left behind on the mantelpiece all the photographs of my little girls and boys, which had accumulated over the last five years as they grew up.

A last look at the handsome room, with the sunshine streaming in from above Downing Street. It looked clean and empty. Yet I still felt part of it. A great chapter of my life has been spent sitting here. Five years and two months, usually ten to twelve hours a day. Excitements and miserable times. Battles, victories and defeats. But always learning and always conscious of how lucky I was to share the privilege.

Despite all the mistakes and failures, we did not do a bad job. Much was beyond our power and influence, for good or ill. Governments and Prime Ministers can achieve much less than their electors believe. Expectations are doomed to disappointment. Prospects for the future of our country do not encourage me. Not because it is a Conservative government in power. They will do their best, and the policy differences will be at the margin. And unless our British people regain their elan, their energy, their will to succeed, that stream will continue to flow in a troubled way, to no great purpose or final objective.

I left for the last time just before 3 o'clock through the black front door with no outside handle into the glorious sunshine and the crowded clamour of Downing Street. I was with Tom McCaffrey and Roger Carroll. Nobody noticed, recognised or acknowledged our departure. No reason why they should. We were the defeated past.

We went to Transport House for Mr Callaghan's farewell talk to staff and his final press conference. He was dignified and moving, answering a questioner who asked what he would do now, by saying that his grandson had told him over the phone yesterday that he hoped Labour would lose so that he would see more of his grandfather. My children share that view. In the background was a TV screen showing Shirley Williams being interviewed after losing her seat. I was personally shattered at this news, as I love Shirley in the simplest, most innocent way.

Then Jim was off to the farm. The few journalists who had come – most were with the new Prime Minister – drifted away. The No. 10 people decided to have tea together. But I declined and slipped off alone. As I walked across Horse Guards Parade to get my car from its privileged parking space for the last time, I was held up by a speeding cavalcade of black cars. Mrs Thatcher automatically waved to me, unseeing, as she flashed by towards Whitehall. A second car was full of police. A third was the familiar Rover driven by Jim's former driver Ken Godber. The latter peeled off across Horse Guards to the back of No. 10 and Ken Stowe leaped out and sprinted through the back gate of No. 10 in order to be there, waiting inside the front door, with the applauding lines of staff, greeting his new Prime Minister.

I climbed into my battered little old Ford Escort and drove slowly home to Kentish Town. Difficult times lie ahead – for Mrs Thatcher, for Britain and certainly for me personally.

List of Persons Mentioned in the Diary

(Names with biographies are marked with a star in the Diary.)

Abel-Smith, Professor Brian
(1926–96) Professor of social administration at LSE. Special adviser to Secretary of State Social Services, 1974–78; to Secretary of State for Environment, 1978–79.

Adley, Robert
(1935–93) Conservative MP for Bristol, 1970–74, and Christchurch, 1974–93.

Aitken, Jonathan
(1942–) Conservative MP for Thanet East, 1974–83, and for Thanet South, 1983–97. Chief secretary at the Treasury, 1994–95.

Allen, Alfred (later Lord Allen)
(1914–85) General secretary, Union of Shop, Distributive and Allied Workers, 1962–79.

Allen, Sir Douglas (later Lord Croham)
(1917–) Permanent secretary at the Treasury, 1966–74; head of the Civil Service, 1974–77.

Allen, John Schofield
Worked for Wilson in 1964–70 government and courtier of Marcia Williams.

Allen, Philip (later Lord Allen)
(1912–2006) Permanent secretary at the Home Office, 1966–72. Chairman of many committees and commissions in 1970s and 1980s.

Armstrong, Robert (later Lord Armstrong of Illminster)
(1927–) Principal private secretary to Edward Heath (as Prime Minister),
1970–74, and to Harold Wilson, 1974–75; deputy under-secretary at the
Home Office, 1975–77; secretary of the Cabinet, 1979–87.

Armstrong, William (later Lord Armstrong of Sanderstead)
(1915–80) Official head of Home Civil Service, 1968–74; chairman of
Midland Bank, 1975–80.

Ascherson, Neil
(1932–) Journalist and author.

Ashley, Jack (Lord Ashley)
(1922–) Labour MP for Stoke-on-Trent S, 1966–92; PPS to the Secretary
of State at the DHSS, 1974–76.

Astaire, Jarvis
(1923–) Boxing promoter, businessman and Muhammad Ali's tour manager
in the 1960s and 70s; former deputy chairman of Wembley plc and Labour
Party donor.

Atkinson, Sir Fred
(1919–) Chief economic adviser to the Treasury, 1977–79.

Atkinson, Norman
(1923–2006) Left-wing Labour MP for Tottenham, 1964–87; treasurer of
the Labour Party, 1976–81.

Attlee, Clement
(1883–1967) Prime Minister of Great Britain, 1945–51.

Baker, Kenneth (later Lord Baker)
(1934–) Conservative MP for St Marylebone, 1970–83, and for Mole Valley,
1983–97. Secretary of State for the Environment, 1985–86; Education,
1986–89; Home Secretary, 1990–92.

Bancroft, Sir Ian (later Lord Bancroft)
(1922–96) Second permanent secretary CSD, 1973–75; permanent secretary for the Environment, 1975–77.

Barclay, Clifford
Accountant, educationalist and close friend of the author.

Barnett, Joel (later Lord Barnett)
(1923–) Labour MP for Heywood and Royton, 1964–83; Opposition Treasury spokesman, 1970–74; chief secretary to the Treasury, 1974–79; vice-chairman of the BBC, 1986–93.

Benn, Tony
(1925–) Labour MP for Bristol SE, 1950–60, and for Chesterfield, 1984–2001; Secretary of State for Industry, 1974–75; Secretary of State for Energy, 1975–79.

Bennett, Alan
(1934–) Distinguished English dramatist, author and actor. Friend and Oxford contemporary of the author.

Benson, Henry (later Lord Benson)
(1909–95) Accountant partner at Cooper Bros.; adviser to Bank of England, 1975–83.

Berrill, Sir Kenneth
(1920–) Chief economic adviser to the government, 1973–74; head of Central Policy Review Staff, 1974–80.

Biffen, John (later Lord Biffen)
(1930–2007) Conservative MP for Salop, 1961–83, and for Shrops. N, 1983–97. Secretary of State for Trade, 1981–82; Lord President of Council, 1982–83; Leader of the House of Commons, 1983–87.

Bindman, Geoffrey
(1933–) Radical solicitor.

Birk, Alma (later Baroness Birk)
(1917–96) Journalist and parliamentarian; under-secretary for the Environment, 1974–79.

Blackstone, Tessa (later Baroness Blackstone)
(1944–) Lecturer, LSE, 1966–75; advised Cabinet Office, 1975–78; Minister of State for Education and Arts, 1997–2003.

Bonham-Carter, Mark (later Lord Bonham-Carter)
(1922–94) Liberal MP for Torrington, 1958–59. Chairman of Community Relations committee, 1971–77.

Booth, Albert
(1928–) MP for Barrow in Furness, 1966–83; Minister of State at the Department of Employment, 1974–76; Secretary of State for Employment, 1976–79.

Boothroyd, Betty (later Baroness Boothroyd)
(1929–) MP for West Bromwich, 1973–92; Speaker in the House of Commons, 1992–2000.

Bottomley, Arthur (later Lord Bottomley)
(1907–95) Labour MP, 1945–83, for Teesside, 1974–83; Secretary of State for Commonwealth Affairs, 1964–66; Minister of Overseas Development, 1966–67.

Bottomley, Peter
(1944–) Conservative MP for Woolwich W, 1975–83, for Eltham, 1983–87, and for Worthing W, 1977–.

Boyle, Edward
(1923–81) Conservative MP for Handsworth, Birmingham, 1950–70; Minister of Education, 1962–64; vice-chancellor of the University of Leeds, 1970–79.

Bragg, Melvyn (later Lord Bragg)
(1939–) Distinguished novelist and broadcaster. Friend of the author.

Brittan, Sir Samuel
(1933–) Economic journalist.

Brzezinski, Zbigniew
(1928–) United States National Security adviser, 1977–81.

Burnet, Alastair
(1928–) Editor of *The Economist*, 1965–74; editor of the *Daily Express*, 1974–76; broadcaster at ITN thereafter.

Burns, Arthur
(1904–87) Chairman of the US Federal Reserve Board, 1970–78.

Butler, David
(1924–) Fellow, dean and senior tutor at Nuffield College, Oxford, 1956–64; author of many works on British general elections and the British political climate.

Butler, Sir Michael
(1927–) Head of European Community Affairs FCO, 1974–76; deputy under-secretary, FCO, 1976–79.

Butler, Robin (later Lord Butler)
(1938–) Private secretary to Edward Heath, 1972–74, and to Harold Wilson, 1974–75; Treasury, 1975–88; secretary of the Cabinet, 1988–98; master, University College, Oxford, since 1998.

Byers, Frank (later Lord Byers)
(1915–84) Liberal MP for North Dorset, 1945–50; Liberal leader in the House of Lords, 1967–1984.

Callaghan, James (later Lord Callaghan)
(1912–2005) Labour MP for South Cardiff, 1945–50, and SE Cardiff, 1950–83; Chancellor of the Exchequer, 1964–67; Home Secretary, 1967–70; Foreign Secretary, 1974–76; Prime Minister, 1976–79.

Callaghan, William
(1948–) Assistant secretary TUC, 1974–77; Economics Department, 1977–99.

Carter, Jimmy
(1924–) President of the United States, 1977–81.

Castle, Barbara (later Baroness Castle)
(1911–2001) Labour MP for Blackburn, 1944–79; Employment Secretary, 1968–70; Secretary of State for Social Services, 1974–76.

Chapple, Frank (later Lord Chapple)
(1921–2004) General secretary Electrical and Plumbing Union, 1966–84.

Charkham, Jonathan
(1936–2007) Cabinet Office civil servant in 1970s.

Cleave, Maureen
(1939–) Irish friend of author at Oxford, later a journalist.

Cleese, John
(1939–) Writer and actor.

Clegg, Professor Hugh
(1920–95) Professor of industrial relations at Warwick University, 1967–79. Chairman Commission on Pay Comparability, 1979–80.

Coates, Ken
(1930–) Left-wing academic and proponent of 'worker's control'.

Cooper, Sir Frank
(1922–2002) Permanent under-secretary at the Northern Ireland Office, 1973–76; Defence, 1976–82.

Corbett, Robin (later Lord Corbett)
(1933–) Labour MP for Hemel Hempstead, 1974–79, and for Erdington, 1983–2001.

Cordle, John
(1912–2004) Conservative MP for Bournemouth, 1959–77. Friend of Lady Falkender.

Corston, Jean (later Baroness Corston)
(1942–) Labour regional organiser, 1976–86; Labour MP for Bristol, 1992–2005.

Cosgrave, Liam
(1920–) Irish Prime Minister, 1973–77.

Couzens, Sir Kenneth
(1932–2004) Deputy secretary, Incomes Policy and Public Finance, Treasury, 1973–77; second permanent secretary, Treasury, 1977–82.

Crewe, Sir Ivor
(1945–) Professor of government, Essex University; vice chancellor, 1995–.

Crosland, Anthony
(1918–77) Labour MP for South Gloucestershire, 1950–55, and for Grimsby, 1959–77; Secretary of State for Education and Science, 1965–67; president of the Board of Trade, 1967–69; Secretary of State for Local Government, 1969–70, and for the Environment, 1974–76; Foreign Secretary, 1976–77.

Crowther-Hunt, Norman (later Lord Crowther-Hunt)
(1920–87) Fellow and lecturer in politics, Exeter College, Oxford, 1952–82;

member of the Commission on the Constitution, 1969–73; Minister of State for Education, 1974–76; Privy Council Office, 1976.

Cubbon, Sir Brian
(1928–) Cabinet Office, 1971–75; permanent secretary Northern Ireland Office, 1976–79.

Cudlipp, Hugh (later Lord Cudlipp)
(1913–98) Editor of various popular newspapers; chairman International Publishing Corporation, 1968–73.

Cudlipp, Michael
(1934–2004) Journalist for *The Times* and the *Sunday Times*; consultant on PR to the Northern Ireland Office, 1974–75; National Enterprise Board, 1975–78.

Cunningham, George
(1931–) Labour MP for Islington SW, 1970–74, and for Islington S, 1974–83 (SDP, 1982–83).

Cunningham, John
(1939–) Labour MP for Whitehaven, 1970–83, and for Copeland, 1983–; PPS to James Callaghan, 1972–76; party under-secretary for Energy, 1976–79; Minister for Agriculture, 1997–98.

Curran, Sir Charles
(1921–80) Director General BBC, 1969–77.

Dahrendorf, Professor Ralf (later Lord Dahrendorf)
(1929–) Director of the LSE, 1974–84; warden of St Anthony's College, Oxford, 1987–97.

Davies, Gavyn
(1950–) No. 10 Policy Unit, 1974–79; chief UK economist and partner at Goldman Sachs, 1986–93; chairman BBC, 2001–04. Friend of the author.

Dayan, Moshe
(1915–81) Minister of Defence and then Prime Minister of Israel.

Deakins, Eric
(1932–) Labour MP for Walthamstow, 1970–87; parliamentary under-secretary at the Department of Trade, 1974–76; DHSS, 1976–79.

Dearing, Ronald (later Lord Dearing)
(1930–) Under-secretary at the Department of Industry, 1972–80; chairman of the Post Office, 1981–88.

Dell, Edmund
(1921–99) Labour MP for Birkenhead, 1964–79; Paymaster General, 1974–76; Secretary of State for Trade, 1976–79.

Denham, Jean
(1939–) No. 10 Press Office, 1974–76. Press officer for Labour Party.

Devlin, Paddy
(1925–99) Northern Ireland politician.

Dewar, Donald
(1937–2000) Labour MP for South Aberdeen, 1966–70, and for Glasgow, 1978–2000; Scottish Secretary, 1997–99; Scottish First Minister from 1999 until his death.

Dierkes, Meinholf
(1935–) Distinguished German social scientist and friend of the author.

Donnison, Professor David
(1926–) Professor of social administration at LSE, 1961–69. Chairman Supplementary Benefits Commission, 1975–80.

Dow, Christopher
(1916–98) Economist. Director of the Bank of England, 1973–81.

Downey, Sir Gordon
(1928–) Treasury, 1952–81 (on loan to CPRS, 1978–81).

Duffy, Maureen
(1933–) Writer.

Eban, Abba
(1915–2002) Israeli minister of Foreign Affairs, 1966–74.

Emery, Fred
(1933–) Journalist for *The Times* and broadcaster.

English, Michael
(1930–) Labour MP for Nottingham W, 1964–83.

Ennals, David (later Lord Ennals)
(1922–95) Labour MP for Dover, 1964–70, and for Norwich N, 1974–83; minister at the FCO, 1974–76; Secretary of State for Social Services, 1976–79.

Evans, Sir Harold
(1928–) Editor of the *Northern Echo*, 1961–66; editor of the *Sunday Times*, 1967–81; editor of *The Times*, 1981–82; close friend of the author.

Ferguson, Sir Euan
(1932–) Private secretary to Foreign Secretary, 1975–78. Assistant under-secretary FCO, 1978–82. Ambassador to France, 1987–92.

Fisher, Alan
(1922–88) General secretary National Union of Public Employees, 1968–82.

Fitt, Gerry (later Lord Fitt)
(1926–2005) SDLP MP for West Belfast, 1970–83; SDLP leader, 1970–79.

Fitzgerald, Garrett
(1926–) Fine Gael MP for Dublin SE, 1969–92; Irish Minister for Foreign Affairs, 1973–77; Taoiseach, 1981–82 and 1982–87.

Foot, Michael
(1913–) Labour MP for Devonport, 1945–55, for Ebbw Vale, 1960–83, and for Blaenau Gwent, 1983–92; political columnist, author, biographer and critic; Secretary of State for Employment, 1974–76; leader of the House of Commons, 1976–79; leader of the Labour Party, 1980–83.

Ford, Gerald
(1913–2006) President of the United States, 1974–77.

Foster, Sir Christopher
(1930–) Economist at Oxford and LSE; special economic adviser, DoE, 1974–77.

Fowler, Professor Gerald
(1935–93) Lecturer at Oxford, 1958–1965; Labour MP for the Wrekin, 1966–70 and 1974–79; Minister for Education, 1969–70 and 1974–76; close friend of the author.

Franklin, Sir Michael
(1927–) Director General Brussels, 1973–77; Cabinet Office European secretariat, 1977–81; permanent secretary Ministry of Agriculture, 1983–87.

Frost, Sir David
(1939–) Television producer and presenter.

Galbraith, John Kenneth
(1908–2006) Distinguished US economist.

Gibbings, Sir Peter
(1929–) Chairman of the *Guardian* newspaper, 1973–88.

Giscard d'Estaing, Valéry
(1926–) French Minister of Economics and Finance, 1969–74; President of France, 1974–81.

Gladwyn, Derek (later Lord Gladwyn)
(1930–2003) Southern-region secretary of the General Municipal Workers Union, 1970–90.

Goldsmith, Sir James
(1933–97) International financier, right-wing politician and friend of Lady Falkender.

Goodman, Arnold (later Lord Goodman)
(1913–95) Senior partner, Goodman, Derrick solicitors; legal and general adviser to Harold Wilson; chairman of the Arts Council, 1965–72, and of the *Observer* Trust, 1967–76.

Goodman, Geoffrey
(1921–) *Daily Mirror* journalist.

Graham, Andrew
(1942–) Senior economic adviser in No. 10 Policy Unit, 1974–76. Economics fellow, Balliol College, Oxford, 1969–2001; master of Balliol College, Oxford, 2001–.

Graham, Doctor Nori
(1936–) Expert on Alzheimer's disease and friend of the author.

Graham, Professor Philip
(1932–) Distinguished child psychiatrist and friend of the author.

Grant, Bruce
(1925–) Distinguished Australian journalist.

Greene, Graham Carleton
(1936–) Publisher, nephew of the author Graham Greene; chairman of Chatto, The Bodley Head and Jonathan Cape, 1970–88; trustee of the British Museum, 1978–2004; close friend of the author.

Griffin, Ken
(1928–) Industry adviser to the Department of Industry, 1972–74; deputy chairman of British Shipbuilders, 1977–83.

Haines, Joseph
(1928–) Political correspondent for the *Sun*, 1964–68; Harold Wilson's chief press secretary, 1969–70 and 1974–76; leader writer, *Daily Mirror*, 1978–90; close friend of the author.

Hale, Professor John
(1923–99) Professor of Italian history and art and tutor to the author on Italian Renaissance at Oxford.

Harrington, Illtyd
(1931–) London local-government councillor, 1959–90. Friend of Lady Falkender.

Harris, John (later Lord Harris of Greenwich)
(1930–2001) Special adviser to Roy Jenkins, 1965–74; Minister of State at the Home Office, 1974–79.

Hart, Judith (later Baroness Hart)
(1924–91) Labour MP for Lanark, 1959–83, and for Clydesdale, 1983–87; Minister of Overseas Development, 1969–70 and 1974–79.

Hattersley, Roy (later Lord Hattersley)
(1932–) Labour MP for Birmingham Sparkbrook, 1964–97; Minister of State at the FCO, 1974–76; Secretary of State for Prices and Consumer

Protection, 1976–79; deputy leader of the Labour Party, 1983–92. Later a writer, historian and media celebrity.

Hayhoe, Bernard (Barney) (later Lord Hayhoe)
(1925–) Conservative MP for Brentford, 1974–92. Conservative Party spokesman on Employment, 1974–92. Minister of State CSD, 1981; Treasury, 1981–85.

Hayman, Helene (later Baroness Hayman)
(1949–) Labour MP for Welwyn and Hatfield, 1974–79. Minister of State for Agriculture, 1999–2001. Speaker of the House of Lords, 2006–. Friend and neighbour of the author.

Hayward, Ron
(1917–96) General secretary of the Labour Party, 1972–82.

Healey, Denis (later Lord Healey)
(1917–2005) Labour MP for Leeds, 1952–92; Defence Secretary, 1964–70; Chancellor of the Exchequer, 1974–79.

Heath, Sir Edward
(1916–) Conservative MP for Bexley, 1950–2001; leader of the Opposition, 1965–70 and 1974–75; Prime Minister, 1970–74.

Heffer, Eric
(1922–91) Labour MP for the Walton Division of Liverpool, 1964–91; Minister of State at the Department of Industry, 1974–75.

Hennessy, Peter
(1947–) Journalist on *The Times*, 1974–76, 1982–83; author; professor of contemporary British history, University of London, 1992–.

Herbecq, Sir John
(1922–) Second permanent secretary Civil Service Department, 1975–81.

Hill, David
(1948–) Political adviser to Roy Hattersley, 1972–79, and to Department of Prices and Consumer Protection, 1976–79. Director of Communications for the Prime Minister, 2003–07.

Himmelweit, Professor Hildegard
(1918–89) Professor of social psychology at LSE, 1964–83. Friend of author.

Hodge, Sir Julian
(1904–2004) Welsh merchant-banker friend of James Callaghan.

Hogg, Sarah (later Baroness Hogg)
(1946–) Journalist on *The Economist*, 1967–81. Head of Prime Minister's Policy Unit, 1990–95.

Hopkin, Sir Brian
(1914–) Chief economic adviser to the Treasury, 1974–77.

Howe, Geoffrey (later Lord Howe)
(1926–) Conservative MP for Bebbington, Reigate, Surrey E, 1964–92; Chancellor of the Exchequer, 1979–83; Foreign Secretary, 1983–89.

Howell, Denis (later Lord Howell)
(1923–98) Labour MP for Birmingham All Saints, 1955–59, and for Birmingham Small Heath, 1961–92; Minister of State for Sport, 1969–70 and 1974–79.

Hughes, Cledwyn (later Lord Hughes)
(1916–2001) Labour MP for Anglesey, 1951–79. Chairman PLP, 1974–79. Leader of the Opposition in the House of Lords, 1982–92.

Hughes, Mark
(1932–93) Labour MP for Durham, 1974–83.

Hunt, Sir John (later Lord Hunt)
(1919–) Second permanent secretary at the Cabinet Office, 1972–73; Cabinet Secretary, 1973–79.

Jackson, Margaret (later Beckett)
(1943–) Labour MP for Lincoln, 1974–79, and Derby S, 1983–; PPS to the Minister for Overseas Development, 1974–75; assistant government Whip, 1975–76; under-secretary at the DES, 1976–79; leader of the House of Commons, 1998–2001; Secretary of State for Environment, Food and Rural Affairs, 2001–05; Foreign Secretary, 2005–07.

Jacobson, Sydney (later Lord Jacobson)
(1908–88) Journalist at the *Daily Mirror, Daily Herald* and the *Sun*; editorial director at IPC, 1968–74.

Jay, Peter
(1937–) Economics editor of *The Times*, 1967–77; Ambassador to Washington, 1977–79. Married daughter of James Callaghan. Friend of the author.

Jeger, Lena (later Baroness Jeger)
(1915–) Labour MP for Holborn, 1953–59 and 1967–79.

Jenkins, Clive
(1926–99) General secretary of the Association of Scientific, Technical and Managerial Staffs, 1970–88; on the general council of the TUC, 1974–89.

Jenkins, Peter
(1934–92) *Guardian* journalist.

Jenkins, Roy (later Lord Jenkins)
(1920–2003) Labour MP for Southwark and Birmingham Stechford, 1948–76; SDP MP for Glasgow, Hillhead, 1982–87; Minister of Aviation, 1964–65; Home Secretary, 1965–67 and 1974–76; Chancellor of the Exchequer, 1967–70; deputy leader of the Labour Party, 1970–72; President of the EC, 1977–81; leader of the SDP, 1982–83.

Jones, Alec
(1924–83) Labour MP for Rhondda, 1974–83.

Jones, David
(1923–) Deputy secretary Department of Industry, 1973–76; Cabinet Office, 1976–77; Department of Energy, 1978–82.

Jones, Elwyn (later Lord Elwyn-Jones)
(1909–89) Labour MP for West Ham and Newham, 1945–74; Lord Chancellor, 1974–79.

Jones, Fred
(1920–) Deputy secretary Treasury, 1975–80.

Jones, Professor George
(1938–) Lecturer and professor at LSE, 1966–99; close friend of the author and with him co-author of a biography of Herbert Morrison.

Jones, Jack
(1913–) General secretary of the TGWU, 1969–78.

Joseph, Sir Keith (later Lord)
(1918–94) Conservative MP for Leeds NE, 1956–87; Secretary of State for Health, 1970–74, and for Education, 1981–86.

Jowell, Tessa
(1947–) Assistant director MIND, 1974–86. Labour MP for Dulwich, 1992–. Secretary of State for Culture, Media and Sport, 2001–07. Close friend and neighbour of the author.

Judd, Frank (later Lord Judd)
(1935–) Labour MP for Portsmouth W, 1966–79; PPS to Harold Wilson, 1970–72; under-secretary for Defence, 1974–76; Minister of State, ODM, 1976–77, FCO, 1977–79.

Kagan, Joseph (later Lord Kagan)
(1915–95) Chairman and managing director of Gannex Textiles; financed the political office; later imprisoned for tax offences.

Kaufman, Gerald
(1930–) Labour MP for Manchester Ardwick, 1970–83, and Manchester Gorton, 1983–; parliamentary under-secretary at DoE, 1974–75; Minister of State at DTI, 1975–79.

Kedourie, Elie
(1926–92) Professor of politics at LSE.

Kinnock, Neil (later Lord Kinnock)
(1942–) Labour MP for Bedwellty, 1970–83, and Islwyn, 1983–95; leader of the Labour Party, 1983–92; MEP, 1995–; European commissioner, 1999–2004.

Kissin, Harry (later Lord Kissin)
(1912–97) Chairman and director of various public and private companies in the City; adviser to Harold Wilson and financier of the political office; introduced the author to Harold Wilson.

Kissinger, Henry
(1923–) US Secretary of State, 1973–77.

Knight, Andrew
(1939–) Editor of *The Economist*, 1974–86; director of News Corp, 1990–.

Knox, Brian
(1933–) Stockbroker partner and colleague of author at Grieveson Grant.

Kreisky, Bruno
(1911–90) Chancellor of Austria.

Lamont, Norman
(1942–) Conservative MP for Kingston upon Thames, 1972–97. Chancellor of the Exchequer, 1990–93.

Lancaster, Terry
(1925–2007) *Daily Mirror* journalist.

Lankester, Sir Tim
(1942–) Treasury, 1973–78; private secretary to Prime Ministers James Callaghan and Margaret Thatcher, 1978–81. President, Corpus Christi College, Oxford, 2001–.

Lapping, Anne
(1941–) Independent television producer.

Layfield, Sir Frank
(1921–2000) Chairman of committee inquiry into Local Government Finance, 1974–76.

Lea, David (later Lord Lea)
(1937–) Secretary of the TUC economic department, 1970–77; assistant general secretary, TUC, 1977–99.

Le Carré, John
(1931–) David Cornwell, distinguished writer.

Leonard, Dick
(1930–) Journalist and broadcaster; Labour MP for Romford, 1970–74; PPS to Anthony Crosland, 1970–74; assistant editor, *The Economist*, 1974–85.

Lester, Anthony (later Lord Lester)
(1936–) Distinguished lawyer and special adviser to the Home Secretary, 1974–76.

Lestor, Joan (later Baroness Lestor)
(1931–98) Labour MP for Eton and Slough, 1966–83, and for Eccles, 1987–93; under-secretary at the Foreign Office, 1974–75, and Department of Education, 1975–76; Labour NEC, 1967–82.

Lever, Harold (later Lord Lever)
(1914–95) Labour MP for Manchester Central, 1945–79; Paymaster General, 1969–70; Labour spokesman on Europe, 1970–72; Chancellor of the Duchy of Lancaster, 1974–79. The author was special adviser to Mr Lever, 1970–74.

Liddell, Helen
(1950–) Economist for the Scottish TUC, 1971–76; secretary of the Scottish Labour Party, 1977–88; Labour MP for Monklands, 1994–2005; Secretary of State for Scotland, 2001–03; High Commissioner, Australia, 2005–.

Lipsey, David (later Lord Lipsey)
(1948–) Journalist and author; special adviser to Department of Environment, 1974–76, and to FCO, 1976–77; member of No. 10 Policy Unit, 1977–79; worked on *The Economist*, 1992–99.

Littler, Sir Geoffrey
(1930–) Treasury, 1954–83; deputy secretary, 1977–83.

Lord, Alan
(1929–) Principal finance officer to DTI, 1973–75; second permanent secretary, HM Treasury, 1975–77.

Lovell-Davies, Peter (Lord)
(1924–2001) Public-relations adviser to Harold Wilson, 1962–74; Minister of State for Energy, 1975–76.

Lyall, Gavyn
(1933–2003) Author and journalist.

Lynch, Jack
(1917–99) Irish Leader Fianna Fáil, 1966–79. Taoiseach, 1966–73, 1977–79.

Lyon, Alexander
(1931–93) Labour MP for York, 1966–83. Minister of State for the Home Office, 1974–76.

Lyons, John
(1926–) General secretary of the Electrical Power Engineers Association, 1973–91.

Mabon, Dickson
(1925–) Labour MP for Greenock, 1955–83. Minister of State at the Department of Energy, 1976–79.

MacArthur, Brian
(1940–) Journalist on *The Times*, *Evening Standard* and *Sunday Times*.

McCaffrey, Sir Tom
(1922–) Head of News at FCO, 1974–76. Chief press secretary to Prime Minister, 1974–79.

McCarthy, Sir Callum
(1944–) Civil servant in Department of Industry, 1972–85. Chairman of Financial Services Authority, 2003–.

McCarthy, William (later Lord)
(1925–) Academic specialist on industrial relations. Special adviser to Secretary of State Social Services, 1975–79.

MacDonald, Margot
(1943–) SNP MP for Glasgow Govan, 1973–74. Vice chairman Scottish National Party, 1972–79.

McElhone, Frank
(1938–82) Labour MP for Glasgow Gorbals, 1969–82; parliamentary secretary for the Scottish Office, 1975–79.

Macintosh, Andrew (later Lord Macintosh)
(1933–) Labour councillor and leader of the Greater London Authority, 1973–83. Minister of State DCMS, 2003–05.

Mackintosh, John
(1928–78) Labour MP, 1966–74, and a professor of politics.

Maclennan, Robert (later Lord Maclennan)
(1936–) MP for Caithness, 1966–97. Parliamentary under-secretary at the Department of Prices and Consumer Protection, 1974–79.

McMahon, Sir Christopher (Kit)
(1927–) Adviser to the Bank of England, 1966–70; executive director, 1970–80.

McNally, Tom (later Lord McNally)
(1943–) Political adviser to the Foreign Secretary, 1974–76 and to the Prime Minister, 1976–79; MP for Stockport S (Labour 1979–81, SDP 1981–83); leader of Liberal Democrats in the Lords, 2004–.

Maguire, Frank
(1929–81) Independent MP for Fermanagh and Tyrone S, 1974–81. Publican at Frank's Bar, Linaskea.

Marquand, David
(1934–) Historian; Labour MP for Ashfield, 1966–77; Oxford contemporary of the author.

Mason, Roy (later Lord Mason)
(1924–) Labour MP for Barnsley, 1953–83; Defence Secretary, 1974–76; Secretary of State for Northern Ireland, 1976–79.

Maudling, Reginald
(1917–79) Conservative MP for Barnet, 1950–74; Chancellor of the Exchequer, 1962–64; Home Secretary, 1970–72.

Maynard, Professor Geoffrey
(1921–) Chief economic adviser to the Treasury, 1972–77. Professor of economics at Reading University, 1968–.

Maynard, Joan
(1921–98) Extreme left-wing Labour MP for Sheffield Brightside, 1974–87; Labour Party NEC, 1972–82, 1983–87.

Mayne, Richard
(1926–) Writer, broadcaster and European specialist.

Meacher, Michael
(1939–) Labour MP for Oldham W, 1970–. Parliamentary secretary for Department of Industry, 1975–76; Trade, 1976–79.

Mellish, Robert (later Lord Mellish)
(1913–98) Labour MP for Bermondsey, 1946–74, and for Southwark, 1974–82; Opposition Chief Whip, 1970–74; Chief Whip, 1974–76.

Metcalf, Professor David
(1942–) Special adviser to Secretary of State Social Security, 1976–79. Professor of industrial relations at LSE, 1985–. Friend of the author.

Middleton, Sir Peter
(1934–) Treasury press secretary, 1972–75; under-secretary, 1976; permanent secretary, 1983–91. Director and chairman of Barclays Bank, 1991–2004.

Mikardo, Ian
(1908–93) Labour MP for Reading, 1945–59, for Poplar, 1964–74, for Tower Hamlets, 1974–83, and for Bow and Poplar, 1983–87; chairman of the International Committee of the Labour Party, 1973–78; chairman, PLP, 1974.

Millan, Bruce
(1927–) Labour MP for Glasgow Craigton, 1955–83; and for Govan, 1983–88. Minister of State for the Scottish Office, 1974–76; Secretary of State for Scotland, 1976–79.

Miller, Sir Eric
(1924–77) Chairman of Peachey Properties, close friend of Lady Falkender and financier of the political office; committed suicide in 1977 while under official investigation for financial irregularities.

Mitchell, Sir Derek
(1922–2006) PPS to PM Harold Wilson, 1964–70; second permanent secretary at the Treasury, 1973–77.

Molloy, Mike
(1940–) Assistant editor, deputy editor and editor of *Daily Mirror*, 1970–85.

Molyneaux, James (later Lord Molyneux)
(1920–) Ulster Unionist MP for Antrim S, 1970–83, and for Lagan Valley, 1983–97. Leader of the Ulster Unionist Party in the House of Commons, 1975–95.

Monck, Sir Nicholas
(1935–) Treasury, 1962–92. Principal private secretary to Chancellor of the Exchequer, 1976–77; under-secretary, 1977–84; permanent secretary for Employment, 1993–95.

Moore, Philip (later Lord Moore)
(1921–) Private secretary to HM the Queen, 1977–86.

Morgan, Gwyn
(1934–) Former assistant general secretary of the Labour Party; Head of the Welsh Information Office, EEC, 1975–79.

Morgan, Janet (later Lady Balfour of Burleigh)
(1945–) Writer and company director. Lecturer in politics at Oxford, 1974–78. Member of CPRS, 1978–81.

Morrell, Frances
(1937–) Special adviser to Tony Benn at Departments of Industry and Energy, 1974–79.

Morris, Alf (later Lord Morris)
(1928–) Labour MP for Manchester, Wythenshawe, 1964–97; under-secretary at the DHSS with special responsibility for the disabled, 1974–79.

Moser, Professor Claus (later Lord Moser)
(1922–) Professor of statistics at the LSE in the 1950s and 60s; head of the Governmental Statistical Service, 1967–78; warden of Wadham College, Oxford, 1984–93.

Muldoon, Sir Robert
(1922–92) Prime Minister of New Zealand, 1975–84.

Mulley, Fred (later Lord Mulley)
(1918–95) Labour MP for Sheffield, 1950–83; chairman of the Labour Party, 1974–75; Minister for Transport, 1974–75; Secretary of State for Education, 1975–76; Defence Secretary, 1976–79.

Murray, Albert (later Lord Murray)
(1930–80) Labour MP for Gravesend, 1964–70; Minister of State at the Board of Trade, 1966–68, and at the Board of Technology, 1968–70; private secretary to Harold Wilson, 1974–76.

Murray, Len (Lionel) (later Lord Murray)
(1922–2004) Assistant general secretary of the TUC, 1969–73; general secretary, 1973–84.

Nairne, Sir Patrick
(1921–) Second permanent secretary, Cabinet Office, 1973–75; permanent secretary DHSS, 1975–81.

Newsom, Sir Peter
(1928–) Education Officer ILEA, 1972–82.

O'Brien, Edna
(1930–) Irish writer.

O'Kennedy, Michael
(1936–) Fianna Fáil member for Tipperary, 1969–80. Foreign Minister, 1977–79.

Oldfield, Sir Maurice
(1915–81) Diplomatic Service, 1947–80. Security coordinator for Northern Ireland, 1979–80.

Orme, Stan (later Lord Orme)
(1923–) Labour MP for Salford W, 1964–83; Minister of State at the Northern Ireland Office, 1974–76; Minister of State at the DHSS, 1976–79.

Ortoli, François-Xavier
(1925–) President of EEC, 1973–76; financial vice president, 1977–84.

Owen, Dr David (later Lord Owen)
(1938–2005) MP for Plymouth Sutton (Labour 1966–81, SDP 1981–92); under-secretary for Defence, 1968–70; Minister of State at the DHSS, 1974–76; Foreign Secretary, 1976–79; one of the 'Gang of Four' founders of the SDP in 1981 of which he was leader, 1983–87 and 1988–92.

Paisley, Reverend Ian
(1926–) Democratic Unionist MP for North Antrim, 1974–85, 1986–. Member of Northern Ireland Assembly, 1998–. First Minister of Northern Ireland, 2007–08.

Palliser, Sir (Arthur) Michael
(1922–) Ambassador and permanent representative to the EC, 1973–75; head of the Diplomatic Service, 1975–82.

Pardoe, John
(1934–) Liberal MP for Cornwall N, 1966–79.

Parker, Sir Peter
(1924–2002) Chairman of the British Tourist Authority, 1969–75; chairman of British Rail, 1976–83.

Part, Sir Anthony
(1916–80) Permanent secretary at the Department of Trade and Industry, 1970–74; Industry, 1974–76.

Peart, Fred (later Lord Peart)
(1914–88) Labour MP for Workington, 1945–76; Minister of Agriculture, Fisheries and Food, 1964–68 and 1974–76; leader of the House of Lords, 1976–79.

Pendry, Thomas (later Lord Pendry)
(1934–) Labour MP for Stalybridge, 1970–2001. Government whip, 1974–77. Parliamentary under-secretary at the Northern Ireland Office, 1978–79.

Peri, Yoram
(1944–) Representative in London of Israeli Labour Party.

Peston, Maurice (later Lord Peston)
(1931–) Special adviser to Secretary of State for Education, 1974–75, and to Secretary of State for Prices and Consumer Protection, 1976–79. Professor of economics at Queen Mary College, University of London, 1965–88.

Piachaud, Professor David
(1945–) Professor of social policy at the LSE since 1987. Member of the Policy Unit, 1974–79.

Pitt, Terence
(1937–86) Head of Labour Party research, 1965–74. Special adviser to Lord President of the Council, 1974.

Plietzky, Sir Leo
(1919–99) HM Treasury, 1950–77; second permanent secretary, 1976–77; permanent secretary for Trade, 1977–79.

Plowden, William
(1935–) Lecturer in government at the LSE, 1965–71; member of the Central Policy Review Staff, 1971–77; director-general, RIPA, 1977–88.

Porchester, Lord (later 7th Earl of Carnavon)
(1924–2001) Held various senior positions in local government and on bodies governing horse racing; racing manager to HM the Queen, 1969–2001; close friend of the author.

Poulson, John
(1910–93) Architect involved in corruption scandals in local government in north-east England.

Powell, Enoch
(1912–98) Conservative MP for Wolverhampton, 1950–74; Minister of Health, 1960–63.

Prentice, Reginald (later Baron Prentice)
(1923–2001) MP (Labour) for East Ham N, 1957–74, for Newham NE, 1974–77, (Conservative) for Newham NE, 1977–79, for Daventry, 1979–87; Minister of Overseas Development, 1967–69 and 1975–76; Education Secretary, 1974–75.

Preston, Peter
(1938–) Editor of the *Guardian*, 1975–95.

Radice, Giles (later Lord Radice)
(1936–) Author and Labour MP for Chester-le-Street, 1973–83, and for Durham N, 1983–2001.

Rampton, Sir Jack
(1920–94) Permanent secretary at the Department of Energy, 1974–80.

Ramsbotham, Sir Peter
(1919–) British Ambassador to Iran, 1971–74 and to Washington, 1974–77; Governor of Bermuda, 1977–80.

Rawlinson, Peter (later Lord Rawlinson)
(1919–2005) Conservative MP for Epsom and Ewell, 1955–78; Attorney-General, 1970–74.

Rayne, Max (Lord Rayne)
(1918–2003) Businessman and philanthropist.

Rees, Merlyn (later Lord Merlyn-Rees)
(1920–2005) Labour MP for South Leeds, 1963–83; Secretary of State for Northern Ireland, 1974–76; Home Secretary, 1976–79.

Reisz, Betsy (Betsy Blair)
Hollywood Oscar-nominated wife of the film director Karel Reisz.

Richard, Ivor (later Lord Richard)
(1932–) Labour MP for Barons Court, 1964–74. UK permanent representative to UN, 1974–79. Leader of the House of Lords, 1997–98.

Richardson, Gordon (later Lord Richardson)
(1915–) Governor of the Bank of England, 1973–83.

Ridley, Sir Adam
(1942–) Member, CPRS, 1971–74. Economic adviser to Shadow Cabinet, 1974–79.

Robbins, Lionel (later Lord)
(1898–1984) Distinguished economist; professor of economics at LSE, 1929–61; chairman of LSE, 1968–74.

Robinson, Geoffrey
(1938–) Labour MP for Coventry NW, 1976–. Chief executive, Jaguar Cars, 1973–75. Paymaster General, 1997–98.

Rocard, Michel
(1930–) French socialist politician. Prime Minister of France, 1988–91.

Rodgers, William (later Lord Rodgers)
(1928–) MP for Stockton-on-Tees (Labour 1962–81, SDP 1981–83); Minister of Defence, 1974–76 and for Transport 1976–79; one of the 'Gang of Four' founding members of the SDP in 1981; leader of the Liberal Democrats in the House of Lords, 1997–2001.

Rogaly, Joe
Journalist on the *Financial Times*.

Roll, Eric (Lord Roll)
(1907–2005) Economist. Director of the Bank of England, 1968–77, and Times Newspapers, 1967–80.

Rooker, Jeff (later Lord Rooker)
(1941–) Labour MP for Birmingham Perry Bar, 1974–2001; Minister of State MAFF, 1997–99; DSS, 1999–2001; Home Office, 2001–02; Office of the Deputy Prime Minister, 2002–05; Northern Ireland, 2005–06; DEFRA, 2005–. Deputy Leader of the House of Lords, 2005–.

Ross, Willie (later Lord Ross)
(1911–88) Labour MP for Kilmarnock, 1946–79; Scottish Secretary 1964–70 and 1974–76.

Rothschild, Lord Victor
(1910–90) Director-general of the Central Policy Review Staff, 1971–74; chairman of N. M. Rothschild & Sons, 1975–76.

Ryder, Don (later Lord Ryder)
(1916–2003) Director of IPC, 1963–70; chairman and chief executive of Reed International, 1968–75; chairman of the National Enterprise Board, 1975–77.

Sainsbury, David (later Lord Sainsbury)
(1940–) Director of J. Sainsbury plc, 1973–90; chairman, 1992–98; parliamentary under-secretary at DTI, 1998–2006.

Sarbanes, Paul
(1934–) United States senator for Maryland until 2006. Long-standing friend of the author.

Scanlon, Hugh (later Lord Scanlon)
(1913–2004) Member of the TUC General Council and president of the Amalgamated Union of Engineering Workers, 1968–78.

Scargill, Arthur
(1938–) Socialist president of the National Union of Mineworkers during the destruction of the coal industry and the diminution of his union.

Schlesinger, James
(1929–) United States secretary for Energy in the Carter Administration.

Schmidt, Helmut
(1918–) German Minister of Defence, 1969–72; German Finance Minister, 1972–74; Chancellor of Germany, 1974–82.

Scott, Derek
(1947–) Special adviser to Chancellor of the Exchequer Denis Healey, 1977–79. Economic adviser to Prime Minister Tony Blair, 1997–2003.

Sedgemore, Brian
(1937–) Labour MP for Luton, 1974–79, and for Hackney, 1983–2005.

Sherman, Sir Alfred
(1919–2006) Iconoclast ex-communist adviser to Margaret Thatcher. Colleague of the author at *Sunday Telegraph* and remained friendly.

Shore, Peter (later Lord Shore)
(1924–2001) Labour MP for Stepney, 1964–74, for Stepney and Poplar, 1974–83, and for Bethnal Green, 1983–92; Secretary of State for Trade, 1974–76, for Environment, 1976–79.

Short, Edward (Ted) (later Lord Glenamara)
(1912–) Labour MP for Newcastle on Tyne, 1951–76; Education Secretary, 1968–70; leader of the House of Commons, 1974–76; deputy leader of the Labour Party, 1972–76.

Short, Renée
(1919–2003) Labour MP for Wolverhampton NE, 1964–87; member of the National Executive Committee of the Labour Party, 1970–81, 1983–88.

Silkin, John
(1923–87) Labour MP for Deptford and Lewisham and Deptford, 1963–87; Minister of Local Government, 1974–76; Agriculture, 1976–79.

Silkin, Sam (later Lord Silkin)
(1918–88) Labour MP for Camberwell, 1964–74, and for Southwark, 1974–83; Attorney-General, 1974–79.

Skinner, Dennis
(1932–) Labour MP for Bolsover, 1970–.

Smith, Sir Cyril
(1928–) Liberal MP for Rochdale, 1972–92. Liberal Party Chief Whip, 1975–76.

Smith, John
(1938–94) Labour MP for Lanarkshire N, 1970–83, and for Monklands E, 1983–94; Minister at the Department of Energy, 1975–76 and at the Privy Council office, 1976–79; leader of the Labour Party, 1992–94.

Snell, Gordon
(1933–) Writer, humorist and long-time Oxford friend of the author.

Soames, Sir Christopher (later Lord)
(1920–87) Conservative MP for Bedford, 1950–66. Ambassador to France, 1968–72. EC Commission, 1973–77. Leader of the House of Lords, 1979–81.

Sonnenfeldt, Helmut (Hal)
(1926–) Assistant to Henry Kissinger, US Secretary of State, 1973–77.

Spiers, Ron
(1925–) United States Embassy official.

Steel, David (later Lord Steel)
(1938–) Liberal MP for Roxburgh, Selkirk and Peebles, 1965–83, and for Tweeddale, Ettrick and Lauderdale, 1983–97; leader of the Liberal Party, 1976–88; first presiding officer of the Scottish Parliament, 1999–2003.

Stewart, Michael
(1933–) Economist and economic adviser to Foreign Secretary David Owen, 1977–78.

Stone, Joe (later Lord Stone)
(1903–86) Doctor to Harold Wilson and Marcia Falkender.

Stonehouse, John
(1925–88) Labour MP for Wednesbury, 1957–74, and for Walsall N, 1974–76; Postmaster General, 1968–69.

Stott, Roger
(1943–99) Labour MP for Westhoughton, 1973–83, and for Wigan, 1983–99; PPS to the Secretary of State for Industry, 1975–76 and to the Prime Minister, 1976–79.

Stowe, Sir Kenneth
(1927–) Assistant under-secretary at the Cabinet Office, 1973–75; principal private secretary to the Prime Minister, 1975–79; permanent secretary, DHSS, 1981–87.

Straw, Jack
(1946–) Labour MP for Blackburn, 1979–; political adviser to the Secretary of State for Social Services, 1974–76; special adviser to the Environment minister, 1976–79; Home Secretary, 1997–2001; Foreign Secretary, 2001–05; Leader of the House of Commons, 2006–07; Lord High Chancellor and Secretary of State for Justice, 2007–.

Stuart, Nicholas
(1942–) Private secretary to the Prime Minister, 1973–76; deputy secretary for Education, 1976–92.

Summerskill, Dr Shirley
(1931–) Labour MP for Halifax, 1964–83. Parliamentary under-secretary at the Home Office, 1974–79.

Tebbitt, Norman (later Lord Tebbitt)
(1931–) Conservative MP for Epping and Chingford, 1970–92; Secretary of State for Employment, 1981–83; DTI, 1983–85; chairman of the Conservative Party, 1985–87.

Thatcher, Margaret (later Baroness)
(1925–) Conservative MP for Finchley, 1959–92. Leader of the Opposition, 1975–79. Prime Minister of Great Britain, 1979–90.

Thorpe, Jeremy
(1929–) Liberal MP for Devon N, 1959–79; leader of the Liberal Party, 1967–76.

Trelford, Donald
(1937–) Deputy editor of the *Observer*, 1969–76; editor, 1975–93.

Trudeau, Pierre
(1919–2000) Prime Minister of Canada, 1968–79.

Underhill, Reginald (later Lord Underhill)
(1914–93) National agent for the Labour Party, 1972–79.

Urwin, Charles (Harry)
(1915–96) Deputy general secretary, Transport and General Workers Union, 1969–80.

Varley, Eric (later Lord Varley)
(1932–) Labour MP for Chesterfield, 1964–84; PPS to the Prime Minister, 1968–69; Minister of Technology, 1969–70; Secretary of State for Energy, 1974–75; Secretary of State for Industry, 1975–79.

Walden, George
(1939–) Conservative MP for Buckingham, 1983–97. First secretary in the Paris Embassy, 1974–78. Principal private secretary to Foreign Secretary, 1978–81.

Walker, Peter
(1932–) Conservative MP for Worcester, 1961; Secretary of State for the Environment, 1970–72, and for Trade, 1972–74; Opposition spokesman, 1974–75.

Wass, Sir Douglas
(1923–) Permanent secretary at the Treasury, 1974–83.

Weidenfeld, George (later Lord Weidenfeld)
(1919–) Founded the publishing firm of Weidenfeld & Nicolson, in 1948.

Weinstock, Arnold (later Lord Weinstock)
(1924–2002) Managing director, General Electric plc, 1963–96.

Whitehead, Phillip
(1937–2006) Television producer and Labour MP for Derby N, 1970–83.

Whitelaw, Viscount William
(1918–99) Conservative MP for Penrith, 1955–83; Secretary of State for Northern Ireland, 1972–73; deputy leader of the opposition, 1975–79; Home Secretary, 1979–83; leader of the House of Lords, 1983–88.

Whittome, Sir Alan
(1926–2001) Director of the European Department of the International Monetary Fund, 1964–86.

Wicks, Sir Nigel
(1940–) HM Treasury, 1968–75. Private secretary to PM, 1975–78; second permanent secretary at the Treasury, 1989–2000.

Williams, Marcia (later Baroness Falkender)
(1932–) Personal and political secretary to Harold Wilson, 1956–83.

Williams, Philip
(1920–84) Fellow of Nuffield College, Oxford, 1958–84.

Williams, Shirley (later Baroness Williams)
(1930–) Labour MP for Hitchin, 1964–74, and for Hertford and Stevenage, 1974–79; SDP MP for Crosby, 1981–83; Opposition spokesman on home affairs, 1971–73; Minister of Education, 1976–79; founder and president of the SDP, 1981–88; leader of Liberal Democrats in the House of Lords, 2001–04.

Wilson, Harold (later Lord Wilson of Rievaulx)
(1916–95) Labour MP for Ormskirk, 1945–50, and for Huyton, 1950–83; leader of the Labour Party, 1963–76; Prime Minister, 1964–70, and 1974–76.

Wise, Audrey
(1935–2000) Left-wing Labour MP for Coventry SW, 1974–79, and for Preston, 1997–2000.

Witteveen, Dr Johannes
(1921–) Dutch business economist and Netherlands minister for Finance, 1963–65, 1967–71. Managing director of the International Monetary Fund, 1973–78.

Wood, Philip
(1946–) Private secretary to Prime Minister James Callaghan, 1975–79. Under-secretary, deputy secretary at the Department of Transport, 1986–97.

Worcester, Sir Robert
(1933–) Chairman of MORI since 1973, which carried out Wilson's and Labour Party opinion polls.

Wright, Patrick (later Lord Wright)
(1931–) Head of the Middle East Department at the FO, 1972–74; private secretary for overseas affairs to the Prime Minister, 1974–77; deputy under-secretary, FCO, 1982–84; head of FCO, 1986–91.

Wright, Vincent
(1937–99) Lecturer at LSE, 1973–79; fellow, Nuffield College, 1977–99.

Zander, Professor Michael
(1932–) Professor of law at LSE, 1977–98, and friend of the author.

Index

BD – Bernard Donoughue; HW – Harold Wilson; JC – James Callaghan

Abbado, Claudio 481
Abel Smith, Brian 195
abortion 244–5, 250, 301, 302, 308–9, 312, 313, 340–41, 492
Abse, Dannie 391
Adley, Robert 25
Admiralty House 276
AEU *see* Amalgamated Union of Engineering Workers
Agee, Philip 152–3, 391
Aherne, Bertie 336
air traffic controllers' strike (1977) 231
aircraft industry 317, 326, 340, 345, 348, 354, 374, 444
Airey, Lawrence 220, 278, 306
Aitken, Ian 499
Aitken, Jonathan 61
Albert, Michel 328–9, 482, 484
Aldington, Lord (Toby Low) 387
Alexander, Ken 179, 337
All the President's Men (film) 27
Allen, Sir Douglas: and child benefits press leak 41–2, 47; chairs industrial democracy committee 75, 87; ideas on Civil Service College 77–8; and Treasury 87, 149; and William Armstrong 87, 153; good at Civil Service College meeting 154; weekly lunches 241; need to replace 243; discusses changes in Civil Service 255, 256; disappointed with CSD job 256, 258; stresses importance of strengthening Treasury officials 261; and Brookings initiatives 296, 338
Allen, Alfred (*later* Lord) 434
Allen, John Schofield 74, 144
Allen, Philip 36
Amalgamated Union of Engineering Workers (AUEW; AEU) 73, 369, 370
Amin, Idi, President of Uganda 52
Amnesty International 334
Andreotti, Giulio 391, 392
Anglo-American Conference on Peace and the Law (1977) 205

Anglo-Irish parliamentary football match (1978) 313, 316, 332, 335, 336
Annan Report on Broadcasting 138; rejected by Home Office/Rees 280, 294, 295, 304; Cabinet committees on 295, 301–2, 338; discussed by Elstein 324; and Home Office negotiations 324–5, 329, 330, 332–3, 337, 342, 347
Apple, Johnny 202, 214, 277, 282, 316, 337, 361, 392, 443
Armed Services pay 315, 319
Armstrong, Anne 30, 146
Armstrong, Robert 126; on slackness in Home Office 44; on HW 44, 93; on 'secrets case' 152–3, 391; on William Armstrong 153; on Kagan 154; and police pay talks 157; as permanent secretary at Home Office 167, 200; 'a big man' 200; on Hunt 214; on HW's 'MI5 mistakes' story 223; 'equable' 233; opposed as Hunt's successor 246, 259, 479; keeps BD up to date on scandals 247–8; embarrassed by Rees 290; on Rees and BBC 304; on Thorpe case 329; on problems in Home Office 404; clashes with Hunt 446; at Unit farewell party 499
Armstrong, William 87, 121, 153, 296, 395, 459
Arnott, Liz 34, 82, 153, 383, 418
Ascherson, Neil 344
Ashfield by-election (1977) 182
Ashley, Jack: recommended by BD 16; marvellous company 28; and Palantype machine 40, 58; and vehicles for the disabled 53; manoeuvred off NEC 87–8; visits Germany 136; at RNID conference 143; and whooping cough vaccine campaign 155, 184, 199, 302; socialises with BD 183, 226, 326
Aspen Institute 433, 450
Astaire, Jarvis 30, 36
Atkinson, Fred 206–7
Atkinson, Norman 21, 73, 169
Attlee, Clement: JC's speech on 120, 122, 123, 124, 125

Aubrey, Gabriel 391
AUEW *see* Amalgamated Union of Engineering
    Workers
Ayckbourn, Alan: *Ten Times Table* 416

Bacon, David 211, 315
Bailey, Alan 421
Bain, Margaret 204, 207, 339
Bakash, Al 367
Baker, Kenneth 302
Bancroft, Ian 133; pro Brookings Institute 278;
    'rather fey' 284; backs Shirley Williams on
    public appointments 321; and Mrs Thatcher
    478
Banda, Hastings 196, 314
Bank of England: incompetence 26; objects to
    honours for Goldsmith 36; and sterling crisis
    (1976) 37, 57, 66, 67, 73; nationalisation
    discussed 69–70; constructs monetary package
    with Treasury 75–6; against IMF loan 80;
    touchy about JC's criticisms 100; and National
    Westminster Bank's financial difficulties 127;
    and interest rates 137, 179, 180; rescues Slater
    Walker 202; and BP shares sale 198, 209, 253,
    339; relationship with Treasury 220–21; tech-
    nical incompetence 226, 227; policy of high
    interest rates 248–9; and monetary seminar
    249, 250–51; 'negative treachery' over interest
    rates 268–9, 270–71; lifts MLR 322; economic
    'package' 333, 334, 335; sells out of gilts
    335–6, 337, 338; excluded from EMS briefing
    375, 376; raises lending rate 386; against EMS
    393; *see also* Richardson, Gordon
Bank of International Settlements scheme 120,
    123
banks, nationalisation of 69–70, 74
Banqueting House, Whitehall: concert 330
Barclay, Clifford 140, 155
Barker, Tony 320
Barnetson, Lord 41, 62
Barnett, Joel: uncharacteristically weak 20;
    constructive over fees for overseas students
    40; and cuts in disabled services 48; briefs JC
    on public expenditure 53; pessimistic about
    cuts 93, 94–5; wants JC to make his position
    clear 111; on Treasury taxation plans 122; and
    Lib–Lab deal 174; at economic seminar 180;
    and social security uprating 190; and family
    support 208; and Polish shipping order 235,
    237; at seminar with Bank of England 250;
    and steel industry cuts 263; clashes with
    Lever 309; on Contingency reserve 375; paper
    rejected in Cabinet 445
Basnett, David: and No. 10/union liaison 24, 34,
    42; discusses public expenditure cuts 42–3;
    agrees to support JC on industrial democracy
    135; depressed about wage policy 141, 152;
    puzzles Healey 141; optimistic about deal 177;
    discusses reorganisation of Labour Party 237;

at Blackpool 369; suggests deal for local
    authority unions 405; and pay negotiations
    431, 434
BBC (British Broadcasting Corporation): and
    Harry Evans 78, 88; and HW's pursuit of
    South African spies 93; reorganisation of *see*
    Annan Report on Broadcasting; disliked by JC
    295, 300; sued by Shrimsley 301; attacked by
    Benn 302; broadcasts Questions 308; and
    White Paper 337–8, 367, 377, 405; and elec-
    tion campaign 481–2
Beckett, Margaret (*née* Jackson): 'will go far' 19;
    and BD 38; hard going against civil servants
    51; at Blackpool Conference (1976) 72; and
    the left's plans over economic package 112,
    126; and NEC 151, 155, 258; scathing about
    Shirley Williams's White Paper 199
Beer, Professor Sam 467
Beevers, Donald 234, 259
Begin, Menachem 278, 366
Benn, Anthony (Tony) Wedgwood 8; accepts
    Energy 17–18; at JC's first Cabinet committee
    20; wants inquiry into BP bribes 26; ticked off
    by JC 27; and import controls 39, 71, 94, 108,
    264, 310, 311; opposes nuclear energy 40, 156,
    178, 183, 190, 277; and privatisation of BP 42;
    opposes public expenditure cuts 49, 50, 54,
    56, 87; gives Herbert Morrison memorial
    lecture 51; threatens resignation over cuts 58;
    toes the line 58; supports Unit's national plan
    paper 98; puts in 'crafty' paper 106; alterna-
    tive strategy debated 109, 110; defends
    appointment of Trotskyite 113; 'cowardly' 115;
    pleased with paper on Marxism 122; 'a
    canting hypocrite' 122; fails to produce
    coherent policy 123–4; his defects as minister
    124–5; on the stamina needed for politics 137;
    proposes company working parties 138; on
    unemployment 155; and Lib–Lab deal 167,
    170; organises left-wing rebellion 170–71;
    ordered by JC to 'unsign' or resign 172;
    private meeting with JC 191; on fighting
    Whitehall 192; and EEC 195; his 'Workers'
    Control' view 202; discusses politics with BD
    202–3; quotes BD's book on Morrison 211;
    supports trade unions over pay 216, 220;
    scheme for BNOC 226; put on the spot over
    Europe 231; lack of ministerial power 243;
    and power strike 258, 260, 261; good paper on
    energy conservation 259; and North Sea oil
    revenues 261, 262; tries to mobilise anti-EEC
    ministers 266; Varley on 266; attacks relax-
    ation of exchange controls 273; and IMF
    letter 276; votes against PR 276; attacks
    'mandarins of TUC' 279; forced to compro-
    mise on nuclear energy 282; behaves badly
    283; and BBC 295, 302; and public appoint-
    ments 321; clashes with JC 322, 384, 388, 405;
    objects to economic package 335; supports JC

on Annan 338; makes sweeping demands 367; praises JC for Conference speech 370; blames motor industry management 379; clashes with JC over nuclear power 384, 388; supports Sedgemore 385, 387; criticised for disloyalty 390; and microprocessor revolution 392; 'courting martyrdom' 395; further clashes with JC 405; irrelevancy 423; and negotiations with unions 432, 435, 439; votes against government over sale of Harriers 444; long discussion with JC 444, 447; in favour of higher income tax 451–2; implied rebuke 455; and *Times* dispute 456; has done nothing about nuclear policy 458; wants to make civil servants 'accountable' 478; wants to abolish House of Lords 479

Bennett, Alan 173, 196; *The Old Country* 234; screenplay on Orton 373

Benson, Henry 25

Berlin: BD's visits 396, 433, 442

Berrill, Ken: and CPRS 46–7, 58, 59; lunches with BD 66; and economic crisis 79; introduces CPRS paper 98, 99; 'cool and detached' 99; and national recovery programme 100, 123, 128–9; admits CPRS responsible for Unit's troubles 134; disliked by Tessa Blackstone 137; tones down CPRS report on Foreign Office 189; attacked by Benn 202; excluded from Strategy Cabinet 205; angry at meeting on family support 208; at monetary seminars 250, 254; and CPRS report on overseas representation 255; on Bank of England 270; and Cabinet standing committees 283; disagrees with CPRS report on unemployment 285, 303; and counter-inflation policy 429

Berry, Halle 391

Berwick by-election (1978) 381

Bessell, Peter 241, 242

Betjeman, John 263

Bevan, Andy 113, 122, 123

Biffen, John 101, 186

Billington, Jim 338

Bindman, Geoffrey 279, 386, 387

Bingham Report on Rhodesia 354; and subsequent inquiry 365, 367–8, 372, 373, 382–3, 386, 398, 402, 448

Birk, Alma 52

Birmingham: NEC Motor Show (1978) 377

Birt, John 495, 497

Black, Jack 262

Blackpool: Labour Party Conferences 72–5, 81 (1976), 368–71 (1978)

Blackstone, Tessa: produces CPRS study on Foreign Office 137, 140, 188; and Berrill 137, 278; attacked by press 188; and discussions on NHS 303, 304, 329, 361; and election campaign 488, 493

Blake, Lord 72

Blumenthal, Michael 131, 160

Blunden, Sir George 225

Blunt, Sir Anthony 238, 259

BNOC *see* British National Oil Corporation

Bohm, Karl 277

Bonds, Denis 326

Bonham Carter, Mark 98

Bonn: World Economic summit (1978) 348

Booth, Albert: recommended by BD 15–16, and Foot 16; nervous in No. 10 17; and pay negotiations 25, 26, 27, 28; and import controls 94; at Janet Davies's farewell party 103; supports Benn/Shore alternative strategy 110; and unemployment 155; has 'grown in the job' 165; and industrial democracy 191, 200, 202; on child benefits 208; and air traffic controllers' strike 231; 'wooden' 233; votes against PR 276; and Civil Service appointments 321; and *Times* dispute 395, 456; and strikes 418, 426, 428: and industrial democracy 461

Booth-Clibborn, Edward 479, 480, 481, 483

Boothroyd, Betty 16, 151, 155, 369

Boston, Terry (Lord) 475

Bottomley, Arthur 38, 56, 301

Bottomley, Peter 341

Bourne, Peter 105, 200

Boyd, John 369

Boyle, Edward (Lord) 98, 129–30, 173, 226, 327, 378

Boyson, Rhodes 84

BP *see* British Petroleum

Bragg, Melvyn 95

Brazil, Jimmy 286, 313

Bremen: EC summit (1978) 343, 344, 345, 347

Brewster, Kingman 195

Bridges, Tom (Lord) 162, 208, 479

Brighton: Labour Conference (1977) 242–4, 245; TUC Conference (1978) 355, 356

British Aerospace 317, 374

British Airways 317, 354, 374

British Council 260

British Leyland: faulty cars 40, 353–4; in decline 155, 156, 163; 'slush fund' scandal 191, 192; to be closed down 363, 379, 380, 398; workers vote Tory 500

British National Oil Corporation (BNOC) 226

British Petroleum (BP): and bribes 20, 26; partial privatisation sale of shares 42, 104, 118, 178, 198, 200, 209, 253, 339

British Steel Corporation *see* steel industry

Brittan, Sam 192, 374

Brixton/Lambeth by-election (1978) 315, 316

Brookings Institute, European: discussions on 83, 98, 142, 264, 278, 291; backed by JC 267–8, 273, 274–5, 285, 308; and Ford Foundation 282, 296, 297, 309; and petty squabbles 292–3; Belgian input on 324, 339; and Civil Service briefing 326; Paris conferences (1978) 328, 340, 349; further support for London siting

344; and EEC Commission 297, 382, 387–8, 392, 398, 399, 429, 440, 451, 454, 462, 466
Brooks, Johnnie 176, 326
Broughton, Sir Alfred 470, 471, 472, 473
Brown, George 387
Brown, Lesley 40
Brown, Tina 88, 190
Brown (David) Tractors 139
Bryant, Gyude 296
Brzezinski, Zbigniew 160
Budgets: March 1977 156, 164, 165, 173–4, 177, 197, 208; October 1977 238, 241, 245, 253, 254; March 1978 299, 301, 303, 305, 306, 307, 308, 310–11, 312, 313, 314; strategy for 1979 448, 451–2, 458, 462; papers left on Tube 457
Bullock Report on Industrial Democracy 75, 87, 90, 124, 134, 138, 191, 202
Bundy, MacGeorge 268, 275
Burmah Oil 104
Burnet, Alastair 89, 475, 499, 500
Burns, Arthur 100, 120, 131, 162
Burton, Humphrey 143
Busby, Matt 249
Butler, Bishop Christopher 301
Butler, David 84, 290, 321–2
Butler, Michael 83, 131, 159
Butler, Robin: on the Treasury 26, 95; sets up computer monitoring in Treasury 95; lunches with BD 124; nearly runs him over 126; on HW 199; on the Treasury and public expenditure 240, 249, 452; aware of weaknesses among colleagues 285; on lack of loyalty in Civil Service 316; 'superb as ever' 334; joins BD in Suffolk cottage 363, 364; socialises with BD 394, 397–8; at German Embassy dinner 421; 'too young' for promotion 452; at Unit farewell party 499
Butt, 'Fatty' 89
'Buy British' campaign 287, 290, 310, 312
Byers, Frank 272

Cairncross, Frances 448
Callaghan, Audrey 3, 23; against living in US (1972) 158; on Canadian trip 66, 69; gives dinner party 83; at JC's Ruskin College speech 84; talks sense at Fabian Society dinner 95; nurses JC 118, 119; at Christmas lunch 127; and Crosland's death 146; on US trip 158, 161; farewell dinner for Patrick Wright 227; and JC's speeches 233; and Indian trip 271; illness 295; supports JC in the House 296; at Labour Party Conference 370, 371; presses for more money for NHS 375; coffee with BD 394; at PMQs 424; organises party for JC 469; at confidence vote 471, 472; 'marvellous' 482; at 'last supper' 502
Callaghan, Bill 265
Callaghan, James
    age and appearance 18, 20, 244; character and

personality 2, 3, 4, 29, 66; chauvinism 244; comparisons with HW see Wilson, Harold; and economics 7; as family man 3, 39, 304; as Home Secretary 139, 364, 373; hymn singing 2, 399; on immigration 153; intellectual capabilities 4–5, 15, 74; Irish blood 2–3, 149; and the media 65; and money 13; morality 19, 20; naval career 2, 3; prime ministerial style 1–2, 3–4, 13, 14–15, 18, 19, 22, 35, 176–7; and Prime Minister's Questions 5, 13–14, 50, 449; prudery 2, 363, 435–6; and religion 2; speeches 5, 23, 24, 233; Sussex farm 24; television broadcasts 5; television watching 362

April–December 1976
    and Policy Unit 13, 15, 18, 25–6, 27; forms Cabinet 7–8, 14, 15–16, 17–18, 20, 21; and BD's Israeli trip 18; praises BD 19; gives superb speeches 19; makes junior appointments 19; first Cabinet committee 20; USDAW Conference speech 21, 22, 23–4; dingy flat 24; prepared to retire 24; and top salaries 25, 36, 88; dominant at Questions 25, 27, 30; and TUC negotiations 26, 27, 28–9; and bad local election results 31; sees ministers individually 27, 31, 39, 55; grumpy at Questions briefing 32; and NEC 32, 43, 60, 69, 72, 73, 85, 86, 88, 122; and child benefits 34–5; attacked over Cyprus 35; and Hunt 36; and sterling crisis 37, 46; and vote of censure 37; and flat at No. 10 38; and import controls 39, 40; at Trooping the Colour 38; at TUC Labour Party committee 42; and Benn 42; and Giscard 43; and public expenditure cuts 43, 47, 55, 58, 59, 61, 86, 91, 94; visits Northern Ireland 49; and special advisers 50–51; hates Questions 50; furious at Foreign Office appeasement of Amin 52; receives honorary degree 57; dislikes devolution 59, 85; patronises Mrs Thatcher 59; and Official Secrets 61, 62; enjoys Balmoral 65; and *Observer* 65; has 'gone off' Crosland 56; loses secret papers 66; and Bank of England 66; and seamen's strike 67; Cabinet reshuffle 67–8; Canadian trip 66, 67, 68–9; and nationalisation of banks 69–70; at Blackpool Conference 70, 72–5; and economy 76, 77, 78, 79, 80, 86, 87, 92, 94; and deputy leadership 81, 82; and Shore 82, 83; hosts dinner party 83; education speech (Ruskin College) 82, 83, 84, 204; and Poulson affair 85–6; crushes Churchill 90; and media campaign 91; approves Unit's national plan 91, 96, 97; and disastrous by-elections 95–6; 'knocks Thatcher around' 98; secret meeting with Treasury 98, 100; critical of Bank 100; meeting with Giscard 101; and PSBR 102–3, 104, 105–6; at European heads meeting 106, 108; and IMF negotiations

over cuts 108, 110, 111, 112, 113, 115–19; ill 114, 115, 116, 117, 119; and IMF Letter of Intent 117, 118–19, 120; and devolution debate 120–21; secret meeting with trade unionists 122; leaves Crosland to entertain Poles 122; on Benn 122; optimistic about exchange rate 123; deflates Hattersley 124; Attlee speech 122, 123, 124, 125; hosts Christmas lunch 127; wants to work on memoirs with BD 127, 128, 130, 137

January–July 1977
initiative on unemployment at World Economic summit 129, 131; and economic policies 131, 132–3, 134, 135, 137; and industrial democracy 134, 135, 138, 139; and Unit's national recovery programme 130, 134–5; at NEB 135; and immigration 135, 138, 139, 140, 141, 143, 151, 152; and Scottish devolution 136, 149, 152–3; asks Hattersley to write draft of national recovery programme 138; sings with Mondale 139; in Huddersfield and Harrogate 139; on Carter 141, 157, 186, 452; at RNID 143; on future overseas visits 142; and Haines's book 142, 145, 146, 147; plans to split Treasury 147, 149, 150; and SAS soldiers 148; defends Haines 155; worried how to approach Carter 157; talks to Thatcher about devolution 157; and HW's removal of Marcia Falkender from Film committee 157; in Washington and Ottawa 158–64; and public expenditure White Paper 165; does deal with Ulster Unionists 167, 168, 169; and Lib–Lab pact 166, 168–70, 171, 172, 174, 178; *even* opens drinks cupboard 172; orders Benn to withdraw name or resign 172; at secret birthday party 173; anniversary celebration 176; pay talks with trade unionists 177, 179; and Prince Charles 178; on pay policy 179, 180, 181; more positive on devolution 183; with Carter in North-East 184; and World Economic summit 182, 183, 184–7; and Jay's appointment as ambassador 188, 189; delays decisions on industrial democracy 190, 191; and nuclear contract with Japanese 190; snaps at BD over British Leyland 191; dinner with Neddy Six 191; and *Mail* error over British Leyland 192; dinner with the Queen 192; and inquiry into Engineering 193; and mortgage rates 193, 195; and Fraser 195; at Commonwealth heads meeting 196, 198; and BP shares sale 198; railroads Rodgers's White Paper through 199; 'avuncular complacency' in Questions 199; in fighting form 201–2; and Shirley Williams's education paper 204; at Chequers Strategy Cabinet 205–6; at Spithead review 207; likes CPRS report on Foreign Office 211; handles seminar with Governor and

Chancellor brilliantly 212; and pay negotiations with unions 213, 215–16, 217, 218–19, 220, 221; Durham miners speech 221–2; 'confidence' speech 223; and NEC meeting 226; and Richardson's threatened rate rise 227; and unemployment 227

August 1977–March 1978
and Booth's capitulation 231; forces Benn into collective responsibility 231; in Scotland 231; at TUC Conference 232, 233; and Christmas bonuses 233; on HW 233; discusses Cabinet members with BD 233–4; uninterested in polls 234; and Healey's reflation packages 234, 236; takes a holiday 236; friendly meeting with Steel 237; opens Brighton Conference Centre 237; in Italy 238, 239; and tax 241–2; at Labour Conference 241, 242–3, 244; criticises Varley and Rodgers 243; wants study on Civil Service reform 243, 244, 246; mentions possibility of election 245; critical of Healey's paper 245; angry at lateness of Cabinet Office report on Rhodesia 245–6; dislikes tree in No. 10's garden 246; discusses Treasury split 246; furious with Healey 247; approves Unit's economic briefs 247; visits Schmidt 248; makes moving speech at Spanish lunch 249; and public expenditure 250; at monetary seminars 251, 254; briefed on 'scandals' 252; optimistic 253–4; supports reform of Foreign Office 255; discusses changes in Civil Service 255–6; and miners 256, 257; speech on the Address 256, 257–8; and power strike 258, 259, 260, 261; and North Sea divers' taxation 261, 262; and steel industry 263, 267, 282; concerned about de-industrialisation 264; and firemen's strike 264, 266, 268; further seminars 264, 265; threatens to sack Benn 266; angry with Bank of England 269; and pay policy 270, 278, 279; criticises BD for meanness to his children 270; pleased with EEC meeting 271; and Treasury 272, 274, 275; and exchange controls 273; supports Brookings Institute 274, 285; tough with Steel over PR 276; in Northern Ireland 278; at Christmas party 279; discussion with Healey 280; and North Sea oil White Paper 281, 283, 289, 297; and further trouble from Benn 282, 283; accused in press of being rich farmer 284; and racist issues 284, 285; favours special advisers 286; economic discussion with Unit 287; and Jay 288; and Mrs Thatcher and immigration 288, 289–90, 291, 292, 293; supportive of CPRS 291; swears about Rees 292; criticised for 'gloomy' statement about economy 292, 294; and Windscale 294; and BBC 295, 302;

opposes Rees 295; worried about wife 295; re-establishes himself at Questions 296, 297, 299; pleased with poll 297–8; and Ireland 298–9, 300; and public expenditure 299

March–October 1978
and Budget 299, 301, 303, 305, 307, 308; meets Tito 300; in Bonn 301; ITV appearance 300; speaks at *Guardian* Businessman of the Year lunch 302; at Election Campaign committee 304; talks to Steel about election 305; against Owen on Middle East 305; Washington trip 304, 306; introduces North Sea oil White Paper 305–6; on inflation 307; and Lib–Lab pact 307, 317; sings at reception for Welsh rugby team 307; and broadcast of PMQs 308, 309; at Windsor 310; and Copenhagen EEC summit 308, 310; on economic options 311; big speech on 'Buy British' 312; reduces workload 313, 323; and Hastings Banda 314; talks with Schmidt 316, 318; moans about inadequacy of briefing 316; pleased about aircraft policy talks 317; attacks Defence 319; and lack of speechwriter 321; clashes with Benn 322; and Finance Bill 322; grumpy with Moshe Dayan 323; therapeutic meetings 324; on *Private Eye* 324; and BBC governors 325; and autumn election 325, 326, 327; too many foreign visitors 326, 328; treats Moser well 328; speaks on 'the family' 329; oozes confidence 330; and end of Lib–Lab pact 331, 453; makes impact at NATO meeting 332; and Indian prime minister 333; and Bank/Treasury crisis package 333, 334, 335, 336–7; and inquiry into selling gilts 339; receives US award 340; meeting with Liberals over employers' insurance premium 341; pay talks with unions 341; very tired 342; and top salaries 343–4; backs Healey 344–5; and Bremen EEC summit 343, 345, 346, 347; robust on public sector pay 346; bored with Questions 347; at NUR Conference 347; at Bonn summit 348; sees CBI 348; defeats Mrs Thatcher 349, 350; problems with new cars 353–4; Brighton TUC speech 353, 355, 356, 357; defers election 354, 359–60, 361–2, 364, 366, 412, 461; and Rhodesian sanctions 358, 365; and 'Themes and Initiatives' 361, 362, 363; on British Leyland 363, 379, 380; Nigerian trip 366; Blackpool Conference 364, 365, 368, 369–71; and EMS 372, 373, 374, 375, 392, 393, 394; and pay policy 375, 380, 383–4, 386, 387, 388, 391; and collapsing dollar 381; quizzes Mason on Northern Ireland 381

November 1978–May 1979
Queen's Speech 367, 368, 373, 382; at Wick's farewell dinner 383; clashes with

Weinstock 384; sacks Sedgemoor 384, 385, 387; at monetary seminar 385; attacks EEC budgetary system 388; and failure of TUC talks 389; entertains Portuguese prime minister 389, 390; and Giscard 391, 392, 394; shocked by shipbuilding crisis 395; and devolution referenda 395; at EEC summit on EMS 397, 398, 400; and pay sanctions vote 398–9, 400–2, 403; 'knocked off course' 404; sends union man away with 'flea in his ear' 405; clashes with Benn 405; at No. 10 Christmas party 405; meets with public service ministers 406; on pay policies and current disputes 412–14; Caribbean trip 412, 415, 416–17, 418, 422, 423; on counterinflation policy and public sector pay 420; and strikes 420, 421–3, 424–5, 426, 427–8, 429, 430, 431; and trade unions 431, 432, 433–4, 436–8, 442; enjoys *Evening Standard* drama awards 435; speaks at local authority conference 438, 439–40; fails to discuss strategy 440; popularity in decline 441; on his broadcast 442; throws out Healey's crisis package 442; opens devolution campaign in Scotland 442; holds firm against unions 443; and Prince Charles's visit to No. 10 443; announces concordat with TUC 444; turns down Murray's compromise proposal 445, and Shore's 'solution' 447; annoyed with Ennals and Shore 447, 455; opens new Institute of Policy Studies 448; and devolution 448, 456, 457–8; TV appearance 450; and Cabinet reshuffle 451; and Civil Service pay claim 452, 453; gives lunch for *Mirror* journalists 452; tired and grumpy 454, 455; instructs Benn not to address *Times* workers 456; at EEC heads of government meeting 457; tells Benn off for lack of energy policy 458; and election 458–9, 462; aggressive in PMQs 460; against wheeler-dealing 461, 464, 465; statement on devolution 464, 465; TV broadcast 465, 466; and loss of drive 466; and confidence vote 467–9, 470–73; surprise birthday party 469; and the Queen 473; and election campaign 474, 475, 476, 477, 478–9, 480, 481, 482–4, 485–6, 487, 488, 489, 490–92, 493, 494–7, 498, 499; last hours at No. 10 502–3; farewell talk at Transport House and final press conference 504

Callaghan, Michael 469, 481, 486, 493, 495, 502
Campbell, John 366–7, 470
Cape (publishers) 33; parties 116, 396
capital punishment 492
car seat belts 380
Caradon, Lord 358
Cardon, Richard 440
Carey, Peter 154, 263, 284
Carmichael, Kay 477

Carroll, Roger: joins Labour election team 339; speechwriting in Political Office 353, 356, 367; and postponement of election 359; and election campaign 467, 475, 476, 478, 479, 480, 481, 483, 484, 485, 486, 487, 489, 493; departs No. 10 504

Carter, Charles 292

Carter, Jimmy, US President 91; inaugural ball 136–7; JC's views on 141, 157, 186, 452; and JC's Washington visit 159–60, 161, 162; in North-East with JC 184; at World Economic summit (1977) 185–6; his advisers 200; Sonnenfeldt's view on 234; 'summit' meeting with JC 304; volte-face on neutron bomb 308; criticised for lack of strategy 309; discussion on his first year 313; criticised by JC at NATO meeting 332; and World Economic summit (1978) 348

Carter, Rosalynn 161, 162

Carter, Ray 16

Cartledge, Brian 208, 476, 502

Carvel, Robert 91

Carver, Lady 30

Casablanca (film) 381

Castle, Barbara 7, 100, 146; not included in Cabinet 16, 17, 20; angry at being dropped 71; asks BD to dance 75; diaries 81; and Thorpe scandal 247–8

Catholic Church 124, 125; and abortion 244–5, 301, 302, 308–9, 312, 340–41; relations with Labour 324, 325

CBI *see* Confederation of British Industry

Central Electricity Generation Board (CEGB) 260, 261

Central Policy Review Staff (CPRS): under Berrill 46, 58, 59, 79; and national recovery programme 91, 96, 98, 99, 105, 121, 123, 125, 128; responsible for Unit's troubles 134; report on FCO 53, 54, 137, 140, 142–3, 162, 188–9, 193, 200, 205, 206, 210–11, 255, 324; under Hunt's control 214; paper on unemployment 283, 285, 303; JC supportive of 291; 7th birthday party 348; and pay policy 429, 431

Central Statistical Office (CSO) 33, 175, 194, 201

Channel Tunnel 216, 362–3

Chapman, Jill and Robin 342

Chapple, Frank 223, 273–4, 390, 434, 438–9, 441

Charkham, Jonathan 55, 120, 316–17

Charles, Prince of Wales 33, 178, 306, 391, 443

Charteris, Martin 267

Chatto & Windus 331

child benefits 6; new scheme deferred 30, 34, 35, 37; and immigrants 26, 27, 30; press leak of Cabinet minutes 41–2, 45, 47–8, 84–5; no more money for 191, 210; trade unions want increase 208; Unit's scheme dropped 213; and public expenditure cuts 213, 275; BD writes brief on 285; and Budget (1978) 307, 312, 329

Christmas bonus for pensioners 233, 240, 246, 373

Chrysler Motors 110

Churchill, Winston 90, 387

CIA 33, 223

City Royal Commission 451

Civil Contingencies Unit 447

Civil Service 241; and cuts 33, 44, 51, 53, 107, 121, 122; English committee/report on 38, 236, 238; BD's secret brief on 243, 244, 245; hostility to Unit and special advisers 128, 132, 355; and appointments 321, 322; and pay 264, 339, 398, 449–50, 452, 459, 460, 463–4, 466; strikes 315, 449; sick leave negotiations 446; *see also* Civil Service Department

Civil Service College 77–8, 154, 284

Civil Service Department 107, 256, 258; response to English Report 283, 286, 333

Clarke, Percy 304, 355, 462, 480

Clarke, Phyllis 304

Clarke, Senator Richard (Dick) 160

Cleave, Maureen 156

Cleese, John 95

Clegg, Hugh 390

Clough Brian 266

Coates, Ken 202

Cocks, Michael, Chief Whip 54, 468, 469, 473

Cohen, Jack 429

Cole, John 341

Colley, George 394

Commonwealth Prime Ministers' Conference (1977) 196, 198, 199

Community Relations Commission 55

community service award scheme 226

Confederation of British Industry (CBI) 25, 31, 87, 90, 134, 138, 141, 191, 195, 348, 375, 378

Connelly, Tom 55

Conservative Party: attacks on dealings with Russia 90; and American bankers 92; fails to attack 167; 'cock-a-hoop' over by-election result 176; no serious threat 197; and devolution 197; and Cordle's expulsion 225; getting jittery 232; embarrassed by leak on use of troops 314; contributes to constructive debate 330; ahead in polls 347; in high spirits 426; subdued 444; wins confidence vote 462, 474; election campaign 481–2, 488, 490, 491; victory 501; *see also* Heath, Edward; Thatcher, Margaret

Contingency Reserve 26, 30, 240, 375

Conway, Father Michael 181, 291

Cook, David, Lord Mayor of Belfast 394

Cook, Peter 78

Cooper, Frank 192, 195, 315

Cooper, Richard (Dick) 391

Corbett, Robin 81

Cordle, Sir John 225, 226, 250

Corr, James (Jim) 153, 217, 398, 421, 430, 485, 500

Corston, Jean 75, 97, 223
Cosgrave, Liam 89, 241
council houses: sale of 6, 29, 32, 33, 327, 336,
    481; lack of insulation 259
Couzens, Ken: and pay negotiations with unions
    179, 210, 217, 219, 220–21; put in charge of
    overseas finance 185, 210; and Treasury
    'bounce' 275; on Schmidt and German
    economy 320; appearance 320; opposed to
    EMS 393; and Irish innocence over EMS 394
Covent Garden Opera 277, 303
Cowans, Harry 311
Cox, Michael 54
CPRS see Central Policy Review Staff
Crathorne, Lord 28
Crawford, Danny 369
Crewe, Ivor 320
Cripps, Francis 106, 203
Croker, Cathy 315, 331
Croker, Ted 193, 238, 266, 315, 331, 481
Crosland, Anthony (Tony) 7–8; appointed to
    Foreign Office 16, 17; leaves problems
    unsolved 30; and Iceland 34, 35; and import
    controls 39; at Chequers 45–6; opposes cuts
    49; and Amin 52; looks ill 52–3; no time to
    read CPRS report 53; and public expenditure
    cuts 54, 66; cuts nose in Washington 54; 'very
    sour' 56; and Franks Report 61–2; and
    economy 80, 82; puts in excellent memo to JC
    92; at JC's emergency meeting 92; supports
    Unit's national plan paper 99; critical of
    Healey 99, 104; 'near end of the road' 99;
    threatens resignation 108; against cuts 109,
    110; entertains Poles 122; preoccupied with
    Rhodesia 137; stroke 146; and Tories' refusal
    to pair 149; praised by Giscard 150; death and
    funeral 150
Crosland, Susan 54, 146
Crossman, Anne 44
Crossman Diaries, The 311
Crowe, Brian 440
Crown Agents, inquiry into 271, 272
Crowther-Hunt, Norman 19
CSD see Civil Service Department
CSO see Central Statistical Office
Cubbon, Brian 376–7, 378, 479
Cudlipp, Hugh 40
Cudlipp, Michael 33, 40, 457
Cunningham, George 37
Cunningham, John 14, 32, 37, 56, 61, 72–3, 168,
    243, 469
Curran, Charles 93
Cyprus 35, 151, 305

Dahrendorf, Ralf: makes 'final offer' to BD 28;
    dines with BD 33; 'still very good' 42; and
    Brookings Institute 83, 98, 141–2, 292; asked
    by JC to arrange economic seminar 99;
    reports on breakfast with Schmidt 108; bril-

liant speech 393; discusses future plans with
    BD 462
Daily Express: and Howell 88; in crisis 180; polls
    257, 297, 387, 441, 491; Tory 'lines' 482
Daily Mail 30; and Kagan 154; on British
    Leyland 'slush fund' scandal 191, 192; and
    Liberal's 'Special Seats Fund' 272; on JC as
    rich farmer 284; protests about Roger
    Carroll's appointment to election team 339;
    photographs 'joggers' at Blackpool 370; poll
    415; a Tory paper 481, 482, 493
Daily Mirror/journalists 27, 65–6; ex-Wilson men
    thrown out of reception 74; serialises Haines's
    book 140, 142–3, 144, 148; and Thorpe
    scandal 241, 275; excluded by McCaffrey 284,
    297, 300, 347; Cabinet spy story 285, 286;
    sensible suggestions 307; and impending elec-
    tion 347, 349, 354, 356, 370; Blackpool parties
    370, 371; Christmas party 405; and Kagan
    scandal 417, 429; depressed over Labour elec-
    tion prospects 438; given lunch by JC 452;
    sycophantic 489; gloomy over election 498;
    blames unions 498
Daily Telegraph: polls 236, 296, 491; Tory 'lines'
    482
Davies, Anne 492
Davies, Bryan 500
Davies, Gavyn: Unit briefs and speeches 28, 31,
    33; on public expenditure 43, 44, 49, 50, 52,
    82, 83; on unemployment 65; and economic
    squeeze 76, 77; discussions and drafts 89, 94;
    thinks of clever ways of cutting PSBR 105;
    grilled by JC 105–6; and IMF Letter of
    Intent 113, 116, 117–19; Budget paper 145,
    147; pay policy brief 150; bets on Labour
    victory in House 168; brilliant paper on prices
    policy 175; and possible computer facilities
    194, 201; and Cabinet strategy paper 194, 203;
    at lunch with Lever 211–12; and T&G rejec-
    tion of pay policy 214; redrafts White Paper
    217, 218, 219; pessimistic about economy 224;
    drafts Budget papers 238, 241, 245; called to
    Brighton 243; monetary seminar briefs 247,
    251, 254, 264–5; and Budget 286, 287, 303;
    public expenditure brief 298; and Bank and
    Treasury's crisis package 333–4; further
    papers 336, 362, 364, 366, 272; football with
    BD 365; discusses monetary policy with BD
    384; papers on TUC agreement 387, British
    Leyland pay 398, Price Commission 404, the
    dollar 406–7; and pay situation 418, 421–2; on
    trade unions 423; plans brief on tax law 457;
    angry at being refused papers on civil
    servants' pay 463; and election campaign 480,
    485, 486, 487, 490, 491, 497, 500; future
    prospects 493
Davies, Janet Hewlett 41, 103
Day, Graham 116–17
Day, Robin 281, 496

Dayan, Moshe 323
Deakin, Nick 75
Deakins, Eric 15, 340
Dearing, Ron 239
de Chabris, George 451
Defence, Ministry of 55, 57, 93, 151, 225, 305, 319, 326, 319, 326, 456–7, 459
Delfont, Bernard 30
Dell, Edmund: recommended by BD 15; rescues Barnett at Cabinet 20; chairs Statistics Committee 32; and import controls 39, 71, 119; on British cars 40; supports Jenkins 61; supports Healey 104, 110, 114; and JC's plan to split Treasury 147; and industrial democracy 190, 191, 200, 202, 311; argues against sterling appreciation 254; defends Foreign Office 255; resigns from Cabinet 389
Democrats Abroad 135
Denham, Jean 83, 304, 321, 476, 480
DES *see* Education and Science, Department of
Desai, Maraji 285, 333
Devlin, Paddy 237
Dewar, Donald 59–60
DHSS *see* Health and Social Security, Department of
Dierkes, Meinolf 147, 198, 442
Dirkes, David 131
disabled, vehicles for the 48, 53, 223, 238, 240, 246
Divertimenti, the 464
Dixon, Michael 93
Dobbs, Maurice 234
DOE *see* Environment, Department of the
Donnett, Charles 436
Donnison, David 323
Donoughue, Clem 33, 37, 119, 288, 306, 374, 404, 405, 407, 411; end of marriage 231, 238; emigrates to France 330, 333, 334
Donoughue, Katie: on JC 38; sleeps in tent 50; and the press 144; remembers BD's birthday 360; theatre with BD 453; 12th birthday 459; lunches with BD 483, 488
Donoughue, Paul 256, 412, 453, 494
Donoughue, Rachel 28; sleeps in tent 50; BD at her school events 55; 86; at State Opening of Parliament 105; school show 221; at the theatre with parents 374, 416; 14th birthday 482; lunch with BD 483
Donoughue, Stephen 194, 443, 494, 500–1
Dow, Christopher 133
Downey, Gordon 275, 429
Drain, Geoffrey 431
Drax B power station 217
Driberg, Tom 435
Ducci, Roberto 291, 391
Duffy, Maureen 188
Duffy, Terry 369, 370, 431
Dupuy, Pierre 163
Dworkin, Ronald 386–7

Eanes, Antonio, President of Portugal 389–90
Eban, Ebba 259
Ecevit, Bülent 326
economic policies *see specific issues, e.g.* Budgets; import controls; inflation; mortgages; pay policies; public expenditure; sterling crises
Economist, The 31, 142–3, 267
Edge Hill by-election (1979) 469, 472, 474
education 20; and 16–18-year olds 66, 325; JC's speech on (1976) 82, 83, 84; Shirley Williams's Green Paper on 199, 201, 202, 203, 211, 212, 215, 225; private 292; and Inner Cities Partnership Scheme 317–18; *see also* Education and Science, Department of; National Union of Teachers; universities
Education and Science, Department of (DES) 31, 35, 40, 51, 55, 59, 68, 70, 330–31; accuses BD of leak 93
Edwards, Bob 488
EEC *see* European Economic Community
Eisenstadt, Stuart 161, 200
Electrical Power Engineers' Association 61; *see also* Lyons, John
Electrical Trades Union 224, 273–4, 441
Elizabeth II, Queen: ceases to see ministers 38; Jubilee (1977) 193, 196, 197; reviews fleet 207; and Civil List 310; sees JC 361; gives him paperknife 473
Elstein, David 324
Emery, Fred 323, 368
employers' National Insurance contributions 56, 334, 341
EMS *see* European Monetary System
English, David 481
English (Michael) Committee/Report on Civil Service 38, 236, 238, 243; CSD response to 283, 286, 333
Ennals, David 146; as Minister of Health 20; abroad 22; and mobility allowance 48, 223; wants 'a monopoly of concern' 99–100; and PSBR 104; against cuts 108, 109, 110; on immigration 135; and Nairne 151; and compensation for vaccine-damaged children 155, 183, 184, 199; and pensions uprating 188; puts in 'terrible' paper 190; not on ministerial committee 195; at Strategy Cabinet 205; and doctors' pay dispute 224; criticised by Moser 237; and Thorpe scandal 241, 250, 252; bad paper on NHS expenditure 303; and public appointments 321; discusses NHS with JC 374–5; 'no balls' over pay policy 419, 431–2, 434–5, 437, 438; 'a human fart' 437, 439; weak on pay negotiations 443, 447, 450, 455
Environment, Department of the (DOE) 29, 32, 83; *see also* Shore, Peter
Escargot, L' (restaurant) 470, 482, 484
Essex University, Colchester 319–20
European Economic Community (EEC) 99, 147, 271, 282; and import controls 71; direct

elections 25, 195, 170, 197, 198; and the left 196, 266; summits 208 (1977), 308, 310, 343, 344, 345, 397 (1978); finance ministers' meetings 264 (1977), 375–6 (1978); and Brookings Institute 297, 382, 387–8, 392, 398, 399, 429, 440, 451, 454, 462, 466; budgets 373, 388; heads of government meeting (1979) 457

European Monetary System (EMS) 6, 372, 373, 374, 375–6, 382, 385, 392, 393–5, 397, 398, 400

Evans, Alan 125

Evans, Geraint 307

Evans, Harry 102; and peerage investigation 22, 27; angling for BBC post 78, 88; tells BD source of leaks 88; on Haines's book 145; lunch with BD 204; buys BD champagne 234; on pre-war communist recruitment 234; offers BD job 293; fed up with unions 312; tells BD of poll 328; shows BD draft on IMF negotiations 332; on Goldsmith's knighthood 347; depressed by events at *Sunday Times* 385–6, 423; on possibility of compromise settlement 456; at dinner for Sonnenfeldt 483; depressed by unions 488

Evans, Moss: pay policy negotiations 369, 378, 380; and transport strike 419, 420, 424; and secondary picketing 425, 426, 430; supports pay 'norm' 431; role in Labour's defeat 498, 503

Evans, Richard 301

Evening News 249, 251

Evening Standard 91, 144, 376, 438; drama awards 435

Fabian Society dinner (1976) 95

Falkender, Lady Marcia 13, 32; after 1964 election 47; relationship with Arnold Goodman 222; and Torrode and Sue Lewis 379; cancels Private Office dinner for HW 22; has never voted in the Lords 94; taken off Film Industry committee 157, 175; leading 'an incredible life' 403

Faulkner, Richard 391

Fay Report on Crown Agents 271, 272

Ferguson, Euen 267, 307, 323

Field, Peggy 140, 223

Film Industry committee 157, 175

Finance Bill (1978) 317, 322, 323–4, 325, 333

Financial Times 72, 114, 308, 313, 318, 393; journalists 192, 301, *see also* Rogaly, Joe

Finney, Tom 461

firemen's strike (1977) 259, 264, 266, 268, 273

Fisher, Alan 414, 434, 437, 443, 445, 487, 503

Fisher, Sammy 403

Fitt, Eileen 400

Fitt, Gerry: supports government 169, 171; on Devlin 237; opposes Speakers Conference 237, 299, and Northern Ireland Representation Bill 314, 403; and vote of confidence 469, 470, 471, 472, 473

Fitzgerald, Garett 148, 241

Flannery, Martin 401

Fleet, Kenneth 209

Fleming, Robert 223

Foot, Michael 8; and JC's Cabinet appointments 16, 17; winds up Budget debate 18; and pay policy discussions 25, 26, 28; falls asleep at Cabinet committee 49; and public expenditure cuts 49, 53, 56; announces scheme to guillotine bills 54; and devolution 58, 123, 149, 150, 152, 189; and incomes policy 70; and deputy leadership 81, 82, 88; and import controls 94; illness 94; supports Benn/Shore alternative strategy 110; supports BD on recovery programme 134, 136; shares BD's love of India 143; and Lib–Lab deal 170, 174; reneges on promise to support Government Bill 197; and PMQs 199, 207; not given chance to speak in Cabinet 199; praises Unit strategy paper 205; and Official Information Bill 225; against Cordle's expulsion 225; has 'lost ground' 233; at lunch for Spaniards 249; and police pay 251–2; at Freyne's supper party 253; on miners and steel industry 256, 263; briefed by BD on North Sea oil 282; and BBC 295; worried about Official Secrets Act 329–30, 331; negotiates with Welsh Nationalists over vote 337; wants election delayed 354, 357, 362; chairs 'Themes and Initiatives' committee 367; persuades JC to intervene in *Times* dispute 395; wants free vote on Rhodesian sanctions inquiry 398; and pay sanctions debate 399, 401; 'totally unrealistic' 418; unrewarding talk with Moss Evans 419; hosts left-wing dinners 428; and pay negotiations 430, 431–2, 433, 437; preferred election day 462; does 'the crudest deals' 467; gives marvellous winding-up speech 471

football: Commons v. Belgian Parliament 118; BD marks ex-professionals 176, 326; European Cups 193, 325; Commons v. German Bundestag 280; Commons v. Crystal Palace 290–91; Anglo-Irish parliamentary match 313, 316, 332, 335, 336; Brazil v. England (1978) 314; England v. Hungary 331; World Cup (1978) 339, 348; charity (v. Jimmy Greaves XI) 396–7; England v. Northern Ireland 441; Commons v. Press Gallery 442; Professional Footballers' dinner 461; charity match (Wimbledon) 474

Ford, Gerald, US President 57, 91, 108, 110, 116, 120

Ford Foundation: and Brookings Institute 223, 263, 264, 282, 296, 297, 309

Ford Motors: strike (1978) 366, 368, 372; Motor Show rep 377; sanctions against 393, 395, 419

Foreign Office 80, 255; Jenkins fails to be appointed Minister 15, 17, 20, 21, 38; and

Amin 52, 53; and CPRS report *see* Central Policy Review Staff; and Jay's appointment 188, 189; homosexuals and 'fellow travellers' 200; and Official Secrets 225; and loss of shipbuilding orders 235; free-traders 265; *see also* Owen, David

Forman, Nigel 332

Foster, Chris 29–30

Fowler, Gerald (Gerry) 61; and overseas students' fees 37, 40–41; on incompetence in his department 59; dropped from Cabinet 68, 70, 71; agrees to make 'generous' speech 74; drinks with BD 81, 125, 177, 213, 225; abstains in vote on economics package 126; has meal with Donoughues 187; looking for job outside politics 296; savage about NUT behaviour 395

Fox, Paul 384

France/the French 101, 106, 253; and aircraft industry 374, 391; and EMS 375, 391, 397; *see also* Giscard d'Estaing, Valéry; Paris

Franklin, Michael 296

Franks, Richard (Dickie) 443

Franks Report on Official Secrets 54–5, 61, 143, 225

Fraser, Lady Antonia 188

Fraser, Malcolm 195

Freud, Clement 472

Friends of the Earth 190

Frolik, Josef 277

Frost, David 36–7, 173, 184, 210, 222

Fulton, Lord 448

Galbraith, J. K. 95

Galway, James 323

Garrett, Ted 177

Garscadden (Glasgow) by-election (1978) 308, 312, 322

Gavron, Bob 291

GEC *see* General Electric Company

General & Municipal Workers' Union (GMWU) 42, 304, 436, 445; *see also* Basnett, David

General Electric Company (GEC) 217, 384, 387

Geraghty, Father 181

Germans/Germany 341, 421; and British economy 90, 123; terrorism 235, 248; opposes Brookings Institute 296, 297; economic summits 343, *see also* Bonn, Bremen; 'swap agreement' with US 300; *see also* Schmidt, Helmut

Gibbings, Peter 83, 138, 239, 357

gilts (Government stock) 75, 80, 127–8, 135, 181, 247, 268, 449, 457; Bank of England sells out of 335–6, 337, 338

Gingerbread 18, 245

Giscard d'Estaing, President Valéry: talks with JC 43, 57, 101; praises Crosland 150; and World Economic summit (1977) 150, 185, 186; meeting with JC 274, 275; at European summit (1978) 310; and EMS 375, 394, 397; receives cool response from JC 391

Gladwyn, Derek: and election campaign (1978) 304, 321, 327, 346; as replacement for Hayward 355; and election campaign (1979) 476, 478, 480, 481, 486, 492, 494, 495

Glasgow 124, 140, 154, 182; *see also* Garscadden

Glasgow Herald 245

Glyn, Tom 473

GMWU *see* General & Municipal Workers' Union

Godber, Ken 504

Goldsmith, Lady Annabel 269

Goldsmith, James: knighthood 32, 36, 347; a 'dynamic and fascinating animal' 269

Gommon, David 132

Goodman, Lord Arnold: and HW's honours list 22, 25, 222; talks with JC about *Observer* 65, 66, and *Express* 180; on HW's 'shabby' friends 180; on his relationship with Marcia Falkender 222

Goodman, Geoffrey 277, 284, 347, 354, 438

Goodman Derrick (law firm) 247, 252

Goodwin, Professor Cranford 223

Goossens, Marie 212

Gore-Brown (broker) 209

Gormley, Joe 218, 434

Goulden, Richard 374

Goven shipyard 239

Gowland, David 76, 79, 96

Graham, Andrew 19, 76, 77, 96, 172, 211, 451

Graham, Nori and Philip 21, 49, 58, 80, 145, 191, 226, 286, 344, 388, 493

Grant, Bruce 140, 165, 173

Grant, George 311

Greaves, Jimmy 396–7

Greene, Alexander 296, 342, 444

Greene, Graham 9; discusses Haines's book 33, 41; socialises with BD 174, 212, 240, 252–3, 260, 415, 441; discusses BD's job possibilities 202, 296, 331, 355, 458

Greenhall, Stella 93

Greenwood, Ron 266

Grieveson Grant (stockbrokers): BD's lunches at 28, 47, 61, 78, 132, 148, 191, 277, 294, 368, 402, 449; on BP sale 200; Sutherland's memorial service 213; critical of Bank of England 235, 256, 319

Griffin, Ken 24

Grimsby by-election (1977) 169, 182

Guardian: and Treasury leak 72; DES policy document given to 93; attacks HW's peers 93–4; and collapse of government 197; on BP shares 209; Businessman of the Year lunch 302; article on unemployment 366; *see also* Gibbings, Peter; McKee, David

Guinea Club, the 301

Guinness, Alec 234

Guinness Mahon 355, 359, 375

Haines, Joe: HW cool towards 19; on HW and peerage investigation 22, 30; on HW's 'South African plot' 32–3, 34; his 'explosive book' (*The Politics of Power*) 33, 62, 150; pressurised by HW over book 41; HW shifty about 62; relationship with BD 72; at Janet Davies's farewell party 103; depressed at being unemployed 126; on chancellorship 126; book published 140; serialisation in *Mirror* 142, 143, 144, 148; book disparaged by Healey 146–7; defended by JC 155; not enough to do at *Mirror* 190; BD plans to use in election 210; on Thorpe scandal 241, 242, 243; helps draft JC's Brighton speech (1977) 243; interviewed by Fraud Squad 248, 250, 252; miserable at *Mirror* 263; on strike 266; at *Mirror* lunch 284; gaining influence 297; as chief leader writer 312; election discussions 321, 327; lunches with BD 331, 334, 345, 347; and Roger Carroll 339; blames McNally regarding election date 359; depressed by news of HW's planned appearance in Morecambe and Wise Show 367; at Blackpool Conference 368, 370, 371; discusses Marcia Falkender 379; 'good company as ever' 382, 385; asks about McCaffrey's brief on pay 389; depressed by industrial troubles in Fleet St 405; thinks JC should return from Caribbean 417; on Kagan case 417, 429; on HW and honours 428; depressed over Labour election prospects 438, 440; on Defence Ministry scandal 456–7, 459; on JC's deferment of election 461; discusses *Mirror*'s use to Labour Party 477; on Labour campaign 489–90; keen that BD should not go into the City 498; attacks 'amateurism' of Political Office 499

Hale, John 33, 99, 469
Hale, Sheila 33
Hall, Peter 277
Halls, Michael 223, 403
Hamilton, Jim 154, 201, 211, 284, 294
Hamilton by-election (1978) 322, 332
Hammers, Giselle 398, 451
Hampden Park football ground 317
Harewood, Lord 173, 315
Harraree, Haya 49
Harriman, Averell 161
Harriman, Pamela (*formerly* Churchill) 160
Harrington, Illtyd 36, 144
Harris, John 239
Harris, Richard 61
Harrison, Elizabeth 61
Harrison, Rex 234
Harrison, Walter 465–6, 473
Harrogate 139
Hart, Judith 21; blames HW for dismissal 126; and NEC 151, 164; JC's plans for 152; and Lib–Lab deal 170–71; and Benn's job 171, 172; critical of 'new left' 201–2; and MI5 222,

223; discusses reorganisation of Labour Party 237; and White Paper on Civil Service 286; and employment of deputy secretary 333; hosts dinner for left-wing ministers 428
Hartman, Art 99, 160
Hattersley, Molly 146
Hattersley, Roy 8; recommended by BD 15; lunches with BD 52, 53; Minister for Prices and Incomes 67; fails to show up for run 73; and cuts in public spending 94, 103, 104, 108, 109, 110, 111; deflated by JC 124; thinks government about to collapse 126; and national recovery programme 134, 138; suggests prices freeze 157; at Strategy Cabinet 205; discussion with Healey 207; at Freyne's supper party 253; on BBC 295, 302; pay policy scheme 376, 377, 378, 379–80; gives poor speech 402; 'a bit flash' 414; and pay policy 415, 419, 420, 432, 439, 440, 463; in favour of reshuffle 449; asked to sit in on pay negotiations 453, 455; swings Fitt to Labour side 469
Hawkins, Hector 214
Hawser, Lewis 269
Hayek, Friedrich 393
Hayes, Maurice 323
Hayhoe, Barney 341
Hayman, Helene 114, 126
Hayward, Ron: sees JC 20; attacked regarding Trotskyites in party 83; 'exhibits vanity on TV' 94; reports on Benn 172; Liddell preferred to 187; 'pathetic' 279; and election campaign (1978) 304; wants to give up as general secretary 354; worst general secretary in history 371; and election campaign (1979) 427, 480, 481, 489; wants colonial governorship 481; and Political Office 499
Healey, Denis: 8, 18; and pay negotiations with TUC (1976) 22, 23, 25, 26, 28; and sterling crisis 37; critical of advisers 38; against import controls 39, 71; and public expenditure cuts 39–40, 44, 45, 46, 47, 49, 50, 53; produces bombshell on employer's NI contributions 56; and Franks Report 61; irreplaceable 66; on floating rate 66; 'The Next Steps' 71; leaks to press 72; emergency talks 73; Blackpool speech on IMF loan 74; and Treasury squeeze 76, 77, 78, 79; import deposit scheme 82; and Scottish devolution 85; and sterling crisis 86; dishonest about public expenditure cuts 87; exhausted 88, 91; at JC's emergency meeting 92; depressed by JC's lack of support 93, 97; more buoyant 94; needs personal staff 97–8; and Lever's Washington trip 100; on PSBR cuts and IMF 103, 104, 106, 109, 110, 111, 112, 114; drink with Sonnenfeldt 117; and Letter of Intent 118, 121; and sterling 'safety net' 120, 131; 'flabby and rambling' statement 122; JC's plans to replace 126, 155; and JC's

plans for Treasury 132, 147; 'bugger the Party' 134; speaks against national recovery programme 134; on his shingles cure 136; on trade unionists 141; and Haines's book 146–7; reports on pay policy 148; on Owen 151; on Hunt 155; plans 'big giveaway' 156; and Budget (March, 1977) 157, 164, *see* Budgets; meetings with trade unionists 177; shown 'dumb insolence' by Bank of England and Treasury 179; sets out policies at seminar 180–81; on recession 182; on special advisers 183; praises Rodgers's transport White Paper 190; and interest rates 194–5; against cancellation of BP shares sale 198; at Strategy Cabinet 205; accepts Unit's reflation programme 206; more sympathetic than usual 207–8; at seminar on reserves 212; 'a bully, a tank' 214; offers 'sweeteners' to trade unions 215, 216, 217–18, 221; and Official Information Bill 225; on sterling 226; praised by JC 233; reflation plans 234, 236; bad relations with Richardson 239; paper criticised by JC 245; 'through his bad period' 246; incurs JC's wrath 247; at seminars with Bank of England 250, 251, 254, 265; and North Sea oil revenues 261, 262; 'talks the market up' 267; proposes relaxation of exchange controls 267, 273; and IMF Letter of Intent 275; under severe pressure 276; supports Bank's views 280; gives vague speech 285–6; irritated by Jay 288; and discussions on Official Secrets White Paper 291; opposes legislation on Ulster Unionists 299; bullies Liberals 313, 317; lectured by JC on 'playing it cool' 322; and Bank's 'package' 334, 335; and inquiry into selling gilts 339; pro EEC proposals 343; White Paper on pay policy 340, 346; backed by JC 345; and election timing 354, 357; at Party Conference (1978) 369, 370; and EMS 372, 375, 393; and 'open government' 373; chairs meeting with TUC 377, 378; reports on Finance ministers' meeting 392; discusses pay policy with BD 397; and pay sanctions 402; grossly offensive to Lever 411–12; told to get on with things by JC 413–14; belligerent with BD 417; pay negotiations with unions 417, 418–19, 420, 433–4, 439, 440; and statutory incomes policy 424; crisis package thrown out 442; told to give way on pay 447; and election campaign 495

Healey, Edna 146, 303

Health and Social Security, Department of (DHSS) 20, 330; and pensions uprating 187, 188; and public appointments 320, 321; and the 'family' 332, 344; *see also* disabled, vehicles for the; Ennals, David; National Health Service

Heath, Edward: and William Armstrong 87, 153, 459; and miners (1973–4) 130, 261; and

Conservative Party finance 147; looks uncomfortable in PMQs 284; lack of contact with Tory whips 325; and polls 387, 391

Heffer, Eric 21, 169

Heinz, Teresa 162

Henderson, David 288, 326

Henderson, Sir Nicholas 469

Hennessy, Peter 61, 102, 149, 238, 259

Herbecq, Sir John 107

Heseltine, Michael 500

Hicks, Sir John 393

Higgins, Ron 333

Higham, David 52–3, 154

Highlands and Islands Board 179, 181, 337

Hill, David 195, 376, 472

Himmelweit, Professor Hilde 106, 138

Hinchelwood, Martin 474

Hindell, Keith 448

Hodge, Julian 302

Hogg, Sarah 31

Holden, Anthony 306

Hollis, Pat 492

Holt, David 502

Home Office: and BBC *see* Annan Report on Broadcasting; and law and order 362; and Agee/Hosenball 'secrets' case 391; and 'open government' 446

Hopkin, Bryan 33, 183

Hosenball, Mark 152–3, 391

Houghton, Douglas 417

Housden, Bill 294, 403

Howe, Geoffrey 66, 221, 478

Howell, Denis: at Wembley with BD 32; as troubleshooter 69; and police investigation 88, 101; Hilton dinner for 191–2; worried about Bryant corruption trial 296; wants to sue *Private Eye* 324; socialises with BD 57, 155, 241, 266, 461

Hughes, Cledwyn 144, 167, 169, 322, 430, 500

Hughes, Mark 81, 99

Hume, Cardinal Basil 301, 302, 325

Hunt, John: warns HW off Crosland 53; diary meeting with JC 13; rivalry with Wass 26; and TUC pay negotiations 29; and nationalised board salaries 35, 36; disliked by JC 36; must be controlled 36; and public expenditure 44, 45, 46; stops BD from going to Social Affairs committee 50; and Franks Report 54–5, 61; on Civil Service reform 70; analysed by BD 70–71; and industrial democracy 75; and Treasury plan 77, 78; 'not very subtle' 87; and Unit's paper on national plan 91–2, 96, 98, 99, 101; and committee on unemployment 132, 133; and scheme to split Treasury 133, 147, 149, 150, 154; unemployment committees 137, 138, 140, 142; repartee with BD 145; on US trip 158; moves like lightning over BP shares 178; at economic seminar 180; and Derek Mitchell 183; against Commons proposal for select committee on foreign affairs 189; on FCO's reception of CPRS report 200; delighted to put 'stick of dynamite' under Treasury 201; writes covering note for Unit paper 204; excluded from Strategy Cabinet 205, 207, 214; and computer model 207; and CPRS 214; resents being excluded 214; upset by article on Armstrong 214; and Unit's redrafting of White Paper on pay 217; suggested for Governor of Bank of England 227; on meetings between Richardson and Healey 227; welcomes 'Wreckers' 236; weekly lunches 241; Stowe's subordination to 245; against Armstrong succeeding him 246; at monetary seminars 250, 254; among Roman Catholic mafia 255; at discussion on Civil Service changes 255, 256; as head of Civil Service 258; and meeting on Brookings Institute 278; and draft North Sea oil White Paper 281, 283, 286, 297; and Cabinet Standing committees 283; and National Front march 290; and Northern Ireland 300; and Rhodesian oil sanctions 358, 365, 368, 374, 387, 448; and election postponement 359, 360; agitated about HW 383; demands no more meetings between ministers and trade unionists 438; angry with Armstrong 446; reveals machinery for pay negotiations 453; supported by BD as National Gallery trustee 469; enjoys change of government 499

Hurd, Douglas 440, 466
Hussein, King of Jordan 362

IBA see Independent Broadcasting Authority
Ilford by-election (1978) 291, 293, 294, 296–7, 301, 302; Rees's speech 290, 291, 292
IMF see International Monetary Fund
immigrants/immigration: and child benefits 26, 27, 30; controls needed 135–6, 138–9, 140, 141, 143, 151; JC's views 152; and Mrs Thatcher 284, 288, 289; positive response to Commons report needed 299, 300–1
import controls 39, 40, 70, 71, 72, 85, 94, 264; and 'protectionism' 310, 311, 312, 313, 320, 325
Independent Broadcasting Authority (IBA) 324, 330, 384, 448
India: BD's trips 103–4, 105 (1976), 279–80 (1978)
industrial democracy 6; Bullock Report on 75, 86–7, 90, 124, 134, 138, 191, 202; Unit draft on 126, 134; Cabinet meeting on 134; Basnett to support JC on 135; discussed at Guardian lunch 138; JC's speech on 139; JC delays decisions on 189–90; Cabinet committee on 191; gap between TUC and CBI 195, and between Dell and Booth 200, 202; White Paper delayed 227; further disagreements on 279; trade

unionists reject compromise 295; progress on 311–12; White Paper 318, 322, 330; unsupportable TUC position on 431; and disagreement between Booth and Shirley Williams 461
Industry, Department of 331, 361; see also Varley, Eric
inflation/counter-inflationary measures 6, 44, 179, 180, 195, 217, 224, 307, 340, 348, 405, 407, 416, 420, 431, 444
Inland Revenue: Conference 31; and allowances 239; and North Sea divers 248, 252, 266
inner city policies 36, 55, 71, 174, 317–18
Innes, Judy 403
Institute of Policy Studies 448
Institute of Production Engineers 268
interest rates 66, 75, 79, 135, 136, 137, 180, 181, 194–5, 212, 227, 228, 265, 268–9, 270–71, 280, 322, 334, 384–5, 386, 441
International Monetary Fund (IMF): British loan negotiations (1976) 5, 37, 39, 71, 73, 74, 76, 86; afraid to impose 'stern' regime 98; secret visitation 102; and PSBR 103, 104, 105, 106, 107, 108; pressurises JC for cuts 108, 110, 111, 112; Letter of Intent (1976) 113, 116–18, 119–20, 121; accepts package in principle 115; Letter of Intent (1977) 271–2, 274, 275, 276
IRA: murder of ambassador 56; BD sets up meeting with defector 192–3; restaurant bombing 298; prisoners on strike 376, 377, 378; bombing 405, 406; Neave's assassination 474
Iran 367, 449, 462
Ireland: ambassadors to London 336, 400; and EMS 394, 397, 400; and Conservative government 470; see also Anglo-Irish football match; Irish Embassy; Lynch, Jack
Irish Embassy 336, 366, 400, 460
Irving, Sidney 473
Isherwood, Christopher: Mr Norris Changes Trains 454, 461
Israel/Israelis 18, 72, 75, 259, 278, 323, 366
ITV 300, 338, 371, 384

Jackson, Colin 81
Jackson, Margaret see Beckett, Margaret
Jacobson, Sidney 27
Japan/Japanese 70, 71, 166, 190, 264, 265, 304
Jarvis, Fred: and Carol Donoughue 189, 242, 290, 319
Jay, Margaret (née Callaghan) 304, 364, 502, 503
Jay, Peter 33, 73, 160, 187–8, 288, 304
Jeger, Lena 151, 494
Jenkins, Clive 233
Jenkins, Peter 45, 72, 209, 239, 401
Jenkins, Roy (later Lord Jenkins) 7; not appointed to Foreign Office 16, 17, 20, 21, 38; relations with JC 19, 27, 74, 129; happy and relaxed 25, 26; tells BD Crosland is ill 53; bored at Cabinet 54; and Franks Report 61; final visit

to No. 10 68; as President of Europe 99, 125; blamed by JC for lack of action on immigration 141; and World Economic summit 184, 186; and Bremen summit 343

'job-swap' scheme 60

John Paul I, Pope 368

Johnny's Café, Covent Garden 372, 373, 388, 392, 450, 455, 483, 488

Johnson, Paul 492

Jones, Alec 60

Jones, David 42, 341

Jones, Elwyn 25, 110, 175, 299

Jones, Fred 32

Jones, George 51, 182, 225, 299, 363

Jones, Jack 20, 141; security clearance 277; and pay negotiations 22, 29, 96; and *Observer* 66; secret meeting with JC 122; sharp exchange with CBI man 141; power ebbing 152; loses temper with Healey 166; and pay negotiations 177, 179, 210, 212, 216, 217–19; at lunch for Spaniards 249

Joseph, Keith 81, 92, 156, 188, 330

journalists' strike (1977) 266

Jowell, Jeffrey 386

Jowell, Tessa: as Orme's special adviser 89, 144; and Ilford by-election 291, 294, 296; brilliant on housing 363; marries 462; loses seat 500

Judd, Frank 153, 298

Kagan, Lord Joseph 154, 379, 401, 403, 417, 429

Karajan, Herbert von 433

Karamanlis, Konstantinos 282

Kaufman, Gerald 61; a 'snake' 116, 144; against doing a deal with Liberals 168; and Varley 263, 278; disliked by JC 263; accused of misleading House 292; and shipbuilding crisis 395

Kaunda, Kenneth 326, 366

Keaton, Buster: *The General* 449

Kedourie, Professor Elie 78

Keegan, Bill 341

Kennedy, Eamonn 400

Kettering by-election (1977) 277

Kinnock, Neil 16, 172

Kirby, Bonnie 69, 105

Kirby, Mike 69, 105, 295

Kirkwood, Archie 262, 313, 314, 347

Kissin, Lord Harry 25, 291–2, 359

Kissinger, Henry 44, 65, 71, 85, 99, 117, 255, 396

Knight, Andrew 31, 267

Knight, Doris 471

Knight, Victor 489

Knox, Brian 45, 200, 342

Konstant, Bishop David 302, 308–9, 324

Koschnik, Hans 90

Kreisky, Bruno 344

Labour Party Conferences 72–5, 81 (1976), 242–4, 245 (1977), 368–71 (1978)

Lamont, Norman 344

Lancaster, Terry: lunches with BD 284, 327, 334, 347; told election is postponed 359; at Christmas party 405; and forthcoming election 438, 452, 489, 498

Lankester, Tim 411, 416, 421, 455, 458, 464, 479, 491; at 'last supper' 502

Lapping, Anne 31

Latham, Arthur 401

law and order 246, 289–90, 362, 364

Layfield, Sir Frank 182; report on local government 60, 182, 183

Lea, David 124, 218, 265, 346, 444

'leaks' 102; *see also* child benefits; special advisers

Le Carré, John 342

Leonard, Dick 31, 142

Lester, Anthony 27, 154, 279

Lestor, Joan 234, 471

Lever, Diane 101, 477

Lever, Harold: and BP shares 42; and IMF loans 73, 76, 77, 78, 80; on Crosland 82; and public expenditure cuts 82; depressed 86; at JC's emergency meeting 92; attacked by officials 100; Washington trip 100, 102; a 'happy meal' with BD 101; threatens resignation over devolution 108; and public expenditure cuts 109, 110, 111; optimistic 115; and reports of JC taking over direction of the economy 132; supports BD 134; and Haines's book 144; sees JC about something 'personal' 165; agrees on need for counter-inflation policy 174; ready to quit 175; furious with Treasury and Bank of England 179, 180; warns BD of meeting with building societies 194; and BP shares sale 198; at Strategy Cabinet 205; clashes with Governor of Bank of England 212; suggested as his successor 225; and Polish shipping order 235–6, 237, 239; praises BD 253; and sterling appreciation 254; plans next move for dealing with Bank 270; and IMF letter 276; briefed by BD on North Sea oil 282; plans not to stand for Parliament again 282; at monetary seminar 288; battles over tax relief for small firms 309; and Unit's minute on financing public debt 336, 337; accuses JC of being afraid of upsetting Governor 336; at meeting over inquiry into selling gilts 339, 340; at seminar on monetary policy 343; wants election delayed 357, 362; and EMS 374, 393; demolishes Governor's arguments on interest rates 385; attacks negativism of Treasury 411; upset by Healey 411–12; at opera with BD 416; on JC 441; depressed 451, 479; at dinner for Sonnenfeldt 483; pessimistic about election 492

Lewis, Sue 379

Lewis, Tony 205

Liberal Party: suicidal 167; Lib–Lab pact 168–9,

170, 175, 176, 197, 203, 221, 223, 237; beaten by National Front 175, 315; pay policy 213; buying of honours 252, 272, 275; and vote on PR 276, 305; and Budget (1978) 313, 314; and end of Pact 328, 331, 455; wins by-election 474

Liddell, Helen: as secretary of Scottish Labour Party 152, 181, 187; meetings with BD 196, 212; and shipping 237; and abortion issue 244, 308; meets with BD on devolution 289; and Garscadden by-election 312, 322; as replacement for Underhill 355; at Blackpool conference 370, 371; optimistic about Berwick by-election 381; pregnant 382; reports on JC 442; on devolution 452; 'too young' for promotion 452

Liesners, Hans 194, 400, 421

Lippitt, John 278, 361

Lipsey, David: and special advisers' salaries 52; liaises with BD over economic policy 92, 'a very clever young man' 99; discusses IMF package 105; and Treasury victory 110; 'perceptive' 130; joins Unit 152, 178, 180; speech-writing for JC 178; excellent work on strategy paper 194; writes JC's Welsh speech 211; redrafts pay policy White Paper 217; briefs on North Sea oil revenues 261, 262; works on public expenditure brief 298; at election campaign meeting 304; and Annan discussions 337; and Bremen summit 344; helps to run Political Office 353, 356; and postponement of election 359; drafts brief on TUC pay agreement 387; pessimistic about economy 407, 418; works on low pay 421; plans brief on tax law 457; and election campaign 467, 475, 476, 478, 480, 486, 497; weeps at JC's departure 503

Littler, Geoff 249, 264, 272, 418

local authorities/government: excessive expenditure 32, 58; Layfield Report on 60, 182, 184; elections (1978) 323; pay talks 390–91, 414; 'scroungers' 411; strikes (1978) 400, 405, 413, 414, 428, 430, 436; pay settlement 429, 443, 438, 442, 445, 447, 448, 449

London Business School: conference (1978) 326

London School of Economics (LSE) 28, 177; Strand House library building 42; BD resigns from 77, 78, 80, 91, 128; and European Brookings Institute 83, 98, 142, 292; hosts French economists 106, 116; BD disappointed with economists from 133–4; dinner for George Jones 182; BD's lunch with visiting American 298; 'dead and reactionary' 363; Zander's lecture 386–7; and Dahrendorf 462

Lord, Alan 78, 97, 98, 180, 200

Lovell-Davis, Peter 19, 144, 145

Lyall, Gavyn 251

Lynch, Jack 240–41, 298, 299, 300, 394

Lynes, Tony 41, 42, 50

Lyon, Alex 19, 60

Lyons, John 60–61, 96, 113, 223, 258, 259, 273–4, 390

'M' see Oldfield, Sir Maurice

Ma Cuisine, Knightsbridge 392

Mabon, Dickson 152

MacArthur, Brian 88, 259, 376, 438

McCaffrey, Tom 17; and JC 20; and leak over HW's honours list 28; and TUC pay negotiations 29; at Chequers 46; against CPRS report on Diplomatic Service 54; and Observer 65; clashes with BD over JC's Canadian trip 67, 68; at JC's Ruskin College speech 84; and lack of information from No. 10 114, 115–16, 129; not happy 127; at ball for Carter's inauguration 136; meetings on immigration 138, 139; attacks Haines 143; behaves oddly 143; on plan to split Treasury 150; on Judith Hart 152; in Washington 158, 162; and Lib–Lab deal 168; and Benn's resignation 172; at JC's anniversary celebration 177; and Jay's appointment as ambassador 187; 'dirty briefing' of press 188; first row with press 189; helps draft JC's Brighton speech (1977) 243; supports Benn over power workers' strike 261; excludes Mirror from briefings 284, 297, 300; attacks Unit North Sea oil White Paper 289; not a team man 346; hated by Mirror 347; and postponement of election 360; briefs on pay agreement with TUC 389; pessimistic about economy 407; panics over strikes 424–5, 427, 434; and Cabinet reshuffle 449; and Labour defeat 465; critical of JC 469, 470; little humour and flair 470; and election campaign 478, 479, 480, 481, 489; shares room with BD 496; at 'last supper' 502; departs No. 10 504

McCarthy, Bill 390

McCarthy, Callum 207

McCusker, Harold 471, 472

MacDonald, Margot 168

MacDougal, Donald 458

McElhone, Frank 60, 74, 140, 153, 177, 181, 330, 337, 344

Macfadean, Frank 98

Macintosh, Andrew and Naomi 46

McKie, David 138, 435

Mackintosh, John 33, 142, 338

Maclennan, Robert (Bob) 16

McMahon, Kit: attacks Lever 100; 'clever and interesting' 100; touchy about JC's criticisms of Bank 100; views on economy 100–1; in Washington for 'consultations' 131; at meetings and seminars 180, 212, 253; no longer 'independent-minded' 250; will not discuss BP shares 253; on Bank's targets 270–71; on public expenditure 300; argues for stiff Budget 376; and EMS 385, 395

McNally, Tom: on JC's first day 13; and setting up of Political Office 14; and JC's failure to appoint Jenkins 16, 17; passes on JC's praise to BD 19; and JC as PM 20; 'very sensible' 26; with BD at film premiere 27; plans future work together 27; on immigrants' child benefits 30; and trips abroad 37, 41; at Chequers 45, 46; sees JC about special advisers 49, 50, 51; backs CPRS report on reforming Diplomatic Service 54; at JC's talk on cuts 56; on Kissinger 65; and *Observer* 65; opposes JC's Canadian trip 67; and bank nationalisation 69; relationship with BD 72; fed up with attacks on special advisers 85; optimistic about by-elections 94; on NEC 96; at JC's dissection of Unit paper 105–6; thinking of becoming an MP 112; feels squeezed out 127; cheered up by future plans 127; agitated by Bank's 'political' policies 127–8; at ball for Carter's inauguration 136; meetings on immigration 138, 139; and attacks on Haines 143, 144; plan for NEC 151; on American trip 158, 159, 161, 162, 163; and Lib–Lab deal 168, 169, 174; at JC's anniversary celebration 177; plans to stand for Parliament 207, 277, 282; drafts JC's Brighton speech (1977) 243; discusses ministerial changes 248; briefs JC on CPRS report on overseas representation 255; on NEC 279; at *Mirror* lunch 284; sees Rees over law and order speech 289, 290; and election campaign 301, 304, 346; sleeps during Budget speech 310–11; and Haines 321, 327; malicious press campaign waged against 342; and Stockport nomination 353; working in Political Office 356; row with JC over going to Brighton 356; and postponement of election 359, 360, 412; in Stockport constituency 363; provided with money by unions 379; refuses to go to West Indies 383; on JC's hostile reception 423; and strikes 426, 427, 430, 440; on Cabinet reshuffle 451; and devolution referendum results 453; on Civil Service control of prime ministers 459; prints election address 464; works on election manifesto 467; first draft of JC's speech dropped 467; criticises JC 468–9; and election campaign 475, 476

McNee, Sir David 290, 291
McVicar, John 139
Maguire, Frank 169, 171, 403, 470, 471, 472, 473
Mahon, Bishop John 301
Manchester Corporation Works Department 330
Manpower Services Commission 366
Margach, James 80–81, 145
Margaret, Princess 310
Marquand, David 22, 74, 112; *Ramsay MacDonald* 178
Marriage of Figaro, The 277, 419, 422
Marsh, Richard (Dick) 357
Marshall, Jim 322, 473
Martin, Paul 69, 163

Masefield, John 444
Mason, Roy: and Turkish invasion of Cyprus 35; reprimanded at first appearance as Secretary of State for Ireland 89; with JC on cuts 110, 115; meeting on Ulster with JC 135; and arrest of British troops in Ireland 148; reports on political/military situation in Ulster 176; at Strategy Cabinet 205; scheme for consultative committee 272; as 'spokesman of the Protestants' 298, 299, 300, 314, 315, 334–5; pleased with 'low profile' policy 371; quizzed by JC 381; wants to talk to Powell 461; told not to negotiate with Ulster Unionists 468; pro-Unionist policies alienate Fitt and Maguire 470, 472
Massion, George 421, 458
Masterton, Valerie 493
Maudling, Reginald 20, 448, 456
Maynard, Geoffrey 131, 133, 207
Maynard, Joan 114, 155, 325, 369
Mayne, Richard 237
Maze prison/Long Kesh 334; strike 372, 376–7, 378
Meacher, Michael 266
Meade, James 393
Mellish, Robert (Bob) 59–60, 125, 403
Mendelson, John 122
Mercer, Joe 461
Metcalf, David 94, 134, 195
Methuen, John 138
microprocessors 374, 392
Middleton, Peter 88, 204, 220–21
Mikardo, Ian 96, 170
Miles, Tony 300, 438
Milhench, Ronald 417
Millan, Bruce 51, 110, 146, 152, 170, 245, 306, 420
Miller, Eric: and Peachey Property scandal 179, 181, 247–8, 249–50, 252, 304; and Hayward 354; suicide 239
miners 55, 130, 256, 257, 258–9, 261, 273
Mitchell, Derek 45; and Marcia Falkender 47; at secret meeting 100; in Washington for 'consultations' 120, 131; nearly gets sack over IMF negotiations 166; meets with BD 165–6; at economic seminar 180; pleased to leave Treasury 183; at World Economic summit 185; and Plietzky 200; critical of Wass 247
Mitterrand, François 253, 328
Molloy, Mike 304, 347, 405, 438, 498
Molyneaux, James 167, 298
Monck, Nicholas 119–20, 219
Mondale, Walter, US Vice President 139
Moore, Henry 374
Moore, Philip 38
Morel, Jean-Claude 382
Morgan, Gwyn 237
Morgan, Janet 311
Morrell, Frances 47, 459

Morris, Alf 146; recommended by BD 16; 'marvellous company' 28; considering resignation 48; and vehicles for the disabled 53, 223; with JC on cuts 110; meets German Embassy staff over the disabled 156; and pay talks 439

Morris, John 263, 267, 320, 321

Morris, Quentin 178, 198, 209, 339

Morrison, Herbert 113, 259

mortgages 75, 77, 79, 190, 193, 194–5, 388

Moser, Claus: at opera 143; gives party in CSO 175; sympathetic to Unit's proposal to run model of economy through computer 201; discusses statistical needs with ministers 237; tells BD about senior civil servant meetings 241; at opera 303; becomes deputy chairman of Rothschilds 319; treated well by JC 328; ill 364; on advisory council for music group 464

Mostyn-Owens, the 143, 303, 337, 480

motor industry 379, 380; see also British Leyland; Ford Motors

Mountbatten, Louis, Earl 20

Mountfield, Peter 217

Moyle, Roland 469

Moyle, Shelagh 470

Muldoon, Robert 19, 20, 319

Mullen, Mick 372, 376

Mulley, Fred 146; and leadership vote 47; meeting with JC 31, 35, 39; at Education 55; goes to Defence 68; on Fowler 71; supports Healey 114; lunch with BD and Crosland 137; and trial of SAS soldiers 148; and Official Information Bill 225; and leak of details on Armed Services pay 319

Murdoch, Rupert 83, 488

Murphy, John, Archbishop of Cardiff 491–2

Murphy, Lesley 308

Murray, Albert 32, 275

Murray, Len: and pay negotiations 22, 29; on TUC support for government 104; secret meeting with JC 122; tries to be helpful 216; and air traffic controllers' strike 231; promises a million majority 233; at lunch for Spaniards 249; and TUC pay negotiations 348, 434, 440; and strikes 425, 426, 432; long discussion with JC 442, 445; and TUC 'concordat' 444; told by BD that unions have destroyed Labour 477

museums, provincial: cuts 52

Nairne, Sir Patrick (Pat) 38; on Ennals 151,184, 286; on Owen 151; critical of English Report 238; as possible Cabinet Secretary 246; on DHSS opposition to voluntaryism 330, 332; discusses NHS with JC 374–5

Nally, Dermot 394, 451

'Nannas, the' (the Misses Knight) 340, 342

Napoletano, Pasqualina 337

National Economic Development Council (NEDC; 'Neddy') 42, 51, 93, 97, 141; union leaders ('Neddy Six') 29, 43, 177, 191, 210, 377, 378, 379–80, 477

National Enterprise Board (NEB) 135, 207, 308, 346

National Executive Committee (NEC): votes against social contract 43; trade unionists defeat left 58, 60; and nationalisation of banks 69; and Varley and Shirley Williams 73, 85; and Ashley 88; supports demonstration against government 88; lack of good men 96; appoints Trotskyite 122, 123; BD's plan 151, 155; and Judith Hart 165; and polls 234; reorganisation of 237; and Margaret Jackson 151, 155, 258; pathetic membership 279; and Benn 283, 395; women members 369; works on election manifesto 479

National Farmers' Union 330

National Front 175, 284, 290, 291, 315, 490

National Gallery 469

National Health Service: pay beds 57; and public expenditure 303–4, 327–8, 329, 344–5, 374–5; as 'theme' 361, 363; pay talks 419; and NUPE strike 436, 437; pay settlements 438, 445, 447, 449, 459

National Theatre 129, 277

National Union of Public Employees (NUPE) 434, 436, 437, 443, 445, 449

National Union of Railwaymen (NUR) 296, 347, 370, 423–4, 425, 434

National Union of Teachers (NUT) 37, 70, 201, 225; Carol Donoughue and 31, 52, 90, 91, 123, 148, 189, 240, 242, 290, 306, 319; and pay 435, 463, 464; strike 498

National Westminster Bank 127

nationalised industries 211, 278; top salaries 25, 35, 36, 82, 88

NATO meeting (1978) 332

Neave, Airey 474

NEB see National Enterprise Board

NEC see National Executive Committee

NEDC/'Neddy' see National Economic Development Council

Neild, Paul 385, 491

Nene College, Northampton 365

New Society 41, 339

New Statesman 202, 293, 306

New York Times 202, 205, 246; see also Apple, Johnny

Newcastle by-election (1976) 94, 95

Newsom, Sir Peter 317–18

Newspaper Proprietors Association 357

NHS see National Health Service

Nixon, Richard 184

Noble, Michael (Mike) 471, 472

North St Pancras Labour Party 43, 240

North Sea oil 6, 167, 241, 243, 253–4; taxation of divers 248, 252, 266; revenues from 257, 260, 261, 262, 263; White Paper 281, 283, 284, 285, 286, 288, 289, 297, 305

Northern Ireland/Ulster: JC's visit (1976) 49; Protestant terrorism 72, 89, 124; and Mason as Secretary of State 89, 135, 298, 299, 300, 334–5, 381; BD's ideas and suggestions 149, 367, 377, 460; political/military situation 177, 323; JC's visit 278; *see also* IRA; Maze Prison; Ulster Unionists

Northern Ireland Representation Bill 299, 314, 401, 403

Nossiter, Bernard 175

nuclear energy 6; opposed by Benn 40, 156, 178, 183, 190, 277, 282; waste reprocessing 190; new power station 217; Windscale 294; policy 326, 458

Nuffield College, Oxford: Anglo-French seminar 380, 381

NUPE *see* National Union of Public Employees

NUR *see* National Union of Railwaymen

NUT *see* National Union of Teachers

O'Brien, Edna 343, 344

O'Brien, Leslie 250

Observer: in financial trouble 65–6, 79, 83, 97; and BD's memoirs 149; HW's attack on security service 222, 233, 251; serialisation of 'Penrose' book 241; and Thorpe scandal 242; and Treasury leaks 253, 255; BD lunches with journalists 341; Hurd's memoirs 440; polls 480, 489; *see also* Raphael, Adam; Trelford, Donald

Official Secrets Act, reform of 224–5, 273, 291, 329–30, 331–2, 373; *see also* Franks Report

O'Halloran, Michael 332

oil tanker drivers' strike (1979) 399, 404, 405, 406, 415, 416, 417, 418, 420

O'Kennedy, Michael 240–41, 299

Oldfield, Sir Maurice 286

Open University 362, 462

Oriel College, Oxford: BD lecture 345

Orme, Stan: recommended by BD 15–16; not Cabinet material 68; and special advisers 89, 94, 134, 144; supports Benn/Shore alternative strategy 110; and Lib–Lab deal 167, 170; at Strategy Cabinet 205; impassioned statement at family support meeting 208; discusses child benefits with BD 213; liked by JC 233; worried about Mason 314; and pay policy talks 431–2, 433, 437, 439; and Fitt and Maguire 472

Ortoli, François-Xavier 99

O'Shea, Kevin 286, 313, 450

O'Toole, Peter 61

Otten, Alan 462

Outer Circle Policy Unit 345

Owen, David 8; recommended by BD 16; battles with Health Department 43; made to feel guilty 73; against economic policy 80; drafts memo on sterling 92; involved in Foreign Office's economic activities 104; shut out of IMF negotiations 126; 'ambitions showing' 136; takes over at Foreign Office 146, 151–2; 'pale and strained' 151; and Nairne 151; proposes new initiative for Rhodesia 157, 198, 206, 222–3, 235; on Carter 157; with JC in America 158, 160, 162–3; interested in economic policy 164; happy with Lib–Lab deal 171; spartan lunch with BD and Stewart 182; good economic suggestions 182; exhausted by travelling 183; proposes Jay as ambassador 187; and reprocessing of nuclear waste 190; and the economy 198, 235; and Strategy Cabinet 204–5, 206; defends Foreign Office 211; clashes with Healey 214; and Official Information Bill 225; expects to replace Healey 235, 257, 265; gets large NEC vote 243; attacks CPRS proposals 255; angry at revaluation of sterling 255, 257; hawkish over Japanese threat 265; gives American Embassy lecture 266; votes against PR 276; wants election delayed 279, 318, 325, 354, 362; on Civil Service White Paper 286; praises North Sea oil White Paper 286; sensible at monetary seminar 288; and discussions on Official Secrets White Paper 291; statement on Rhodesia 297; wants involvement in Middle East UN peacekeeping operation 305; and import controls 310, 311, 320, 325; and Rhodesian oil sanctions scandal 354, 358; against early election 420, 434, 439; and EMS 372, 373; critical of Ennals 434–5

Owen, Deborah 152, 158, 160, 162, 163, 171, 243

Owen, Will 223

Oxford University 81, 84, 156, 345, 404

Page, Bruce 306

Paisley, Reverend Ian 165

Palliser, Sir Michael 53, 78, 80, 151, 188, 241, 257, 479, 483

Pardoe, John 171, 203, 237, 313, 314, 317, 341, 455–6

Paris, BD in 264, 328, 340, 349, 474

Parker, Peter 98

Parliamentary Labour Party (PLP) 53, 73, 82, 188, 192, 201–2, 214, 276, 322, 399

Parsons (nuclear manufacturer) 217, 384

Parsons, Anthony 483

Part, Sir Anthony 98

Patterson, Michael 479, 491, 502

pay policies: and union negotiations 22, 23, 26–7, 28–9, 42, 61, 96 (1976), 141, 148, 166, 177, 179, 181, 191–2, 195, 208, 210, 215–20, 224, 259–61, 266, 270 (1977), 341, 342, 348, 369–70, 378, 379–80, 386–90 *passim* (1978), 406, 413–14, 417–49 *passim* (1979), *see also* Civil Service; national plan 70, *see under* Policy Unit; sanctions on employers 240, 398–9, 400, 401–2; Conservatives' 213, 501; and the low paid 383, 433–4; *see also* public expenditure; social contract; top salaries

Peachey Property Co. 179, 181, 252

Pearson Report on Compensation for Accidents 302

Peart, Fred 110, 146, 208, 455, 460

'Pencourt' book 241, 252, 286

Pendry, Tom 37

pensions 38, 107, 121, 122, 187, 188

Peri, Yoram 90

PESC see Public Expenditure Survey Committee

Peston, Maurice 109, 172, 207

Peterson, Colin 479, 502

Peterson, Susan 323

petrol, tax on 174, 175, 176

Philip, Prince, Duke of Edinburgh 38, 65

Phillips, Hayden 309

Piachaud, David: drafts JC's USDAW speech 21; returns to LSE 34; and child benefits leak 47; as economic consultant 43, 76, 77, 96; paper on Price Commission 404; and election 477, 496

Pickering, Sir Edward 65–6

picketing 424, 425, 426, 430–31

Pitfield, Michael 163

Pitt, Terry 74, 144

Plietzky, Leo: worried about local authority spending 32; and public expenditure cuts 42–3, 70, 83, 93, 95, 106–7; garrulous 43, 102; accuses BD of prejudice against Civil Service 107; on Treasury co-operation 157; moves to Trade 180, 187, 200, 272; against EMS 400

Plowden, Lady Veronica 247, 302

Plowden, Sir William: 'eternally restless' 27; on CPRS 59, 121, 123; at shows with BD 128, 247; and Brookings Institute 142; on US lecture tour 167; thinking of leaving Civil Service 196; not happy at Department of Industry 237, 285, 309; celebrates new job 437

PLP see Parliamentary Labour Party

police pay 156–7, 247, 252

Policy Unit: continues under JC 13, 15, 21, 26, 27; staffing worries 27; briefs praised by JC 39, 50; based on French 'Cabinet' system 43; papers on public expenditure 43, 45–6, 48, 49, 82; undermined by Civil Service 48, 128; accused of 'leaks' 49; 'Stabilisation and Recovery Programme 1977–80' (national plan) 70, 83, 91–2, 96, 97, 105, 125, 130, 132, 134, 150; 'family initiatives' 175, 176–7, 178, 195, 208, 341, 344, 383; Cabinet Strategy paper 193, 194, 195, 203–4, 205, 206; public expenditure papers 212, 249, 398; discussion of future plans 271; briefs on North Sea oil 257, 260, 261, 281, 283, 284, 286, 288, 289; on 'protection' 335; revitalised 361, 362; on housing 363; Hurd's views on 466; election briefing 473–4, 475, 477, 478, 480, 489, 496; farewell party 498, 499; files shredded 501; memos archived 501; see also Davies, Gavyn; Lipsey, David

Political Office (No. 10) 14, 353, 356, 499; see also McNally, Tom

polls 328, 347, 391, 477, 480, 483, 486, 487, 489, 492, 495, 497, 501; Gallup 254, 296, 380, 445, 446, 480, 489, 491, 494, 497, 501; MORI 486, 497; see also Daily Express; Daily Telegraph; Worcester, Robert

Polsby, Professor Nelson 298, 327

Pomavivev (ex-Stalinist) 90

Porchester, Lord Henry 114, 269

Porchester, Lady Jeannie 114, 475

Poulson, John: corruption scandal 20, 85–6, 225

Powell, Carla 291, 388

Powell, Charles 388

Powell, Enoch 101, 165, 167, 213, 298, 324, 458, 461, 466

Powell, Steve 121, 123

Power Engineers see Lyons, John

power station strike (1977) 258, 259, 260–61

Prentice, Reginald 54, 104, 110, 114

Price Commission 404, 489

Private Eye 243, 324, 347

Profumo affair (1963) 154

PSBR see Public Sector Borrowing Requirement

public expenditure: cuts (1976) 40, 42–9 passim, 53–9 passim, 62, 82, 83, 93, 94–5, 121; White Paper 165, 166; Treasury worries 210, 240; Unit papers 212, 249, 398; extra money for 250; JC lectures Cabinet on 299; 'shortfall' 307; Treasury concedes on 340; approved by Cabinet 344–5; City experts on 381; see also Civil Service; local authorities; National Health Service; pay policies; Public Sector Borrowing Requirement

Public Expenditure Survey Committee (PESC) 95, 327, 344–5

Public Sector Borrowing Requirement (PSBR) 78, 88, 91, 95, 100, 102–3; and IMF 103, 104, 105, 106–12 passim, 115

Publishers Association party 471

Puerto Rico summit (1976) 37, 42, 44, 45, 46, 47

Pym, Francis 189

Radice, Giles 59

rail strikes 296 (1978), 416, 423–4, 425, 428, 430 (1979)

Rampton, Jack 124–5

Ramsbotham, Peter 162, 188

Raphael, Adam 306, 494

Rawlinson, Sir Anthony 185, 210, 220, 240, 249, 340, 374, 421

Rayne, Max (Lord) 44

Read, Celia 286, 307, 363, 405, 419, 422, 477

Read, Tom 286, 307, 363, 405

Rees, Colleen 83, 259, 470

Rees, Merlyn 22, 175; moved to Home Office 68; and cuts 110; and immigration 135, 136, 141, 143, 290, 299, 300–1; and Scottish devolution 150; chairs meeting on family support 208;

dissociates himself from Home Office paper 225; and police pay 247; on Morrison 259; unhappy with Mason's scheme 272; and Annan Report on BBC 280, 295, 302, 304, 325, 338; Ilford speech on law and order 290, 291, 292; opposes legislation on Ulster Unionists 299; has 'lost his nerve' 304; gives negative statement on immigration 310; worried about Mason 314; dinner with BD 326; and election 357, 362; chairs 'emergency' meetings on strikes 417, 418; deserted by civil servants 431; 'permanently puzzled' 439; at JC's birthday party 469

Rees-Mogg, William 238, 259

Reisz, Betsy 49, 270

Reisz, Karel 49, 270, 342

retirement ages 332

Revie, Don 193, 238, 249

Rhodesia: and talks with Kissinger 65, 71, 85; and Ivor Richard 97, 137; Owen's initiative on 157, 198, 206, 222–3, 235, 297; and South Africa 234; Cabinet Office report on sanctions against 245–6; and Bingham Report on violations of sanctions 354, 357–8, 365, 367; sanctions and HW 355, 357; and inquiry into sanction breaking 365, 367–8, 372, 373, 382–3, 386, 387, 398, 402, 448; Churchill sacked in rebellion against sanctions 387

Richard, Ivor 97, 137, 157

Richardson, Gordon (Governor of Bank of England): walks in on William Armstrong's 'crack-up' (1974) 153; JR refuses to see 37; on public borrowing 47; opposes JC on supporting sterling 66; at secret meeting with Treasury 100; negotiates with Americans 120; at economic seminar 180; and BP shares sale 198, 209; a total monetarist 212; plans reported to BD 220; criticised 225, 226–7; threatens interest rate rise 227; relations with Healey 239; at monetary seminars 250–51, 254, 265; woken in night by JC 269; clashes with JC 288, 385; at Robbins's birthday dinner 393; praised by BD 412; *see also* Bank of England

Ridley, Adam 437, 498

RNID *see* Royal National Institute of the Deaf

road haulage dispute (1979) 413, 414, 415, 416, 417, 418, 420, 423, 427, 428; settlement 436; *see also* oil tanker drivers' strike

Robbins, Lionel 361; 80th birthday dinner 392–3

Robertson, Lewis 199

Robinson, Geoffrey 168, 183

Rocard, Michel 253, 264, 328–9, 474

Rockefeller, Nelson 149

Rodgers, William (Bill) 8; recommended by BD 15; refuses post 19; as Minister for Transport 68, 71; warned about Healey 87; on Howell 101; and economic debates 104, 109, 110; on Crosland and Lever 108; Transport White Paper 190, 192, 196, 199; takes JC's swimming

trunks 206; criticised by JC 243; on BBC 295, 302; in Cabinet 309; and Annan Report 338, 347; and election 357, 362; and Channel Tunnel 362–3; slapped down by JC 398; tough on pay 416, 428, 432, 439; on JC's election plans 458–9

Rogaly, Joe 93, 102, 114, 192, 264, 291

Roll, Eric 225, 292

Rolls-Royce 317, 326, 374

Rooker, Jeff 197

Ross, Richard (Dick) 329

Ross, William (Willie) 16–17, 20, 146

Rothschild, Lord Victor 44, 58, 98, 234, 290

Royal Commission on Gambling 44, 98

Royal Commission on Legal Services 25, 34, 142, 386

Royal Commission on the Press 209

Royal Institute for Public Administration 309, 437

Royal National Institute of the Deaf (RNID): conference (1977) 143

Ruskin College, Oxford University: JC's education speech (1976) 80, 82, 83, 84, 204

Russia/Soviet Union 85, 90, 259, 322, 332

Ryder, Don 192, 207

Ryder, Richard 498

Saffron Walden by-election (1977) 203

Sainsbury, David 195, 390

St Ermin's Hotel, London 494, 495

Sanders, Nick 468, 476, 479, 502

Sarbanes, Senator Paul 105, 160, 162

Sargan, Denis 133–4

SAS 148, 248

Scanlon, Hugh 141, 152, 166, 177, 210, 216, 233

Scargill, Arthur 273

Schlesinger, James 160, 396

Schmidt, Helmut 27; and Britain's financial situation 57, 78, 80, 90, 92, 108, 110, 116; talks with JC 137; and Giscard 150; opposes reflation 158; at World Economic summit (1977) 185, 186; and terrorists 248; economic discussion with JC 301; at European summit (1978) 310; further talks with JC 315, 316, 318; possible thyroid trouble 320; on Bremen summit 345; and World Economic summit (1978) 348; JC prepares for meeting with 374, 375; and EMS 385, 397, 398

school meals 107, 275–6

Scotland: BD's visits 178, 181 (1977), 337 (1978); JC in (1978) 231; abortion issue 244–5; *see also* Glasgow; Scottish devolution; Scottish National Party

Scott, Derek 275, 463

Scott, Norman 241, 247, 249, 250, 251

Scott, Paul 199

Scottish Development Agency 181, 199

Scottish devolution 6; and John Smith 15, 57, 58; JC's views 59, 85; and Scottish nationalism 107; Commons debate 119, 120–21; Cabinet

discussions on referendum 123, 136, 147;
  Smith less optimistic 149; Bill defeated 150,
  152, 156, 157, 183; and inter-party talks 154,
  189, 197–8; Smith still hopeful 192; and
  taxation powers 195, 204; and Scottish
  Nationalists 207; Smith changes Bill 213;
  guillotine vote 263; Bill progressing well 276;
  referendum discussions 305, 382, 395;
  campaign and polls 442, 450, 452, 453; referendum result 453–4, 456, 457, 460, 461; and
  vote of confidence 448, 457–8, 464–6
Scottish Labour Party 152, 182, 187
Scottish National Party (SNP) 140, 168, 178; and
  inter-party talks on devolution 197; vote of no
  confidence 207, 211; and devolution vote 263;
  and Hamilton by-election 322, 332; votes against
  pay sanctions 401; and devolution 457–8, 458,
  464, 465; and motion of censure 465–6
seamen's strike (1976) 67, 68
Sedgemoor, Brian 16, 243, 384, 385, 387
Seligman, David 461
Shapiro, David 35
Sharpe, Ruth 83, 127, 358
Shaw, George Bernard: *The Philanderer* 450
Shawcross, Hartley 377
Sherman, Alfred 188
shipbuilding industry 61; and nationalisation 107,
  116–17; collapse of Polish deal 235, 236, 237,
  239, 265, 273; crisis in 395, 457
Shore, Peter: and Michael Stewart 145; and
  immigrants' child benefits 27; 'frightened of
  immense tasks' 29–30; and sale of council
  houses 32, 327, 336; and import controls 39,
  71, 94; against public expenditure cuts 50, 56,
  87; dislikes Layfield Report 60; housing plans
  71; discusses DoE with JC 83; against any
  national recovery paper 99; and PSBR 103;
  alternative strategy debated 109, 110; and JC's
  plan to split Treasury 147; and Lib–Lab deal
  170; presents paper on inner cities 173; and
  nuclear waste 190; and mortgage relief 190,
  193; and direct elections 197; 'quite mad' on
  Channel Tunnel 216, 363; too 'wildly rhetorical' 233; explodes over exchange controls 273;
  and IMF letter 276; votes against PR 276; and
  Windscale 294; 'totally conservative' 320–21,
  327; fails to support Foot on Official Secrets
  331; and mortgage rate increase 388; opposes
  Shirley Williams's education scheme 390; more
  human than usual 419; at left-wing dinner 428;
  and pay talks 435, 437, 438, 439, 447, 450, 455
Short, Edward (Ted) 15, 20, 47, 146
Short, Renée 155
Shrimsley, Anthony 89, 301
Silkin, John: as chief whip under HW 473;
  accepts Cabinet appointment 17; and immigrants' child benefits 27; not Cabinet material
  68; supports Benn/Shore alternative strategy
  110; and state of emergency 425; at left-wing

dinner 428; and pay policy 431–2; devious
  over use of troops 432; plays left-wing union
  card 432, 439; as possible Chancellor 451; and
  election campaign 494
Silkin, Sam 20, 61, 85, 357
Simon, Julian 79
Skinner, Dennis 147
Slater Walker (firm) 202
Smith, Cyril 272, 464, 467
Smith, Geoffrey 390
Smith, Gordon 163
Smith, Ian 223, 234
Smith, John 8; recommended by BD 15; sees JC
  17; and Scottish devolution 57, 58–9, 81, 149,
  150, 152, 177, 192, 213, 221, 276; on HW 178;
  with Benn on fighting Whitehall 192; promoted
  to Cabinet 389; and devolution vote 457
Smithsonian Institution, Washington 338
Snape, Peter 473
Snell, Gordon 61, 345, 400
SNP *see* Scottish National Party
Soames, Christopher 267
social contract 43, 86, 109, 124, 180, 260
social security benefits uprating 107, 187, 190
Society for the Protection of the Unborn Child:
  abortion campaign (1978) 301, 302, 308
Sonnenfeldt, Hal 44–5, 117, 234, 309, 483
Soskice, Frank 241
Southall: race riots (1979) 490, 491
Soviet Union *see* Russia
special advisers 89, 109, 203, 286; accused of leaks
  41, 42, 45, 49, 51, 84, 93; salaries 49, 52, 278,
  355, 298
Spectator, The 202
Spiers, Ron 33, 85, 151, 208
spies/spying: pre-war Cambridge 234, 238, 259;
  Judith Hart 223; Will Owen 223; trade
  unionist 277; and 'Pencourt' story 286; and
  Cyprus 151–2
Sports Council 295, 315
SPUC *see* Society for the Protection of the
  Unborn Child
Stallard, Jock 171, 403
Stanley, John 468
Stassinopoulos, Arianna 374
State Opening of Parliament 105, 257–8, 382
Stechford by-election (1977) 169, 173, 174, 175
Steel, David: and Lib–Lab pact 168, 169, 170,
  171, 174, 176, 197, 214, 237, 280; uninformed
  on devolution 177; praised by JC 178; and
  Thorpe scandal 249; tea with BD 262; and PR
  276; discusses election with JC 305, 307; and
  Budget (1978) 313; and Finance Bill 317;
  cannot control Pardoe 317; and end of
  Lib–Lab Pact 331, 455; and employers' insurance premium 341; low in morale 347;
  worried about Thorpe trial 435; on Thorpe's
  drinking 455–6; compared with Pardoe 456;
  and devolution 460, 464; and election 496, 497

steel industry 256, 262–3, 267, 282, 292, 294, 298
Stephens, David 325
sterling: crises 37, 58, 66, 67, 71, 73, 86, 87, 88–9; and 'safety net' negotiations 115, 116, 120, 121, 122, 123, 131; appreciation 250–51, 254, 255, 256, 257
Stern, Isaac 442
Sternberg, Rudi 354
Stevens, Caroline 498
Stevens, George 161
Stevens, Liz 161
Stewart, Donald 457, 458
Stewart, Michael 92, 132, 145, 182, 203; discussions on 'protection' 310, 311, 312, 320, 325
Stobbe, Dietrich 396
Stone, Joseph (Lord) 93–4
Stonehouse, John 277
Stoppard, Tom: *Jumpers* 128; *Dirty Linen* 374
Stott, Roger: on American trip 158, 159, 161, 162, 163; and Lib–Lab pact 168, 169; at anniversary celebration 177; tells JC off 292; refuses to go to West Indies 383; shocks JC 435–6; hostile reception in constituency 423; pessimistic 425; and devolution debate 465; organises surprise party for JC 469; tells BD election date 472
Stowe, Ken 4, 13; and peerage investigation 28; and TUC pay negotiations 29; on Hunt 35; and leak on child benefits 41; on public expenditure cuts 47; brilliant additions to JC's education speech 83; on police investigation of Howell 88; puts CPRS and Unit papers to JC 96; 'open and helpful' 102; on JC and President Ford 110; refuses to impart information 113–14; lunch at No. 10 116; on Varley and Kaufman 116; on Treasury stupidity 123; 'a decent machine man' 127; thinks government is going to fall 128; on radicals in CPRS 140; rejects BD's ideas for Ireland 149; on US trip 159, 161; drafts letter for Lib–Lab pact 169; and Benn's resignation 172; accused of leaks by HW 175; and exclusion of civil servants from Strategy Cabinet 205; in flap over BD's leak about BP shares 209; and HW's 'MI5 mistakes' article 222, 223; on Budget package 245; discusses reform of Civil Service 246; against Armstrong becoming Cabinet Secretary 246; discusses Brookings Institute with BD 267–8; and Richardson 269, 270; asked by JC to stay on 274; and Civil List 310; and JC's Rovers 354; and Rhodesian oil sanctions 358, 365, 383; on HW's heart attacks 371; 'absolutely right' for JC 407; and strike crisis 426–7, 429; worried about JC's frame of mind 433; and union negotiations 438, 443; on JC and Healey's latest strategy 448; on Cabinet reshuffle 451; on imminent change of government 461; and Civil Service pay claim 463, 464; on Cyril Smith 464; on

Foot 467; in regular touch with Tories 468; worried about inexperience of election team 475, 478; looks older 479; future posting 479; on election result 496–7; shows Mrs Thatcher's staff around 498; at 'last supper' 502; greets new Prime Minister 504
Straw, Jack 28, 71, 203
Streeter, Ed 289, 382
Stuart, Nicholas (Nick) 14, 19, 55, 124, 215, 499
Suarez, Adolfo 146, 249
Sultzer, Jack 266
Summerskill, Shirley 369
Sun 42, 301, 339, 482, 492, 493
Sunday Mirror 488
Sunday Telegraph: poll 489
Sunday Times: investigation into HW's peerage lists 22, 25, 27, 60; article on sterling 86, 88; and BD's alleged leak 127; articles on Haines's book 144, 147; accuses BD of 'muck-raking' 209; on Armstrong 215; on BD getting editorship of *New Statesman* 293; and lack of press release from Transport House 488; polls 489, 494; journalists *see* Evans, Harold; Holden, Anthony; Young, Hugo
Sutherland, Arnot 213
Swain, Tom 473
Swan Hunter 239

T&GWU *see* Transport & General Workers' Union
Taylor, Ann 322, 430, 472, 473
Taylor, Ronald 444
teachers *see* National Union of Teachers
Tebbit, Norman 25, 155
textile industry 244, 247
Thatcher, Margaret: 'gracious' at Questions 14; dominated by JC in the House 5, 37, 59; blames BD for prolonged Parliamentary session 59; cancels pairing of the sick 60; gives very good speech 81; and media attack on government 89; and Cosgrave 89; worries JC 96; 'knocked around' at Questions 98; brilliant dissection of Devolution Bill 120–21; and Attlee memorial statue 125; financing of 147–8; discusses devolution with JC 157; announces no-confidence motion 166; gives poor speech 171, 172; JC's view of 186; and *Mail* 192; slapped down by JC 200; lack of humour exposed 211; good at ad-libbing 224; behind JC in polls 236, 254; at State Opening of Parliament (1977) 258; views on immigration and race relations 284, 288, 289, 290; Labour attacks on 291, 292, 293, 299; and *Sun* 301; at first Questions to be broadcast 308; and leak on use of troops 314; not happy 315; and pairing of Heath 325; angry intervention about economic 'package' 335; defeated by JC in censure debate 349–50; quite effective in debate on Address 382; sacks Churchill 387; scores points off JC 390; behind

Heath in polls 391; poor performance in House 402, 403; and strikes 424, 432, 437, 452; subdued 460, 465; effective TV broadcast 465, 466; confidence vote speech 471; hated by Heathites 475; declines to go against JC on TV 477; and civil servants 478; JC's views on 480, 484, 490, 493; election campaign 485, 488, 489, 493, 496, 499; in favour of hanging 492; party political broadcast 495; problems facing 503; bypasses Cabinet 2; radical reforms 6; and council house sales 6; and 'Thatcherism' 7

Thomas, George, Speaker 14, 54, 60, 90, 155, 470; and Thorpe scandal 241, 242, 252

Thornton (Board of Trade) 32

Thorpe, Jeremy 125; slapped down by JC 155; and murder case 241, 242, 243, 247–8, 249, 250, 252, 272, 275, 329, 354, 361; and Liberal's 'Special Seats Fund' 272, 275; trial scheduled 435

Times, The 33, 115, 149, 259; on BD leaving LSE 80; DES policy document given to 93; sympathetic to Haines 144; on Tories using troops as strike-breakers 314; offered exclusive on Rhodesia by HW 355; dispute 395, 456, 457; journalists 88, 89, 102, see also Hennessy, Peter

Tito, President Josip Broz 300

top salaries 22, 227; in nationalised industries 25, 35, 36, 82, 88; civil servants 339, 341, 343–4

Torode, John 366, 379

trade unions: and NEC demonstration against government 88; Neddy Six see National Economic Development Council; strikes and picketing 5–6, 417, 418, 419, 423, 424, 425, 426, 430–31, 439; and Mrs Thatcher 432, 452; and Labour's election defeat 419, 498–9; see also industrial democracy; pay policies; social contract; Trades Union Congress; and specific unions

Trades Union Congress (TUC): and import controls 39; supports government 58, 104; and industrial democracy 195, 311–12, 431; Conferences 232, 233 (1977), 355, 356, 357 (1978); and election campaign 346–7; BD's Charter for 436; 'concordat' with government 439, 440, 441, 443, 444, 462

Transport & General Workers' Union 212, 213, 215, 258, 369, 420, 424, 425, 432; see also Jones, Jack

Transport House 304, 322; and election campaigns 327, 346–7, 480, 481, 483, 488, 494, 495; JC's farewell talk 504

transport strikes see oil tanker drivers' strike; rail strikes; road haulage dispute

Treasury: rivalry with Cabinet Office 26; and public expenditure 32, 37, 42–3, 44, 45–6, 48, 55; leaks to the press 47, 72; and report on economic indicators 33; and overseas students' fees 40; and vehicle excise duty 60; constructs monetary package with Bank of England 75–6;

against IMF loan 76, 78, 80; traditional 'squeeze' 77; 'primitive monetarists' 79; and IMF loans 80, 97; dishonesty 87; terrible forecasts 88; PSBR and public expenditure cuts 91, 95, 102–3, 104; computer monitoring 95; 'at sixes and sevens' 106; and school meals 107; wants Cabinet minutes rewritten 111; 'bounce' of all time 116–17; 'stupidity' 123; 'defeatist' on sterling 131; and unemployment 131; and industrial strategy 136; and plans to split 132–3, 147, 149, 150, 154, 246, 285; and Policy Unit 157, 240; and pay policy 179, 210, 217, 240; and interest rates 179, 180, 194–5; removal of permanent secretaries 180–81; and IMF 200; gloomy assessment 200; computer model for economy 201, 205, 207; relationship with Bank of England 220–21, 249; and Healey's 'sweeteners' 221; ignores ministers 249; and monetary seminar 249, 250–51; leaks 253, 255; quality of officials 261, 285; and IMF Letter of Intent 271–2, 274, 275, 276; crisis package 333; and union pay negotiations 378; and public expenditure cuts 381; against EMS 393; and price legislation 404, 429; negativism attacked by Lever 411; on cash limits 449; see also Barnett, Joel; Couzens, Ken; Healey, Denis; Mitchell, Derek; Plietzky, Leo; sterling crises; Wass, Douglas

Trelford, Donald 60, 149

Trethowan, Ian 89, 377

Tribune Group 24, 134, 202, 400, 401, 472

Trudeau, Margaret 162, 163, 164

Trudeau, Pierre 69, 162, 163, 164, 185, 186, 295, 399

TUC see Trades Union Congress

Uganda 52

Ulmann, Dick 246

Ulster see Northern Ireland; Ulster Unionists

Ulster Unionists: co-operation with Labour 165, 167, 168, 213; and Speakers Conference 237, 299; and Mason 298; and Northern Ireland Representation Bill 299, 314, 401, 403; against Finance Bill 323–4; against pay sanctions 401; and devolution 458, 461; and vote of censure 462, 466, 468, 470, 471; and Tory victory 501

Underhill, Reg 304, 355

unemployment: and economy 46, 65, 75, 76, 88, 94, 118; JC's initiative at World Economic summit 128, 129; interdepartmental committees on 131, 138, 140, 142, 143, 155; in construction industry 216; in shipbuilding industry 235; and inflation 224; CPRS paper on 283, 285, 303; JC's views 228, 307; and Tory attack 315; in Germany 318; as 'theme' for Unit 361; long-term 364, 366, 374; and CBI opposition 375

United States: elections 33; and British economy

45, 85, 92, 99, 108, 120, 123, 126, 131, 166; and Rhodesia 65, 71, 85; and Owen's appointment 152; British visit (1977) 158–63; and BP shares 209; 'swap agreement' with Germany 300; and collapsing dollar 381, 382, 391; aircraft industry 317, 326, 340; *see also* Carter, Jimmy; Ford, Gerald

universities: overseas students' fees 37, 40–41, 48; teachers' pay 91; demoralisation 225; Boyle's lecture on 327; as employers 355

Urwin, Charles (Harry) 434

USDAW: Blackpool Conference (1976) 21, 23–4

Vaisey, Lord John 290

Value Added Tax (VAT) 122, 233, 239, 333, 334, 335, 484, 487

Vance, Cy 160

Varley, Eric: nervous at meeting with JC 39; and import controls 39; beaten by Atkinson for treasurership 73; and rise in interest rates 79; complains about industrial strategy 89; wants cuts in social programme 94; unwilling to show hand 109–10; depressed and petulant 110–11; ignored by his officials 113, 125; and nationalisation of ship repairing 116; JC disappointed by 119; and industrial strategy 136; and British Leyland 192; and inquiry into Engineering 193; at Strategy Cabinet 205; and Ryder's resignation from Enterprise Board 207–8; and Polish shipping order 235, 237, 239; criticised by Moser 237, and JC 243; and steel industry cuts 262, 263; relationship with Kaufman 263, 278; on Benn's lack of credibility 266; 'psychological weaknesses' 278; accused of misleading House 292; 'clapped-out' 361; and British Leyland 363, 379; at Party Conference (1978) 369; asked to help 'educate' trade unions on microprocessors 392; and public pay policy 420, 423

Varracatt, Gerry 163

VAT *see* Value Added Tax

vehicle excise duty 60, 174, 364

Vickers, Alfred: painting sold 242

Villiers, Sir Charles 292

Waddell, Willie 181

Walden, George 311

Wales: devolution 120, 123, 382, 395, 453, 466

Walker, Peter 284

Wall Street Journal 462

Walsall by-election (1976) 94, 95, 97

Warnock, Mary (*later* Baroness) 344

Wass, Douglas: rivalry with Hunt 26; and public expenditure discussions 45, 66; lacking 'grit' 87; on Healey 88, 91, 97; at JC's emergency meeting 92; at LSE meeting 98; on IMF 98; and Mitchell 183, 247; at JC's secret meeting 100; lunches with BD 149–50; and plan to split Treasury 133, 150, 154; on Healey's 'big

giveaway' 156; on the Budget 174; at economic seminars 180, 212; agrees to computer model for economy 206; 'worn out' 220; worried about pay policy 226; on reflation 232; weekly lunches 241; blames Healey for not informing JC about gilts 247; criticised by Mitchell 247; at monetary seminar 250, 251; at discussion on changes in Civil Service 255, 256; criticised by Allen 258; in a minority 264–5; doubtful about Brookings Institute 278; sees Howe 478

water workers' strike 399–400, 424, 426, 427

Waterhouse, Keith 498

Watkinson, Harold 141

Watt, David 192, 437

Waugh, Evelyn: *Brideshead Revisited* 430, 451

Webster, David 294, 367, 377

Weedon, Kenneth 168

Weidenfeld, George (*later* Lord) 30

Weighell, Sid 370, 434, 438

Weinstock, Arnold 384, 387, 412

Welsh Nationalists 466, 468

Welsh Rugby team 307

West, Harry 298, 461

West, Trevor 316, 372, 376, 400, 493

Westminster by-election (1977) 154

Wheatcroft, Stephen 103

White, Frank 498, 502

White, Richard (Dick) 259

White, William (Willie) 400

Whitehead, Phillip 16, 22, 81

Whitelaw, William 284

Whitlam, Gough 326

Whittome, Alan 108

whooping-cough vaccine 155, 183, 184, 199, 302

Whyte, Robert 160

Wicks, Nigel: drafts JC's USDAW speech 21; debriefs BD on economic committee 28; and Treasury 'squeeze' 76; and Treasury 'bounce' 116–17, 118–20; warns BD of enemies 123; on Healey 134; hears BD's 'voice' in JC's arguments 136; drafts JC's speech 167; at economic seminar 180; on JC's TUC speech 232; gets copy of Healey's Letter of Intent for Unit 275; and discussion on incomes policy 287; dictates JC's brief for Healey 337; and JC's support for Healey 345; on EEC 346; farewell dinner 383

Williams, Bernard 400

Williams, Philip 48

Williams, Shirley 8; on joining Cabinet 16; and pay negotiations 26, 29; chairs discussion on vehicles for the disabled 48; falls asleep at Cabinet committee 49; supports Jenkins 61; becomes Minister for Education 68; welcomes JC's new toughness 70; loses AEU votes for NEC 73; opposes rise in interest rates 79; and deputy leadership 81–2, 85; plans for education 85; warned about Healey 87; supports Crosland 104, 108, 109, 110; advised by BD on special advisers 108, 113; entertains 125–6; and immigration 135; and NEC 151; and unemployment 155; good in economics discussion 157; Green Paper on education 199, 201, 202, 203, 204, 211, 212, 215, 225; at Strategy Cabinet 205; JC concerned about 233; and abortion issue 250, 301, 302, 308, 309, 313, 340–41; coffee with BD 267; and IMF letter 276; taken to lunch by BD 276–7; and private education 292; late for No. 10 294–5; on BBC 302; 'quite delightful' 309; compromises on industrial democracy 311; and public appointments 320, 321; discussion with Bishop Konstant 324; gossips with BD 328; and McElhone 337; supports JC on Annan 338; praised by BD 342; ready to quit 347; and election 357; reads lesson in Blackpool 369; persuades unions to reconsider votes on pay policy 369; in favour of EMS 382, 393; and educational maintenance allowances 389, 390, 393; hi-fi to be mended by BD 400; and public pay policy 419; and teachers' pay claim 435, 492; complains about civil servants' pay rise 459–60; and industrial democracy 461; and election campaign 477; comes close to resignation 479; at ITN election party 500; loses seat 504

Willis, Ted 249

Wilson, Harold: at University 365; arrival at No. 10 (1964) 47, 497; comparisons with JC 1, 2, 3–4, 14–15, 16, 18, 19, 22, 23, 24, 29, 31, 38, 40, 53; and JC's loyalty 257; illegal bank deposit 199; and trade-union spies (1974–5) 277; and Judith Hart (1975) 126; heart attacks (1975–6) 371; sacrifices Varley 109–10; controlled by Hunt 459; memoirs not written from memory 137; 'cool' with Haines (1976) 19; Private Office dinner cancelled by Marcia Falkender 22; and honours list 14, 22, 25, 28, 30, 32, 36, 44, 60, 145, 147, 222, 428; paranoid delusions 32, 34; worried about Haines's book 41; at No. 10 reception 61–2; shifty about Haines 62; gets 'alpha' for new book 71–2; involves BBC in pursuit of spies 93; uses Rothschild as intermediary with BD 98; offered Treasury by JC 154; and Higham 154; continues to deny various allegations 151; 'shrunk' and 'shabby' 164–5; and Marcia's

removal from Film Industry committee 157, 175; distracted 180; and Eric Miller/Peachey scandal 181; at Locketts with Marcia and Frost 210; house for sale 213; attacks MI5 in press 222, 223; asked to shut up by JC 233; has long chat with BD 250; and 'Pencourt' spy story 286; on trip to Israel with Kissin 291–2; on his drinking 343; advises BD on election timing 349; and Rhodesian oil sanctions 355, 356, 358, 368, 383; to appear on Morecambe and Wise Show 367; meets Kagan in Israel 401; drinking too much 403; his golden rule 422; attacks JC in press 446; as chairman of City Royal Commission 451; on Mary Wilson voting for Mrs Thatcher 493

Wilson, Mary 292, 493

Windscale nuclear plant 294

Winterbottom, Walter 295

Wise, Audrey 169, 197, 202

Witteveen, H. Johannes 108, 110, 111, 140

Woestner, Bill 165

Wood, Philip 139; on North Sea oil 253; lectured by JC 269; drafts JC's speeches 401, 468; and devolution 454, 464, 465; farewell celebrations 476, 479

Woolf, Bob 177

Worcester, Robert (Bob) 91, 136, 174; presses for Labour to commission polling 184, 198, 234; runs polls 256–7, 297, 312, 315, 412; socialises with BD 279, 306; presentations 314, 452; election polls 487, 494, 495, 497

Workington by-election (1976) 94, 95

World Economic summits: London (1977), 128, 129, 166, 182, 183, 184–7; Bonn (1978) 308, 348

Wright, Patrick 18, 52, 135, 142, 161, 193, 208, 227

Wright, Sheila 137

Wright, Vincent 189

Wright, Virginia 208

Writers' Guild 188

Yeo, Ed 76, 79, 131

Young, Hugo 340, 386, 482

Ypersele, Jacques van 324, 392, 399, 451

Zander, Michael 34, 142, 386, 387

Zukerman, Pinchas 442